About the Author

Mark S. Smith is Skirball Professor of Bible and Ancient Near Eastern Studies at New York University. His publications include *The Pilgrimage Pattern in Exodus* (1997), *The Ugaritic Baal Cycle* (1994), *The Early History of God* (1990), as well as several other books on the Hebrew Bible, the Dead Sea Scrolls, and West Semitic mythology and literature.

The Origins of Biblical Monotheism

THE ORIGINS OF
BIBLICAL MONOTHEISM

*Israel's Polytheistic Background and the
Ugaritic Texts*

Mark S. Smith

OXFORD
UNIVERSITY PRESS
2001

OXFORD
UNIVERSITY PRESS

Oxford   New York
Athens   Auckland   Bangkok   Bogotá   Buenos Aires   Calcutta
Cape Town   Chennai   Dar es Salaam   Delhi   Florence   Hong Kong   Istanbul
Karachi   Kuala Lumpur   Madrid   Melbourne   Mexico City   Mumbai   Nairobi
Paris   Shanghai   Singapore   Taipei   Tokyo   Toronto   Warsaw

and associated companies in
Berlin   Ibadan

Copyright © 2001 by Mark Smith

Published by Oxford University Press
198 Madison Avenue, New York, New York 10016

Oxford is a registered trademark of Oxford University Press

Library of Congress Cataloging-in-Publication Data

Smith, Mark S., 1955–
The origins of biblical monotheism : Israel's polytheistic background and the Ugaritic
texts / Mark S. Smith.
p. cm.
Includes bibliographical references and indexes.
ISBN 0-19-513480-X
1. God—Biblical teaching.   2. Ugaritic literature—Relation to the Old Testament.   3.
Bible. O.T.—Criticism, interpretation, etc.   4. Gods, Semitic.   5. Polytheism.   6.
Monotheism.   I. Title.

BS1192.6.S555   2000
296.3'11'0901—dc21   99-058180

2 4 6 8 9 7 5 3 1
Printed in the United States of America
on acid-free paper

For Liz

To the nut grove I went down,

To see the fruit of the vale,

To see if the vines had blossomed,

If the pomegranates had bloomed.

Song of Songs 6:11

Acknowledgments

But I should have liked to write a poem strong
And beautiful as mercy, and as long.

Elliott Coleman, One Hundred Poems,
June Sonnets #6

This book was produced largely thanks to a fellowship at the Center for Judaic Studies of the University of Pennsylvania in 1997–98. During the year, which was dedicated to the topic of Israelite religion, I took up the fundamental question of what divinity is. My earlier book *The Early History of God* discusses many different deities, but it does not define the more basic issue of what divinity is. Nor does that book address the categories, structures, or characteristics of deities. For quite some time I had given thought to this area of inquiry so that when I was given the opportunity to spend a year at the Center for Judaic Studies, I selected it as my topic. This book is the basic result of my year's research at the Center. So before I offer any other acknowledgments, I am happy to thank the director of the Center, Professor David Ruderman, the Associate Director, Dr. David Goldenberg, and all the staff and fellows at the Center for Judaic Studies for contributing to an enjoyable and stimulating year. They helped me in so many ways with the work represented by this book. My thanks go in particular to a co-fellow, Professor Ted Lewis, for reading the entire manuscript and offering detailed comments. His remarks greatly improved this study.

Part I (chapters 1–4) represents a developed version of my paper delivered at the Center's symposium at the conclusion of the year. Part II (chapters 5–6) benefitted from a variety of family and colleagues. Comments contributed by Professors Tikva Frymer-Kensky, Saul Olyan, Benjamin Sommer, and Irene Winter were especially helpful. In September 1997, the Antiquity Colloquium at Saint Joseph's University survived a presentation of an early draft of chapter 5. I am grateful for participants' many helpful comments. My departmental colleague Professor David Carpenter was particularly gracious in providing me with written comments on the paper; these are reflected in additions and reformulations at the end of the chapter. For chapter 5, I am grateful also to my daughter, Shulamit, who discussed with me several questions relevant to the characteristics of divinity; her contribution is reflected in the final section of chapter 5. The research for chapter 6 was presented before the Center for Judaic Studies, to the Department of Bible of the Hebrew University, and at the Old Testament Colloquium (Conception Abbey). I wish to express my thanks for the suggestions that members of these three bodies generously offered. For the research on this chapter, I especially grateful to my co-researcher, co-fellow (at the Center for Judaic Studies in 1997–98), and wife, Dr. Elizabeth (Liz) Bloch-Smith, and to Professors Ron Hendel, Ted Lewis and Philip Schmitz for commenting on an earlier draft of this essay. I am indebted in particular to Professor Schmitz for checking the discussion of the Phoenician and Punic evidence. My thinking on the Mesopotamian material benefitted from discussions with Dean Karel van Toorn during my visit to Leiden in December 1998. I am grateful to the *Scandinavian Journal for the Old Testament* for publishing an earlier version of this study. I also wish to reserve a special word of thanks for Professor Tryggve Mettinger regarding the subject of chapter 6. I have deeply appreciated the great interest he has taken in my research, both on this subject and other projects.

Part III (chapters 7–10) benefitted from help from many quarters. Chapter 7 originated as a summary piece on the god El for the *Eerdmans' Dictionary of the Bible*. I have revised the piece to highlight the questions of El as the original god of Israel and as the original divine patron of the Exodus from Egypt. This presentation of this material was enhanced by my discussions with Ted Lewis, who traded his draft of research on El for mine; mine benefitted especially from his reminder about the importance of Numbers 23–24 for the issue of El as the god of the Exodus. Chapters 8 and 10 originated as a lecture delivered at the Department of Near Eastern Studies of the University of California, Berkeley, in February 1998. I thank Professors Carol Redmount, Anne Kilmer, and Robert Alter for hosting my visit. I was especially grateful for the helpful comments offered in reaction to the presentation, in particular thoughtful questions raised by Professor Erich Gruen. I recall this visit with a particular fondness afforded by the tremendous interest shown in my work, by the many engaging students and faculty there, and by the sheer beauty of the place (cf. Proverbs 3:17). Some of the points made in chapter 8 were presented in a lecture before the International Organization for the Study of the Old Testament in Oslo in August 1998. I am deeply grateful for the invitation from Professor Hans Barstad to offer thoughts on the Ugaritic texts and the Bible. In particular, I wish to thank Professor Phyllis Bird for her reactions to some of my suggestions offered in chapter 8; I have modified and clarified points accordingly. Chapter 10 draws on current research on pertinent Mesopotamian textual and iconographic material, especially the "mouth-opening" (*pit pî*) and "mouth-washing" (*mīs pî*) rituals. I am hardly a specialist in Mesopotamian religion and texts, and here I have been particularly guided by the research of Michael Dick and Victor Hurowitz. Professor Dick placed some of his unpublished work on the subject at my disposal; this work has fortunately appeared in print. All of these chapters in this book represent an effort at synthesis; accordingly, it is deeply indebted to the work of many scholars.

I also wish to expression my deep appreciation to the institutions in Jerusalem that supported my research. I am grateful to the Hebrew University of Jerusalem. Much of the groundwork for this study was laid in the summer of 1997 when I served as a Lady Davis Visiting Professor there. I thank the university and its many faculty who took an interest in my work, especially Professors Avi Hurvitz and Shalom Paul for their sponsorship. The staffs at the William Foxwell Albright Institute and the École Biblique were gracious to me, and I benefitted many times over for their generosity. The library staffs at these two institutions deserve special note. At home, Saint Joseph's University was exceptionally supportive in all of my presentations. I am especially grateful for the support given me by the chair of the Department of Theology, Professor Paul Aspan, and by the Dean of the College of Arts and Sciences, Professor Judi Chapman. The interlibrary loan staff at Drexel Library of Saint Joseph's University has worked overtime to acquire all of the exotic items I have requested; I am happy to thank all of the library staff for their generosity and good humor, in particular Mary Martinson, Patrick Connelly, Rebecca Reilly, and Naomi Cohen. I am very much indebted to the many students who worked with me on the course on Israelite religion. Over the past five years, this course has increasingly taken up the themes of this book. Saint Joe's students often served as the first sounding boards for my material. They asked questions that helped me to keep clarifying the evidence and the analysis. In 1994–95 and 1998–99 I taught Ugaritic at the University of Pennsylvania. My thinking benefitted from my reading of some of the Ugaritic texts treated in this book. I thank two scholars who sent me copies of their dissertations, Dr. Terje Stordalen of the Lutheran School of Theology in Oslo, and Dr. Lourik Karkajian of the University of Montreal. I am also pleased to acknowledge the support and warm reception by new colleagues at New York University, especially Dan Fleming and Larry Schiffman. Finally, I am grateful to Oxford University Press for publishing this book, and to its staff, especially Cynthia Read and Robert Milks, for shepherding it through the publication process.

I close this list with mention of two people who have been instrumental to my happiness. The topic of divinity was Marvin Pope's lifelong passion, and in retrospect his spirit very much permeated my days working on this book. Many readers will recognize Marvin's guidance both in his writing and teaching, and I am happy to acknowledge my debt to him (still, always). Finally, I dedicate this book to my wonderful wife, Liz. As my "fellow fellow" at the Center for Judaic Studies in 1997–98, she accompanied me along the way through this book, and her presence through our years together is a rare and irreplaceable companionship, at once personal and intellectual. "Our secret garden" (as our daughter Rachel calls it) winds down the side of our house and into our small, secluded backyard; it is hardly the only echo of our life that I hear in Song of Songs 6:11.

Department of Hebrew and Judaic Studies   M. S. S.
New York University
July 2000

Contents

Abbreviations, Terms, and Sigla

The abbreviations, listed in *Journal of Biblical Literature* 107 (1988), 584–96, and *The Assyrian Dictionary, Volume 15 S* (ed. E. Reiner et al.; Chicago: Oriental Institute, 1984), vii–xxii, are used with the following additions, changes, and sigla. Second Temple works besides the Dead Sea Scrolls cited in this study may be found in James H. Charlesworth, ed., *The Old Testament Pseudepigrapha* (two vols. Garden City, NY: Doubleday, 1983, 1985).

Books, Journals, and Series

Abbreviations used here beyond standard ones are:

ABD   *The Anchor Bible Dictionary.* Ed. D. N. Freedman. Six volumes. New York: Doubleday, 1992.

ANET   *ANET*. Third edition.

AO   *Aula Orientalis.*

BOS   U. Cassuto, *Biblical & Oriental Studies. Volume 2: Bible and Ancient Oriental Texts.* Trans. I. Abrahams. Jerusalem: Magnes, 1975.

CAT   M. Dietrich, O. Loretz, and J. Sanmartín, *The Cuneiform Alphabetic Texts from Ugarit, Ras Ibn Hani and Other Places* (KTU: 2nd, enlarged edition). ALASPM 8. Munster: Ugarit-Verlag, 1995.

CMCOT   R. J. Clifford, *The Cosmic Mountain in Canaan and the Old Testament.* HSM 4. Cambridge, MA: Harvard University Press, 1972.

CMHE   F. M. Cross, *Canaanite Myth and Hebrew Epic.* Cambridge, MA: Harvard University Press, 1973.

CML   J. C. L. Gibson, *Canaanite Myth and Legends.* 2nd ed. Edinburgh: T. and T. Clark, 1978.

DDD   *Dictionary of Deities and Demons in the Bible (DDD)*. Ed. K. van
der Toorn, B. Becking, and P. W. van der Horst. Second ed.
Leiden: Brill, 1999.

DLU   G. del Olmo Lete and J. Sanmartín, *Diccionario de la lengua ugar-
ítica: Vol. I. '(a/i/u)-l.* Aula Orientalis—Supplementa 7. Bar-
celona: Editorial AUSA, 1996.

DW   P. D. Miller, *The Divine Warrior in Early Israel.* HSM 5. Cambridge, MA: Harvard University Press, 1973.

EA   El-Amarna letters.

EHG   M. S. Smith, *The Early History of God: Yahweh and the Other Deities in Ancient Israel.* San Francisco: Harper & Row, 1991.

Emar   D. Arnaud, *Recherches au pays d'Aštata. Emar VI: Tome 3. Texts
sumériens et accadiens. Texte.* Paris: Editions Recherche sur
les Civilisations, 1986. Cited by text number.

EUT   M. H. Pope, *El in the Ugaritic Texts.* VTSup. 2. Leiden: Brill,
1955.

GA   U. Cassuto, *The Goddess Anath.* Trans. I. Abrahams. Jerusalem:
Magnes, 1971.

KAI   H. Donner and W. Röllig, *Kanaanäische und aramäische Inschriften.* Wiesbaden: Harrassowitz, 1964–68.

KTU   M. Dietrich, O. Loretz, and J. Sanmartín. *Die Keilalphabetischen
Texte aus Ugarit.* AOAT 24/1. Kevelaer: Verlag Butzon &
Bercker; Neukirchen-Vluyn: Neukirchener, 1976.

Lane   E. W. Lane, *An Arabic-English Lexicon.* In eight parts. London:
Williams and Norgate, 1863–1893. Reprinted, Beirut: Librairie du Liban, 1968.

LAPO   *Littératures anciennes du Proche-Orient.*

MARI   *Mari Annales de Recherches Interdisciplinaires.*

MLC   G. del Olmo Lete, *Mitos y leyendas de Canaan segun la Tradicion
de Ugarit.* Institucion San Jeronimo para la Ciencia Biblica
1. Madrid: Ediciones Cristiandad, 1981.

PE   Eusebius, *Praeparatio evangelica*, cited according to H. W. Attridge
and R. A. Oden, Jr., ed. *Philo of Byblos The Phoenician History: Introduction, Critical Text, Translation, Notes.* CBQMS
9. Washington, DC: Catholic Biblical Association of America, 1981.

RHA   *Revue hittite et asianique.*

RNAB   Revised New American Bible.

SPUMB   J. C. de Moor, *The Seasonal Pattern in the Ugaritic Myth of Baʻlu:
According to the Version of Ilimilku.* AOAT 16. Kevelaer:
Butzon & Bercker; Neukirchen-Vluyn: Neukirchener, 1971.

SEL   *Studi Epigrafici e Linguistici.*

TO 1   A. Caquot, M. Sznycer, and A. Herdner, *Textes ougaritiques I.
Mythes et legendes.* LAPO 7. Paris: Editions du Cerf, 1974.

TO 2   A. Caquot and J. M. de Tarragon, *Textes ougaritiques: Tome II.
Textes Religieux and Rituels*, and J. L. Cunchillos, *Correspond-
ance.* LAPO 14. Paris: Cerf, 1989.

UBC   M. S. Smith, *The Ugaritic Baal Cycle: Volume 1. Introduction with Text, Translation and Commentary of KTU 1.1–1.2.* VTSup 55. Leiden: Brill, 1994.

UBL   Ugaritisch-Biblische Literatur.

Ug V   J. Nougayrol, E. Laroche, C. Virolleaud, and C. F. A. Schaeffer, *Ugaritica V.* Mission de Ras Shamra XVI. Paris: Imprimerie Nationale Librairie orientaliste Paul Geuthner, 1968.

UNP   M. S. Smith et al., *Ugaritic Narrative Poetry.* Ed. S. B. Parker. SBL Writings from the Ancient World Series. Atlanta, GA: Scholars, 1997.

UT   C. H. Gordon, *Ugaritic Textbook.* AnOr 38. Rome: Pontifical Biblical Institute, 1965.

WUS   J. Aistleitner, *Wörterbuch der ugaritischer Sprache.* Ed. O. Eissfeldt. 3rd edition. Berlin: Akademie-Verlag, 1967.

YGC   W. F. Albright, *Yahweh and the Gods of Canaan: A Historical Analysis of Two Contrasting Faiths.* New York: Doubleday, 1968. Reprinted, Winona Lake, IN: Eisenbrauns, nd.

Terms

Languages and Dialects

BH   Biblical Hebrew
ESA   Epigraphic South Arabic
Heb.   Modern Hebrew
MA   Middle Assyrian
MB   Middle Babylonian
NA   Neo-Assyrian
NB   Neo-Babylonian
OB   Old Babylonian
PS   Proto-Semitic

Grammatical Terms

acc.   accusative case
C   causative stem (BH "hiphil")
cst.   construct state
D   double stem (BH "piel")
DN   divine name
Dt   double stem with -*t* reflexive or reciprocal (BH "hithpael")
fem.   feminine gender
G   ground or simple stem (BH "qal")
Gt   ground stem with -*t* reflexive or reciprocal
impf.   imperfect or prefix tense
impv.   imperative
inf.   infinitive
masc.   masculine gender

N	N-prefix stem (BH "niphal")
p	person
pl.	plural number
pass.	passive voice
perf.	perfect or suffix tense
pl.	plural
PN(s)	proper names(s)
prep.	preposition
ptcp.	participle
sg.	singular
Št	causative stem with -t reflexive or reciprocal

Other Terms

EA	El-Amarna
LXX	Septuagint
MT	Masoretic Text
n.	note
nn.	notes
RIH	Ras ibn-Hani (text number)
RS	Ras Shamra (text number)

Sigla

ʾ	ʾaleph (e.g., in Hebrew and Aramaic)
d	Ugaritic sign 16
ʿ	ʿayin
*	hypothetical form or root
<>	restored letters
//	parallel terms or lines

The Origins of Biblical Monotheism

Introduction

All this was a long time ago, I remember,
And I would do it again, but set down
This set down
This: were we led all that way for
Birth or Death?

> T. S. Eliot, "Journey of the Magi"

Now, at the turn of the millennium, God remains a central question in Western culture. Through the Middle Ages, the Renaissance, and the Reformation, the notion of God could be assumed. People may have seriously questioned the justice or nature of God, but the "existence" of God was a given. In the wake of massive religious wars and the Enlightenment came more critical analysis of religion, specifically religion as human artifact. Feuerbach, Marx, Nietzsche, Durkheim, Freud, Geertz: their powerful analyses cumulatively put belief in God first in jeopardy and then in flight before an increasingly secular Western culture. The crisis-point in many intellectual circles has long passed.[1] Numerous studies of God treat the divine largely as a social construct, psychological projection, or literary figure. Now in religious studies departments, theological discussions question the intelligibility of either God or the act, concept, and structure of faith ("what does it mean to believe in God?"). Yet the "flight of God" from American universities is hardly a uniform phenomenon. Although discourse about God and the notion of belief has become increasingly problematic in departments of religion and divinity schools, theists elsewhere in the university are scarcely in full retreat. For example, a survey of American scientists on one campus, the University of Georgia, conducted by the Pulitzer Prize–winning historian of science Edward Larson,[2] hardly indicates complete lack of belief; if anything, the opposite is the case. Moreover, the topic of God has enjoyed a remarkable resurgence in contemporary Western culture by way of the field of physics. Recent works exploring the divine and physics include Mark Worthing's *God, Creation and Contemporary Physics*.[3] So, at the start of the new millennium, faith is increasingly questioned in religion and divinity faculties even as it is affirmed in other quarters of American universities.

This range is evident as well in recent studies of God in the Bible. Within the fields of theological and biblical studies, traditional theological studies of God remain a standard feature of the landscape. The field also continues to witness interest in the historical study of God and monotheism, for example in the recent popular book *Aspects of Monotheism: How God Is One*.[4] From the religious side, Robert K. Gnuse's *No Other Gods: Emergent Monotheism in Israel* attempts to mediate between traditional historical study of biblical monotheism and scientific study.[5] Following its fine survey of current scholarship, the book describes the contribution of monotheism to Western civilization, in particular the evolution of humanity and the cosmos. Other recent books have departed from traditional theological expositions about God or from analysis of the religious history of Israel's national deity. Jack Miles has offered *God: A Biography*, an engaging "literary study" of God as a character over the course of the biblical books.[6] Despite its purported purpose as a literary study, the book makes many historical assumptions. As a result, the book demonstrates the need for historical context for the study of texts. The same point applies to the divinities mentioned in the Bible as well. Regina Schwartz's book *The Curse of Cain: The Violent Legacy of Monotheism* offers a secular sermon on the dangers of the post-biblical careeer of biblical monotheism and consequently calls for a rejection of the Bible: "The old 'monotheistic' Book must be closed so that the new books may be fruitful and multiply."[7] The book is likely to convince primarily a congregation that has already heeded its message about the "old Bible." Perhaps as an effort to combat secular attacks on one side and conservative theological discourse on the other, some have recently emphasized the virtues of biblical monotheism.[8]

In the face of contemporary attitudes toward God and biblical monotheism, interest in these topics clearly shows no signs of abating. All of the works mentioned thus far point to a broadly felt need for an exploration of divinity in the Bible. "God-talk" retains an interest for people, whether for their faith, their quest for spirituality (whether traditional or nontraditional), or their desire to understand Western culture. All interested parties deserve access to the increasingly richer harvests from the ancient texts to which modern communities of scholarship and faith lay claim. The picture of biblical monotheism is complex. The Bible provides a basic narrative account of human knowledge of the monotheistic God. According to the story of the Bible, monotheism was not the original condition of the world. Instead, it stepped onto the world stage with the appearance of Israel. For when Israel's god, Yahweh, was revealed first to the patriarchs and then definitively to Moses and the Israelite people on Mount Sinai, the central moment in world history occurred: the revelation of the one God known by the one name of the Tetragrammaton. Thanks to the biblical picture, the monotheism of ancient Israel has been regarded as a revolution against the religious thought of its neighbors. Such a view can be found today not only in the general culture but also in scholarly circles as well.[9]

However, over the last half-century numerous scholarly studies have sought to locate the biblical foundational story of monotheism within its larger cultural context. In part, this endeavor has occurred through scrutiny of the biblical sources themselves. Various passages in the Bible suggest a more complicated picture lying behind the more dominant narrative of Israelite monotheism. Signs of polytheism are apparent. For example, Moses and the people ask: "Who is like You among the gods, O Yahweh?" (Exodus 15:11); the question rather neutrally implies the existence of other deities. Other biblical passages contain vestiges of Israelite polytheism. The complex relations between Israelite monotheism and polytheism were not always an issue of conflict, as the bulk of biblical narratives have strongly led readers to believe. Instead, it has become clear that Israel knew some sort of polytheism; how to reconcile signs of such a religious situation within the larger framework of monotheism in the Bible has been a major topic of scholarly discussion for some time. Extra-biblical sources have also affected the discussion of biblical monotheism. Discovery of ancient inscriptions has added greatly to the scholarly knowledge of deities mentioned in the Bible. Moreover, archaeological research has accumulated a massive amount of information pertinent to the understanding of ancient religion. In recent years pictorial art has come to the fore as a major source for studying ancient deities. In short, only in the twentieth century did the scholarly community come to know these deities on their own terms, namely from the vantage point of their own adherents, rather than from biblical polemics directed against them. These discoveries have inspired a renewed investigation into biblical religion, in particular biblical monotheism and its relations to polytheism in ancient Israel and neighboring cultures.

This book represents a synthesis that focuses not so much on specific deities as on the concepts that the ancients used to understand them. In other words, I am interested not only in describing Israelite monotheism but also in examining the conceptual unity and coherence of its religious congener, Israelite polytheism, as well as the religious unity expressed in the polytheism revealed in the largest cache of relevant extra-biblical texts, namely the myths and rituals from the ancient city of Ugarit (modern Ras Shamra). Located on the Mediterranean coast of modern Syria about a hundred miles north of Beirut, this city flourished during the late Bronze Age. Since 1928, this site has yielded scores of texts and artifacts detailing its religious practices and notions, including a full-blown polytheism with narratives and rituals involving many of the deities known from the Bible (except Yahweh). Thanks especially to the Ugaritic myths, there is material to probe the indigenous understanding of the deities and their interrelations. Of all the ancients texts found in the Levant containing this kind of information, the Ugaritic texts are also most proximate in time and place to ancient Israel.[10] This situation stands in contrast to the many texts from the now famous sites of Ebla, Mari, and Emar. The vast number of texts discovered at Ebla provide considerably less background information about the Israelites' conceptualization of deities and divinity,[11] as they lie at a greater geographical and temporal distance from the Bible. Mari[12] and Emar[13] have also provided important information about the Levant during the Bronze Age. They also illuminate aspects of ancient Israel, and they are, roughly speaking, as proximate to Israel as Ugarit. However, for the study of divinity in the Hebrew Bible, these two sites have yielded less information than Ugarit.

Thanks to the Ugaritic and Israelite texts, the polytheisms attested in these cultures, as well as Israelite monotheism, can be described with deeper understanding. Such an approach to divinity in the Bible has been slow to emerge in biblical studies. Such issues have been raised about the conceptual coherence of other polytheisms but not for Israel and relatively little for Ugarit. Researchers in Egyptology[14] and Assyriology[15] have broached these issues. So have scholars working on Hinduism and Greek religion. For example, a 1989 volume entitled *Polytheistic Systems* offers some interesting studies on conceptual structures in Hinduism and Greek religion. However, the essay on ancient Israel treats only the issue of monotheism in the Bible, and the author of the essay, a well-known expert on Ugaritic, ignores polytheism.[16] Perhaps owing to the special position of the Bible and its pictures of monotheism, no overall investigation[17] has been undertaken for the conceptual unity of West Semitic polytheisms; this book aims to redress this lack. In addition to investigating these aspects of Ugaritic and Israelite polytheism, I will also ask questions about the ancient circumstances of biblical monotheism. What religious issues did it address? How did it answer them? Why did biblical monotheism make sense at the time of its emergence within the context of Israelite polytheism and against the larger backdrop of West Semitic polytheism from which Israelite polytheism emerged and of which Ugaritic polytheism was another, yet more articulated "relative"?

1. The Scope of This Study

Some years ago my friend and professorial colleague Victor Hurowitz posed a question that provided part of the impetus for this book. When he read a draft of my earlier book *The Early History of God*,[18] he scribbled in the margin of one page, "what is an *ilu*?" (This is the Akkadian word for "god.") Professor Hurowitz was quite right; this question is absolutely central.[19] *The Early History of God* discusses many different deities, but it does not address the more basic issue of what divinity is. To answer Victor's question might seem a relatively simple task. A basic approach to this question would be to take an inventory of figures called "divine" (Akkadian *ilu*, Ugaritic *'il*, BH *'ēl*).[20] Such a list in different Semitic languages would turn up not only major deities but also a wide variety of other phenomena: monstrous cosmic enemies[21]; demons[22]; some living kings[23]; dead kings[24] or the dead more generally[25]; deities' images[26] and standards[27] as well as standing stones[28]; and other cultic items and places.[29] In addition to words for "divine," Akkadian uses a special sign (called a "determinative") to mark divinity.[30] The special sign for divinity applies not only to deities but also to many other phenomena such as demons, stars,[31] the images of monstrous creatures,[32] the determined order (*šimtu*),[33] and legendary human heroes of old, such as Gilgamesh and Enkidu.[34] On the whole, such an inventory suggests that divinity was attributed not only to major and minor deities but to a whole host of associated phenomena. It is further evident that distinctions were recognized among the figures and phenomena called "divine."

In this inventory one feature stands out: apart from cult objects and places, divinity seemed to betoken status or being significantly greater than that of human beings. In general, to be divine is not to be human. So the Mesopotamian god Erra is accused of behavior inappropriate to his assigned status: "You changed your divine nature and made yourself like a mortal."[35] Yahweh reminds Hosea's audience (Hosea 11:9): "For I am a god and not a man" (*kî 'ēl 'ānōkî wĕlō'-'îš*; cf. 1 Samuel 15:29; Isaiah 31:3, Ezekiel 28:2, 9, Job 9:32). Deities and people generally constitute two different divisions within reality (Akkadian *ilū/ilāni u amelūtu*[36]; Ugaritic *'ilm wnšm*, CAT 1.4 VII 51; BH *'ĕlōhîm wa'ănāšîm*, Judges 9:9, 13; Qumran Hebrew *'lym w'nšym*, The War Scroll, 1QM 1:11). That humanity and divinity fall in two generally incommensurate categories[37] represents only a beginning point for understanding either one. In one sense we are never too far from this point in discussing divinity in the ancient Middle East. We often see how divinity and humanity are distinguished and yet treated as analogous. In itself, this approach will take us, however, only a certain distance in the discussion of divinity.[38]

The question of divinity may be approached also etymologically. This time-honored method yields controversial results for the word "god" (Akkadian *ilu*, Ugaritic *'il*, BH *'ēl*). A common scholarly view holds that the term derives from **'y/wl*, "to be pre-eminent, strong."[39] It is not uncommon to relate the Hebrew word, *'ayil*, "leader" or "chief," to this word (this word is sometimes taken to be related to BH *'ayil*, "ram," but then again this word too is at times thought to be related to **'y/wl*). This word (root) in Hebrew may also underlie **'eyāl*, "strength" (for example, in Psalms 22:20, 88:5).[40] This root has also been thought to underlie the BH idiom, *yeš/'ên lě'ēl*, "it is/is not in the power (of X to do Y)," attested in Genesis 31:29 and Deuteronomy 28:32 (cf. Ben Sira 14:11 A).[41] However, W. G. E. Watson has criticized this interpretation of this expression.[42] Seeing the West Semitic word **l*, "power" here, Watson reparses the consonants of the expression to **yn l' lyd-*, "there is no power to the hand of . . .", thus removing **'ēl* from the expression altogether. Watson's reinterpretation of this idiom may be doubted, since **l'y* is hardly a productive root with this meaning in BH; in fact, the opposite meaning is found in BH. Even so, the interpretation of **'ēl* in the expression *yeš/'ên lě'ēl* clearly remains debatable.[43] Similarly, to find an example of the Ugaritic noun in the meaning of "strength" or the like, one might appeal to Ugaritic *'ul* in CAT 1.14 II 35 (see also 1.14 IV 15) or *'awl* in 1.12 II 57. The former may mean "army" instead (though possibly based on an older sense, "strength"), while the latter word has been read alternatively as *l'akl* by S. B. Parker.[44] Even if these possible attestations of the word Ugaritic *'il*/BH *'ēl* were admissible as evidence, it would be clear that **'y/wl*, "to be strong," was not a productive root in either Ugaritic or Hebrew.[45] This fact hardly resolves the issue against this etymology, but it may suggest that the meaning "strength" was not a particular connotation of the nominal forms for "god" (Akkadian *ilu*/Ugaritic *'il*/BH *'ēl*). It is true that such a meaning would very well suit the point made earlier that deities were considered greater than humans in a number of respects, but without other examples of the word in this meaning it is hard to insist on this conclusion. Moreover, the etymology itself is hardly a matter of general acceptance. So M. H. Pope comments: "There is little point in entering into further discussion of these and other proposals. None of them carries conviction or appears to have any considerable degree of probability."[46] Finally, D. Pardee has noted some counterindications to this theory.[47] In sum, we should exercise great caution before accepting and using this etymology.

A third approach to divinity is to list and study individual deities from Ugarit and perhaps to coordinate this information further with data derived from other West Semitic inscriptions, the Bible, and other corpora from sites in Syro-

Mesopotamia. The covert, or not so covert, purpose of these operations is to recover information that advances the understanding of Israel's chief deity. (This is the overall thrust, for example, in *The Early History of God*.[48]) Although this approach emphasizes paying great attention to both philological and historical details, it tends to lack a larger coherent strategy for approaching the more general picture of divinity in any given ancient culture.

This atomistic approach may be contrasted with a fourth approach, namely a large-scale comparative approach that ventures a typology of divinity. In one of his contributions to *The Encyclopedia of Religion*, the historian of religion T. M. Ludwig discusses two types of typologies, the first a cosmic typology based on geography or realms (deities of sky, meteorology, earth, and underworld), and the second a social typology based on functions of vital interest to humanity (creation and guardians of society and order; protection and war; fertility and prosperity; home and community; healing, sickness and death; and esoteric knowledge and magic).[49] This approach runs the risk of categorization without sufficient attention to the specific cultures under examination.

This book attempts to combine the advantages of these approaches in examining the major indigenous conceptual structures that ancient Ugaritic and Israelite societies used to construct their religious reality. Part I approaches the issue of divinity by examining different groupings of divinity in the Ugaritic texts from the largest collectivities down to the smallest units. Chapter 1 diagrams the basic contrast between anthropomorphic deities and monstrous divine creatures. Here F. A. M. Wiggermann has provided a very helpful typology,[50] which, modified for Ugaritic literature, helps us to sketch the religious mapping of the cosmos. Chapter 2 examines the basic concept used to refer to the polity of deities, namely the divine assembly, studied in particular by E. T. Mullen and L. K. Handy.[51] This organization was ancient already by the time of the Late Bronze Age texts of Ugarit. Ugaritic literature develops a further conceptual coherence of divinity through the notion of the divine family. Working with the study of Ugaritic society offered by J. D. Schloen,[52] chapter 3 lays out the correspondence between the four tiers of the pantheon examined in chapter 2 and the four levels of the family household in Ugaritic society. This correspondence, and the widespread attestation of familial terminology for the pantheon, would point to the patrimonial household as the fundamental image that provided a conceptual unity for the wide variety of divinities and their multiple relations. Chapter 4 discusses different sorts of divine intersections or interrelations, including pluralities and pairings of deities. Part I attempts to show the multiple levels and types of interrelationality within divinity, or what moderns might call the "godhead." This interrelationality gave divinity its integrity or "oneness." The notion of the family household perhaps provided polytheism with the sort of "oneness" that monotheists associate with monotheism. Indeed, in a society where the highest level of social association and identification was the family and not the individual, the polytheism of a divine family would have been far more intelligible than any notion of monotheism. Stated differently, the divine family was for polytheism a sort of "mono-theism." Only through exploring all the different divine relations can polytheism be approached on its own terms. In contrast, biblical Israel has been shorn of such a divine family, leaving divinity to be imaged largely in terms of a royal organization headed by an absolute monarch.

Part II treats divine characteristics of deities by looking at their general characteristics of strength and size, body and gender, holiness and life (or deathlessness). Chapter 5 asks what characteristics deities generally share. Or, put differently, what terms do the texts use to express what deities are? Chapter 6 addresses a particularly unusual case of divine death. This exception is the god Baal, considered a classic example of Sir James George Frazer's category of "dying and rising gods." Chapter 6 addresses the methodology and viability of Frazer's claim as it has been applied to Baal of Ugarit. Here I have been influenced by Jonathan Z. Smith's massive critique of Frazer's category of dying and rising gods[53] as well as recent studies on ritual and myth. Chapter 6 also ventures a constructive step in the interpretation of Baal's death. In other words, if Baal is not to be regarded as a dying and rising god, what is the significance of his death and return to life?

Part III treats one of the most important topics in the modern study of Israelite religion, its monotheism. Chapter 7 begins the discussion by noting the deep impact on Yahweh of the god El. The formative traditions of Israel, now largely lost in the mists of time, camouflage a complex relationship between El and Yahweh. Chapter 7 in particular turns to a seminal question in the religion of ancient Israel: who was the original chief god of Israel? Thanks to the pioneering work of B. A. Levine on El traditions in Iron Age Transjordan,[54] it is possible to explore further old traditions about El in early Israel. Because the name of the god El appears as the divine element in the name of Israel, it has been supposed that El was the original god of Israel. Some evidence may point to El as the god associated with the Exodus from Egypt in some early biblical tradition. The implications for the religious origins of ancient Israel are profound, and they raise basic questions for anyone, scholar and nonscholar alike, who takes seriously the complexity of the biblical witnesses to the god of Israel. This chapter also addresses the origins of Yahweh and the problems surrounding reconstructing them.

Chapter 8 addresses monotheism in the context of the polytheisms of ancient Ugarit and early Israel. Within the Bible, monotheism is not a separate "stage" of religion in ancient Israel, as it is customarily regarded. It was in fact a kind of ancient rhetoric reinforcing Israel's exclusive relationship with its deity. Monotheism is a kind of inner community discourse[55] using the language of Yahweh's exceptional divine status over and in all reality ("there are no other deities but me") in order to absolutize Yahweh's claim on Israel and to express Israel's ultimate fidelity to Yahweh in the face of a world where political boundaries or institutions no longer offered sufficiently intelligible lines of religious identity. In its political and social reduction in the world (first because of the rise of foreign empires in the seventh century followed by its exile in 587–538), Israel elevated the terms of its understanding of its deity's mastery of the world. (All dates in this book are BC [BCE], unless otherwise noted.) Put summarily: Israel was now no nation, but the gods of other nations, including the greatest powers, were not really gods; and Yahweh was the sole force over both. Chapter 9 examines the monotheistic theologies in the priestly work of Genesis 1, the wisdom of Proverbs 1–9, and the apocalyptic of Daniel 7. Chapter 10 offers a study of the monotheistic rhetoric in what is considered the most prominent evidence of this language, namely Isaiah 40–55. The language of monotheism in this section of the Bible particularly illustrates that monotheism is hardly a "religious stage" at this point but rather a rhetorical strategy designed to persuade its audience of the reality of Yahweh's absolute power in a world where a foreign empire holds sway over Judah.

Throughout this work I emphasize the Ugaritic material. I beg readers' indulgence for the number of citations of primary and second literature, but the view expressed almost a half century ago by the greatest scholar of Ugaritic ever, H. L. Ginsberg, still applies today: "The specialist can not yet dispense with conscientious sifting of all the better writers on Ugaritica since the birth of this discipline."[56] In part, I have presented a good deal of Ugaritic material in order to present Ugaritic divinity on its own terms and in part to use the Ugaritic material as a backdrop or *Gestalt* for viewing the biblical material. Most chapters therefore contain some discussion of comparable biblical texts and ideas. One of the major roadblocks in comparing Ugaritic and biblical material involves modern presuppositions about monotheism and polytheism.

2. Issues in Discussing Monotheism and Polytheism

Modern students of ancient Middle Eastern societies and religions stand on one side of an incalculable divide, while the subject they study stands on the other. Standing between the two is the Bible and the three "religions of the Book" that it influenced. Almost all, if not all, students of the Bible have been long exposed directly or indirectly to either Judaism, Christianity, or Islam, traditions that have anchored their identity in the belief in only a single deity, however differently these three religions may define this deity. This belief, labeled "monotheism" in the modern era, separates modern scholars from the "polytheistic" religions of the ancient Middle East that they study.[57] Monotheism appears clearly in biblical texts dating to the sixth century, and it is possible to push back this date by a century depending on how the point is argued; in either case, monotheism seems to represent an inner-Israelite development over hundreds of years, not a feature known from Israel's inception.[58] Polytheism, in contrast, is represented by many different bodies of texts from ancient Mesopotamian cities such as Assur and Babylon; many sites in Syria including the Bronze Age cities of Ebla, Ugarit, Mari, and Emar; and finally, early Israel itself as well as its Iron Age neighbors. The timing of the emergence of Israelite monotheism in the late Iron Age fits what has been called the "Axial Age" by the philosopher Karl Jaspers and his followers, a period in world history (ca. 800–200) that "witnessed the emergence of revolutionary new understandings of human understanding," including the awareness of "the separation between transcendant and mundane spheres of reality."[59] This periodization of intellectual and spiritual horizons represents a broad generalization, but it illustrates how the religious worldview of early, pre-monotheistic Israel (ca. 1200–800) may share as much, if not more, with the religious outlook expressed in the texts from Ugarit (ca. 1350–1150) than with later Israel (ca. 800–200) and the monotheistic faith it eventually produced. Moreover, chapters 8 and 9 demonstrate just how central "the separation between the transcendant and mundane spheres" was to the development of the monotheistic outlook in a number of biblical texts.

Because of this great historical divide, it is difficult to remember that comparing ancient polytheistic religions with a monotheistic one is anachronistic, as the term "polytheism" only has any meaning or sense because it is contrasted with monotheism.[60] Accordingly, monotheism and polytheism in themselves hold little meaning for the ancients apart from the identity of the deities whom they revered and served. No polytheist thought of his belief-system as polytheistic per se. If you asked ancient Mesopotamians if they were polytheists, the question would make no sense. If you asked them if they or other people they knew acknowledge a variety of deities, that's a different question, because for them the deities in question mattered, not the theoretical position of polytheism. This point applies to monotheism as well. If you asked ancient Israelites around the Exilic period (587–538) if they were monotheists, they would not have understood the question. If you asked them if there is any deity apart from Yahweh, then that's also another question, because for them what mattered was the exclusive claim and relationship of the Israelite people and their deity.

The concept of monotheism reflects our modern situation as much as the circumstances of ancient Israel or the Bible, for monotheism is largely a modern concern. Monotheism's importance perhaps derived in part from contact between modern Europeans and non-Westerners, as a way of defining the Western religious traditions in contrast to non-European cultures.[61] There is a further aspect to monotheism's prominence in Western religious discourse. In the wake of the great religious conflicts since the Reformation, Western culture has learned to live with religious plurality as well as nonreligious sensibilities. Even if Christianity plays a decreasing role in people's beliefs or practice, its monotheism has continued to play a crucial role. On one hand, it has served an apparently positive social role in binding members of different Western religions and increasingly secularized people formerly of Christian backgrounds to a common "civil religion." Monotheism has served as the "sublime idea" in Western civilization in contrast to (or to avoid?) the contentious differences in actual beliefs and practices. For an increasingly secularized culture, monotheism could serve as a substitute for religious beliefs and rituals, some of which might be seen as primitive for some highly "cultured" Westerners. In the important works of the biblical scholars T. Frymer-Kensky, E. Gerstenberger, and R. Gnuse,[62] monotheism in part serves an essentially liberal point of view (theologically and politically speaking), with little connection to explicit religious tradition or praxis.

On the other hand, perhaps as part of the effects of secularity, monotheism in itself has come to be blamed for the religious problems in the West. In the twentieth century, monotheism has been criticized as a totalizing discourse that tends toward an exclusivity of others and consequently a potential for inducing violence.[63] These viewpoints, no matter where they stand on the merits and deficiencies of monotheism, assume that monotheism is a cultural or religious phenomenon in itself. These discussions have reified the idea of monotheism and disconnected it from its larger religious context. As a result, monotheism has apparently achieved a status in modern discourse that it never held in ancient Israel, where it functioned as a rhetoric expressing and advancing the cause of Israelite monolatrous practice.[64] The specifics of the practice and the accompanying dimensions of belief were considered every bit as important, if not more so, as the monotheistic rhetoric. The theoretical terms polytheism and monotheism then represent a way to pose some of the theoretical issues, and we should remain aware of this point. In this study I use the terms monotheism and polytheism as an entry point. We can then begin to ask questions about specific religions in particular times and places that involve multiplicity of deities and singularity of godhead. Accordingly, these terms serve only as a beginning for describing divinity.

During the twentieth century, it was common practice for biblical scholars to elevate ancient Israel's monotheism at the expense of the polytheism of its neighbors (especially expressed in the Late Bronze Age texts from Ugarit). Differences noted between biblical and extra-biblical literatures seem to exalt Israelite monotheism and to denigrate non-Israelite polytheism and to ignore or at least minimize, Israelite polytheism as well.[65] For example, Scholars have portrayed Israelite monotheism as a historical religion and polytheism as a nature or fertility religion,[66] or claimed Israel an ethical religion and polytheism as a pagan "deification of power and process of material production."[67] The myth of Canaan (putatively exemplified by the Ugaritic texts) contrasts with the narrative of Israel.[68] A more sophisticated analysis saddles polytheism with an order to which the gods themselves are subject, in contrast to the monotheistic deity's control over all.[69] But there is little, if any, evidence for an independent order having mastery over deities in either Ugaritic or Mesopotamian mythologies.[70] Moreover, no idea of such an independent order of "fate" exists in ancient Middle Eastern mythologies. Ugaritic lacks a word even approximating this notion, and Akkadian *šimtu*, usually taken to mean "fate," refers to a "determined course" that can be changed.[71] No hard evidence supports the further claim that polytheism involves "a vast, dark and uncomfortable world."[72] In sum, earlier generations of biblical scholars championed—as historical judgments—the very religious views to which they largely subscribed personally.[73] The religious posture of interpreters is in itself no argument against their views. However, there is little or no basis for these contrasts distinguishing monotheism from polytheism, nor is there a firm basis for the theological weight attached to biblical monotheism itself, a weight that the Bible itself hardly reflects (as discussed in chapter 8). Some of the more recent approaches to polytheism also raise questions. In a recent treatment, the polytheism that preceded monotheism of the Bible becomes immoral and impotent, reflecting a "pessimism" and even a religious crisis questioning polytheism itself, "a pantheon of disillusion."[74]

In all of these presentations polytheism stands not only as the backdrop to biblical monotheism; it serves further as a negative foil to the biblical monotheism championed by these authors. This is apologetics, not history (or history of religion). Fortunately, things have improved in recent decades. Many scholars now recognize their religious suppositions and try to set aside their own views. Accordingly, they attempt to study polytheism on its own terms. In part as a result of the more positive definitions of myth, the dichotomies drawn between myth, on the one hand, and theology and history, on the other, have been eroding. Some biblical scholars have used the label "Israelite 'myth'" for Israelite material paralleled by the Ugaritic myths,[75] and virtually equate "Israel's religious «myth»" with its "theology."[76] "Theology," a label often restricted to texts sacred to modern religious tradition, has been applied more recently to ancient Near Eastern texts besides the Bible. The Ugaritic Baal Cycle has been said to reflect a "theology,"[77] and the authors of the great conflict-myth, Enuma Elish, have been called "Babylonian theologians."[78] Similarly, biblical studies for at least two decades have recognized that history and myth do not constitute two separate categories in either biblical or extra-biblical texts. In the words of J. D. Levenson, the two "reinforce each other: history concretizes cosmology, and cosmology lifts history above the level of the mundane."[79]

Yet I have wondered if we now regard polytheism appropriately. Views of ancient polytheism seem to labor still under simplistic notions, such as the idea that polytheism was a system of division of powers corresponding to different deities.[80] In this view, each deity has a prime characteristic or profile (e.g., Baal as a storm-god) and these characteristics, or at least the positives ones, cumulatively equal the total that monotheism claims for its single deity. In other words, polytheism is simply monotheism multiplied by number of divinities and their functions. Monotheism apparently continues to affect the way we think about polytheism. This book is my initial attempt to appreciate the particular polytheism known from ancient Ugarit and the coherent understanding of reality it provided. As a product of, and adherent to, one of the three religions of the book, I too am susceptible to errors in describing polytheism in the biblical world (specifically in the Ugaritic texts); indeed, scholars will need to correct any false assumptions they detect here.

In general, my concerns in this book are twofold. I am interested in describing the indigenous notions of divinity presented by the texts discovered at Ugarit. What ideas of divinity lie behind different presentation of the pantheon? What sense of reality inheres in the descriptions of the pantheon? Only after a sympathetic reading of the Ugaritic texts will I try to use them as a backdrop to highlight comparable biblical texts. Ancient texts, both biblical and nonbiblical, provide pictures of reality[81] in narrative and other forms. We might think of the narratives or myths as communicating a picture of reality through moving pictures, of ritual and prayer as expressing a picture of reality through performative interaction, and of letters manifesting a picture through written monologue. All of these ancient texts presume and, to some extent, express an understanding of reality often couched in terms of gods and goddesses as its main figures. In short, such pictures are expressions of the "theology" of the ancient writers, the theology which they inherited and in some cases expanded to capture the nuances of their understanding of reality. From this point of view, the descriptions of divinities reflect various mappings of reality. Such descriptions afford modern scholars an opportunity to understand how reality worked for the ancients, but only if polytheistic texts can be given as much "credence" as the monotheistic texts of Israel.

I also use the Ugaritic texts to help identify and rectify stereotypes about monotheism in ancient Israel. In other words, this study uses a sympathetic reading of polytheism in the Ugaritic texts to bolster the discussion of Israelite monotheism with better theoretical foundations. I would like spell out this point. This study focuses attention on the common assumptions about divinity made by different West Semitic peoples, including Israelites and their contemporary neighbors (such as the Phoenicians, Moabites, and Edomites) as well as their predecessors to the north, especially the now well-documented people of the city-state of Ugarit. All of these peoples in the Levant, despite distances in time and space, shared many views of what deities were in general expected to be and do, although these peoples may have developed perceptions of deities specific to their cultures. As a consequence of this approach to studying deities, this book situates the religious culture of Israel within the larger setting of West Semitic religion (or what some scholars would call "Canaanite" religion). For some time now, scholars have challenged the claims made in the Bible, and often championed by its modern adherents, that Israel was originally separate from its Canaanite neighbors and that Israel's religion, so centered around the one god Yahweh, was completely different from its neighbors' religious practices and deities. Research summarized in *The Early History of God* indicates that, while early Israel recorded some traditions not shared by its neighbors, these distinctive features are relatively rare and hardly indicate a wholly different culture or religion. Indeed, the prophets seem to have been quite right in observing that Israel maintained religious practices quite like the ones conducted by its neighbors. But while the prophets thought this trend to be of secondary influence, it would seem that in fact these practices were old ones in Israel. Israel's perception of itself as a separate culture and religion destined to a covenantal life only with Yahweh grew over a long period of time. It did not leap into being on Mount Sinai at the beginning of Israel's existence as a people as recorded in the book of Exodus. Indeed, the pristine picture of Israel's relationship with Yahweh at Sinai was itself part of a later effort to clarify a distinctive religious identity for Israel, one no earlier than the ninth century as far as we know, and in the view of many scholars, hardly even this early. The Sinai narratives, largely a product of the monarchy and later periods,[82] reflect Israel's long historical struggle to understand itself as a priestly people and a people set apart for the service of a single deity, in short, a monotheistic one. With this understanding of Israel's so-called "Canaanite" heritage, in language, literature, and religion, this book works with a model of Israelite religion that developed in many diverse ways from a larger West Semitic background, or a "Canaanite" background. This term has engendered a great debate; I will therefore discuss it in the next section.

3. Problems with the Term "Canaanite"

Despite the widespread scholarly use of the term "Canaanite," I want to warn readers that I have largely avoided it in this study. It is a misleading term that often clouds analysis. In the current scholarly environment, it is impossible to escape the debate over the relations between "Canaanite," "Ugaritic," and "Israelite," as well as "Amorite." The labels "Ugaritic" and "Canaanite" have been a matter of discussion since the discovery of the Ugaritic texts. In the 1960s, A. Rainey argued that Ugaritic is not Canaanite, because one Ugaritic text refers to a Canaanite with other foreigners, specifically an Egyptian and someone from Ashdod (CAT 4.967).[83] Rainey also cites an Akkadian text from the site of Ugarit that refers to "the sons of Ugarit" and "the sons of Canaan." Following Rainey's lead, D. R. Hillers[84] has suggested that the Ugaritic texts cannot be used to establish a Canaanite culture with which to compare developments in Israel. The denial of the equation of Ugaritic and Canaanite is correct, strictly speaking, but on the basis of linguistic criteria it is possible to defend a strong relationship betwen the two.[85] I will return to this issue later.

Preferring the term "West Semitic" to "Canaanite," N. P. Lemche goes farther than Rainey or Hillers.[86] He disputes Rainey's arguments that Ugarit was not part of Canaan. According to Lemche, one letter from the king of Tyre (EA 151) includes Ugarit in the land of Canaan; yet Rainey has seriously questioned this interpretation.[87] There is the further issue of the historical significance of the term "Canaanite." Lemche argues that "Canaanite" never appears in records used by "Canaanites" themselves: "to the scribe of ancient Western Asia 'Canaanite' always designated a person who did not belong to the scribe's own society or state, while Canaan was considered to be a country different from his own."[88] Lemche sees the biblical use "Canaanite" as an artificial construct largely deriving from the post-exilic period. Lemche takes the conflicting descriptions of Canaanites in biblical and other Near Eastern texts as evidence that no such people or culture existed. In effect, Lemche relies on an argument from silence. Moreover, Lemche claims: "The Canaanites of the ancient Near East did not know that they were themselves Canaanites."[89] However, it seems odd to suppose that foreign courts from Egypt to Hatti to Mesopotamia used the term "Canaanite," but the people whom others designated with this term never knew themselves by it. Perhaps this term did not function as the primary self-designation of people from "Canaan" (perhaps their individual clan units, cities, towns, or sub-regions were the primary self-designations).[90] However, the evidence does not establish Lemche's claim.[91] Moreover, "Canaanite" has a certain utility as a geographical term essentially designating the coastal areas south of Ugarit and Alalakh as opposed to inland Syria. However, the problem is difficult, and perhaps the question of what constitutes an ancient culture deserves a re-examination in light of Lemche's study. In the meantime, because too little is known of a clearly identifiable and coherent Canaanite culture (at least from a textual perspective), perhaps it is preferable to use the broader term "West Semitic."

A similar problem of definition applies to the terms "Ugaritic" and "Amorite." This question has a long lineage, going back at least to A. Goetze in 1941,[92] and continued later by his student J. C. Greenfield[93] and most recently by R. Zadok.[94] Zadok defines Ugaritic in relation to Amorite: "Amorite is understood here as a dialect cluster extending from Mesopotamia to northern Syria. Ugaritic, which has intensive lexical correspondences with Canaanite, is not a straightforward Canaanite dialect and may therefore be regarded the westernmost dialect of 'Amorite' type."[95] In the "'Amorite' type" Zadok includes material from Babylonia, Mari, Emar, and Munbaqa, as well as Ugarit. Zadok's "Amorite" is the West Semitic material from Syro-Mesopotamian cuneiform sources in the second millennium. From the modern perspective, Amorite language and culture are particularly difficult to evaluate as grouping. The evidence varies tremendously, from the rich textual evidence of Ugarit and Emar to the Mari texts wherein the Amorite shines through the veneer of the standard East Semitic language (standard Akkadian) to the more occasional item in the record from Babylonia proper. However, Ugaritic literature shows cultural contacts with the West Semitic Amorite traditions known in Akkadian sources. In the words of A. Caubet, "Ugarit had maintained close ethnic, cultural and economic ties with the Middle Euphrates and Babylonia, particularly well documented at Mari for the early second millennium."[96] To cite one known example, both the Kirta narrative and the genealogy of the Hammurabi (Hammurapi) dynasty mention a common ancestral background.[97] The apparently shared tradition then links the Ugaritic material with those whom the urban elites of Syro-Mesopotamia knew as Amurru. Such a picture also helps to explain better the influence of West Semitic motifs that have made their way into Mesopotamian literature; witness T. Jacobsen's brilliant insight that the West Semitic conflict myth influenced the presentation of Marduk and Tiamat in Enuma Elish.[98] (This view has not been wholly welcomed by the Assyriological community, a reaction due less to scholarly arguments than to reasons involving the modern history of Assyriology and its famous Bibel/Babel controversy.[99] Yet to anticipate a point made later, if Assyriology has at times shunned biblical studies, Ugaritic studies has perhaps suffered from the opposite tendency.) Indeed, it is not clear linguistically why Ugaritic or Amorite should be clearly delineated from the West Semitic evidence of "Canaan" known from the Amarna letters. A handful of isoglosses might be invoked, such as the classic "Canaanite shift,"[100] but even such a criterion has been a matter of debate. While one can argue that this feature does not exist in Ugaritic,[101] it may also be lacking in what might be called "north Canaanite." W. F. Albright, for example, called this feature the "south Caananite shift." Thus, at this point the field can probably do little better than categorize Ugaritic, Amorite, and Canaanite material all under the rubric of West Semitic. There are linguistic and cultural advantages to keeping these terms separate, and this approach avoids the historical problems of identifying Ugaritic, Canaanite, and Amorite. In the end, perhaps we should drop the term "Canaanite" as a modern category of analysis and just pay attention to its ancient uses.

Recently, many have remarked that Ugaritic religion should not be included in discussions of "Canaanite" or Israelite religion, since it is not "Canaanite" or because it stands at such a temporal and geographical distance from Iron Age Israel and Judah. For example, O. Keel and C. Uehlinger correctly assert that the Ugaritic texts "are not primary sources for the religious history of Canaan and Israel,"[102] but such a view hardly precludes seeing the Ugaritic texts as providing some of the larger background behind the development of Israelite religion. The two societies that produced these literatures show many cultural differences: ancient Ugarit's literature was generally far more ancient (ca. 1350–1150), its kingdom far more urban, cosmopolitan, and centralized. In contrast, ancient Israel was far more rural, was far more diverse topographically and territorially, and had a lengthier history of extant literature (ca. 1150–160). This area lacked a centralized monarchy in the Iron I period and remained far less centralized even when the monarchies manage to imprint themselves on their agrarian, clan-based cultures. No matter how this cultural relationship is resolved, the diversity of later reflexes of material in the Ugaritic texts shows that mythic narratives were transmitted in the areas known in the Bible as Canaan and Israel.[103] These later sources include some Phoenician inscriptions and classical sources on Phoenician culture; biblical and rabbinic texts describing different versions of the West Semitic conflict myth; Aramaic monumental and bowl inscriptions; and late classical sources.[104] On the basis of parallels between the Baal Cycle and other second millennium texts on one hand, and the Hebrew Bible, Philo of Byblos, and other later sources on the other hand, a number of scholars have argued that the Levant, including ancient Israel, enjoyed a wide body of creation and battle myths.[105] As J. Day has recently demonstrated,[106] specific proper names and terms common to both the Ugaritic and biblical texts indicate that the Ugaritic texts remain germane to the study of ancient Israel, even if Ugarit is neither proximate to Israel nor equivalent to "Canaanite." Such specifics include references not only to deities in general terms but also to the names of their abodes (such as Baal's home, Mount Sapan, mentioned in Psalm 48:3) or enemies (such as Baal's enemies, including Leviathan and Tannin).[107]

In this connection, Ugaritic mythic material does more than refer to "Canaanite" sites (such as Tyre, Sidon,[108] and *šmk*, that is, Lake Huleh[109]). The Ugaritic corpus also contains traditions associated with "Canaan," such as the mention of Ashtaroth and Edrei, two Transjordanian sites (CAT 1.108.2–3). Vocabulary found in Israel's oldest poems and the Ugaritic texts suggest continuity in the literary tradition between these corpora.[110] In sum, the broader literary tradition between the Late Bronze Age Levant and biblical material includes the Ugaritic texts as well as material in the Amarna letters from "Canaan."[111] It is evident that ancient Ugaritic and early Israelite literatures were not completely different, especially in the general parameters of language, social structure, religious terminology, and religious practices (prayer, sacrifice, and religious experience), and even conceptualizations of divinity.[112] None of these points of contact between Ugaritic literature and "Canaanite" culture should be construed as suggesting a simple equation between them. Even so, their complex literary traditions can hardly be separated. Analysis of specifics will include similarities as well as differences but perhaps more important at this stage of research are the differences within the parallels.[113] It is precisely the differences within their larger similarities that sharpen our understanding of Israelite religion, particularly its differentiation from the larger West Semitic culture for which the Ugaritic texts constitute the single greatest extra-biblical textual witness. These distinctions do not diminish the significance of the parallels; rather, they more precisely define them. The same point applies to religion. These specific points of contact between Ugaritic and Israelite religion need not be understood as pointing to a single or "same" religion, but they do point to a larger religious tradition shared broadly by West Semitic peoples, including the Israelites.[114] Many people like to contrast the polytheism of a site like Ugarit with Israel's monotheism, but this monotheism emerged only midway through Israel's history. It was heir and reaction to a long tradition of Israelite polytheism.[115] In sum, the Ugaritic texts remain pertinent despite significant differences. Although the Ugaritic texts are not to be labeled Canaanite, late reflexes of material attested in the Ugaritic texts show that mythic narratives were transmitted in the areas known in the Bible as Canaan and Israel during the Iron Age.[116] The biblical texts also show the imprint of this mythic material and show its existence among the people of the coast in what was regarded as Canaan by the biblical authors.

4. More Cautionary Notes: Literature, History, Theology, Myth

The issue of the literary and cultural relations between the Ugaritic texts and the Bible is not the only methodological problem involved in this study. This section addresses further assumptions sometimes made by students of the Bible and the ancient Near East. An investigation into biblical and Ugaritic statements about deities assumes their validity as historical generalizations for the cultures involved, on some level. Such statements are taken to represent perceptions prevalent among those segments of society that produced them. In turn, one might infer further that the scribal groups that produced these texts were sharing viewpoints held by nonwriters, either by virtue of a shared wider worldview or by scribal groups' influence upon nonwriters, or vice versa.[117] In any event, any analysis stands at a great remove from the actual religious situations, for so little is known of them. Scholars of the Bble and ancient Middle East largely investigate vestiges of ancient religious situations behind texts, many of which remain largely impervious to confident historical reconstruction. Many critics of an earlier book of mine, *The Early History of God*, persuasively argued that the book should have grounded the religious information in it in more concrete historical or social circumstances. I have attempted to address this weakness here, but I also remain deeply suspicious of further reconstructions. It is for this reason that this work, to some extent like *The Early History of God*, stands at a greater threshhold of generalization in positing historical backgrounds to texts. There is nothing wrong with admitting the possible impossibility of a "thick description," to use Clifford Geertz's term[118]; perhaps even a thin description may be impossible. And there is nothing wrong with such a lesser enterprise; it is all that we have. And even so, it is difficult to be too careful. (So T. S. Eliot's helpful reminder from "Gerontion": "History has many cunning passages, contrived corridors / And issues, deceives with whispering ambitions, / Guides us by vanities.")

In this study, I offer a central cautionary note about highly specific historical statements correlating what deities were and did and what ancient peoples believed and acted on.[119] A glance through a journal such as *Historical Methods: A Journal of Quantitative History and Interdisciplinary History* should stop biblical scholars from offering historical conclusions marked as little more than educated guesses or working hypotheses. Even the more thematically and less quantitatively oriented journal *Comparative Studies in Society and History* should arrest our impulse to generalize.[120] Similarly, a perusal of work in historical sociology will reveal the dearth and jagged contours of the religious data available to us.[121] (Or, to twist the train of Eliot's words from his *Four Quartets*, "These are only hints and guesses / Hints followed by guesses; and the rest is prayer, observance, discipline, thought and action."). Our limited data force a sense of historical fragility: even as I nurture interpretation, I continually run the risk of creating it in my own image.[122] General considerations about deities are like dots that I am pinpointing and connecting. Deities are worthy subjects of traditional scholarship (*Wissenschaft*), yet all scholars face the same historical problem when we attempt to interpret a dataset.

For the historian or historian of religion trying to understand a wider historical context such as Israel and the ancient Near East, for the theologian attempting to understand who God was and is within a wider theological landscape such as the Bible, the methodological issue is the same. In short, my own historical interests as well as religious and theological concerns—and our guild's as well—drive this study and others like it. Because of Western historical consciousness since the Enlightenment, one cannot pose such an issue without historical context. As the Bible itself suggests, the historical context for understanding the biblical God includes other gods and goddesses. This book reflects this fundamental problem for students of divinity in the world of ancient Israel as reflected in the Bible. As a result, this study straddles the line between theology and the academic study of religion.[123] Theology generally asks normative questions of what should be believed and, correspondingly, who God was and therefore is. Theology usually works on the assumption that the identification or study of the deity is championed in some sense by the investigator. In contrast, the study of religion asks descriptive questions about what people believed, and further about what goddesses and gods including Yahweh were or were considered to do and be. Religious research may presuppose that the investigator at least sets aside her or his belief in the object of inquiry. Lately there has been a great deal of crossover between theology and religion. Perhaps they now share greater common ground after an initial history of conflict between the two fields. Moreover, theology can benefit from historical study of ancient religion that precisely profiles the biblical text, viewed as the abiding theological witness to the divine choice of Israel. The religious struggles underlying the development of the Bible are better understood as a result of historical study. The study of religion in this book should hold potential value for theology, as it explores some of the choices that Israel's eventually normative traditions rejected and selected over time.

Finally, I noted earlier that the capacity to link general statements (including those about deities) to historical *contexts* is a well-known and often rehearsed problem,[124] but doing so without wading into the current (or "post-modern") debate about theory[125] perhaps betrays a failure to engage the philosophical issues and presuppositions of our discipline. (My own work, *The Early History of God*, is a fine example.) However, this debate deserves its own separate, complete treatment. For now, suffice it to say that I attempt to describe religious reality expressed in the Ugaritic *and* biblical texts. I try to render the two without giving an implicit or explicit higher value judgment to biblical monotheism, even though I am a product of a tradition that champions it. I try to understand the perceptions and visions of reality in both sets of texts. (And I do not assume uniformity within either set of texts; there is variation in conceptualization and historical setting and development.) I know that such studies are driven by contemporary needs and traditional questions of theology. I realize that such study then is not without valuation (what study is?), yet I have tried not to "choose sides" in the descriptive and analytical task.

Given the issue of situating my own intellectual point of standing, it would be appropriate to return to the modern intellectual critics of God and belief. These figures have provided students of religion with a wide array of weapons. Their analyses are powerful, *necessary* tools in the intellectual arsenal of anyone interested in the study of religion, believer and nonbeliever alike.

> What a Marx or a Nietzsche or a Freud offers the believing community is a panoply of iconoclastic devices for smashing the idols of belief naively unaware of its origins in certain systemic distortions—be those distortions economic, philosophical, or pyschodynamic. But "to smash the idols is to let the symbols speak." . . . The burden of faith is to evoke a refined passion for the possible by way of an excavation of the distortions at the base of its origins.[126]

The tools offered by these modern icons (or idols?) pierce deeply to the human dimension in religion, and it is the task of scholars, whether they are believers or not, to offer an "excavation of . . . origins" that clarifies the ancient context of religion and ultimately the modern religious situation as well.

Believers may worry that with these tools one could claim that religion can be "explained" as human projection. However, this view represents only that, a claim or a hypothesis, validated by no more or less evidence than the conviction that religious expression reflects more than a human monologue only masquerading as a human-divine dialogue. For example, J. S. Preus's book *Explaining Religion*[127] admirably surveys the modern history of discussion about religion but finally concludes that religion can be "explained" (really in the sense of being "explained away"). Preus combines Freud's psychological views on religion with sociobologists' more societally oriented understandings of human beings. For Preus, the two add up to individual and social explanations for religion qua projection. All this is in the spirit of our age, but even a detour through Gordon Allport's critique of Freud[128] on religion is sufficient to warn students about making claims about religion as a matter of purely human projection.[129] It is unclear from any modern critique of religion that anyone is in a position to disprove the reality of religious mystery expressed in the ancients' texts, even if we probe that mystery. Modern affirmations of such faith as well as denials of it are acts of faith. Yet these critiques of religion bring us closer to understanding the human side of divine-human relations. And this is what believers and nonbelievers, believing and unbelieving theologians and historians of religion share: a desire to understand the human side of the equation in religious traditions.

Moreover, modern believers perhaps have a critical contribution to make in the study of ancient texts. Even if the structure of belief or notion of belief or divinity is radically removed from the ancient texts to which believers lay claim, they are more prepared to accept ancient religious experience, concepts of divinity, and religious tradition as valid; sometimes nonbelievers do not take seriously ancient claims made about divinity or the experience of it. I may be wrong in this view, but much of the study of Israelite religion or West Semitic religion in graduate schools hardly broaches the subject of religious experience. Yet out of experience comes literature, and out of religious experience comes religious literature. Some appreciation of religious experience perhaps then is a helpful aid in the quest to understand both biblical and extra-biblical texts. These religious texts are replete with language for the divine. Deconstruction, in S. McFague's words,[130] means that discourse is nothing but metaphor, and in religious discourse, there is nothing but metaphor.[131] Yet Ugaritic and biblical texts hardly constituted language or metaphor devoid of context. Ancient religious metaphor and experience mediated one another and both partook at once of mystery[132] and the personal.[133] The visions of religious reality reflected in the ancient texts were expressions of hope informed and focused by tradition, experience, and imagination.[134] In this experience ancients and moderns have identified "God," thanks in part to the biblical tradition. Ancient and modern religious experience has involved climbing the mountain of biblical metaphors that in turn have given shape to that experience.[135] Religious faith and practice are generated by and generate mystery, which conceals even as it continues to reveal.

Finally, I must address the potentially misleading term "myth," for the Ugaritic narratives are regarded as myth whereas biblical narratives about the Israelite god are considered historical. Many, if not most, people today think of myth as untrue and history as true. Furthermore, past attempts to identify or list myths in the Bible according to a theoretical definition, such as that found in B. Otzen, H. Gottlieb, and K. Jeppesen's *Myths in the Old Testament*,[136] are problematic because of the divergent use of the term "myth" in biblical studies since the last quarter of the eighteenth century.[137] Before discussing myths in Ugaritic and Israelite literatures, I would like to examine, at least in a cursory manner, the definitions of myth as well as their limits. My purpose is not to discuss the theoretical issues in their entirety, an impossible goal in any single essay, but to establish a minimal starting point from which to discuss the social and political uses of myth in Israelite society and the so-called demise of myth in Israel.

Today myths represent untrue stories for many people. For a modern audience, myth conjures up the world of Greek, Roman, or Norse deities, and this mythology is often considered a quaint, but untrue area of antiquarian interest. Some scholars, such as R. A. Oden, argue that the modern attitude, which is so critical of myth, derives from negative stereotypes of myth partially inherited from Christian tradition.[138] The modern academic fields of theology and philosophy, based on traditional antipathy toward myth and the post-Enlightenment exaltation of history, have at times diminished the value or truth of myth.[139] Older critical definitions of myth in the work of biblical scholars such as H. Ewald and H. Gunkel reflected this negative assessment in their formal definition of myth as stories about deities but not the Deity of Israel.[140] This view represents a Christian modification of the Grimm brothers' definition of myth as stories about deities, a definition echoed in the work of modern folklorists such as Stith Thompson.[141]

Although myth still carries a decidedly negative connotation in general culture, some modern philosophers and theologians,[142] psychoanalysts,[143] and anthropologists and historians of religion[144] have re-examined myths in a more positive manner. For anthropologists, for example, myths reveal important values about the societies that produce them. Accordingly, anthropological approaches toward myth tend to address their functions in societies rather than their formal characteristics. Unlike formal definitions, functional definitions assert what myths "do," such as "explain things." Or, for some anthropologists, myths reflect social structure or resolve social conflict.[145] Based on work in history of religions, M. Eliade[146] combines formal and functionalist criteria in his definition of myths as stories about supernatural beings; these stories are considered true because they refer to realities and sacred because they involve supernatural beings. For Eliade, myths describe origins of realities manifest in the world, and people who "live" the myths are able to affect these realities through knowledge of myths. Oden offers a similar definition of myths containing four elements:[147] (1) myths are narratives; (2) they are traditional, that is, transmitted almost always orally within a communal setting and for a long time; (3) they contain characters who are more than human in some way; and (4) they relate events from remote antiquity.[148] According to Oden's definition, virtually any biblical narrative with a long history of transmission placing Yahweh or other divine beings in the distant past is a myth.[149] Thus, on the Ugaritic side, the Baal Cycle, Keret and Aqhat, and many other texts are myths, and on the biblical side, virtually all of the Pentateuch, the Deuteronomistic History, the books of Chronicles, stories in the prophetical books, and many other texts would fall under the rubric of myth.[150] For Oden, any story mentioning Yahweh, the heavenly council, or an angel constitutes a myth. These approaches to myth are consonant with the recent erosion of dichotomies drawn between myth on the one hand, and theology and history on the other (mentioned earlier). Indeed, as I mentioned, it has been recognized for at least two decades that history and myth do not constitute two separate categories in either biblical or extrabiblical texts.[151]

Nonetheless, there are difficulties with Oden's definition. This definition does not differentiate myth from folktales, legends, and sagas, although this distinction proposed by the Grimm brothers has been maintained in biblical studies at least since J. P. Gabler in the late eighteenth century.[152] Like myths, folktales, legends, and sagas are also narratives thought to hail from remote antiquity and containing characters who are in some way more than human.[153] Ugaritic texts such as Keret and Aqhat are sometimes considered myths, but the label of myth is controverted in these cases, and O. Eissfeldt and others have regarded them instead as saga.[154] Some scholars categorize narratives focusing on human deeds of remote antiquity as legend even though deities appear in them, whereas narratives focusing on deities are considered myths.[155] With Oden, one might widen the definition of myth to include narratives involving Yahweh or divine beings and not just ones centering on divine beings, especially since, as Thompson notes, many cultures do not draw such a fine distinction.[156] And when one needs to make such a fine distinction, the validity of the definition might be questioned. Both older and newer definitions appear dictated by the discipline or intellectual traditions to which the definer belongs.[157] This state of affairs might lead to jettisoning use of myth as a literary category.

Nonetheless, a narrow, formal definition retains a certain utility on three fronts. First, Thompson and folklorists begin with a definition of myth as narrative centering on divine beings before defining the functions of these myths or including other works such as folktales with divine beings under the rubric of myth. In such a narrower, formal definition rather than a functional one, myths can be identified first and then classified by functions according to different approaches, whether form-critical, myth and ritual, anthropological, structuralist, or something else. The insights to be gained from these disciplines are by no means minimal, but for ancient societies accessible chiefly through literary and archaeological remains, a definition for the literary category of myth is a helpful starting point prior to larger claims about different myths in relation to their wider cultural contexts. Second, the narrower definition accords with the minimum view traditionally accepted in ancient Middle Eastern studies, although this situation is changing. Third, rather than regarding all depictions of Yahweh as myth, this approach does not obscure an important difference between myths, that is, narratives, and "mythic imagery," which is more prevalent in biblical texts than myth. A minimum view may begin therefore with the circumscribed definition of myth as narratives about divine beings, but without excluding narratives with only one deity such as Yahweh. For Ugaritic and biblical studies, the Baal Cycle (CAT 1.1–1.6) may serve as a useful standard for myth.[158] If there is one text that all scholars can agree is a myth, it is the Baal Cycle.[159] And if the Baal Cycle is a myth, then biblical narratives about the storm-god Yahweh are mythic.[160] As a working definition, biblical narrative considered to relate events of remote antiquity and centering on the action of at least one divine figure comparable to narrative in the Ugaritic Baal Cycle is "myth," and biblical material using divine imagery comparable to divine imagery known from the Baal Cycle may be characterized as "mythic imagery."[161] As a further distinction, I will use the term "mythic material" in this study for both "myth" and "mythic imagery."

Using the Baal Cycle as a standard, one may apply the term myth to a limited number of biblical passages including the following texts: Genesis 1–2; Genesis 6: 1–4; Exodus 15;[162] Deuteronomy 32:8–27, 33:2–5 (cf. Judges 5:4–5; Ps 68:7–8); Joshua 2:2–5 (cf. Judges 6:11–18); Job 1:6–12 and 2:1–6 (cf. Job 38–42:6); Psalms 74:12–17 (cf. 29: 3–8; 89:9–10; 104:5–9), 78:21–72; 82:1–7; 105:12–45 (cf. 106: 6–46; 107; Lamentations 2:1–8); 135:5–12 (cf. 136); Isaiah 14:12–15; Ezekiel 28: 11–19 (cf. 28:1–10); Habakkuk 3:3–15; and Daniel 7–12. Some scholars might balk at such an idea of biblical myth in the context of prayers and other biblical texts, but few scholars would deny the historical dimensions of the recitation of Israel's foundational events in Psalms 78, 105, and 106. If these psalms can be seen as containing "narrated history" in liturgical form, then so too the passages listed in this paragraph can be regarded as "myth." Like the Baal Cycle, many biblical texts reuse or reformulate older narratives about the divine warrior (e.g., Judges 5:4–5; Deuteronomy 33:2–5; Psalms 29 and 68:7–8; Habakkuk 3:3–15). While old myths were commonly readapted in ancient Israel, new myths are rarely attested. Stith Thompson remarked of new myths: "It is always easier to borrow a myth or tale than it is to construct one."[163] Israel generated relatively few new myths, and the majority of them drew on older mythic material, including the Garden of Eden and the personifications of wisdom; these are addressed in chapter 9. According to M. Himmelfarb, the tour of heaven provided by an angelic guide was an Israelite innovation.[164] In short, it may be preferable simply to regard both Ugaritic "myths" and biblical material as different ways of presenting the divine. If there is any contrast to be drawn, we might say that the Ugaritic myths offer a continuous narrative, like a modern film, whereas the biblical sources provide a series of glimpses, a handul of snapshots or frames; both derived from the same tradition of continuous narrative. Furthermore, Ugaritic myths and biblical texts present largely differing perspectives: the myths tend to focus on a divine world with little representation of humanity's participation in witnessing this divinity; in contrast, the biblical prayers and other texts with mythic imagery view divinity from the human perspective. Of course, this contrast is a matter of genre: Ugaritic prayers (such as CAT 1.119) also offer a human viewpoint on divinity.

All this by way of introduction to the many, complex methodological difficulties entailed in exploring divinity in the Bible and the Ugaritic texts.

PART I

THE STRUCTURES OF DIVINITY

Anthropomorphic Deities and Divine Monsters

There's no place like home.

The Wizard of Oz

What do Ugaritic texts and iconography tell us about the representation of divinity? This inquiry begins with the groupings of divinity in the Ugaritic texts. This initial chapter focuses on the most basic structural division in divinity in the Ugaritic texts, namely, the main distinction between anthropomorphic deities and monstrous divine creatures. Following a long line of discussion by anthropology and ancient Middle Eastern studies, especially in the 1970s and 1980s,[1] the Assyriologist F. A. M. Wiggermann has applied to the Mesopotamian organization of the cosmos an important and basic spatial distinction well-known in anthropological research: the "periphery" as opposed to the "center" (or "home").[2] This general division informs a series of correlations in urban elites' conceptual organization of time and space, between their perception of culture and the cultivated on the one hand, and uncultured and the uncultivated on the other. J. D. Schloen describes the relationship between center and periphery in Ugaritic literature in these terms:

> [T]he social "center" is thus "the center of the order of symbols, of values and beliefs, which govern the society"; thus the terms "center" and "periphery" do not necessarily imply spatial separation. For Ugarit, however, it can be argued that the social center was focused in the physical center of the kingdom at Ras Shamra, which appears to have been the main locus of administration, or ritual, and of literary activity. In this case, then, "urban-rural" is more-or-less synonymous with "center-periphery."[3]

At the heart of the center lies the household, which connotes safety and protection as well as familial patrimony and land,[4] the site denoting not only family safety but also domestic conflict. The periphery stands as a transitional zone between the center and the distant realms of the cosmos lying beyond human experience and control. Accordingly, one might prefer to propose three zones: center, periphery, and beyond the periphery (beyond the organized cosmos).

Although these general categories have been well delineated for ancient societies, scholars—with the exception of Wiggermann and Schloen—have not extended these categories to the presentation of the cosmos (or universe) in ancient
mythological material. Allowing for some flexibility, I attempt in the following
section to apply these categories to divinity and the cosmos in the Ugaritic texts.[5]
These categories may be applied to deities as well as divine geography and topography based on indigenous terminology and distinctions. Within the center, we
may note a further distinction between home and foreign. And within the periphery, what is in the periphery and experienced by humans is different from what
is beyond the periphery and beyond human experience. These subdivisions are
primarily expressed in terms of space and place.

1. Place: Near, Foreign, and Far

In accordance with this scheme, deities inhabit "near" places whereas "monsters"
or "demonic forces" do not. The division of divinity between deities and demons,
so to speak, corresponds to the mapping of divine space. CAT 1.23.65–69 expresses
a contrast between the center versus the periphery in agrarian terms, the "sown"
(*mdrʿ*) versus the "outback, steppe" (*mdbr*).[6] According to this text, the sown
contains plenty of food and wine (1.23.70–76). This use of "sown" appears also in
administrative lists, twice for royal workers (4.141 III 16 and 4.618.6), and once
for a record of wine (4.149.16). This last reference (4.149.14–16) is of further
interest, as it shows cultic devotion in the "sown": "five (jars of) wine for the
sacrifice of the queen in the sown" (*ḥmš yn bdbḥ mlkt bmdrʿ*).[7] Failing vegetation
is the object of Danil's verbal expression (ritual "prayer"?) in 1.18 II 12–25. Fields
(*šd*) are subject to both human cultivation (e.g., CAT 4.39.1–7, 4.72.2–20) and
divine ownership (1.23.28).[8]

Within the center or area of human cultivation and civilization, deities are
accorded sacred mountains or cult sites,[9] but cosmic enemies are not. One of the
Ugaritic snake-bite incantations lists the following divinities with their mountains
or cult-sites: El on mount *ks*, Baal on *ṣpn* (1.100.9), Anat and Athtart on *ʾinbb*
(1.100.20); and Dagan at *ttl* (Tuttul, 1.100.15), Resheph at *bbt* (1.100.31), Athtart
at *mr* (Mari, 1.100.78)[10] and perhaps Mlk at *ʿttrt* (Ashtarot, 1.100.41), Yarih at
lrgt (1.100.26), and ẒẒ and KMT at *ḥryth* (1.100.36).[11] The Ugaritic texts recognize
a distinction between home and foreign divinities and home and foreign cult-sites.
Although Kothar wa-Hasis's activities of weapon making (1.2 IV) and palace building (1.4 V–VII) clearly take place in the center, he has no mountain as his abode.
Instead, he is said to dwell in Memphis and Caphtor (1.100.46), perhaps a reflection of the center of foreign culture and system of trade that brought artisans at
Ugarit the materials necessary for their craft. Indeed, given Ugarit's location as a
crossroad for land and sea trade across the eastern Mediterranean, the Levant, and
Syro-Mesopotamia, it is hardly surprising to see such locales reflected in the mythological presentation of the outer reaches of the zone of civilization tied to the
home. Ugarit's trade may constitute the basis for the mythological rendering of
the connections between home and foreign within the center, with its agricultural

life, its "sown," at the heart of its basic sense of home. In short, the mythlogical center manifests a subdivision between home and foreign space.

Within this general home of human and divine order is a center point, Baal's mountain, Mount Sapan.[12] This conceptualization is evident from the description of Baal's palace on the mountain in the Baal Cycle and from the heading of one list of deities as "the gods of Sapan" (*'il ṣpn* in 1.47.1), as well as the superscription of a ritual text, "the feast of Sapan" (*dbḥ ṣpn* in 1.148.1; 1.91.3).[13] Baal's mountain is also called "pleasant place" (*n'm*), perhaps garden language that, in biblical texts, is a recurring motif for the center point of the cosmos.[14] Later West Semitic cosmology, for example in the Bible (Genesis 2–3 and Ezekiel 28), represents this sown as a garden,[15] a reflection of the divine fructification of the center. For this reason the mountain of the gods is also regarded as a garden. However, this notion of garden is scarcely developed in the Ugaritic texts.[16] In sum, the sown is the region of human habitation and cultivation; within it lies the realm of cultic activity devoted to beneficial deities. These distinctions for center may be schematized in the following manner:

PLACE HORIZONTAL SPACE

HOME	FOREIGN
'ugrtym (2.81.27, 28)	Egypt/Crete
local cultivation (e.g., Baal)	foreign culture and trade (e.g., Kothar)

SUPERNATURAL

Home Deities	Foreign deities
Cult/blessing	No cult/with blessing

Just as the center bears a subdivision, the periphery likewise shows a distinction between what humans experience in the periphery and what lies beyond this periphery. This distinction is also expressed spatially:

Periphery	Beyond the Periphery
Unpopulated zones (outback)	Underworld (*'arṣ*)
mdbr, "outback"	Netherworld (e.g., Mot[17]),
Near surface waters	Waters beyond (*thmtm*; e.g., Yamm)

In contrast to home, the periphery, or "outback," is characterized as a terrain of "rocks and brush" (*l'abnm wl'ṣm*,1.23.66).[18] The outback marks a marginal or transitional zone and the site of human activities such as grazing and hunting (for the latter, see 1.12 I 34–35, 1.92.3); here begins the area of dangerous forces. Accordingly, in the cosmic geography of the Baal Cycle, *dbr*, "outback," is part of the designation for the locale where Baal meets Mot, the god of "Death" (1.6 II 20; cf. 1.5 VI 6, 29); this place appears to be the edge of the underworld (1.6 I 8– 14). The *mdbr* is also the site where Baal's foes are to confront him in 1.12 I 19– 22.[19]

Unlike the beneficent gods, Yamm, Mot, *tnn*, and the other cosmic enemies do not have holy mountains. Furthermore, the departures from this divine topography are perhaps as interesting as the general pattern itself. For example, one divine enemy, Mot, is associated with a mountain called *knkny* (1.5 V 13). However, Mot does not live on top of his mountain. Instead, the mountain is the entrance to the underworld. The homes of the astral deities, Shahar and Shalim, understandably are in the heavens (*šmmh*, 1.100.52). Athirat has no divine mountain, although one might argue that she shares her divine husband's home (at least on a part-time basis.[20]) El's home is also of further interest. The mythological texts present it in terrestrial terms as a mountain located at "the channels of the Double-Deeps" (*'apq thmtm*, 1.4 IV 21–22; cf. 1.3 V 6–7, 1.17 VI 47–48), but one of the snake-bite incantations (1.100.3) mentions the same abode in terms of the same waters, this time identified in cosmic terms, at "the meeting-place of the Double-Deeps" (*b'dt thmtm*). As the expression in the snake-bite text indicates, El's home apparently lies at the edge between "near" and "far." Therefore, none of the locations listed in 1.100 lies beyond the orbit of what would have been considered culturally "far." Yet even with the exceptions, the pantheon as a whole is marked by the topography of the sacred mountain, for it meets on Mount ll, a peak named only in one passage of the Baal Cycle (1.2 I 20).[21] Hence, the family of the gods is located within the "near" space of a holy mountain.

A further divine mapping involves realms, a feature confined to the second tier of competing male gods and their enemies.[22] The Baal Cycle includes and builds on this divine topography of mountains and cult sites by organizing divine space additionally according to realms ruled by the second tier of the pantheon held by Baal, Yamm, and Mot. More specifically, realms are attributed only to Baal (sky), Yamm (sea), Mot (underworld), and possibly Athtar (earth?).[23] Space therefore is used in two different ways: mountains to mark proximity of deities enjoying cult and bestowing blessing of various sorts, and realms to mark cosmic competition.

2. Blessing at Home and Abroad versus Destruction

Divisions apply not only to cosmic space but also to divine powers. The first and fundamental division marks deities who meet human need and functions versus divinities who pose a human threat or destruction. This point applies across a number of genres. This distinction operates in the myths where deities largely aid humans or the natural world on which they depend. Many letters include opening greetings that invoke the gods (*'ilm*) to provide well-being (**šlm*) and to protect (**nǵr*) the addressee.[24] One letter also asks the gods to strengthen the addressee (**'zz*, CAT 2.4.4–6; see also the blessing in 1.108.19–27). Another letter specifically asks for "the gods of Ugarit" (*'ily 'ugrt*, 2.176.4–6) to bestow blessing. Although the language in these letters is stereotypical, 1.15 II provides a glimpse into one way that the divinities' blessing was thought to transpire. In this scene, Baal asks El to confer his blessing upon King Kirta,[25] with the other deities in attendance. Divine blessing apparently includes the deceased royal ancestors. CAT 1.161 invokes blessing in a ritual context involving the deceased heroes and kings, also called "god" or "divine" (*'il*) in 1.113.14–26.[26] Finally, personal names show divine benevolence. According to A. Caquot, Ugaritic personal names express a desire for health and blessing, protection and favor from deities, even though the names of the deities vary widely.[27] Some deities, especially in their capacity as patrons of one group, may undertake the destruction of others. So, for example, Anat defeats human enemies in 1.3 II, El supports Kirta's campaign against King Pabil in 1.14–1.15, and Horon is invoked by Kirta to smash his rebellious son's head in 1.16 VI. These cases, too, may be understood as expressions of blessing for humans, because they aid some people at the expense of others. Some cases, such as the mythic rendering of Anat's murder of Aqhat in 1.18, might seem to counter the notion of the deities as generally benevolent, yet this case represents human disobedience and divine punishment. It is also one of the relatively rare exceptions to the rule in Ugaritic mythic narratives. In sum, well-being, including fertility at various levels,[28] was to derive from a number of deities.

In contrast, monstrous divine powers were thought to provide no benefit but only a threat to human well-being from the periphery. Yamm, for example, is connected with the demise of Kirta's household (CAT 1.14 I 19–20). Mot is known for his destruction as well (1.127.30–32:[29])

If the city is (has been) taken,	*hm qrt t'uḫd*
(or) if Mot should attack man,	*hm mt y'l bnš*
the house of the son(s) of mankind will (should) take a goat	*bt bn bnš yqḥ 'z*
and will (should) look to the future (lit. afar).	*wyḫdy mrḥqm*

Here monstrous forces can enter the sown from beyond the periphery to threaten human life, a view expressed in equal conviction in Israelite sources. Pestilence is once interpreted as death personified entering human habitations (Jeremiah 9: 20).[30] One Ugaritic myth, CAT 1.23, narrates how so-called beautiful (but actually monstrous) divinities (*'ilmm n'mm*) roam the steppe until they come upon the sown realm, which provides them with plenty. Unfortunately, the precise import of this text has not yet been determined: does it parallel a similar pattern of threatening divinities reflecting a situation such as drought or famine? In any case, threatening demonic forces may impinge upon the center from the periphery, but they are not "at home" in the center. As a general indicator of this distinction, unlike benevolent deities, monstrous divine forces generally do not receive cult.[31]

The Ugaritic texts show a further division between the home deities who provide blessing and foreign deities who also bless. Ugaritic letters distinguish between home gods and foreign gods: "the gods of Ugarit" (*'ily 'ugrt*) in 2.16.4–6 versus "the gods of Egypt" (*'il mṣrm*) in 2.23.22 and "the gods of Alashiya" (*'il alty*) in 2.42.8. In 2.42, the gods of Alashiya follow a list of Ugaritic deities invoked in lines 6–8. Opening greetings in these letters invoke both home gods and foreign gods to bestow blessing on the addressee. The home deities may be reflected also in the heading given to the list of deities in 1.47.1 (absent from 1.118), namely, *'il ṣpn*. This expression evidently refers to the "gods of Sapanu,"[32] the home deities of the kingdom of Ugarit, perhaps identified by the mountain of Baal, the divine patron of the Ugaritic dynasty. The ritual texts further reflect the dichotomy between home and foreign gods in the title of a ritual, "sacrifice of the gods of the country (*dbḥ 'il bldn*) in 1.162.1, a heading evidently reflected in 1.91.6, "[the one] of the gods of the country" (*'il bldn*).[33] Foreign deities could stand parallel to home deities through scribal texts listing them in parallel columns, as in 1.47 (and its ritual counterpart, 1.118) and RS 20.24.[34] Or a home god and a foreign deity may have a mythical relationship. The concept of the divine family (the topic of chapter 3) could be used to represent the relationship of foreign deities. CAT 1.24 not only attests to deities with foreign names, but the relationship of a foreign deity to an indigenous one is expressed through the family metaphor of marriage. The Mesopotamian moon-goddess Nikkal (Sumerian nin-gal, "great lady") is to be wed to her West Semitic male counterpart, Yarih (CAT 1.24). Implicit in this marriage is an identification of the two as moon-deities. The text makes a point of mentioning Nikkal's family, referring to her father, mothers, brothers, and sisters (1.24.33–37). In this case, the divine family provides conceptual coherence in the face of an outsider deity through the family metaphor of marriage, the one ritual that extends family relations.

3. Animals: Domesticated versus Monsters

Benevolent deities are often rendered anthropomorphically, whereas destructive divinities appear as monstrous in character. Moreover, theriomorphic representations reflect the dichotomy between deities and cosmic enemies. Whereas cosmic enemies are monstrous or undomesticated, the animals associated with benevolent deities ("attribute animals")[35] lie within the orbit of cultural domestication.[36] This fundamental set of distinctions may be schematized in the following manner:

Benevolent Deities	Destructive Divinities
Anthromorphism	Animal gods, monsters
Domesticated species	Undomesticated species
emblematic of deities:	emblematic of monsters:
bull, calf, bird, cow	snake, serpent

El often bears the title, "Bull" (CAT 1.1 III 26, IV 12, V 22; 1.2 I 16, 33, 36, III 16, 17, 19, 21; 1.3 IV 54, V 10, 35; 1.4 I 4, II 10, III 31, IV 39, 47; 1.6 IV 10, VI 26, 26; cf. 1.128.7). In this connection, the personal name *'iltr*, "El is Bull," may be noted (4.607.32).[37] Baal is presented as a bull-calf (1.5 V 17–21; 1.10 II–III, esp. III 33–37; cf. 1.11; see more later), and here we may note P. Amiet's characterization of the bull as the storm-god's "attribute animal" in Syrian glyptic.[38] In this connection, the bull or bull-calf mentioned in the Bible may reflect the iconography associated with El and Baal. El's iconographic representation may underlie the image of the divine as having horns "like the horns of the wild ox" in Numbers 24:8, for this passage shows other marks of language associated with El. Many scholars are inclined to see El's rather than Baal's iconography behind the famous "golden calf" of Exodus 32 and the bull images erected by Jeroboam I at Bethel and Dan (1 Kings 12),[39] but this iconography has been traced back to Baal as well.[40] Here we might include not only the depiction of Baal in the Ugaritic texts but also the "fierce young bull" (symbol) of the storm-god, Adad.[41] Nonetheless, the tradition in ancient Israel favors Bethel originally as an old cult-site of the god El (secondarily overlaid—if not identified—with the cult of Yahweh), perhaps as the place-name Bethel (literally, "house of El") would suggest (Genesis 28:10–22).[42]

The case of Anat as a bird is particularly interesting as the evidence is both textual and iconographic.[43] In CAT 1.108.8, the goddess bears the title of "flyer of flyers, she who soars" (*d'i d'it rḫpt*).[44] And 1.18 IV presents Anat hovering (*rḫb*) among a flock of birds over her prey, the hero Aqhat. As he sits down to eat, she releases her air-to-ground missile in the form of her hired warrior, YTPN. In these two instances, the textual evidence is explicit. Thanks to iconographic evidence, we know that Anat's form of a bird underlies also the description of her travel to El's watery home in 1.4 IV III–IV. This text does not mention her theriomorphic form, but a drinking mug excavated from Ugarit depicts this scene at El's abode: Athirat stands before the seated El; behind his throne is a fish, signaling the water, and behind Athirat is a bird, Anat.[45] The reason for Anat's presentation as a bird may not be obvious but may be related to her depiction as a winged warrior goddess. B. Tessier remarks on the iconography of Baal and Anat depicting them together on seals: "On Syrian seals the weather god is very often associated with a winged and armed goddess, and a similar association of the weather god and a warlike goddess, Anat, is found in the mythological literature from Ugarit."[46] These scenes sometimes contain either a bull, Baal's attribute animal,[47] or Anat's, a bird.[48]

In contrast to these deities' animal forms, a number of the cosmic enemies are snake-dragons.[49] The language of dragons, known from Ugaritic and biblical texts, denotes their monstrous form. The Bible contains literary references to the multi-headed dragon of ancient Israel (Psalm 74:13, 14; cf. Job 26:13; Revelation 12:3, 13:1). CAT 1.3 III 40–42 describes Tunnanu (or less likely an unnamed cosmic enemy) as a snake-dragon:

> Surely I bound Tunnanu and destroyed (?) him.
> I fought the Twisty Serpent,
> The Potentate with seven Heads.

The god Mot reminds Baal of his defeat of Leviathan in similar terms (CAT 1.5 I 1–3):

> . . . [Y]ou killed Litan, the Fleeing Serpent,
> Annihilated the Twisty Serpent,
> The Potentate with seven heads . . .

Glyptic from Ugarit attests to the anthropomorphic warrior-god with a snake in either hand.[50] Such divine opponents are manifest in incantations as enemies of humans (as in CAT 1.82.1),[51] whereas mythological contexts describe divine opponents in the same forms yet on a cosmic scale.

4. The Head God and His Beloved Monsters

The biblical hymn of Psalm 148:7 calls on the cosmic sea creature Tannin to join in praising Yahweh. Mesopotamian culture, too, regarded monstrous creatures as subservient to deities,[52] so the kindly attitude toward cosmic monsters may not be an Israelite innovation. Indeed, this view of the monstrous enemies recalls El's special relationship with these foes, expressed through various "terms of endearment" and other nomenclature. The Ugaritic material is especially rich in terms of endearment between El and the cosmic enemies. The *locus classicus* for this phenomenon is Anat's speech to Gpn w-Ugr in CAT 1.3 III 36–1.3 IV 1:

> Why have Gapn and Ugar come?
> What enemy rises against Baal,
> What foe against the Cloud-Rider?
> Surely I fought Yamm, the Beloved of El (*mdd 'il*),
> Surely I finished off River, the Great God (*'il rbm*),
> Surely I bound Tunnanu and destroyed (?) him,
> I fought the Twisty Serpent, the Seven-headed Potentate.
> I fought Desi[re] (*'arš*), the Beloved of El (*mdd ilm*),
> I destroyed Rebel (*'tk*), the Calf of El (*'gl 'il*).
> I finished off Fire (*'išt*), the Dog of El (*klbt 'ilm*),
> I annihilated Flame (*dbb*), the Daughter of El (*bt 'il*)
> That I might fight for silver and inherit gold.

Different images are used for the monstrous cosmic forces' relationship to El. Here Yamm and Arsh are called his "beloved" (*ydd 'il*/*mdd 'il*). Like these cosmic monsters, Mot is cast with the same title elsewhere.[53] This title bears a particular cultural freight and association. Commonly taken as an expression of El's preferred feeling for Yamm, the word may more precisely denote El's legal selection of Yamm over the other gods in his family. H. Z. Szubin has insightfully commented on the legal force of the term in biblical literature:[54]

> This status invested the chosen "beloved" designee with power, authority and title and bestowed upon him special rights and privileges. In the areas of adoption, matrimony, inheritance and succession, such designations were of paramount importance for they not only determined the validity of transfer of valuable property such as ancestral estates, but also the legitimacy of transmission of office, rank and title.
>
> In controversial and disputable cases the designation of a "beloved" functioned to silence also claims and potential jactations which challenged the legitimacy of the lawfully chosen "righteous" son, king, disciple or teacher in a manner similar to the intended purpose in Solomon's appellation Jedidiah—"beloved of the Lord."

The name of this royal heir signifies Solomon's publicly taken action that legally defines this son as his heir. The titles of Yamm and Mot, *ydd 'il* and *mdd 'il*, have been compared to the name of Jedidiah,[55] but their possible legal force has gone unnoticed. These epithets mark not only El's preference for them over the other gods but also their status as his publicly designated successors. They hold a claim to divine kingship from the perspective of divine patrimony. In the context of the narrative, this preference comes at the expense of Baal, whose paternity marks him as an outsider to the divine family.[56]

Two of the other figures mentioned in Anat's speech quoted previously have animal terms associated with them. Fire[57] and Rebel are El's "pets," specifically "calf" (*'gl*) and "dog" (*klb*), while Flame is called his "daughter." The two phrases, *'gl 'il* and *klbt 'ilm*, are terms of endearment, like the expression "beloved of El" and the family term "daughter."[58] The animal nouns are very clearly understood as *'gl*, "calf"[59] and *klbt*, a female dog ("bitch"),[60] but the further significance of these two terms has received very little attention.[61] Texts proximate in time and space to CAT 1.3 III 44–45 use "dog" and "calf" to denote subservient status. The El-Amarna correspondence standardly uses *kalbu*, "dog," to express vassalage to Pharaoh.[62] The juxtaposition of this title with "servant" (*ardu*) especially indicates of this understanding of "dog": "What is Abdi-Ashirta, servant and dog, that he takes the land of the king for himself?" (EA 71:16–19; cf. 60:1–9; 88:9–11). The question implicitly compares Abdi-Ashirta to a dog that is supposed to be obedient to its owner. The same usage appears in the Lachish letters (KAI 192:3–4; cf. 195:3–4, 196:3) and 2 Kings 8:13. Certainly, "dog" was used as a term of derision for a disobedient servant as well; the point of both usages is servitude.[63] Proper names also attest to this usage for both dog and calf. Ugaritic, Hebrew, and Phoenician names containing the element **klb*, "dog," are understood in the similar sense of "servant, slave."[64] An analogous usage may underlie Ugaritic *'gl 'il* in the same context. Akkadian proper names include *A-ga-al-ᵈMarduk*, "calf of Marduk."[65] As further evidence for this notion of "calf" as a term of subservience, one may point also to personal names that use Akkadian *būru*, "calf," plus divine name.[66]

If this approach to *'gl* and *klbt* is correct, Anat's foes, *'tk* and *'išt*, are said to stand in a subservient relationship to El. Apart from support for this interpretation of *'gl* and *klbt*, this view also lends coherence to the list of enemies in 1.3 III 38–46, who would seem generally to bear a special relationship to El. For example, lines 38–39 apply to Yamm the epithet, *mdd 'il*, "darling of El." This relationship is given some context in CAT 1.1 IV, where El seems to select Yamm as the champion of the gods; this deputation takes place clearly at Baal's expense. Although no such context is provided for *'tk* and *'išt*, a comparable understanding may be involved: these cosmic enemies opposing Anat and Baal are considered the beloved servants of El. The words *'gl* and *klbt* then may connote not only animal form but also subservience, service, perhaps even endearment. Even though dogs could be a potential problem (Exodus 11:7; Psalms 22:17, 59:6, 14), the use of dog as well as calf derived from their domestication; under normal conditions, they are safe and pliable servants. Dogs helped humans care for their flocks (Job 30:1) and accompanied them on journeys (see Tobit 6:1).[67] Humans were also served by calves as beasts of burden (1 Samuel 28:24).[68]

Finally, some of the Ugaritic cosmic enemies are associated with Yamm, others with El. Within the narrative of the Baal Cycle, Yamm and El share a common trait: both are opponents of Baal up through CAT 1.2 I. Perhaps this division of cosmic characters highlights El's relationship with Yamm. Yamm, at least in the Baal Cycle, is the premier figure of El's favor. The situation is quite different in the Bible. Yamm has little mythology left in the extant biblical corpus. The other monstrous enemies survive as symbols of worldly powers in Jewish apocalyptic.[69]

5. Israelite Cosmic Enemies Tamed and Denied

At this juncture, we may take stock of the Mesopotamian and Ugaritic traditions and the comparable material in the Bible pertaining to the cosmic enemies. First of all, ancient Israel inherited the names of some of the cosmic enemies from West Semitic culture (which it shares with Ugarit). Baal confronts four foes with basically the same names in the Ugaritic material and Yahweh in the Bible: Sea (Hebrew *yām*, Ugaritic *ym*);[70] biblical Leviathan (*liwyātān*) and Ugaritic *ltn*;[71] biblical *tannīn*, Ugaritic *tnn* (*tunnanu* in the Ugaritic polyglot,[72] spelled Tunnanu in the English translation later); and biblical Mawet and Ugaritic Mot, both literally meaning "Death."[73] For Baal, most are enemies of old, but Sea (Yamm) and Death (Mot) are ongoing threats, a notion entirely missing from most biblical or Mesopotamian conflict stories, though not from biblical apocalyptic and other genres.

Second, just as these cosmic enemies are mentioned as Baal's or Anat's old enemies, they are known in Israelite tradition as enemies of Yahweh, the warrior god. Three of these enemies appear in Psalm 74:12–17:

> Yet, O God, my king from of old,
>   Maker of deliverance throughout the world,
> You are the one who smashed *Sea* with your Might,
>   Cracked the heads of the *Tannin* in the waters;
> You are the one who crushed the heads of *Leviathan*,
>   Left him as food . . .[74]
> You are the one who broke open springs and streams,
>   You are the one who dried up the Mighty Rivers.
> To You belongs the day, Yours too the night,
>   You are the one who established the Light of the Sun.
> You are the one who fixed all the boundaries of the world,
>   Summer and winter—it was You who fashioned them.

Here the cosmic enemies' defeat serves as prelude to creation. In contrast, Isaiah 27:1 presents Leviathan's defeat as a sign of the end-times. Isaiah 25:8 likewise proclaims a reversal of the power of the cosmic enemy, Death. The image of God there swallowing up Death reverses the comparable image of Death's demanding to swallow Baal in Ugaritic (CAT 1.5 I 6–8, II 2–6).

Third, biblical texts attest to the cosmic forces as the chief-god's domesticated beasts. The book of Job knows these cosmic enemies both as human foes and divine playthings. So Job himself expresses the understanding of these figures as hostile powers, when he complains against God: "Am I Sea or Tannin that You set a watch over me?" (Job 7:12; see the reference to Leviathan in Job 3:8 and the mention of the Sea and the serpent in 26:13). Yet the book of Job later declaws these enemies by rendering them not as Yahweh's enemies but as objects of divine domestication. So God responds to Job that he treated Sea at creation not as an enemy but as a new-born babe (Job 38:8–11). Leviathan is the sea creature caught by God's "fishhook" (40:25, NJPS), drawn by a rope and nose-ring. God asks Job: "Will you play with him like a bird . . . ?" (40:29). Psalm 104:26 similarly identifies this figure as a creature made for play: "Leviathan whom you formed to sport with." This view of Leviathan as a tamed pet may counter the expectation of an Israelite audience, which knows Leviathan primarily as a monstrous enemy,[75] as in the Ugaritic texts that pit Baal or Anat against such figures. However, the biblical texts treating the monstrous figures instead as pets may echo their "beloved" relationship with El. Just as the biblical material coalesced the differing imagery involving El and Baal with the national god of Yahweh,[76] so too the differing roles of the cosmic forces as foes and beloved of the divine perhaps coalesced, issuing a different configuration than what appears in the Ugaritic texts.

The Ugaritic material, however, differs from some biblical passages in a number of respects involving the cosmic enemies and the gods connected with them. First, there is the matter of whether these forces are considered divine or not. In Ugaritic, these figures are at a minimum treated as equal in power to the deities who fight them. Note the stalemate between Baal and Mot in 1.6 VI 16–22, as well as the depiction of Baal apparently slumped beneath Yamm's throne in 1.2 IV 6–7. Moreover, some of the texts mentioned before treat the cosmic enemies explicitly as divinities. For example, River (a title of Yamm) apparently bears the further epithet, "Great God" (*'il rbm*) in 1.3 III 39.[77] Included in the same list (1.3 III 38–47) as Yamm are El's beloved or pets, the other cosmic enemies; in this context it would appear that they are comparable in rank or status to Yamm. In 1.14 I 18–20 Yamm's destruction is paralleled with the havoc caused by another god, Resheph. In 1.4 VIII 45–46, Mot receives the title *bn 'ilm* (either "son of El" or "son of the gods"), the same title used elsewhere for members of the pantheon (for example, in 1.4 III 14). I mention again the destructive "beautiful gods" (*'ilm n'mm*) of 1.23. Finally, the personal name *ym'il*, "Yamm is god" (CAT 4.75 V 14, 4.183 II 2; cf. 4.588.2), likewise points to the divine character of Yamm.[78] Thus, the Ugaritic texts present these figures at least as divine in rank and power, if not in formal designation.

In contrast, many biblical passages do not accord them a status comparable to a god. Yet at one time in Israel, such cosmic foes may have been regarded as divine, and only in the attested corpus do they appear in their reduced state. For example, the personal name Yemuel (Genesis 46:10; Exodus 6:15) may well be the biblical Hebrew equivalent of Ugaritic *ym'il*, "Yamm is god."[79] However, such evidence is scant at best, and the biblical corpus shows a marked remove from the divine status that such cosmic foes could well have held in early Israel. Some examples will help to illustrate the contrast. In Psalm 74, when the enemies fight against Yahweh, they hardly compare in power with Yahweh.[80] (Contrast Baal's initial setback in his conflict with Yamm in CAT 1.2 IV, followed by victory, thanks only to magical weapons made by Kothar, the craftsman-god.) Psalm 104 mentions the cosmic waters, but they are akin to the other raw material of creation. Psalm 104 omits an account of cosmic conflict before creation, instead making the divine rebuke of the waters (a battle motif) in verse 7 part of the process of creation. No longer here are the waters the opposing monster before creation; instead, another element needs to be put in its proper location in order to play its proper part in the order of creation. The waters now in their place play a beneficial role in the divine plan. They supply drink for the beasts in verses 10–13 and presumably for the world's crops in verses 14–18. According to verses 25–26, the waters, too, provide ships with a "sea-road" (to echo a kenning in Beowulf) as well as a home for all the creatures of the sea, including Leviathan, mentioned in passing in verse 26, now as a divine plaything.

Genesis 1 likewise minimizes the cosmic waters as a divine enemy. The audience of the creation story of Genesis 1 is prepared for a cosmic conflict by the opening references to enemies in verse 2. In this passage the lack of any conflict, or even any personification of the cosmic oceans or waters, heightens the picture of a powerful God who but speaks and the divine will is accomplished. So too the passing generic reference to the *tannînîm,* contained in the created order in Genesis 1:21, conveys the notion that this God is beyond opposition, beyond any other power. Such a presentation carries an especially powerful conviction for an audience that knows and presumes the traditional stories of its warrior-god's victories over the ancient cosmic enemies.[81] Indeed, such a presentation assumes that the audience knows how such stories convey its deity's mastery over the universe.[82] Genesis 1 plays on this knowledge and thereby extends the theme of divine mastery.

Yet there is more to this passage. Not only is the conflict role eliminated in Genesis 1; even the old role of cosmic forces as domesticated has been downplayed, even depersonalized. These cosmic monsters are no longer primordial forces opposed to the Israelite God at the beginning of creation. Instead, they are creatures like other creatures rendered in this story. The narrative encloses the order of the divine creation around these monstrous enemies and, by omission, transforms them into another part of creation. This transformation in the character of the divine foe involves an alteration of theme as well as literary order. Accordingly, in placing the *tannînîm* within the narration of the created order in verse 21 instead of at the beginning of the account, the literary order of Genesis 1 contributes to a monotheistic vision. The text manifests a "monotheistic poetics,"[83] which alters the perception of reality with its created order. This reading applies not only to these sea creatures; it also works for the sun and the moon, called only "the greater light" and "the lesser light" (Genesis 1:16), titles not necessarily polemical as such but quite traditional (cf. "great light," *nyr rbt,* for the Ugaritic sun-goddess in CAT 1.161.19,[84] and "light of the heavens," *nrt šmm,* for the Ugaritic moon-god in 1.24.16, 31). In Genesis 1 these figures are no longer divinities.[85] Instead, like the sea creatures, they appear within the created order. Here, ambiguity between Creator and creatures is resolved; there is no middle ground left in Genesis 1's "monotheistic poetics."

As this discussion indicates, Genesis 1 shows some displacement from the traditional picture of both the chief god and the monstrous forces. The book of Job, too, shows some important differences. The book does not simply echo the earlier roles in the Ugaritic texts, at least for the chief god. For Job modifies the portrait of God compared to that of either El or Baal. In Job 38:1 this god appears not in westerly storm-cloud, a traditional locus of Baal's theophany (or in human dreams, El's usual medium of communication with humans). Instead, God appears in the storm of the dust-cloud, the "whirlwind" (*haśśĕʿārâ,* Job 38:1), the dessicating wind of the eastern desert, a natural force (associated mythologically, if anything, with Mot, the god of death). This motif in Job signals that God rules not only the domesticated human sphere but also realms undomesticated, even unknown by humans; therefore, the divine cannot be controlled or tamed by human assumptions.[86] For humans, the divine is accessible and therefore to that extent domesticated, yet this God moves about in the unknown reaches of the universe. This God knows the known and unknown; this God belongs not only to the center but also to the periphery and well beyond. And so God is the God Job knew not only from of old but also met for the first time (Job 42:5). "Home is where one starts from," we are told by T. S. Eliot (*Four Quartets*), and the point applies to human perception of the divine. To know the God of Job starts at home but requires visiting realms beyond the home, as Job shows in his discovery of the divine in the whirlwind.

I would like to end this chapter with a comment on a remark made by G. E. Mendenhall: "Dualistic mythology is always essentially political."[87] Mendenhall meant polytheistic mythologies of power, but if such a comment applies to a polytheistic mythology such as the Baal Cycle or Enuma Elish, it may apply as well to biblical presentations of such conflict. Such mythological conflicts may involve either divine strength or power, or its lack. For example, in Enuma Elish, Marduk's defeat of Tiamat, a foe at the outset presented in majestic terms, is definitive, and his mastery over the cosmos is complete. As I noted before, Yahweh's dominion in Genesis 1 is so great that conflict is assumed and transcended. We might be content to say that deities' mastery over their enemies expresses the well-being of those who composed such a plot. Most of these texts are political expressions about deities rendered through mythological narrative and paralleled by the human experience that inspires such narrative.

However, "dualistic mythology," to use Mendenhall's expression, expresses not only political power; it clearly has the flexibility to express political or communal weakness, even desperation. Psalm 74 presents a recollection of divine victory of the past at a time of human powerlessness. Psalm 74:12–17 in particular appeals to divine strength at a moment of perceived divine weakness or indifference. In this case, Yahweh's mastery is not fully realized; for ancient Israelites, this divine dominion is in fact a debatable matter. So, too, in passages such as Isaiah 27:1, where the prospect of divine victory is held out for a future time. Yahweh here has not yet exercised complete mastery over the cosmos. Isaiah 51:9–11 likewise can proclaim the power of Yahweh over the cosmic enemy as an expression of hope and herald to human weakness at the time of exile. If Genesis 1 is to be situated against the backdrop of foreign empires' imposing their power upon Judah,[88] then again divine mastery stands in inverse relation to the political status of the text's author(s). Such a lack of divine mastery is also apparent in Baal's need for help from other deities and his lack of definitive victory over Sea and Death.[89] In these cases, we might reverse Mendenhall's comment. Here "dualistic mythology" stands contrary to the political condition of the author's community. Divine power can encode human power as well as human powerlessness. This, too, is a political statement that a community retains a sort of control over its identity despite its political powerlessness. The conflict between the divine hero and the divine enemy may encode the condition of the human community against a terrestrial threat that may be overwhelming. Finally, these mythologies, monotheistic and polytheistic, are ultimately not "dualistic." Instead, various lines subtly connect the deities and their blessing and the divine monsters. No hero is great without a great enemy to defeat, and few cosmic enemies exist without a hero to vanquish them. Accordingly, pure political power is not the essence of dualistic mythology. Instead, narratives of divine conflict composed at moments of political power or powerlessness are expressions of vision or hope. Some conflict narratives present either an existing political order (hence Mendenhall's sentiment) or an emerging order or even a nonexistent order that is hoped for. This order, real or unrealized, is a source of blessing, or at least it expresses hope for blessing as of yet unknown, of things unseen. Hope then seems to be the key trope in these texts.[90]

The Divine Council

> Well ye have judged, well ended long debate,
> Synod of gods, and, like to that ye are,
> Great things resolved
>
> John Milton, *Paradise Lost*,
> Book II, 390–92

1. The Language of Council

It is not uncommon for Bronze Age texts from Mesopotamia and Syria to refer to the general collectivity of deities as a "council" or "assembly." Indeed, this divine social structure seems to be the dominant way to refer to the gods and goddesses as a group.[1] Mesopotamian literature attests to "the assembly of the gods" (*puḫru ilāni*) in a number of different contexts.[2] The Ugaritic texts also use this language extensively to refer to the deities.[3] Apart from the expression "meeting of the gods" (*'dt 'ilm*), which is confined to one section of Kirta (1.15 II 7, 11), the terminology for the general assembly involves the root, **pḫr*. The usages with this term might be divided into three categories:

- "the assembly of the gods," *pḫr 'ilm* (1.47.29, 1.118.28, 1.148.9)
- "the assembly of the divine sons," *pḫr bn 'ilm* (1.4 III 14)
- "the assembly of the council," *pḫr m'd* (1.2 I 14, 15, 20, 31)

The meaning of Ugaritic *pḫr* is suggested not only by the ample attestation of its cognate term *puḫru* in Akkadian[4] but also by its use in the Ugaritic texts. In 1.23.57 the word refers to a group: "and the assembly sings" (*wyšr pḫr*). In 1.96.9, 10, the word is apparently parallel to "gate" (*ṯġr*). These passages illustrate the sensibility of what Ugaritic *pḫr* designated, namely, a group (1.23.57) and perhaps the location where that group meets (1.96.9–10?). The contexts of the other non-divine attestations are unclear (1.84.41; 4.17.2). In the cases listed, the word might denote the pantheon as a generic whole without reference to any particular deity. The word *'ilm* in this first category may mean either "gods" or the name "El" with final *-m*. In favor of the first option,[5] we might contrast the expression, "the assembly of the sons of El," *mpḫrt bn 'il*, where the lack of *-m* on the final word marks it as a singular noun and hence the god's name. Accordingly, one might not be inclined to view these expressions of assembly as El's assembly as such. To put the point differently, the mythological texts may present El as the head of the divine assembly, but the terminology embedded in the expressions for assembly here might not refer specifically to him.[6]

Accordingly, the word "assembly" (*pḫr*) may refer to more restricted groupings of deities centered around particular gods. In contrast to the more inclusive expressions noted thus far, these expressions clearly name a specific god:

El

"the assembly of the sons of El," *mpḫrt bn 'il* (1.65.3; cf. 1.40.25, 42; cf. 34); cf. *bn 'il* (1.40.33, 41, and its reconstruction in parallel lines in the same text, lines 7, 16, 24; 1.62.7; 1.65.1; 1.123.15).

"the circle of El," *dr 'il* (1.15 III 19)

"the circle of El and the assembly of Baal" *dr 'il wpḫr b'l* (1.39.7; 1.62.16; 1.87.18)

"the circle of the sons of El," *dr bn 'il* (1.40.25, 33–34)

"the assembly of the stars," *pḫr kbbm* (1.10 I 4), possibly parallel to "sons of El," *bn 'il* and "the circle of those of heaven," *dr dt šmm* (1.10 I 3, 5)

Baal

"the assembly of Baal," *pḫr b'l* (1.162.17); cf. *dr 'il wpḫr b'l* (1.39.7; 1.62.16; 1.87.18).

Ditanu

"the assembly of the collectivity of Ditanu," *pḫr qbs dtn* (1.15 III 15; cf. line 4; 1.161.3, 10).

These expressions suggest a more particular organization than the pantheon as a whole, namely, various groupings centered around a specific divine figure. These may represent the families of these patriarchal figures. This paradigm is evident in the case of 1.40.33 where "the circle of the sons of El" (*dr bn 'il*) is preceded by "the sons of El" (*bn 'il*).[7] These examples also show the terms, "circle" (*dr*) and "collectivity" (*qbṣ*).[8] The term *dr* might be rendered either "council" or "circle," or perhaps better "collectivity," based on "the collectivity of priests" (*dr khnm*) in 4.357.24.[9] In sum, the terminology of *pḫr* + divine name reflects different divine "assemblies," one belonging to El, a second to Baal, a third to Ditanu. As the next section claims at greater length, none of these represents the pantheon as a whole.[10] Of the expressions I listed, "the circle of El and the assembly of Baal" (*dr 'il wpḫr b'l*) in 1.39.7 and 1.41.16//1.87.17–18, seem to refer to the pantheon as a whole as the sum of two parties named according to the two chief gods; if correct, it would imply that *dr 'il* does not constitute the pantheon as a whole.[11]

The general Ugaritic pantheon may lie behind the enigmatic expression in 1.47.1, *'il ṣpn*, "the gods of Sapan," given the rather inclusive listing of deities that follows (note also the collective *pḫr 'ilm* in line 29 of this text); if correct, subsuming the deities under the rubric of Baal's mountain would reflect the divine leadership of Baal over the pantheon. F. M. Cross offers a wider definition of the pantheon as a whole (1.3 V; 1.4 IV–V; 1.17 VI): wherever two or more deities with El are present, there the general divine assembly meets, even if the terminology of council is absent from the passage.[12] However, there is no reason to assume that the mythological scenes describing El at his abode involve (even as *pars pro toto*) the general pantheon, perhaps only El's more immediate assembly. Indeed, the language of assembly is missing from these scenes, and their rendering of El's abode differs markedly from the description of the divine council.[13] The issues are admittedly complex and the data debatable, but given these differences in the rendering of El's abode and the site of the divine council, caution in identifying them is in order; the same point may apply to the language of El's council and the pantheon more generally.

2. The Assemblies of El and Baal

In the case of the "circle of El" (*dr 'il*) and "circle of the sons of El" (*dr bn 'il*), there is apparently not much, if any, real difference in the referents of these two expressions: both refer to a group centered around El. In the case of the parallelism of *'ilm//dr 'il* in 1.15 III 18–19, the latter phrase seems to specify the former word, as is common for the parallel "B-term" in Ugaritic poetry. El's assembly seems to be denoted further by "the assembly of the stars," *phr kbbm* (1.10 I 4), since this phrase seems to parallel "sons of El," *bn 'il* and "the circle of those of heaven," *dr dt šmm* (1.10 I 3, 5). To anticipate the next chapter, this text, if correctly understood, adds to the information supporting the view that El's family may be astral in character.

Perhaps the most interesting text involving El and his assembly is 1.65. This text seems to provide a restricted listing of those associated with El's council and family as opposed to the more general divine council:[14]

1	El,[15] the sons of El,	*'il bn 'il*
2	The circle of the sons of El	*dr bn 'il*
3	The assembly of the sons of El,	*mphrt bn 'il*
4	TKMN and SHNM[16]	*tkmn w šnm*
5	El and Athirat	*'il w'atrt*
6	The Mercy of El,[17]	*hnn 'il*
7	The Constancy of El,	*nsbt 'il*
8	The Well-being of El,	*šlm 'il*
9	The god *hš* (?),[18]	*'il hš*
	The god Adad,[19]	*'il 'add*
10	Baal Sapan,	*b'l[20]spn*
10–11	Baal of Ugarit,	*b'l 'ugrt*
12	By the spear of El,[21]	*bmrh 'il*
13	By the axe of El,[22]	*bn'it 'il*
14	By the weapon of El,[23]	*bsmd 'il*
15	By the strength (?) of El,[24]	*bdtn 'il*
16	By the incandescence (?) of El,[25]	*bšrp 'il*
17	By the firmness of El,[26]	*bknt 'il*
18	By the vigor (?)[27] of El:	*bgdyn 'il*
19	The sons of El (?).[28]	*bn 'il*

This cast of characters in lines 1–5 belongs to El's own household, not the company of the pantheon in general.[29] The same limited group, without Athirat, is the object of devotion in the ritual text, 1.40.[30] Athirat is El's spouse, and TKMN and SHNM play the role of the pious sons (as presented in 1.17 I 30–31, II 5–6, 19–20), who hold the hand of the drunken El in 1.114.[31] Despite the many difficulties involved in the interpretation of CAT 1.65, this text provides some further information about the assembly centered on El. CAT 1.65 twice lists "the sons of El" (*bn 'il*), in contrast to *bn 'ilm* known in other Ugaritic texts. Instead, this latter phrase may be understood as "the divine sons." Similarly, *mpḫrt bn 'il* and *pḫr 'ilm* are not necessarily the same; *pḫr 'ilm* denotes the "assembly of the gods" (1.47.29 = 1.118.28), as indicated by the Akkadian equivalent *puḫur ilāni* in RS 20.24.[32]

Finally, CAT 1.65—if correctly interpreted—may suggest the secondary incorporation of Baal into El's family, perhaps reflecting Baal's important place in the pantheon for the Ugaritic dynasty. This text perhaps provides further "mythological information" about El, namely, that within his cult he was considered a warrior (lines 12–14) and that it is his power that shows care for the city of Ugarit. Following G. del Olmo Lete, N. Wyatt compares the weapons in this text with the ritual use of weapons attested at Emar and Mari.[33] Perhaps such an allusion to weaponry in 1.65 suggests the ongoing martial role of El in Ugaritic thought, despite the ascendant position of Baal. Indeed, it has often been claimed that El is a warrior in the Ugaritic texts,[34] but the evidence marshaled to date is so poor that the view has been characterized as "unfounded."[35] However, most, if not all, treatments of this question overlook the possible relevance of 1.65.12–14, but caution is in order here as well, for *'il* in these lines may simply denote each weapon as "divine," in which case they could signify Baal's weapons. In any case, if El ever had any martial role in Ugaritic tradition, Baal's status in the pantheon may have displaced it.[36]

The mythological picture of Baal's dependents would include perhaps his "sister" Anat, his three "daughters" (Pidray, Arsay, and Tallay),[37] his messengers (Gpn w'Ugr), and his meteorological vanguard described in CAT 1.5. V 7–9.[38] Ritual texts (1.47.26, 1.84.8, 1.109.21, 1.118. 25, 1.148.8; cf. 1.84.7, 1.139.6, 1.162.12) refer to *'il t'dr b'l*, "Baal's divine helpers" (cf. the personal name, "Baal is help," *b'lm'dr* in 4.172.3, 4.266.3, and 6.16.1),[39] and these figures might be identified with Baal's meteorological retinue of 1.5 V 7–9. Glyptic supplements the textual evidence. In one scene the storm-god standing astride a quadraped is accompanied by a figure holding weapons; perhaps this figure is a member of Baal's retinue.[40] It is unknown how these collectives may relate to *mhr b'l wmhr 'nt* in 1.22 I 8–9 (cf. 1.22 II 7). Even so, it would seem that somehow these groups serve Baal and Anat. The mythological texts take no interest in identifying either Baal's spouse or the precise terms of his brother-sister relationship to Anat (half-sister?).[41] Then again, the consorts of gods within the pantheon's second tier (described in the next section) are rarely a matter of mythological speculation. As noted in chapter 1, the exception of Nikkal wa-Ib (CAT 1.24) involves marriage of a goddess outside the Ugaritic pantheon to an insider god, Yarih. The ritual texts do not clarify the identity of Baal's spouse.

3. The Divine Council and Its Four Tiers

Clearly one of the main activities of the general assembly is feasting. This activity forms the backdrop to narrative action, (e.g., the assembly's surrender of Baal to Yamm in 1.2 I, the insult suffered by Baal in 1.4 III, and the blessing of Kirta by the assembly in 1.15 II). These scenes confirm deities from four levels in the pantheon.[42] The highest rank is held by El, who shows his status in presiding over the pantheon and in issuing decrees. Both F. M. Cross and E. T. Mullen emphasize El's roles in the general assembly, especially for establishing corporate decisions and actions. With El is his consort, Athirat, who may influence his decisions, as in her petition to El to give permission for the building of Baal's palace in 1.4 IV–V. She may even participate in the decision-making process, perhaps in the selection on a successor to Baal in 1.6 I. It has often been suggested that Athirat in these instances reflects the role of the royal wife (though not the royal mother), who intercedes with her husband in political matters that affect the well-being of her sons.[43] This view is consistent with Athirat's standard title "Lady," *rbt* (e.g., 1.4 I 13, 21, 28, II 28, 31, III 25, 27, 28, 34, IV 31, 40, 53, 1.6 I 44, 45, 47, 53) and with the use of the epithet *rabītu* for royal wives in the Akkadian texts from Ugarit.[44]

The second level of the pantheon includes the royal children, called the seventy sons of Athirat (1.4 VI 46).[45] It is possible that this tier also receives the general designation *'ilm rbm*, "the great gods," which Mullen compares with Akkadian *ilū rabûtum*.[46] According to Mullen, "the Lord of the great gods" (*'adn 'ilm rbm*) refers to El in 1.124.1–2, but this interpretation is open to question.[47] The usage of *'ilm rbm* is quite limited (1.107.2); an interesting detail, 4.149.1–2 refers to *bt ilm rbm*. The deities belonging to the second tier include major figures of the pantheon: Anat, Athtart, Athtar, YD'-YLHN, Shapshu, Yarih, Shahar, and Shalim. Here Baal is an outsider, but despite his status as an outsider, he can claim some sort of familial relation to El; like the other deities (1.3 IV 54; 1.92.15), Baal can refer to "Bull El" as his father (1.3 V 35; 1.4 IV 47; cf. 1.4 I 5).

Combat and conflict generally involve this level of the divine family. References to conflict against cosmic enemies are confined largely to Baal and Anat (cf. 1.83). Similar rank along lines of military prowess is implied for other figures of this rank. Athtar's nomination to Baal's throne suggests a martial view of him, though he hardly measures up to Baal (or at least his throne). Given her military character in Egypt,[48] Athtart would appear also to reflect this martial dimension of the second tier of the pantheon. A further distinctive point about the second tier involves nature. Many deities of the second rank are associated with nature or natural phenomena in the Ugaritic texts. This point extends to Baal, Yamm, Mot, and Athtar, but also to Shapshu, Yarih, Shahar, and Shalim. (Parenthetically, the next chapter explores the astral character of the divine family of El and Athirat more generally, but the astral nature of these two divine parents remains in the background of the Ugaritic texts.)

The issue of natural fertility is also a matter for the second tier. Deities are sometimes thought to have control over (or even "be"!) forces of nature, but in fact such an association in the Ugaritic texts appears to be confined to the second tier. An important caveat: the language of identification of natural "forces" with deities is reductionistic and potentially misleading; perhaps one may say that the terrestrial manifestation of deities in this tier occurs in specific natural realms or phenomena. Indeed, it is important to be careful because nature, though seemingly emphasized in a text like the Baal Cycle, is rarely stressed in either proper names, prayers, or incantations. In iconography, too, Baal's weaponry comes to the fore, although the so-called Louvre stele depicts the storm-god's spear with features of a plant.[49] Without the Baal Cycle, scholarly assessments of Baal would emphasize far more his warrior role than his role as storm-god. The two roles certainly cohere, but across genres and in the iconography the martial role is more prominent.[50]

The third level of the pantheon is poorly represented in the Ugaritic texts, but the figure who comes to mind is Kothar wa-Hasis. He serves the upper two tiers of the royal family; they need his services. He is ordered by El to build a palace for Yamm (1.1 III; 1.2 III). Kothar also makes a weapon for Baal (1.2 IV), and later he builds a palace for him (1.4 V–VII). M. S. Smith suggests that:

> Kothar occupies a "middle" position between the great deities El, Baal, Athirat and Anat, and the lesser deities in the Baal cycle. He performs numerous services for them. His wisdom is superior to that of at least one of his divine superiors, Baal. The god serves him in CTA 4.5.107–110 [= KTU/CAT 1.4 V 45–8], but all the while he acts in the role of divine servant. He is the "general factotum" of the great gods and goddesses of the pantheon, as his services extend beyond craftsmanship into spells, advice, and wisdom.[51]

Like figures in the top two tiers, Kothar may be regarded as royalty, reflected in the personal name, *ktrmlk*.[52] By the same token, his homes in Egypt and Crete signal his place outside the immediate orbit of the upper two tiers and their homes in Syro-Mesopotamia. Perhaps this tier represents a particular development at Ugarit reflecting not only foreign trade, as reflected by Kothar's homes, but also the important place of craftsmen in Ugaritic society. Moreover, as a foreigner, Kothar would be marked as outside the indigenous pantheon.

The fourth level of the pantheon includes minor deities who serve other deities, such as the messenger-gods (discussed in the next chapter). Other minor gods serving in the retinue of major deities might also be placed at this level, such as those collectivities that serve as the military retinue of a major deity. (This question is addressed further in chapter 4, section 1.) Finally, other minor divinities may be placed at this level. The "divine workers [or staff]" ('*inš 'lm*, literally, "men of the gods") are included as recipients of sacrifices (e.g., 1.41.27).[53] A final observation: according to Mullen, the Mesopotamian council would not have included the lower tiers of the pantheon, such as workers or servants: "[T]he gods who constituted the membership of the council were specifically the major gods of the pantheon."[54] Mullen's comment may seem to overgeneralize for ancient Mesopotamia, but it suggests that the Mesopotamian notion of assembly covers fewer levels of divinity than what we find in West Semitic texts.

4. Israel and the Tiers of the Pantheon

One can subject ancient Israelite texts to the same sort of analysis of divine tiers, as the Bible manifests the language of the divine assembly. A number of scholars have discussed the language of assembly, especially in the Psalms and other poetic books.[55] Moreover, the presentation of Yahweh as a king enthroned and surrounded by his heavenly hosts can be found in many biblical passages, such as 1 Kings 22, Isaiah 6, and Daniel 7. L. K. Handy provides a helpful description of the four-tiered pantheon of the Ugaritic texts and the Judean kingdom prior to its fall.[56] At the top of the Judean pantheon stands the divine couple, Yahweh and Asherah. Many scholars believe that the asherah in the Jerusalem temple was none other than the symbol of the goddess (2 Kings 17:16), either a tree or wooden pole, and that the image (*pesel*) was hers ("the image of the asherah/Asherah," 2 Kings 21: 7); this evidence would suggests that Asherah was a goddess venerated in the Jerusalem temple devoted to Yahweh and was therefore regarded as his consort. To this evidence, scholars would add the eighth-century inscriptions from Kuntillet 'Ajrud and Khirbet el-Qom that mention "Yahweh and his asherah."[57] Some commentators simply regard "asherah" here as the name of the goddess, whereas others see it as her symbol, since divine names generally do not take a pronominal suffix. In either case, most scholars who comment on these inscriptions' references to asherah use them to support the idea that Yahweh and Asherah were a divine couple in ancient Israel and Judah. Although such putative "ditheism" was criticized by prophetic critics from the eighth century onward and transmuted into more acceptable forms (such as personified Wisdom rendered also as a tree in Proverbs 3), some argue that this form of worship of Yahweh was well known. Indeed, prophetic condemnations are often taken precisely as evidence for such worship; after all, so goes the reasoning, why condemn something unless it is a problem?[58]

What is clear from biblical criticisms of the asherah is a paradigmatic shift away from the model of the divine couple in charge of the four-tiered pantheon to a single figure surrounded by minor powers, who are only expressions of that divinity's power. This is evident from the information marshaled for the second and third tiers of the pantheon. According to Handy, Yahweh was the king of the heavenly host of deities, with only scattered references to these midlevel deities having survived; more such divinities are now lost due to the editing of later monotheists. In other words, the paradigm of the pantheon went through a process of collapse and telescoping (aspects of a larger process of convergence in Israelite religion). There is no full-scale second tier represented in the extant biblical texts. Instead, there are few references to deities whose names might be recognized from the Ugaritic texts as figures belonging to this tier; and there is little evidence that in ancient Israel they held the roles assigned to them at Ugarit. For example, the names of Resheph, Deber and Astarte are at times little more than generic nouns in the Bible.[59] In other instances, the names of such deities reflect considerably more. For example, the divinities Resheph and Deber appear in Habakkuk 3:5 as part of Yahweh's theophanic retinue.[60] Such a text would seem to reflect already the reduction of other members of the second tier to Yahweh's servants similar to

Baal's theophanic retinue described in CAT 1.5 V 6–9. In general, the evidence that Yahweh headed a pantheon consisting of other figures known from the second tier of the Ugaritic texts is unfortunately vestigial.

One biblical text that presents Yahweh in an explicit divine council scene does not cast him as its head (who is left decidedly mute or undescribed, probably the reason why it survived the later collapsing of the different tiers). This text is Psalm 82,[61] which begins in verse 1:

> God (*'ĕlōhîm*) stands in the divine assembly/assembly of El (*'ădat 'ēl*),
> Among the divinities (*'ĕlōhîm*) He pronounces judgment.

Here the figure of God, understood as Yahweh,[62] takes his stand in the assembly. The name El was understood in the tradition—and perhaps at the time of the text's original composition as well—to be none other than Yahweh and not a separate god called El. In any case, the assembly consists of all the gods of the world, for all these other gods are condemned to death in verse 6:

> I myself presumed that You are gods,
> Sons of the Most High (Elyon),
> Yet like humans you will die,
> And fall like any prince.

A prophetic voice emerges in verse 8, calling for God (now called *'ĕlōhîm*) to assume the role of judge of all the earth:

> Arise, O God, judge the world;
> For You inherit all the nations.

Here Yahweh in effect is asked to assume the job of all gods to rule their nations in addition to Israel.[63] Verse 6 addresses the gods as "the sons of Elyon," probably a title of El at an early point in biblical tradition (cf. El Elyon mentioned three times in Genesis 14:18–20). If this supposition is correct, Psalm 82 preserves a tradition that casts the god of Israel in the role not of the presiding god of the pantheon but as one of his sons. Each of these sons has a different nation as his ancient patrimony (or family inheritance) and therefore serves as its ruler. Yet verse 6 calls on Yahweh to arrogate to himself the traditional inheritance of all the other gods, thereby making Israel and all the world the inheritance of Israel's God.

This family view of the divine arrangement of the world appears also in the versions of Deuteronomy 32:8–9 preserved in Greek (Septuagint) and the Dead Sea Scrolls:

> When the Most High (Elyon) alloted peoples for inheritance,
> When He divided up humanity,
> He fixed the boundaries for peoples,
> According to the number of the divine sons:
> For Yahweh's portion is his people,
> Jacob His own inheritance.

The traditional Hebrew text (Masoretic text, or MT) perhaps reflects a discomfort with this polytheistic theology of Israel, for it shows not "divine sons" (*bĕnê 'ĕlōhîm*), as in the Greek and the Dead Sea Scrolls,[64] but "sons of Israel" (*bĕnê yiśrā'ēl*).[65] E. Tov labels the MT text here an "anti-polytheistic alteration."[66] The texts of the Septuagint and the Dead Sea Scrolls show Israelite polytheism which that focuses on the central importance of Yahweh for Israel within the larger scheme of the world; yet this larger scheme provides a place for the other gods of the other nations in the world. Moreover, even if this text is mute about the god who presides over the divine assembly, it does maintain a place for such a god who is not Yahweh. Of course, later tradition could identify the figure of Elyon with Yahweh, just as many scholars have done.[67] However, the title of Elyon ("Most High") seems to denote the figure of El, presider par excellence not only at Ugarit but also in Psalm 82.

The author of Psalm 82 deposes the older theology, as Israel's deity is called to assume a new role as judge of all the world. Yet at the same time, Psalm 82, like Deuteronomy 32:8–9, preserves the outlines of the older theology it is rejecting. From the perspective of this older theology, Yahweh did not belong to the top tier of the pantheon. Instead, in early Israel the god of Israel apparently belonged to the second tier of the pantheon; he was not the presider god, but one of his sons. Accordingly, what is at work is not a loss of the second tier of a pantheon headed by Yahweh. Instead, the collapse of the first and second tiers in the early Israelite pantheon likely was caused by an identification of El, the head of this pantheon, with Yahweh, a member of its second tier. This development of convergence will be explored further in chapter 7.

This development would have taken place by the eighth century, since Asherah, having been the consort of El, would have become Yahweh's consort (mentioned before) only if these two gods were identified by this time. Indeed, it is evident from texts such as Isaiah's vision of Yahweh surrounded by the Seraphim (Isaiah 6), and especially the prophetic vision of the divine council scene in 1 Kings 22:19 that Yahweh assumed the position of presider by this time. Indeed, prior to the eighth century such a "world theology" suited the historical circumstances in Israel very well. In the world order there were many nations, and each had its own patron god. This worldview was cast as the divine patrimonial household in Deuteronomy 32: each god held his own inheritance, and the whole was headed by the patriarchal god. Other gods in their nations represented no threat to Israel and its patron god as long as they were not imported into Israel. As long as other gods did not affect worship of Yahweh in Israel, they could be tolerated as the gods of other peoples and nations. This state of affairs perhaps began to change in the eighth century when the neo-Assyrian empire presented a new world order. Only after this alteration of the world scene did Israel require a different "world theology" that not only advanced Yahweh to the top but eventually eliminated the second tier altogether insofar as it treated all other gods as either nonentities or expressions of Yahweh's power.[68]

The lowest tier of the Israelite pantheon also went through alterations. As the Ugaritic texts show, the lowest tier involved a number of deities who served in menial capacities. A common task for such gods was to act as messenger, the literal meaning of the English word "angel."[69] Like the middle tiers, this tier went through a change in perspective. Certainly angels are not regarded in later tradition as gods. Instead, they are powers that act only in the name of their patron god and only thanks to the power of that deity. The Dead Sea Scrolls frequently refer to angelic powers as *'lym,* literally, "gods,"[70] but in the wake of the earlier telescoping of the pantheon and the collapse of its middle tiers, this word probably conveyed the sense of heavenly powers (under the One Power) rather than full-fledged deities. So when one of the prayers from the Dead Sea Scrolls (the Hodayot, 1QH 7:28) asks in the same words as Exodus 15:11, "who is like You among the gods?" the question does not carry the same freight; the question in the Hodayot is devoid of its earlier polytheistic context. In sum, in the pre-exilic period (and perhaps as early as the eighth century) Israel enjoyed perhaps a lesser pantheon than that in the Ugaritic texts, but certainly it was considerably more extensive than what the biblical record reports.

Identifying four tiers as levels in a single system of divine polity is a heuristically helpful approach to the pantheon in Mesopotamia and Syria-Palestine. P. D. Miller comments regarding the divine assembly:

> The divine assembly is an image for speaking of a system for divine governance and order that is intimately involved with the world but not coterminous with it. The cosmological structure of the universe is operative in the universe but transcends it. The pious ones of Mesopotamia and Syria-Palestine were convinced that all they could see and comprehend and investigate of the universe about them was not all there was to the world.[71]

Miller proceeds to characterize the divine assembly in Israelite culture:

> In all of the manifestations of the divine council imagery we encounter Israel's way of dealing in a theological and foundational way with the problem of the one and the many and how they they are held together within a single reality that is the cosmos. While in some sense it would seem that that issue was resolved or disappeared with the monotheistic thrust, to assume that is to forget that what took place was a radical centralization of divine power and reality in one deity in whom the complexity and plurality of the universe was not lost but ruled. The plurality and diversity of the experiences and phenomena that make up the creation point to a complex cosmos that is allowed both its complexity and its ordered direction by a fully integrated divine world order whose rule by one is as clear as its social character. The divine assembly of ancient Israel thus holds as one reality a monistic impulse in a pluralistic cosmic structure. That such a dialectic was intentional and at the heart of Old Testament theology and cosmology is nowhere clearer than in the ancient name by which the God of the Old Testament was known and is stilled praised, "the Lord of hosts."[72]

These two statements offer some helpful points for our understanding of divinity in the Bible. Miller's first statement shows an effort to appreciate the theological importance of the divine assembly in texts outside of Israel. According to Miller, the divine assembly expresses at once the relatedness of the divine assembly to the world as well as its transcendance; the relatedness and transcendance belong to an order in the cosmos ruled by divinity. It is the order itself that expresses a certain one-ness of divinity.

Miller's second statement focuses on Israel, first by suggesting—rightly in my view—that the divine assembly in biblical thought provides one means of dealing with the issue of the one and the many. However, I believe this point applies equally well to the divine assembly in the Ugaritic texts. The divine council mediates the problem of the one and the many in Ugaritic and Israelite language alike. Miller discusses the effect of Israel's "monotheistic thrust" on the imagery and language of divine assembly. At first glance, Israelite monotheism would seem theoretically to stand at odds with the imagery of Israelite assembly with its multiplicity of divinities, even if they are minor or subservient to Yahweh as their absolute king. In fact, the divine assembly is not oppositional to monotheistic statements in biblical literature. For example, it is commonly held by biblical scholars (including Miller) that the opening of "Second Isaiah" (Isaiah 40) involves a divine council scene, yet this chapter is part of a larger work that contains the greatest number of monotheistic statements in the Bible (addressed in chapter 10). Divine council language and scenes also appear in the "priestly work" of the Pentateuch and post-exilic books (Zechariah and Daniel), which assumedly are monotheistic. In other words, monotheism requires that one divine assembly headed by one divine ruler, but it makes little or no impact on the language of assembly in itself. Moreover, as noted, it probably reduced and modified the sense of divinity attached to "angels."

The Israelite presentation of the divine council differs little structurally from the Babylonian presentation of Marduk in Enuma Elish. Both Enuma Elish and the Hebrew Bible present a divine ruler surrounded by subservient divinities. Radical divine rulership manifest in these texts polarizes the divine polity into the ruler and his ruled. Viewed in these terms, the "monotheistic thrust" in itself does not alter this general structure of the divine polity. (In contrast, the Ugaritic Baal Cycle manifests more complexity at the top and middle of the pantheon and thus differs from both Enuma Elish and the Bible.) Therefore, one might see a "monistic impulse" at work in both Babylonian polytheism and so-called Israelite monotheism. The definition of monotheism might then apply the Babylonian constructions of the world.[73] However, this conclusion flies in the face of Enuma Elish's own reference to divinities other than Marduk as gods. This approach also seems to reflect an attempt to locate the idea of monotheism in the structure of the pantheon and the basic relationship between one ruler and his subjects, even if they too are divinities. Yet this approach stretches the definition of monotheism beyond recognition. Many (though hardly all) Israelite texts differ from Enuma Elish in neither the notion of assembly nor the radical polarization between Ruler and ruled. Instead, further changes are evident. All but the highest tier of divinities are reduced in status, no longer regarded as deities in any manner analogous to the head of the council; their power is entirely derivative and expresses the dominion of the Divine Head.

There is another basic contrast between Babylon and Israel of the exilic period (587–538). Chapter 9 suggests that with Enuma Elish, Babylon stands at the height of its political power, and its older deities pay homage to its newly exalted divine ruler. In contrast, Israel stands at the bottom of its political power and it exalts its deity inversely as ruler of the whole universe, with little regard for the status of the older deities known from the pre-exilic literary record. In sum, the imagery of the divine assembly represents for both monotheism and polytheism a pliable theological strategy for presenting order with the one and the many of divinity; this divine order may either mirror the conditions of the human world or it may oppose it. Assembly provides one avenue for expressing order and one-ness in the conceptualization of divinity.

Before proceeding to the next chapter, it is necessary to note a further development in the study of the assembly. In a book-length study, L. K. Handy follows a line of scholarly research suggesting that the pantheon should be understood as a bureaucratic system of operation.[74] First, Handy defines the social context in Ugaritic society:

> The monarchs and the scribal schools came together precisely in the area of bureaucratic government; it was necessary for the royal family to place competent members of its own relatives in key positions, as well as to find capable persons for myriads of other scribal posts required by the culture. Some positions in royal court offices were held by people outside the kinship circle of the royal family, by reason of knowing family members or inherited privilege.[75]

Handy then applies Max Weber's category of bureaucracy to the pantheon. In contrast, J. D. Schloen claims that the monarchy did not represent a system of bureacracy in Weber's terms but itself functioned as a patrimonial household, with household workers. Schloen instead asserts that the Ugaritic pantheon reflects the larger patriarchal paradigm or patrimonial society Weber outlined. In other words, Schloen would interpret Handy's a bureaucratic model primarily as a form of patriarchal structure at the royal level. Apart from the theoretical issues in Weber's thought,[76] it is true that the Ugaritic presentation of the pantheon shows few major deities standing outside of kinship groups. One possible example of a major god from Ugaritic literature is Kothar wa-Hasis, the craftsman god. Interestingly, he is also the only deity assigned to the third tier, and he may be regarded as an outsider of sorts because his abodes are not located in the Syro-Mesopotamian heartland, like the homes of the main deities, but in Egypt and Caphtor (probably Crete). Furthermore, there is no typically bureaucratic divine figure such as a scribe in the Ugaritic pantheon nor any other figure apart from a divine craftsman who worked in the royal divine bureaucracy.

The biblical material offers only slightly more evidence of a divine bureaucracy. Handy places considerable weight on the figure entitled "the satan," traditionally called Satan, later identified as the Devil. In the book of Job, he is one of "the divine beings" (*běnê hā'ĕlōhîm*, Job 1:6) who appears as a prosecuting attorney in the heavenly court of God in chapters 1 and 2. Biblical material shows some individuation of divine beings (often regarded as "angels"), which might be added as evidence for a bureaucratic model.[77] However, these are relatively few and the biblical material barely supports a general structure of bureaucracy. In short, the number of such divinities of bureaucracy in either Ugaritic or Israelite literature is minimal, whereas the number of family members in the pantheon in Ugaritic literature is high. Of course, there was a multitude of deities in Israelite polytheism. With the sun, moon, and the hosts of heaven in attendance, the divine assembly of Yahweh is quite full (1 Kings 22:19; cf. Exodus 15:11). In general, the apparent organizational language in Mesopotamian mythology and society does not seem to apply with full force to the Ugaritic presentation of divinity,[78] and the relative absence of the language of the divine family from the Bible may also divert attention from familial terms for divinity in Ugaritic mythology. Accordingly, whatever the functions of "bureaucracy" might be, they may be situated within the divine royal household in Ugaritic myth. These observations point to key differences between Ugaritic and Israelite literatures as presently known. Whereas the Ugaritic texts display a wide variety of relational concepts, the Israelite material manifest in the Bible shows far fewer, and what is largely left in the biblical material is the council of a single god. Although other gods are in this assembly, it is headed by a single ruler: this is one well-attested form of Israelite polytheism, and its conceptual unity lies in the image of Ruler and the ruled of this single assembly.

Divinity involves more than either the economic "cost-benefit" of blessing and protection that deities can provide against threat or political power or subjugation. Divinity also involves one-ness through relatedness, expressed not only in terms of power but also of care and love as in the concept of the family. The case for the family model and its meanings in Ugaritic literature as well as some biblical texts are addressed in the next chapter.

3

The Divine Family

In my Father's house
there are many dwelling places.

John 14:2; RNAB

Beloved, we are God's children now.

1 John 3:2; RNAB

As the end of chapter 2 suggests, the divine council is coterminous in the Ugaritic texts with the divine household, the divine family its main members. The family concept also contains a built-in flexibility to integrate deities not originally "at home" in the main divine household. This chapter explores the central role of the family in expression of interrelations among the Ugaritic deities and also shows how the divine family was deeply grounded in West Semitic societal concepts.

1. The Four Tiers of the Divine Household

One Ugaritic passage (CAT 1.65) uses the terminologies of council and family together, first in the phrase, "the council of the sons of El" (*mphrt bn 'il*) in line 2, and then in line 3, "the circle of the sons of El" (*dr bn 'il*). These juxtapositions are not isolated examples, as they appear also in CAT 1.40.25 (and apparently in lines 8, 17, 34, 42 as well, although the broken condition of these lines must be noted). Likewise, 1.162.16–17 names "the circle of El and the council of Baal" (*dr 'il wphr b'l*) as the recipients of a single sacrifice.[1] Finally, the terminology for "clan" seems also to underlie the Ugaritic word, *hmlt*, used in parallelism with '*ilm*, "the gods" (1.2 I 18, 35). In general, the notion of the family serves as a further feature (beyond the language of divine council) in a cohesive vision of religious reality. Or, in N. Wyatt's apt formulation: "The image of the one family is a classic instance of systematic theology at work."[2]

J. D. Schloen underscores the immense importance of the patrimonial household in both human and divine society in the Ugaritic texts in his lengthy treatment of the patrimonial household in Ugarit. Schloen finally turns to the question of its mythology:

Although little mention has so far been made of the well-known mythological texts from Ugarit, it is worth considering here briefly the structure of authority that is revealed in them. Of course, myths are often murky refractions rather than direct reflections of mundane social realities, but it is striking that a concern for the preservation of the patrilineage is prominent in the Epics of Keret and Aqhat. Furthermore, the household of the gods themselves has the appearance of a typical Near Eastern joint family, complete with rivalries among adult sons and daughters. In the Baal Cycle, a major theme is Baal's desire for a house of his own—as the eldest son and heir he is restless and unhappy under the direct supervision of the aging patriarch, El. The acquisition of his own house does not mean, however, that Baal is totally independent of El or wants to be his rival; indeed, his true rivals are members of his own generation—favorites of El such as Yamm and Mot who want to displace him as heir.[3]

Here Schloen lays out the basic social paradigm for the Ugaritic pantheon as a whole. The pantheon is a large multi-family or joint household headed by a patriarch with several competing sons. Although older studies of Ugaritic religion and literature have recognized the language of the family in Ugaritic myths, its social background perhaps has not been equally appreciated. Since Schloen barely applies his own insight to the divine family (apart from CAT 1.12 and 1.23,),[4] this chapter extends his approach by detailing the applicability of the patrimonial household to the presentation of divinity in Ugaritic texts.[5] At the end of the next chapter, I reflect on this language as a key in the coherence and intelligibility of Ugaritic polytheism.

We may begin here where the last chapter leaves off. The four tiers of the pantheon are analogous with different tiers of the divine household. In the top two tiers of the pantheon are the divine parents and their children; the bottom two tiers of the pantheon consist of deities working in the divine household. El is the father of deities and humanity. Accordingly, El's capacity as ruler of the pantheon expresses his function as patriarch of the family. His wife Athirat (biblical Asherah) is the mother of deities and humanity. El and Athirat are the divine royal parents of the pantheon, and the dominant deities are generally regarded as their royal children. (As R. M. Good quips, "What great god wasn't a king?")[6] These divine children are called in generic terms "the seventy sons of Athirat" (KTU 1.4 VI 46). The narrative of Elkunirsa, a West Semitic myth written in Hittite, gives the number of Ashertu's children as the variant "seventy-seven" (followed in parallelism by "eighty-eight").[7] Seventy is a well-known conventional number for a generally large family group (see Judges 9:5; 2 Kings 10:1; cf. Exodus 1:5).[8] The case of Jerubbaal and his seventy sons (Judges 9:5) is a prime example. Hence, the seventy sons designate not the divine council as a whole, but its leading members. Further, the leading members of Emar are called "the seventy sons of Emar" (Emar 373.37–38). One of the two Tel Dan inscriptions refers to the "seventy kings" faced by the Aramean king.[9] The number of gods perhaps survives in the later Jewish notion of the seventy angels, one for each of the world's putatively seventy peoples (1 Enoch 89:59, 90:22–25; Targum Pseudo-Jonathan to Deut 32: 8;[10] bT. Shabbat 88b; Sukkah 55b).[11] The myths provide descriptions of "domestic scenes" in the household of El. In CAT 1.114 El's three children, Anat, Athtart, and Yarih, help in the preparation of the food for El's feast in his house, and later two of his sons, T̲KMN-wa-ŠNM, carry El when he arrives home "dead-drunk."[12] CAT 1.23 describes how El sires two children, Dawn (Shahar) and Dusk (Shalim). Athirat is clearly the divine mother of the main divine family in the myths. The term "mother" applies also to the divine mother of the outsider goddess, Nikkal (1.24.34).

The second tier of gods can have their own households as well. Athirat's sons are said to have their own houses, according to Baal's complaint (CAT 1.3 IV 48, etc.). El may well be patriarch of the clan, but the family-heads have houses of their own. Within these households are families with a "baal" at their head. Accordingly, every male family authority ideally might have his own house. Baal's house is known not only from the Baal Cycle (1.4 V–VII), but also from 1.119.3, *bt b'l 'ugrt*, "the house of Baal, in Ugarit." The sacrificial offering in the temple of Baal in 1.109.11–15 lists the recipients as Ilib, El, Baal, and Anat of Sapan and Pidray.[13] This list reflects a partial listing of Baal's household after the official deference to Ilib and El. In the mythological material, Baal has his military retinue and also three "daughters" (*bt*) (Pidray, 'Arsay, and Tallay), evidently reflecting his meteorological and chthonic aspects. The designation *bt* may not be merely a term for "woman," as 1.24.26–27 refers to Baal as the father of Pidray. This set of divine relationships may be reflected further in royal cult. Pidray is also the object of a sacrificial ritual, according to the list of 1.91.7.[14] More intriguing yet, 1.132.1–3 seems to include Pidray as part of what has been regarded as a ritual for the enthronement of the new king: "On the nineteenth (day), the bed of Pidray is laid out for the installation of the king" (*btš' 'šrh trbd 'rš pdry bšt mlk*).[15] This text may communicate the understanding that the king becomes related to the divine patron of the dynasty, Baal, through marriage to his daughter, Pidray (perhaps analogous with the marriage mentioned in 1.23.26–27). We may note one further familial construct involving Baal: Mot refers to his own brothers as well as Baal's (1.5 I 22–25, II 21–24; 1.6 V 19–22, VI 10–16); the god's comments apparently point to the households with these two gods as their most prominent members.[16] Finally, the collectivity under Baal's authority may correspond to the designation *phr b'l* in the ritual texts (e.g., CAT 1.39.7: *p[h]r b'l*), although this is uncertain.

One member of the pantheon's second tier generally regarded as El's child does not fit into this family without complication: Anat. She is, at least in general terms, the daughter of El (cf. 1.3 V 25; 1.18 I 16), but the identity of her mother is not clear. Nothing in the texts suggests that she is Athirat's daughter. Anat's status is complicated further by her character. She is a young female, unattached to any male; therefore, her social position is unresolved.[17] She is not fully under the control of patriarchal authority, as she may defy El and she is not beholden to a husband. Moreover, her passion and intensity cannot be controlled. In this respect, Anat presents a demeanor similar to that of Sumerian Inanna (perhaps under the influence of Akkadian Ishtar with whom she was identified), who manifests, in the words of T. Frymer-Kensky, "sheer force, rage, and might, with a physical power, that exists in a somewhat uneasy relationship to the orderly world of the hierarchical pantheon."[18] Finally, there is the question of whether Baal is not only her brother but also her husband, a point made explicitly in the texts.

J. C. de Moor follows a long line of scholarship in asserting that Anat is Baal's spouse and he is therefore El's son-in-law.[19] As discussed in n.41 to chapter 2, this scenario has been challenged by N. H. Walls, Jr., and P. L. Day.[20] Moreover, Egyptian culture imported West Semitic deities, and Egyptian texts attest to Anat as the wife of Seth, commonly understood to be the local Egyptian substitution for Baal. For example, the Egyptian story, "The Contest of Horus and Seth for the Rule," presents Anat and Astarte together as the daughters of Re and the wives of Seth, who was identified with Baal in the Late Bronze Age.[21] Walls (as well as Day) follows Te Velde in challenging the value of this particular text.[22] As his chief argument, Te Velde notes that in this one text Anat is otherwise not called the consort of Seth. The uniqueness of this rendering of Anat as the wife of Seth might favor its authenticity as a witness to the West Semitic tradition. However, Te Velde also retranslates the passage in question, with the result that "the Seed" is said to be Seth's spouse and Anat only intercedes on behalf of Seth before her father Re. A sixth or fifth century Aramaic funerary stele from Egypt perhaps calls Baal "the husband of Anat."[23] The little weight afforded by the Egyptian evidence may yet favor the older view that Anat and Baal were indeed lovers. In general, Ugaritic myth seems considerably more concerned with the status and relations among competing males than among females, so it leaves some relations largely unexplored. This point applies to both Anat and Athtart: their relations to males of the second tier remain unclear.

As noted, the bottom two tiers of divinities are exemplified by Kothar and messengers. Kothar himself is the craftsman hired by different divine royals for their various needs. Analogously, human craftsmen were employed by the Ugaritic dynasty. At the very bottom of the divine society are household workers of the following sorts (textual listings following each term reflect attestations of these words for human workers mostly outside of mythological contexts):

"female servant," *'amt* (cf. 1.14 II 3, II 10, III 25, 37, VI 22; 2.70.19)
    tlš 'amt yrḫ (1.12 I 14–15)
    dmgy 'amt 'aṯrt (1.12 I 16–17)

"messenger," *ml'ak* (cf. 2.17.7, 1.23.5, 2.33.35, 2.36.11, 2.76.3)
    ml'ak ym (1.2 I 22, 26, 28, 30, 41, 42, 44)
    ml'ak šmm (1.13.25–26)
    [m]l'akm (1.62.6)
    ml'akk 'm dtn (1.124.11)

"servant," *'nn*[24] (2.8.4 [?]; cf. 7.125.3 [?])
    Gpn w-'Ugr (1.3 IV 32; 1.4 VIII 15)

"gate-keeper," *ṯǵr* (cf. 4.103.39, 40, 4.224.8, 9, 7.63.6)
    Resheph as gate-keeper to the underworld (1.78.1–3; cited later).
    Yarih (?) as gate-keeper of El's house (1.114.11)

The terms *ṯǵr* and *ml'ak* involve specific tasks apparently assigned only to males. Ugaritic glyptic may supplement the evidence for divine guardians or gate-keepers, as noted by P. Amiet.[25] The word *'amt* is a generic term for a female worker at this rank.[26] The word *'nn* seems to be a general term for servant, either male or female. Employees of divine family members are apparently delineated at least in part according to gender: divine gate-keepers and messengers are evidently male and the domestic servants are apparently female. El's question to Athirat reflects this assumption (1.4 IV 59–62):

"So am I a servant, Athirat a slave?	p'bd 'an 'nn 'aṯrt
So am I servant who wields an 'ulṭ-tool,	p'bd 'ank 'aḥd 'ulṭ
Or is Athirat a maid-servant who makes bricks?"	hm 'amt 'aṯrt tlbn lbnt

The question makes one assumption about gender roles and another about status. Roles are distinguished at the lowest rank, and rank is also clearly demarcated. More specific roles are hardly generic: *dgy* is specific to Athirat's workman Qdš w-'Amrr (1.4 II 31, IV 2–4). Yet this instance would seem to convey his master's specific relationship to the sea.[27] One comment about the social background of these roles: *'bd, 'nn,* and *'amt* all derive from the language of the family household. The word *ml'ak* in the Ugaritic material is less clear, but biblical material shows family messengers (e.g., Genesis 32:4–7) not only messengers of the royal household (e.g., 1 Kings 19:2).[28] In sum, the divine household exhibits numerous structural and linguistics hallmarks of the patriarchal household. This outline of the divine household calls for further reflection on households in West Semitic society.

2. The Royal Patriarchal Household as Model for the Pantheon

It is evident from the language of family relations that the model of the patriarchal household is central to the Ugaritic texts' presentation of divinity.[29] As the basic unit of society, the family household delineated in West Semitic texts could include the patriarch, multiple nuclear families headed by his sons, and other relations as well as workers and slaves.[30] Similarly, El and Baal, as well as other gods of the second tier, may have their own households. The oldest male serves at the top of the social pyramid within the household, mediating relations within the household and mediating between the household and other households or social segments. The patriarch mediates internal, domestic conflict and protects against external threat. The ultimate goals of the patriarchal unit are to preserve the family line, its prosperity, land, and honor (reputation). This patriarchal unit is to be situated within its larger agrarian context. The unit maintained both animals and crops. By physical proximity to the elements and the need to cultivate both herds and crops, family units were highly attuned to the nuances of the seasons and the weather.

This family structure also underlies the relations between El, Baal, and their heavenly subjects. The larger divine household of sons and daughters at the second level is headed by El. Similarly, the joint household may consist of *bn*, "the sons of X," with multiple heads called *b'lm*. Over them may have been a head, the *'adn*. To illustrate social structure as it applies to the divine family, we may turn to an administrative text, CAT 4.360, which lists a number of families (with each section divided by a scribal line, here indicated by a line between units):

The sons of B'LN of BIRY:	bn b'ln b'iry
Three heads[31]	ṯlṯ b'lm

| And their master[32] Bull, | *w ’adnhm tr* |
| and his four daughters. | *w ’arb‘ bnth* |

| YRḤM (together) with his two sons, two heads,[33] | *yrḥm yd tn bnh b‘lm* |
| and three retainers[34] and one daughter. | *w tlt n‘rm w bt ’aḫt* |

| The sons of LWN: six heads. | *bn lwn tlttm b‘lm* |

The sons of B‘LY: six heads	*bn b‘ly tlttm b‘lm*
And one free-man[35]	*w ’aḫd ḫbt*
And four women.	*w ’arb‘ ’att*

The sons of LG, his two sons,	*bn lg tn bnh*
two heads, and his sister(s)	*b‘lm w ’aḫth*
In ŠRT.	*b sȓt*

| ŠTY and his son (s). | *šty w bnh* |

This text follows a standard in its listing of family members: patriarchs (once called *’adn*), sons called heads (*b‘lm*),[36] male servants (either *n‘rm* or *ḫpt*), followed by daughters and women. (The texts do not refer to the wives of the men as such.) The large patrimonial units ("sons of X") mentioned in this text have several households, each with a head (*b‘l*) with various family and nonfamily dependents below him. Both *’adn* and *b‘l* here belong to the terminology of the family. In the first family presented in lines 1–3, the word *’adn* refers to the patriarch of the family, which includes his three married sons and his four daughters.

The mythological evidence exhibits an analogous use of social terminology. El is called *’adn* (1.1IV 17), and it is clear from parallelism with "mother" (*’um*) in 1.24.33–34 that *’adn* may connote "father." Accordingly, this word may be viewed as a familial term both in its application to El and in the listing of various kingship relations in 4.360. Like the god Baal, *b‘l* is a family head, and the name of one household patriarch, "Bull." It is also one of El's titles,[37] perhaps a marker of his premier status.[38] In his own "family," perhaps Dagan is also regarded as "bull" (1.127.22) and father of Baal.[39] The Ugaritic attestation of Baal as *bn dgn* (1.2 I 19, 35, 37, 1.5 VI 24, 1.6 I 6, 52, 1.10 III 12, 14, 1.12 I 39; 1.4 II 25, I 7) and *ḫtk*[40] *dgn* (1.10 III 34) could sustain this understanding of Dagan. The same usage of *tr* may lie behind the designation of the "head *rp’u*" as *tr ‘llmn* in 1.161.7, 23–24.[41] The households enumerated in CAT 4.360 also list three classes of females: sisters (*’aḫt*), daughters (*’aḫt*) and women (*’att*). Similarly, the mythological construction of the divine family lists Anat as one of Baal's sisters (1.4 IV 39, 1.10 II 16, 20) and as El's daughter (1.3 IV 27). Pidray, ‘Arsay, and Tallay are mentioned both as Baal's women (1.3 IV 40) and his daughters (1.3 I 24; cf. 1.24.27); all three are also called "brides" (1.3 VI 15, 1.4 IV 54, etc.). CAT 4.360 does not mention female servants (*’amht*), but other nonmythological texts do (2.70.19; cf. 4.659.7); this category is known in narrative about deities (1.12 I 14–15, 16–17; 1.14 II 3, II 10, III 25, 37, VI 22; cf. 1.4 III 21). Finally, despite the presence of many divine servants in the mythological narratives, *ḫpt* and *n‘r* are not attested in the divine household (cf. 13 I 19).

Equally fundamental to the family unit is the language of parentage, and here divinities strongly show these roles. El's role as father and Athirat's as mother are often emphasized. Yet divine children are themselves fathers and mothers in the divine household. Proper names attribute fatherhood not only to El but also to Athtar, Baal, Ea, Kothar, Rapiu, and Resheph.[42] Similarly, proper names regard not only Athirat as mother but also Anat, Hebat, and even apparently the god, Athtar![43] Furthermore, if proper names reflect a fund of information for popular piety, as D. Pardee has cogently argued,[44] then family roles apply to more deities in popular religious sensibility than in royal prayers, rituals, or other sanctioned Ugaritic texts (such as Baal, Kirta, or Aqhat). Indeed, in proper names after *'il*, words for "father" and "mother" seem to apply to more deities than any other divine roles.

The divine family is modeled on the royal household in particular.[45] The monarchy represents a royal version of the patriarchal household. CAT 4.360 exhibits much of the same social terminology seen in the royal correspondence and the myths.[46] In royal letters *b'l* refers to a social superior and *'adn* to the father of the writer.[47] The royal titulary of 7.63.4 calls the king "upright lord" (*b'l ṣdq*). These titles locate the king at the head of the royal household. As the preceding section shows, even the typical language of monarchy, *'adn* and *'bd*, obtains in nonroyal households. As an aside, the titulary (7.63.6–7) includes a title "gate-keeper of the kingdom" (*ṯġr mlk*). The latter reflects the patriarchal role of protecting the "royal household," namely, the society, against external threats of enemies and mediating domestic conflict. Therefore, in ideological terms, the king is at once the patriarchal provider and protector; he is judge and father to the society, as well as the warrior who battles on its behalf. Moreover, the Ugaritic king showed a concern for maintaining family patrimony.[48]

The concepts of the divine household as well as particular divine roles are founded on the fundamental patriarchal-royal model. The social metaphors for chief deities overwhelmingly reflected the patriarchal experience in households, nonroyal and royal alike. Accordingly, hierarchy is a basic feature of the pantheon in the Ugaritic texts. At times it may take on a specifically royal cast. For example, El's commitment to Sea's (Yamm's) messengers that the gods will render him tribute (CAT 1.2 I 37–38) underscores political hierarchy in the divine realm. The structure of divine society with its multiple households coheres with the socio-political structure of Ugarit itself, with the royal household and the temples it patronized reigning over the other "households" of their domestic cults.[49] The royal household is the "family of families," the top of the social pyramid expressed through the royal palace, which at Ugarit enjoyed a particularly prominent size and position. The royal palace at Late Bronze Age Ugarit was an elaborate architectural achievement covering almost 7,000 square meters including living quarters, archives, courtyards, a throne room, a paved court, a pool, and other spaces; the palace was also situated just inside the western fortified gate.[50] Commenting on the widespread distribution of figurines throughout the city, M. Yon notes:

> The existence of these places of worship found throughout the city is evidence of the presence of religious activities among all the inhabited areas, and not just the areas which were reserved for it. One cannot exclude either the existence of domestic cults, a manifestation of popular religion side by side with frequentation of the great temples, to judge by the number and dispersion in all areas of the

site of small figurines, whether it be pendants in precious metal or the effigy of the goddess (Astarte?) or more humble figurines modeled in terracotta.[51]

The royal "family ideology" is reflected also in a number of later West Semitic inscriptions. The notion that the king serves as the head of the societal household continues in first-millennium West Semitic texts. Accordingly, King Azitawadda can claim: "Ba'l made me a father and a mother to the Danunites."[52] King Kila-muwa of Y'dy claims that "to one person I was a father, to another I was a mother, to another I was a brother. The person who had never seen the face of a sheep I have given him a flock. . . ."[53] With the model of the royal family as background, one may ask whether the divine family in the Ugaritic texts was understood as having any other general features.

3. The Astral Background of El's Family in Ugaritic and Israelite Literatures and Baal's Outsider Status

The Ugaritic texts hint that El's family was understood as astral in character,[54] although the texts rarely stress this feature.[55] To begin, a category of divinities called "star-gods" is attested to in 1.43.2–3 evidently with their own "house" (*bt 'ilm kbkbm*). In general, these deities are not specified.[56] A possible exception is 1.10 I 3–5:[57]

which the sons of El do not know (?)	[ ]*h dlyd' bn 'il*
the assembly of the stars	[ ]*pḫr kbbm*
the circle of those of heaven	[ ]*dr dt šmm*

On the face of it, the three expressions seem parallel.[58] The first may identify the group involved as El's family, but one could render *bn 'il* as "divine sons" and not literally as "sons of El." The other two phrases, "the assembly of the stars" (*pḫr kbbm*) and "the circle of those of heaven" ([ ]*dr dt šmm*), clearly involve astral language (cf. *'ilm kbkbm* in 1.43.2–3). However, the context of 1.10 I 3–5 is broken and not well understood. Given the many difficulties involved in interpreting 1.10.13–15, the hypothesis that El's family is astral requires support from texts that mention El and astral deities. Many astral figures are worthy of consideration: Shahar and Shalim; Yarih; Shapshu, Athtar, and Athtart; and Resheph.

1. Shahar, "Dawn," and Shalim, "Dusk,"[59] are El's two sons, according to CAT 1.23.
2. The moon-god Yarih[60] is evidently identified as *n'mn* [*'i*]*lm*, "the favorite of El," in CAT 1.24.25. In 1.92.14–16 Athtart's hunt provides meat for El and Yarih, presumably as a member of the head god's household.[61] Yarih participates in the cooking of a meal in El's house in 1.114; it is unclear whether or not it is he who serves as El's door-keeper (*ṯǵr*) and rebukes "El, his father" (*b'il 'abh*) in lines 11–14.
3. The sun-goddess Shapshu serves as El's special messenger according to CAT 1.6 VI. Further, the stars (*kbkbm knm*) are generally grouped after her in 1.23.54 (cf. *bt 'ilm kbkbm* in 1.43.2–3).[62] See also the blessing

in 1.102.26–27 paralleling the sun and moon with El: *lymt špš wyrḫ wn'mt šnt 'il.* From these texts thus far, one might presume that the sun, moon, and stars belong to El's family.[63] According to M. Dijkstra, CAT 1.128.13 identifies El with a Hurrian moon-god, Kusuhu; he comments that "the reason for this identification is obscure."[64] The text is indeed difficult and such an identification may be obscure, but if it were correct, one may then ask whether it reflects the astral character of El's family.

4. Athtar and Athtart seem also to belong to El's family, though in different texts. The Baal Cycle indicates that Athtar, unlike Baal, belongs to the family of El and Athirat (1.6 I). Athtart likewise seems to belong to El's family (see 1.92.14–16, noted before). At Emar Athtar is once called ᵈ*Aš-tar* MUL, "Ashtar of the stars,"[65] and Aramaic texts from the ninth century onward attest to *'tršmn*, "Athtar of heaven,"[66] apparently a reference to the god's astral character. References to the astral character of Ishtar in Mesopotamian sources are also commonly used to bolster a case for Athtart as an astral god.[67] Taken together, such textual references lend credence to the old view that Athtar and Athtart represent the morning and evening "star" (Venus).[68] Accordingly, the basis for their relationship to El and Athirat may lie in the astral character of this family unit. Unfortunately, the evidence is meager. Athtart herself is not labeled in an astral manner in Levantine sources.

5. Resheph may be an astral figure. M. J. Dahood and W. J. Fulco have argued for the astralization of Resheph at Ugarit, based on the astronomical omen text, CAT 1.78: *bttym ḥdt ḫyr 'rbt špš tǵrh ršp,* "on day six (?) of the new moon (on the month) of Hyr, the Sun went down, with Resheph (= Mars?) as her/its gate-keeeper."[69] If the identification of Resheph with Mars is correct, then the text provides evidence for the astral character of the god. However, this identification is not assured. Perhaps in support of Resheph's astral character, one may note that 1.107.40 pairs him with Yarih. However, it is also unclear if Resheph belongs specifically to El's family.

It may only be coincidental, but this roster of deities adds up to seven, and seven is the number in the expression "seven stars" (*šb' kbkbm*) in 1.164.15 (if one were to assume that the two words construed together refer to divinities). Beyond the textual evidence, we might appeal further to the iconographic record. O. Keel and C. Uehlinger have argued for a lunar presentation of El on a cylinder seal from Beth-Shean.[70] A. J. Brody has drawn attention to the astral features of Athirat's iconography.[71] By the same token, the textual evidence for the astral character of El[72] and Athirat[73] is admittedly minimal. This paucity of information may reflect the displacement of the family of El and Athirat by the Ugaritic cult of Baal, who does not belong to that family.[74] In sum, one might cautiously suggest that the sun, moon, and the stars were especially associated early with El in West Semitic religion.

The later religion of Israel may have known a cult of El that included a minimum number of these astral deities.[75] Job 38:6–7 may reflect a witness to this notion:

Who set its cornerstone
when the morning stars sang together
And all the divine beings (*bĕnê 'ĕlōhîm*) shouted for joy?

In the verse Yahweh the creator-god (like old El?) asks Job if he was present when Yahweh set the cornerstone of the world's foundations, an ancient event celebrated by the divine beings, here specified as stars. In this passage, the morning stars are clearly parallel to *bĕnê 'ĕlōhm*, and on the basis of this verse, U. Oldenburg connects the astral bodies with El.[76] The god's astral association apparently lies behind the polemic against the king of Babylon in Isaiah 14:13 who attempts to ascend into heaven and exalt his throne "above the stars of El" (*mimma'al lĕkôkĕbê-'ēl*).[77] The astral dimension of such a polemic against a foreign king perhaps lived on in the polemics directed against Antiochus IV Epiphanes in Daniel 8:9–11. The "little horn" grew "even to the host of heaven" and cast some of them down. Although not explicitly connected with El or Yahweh in Israelite religion, Shahar and Shalim seem to continue into Israelite religion. Shahar is known from biblical literature through an allusion to the myth of Shahar ben Helal, the fallen star (Isaiah 14:12).[78] Shahar also appears as an element in Hebrew proper names.[79] Shalem is attested to sporadically in biblical literature, including in the form of proper names such as *'ăbîšālōm*.[80] Proper names with *šlm* as the theophoric element appear also on inscriptions from Arad, Ein Gedi, and Lachish.[81] Given their earlier and later attestation as deities, the sun and moon likely continued as deities at this stage as well.

Furthermore, as part of his identification with El,[82] Yahweh continued to be associated with astral deities in the form of the "host of heaven," as noted by J. G. Taylor[83] and B. Halpern.[84] Taylor points to passages such as 1 Kings 22:19 and Zephaniah 1:5 as evidence for the association of the host of heaven with the cult of Yahweh.[85] And 2 Kings 21:5 mentions Manasseh's construction of "altars for all the host of heaven in the two courts in the house of Yahweh." Perhaps as the last phase in the "career" of astral divinities in Israelite religion, biblical texts criticize astral deities within the cult of Yahweh under the rubric of the "sun, moon and the stars." It is possible that the criticism represented by these prohibitions derived from a perceived threat of the neo-Assyrian astral cult during the Iron II period,[86] but this fact does not diminish the indigenous character of the cultic devotion paid to the sun, moon, and stars.[87] Another possible text associating the sun and moon as part of Yahweh's military host is Joshua 10:12.[88] Some biblical scholars judge El as indigenous and Israelite whereas others view the host of heaven and astral deities as foreign and non-Israelite. Yet given the biblical acceptance of El (under the guise of his identification with Yahweh) and the condemnations of astral deities, one might argue that biblical historiography has influenced the differing scholarly assessments of El and astral deities.

The astral background of El's family versus Baal's background as a storm-god may lie at the root of Baal's status as an outsider to this family. Baal's outsider status is expressed through the family metaphor in CAT 1.24.25–26 where the moon-god Yarih is called the "brother-in-law of Baal." The family metaphor can be extended to include outsider figures through a divine marriage betwen an insider deity and outsider deity. (Unfortunately, the texts do not name the female in El's family Baal is married to, if not to Anat, long thought to be his wife.)[89] Baal's own title, *bn dgn*, "son of Dagan" (1.2 I 19; 1.5 V 23–24) apparently points to his separate paternity from the rest of the divine family.[90] Yet Baal can also stereotypically refer to El as his father, since El is generically regarded as the father of the pantheon. From this discrepancy H. L. Ginsberg deduced that this "may echo a stage of the tradition in which he was not a son of El."[91] Later Levantine tradition, attested in Philo of Byblos's *Phoenician History*, provided a narrative explanation for Baal's problematic paternity: "Thus, Kronos waged war against Ouranos, expelled him from his dominion, and took up his kingdom. Ouranos' favourite mistress, who was pregnant, was also captured in the battle and Kronos gave her in marriage to Dagon. While with the latter, she gave birth to the child conceived by Ouranos, whom she called Demarous."[92] According to this story, Demarous is regarded as a concubine's son sired by Ouranos; the concubine subsequently becomes the wife of Dagon. The old West Semitic divinities behind this account are mostly clear: Kronos is El, Dagon is Dagan, and Demarous is a title of Baal, as attested in the Baal Cycle.[93] Curiously, given the Ugaritic evidence, Dagan is not the "natural" father of Demarous but called his father by "adoption." Ouranos, "Heaven," is credited as the natural father.[94] Ouranos theoretically should be the father of El, a figure unknown from West Semitic mythology. The ritual texts (CAT 1.47.12 = 1.118.11; 1.148.5, 24) attest to the binomial pair "Heaven and Earth" (*šmm w'arṣ*), but the place of Ouranos in this episode may derive from Greek tradition, which witnesses to Ouranos as the father of Kronos and the grandfather of Zeus.[95] What is clear from the Ugaritic texts and later sources is that Baal Haddu stands outside the immediate family of El.[96]

The model of family relations is at work in both the Ugaritic material and the story by Philo of Byblos. Both reflect Baal's status as an outsider to the family of El and Athirat. Philo of Byblos provides a narrative for this relationship, which reflects the common Levantine way to regard such an outsider. The son of a concubine has no legal rights, and the legal wife, as well as her children, may harrass or even expel the concubine or her son from the family. Perhaps Baal's situation as presented by Philo of Byblos is comparable to Jepthah's: he is the son of a prostitute sired by a man whose legal wife and sons drive him from the family; as a warrior he is eventually raised to leadership despite his status (Judges 11). No such familial particulars are spelled out for Baal in the Ugaritic texts apart from his epithets *bn dgn* (1.2 I 19, 35, 37, 1.5 VI 24, 1.6 I 6, 52, 1.10 III 12, 14, 1.12 I 39; 1.4 II 25, I 7) and *ḥtk dgn* (1.10 III 34) and his conventional appeals to El as his father (1.3 V 35; 1.4 IV 47; cf. 1.4 I 5). His mother is never named. However, Baal's family situation behind these pieces of information may parallel Philo of Byblos' comments on his status, for hostility between Baal and Athirat's sons surfaces in the Baal Cycle (see 1.4 II 24–26). This is the same household that Baal invites to his feast in 1.4 VI 46 (there called "the seventy sons of Athirat") and that he attacks in 1.6 V 1. The West Semitic myth of Elkunirsa preserved in Hittite also reflects the animosity between Baal and Athirat and her family. After Baal and Athirat engage in sexual relations, he says to her: "Of thy sons I slew seventy-seven, I slew eighty-eight. Ashertu heard this humiliating word of the Storm-god and her mind got incensed against him."[97] Clearly the initial status of Baal and Jephthah was lower than that of the sons sired by wives. Baal seems to be an outsider of the same generation as the children of El and Athirat. He is in a sense "adopted up" to a status ultimately exalted beyond the rest of the family. This change occurs not because of the circumstances of birth but because of his achievement in his conflict with the god Sea (Yamm). Jephthah, too, does not enjoy acceptance from the family of his father; his status changes also because of his martial prowess. Accordingly, we may note that within the family, whether divine or human, the children of concubines or adoption occupy a lower status. However, the status of these children produced from concubines or adoption can change, a possibility that the wives may fear, as the story of Sarah and Hagar in Genesis 16 illustrates.

If Athtar is an astral figure and full-fledged son of El, his conflict with Baal in the Baal Cycle may provide some insight about Baal and the divine family. The Ugaritic texts and the most proximate comparative evidence from Emar suggests that Athtar was an astral deity who was considered a major warrior deity. The narratives of CAT 1.2 III and 1.6 I 63 stress that Athtar is not powerful enough to be king. Within the Ugaritic texts, Athtar is rendered as a weak god, perhaps a historical reflection of his cult's demise, as reflected in other sources from the Levantine coast. A. Caquot argues[98] that the Ugaritic texts may reflect the historical demise of Athtar's cult at the hands of Baal's cult. Both were warrior-gods, but Baal was the divine patron of the Ugaritic dynasty. The geographical distribution of the cults of Baal and Athtar may clarify the status of Athtar at Ugarit.[99] The historical cult of Athtar may have been generally restricted to inland areas. Apart from the Ugaritic texts, there is no clear evidence for the cult of Athtar on the coast. There is no mention of Athtar in the Amarna letters, Egyptian sources mentioning West Semitic deities, the Bible, or Philo of Byblos. The single Phoenician attestation is debatable. In contrast, the cult of Baal is at home on the coast. It is tempting to view the conflict between Baal and Athtar in terms of the Arabic use of these gods' names for land fed by water. W. Robertson Smith remarks that bt. Baba Batra 3:1 reflects the older use of *ba'l* as land wholly dependent on rain and claims that the original contrast lay between land wholly dependent on rain and irrigated land.[100] The coastal regions received heavy rainfall, which precluded the need for either dry farming or irrigation. At Ugarit, for example, the rains occur over seven or eight months and exceed 800 mm each year.[101] In contrast, many of the inland locales where Athtar is attested practiced either dry farming or natural irrigation. One might argue, then, that in the environment of Ugarit, the god of the coastal storm would naturally supplant the god of natural irrigation. Unfortunately, it is impossible to ground any further speculation regarding Baal and the family of El, but we are left with a contrast between the astral family of El and Baal's role as storm-god.

As this inquiry indicates, the language of family encompasses both divine insiders and outsiders, both the established family and the strong newcomer. The concept of family provides a conceptual unity for Ugaritic divinity. It shows an elasticity that can give expression to a multitude of relations. Finally, the concepts of both council and family also allow a focus on the two main protagonists of the Ugaritic mythological texts, El and Baal. Council in effect points to the holders of power in council. El is the first figure of power in the council (1.2 I), and Baal's rise within the council, with El's consent (1.4 IV–V), highlights his new place in the Ugaritic conceptualization of divinity. The next chapter takes up some of these relations in more detail and in the final section explores further the presence of family language in Ugaritic myth.

4

Pluralities, Pairings, and Other Divine Relations

> This thou perceivest, which makes thy love more strong . . .
>
> Shakespeare, Sonnet 73

Chapter 3 examines familial language for divinity at Ugarit. As the discussion there indicates, the patrimonial household provides conceptual unity for describing divinity. Within the divine household are additional relationships centered on one or two figures. This chapter explores these relationships to illustrate further the root metaphor of the family for Ugaritic divinity. After this survey of relations among the Ugaritic deities, the final section of this chapter explores alterations of divine relations within the presentation of divinity in ancient Israel.

1. Baal, Resheph, Yahweh, and Their Retinues

As chapter 3 observes, the four tiers of the family include the household workers. Here we may note examples of another type of household "workers," the groups of retainers attached to two gods of the second tier. There is some evidence for a group of divine retainers who serve Baal. The best evidence may be the god's meteorological retinue in CAT 1.5 V 6–9. Possibly related, the phrase 'il t'dr b'l, "Baal's divine helpers," occurs in 1.47.26 = 1.118.25.[1] We do not know how this collective may relate to mhr b'l wmhr 'nt in 1.22 I 8–9 (cf. 1.22 II 7). Common to all of them may be the military image underlying them: Baal is the leader of his military retinue. There is also possible evidence for a military retinue revolving around Resheph. Ugaritic attests to both ršpm and to several ršp combined with a place name.[2] However, the plural ršpm in CAT 1.91.11, described as entering bt mlk, the royal palace or royal sanctuary/chapel, probably refers to the procession of cult statues of Resheph.[3] "The Reshephs" are known in Egyptian and Phoenician sources, perhaps warranting the hypothesis that second millennium Levantine religion generally knew this plural collective. A New Kingdom Egyptian text compares Ramses III's army to them: "the chariot-warriors are as mighty as Rashaps."[4] Sidonian inscriptions (KAI 15:2; RES 289:2, 290:3, 302 B:5) mention 'rṣ ršpm, "the land of Reshephs" (cf. 'rqršp in KAI 214:11). Following W. F. Albright, H.

Donner and W. Röllig interpret *ršpm* as a general collectivity of deities like the Rephaim (see the next section).[5] W. J. Fulco renders *'rṣ ršpm* as "Land of the Warriors."[6] Phoenician *ršpm* may designate a martial vanguard. BH *rešep* appears as part of theophanic vanguard (Deuteronomy 32:23–24; Habakkuk 3:5; Ben Sira 43:17–18) and as a generic noun for sparks and fiery arrows (Psalm 76:3; Job 5:7; Song of Songs 8:6; cf. Aramaic *rišpā'*, "flame").[7] Hababkkuk 3:5 mentions Resheph as a member of Yahweh's theophanic retinue.[8] Given the warrior character of both Baal and Resheph, these pluralities would seem to be military retinues of the gods after whom they are named. As members of the second tier of the divine assembly and sons of the divine patriarch, these two gods were in a position to have retainers work for them. Accordingly, these retinues are well within the paradigm of the patrimonial household. The same paradigm of military retainers may underlie Philo of Byblos' comments (*PE* 1.10.20): "Now the allies of Elos, i.e. Kronos, were called 'eloim', as the ones named after Kronos would be 'Kronians' " (*hoi de summachoi Elou tou Kronou Elōeim epeklēthēsan hos an Kronioi houtoi ēsan hoi legomenoi epi Kronou*).[9]

2. Dead Rephaim and Kings, and the Power of Death in Life

The analysis thus far has focused largely on major deities and the organization of divinity as it pertains to the members of the divine assembly or household. This schema does not account for lesser divinities outside the greater household of deities. In Ugaritic literature, dead kings (*mlkm*) and their putative tribal predecessors, the *rp'um* (henceforth Rephaim, after the spelling in English translations of the Bible), constitute two divine groupings possibly centered around a specific divinity. However, the issues are complex and the evidence is tricky. The *mlkm* appear in 1.22 I 17, 1.47.33 = 1.118.32, and they might be related to *mlk 'ttrt* in 4.790.17. The Rephaim occur in 1.6 VI 46, 1.20–1.22 and 1.161.8, 24, and they may be related to *rp'u* in 1.22 I 8, 1.108.1, 19.[10]

These cases of *mlkm* and *rp'um* may carry a comparable pattern of relationship, perhaps analogous seen with Baal and Resheph and their retinues, namely, a god with a retinue named after him. The two sets here may involve a single chthonic character, to be related perhaps in the following manner: *rp'u : mlk:: rp'um : mlkm*. The singular terms, *rp'u* and *mlk*, do not seem to be distinguished in 1.108.1–2, especially given the fact that the title of *rp'u* as *mlk 'lm* in 1.108.1 is perhaps an allusion to his identification with *mlk* known from 4.790.17.[11] Indeed, many scholars have noted that *rp'u* bears the same address of *'ttrt* (1.108.2) as *mlk* (1.107.42; 4.790.17), further suggesting their identification.[12] However, there are problems with relating the plural forms. A difference between two of the plural groups seems evident in CAT 1.161, which appears to delineate the *rp'um* as the older (perhaps tribal?) predecessors of royal ancestors, *mlkm*.[13] As with so many aspects of Ugaritic studies, the evidence supports little more than conjectures. In sum, 1.108.1–2 could reflect the amalgamation of the different singular terms in a single figure,[14] while 1.161 retains some distinction between the older *rp'um*, the older tribal ancestral heroes, and *mlkm*, the more recent deceased monarchs. Despite the nuanced difference, the two plural entities supposedly belonged to two parts of a single line of deceased ancestors of the royal line.

A final point regarding the royal cult of the dead at Ugarit: it might seem prima facie that the cult of the dead ancestors was generally maintained apart from the cult of the so-called "high deities." However, caution is warranted, as *rp'i yqr* appears in line 13 of the admittedly very difficult 1.166, a text that also mentions Dagan and Baal in line 9. Moreover, if *'il'ib* were to be understood as the "ancestral god" (literally, the father who has become god) as K. Van der Toorn has argued,[15] then his place in Ugaritic pantheon lists (1.47.2 = 1.118.1 = ^{d}abi in RS 20.24 and probably to be reconstructed in 1.148.1) suggests how near and dear cultic devotion to deceased ancestors could be.[16] Finally, cultic devotion paid to *rp'u* was not entirely separate from the cult of the so-called high deities. Indeed, both "constituencies" or "assemblies" (*phr*; see chapter 2, section 1) were of central concern to the royal cult, as suggested by El's blessing (in the company of high deities) evoking *rp'um* (1.15 III 2–4, 13–15).

For about a half century scholars have contrasted the biblical attitude toward death with what was seen in the Ugaritic material as a "Canaanite embrace" of death.[17] In the last two decades biblical scholars have proposed that the biblical critique of "Canaanite" customs pertaining to the dead reflects a more popular Israelite devotion to the dead and some priestly and deuteronomic restrictions on such activity.[18] With the publication and integration of important archaeological studies, such as E. M. Bloch-Smith's groundbreaking 1992 study *Judahite Burials and Beliefs about the Dead*,[19] scholars have revised their understanding of the Rephaim in Ugaritic (*rp'um*) and biblical texts (*rĕpā'îm*). Recent studies view the Rephaim in both corpora as the heroic ancestors. However, there is more to this comparison. Both the Ugaritic and biblical views of the Rephaim are the products of their societies. For Ugarit, KTU 1.161 makes it clear that the Rephaim represent the ancient cultural tradition with which the monarchy identified; in short, the Rephaim mark cultural identification for the monarchy (and for other sectors of Ugaritic society). Given the Israelite devotion to the dead, a similar view may have obtained throughout much of Iron Age Israel. But in Israel we see a reaction against popular practice. For example, for deuteronomic texts, the Rephaim represent the ancient cultural tradition of Israel's putative predecessors in the land, the Canaanites; in short, in these texts Rephaim signal cultural distance or "disidentification." The Rephaim then are cultural markers of identity, insiders for the Ugaritic monarchy and society as well as Israelite popular religion, but outsiders for deuteronomic authors. Both the Ugaritic monarchy and authors of deuteronomic works use the putatively ancient cultural tradition of the Rephaim to claim political identity and authority.

Another plurality is the Kotharat (*ktrt*), evidently beneficial in conception (see CAT 1.17 II 24–46; 1.24).[20] and perhaps modeled on the collective of family females who traditionally conveyed a new bride to the wedding-chamber. (These divine females are related only etymologically to the singular form *ktr*, the name of the Ugaritic craftsman-god. The root denotes "skill.")[21] Although Ugaritic attests to a number of other pluralities in the ritual texts, they are poorly attested and little understood.[22] These pluralities and the gods related to them seem to be tied to essential elements of death and life: the Kotharat associated with the beginning of marriage and human conception, and the Rephaim and other related figures associated with human death. Although these deities seem to stand outside of the "mythic mainstream" of the divine household, they are nonetheless important. They appear in Ugarit's myth, not only in its royal ritual. Moreover, at Ugarit the dead were interred in tombs under the houses; clearly death "inhabited" the home. Household matters of both life and death penetrate and permeate the mythology. I contend in chapter 6 that the royal concern for the deceased kings and Rephaim has intensively influenced the longest piece of Ugaritic literature, the Baal Cycle. Baal is cast in the role of dead king and hero in the final two tablets of the cycle. Indeed, nowhere else in the ancient Middle Eastern literature is Death so prominent a divinity as in the Baal Cycle. Thus, death and the realm of death play an integral role in the Ugaritic presentation of the cosmos: death is a part of life and life a part of death.

3. Pairings: Making Associations

Ugaritic literature is conspicuous for its many pairings across genres. I offfer a sampling[23] from ritual and myths:

The Snake-Bite Incantation, CAT 1.100
  a. *'nt w'ttrt 'inbbh*, "Anat and Athtart at Inbb" (1.100.20); Anat and Athtart (1.107.39, 1.114.22–23, 26; parallel in lines 9–10). In 1.16 II 26–28 Athtart is now read instead of Athirat (parallel with Anat, with her name reconstructed but not her epithet *btlt*).[24] The twelfth-century Egyptian story, "The Contest of Horus and Seth for the Rule," presents Anat and Astarte together as the daughters of Re and the wives of Seth,[25] identified with Baal in the Late Bronze Age.[26]
  b. *zz wkmt hryth*, "ZZ and KMT at Hryt" (CAT 1.100.36; see 1.82.42; 1.107.41).
  c. *ktr whss kptrh*, "Kothar wa-Hasis at Kaphtor" (CAT 1.100.46; see 1.1 III 17, 1.2 IV 7, etc.).
  d. *šhr wšlm šmmh*, "Shahar and Shalim in (the) heavens" (CAT 1.100.52; see 1.23.52, 1.107.43, 1.123.11).

Other Ritual Texts
  e. *tkmn wšnm*, "Thakamuna and Shanuma" (CAT 1.39.3, 6; see also 1.65.4; 1.114.18–20; 1.123.8).
  f. *'il w 'atrt*, "El and Athirat" (CAT 1.65.5).
  g. *'ars wšmm*, "Earth and Heaven" (CAT 1.118.11 = 1.147.12, partially reconstructed; 1.148.24).
  h. *grm w['mqt]*, "Mountains and [Valleys]" (CAT 1.118.18, entirely reconstructed in 1.47.19).
  i. *'ttr w'ttpr*, "Athtar and Athtapar" (CAT 1.107.41; cf. 1.123.10 without *w-*).

j. *dgn wbʻl*, "Dagan and Baal" (CAT 1.123.4; cf. 1.107.39).
k. *qdš w'amrr*, "Qudshu and Amrar" (CAT 1.123.26; see 1.4 IV 13; parallel terms in 1.4 IV 16–17; cf. 1.3 VI 11 without *w-*).

Mythological (Narrative) Texts
l. *mt wšr*, "Mot and Sr" (CAT 1.23.8).
m. *'atrt wrḥmy*, "Athirat and Rahmay" (CAT 1.23.13, 28).
n. *nkl w'ib*, "Nikkal and Ib" (CAT 1.24.1).
o. *ltpn wqdš*, "Beneficent and Holy" (CAT 1.16 I 11, 21–22, II 49 [reconstructed]).
p. *gpn w'ugr*, "Vine and Field" (CAT 1.3 III 36; 1.5 I 12; 1.8 II 7–8).

These pairings' distribution is quite strong in 1.100 and other ritual texts.[27] Given this distribution, one might interpret many of them largely as associated pairings for offering sacrificial provisions.

Others associations relate various deities in different ways. Some associations reflect family relations, such as El and Athirat as divine couple, or Dagan and Baal as father and son. Other pairings are apparently "natural," such as "Dawn and Dusk" (Shahar and Shalim), "Heaven and Earth," "Mountains and Valleys," or "Vine and Field." The pairs of "olden gods" (e.g., "Earth and Heaven") are a well-known feature of ancient Near Eastern theogonies, but the Ugaritic material lacks such pairings in any theogonic context.[28] Finally, the binomial pattern is so common that it is used also to denote single deities with two names, as in Kothar wa-Hasis and Nikkal wa-Ib. In these two cases, the second term characterizes the deity named with the first term. Accordingly, Kothar is Hasis, or "wise"; and the Mesopotamian moon-goddess mentioned in CAT 1.24, Nikkal (= nin.gal, "Great Lady," the wife of the moon-god Sin in Mesopotamia), is called Ib, probably related to her Akkadian epithet *ilat inbi*, "goddess of fruit."

For a number of these cases, J. C. de Moor argues for a gradual evolution from two separate deities into one entity.[29] In many cases, we do not possess enough information to confirm or preclude such a conclusion. Do we know that Anat and Athtart are, as de Moor proposes, the "two 'Anatu-goddesses who were regarded as aspects of one divine being"? Is there really enough evidence to indicate that Kothar wa-Hasis was ever regarded as two divinities fused into a single one? Specific cases of "fusion" can be defended,[30] but it is unclear that such an evolution applies generally to double names. G. del Olmo Lete suggests that some double names reflect the syncretism of two pantheons, one "Amorite" and the other "Canaanite."[31] Such a view might work for *bʻl/hdd*, but *'il/dgn* and *'nt/'ttrt*, the two other sets of names del Olmo Lete mentioned, seem to be distinguished at least in the mythological texts.

Despite such questions, the preponderance of binomial names remains an interesting feature of the Ugaritic texts, and perhaps it prompts further consideration of compound divine names in ancient Israel. Some of the Ugaritic compound names sometimes lack the coordinating conjunction "and" (*w-*). Kothar wa-Hasis is once called Kothar Hasis. It is this sort of compound that appears in biblical texts, for example: Yahweh Elohim in Genesis 2:7–9, 15, 18, 19–22; El Elyon in Genesis 14:18–20; and Adonay Yahweh in Ezekiel 2:4, 3:11, 27, 4:14. Most of these instances seem to represent a pattern of divine name followed by a divine title, except in the case of Adonay Yahweh ("Lord Yahweh"), in which the title precedes the name. These biblical titles further reflect high status, rather than function or characteristic (such as "wise," the meaning of the second name of Kothar wa-Hasis). Beyond these observations lies only sheer speculation. I will offer one. Much of the Ugaritic and biblical material containing such binomials belongs to priestly scribal traditions. The cosmopolitan culture at Ugarit attesting to eight languages and a developed literary and religious tradition perhaps draws theological speculation about reality in largely expressed in religious terms. Exploring interrelations in religious reality (e.g., binomials) represents one means for such theological reflection. But Israel is not exactly like Ugarit. Binomials, at least the ones cited, suggest an exaltation of the dynastic and national god. Even El Elyon, possibly an older title of El passed down in ancient Israel, in its attested context in Genesis 14 elevates the national god of Israel. With the examples from Ezekiel, we may also see the sort of priestly combination attested at Ugarit pressed into the particular purpose of exalting Yahweh. Moreover, the examples of Genesis 2 may reflect a priestly redactional hand (the same as the priestly author/redactor of Genesis 1), which added the divine title God (*'ĕlōhîm*) used in Genesis 1 to the divine name Yahweh attested in Genesis 2.[32] An aspect of Genesis 1's "monotheistic poetics" might then extend redactionally to Genesis 2.[33]

4. Divine Possession and the Problem of Yahweh and His Consort

CAT 1.43.13 presents a most intriguing formation in the prepositional phrase *l'nth*. The context, 1.43.9–13, involves offerings made at the royal palace to a number of divinities:

When the Gatharuma enter the palace:	*'lm t'rbn gṯrm bt mlk*
one shekel of gold for Shapshu-and-Yarih,	*ṯql ḥrṣ lšpš wyrḥ*
for Gathru a shekel of pure silver,	*lgṯr ṯql ksp ṭb*
a snout and neck for his (?) Anat.	*'ap w npš (13) l'nth*[34]

This phrase *l'nth* has been interpreted by M. Dietrich and P. Xella as "for his Anat" (so also reconstructed in line 16).[35] The antecedent of the pronominal suffix is taken to be the god *gṯr* mentioned in line 11. If the *-h* suffix were pronominal, as suggested by this translation, then this usage might be regarded as elliptical for "for Anat, his lady" (**l'nt 'adth*) or the like. In this case (and perhaps in the later well-known case of *l'šrth* at Kuntillet 'Ajrud, as Dietrich and Xella both argue), the usage refers to god and goddess as consorts. However, the final letter of *l'nth* has been interpreted quite differently by D. Pardee. Given the exceptional character of *-h* on a divine name, he prefers to regard the *-h* "as a doubly marked adverbial form indicating the recipient of the sacrifice." He suggests: "Without an ancient vocalization, it is impossible to know whether what I have indicated as /-ha/ constitutes 'emphatic' *-h* or 'adverbial' *-h* (i.e. the so-called locative-directive morpheme), or even whether these constituted separate morphemes."[36] But is Pardee's marking any less exceptional than a pronominal suffix on a proper name? As

Pardee's comments suggest, caution is in order for -*h* here: a pronominal suffix of possession is questionable, for Anat is not known as the consort of Gathru. There is a very enigmatic collocation of words '*nt gtr* in 1.108.6, but their meaning is unclear in this context. There is no entirely satisfactory answer to the ending -*h* on *l'nth*. Accordingly, perhaps it is a pronominal suffix expressing a relationship to a god. We simply lack the evidence to exclude this interpretation altogether, despite its difficulties.

This discussion encroaches on a larger issue, one quite central to scholarship on Israelite religion in the last two decades: whether Yahweh had a consort named Asherah in ancient Israel. According to current scholarly discussions of Asherah, the simplest reading of 2 Kings 23:4 suggests that the cult of "Baal, Asherah and all the host of heaven" was supported within the Jerusalem temple in the late seventh century (see also 2 Kings 21:3).[37] This interpretation has been fueled largely (but not exclusively) by the Kuntillet 'Ajrud inscriptions (ca. 800) mentioning "Yahweh and his asherah (*lyhwh . . . wl'šrth*)."[38] Like the Ugaritic evidence just cited, this phrase seems to show a suffix on the name of the goddess Asherah, or at least her symbol denoting her. The inscriptions discovered at the site of the ancient Philistine city Ekron (Tel Miqne) may provide more evidence for the worship of Asherah. The excavations have yielded important evidence of a seventh-century Philistine or neo-Philistine culture,[39] that is, the regional Semitic language with some features that distinguish it from either Phoenician or Hebrew in this period.[40] Found in "an elite area" and sealed in the destruction level dated to 603 B.C.E., some fifteen inscriptions on shards include the prepositional phrases *l'šrt* and *lqdš*.[41] The phrase *l'šrt* appears on a shard restored on the same vessel as a second shard that bears the inscription, *lqdš*. Are these phrases terms for "sanctuary" or cult "place," or do they stand for a goddess, "Asherat," and her putative epithet, *qdš*, "the Holy One"?[42] The excavator, S. Gitin, favors the second alternative and says that "the inhabitants worshiped the goddess Asherah."[43] Phoenician cognates would fit the first interpretation of *l'šrt* and *qdš* as terms for sanctuary, whereas Hebrew cognates suit the second view of these words as terms for the goddess. As Gitin notes,[44] it may be possible to exclude Hebrew as an option because the final -*t* is not the norm for Hebrew feminine singular nouns in the absolute state; rather, final /â/ is the norm in this period.[45] The inscriptions from Tel Miqne are ambiguous. Given the nature of their grammar and script, they attest to a non-Israelite, non-Judean cult.[46] Tel Miqne has also yielded a seventh-century silver medallion with a figure praying to a goddess standing on a lion.[47] The divine figure may be Asherah, if the arguments regarding the association of Asherah and the lion are correct.[48] Finally, the wider polytheistic context of Tel Miqne has apparently been verified by the recent discovery of an inscription reading "for Baal and for Padi."[49] The latter figure is known as a ruler of Iron II Ekron. The inscription was written on a storage jar found in a side room of Temple Complex 650. Thus, the evidence from Tel Miqne may be highly pertinent for the reconstruction of Asherah as a goddess in the region.

The biblical field has generally embraced the view that the inscriptions from Kuntillet 'Ajrud, Khirbet el-Qom, and Tel Miqne and some biblical passages attest to a goddess,[50] regardless of problems attendant with this reconstruction.[51] Those

Judeans who opposed the symbol in the Jerusalem Temple in 2 Kings 23:4 and elsewhere seemed to have regarded it as a symbol for the goddess, but it is not clear whether those Judeans who supported it viewed in it similarly. Complicating matters, the deuteronomistic detractors of the symbol may have engaged in guilt by association, with the god Baal who, as S. M. Olyan has argued,[52] had no primary relationship to Asherah. The symbol as it appeared in the Jerusalem Temple may not have represented a goddess as such. Yet the matter is hardly so simple, for 2 Kings 21:7 also refers to an image of the asherah (*pesel hā'ăšērâ*), and normally an image would point to a deity.[53] If one suspects that the *pesel* is a representation of the symbol of the asherah, one might agree that no goddess is involved. In the past I adopted this view.[54] Other scholars have also since expressed doubt about Asherah as a goddess in the Kuntillet Ajrud inscriptions.[55] Currently, however, most scholars believe that Asherah was a goddess in ancient Israel, possibly even Yahweh's consort. In short, the jury seems still to be out on the issues, which are undeniably complex.

5. Re-presentation of Divinity: Athtart as the "Name of Baal"

The warrior goddess Astarte bears the title "name of Baal," *šm b'l* (CAT 1.16 VI 56; KAI 14:18).[56] The precise religious significance of this title is unclear from the Ugaritic corpus, especially as Baal and Astarte neither act together nor appear as consorts in the mythological texts.[57] Scholars recognize that they are both warriors,[58] but the relationship appears to involve more than a common martial role. Later evidence suggests a relationship between Baal and Astarte. F. M. Cross,[59] E. T. Mullen,[60] P. K. McCarter,[61] and S. M. Olyan[62] interpret the goddess as the name-hypostasis of the god.[63] Philo of Byblos perhaps reflects accurate Phoenician tradition in reporting that Astarte and Baal (*Zeus Dēmarous kai Adōdos*), "king of the gods" (*basileus theōn*), ruled the land together under the consent of El (*kronou*) (PE 1.10.31).[64] Based on this passage, Olyan asserts: "This suggests clearly that she is queen alongside Baal who is king, though the word 'queen' does not occur in the text."[65] Olyan concludes that Astarte was the queen, consort, and ally of Baal. The evidence from Philo of Byblos and Astarte's title *šm b'l* represents the strongest support for Olyan's reconstruction, although the Ugaritic texts do not apply the language of queen or consort to Astarte. As noted in chapter 2, the Ugaritic mythological texts only exceptionally refer to the second tier of the pantheon as married. It may be that the literary descriptions of Baal and Astarte assume this relationship.

The possibility that this Ugaritic usage of *šm* marks a form of cultic presence may be supported by later Israelite attestations to *šēm*[66] in connection with theophany. It has often been noted that the divine "name" *šēm* in biblical sources serves as a sign of divine presence (Exodus 23:20–21). The divine name is also an element in the divine procession of Exodus 23:20–21. According to this text, Yahweh will send his "messenger" (*mal'āk*) with the Israelites, and "my name is within him" (*šěmî běqirbô*). The proclamation of Yahweh's name in the divine appearance to Moses in Exodus 33:19 may be a reflex of this old notion. The divine name acts also as a warrior (Isaiah 30:27.[67]) Similarly, Psalm 29:1–2 alludes to the name as a divine quality with martial qualities, including "radiance" (*kābôd*) and "strength" (*'ōz*), expressed further as "the glory of his name" (*kĕbôd šĕmô*). Most interpreters assume that the *bĕnê 'ēlîm* of Psalm 29:1 are invoked to acknowledge these various divine characteristics. Citing Deuteronomy 32:3 and Psalm 68: 33, C. Kloos comments on the opening of Psalm 29: "The context of these passages indicates, that 'to give greatness' or 'strength' means 'to praise', indubitably by exclaiming that the god is great c. q. strong."[68] In other words, the *bĕnê 'ēlîm* are called to acknowledge the *kābôd* and *'ōz* of Yahweh and the *kĕbôd šĕmô*. The theophany that follows the invocation[69] suggests that the qualities involved are not general abstractions but belong to the divine appearance in the storm. BH *kābôd*, "radiance, effulgence," is no abstraction but comparable to Akkadian *melammu*, the theophanous power accompanying the procession of the deity.[70] Similarly, *kĕbôd šĕmô* in Psalm 29:2 may be no abstraction but the theophanous radiance manifested by the appearance of the name.[71] In short, the name is the focus of Yahweh's martial manifestation. Yet this name-warriorship belonging to a storm theophany proceeds to a sanctuary where it is sighted. The last line of Psalm 29: 9 is often rendered: "and all in his temple say 'Glory!' " (Because glory is seen and not said,[72] and because BH *kullô* is often a postpositive attached to places,[73] it may be more accurate to translate "and in His temple—all of it—radiance appears.") The point is the cultic setting of this glory of the divine name.

As this brief survey indicates, biblical and other West Semitic texts mentioning the divine name share terminological and thematic features. The name designation of Astarte and her martial character and special relationship to the warrior god Baal approximate the martial character of the name and its special relationship to Yahweh the warrior god. The extra-biblical evidence for the name may suggest the background for the name in ancient Israel, otherwise lacking in textual support: the name may have been associated at one time with a goddess in early Israelite religion. In turn, the biblical evidence also provides a possible insight into the West Semitic evidence for the name. The liturgical setting of the name in Israelite sources may support P. K. McCarter's suggestion that hypostases represented the "cultically available presence in the temple" of the god.[74] McCarter makes this point specifically about *'šmbt'l* and *'ntbt'l* as the hypostases of Yahweh at Elephantine, but the point may apply more widely within Phoenician or Ugaritic religion. The biblical evidence suggests an older liturgical setting for West Semitic goddess qua name.

Finally, a further suggestion about Astarte as the *šm b'l* may be offered. The expression *šm b'l* formally approximates a proper name, as in the Ugaritic names *šmb'l*, "name of Baal," and *šm'nt*, "Name of Anat," and in Akkadian names from Ugarit *šu-um-ᵈaddu*, *šùm-a-di*, "name of Haddu," and *šu-um-a-na-ti*, "name of Anat."[75] Amarna personal names include the similar name, *šu-um-ad-da*, spelled also *šum-ad-da* and *šu-mu-ha-di*, "name of Haddu."[76] Accordingly, Athtart's designation as *šm b'l* marks her in a manner similar to a person with the name "name of Baal." This name perhaps then denotes her relationship to the god in a manner analogous to the human person who would bear such a name. One might presume that a worshipper with such a name is dedicated to or associated with the deity named; an analogous sentiment may lie behind Athtart's title and thus her relationship to Baal in the Ugaritic texts.

6. Divinized Qualities of Deities

Apart from Ugaritic *šm*, other divinized nouns may have operated in connection to a deity. In this context we may mention again the binomial name of the Ugaritic craftsman-god, Kothar wa-Hasis, denoting "Skill and Wisdom," two qualities befitting him. This name may then represent both the divinization and personification of craftsmanship. CAT 1.65 presents qualities after a list of deities, perhaps suggesting divinized qualities in connection with El (lines 5–8):

El and Athirat,	*'il w 'aṯrt*
The Mercy of El,	*ḥnn 'il*
The Constancy of El,	*nṣbt 'il*
The Well-being of El	*šlm 'il*

Here the qualities of El are invoked after El and Athirat.[77] CAT 1.65 is not the only text with qualities appearing with a list of deities. CAT 1.123 includes a standard group of deities and then lists the following figures in lines 12–16:

Light and Firmness (?),	*ngh wsrr*
Eternity and Rule (?),	*'d w šr*
Right (and) Justice,	*ṣdq mšr*
Compassion of the sons of El, (?) . . . ,	*ḥn bn 'il dn[*
Glory and Light	*kbd w nr*

The words *ḥn* and *ṣdq mšr* reflect divine qualities; the latter combination is well-known from Philo of Byblos' *Phoenician History* as Misor and Sydyk/Sedek.[78] Three of the other divine terms in 1.123 relate to theophany in biblical contexts: BH *nōgāh*, *kābôd* and *nûr* in 2 Samuel 22:13 = Psalm 18:13; Ezekiel 10:4; and Habakkuk 3:4. As noted in the previous section, Ugaritic *kbd* could reflect in some cases a divine entity or quality,[79] and the Israelite *kābôd* used in various theophanic contexts evidently echoes this older usage.[80] What is striking about a number of these qualities in their biblical contexts (e.g, *kābôd*, *nōgāh*, and *nûr*) is the theophanic or liturgical settings attested for them. Similar usage appears with other divine qualities in biblical texts, such as the divine "light" (**'ôr*) and "truth" (**'ĕmet*) in Psalm 43:3. This listing is binomial, a structural feature favored in 1.123.12–14, as well as the arrangement of divine names in rituals and other contexts noted in section 3. When the divine qualities appear in any larger context in the Bible, whether narrative or prayer, they sometimes assume work associated with divine laborers, specifically, accompaniment. In some instances the accompaniment entails the theophanic retinue of the chief god whom they serve. In Psalm 43:3, they are to accompany the human worshipper of the chief god: " 'Light' and 'Truth' are personified as two of Yahweh's attendants, sent from the divine council as 'guardian angels' to guide the psalmist to the Temple."[81] Many divinized qualities could attach to any number of benevolent deities to express various qualities of those deities to worshippers, especially in liturgical contexts.

7. Extension of Divinity: Cultic Places and Things

By virtue of association with particular deities or their cult sites, particular locales could be regarded as divine. Accordingly, it is well-known that Baal's mountain, Sapan, is labeled "divine" in the Baal Cycle (1.3 III 29, IV 19). This mountain also appears in a list of deities (1.47.32 = 1.118.14) and as the recipient of offerings with other divinities (e.g., 1.41.34 = 1.87.37). Other places divinized or at least sacralized as part of the ritual "center" are the sacred garden and the sacred spring. The sacred garden is expressed in the "mythology" of Genesis 2–3 and Ezekiel 28.[82] The term *bnbk* stands in the syntactical slot expected of a deity in 1.87.35 (reconstructed in 1.41.32), but the syntax seems to militate against such a view:[83] the syntagm literally means "in the spring." This difficulty has not prevented some recent authors from relating this term in the ritual to both the cosmic waters at the site of El's abode (called *mbk nhrm*) and the representations of the cosmic sea in temple courtyards in both Mesopotamia and Israel.[84] From the position in the text, this site might be divinized in some manner. More generic divinized topographical features in Ugaritic are *'arṣ wšmm* (CAT 1.118.11 = 1.147.12, partially reconstructed; 1.148.24) and *ġrm w['mqt]* (CAT 1.118.18, entirely reconstructed in 1.47.19). Cross explains the former binominal pair as "olden gods" belonging to ancient theogony.[85] The latter may follow suit. If so, these sorts of "divine places" derive their divinity in part from their perceived antiquity in the divine unfolding of the creation.

Objects, perhaps by their association with cult, are likewise labeled or regarded as divine: the "lyre," *knr* (1.47.32 1.118.31, a deity-list; see also [d gis]*zannaru* in *Ugaritica* V i 170:6'; cf. 1.148.9, 38).[86] Here note T. Jacobsen's comment: "Prayer appealed to divine compassion by vivid descriptions of suffering, music soothed distress or anger in the gods, and so their bull harps were seen as calming counsellors. Intercession was almost always by gods—even the harps were considered deities."[87] Consumables of cult also appear seemingly in divine terms (*dqt* in 1.102.8; *trt* in 1.102.9). Based on the extension of the rubric of divinity to cult places and objects, one may suggest that divinity was considered to adhere to cult. In other words, as a center for the experience of divinity, cult itself participated in the divinity of the deities to which it was addressed. Cult then becomes for its human maintainers the manifestation of divinity, or at least the context of divine manifestation for the deities whom they worship. By extension cult becomes imbued with divinity. I will address this question again in connection with holiness in the next chapter (section 3).

8. Afterword: The Conceptual Unity of Ugaritic Polytheism

In closing the first part of this study, I would like to make "a plea for polytheism," or, more precisely, a plea for considerably greater understanding and appreciation of how polytheism functioned for its adherents in both Ugaritic and Israelite texts.

The divine council and divine family household are the chief concepts for expressing relationality within divinity. Within this generalization, we can see some differences in Mesopotamia, Ugarit, and Israel. On the whole, Mesopotamia does not use the divine household as a means of achieving conceptual unity to the same extent as Ugaritic myth. I do not intend to overlook the many examples of familial relationships among deities in Mesopotamian literature, only to note the relative importance given to the divine family as a means of characterizing deities. In general, it is my impression that the root metaphor of the family, although well attested for specific relationships between deities, does not extend as strongly to the collectivity of divinities in Mesopotamia. Instead, the language of council and hierarchical relations within this grouping predominates there.[88] In contrast, the divine family is more prevalent in the Ugaritic texts. It may be that the divine assembly was the more established language, at least in Mesopotamia, but it is heavily complemented by familial discourse in Ugaritic myths.

The picture of divinity qua family in the Ugaritic texts may be contrasted in a different manner with the extant Israelite texts. Whereas the language of council continues strongly in ancient Israel, the root metaphor of the divine family has been eclipsed; it also appears in the language of the deity's relations with human devotees (e.g., God as "father").[89] What generally remained is a system headed by the chief god, possibly his consort, lesser or subordinate deities (some as members of his retinue), astral bodies, and servant-messengers. In short, a single assembly with Yahweh as its head is the conceptual unity of Israelite polytheism. Because of the reduction of polytheism in this paradigm as well as its structure, scholars have called this conceptualization of Israelite divinity "henotheism." In this form of Israelite polytheism, there are no other competing major deities or assemblies, and the language of the divine family is at best only vestigial, for example, in a text such as Deuteronomy 32:8–9. The Israelite God is still regarded as father, not to divine family members but to Israel (Deuteronomy 32:6). In further reducing the members in the divine council, later Israelite tradition regarded this structure as a sort of monotheism. In other words, biblical Israel has been shorn of such a divine family, leaving divinity to be imaged largely in terms of a streamlined bureaucracy headed by an absolute monarch. This later monotheism assumes that divinity is tantamount to an individual figure. The loss of middle tiers of the pantheon or of older generations of deities renders Yahweh's status utterly exceptional compared to the descriptions of Marduk or Ashur; these deities are understood as utterly powerful like Yahweh but hardly to the utter exclusion of other deities. With no divine family or middle tiers in the pantheon, the nature of Yahweh's power is without analogy. Even when Marduk's power is absolute, it is patterned on the prior model of Ea's power over Apsu, and Baal's own limited power is analogous to that of other figures such as Athtar whose power is less than his yet nonetheless comparable. Yahweh not only lacks peers within the pantheon; with his genealogy largely erased from the biblical record, he becomes a god not only without peer but also without precedent.

In conceptualization of divinity, the Ugaritic texts express a sense of divine singleness or unity through a series of family relationships. For ancient Ugarit, conceptual religious unity was expressed most strongly in the identification of the divine council as a divine family.[90] This family has inner connectedness not by virtue of a single deity but thanks to a single family of deities whose connectedness is marked by their familial relations. The strongest form of social identity at Ugarit was the family, which was marked by personal names with the form of *bn/bt* + PN (e.g., CAT 4.354). D. Pardee comments: "Generally speaking, the Ugaritians seem to have considered the patronym the most important element to be stated when identifying a person, for it is usually given and may indeed function as the only identifier (CTA 105), both masculine (*bn* PN "son of PN") and feminine (*bt* X "daughter of X"). Long lists, such as CTA 102, rarely omit the patronym."[91]

In the legal documents (such as 4.7, 4.356, and 4.357), land transfers from "the sons of X" to the "sons of Y." Therefore, we may offer a working hypothesis for the application of family language for the deities in the Ugaritic texts: given the prominent familial terminology in the Ugaritic administrative texts, the polytheistic family may have provided what would have been in Ugaritic culture the most "natural" means to express singleness and coherence in "divine society."

In early Israel, a similar family structure long obtained, probably through the period of the monarchy.[92] Throughout this period Israelite texts attest to *naḥălâ* for family patrimony and other indicators of lineage maintenance. However, by the seventh century the lineage system had perhaps eroded, thanks to a variety of factors, including the deleterious effects of royal power on traditional patriarchal authority, the acquisition of traditional family lands by an emergent landed class and the devastating effects of warfare on the countryside.[93] The post-exilic structure called the *bêt 'ăbôt* ("fathers' house")—as opposed to the older and more traditional form known as the *bêt 'āb* ("father's house")—has been thought to be a further witness to the decline of the traditional family structure.[94] Israelite texts dating to roughly the same period as the earliest clear expressions of monotheism (seventh and sixth centuries) proclaim that the righteousness of parents cannot save their children (Ezekiel 14:12–23). This change in perspective might be reflected also in the claims of sixth-century prophets (Jeremiah 31:29–30; Ezekiel 18, cf. 33:12–20) and deuteronomic literature (Deuteronomy 24:16)[95] that children would no longer be punished for the sins of the fathers.[96] We may therefore propose a working hypothesis for Judah: a culture with a diminished lineage system, one less embedded in traditional family patrimonies due to societal changes in the eighth through sixth centuries, might be more predisposed both to hold to individual human accountability for behavior and to see an individual deity accountable for the cosmos.[97] (This individual accountability at the human and divine levels may be viewed as concomitant developments.) Accordingly, later Israelite monotheism was denuded of the divine family, a development perhaps intelligible in light of Israel's weakening family lineages and patrimonies. This is only one dimension of Israelite monotheism, a complex matter that the last chapter of this book addresses in detail.

To end this chapter with Ugarit's polytheism, I might argue that the presentation of divinity provides a map of religious reality. If true, relational polytheism maps a reality marked by diversity linked by relationships at multiple levels of a hierarchy. The Ugaritic texts provide a massive strategy for articulating cohesion and unity in religious reality. For most Ugaritians there is little evidence for a "crisis of polytheism" (to cite J. C. de Moor's phrase);[98] rather, Ugaritic polytheism probably offered its adherents a far more integrated vision of reality than its modern students have ever imagined.[99] It may have been ultimately beyond human comprehension to understand the ways of deities, but this religious sensibility did not simply lead to pessimism. Instead, the texts point to a conclusion that the ways of deities were mysterious and wondrous to behold. That very mystery is conveyed, yet not fully revealed, by the god Baal in his message to his sister Anat (CAT 1.3 III 14–31):

Place in the earth war,	*qryy b'arṣ mlḥmt*
Set in the dust love;	*št b'prm ddym*
Pour peace amid the earth,	*sk šlm lkbd 'arṣ*
Tranquility amid the fields.	*'arbdd lkbd šdm*
You hasten!	*ḥšk*
You hurry!	*'ṣk*
You rush!	*'bṣk*
To me let your feet run,	*'my p'nk tlsmn*
To me let your legs race.	*'my twtḥ 'išdk*
For I have a message I will tell you,	*dm rgm 'it ly w'argmk*
A word, I will recount to you:	*hwt w 'aṯnyk*
Word of tree and whisper of stone,	*rgm 'ṣ w lḫšt 'abn*
The converse of Heaven to Hell,	*t'ant šmm 'm 'arṣ*
Of Deeps to the Stars.	*thmt 'mn kbkbm*
I understand lightning the Heavens do not know,	*'abn brq dl td' šmm*
The word people do not know,	*rgm ltd' nšm*
And earth's clans do not understand.	*wltbn hmlt 'arṣ*
Come and I will reveal it,	*'atm w'ank 'ibġyh*
In the midst of my mountain, Divine Sapan,	*btk ġry 'il ṣpn*
On the holy mount of my heritage,	*bqdš bġr nḥlty*
On the beautiful hill of my might.	*bn'm bgb' tl'iyt*

The mystery, though not directly accessible to humans, is conveyed to them indirectly through the descriptions of how deities tell of such mysteries. This poetic description provides a beauty of imagery and heralds the wondrous prospect of blessing that Baal is poised to bestow upon the cosmos, which by definition embraces human life. This vision, as well as the deities involved, is presented in highly personal terms. To appreciate this polytheistic vision of deities as persons, one must examine the personal features of divinity at Ugarit, the subject of the next major section of this book.

PART II

CHARACTERISTICS OF DIVINITY

5

The Traits of Deities

The previous chapters examine different groupings of divinity in Ugaritic literature, with a glance at the related motifs attested in biblical texts. This chapter
collects and analyzes labels and statements about deities to answer the fundamental
question of what a deity was considered to be. Ancient Middle Eastern literatures
generalize about deities' characteristics and actions abstracted from religious tradition and experience ("second-order discourse"). We have already seen in chapter
3 how the Ugaritic texts stress the idea of the deities as a divine royal family
bound by social hierarchy and family ties. This chapter examines four other common features of deities: (1) strength and size, (2) body and gender, (3) holiness,
and (4) immorality.[1] I address each of these traits[2] in turn, first in Ugaritic literature
and then in Israelite texts.

1. Strength and Size

> Note My might . . .
>
> Isaiah 33:13

The hand of a god denotes divine power, whether for good or for ill. The divine
hand may offer blessing, such as the upraised hand of the seated figure of the El-
type god.[3] A figurine excavated from Ugarit also shows a female standing with an
upraised hand; she is presumed to be a goddess, perhaps Athirat.[4] Alternatively,
the divine hand may denote power exerted against enemies,[5] as with the hand of
the goddess Anat against Aqhat (CAT 1.18 I 14; cf. 1.19 IV 58). The power (yd)
of a god such as Mot (1.4 VIII 23, 1.6 II 25) also suggests a destructive sensibility,
in keeping with his character. With a sense of doom, a letter from Ewari-sharri
reports dire conditions to Pilsiyu (CAT: 2.10.11–13): "The 'hand of the gods' is
here, for Death (here) is very strong" (wyd 'ilm p kmtm 'z m'id).[6] As D. Pardee
observes, the phrase could refer generically to a god or the gods or to a specific
god. Pardee suggests that this is a generic expression for "the hand of a god," "a

divine hand" serving as an idiomatic expression for pestilence. Whether singular or plural, the generic interpretation of the phrase suggests that the image of the divine hand expressed divine strength. Even if the expression here refers to a particular deity, the expression is so widespread in ancient Middle Eastern literature that it seems applicable to many deities. Pardee's examples involve Nergal, Ishtar, Marduk, and Yahweh. So Numbers 11:23 asks about the power of Yahweh: "Is the hand of Yahweh too short?" Job 40:9 poses the issue of divine strength not in terms of Yahweh's hand, but the divine arm: "Do you have an arm like God's?" The "hand" applies to a number of deities and therefore can be viewed more broadly as a divine characteristic of strength.

Just as deities have superhuman strength, they also have superhuman scale.[7] Ugaritic deities are of superhuman size when they travel on foot. At times divinities travel across "a thousand fields, ten thousands hectares" or bow down in obeisance from such distances (CAT 1.3 VI 17–19; 1.4 V 24; 1.4 VIII 24–26). These descriptions evoke deities superhuman in size, striding across massive areas of earth. One case of El's supersize is sexual. The description of his penis, literally "hand,"[8] in CAT 1.23.33–35 implies his super-scale more generally:

El's penis extends like the sea,	*t'irkm yd 'il kym*
Indeed, El's penis, like the flood.	*wyd 'il kmdb*
El's penis extends like the sea,	*'ark yd 'il kym*
Indeed, El's penis, like the flood.	*wyd 'il kmdb*

The superhuman size of the god's body in general is not the point of the text. Instead, it is his love interest. Similarly, 1.4 IV 38–39 uses *yd* in a sexual manner. After Athirat's journey to El, he offers her food and drink and then more:

Or, does the love (*yd*) of El the King excite you,
The affection (*'ahbt*) of the Bull arouse you?

In these passages, clearly it is the god's penis and not the rest of his body emphasized as superhuman in scale. However, the god with the supersize penis was generally accordingly reckoned to be supersize as well.

Baal is also described as superhuman in size. CAT 1.101.1–3 describes Baal as large as his own mountain, Sapan. It has been suggested that this text "describes Baal's sitting on his throne in such a way so as to highlight his enormous size."[9] On the whole, the text seems to identify features of the god with those of his mountain, again implying the god's superhuman size.[10] In the Ugaritic Baal Cycle, Baal is the focus of expressions of strength and size. By implication, Baal's throne and footstool are of superhuman size, so large that not even the divine warrior Athtar can measure up: "his feet do not reach the footstool, his head does not reach the head-rest" (1.6 I 59–61). Baal has a palace that is superhuman in scale (1.4 VI 56–57). Like the distance traveled by deities, the palace covers "a thousand fields, ten thousands hectares." This concept of the divine palace as housing a superhuman-size god is replicated in Syrian temple architecture in the early first millennium. The meter-long footsteps carved into the portal and thresholds leading into the cult niche of the temple at 'Ain Dara suggest a huge deity.[11]

Superhuman divine size was also a part of Israel's cultural heritage. Early Israel understood its deity and cultic appurtenances devoted to the deity in superhuman terms.[12] According to 1 Kings 6:23–28 the throne built for Yahweh in the Temple's "Holy of Holies" or "backroom" (*děbîr*) was 10 cubits high and 10 cubits wide (ca. 5.3 meters square). Only a deity superhuman in scale could take a seat in such a throne. The Temple's courtyard items were also of unusually great size and, in the case of the tank and stands, significantly larger than the adduced ancient Middle Eastern parallels. The pillars, *yākîn* and *bō'az*, rose a total of 23 cubits (ca. 12.2 meters), consisting of a 5-cubit high capital atop an 18 cubit high stem. The immense tank, 10 cubits in diameter (ca. 5.3 meters), held nearly 38,000 liters. Including the height of the wheels and the band that supported the basin, each stand/"laver" measured 4 cubits square (ca. 2.1 meters) and 7 cubits high (ca. 3.7 meters). The basin supported by each of the 10 stands had a capacity of 40 baths (ca. 920 liters). Accordingly, the exaggerated size of the structures in the Solomonic Temple courtyard suggests that they were intended not for human use but for the realm of the divine. The courtyard symbols perhaps conveyed Yahweh's triumphant enthronement. Upon defeating the chaotic forces of nature, as represented by "the Molten Sea," the god of the Israelites accepted the sacrificial offerings (perhaps of constituent groups or tribes represented by the stands) and entered the Temple bestowing blessings on the king and the people, as recorded on the pillars flanking the Temple entrance. Like Baal on his throne in his heavenly palace on Mount Sapan, Yahweh was perceived as assuming his superhuman throne in his palace in the "Holy of Holies," on his mountain, Jerusalem.

Several prophetic and Pentateuchal passages reflect on Yahweh's superhuman size. The vision of the prophet Isaiah draws on the notion of Yahweh's enthronement in the Jerusalem Temple (Isaiah 6:1) and assumes a deity superhuman in scale. The skirt of the divine robe is said to fill the Temple, again evoking the deity's massive scale.[13] Ezekiel 1 seems to build on the prophetic tradition of "seeing God," yet modifies it in substantial ways, by prescinding from identifying the figure as human in form and by minimizing the anthropomorphism of Isaiah 6:1. Ezekiel describes the "likeness" (*děmût*) of God as being "like (*kě-*) the appearance of a human." Here the anthropomorphism is presented as problematic (the text is heavily qualified), but it is recognized nonetheless. More pertinent here, the passage also locates the vision not in the Temple but on the firmament, the heavenly temple or palace, denoting super-earthly or cosmic size. Cosmic size and location suggest a spatial extension of the deity,[14] which may constitute the root of the notion of divine omnipresence, as observed by V. Hurowitz.[15] Such descriptions suggest not only the spatial extension of the god and hence his omnipresence; they sometimes include a description of the deity's four eyes, which, according to D. Schmandt-Besserat, denote divine omniscience.[16] She refers to the description of Marduk's four eyes and ears in Enuma Elish (I:95–98):

> Four were his eyes, four were his ears;
> When he moved his lips, fire blazed forth.
> Large were all four hearing organs,
> And the eyes, in like number, scanned all things.[17]

We might compare the vision of the transcendent in Ezekiel 1, which includes the four creatures, each with four faces. Here the number four denotes movement in four directions at the same time. These cosmic creatures respresent the power and character of the "divine presence" (verse 28), and we might conclude that their features denote both spatial extension and knowledge. In other Israelite texts, divine eyes can indicate watchfulness and knowledge of human activity (Psalms 5:6, 11:4; cf. 9:14, 10:14). The biblical writers and authors of other ancient Near Eastern texts described the divine person in anthropomorphic terms; later tradition defined specific divine traits (omnipresence, omniscience).

Like Isaiah 6 and Ezekiel 1, the Pentateuch reflects on "seeing God." Exodus 24:9–11 straightforwardly informs readers that Moses and others saw God on Mount Sinai. Later transmitters of this tradition evidently thought this simple statement needed some delineation or clarification that would preclude potential simple-minded readings. Such an answer is provided in Exodus 33:18–23.[18] As the culmination of a dialogue between Yahweh and Moses, this passage shows marked theological reflection on Yahweh's size and its implicit anthropomorphism. The leader of Israel asks his deity to let him see the divine face, as a mark of divine presence, protection, and approval. Although Moses has the stamp of divine approval, human experience of the divine is limited. Yahweh offers Moses the experience of seeing the divine "back," which at once serves to express Yahweh's support of Moses and to delimit human experience of the divine. Yahweh instructs Moses in 33:21–23: "See, there is a place near Me. Station yourself on the rock and, as My Presence passes by, I will put you in a cleft of the rock and shield you with My hand until I have passed by. Then I will take My hand away and you will see My back; but My face must not be seen." The divine hand suggests a superhuman appendage that can cover a human being, further pointing to a superhuman sized deity. To judge from these biblical passages, this idea of divine scale may have been quite widespread. The description of the divine throne in the Temple especially implies a general view, for the throne was a public symbol of Yahweh. Isaiah's vision evidently reflects the widespread perception that Yahweh looked human but was superhuman in size. Even as the theological reflection of Exodus 33 limits what humans can experience of the divine, the motif of the divine hand in this passage recalls the older Levantine tradition of describing divinities of superhuman scale. All of these visionary descriptions imply not only great size but also body and gender.

2. Body and Gender

> God is love.
>
> 1 John 4:8

In general, the deities engage in human activities that presuppose human form; these include ritualized behaviors (lamentation, music, intercession), social activity (feasts, hunting, duties of the faithful son, sex), and other human experience (dreams). As in the ancient Middle East,[19] deities in Ugaritic sources typically are marked for sex or gender. Ugaritic iconography is central here, presenting deities mainly in human form. Most textual presentations of deities assume a human form; deities walk, talk, eat, drink, sit on thrones in manners that presuppose human form. It is not always clear whether human or theriomorphic form is involved in sexual relations. On the one hand, as noted in the previous section, old El is considered to have tremendous sexual capacity; his "hand" (*yd*), a well-known euphemism for penis, is said to be as long as the cosmic sea (CAT 1.23.34–35). On the other hand, in one of the more prodigious sexual feats attested from the ancient Middle East, Baal is said to make love with a heifer (*prt*), mounting and having intercourse with her "sixty-six, seventy-seven times" (CAT 1.5 V 18–21). Accordingly, the scene seems to assume that Baal manifests his theriomorphic presentation as bull-calf.[20] He also engages in similar sexual relations in 1.11.[21] Another major exception involves the presentation of Anat in the form of a bird, her theriomorphic presentation or "attribute animal."[22] Finally, as noted in chapter 1, Bull El is a standard title for the divine patriarch in the Ugaritic literary texts, and his iconography adorns him with horns, perhaps reflecting this theriomorphic identification.

Anthropomorphism is quite the norm for descriptions of Ugaritic deities, so much so that J. C. de Moor suggests that "the gods of Ugarit had become too human."[23] De Moor deduces an apparent "crisis" in Ugaritic polytheism from the apparent lack of respect shown to El by Anat (CAT 1.18 I 6–14): "Thus even the head of the pantheon is reduced to the size of man."[24] There are two claims embedded in this view: (1) Anat's disrespect of El in this scene is emblematic of a general situation within the pantheon; and (2) one might interpret such a putative disrespect as indicative of an attitude or view held by the text's author and audience about Ugaritic polytheism. The first point is certainly problematic. Indeed, Anat is the exception to the divine model of respect shown to El.[25] The second point is equally problematic. It represents a psychological reading of the text's audience. Without more explicit evidence, this approach cannot support a claim about a crisis in polytheism, in which the gods had become "too human."[26]

It is commonly thought that anthropomorphism is a general ancient Middle Eastern trait that Israel eventually discarded, unlike the rest of the region. This characterization is inaccurate for both Israel and the rest of the ancient Middle East. Anthropomorphism was subject to various sorts of theological reflection in Mesopotamia and Ugarit. Some texts interpret other deities in terms of features of Marduk, the great Babylonian god. (The phenomenon is not confined to this god.) A few first millennium Mesopotamian texts equate the parts of the bodies of particular deities (Marduk, Ninurta, Ishtar) with other deities, indicating that these individual deities literally "embody" the others.[27] For example, one hymn to Ninurta construes him in the following terms:

> O lord, your face is the sun god, your hair, Aya,
> Your eyes, o lord, are Enlil and Ninlil . . .[28]

Another text identifies different deities as qualities of Marduk; for example, "Shamash is the justice of Marduk."[29] Somewhat similarly, various deities are described as different aspects of Marduk:

Urash (is)	Marduk of planting.
Lugalidda (is)	Marduk of the abyss.
Ninurta (is)	Marduk of the pickaxe.
Nergal (is)	Marduk of battle.

Zababa (is)	Marduk of warfare.
Enlil (is)	Marduk of lordship and consultations.
Nabû (is)	Marduk of accounting.
Sîn (is)	Marduk who lights up the night.
Shamash (is)	Marduk of justice.
Adad (is)	Marduk of rain.
Tishpak (is)	Marduk of troops.
Great Anu (is)	Marduk of . . .
Shuqamuna (is)	Marduk of the container.
[ ] (is)	Marduk of everything.[30]

Finally, the end of Enuma Elish attributes to Marduk fifty names, many belonging to other deities. In these cases Mesopotamian descriptions of the divine do not avoid anthropomorphic language. Instead, they heighten the anthropomorphism to make the deity transcend the basic analogy between humans and deities which the traditional anthropomorphism. In this way anthropomorphism is both affirmed and relativized. Such texts create a new form of anthropomorphism, what R. S. Hendel insightfully calls "transcendent anthropomorphism."[31] Ugarit does not provide much material in this vein, but CAT 1.101, noted in the previous section, is pertinent. This text describes Baal's body in terms drawn from nature and the topography of his mountain,[32] extending the god's size to cosmic proportions. The effect is to relativize the usual sort of anthropomorphism.

Like the Mesopotamian and Ugaritic material, Israelite texts show complex usage of anthropomorphism. To be sure, the Bible often avoids or modifies anthropomorphism.[33] Yet a tremendous amount of biblical literature. Passages assigned in traditional source-criticism to the so-called "Jahwist source," for example, contain a number of highly anthropomorphic statements about Yahweh. Genesis 3:8–9 presents Yahweh walking in the garden of Eden and then asking the man where he is, which on a plain reading implies that Yahweh does not know everything. Genesis 6:6 represents Yahweh as a regretful figure whose heart is saddened by the moral downturn of humans (cf. 1 Samuel 15:29). Genesis 8:21 describes Yahweh smelling the sacrifice that Noah offered to him. It may be that in the time of this so-called Jahwist "source" (dated by scholars variously from the tenth to the sixth centuries B.C.),[34] Yahweh was generally regarded in anthropomorphic terms. Quite striking as well is the anthropomorphism of the weeping Yahweh in Jeremiah 12:7–13.[35] As noted in the preceding section, Isaiah 6 clearly represents the vision of an enthroned anthropomorphic god. Recently scholars have suggested that this portrait includes the stronger anthropomorphism of referring to divine sexual parts. According to Isaiah 6:1, the prophet "saw Yahweh sitting [enthroned] on a throne high and exalted, with 'his train' (*šūlāyw*) filling the Temple." Instead of seeing here the "train" of the divine garment, L. Eslinger takes the word **šûl* in the first verse of Isaiah 6 as the divine genitalia.[36] Despite problems with this interpretation, it is not out of the realm of the possible.[37] M. H. Pope has offered an equally graphic interpretation of Ezekiel 16. He suggests that Ezekiel 16:8–14 recounts Yahweh's courtship, marriage, and sexual relations with Jerusalem, personified as a young woman.[38] God recounts their relationship in first person speech: "Now when I passed you . . . , your time was the time of love, I spread my cloak over you and covered your nakedness . . . and entered into a covenant with you . . . Then I washed you with water, indeed cleaned your blood from you. . . ." Pope interprets the covering of the woman in her time of love as sexual relations, the covenant as marriage, and the blood as the traditional signal for the loss of female virginity. Accordingly, Pope reads this divine speech as a description of sexual relations and marriage on the part of Yahweh and Jerusalem. These explicit inter- pretations of Yahweh's sexual genitalia and behavior remain highly controversial. Equally significant is the rarity of biblical passages that lend themselves to such possibilities. Even if one were to accept the interpretations of Eslinger and Pope, still only two passages are involved.

Israelite anthropomorphism hardly ends with the monarchy. Post-exilic liter- ature, where anthropomorphism might be less expected, is in fact replete with it. Later works belonging even to the priestly tradition continued to transmit an- thropomorphic imagery. Post-exilic priestly texts, such as Zechariah 3, attest to the divine council. Zechariah 3:7 includes the high priest in the ranks of the celestial courts (cf. Zechariah 12:8). Post-exilic apocalyptic circles (Daniel 7) also continued anthropomorphic renderings of Yahweh and the divine council (Daniel 7; cf. Zechariah 14:4; 1 Enoch 14). Indeed, the apocalyptic genre provided fertile ground for mythic material. This genre more than any other expressed mythic content in dramatic form. All of these biblical passages as well as many others (such as Isaiah 27:1) reflect the continuation of old mythic material in post-exilic Israelite tradition. Furthermore, nonbiblical Jewish literature from the fourth to the second centuries, including 1 Enoch and the Book of Jubilees, represents an additional source of anthropomorphic speculation. The anthropomorphic language of Yahweh, other divine beings, and their heavenly realms never disappeared from Israel. Accordingly, it may be regarded as quite traditional in ancient Israel.

By the same token, the archaeological and textual record may point to an anti-anthropomorphic reaction in ancient Israel as well. Because of the relative lack of divine iconography in Israel, some scholars have claimed that Israel was essentially aniconic.[39] Theological reflections of various sorts demonstrate a con- comitant move away from traditional anthropomorphism. Psalm 50:8–15 criticizes the idea that Yahweh actually consumes the offered sacrifices and evidently reflects the more popular conception. The priestly avoidance of anthropomorphism indi- cates that divine corporeality was a general expectation of what a deity was. The priestly texts of Numbers show some tension between the older anthropomorphism of Israel and its own sensibilities about divine "body language." For example, the priestly blessing of Numbers 6:24–26 twice refers to the "face" of God and once to the lighting of the divine face, yet God appears to Moses in a disembodied form in Numbers 7:89 as a voice having itself speak (*haqqôl middābbēr*). The anthro- pomorphic language can be retained in the priestly tradition; in these contexts it is perhaps regarded as expressions of blessing and presence and not a matter of some experience of the divine face.

Another priestly strategy about such anthropomorphism may be seen at work in the description of the human person's creation in Genesis 1. As I noted in the previous section, the prophetic vision of the divine assembly of Isaiah 6:1 renders Yahweh after the fashion of an enthroned human king, and Ezekiel 1:26 modifies this vision. Like Isaiah 6 and Ezekiel 1, Genesis 1:26–28 utilizes the traditional language of the divine council, as manifest for example in the use of the first common plural for divine speech in Genesis 1:26, a feature found also in Genesis 3:22, 11:7, and Isaiah 6:8. The use of *dĕmût*, "likeness," and *ṣelem*, "image,"[40] in Genesis 1:26–28 presupposes the vision of the anthropomorphic god yet reduces the anthropomorphism radically compared to Ezekiel 1:26. In fact, Genesis 1 achieves the opposite effect of Ezekiel 1:26. Whereas Ezekiel 1:26 conveys the prophet's vision of Yahweh in the likeness of the human person, Genesis 1 presents a vision of the human person in the likeness of the Divine. Rather than reducing Yahweh to human terms through an anthropomorphic portrait, Genesis 1:26–28 magnifies the human person in divine terms. What is possibly an old poetic piece embedded in 1:27 has been understood as implying an androgynous God, as the human person in the divine image is male and female.[41] Unfortunately, the examples claimed for divine androgyny in Ugaritic and other ancient Middle Eastern texts are unconvincing; it would be more persuasive to view this language at most as vestigial from an older form of Yahwistic cult that acknowledged Asherah as Yahweh's consort, hence male and female.[42] However, such a sensibility about the divine image could only be imputed to the pre-priestly poetic piece thought to underlie Genesis 1:27, for the so-called priestly tradition represented in Genesis 1 did not understand its God in such ditheistic terms.[43] In its present context in Genesis 1:26–28, any anthropomorphic background is at most muted. Indeed, Genesis 1 draws on the older visionary tradition of the anthropomorphic deity but ultimately transcends it, as it omits any description of the divine. In context, the priestly understanding of the divine image would appear to pose an analogy between God as creator and the first human couple as creators, as the following verse 28 commands them to procreate. Anthropomorphism was evidently quite popular in ancient Israel. Theological expressions in the biblical texts occasionally construed the anthropomorphism in terms differing from the traditional discourse of analogy between deities and humans.

Divine anthropomorphism and the analogy it implies with human nature involve complex historical issues when they involve divine gender roles. Biblical texts show a variety of strategies in handling divine gender.[44] In Deuteronomy 32: 18, Psalm 22:9–10, and Isaiah 46:3, 66:9, and 13, Yahweh was not considered female, either separately or in conjunction with male language for Yahweh. Rather, these passages treat Yahweh as a male deity to whom female imagery was occasionally attributed on a metaphorical level. We can also see the continued use of paternal language applied to Yahweh directly, although it is not very frequent (Deuteronomy 32:6; Jeremiah 3:4, 19; 31:9; Isaiah 63:16, 64:7 [E 8]; Malachi 1:6, 2:10; Wisdom of Solomon 14:3; Ben Sira 23:1, 4; cf. Exodus 4:22; Hosea 11:1). Other images of king, redeemer, warrior, and so on, are considerably more widespread in the Bible and deuterocanonical works. If Yahweh was considered essentially a male deity, then biblical passages with female imagery for Yahweh may have represented an expansion of the Israelite understanding of Yahweh. Such innovation may best explain not only the female images for the Divine in Second Isaiah (Isaiah 42:14; 46:3; 49:14–15; cf. 45:10–11; 66:9, 13)[45] but also the divine lamentation in Jeremiah 12:7–13 and other verses, an anthropomorphic portrait best compared in Mesopotamian literature with the goddess mourning the destroyed city.⁴⁶ "Monotheism" in "Second Isaiah" (Isaiah 40–55)⁴⁷ in no way precludes male or female language for Yahweh. Accordingly, Yahweh both encompasses the characteristics and values expressed through gendered metaphors and transcends the categories of sexuality (cf. Job 38:28–29): monotheism is beyond sexuality yet nonetheless expressed through it.

Attribution of female roles to gods was by no means an Israelite innovation.⁴⁸ Indeed, even specifically female roles for gods (and vice versa?) were posited in proper names, such as Ugaritic *'ttr'um*, "Athtar is mother" (cf. *'ttr'ab*, "Athtar is father"); *'il'nt*, "Anat is (a) god;" Akkadian *ummi-šamaš*, "Shamash is my mother," and *a-da-nu-um-mu*, "lord is mother." Deities in ancient Middle Eastern prayers likewise convey the combination of gender roles. Two examples suffice. In his prayer to Gatumdug, the city-goddess of Lagash, Gudea says:

I have no mother—you are my mother,
I have no father—you are my father,
You implanted in the womb the germ of me,
gave birth to me from out of the vulva (too),
Sweet, O Gatumdug, is your holy name!

The poem combines parental imagery of mother and father. The same juxtaposition appears to underlie Psalm 27:10. Compared to Gudea's prayer, this biblical verse suggests that Yahweh assumes the role of father and mother, thereby affirming divine care. A second millennium Hittite prayer likewise attributes both parental roles to Istanu, a sun god: "Thou, Istanu, art father and mother of the oppressed, the lonely (and the) bereaved person." These examples illustrate the larger ancient Middle Eastern background to the combination of parental roles for Yahweh. They also show that such a combination was already ancient in Middle Eastern literature. Ancient Middle Eastern texts indicate that female metaphors do not imply a female status for a male god. Rather, according to ancient Middle Eastern categories, a male god could be accorded female imagery without implying that he was considered both male and female. The inverse is true as well: male metaphors could be attributed to a goddess without meaning that the goddess was thought to be both female and male. Female imagery could have been attributed to Yahweh without any influence from any goddess. Ancient Middle Eastern literature, including the Bible, did not maintain a strict correlation between gods and putatively male imagery and roles or between goddesses and putatively female imagery and roles. Divine discourse is more elastic, in part perhaps because deities are not human beings.

Monotheistic Yahwism resembled neither a Greek philosophical notion of Deity as nonsexual Being nor some type of divine bisexuality. Instead, Israelite society perceived Yahweh primarily as a god, embodying traits or values expressed by gendered metaphors yet transcending such particular renderings. It is unnecessary and it is not supported by any biblical text to argue that monotheistic Yahweh involved either androgyny⁴⁹ or homoeroticism.⁵⁰ Such views appear eisegetical and seem based on a wooden reading of ancient gender roles as applied to divinities (for theological reasons regarded by B. S. Childs as "the worse kind of literalism"⁵¹).

Many, if not most, of the Israelite gendered presentations of Yahweh are not so concerned with divine sexuality. So T. Frymer-Kensky comments on the sexuality of the monotheistic Yahweh: "God is not a sexual male, and therefore even the erotic metaphor of passion reveals a lack of physicality. God is not imaged in erotic terms and sexuality was simply not part of the divine order."[52] Instead, the issue is divine-human interpersonal relations, as rightly noted by R. S. Hendel.[53]

One may rightly ask about further nuances in the maleness of the divine body. Isaiah sees God at the outset of divine revelation made to the prophet (Isaiah 6). Ezekiel 1's complex, perhaps even seemingly bizarre, rendering of the divine is aimed at prophetic revelation of a god beyond human comprehension. Moses and others see God in Exodus 24:9–11 in order to describe community with the divine, and Exodus 33–34 shows a visionary experience that at once reveals and conceals God to Moses. There is no hint here of sexuality. Indeed, divine sexual relations or some other explicit marker of sexuality is absent from all of these passages, in contrast to the Ugaritic texts on divine sexuality. The biblical texts concern revelation, authority, and a divine capacity and desire to help by revealing the divine will. Revelation is in part a matter of divine authority,[54] which divine maleness serves to convey (as divine authority is expressed by the leading male of the divine social unit, the divine family). As chapter 3 illustrates, the model of divinity is patriarchal, and we may then identify in divine maleness a sensibility of authority and a capacity and will to help.

Given the evidence that Yahweh's maleness does not convey sexuality per se, but personal divine communication, authority, concern, and dedication (perhaps we might say even accessibility to human emotion), it is then hardly surprising that the Bible rarely, if ever, describes divine sexual relations or genitalia. A brief survey of divine body parts in the Bible may help to explain the point further. Different body parts serve commonly as parts for the whole (*pars pro toto*) in order to denote divine attitudes (human body parts show analogous uses of *pars pro toto* to denote various attitudes). Divine eyes denote watchfulness and knowledge of human activity (Psalms 5:6, 11:4; cf. 9:14, 10:14); the divine hand and arm power and strength (Psalm 10:12); the divine nose anger (Psalms 2:11, 18:9); the divine hands and fingers creation (Psalm 8:4, 7) or trapping (Psalm 9:17), the divine ears a capacity to receive human prayer (see Psalm 10:17; cf. 5:2), and the divine face access or presence (Psalms 17:15, 42:3) and blessing (Psalm 4:7), as well as absence (Psalm 10:11). Some divine actions also presuppose a familiarity with divine body language: divine sitting denotes enthronement (Psalm 2:4; cf. 9:5, 8), and divine standing a lack of action or movement toward (i.e., on behalf of) the speaker (Psalm 10:1). We might think that, in contrast, divine genitalia denote no divine action or attitude toward human beings. Divine fatherhood can be expressed to denote patronage or support (see Psalm 2:7), but the body language of genitalia rarely, if ever, comes into play. In sum, the monotheistic picture of Yahweh, the male god without a consort, dominated biblical discourse for the divine, as far as the sources indicate (assuming that these sources correspond reasonably accurately with historical reality). At the same time, male language for Yahweh accompanied less anthropomorphic descriptions for the deity and metaphors occasionally including female imagery or combining it with male imagery.

The value of anthropomorphism deserves fuller consideration. In some contexts it could convey the personal aspects of divinity and its accessibility[55] in the face of a general notion of divine transcendence. If divinity is analogous to humanity, then divinity is perceptible as personal, as the paramount paradigm of personal relations remains human-human interaction. To regard anthropomorphism as little more than a figurative ornament expressing divine-human communication and interaction diminishes the religious expression and experience of the Israelites and other West Semitic peoples. These ancients did not develop abstract metaphysical systems involving philosophical logic. Instead, they represented their theology, their religious reality, through pictures of divinity in narratives and poetry. Even the priestly and deuteronomic works do not entirely dismiss anthropomorphic language. Instead, these sources offer a minimal anthropomorphism designed to modify people's understanding of God. Accordingly, if adherents of biblical tradition wish to appropriate their "God-talk" from the Bible, then they must acknowledge the biblical tension between "maximal" and minimal anthropomorphism, and ultimately its subordination to the transcendent reality represented by Israelite monotheism. Biblical monotheism is expressed through anthropomorphism, through gendered language, yet it relativizes anthropomorphism, perhaps even subordinates it to the divine one known only by the name of Yahweh. However, this view of anthropomorphism and divine sexuality in the Bible may have resulted at least in part from a de facto omission of older, more sexually explicit descriptions of the divine, as suggested in the following discussion of holiness.

3. Holiness

God is light.

1 John 1:5

Deities were generally marked for holiness (*qdš*), as can be inferred from the general designation of deities as "holy ones."[56] The Ugaritic texts refer to the deities collectively as "sons of *qdš*" (CAT 1.2 I 20–21, 38; 1.17 I 3, 8, 10–11, 13, 22; cf. 1.2 III 19–20), literally "sons of holiness" or "sons of the holy one."[57] A Phoenician inscription (KAI 4:4–5) refers to the deities in general as the "holy ones" (*qdšm*). Holiness was also regarded as a special attribute of a particular deity. Ugaritic texts refer to *ltpn wqdš*. The first is the god El's title, "Beneficent," but the second title has been imputed either to El or his wife Athirat.[58] However, one might expect the feminine ending (**qdšt*) if the title belonged to the goddess in Ugaritic literature (see note 42 on page 237). In any case, the title "holy one," belongs to one deity or the other. Athirat's servant bears the compound name, Qdš w-'Amrr. Here again the first part of this double-name means "Holy One."

In the West Semitic world, holiness was a general characteristic adhering to material realia and social processes in shrines,[59] including the appearance of divinity (theophany). By definition, divinity is observable in some sense in these places. They are marked and demarcated for holiness, and divinity is perceived to partake fully of holiness. In turn, the presence of divinity imparts holiness to those places.

From a cultic perspective holiness of deities is a matter of liturgical experience and expression: deities are known in holy places and both are considered holy. By extension, deities' sanctuaries as well as their dwellings on mountains partake of holiness. So Baal's mountain, Mount Sapan, is called "holy" (CAT 1.3 III 30; 1.16 I 7) as well as "divine" (1.3 III 29). Accordingly, temples, as well as their mythic expressions as sacred garden, participate in the deity's holiness.[60]

In a sense, to call deities "holy ones" may seem to constitute a sort of tautology, but further study of the words for "holy" and "holiness" reveals the root metaphor underlying the idea of divine holiness. One of the main Akkadian terms for "holy," *ellu*, denotes not only holiness but also cleanliness[61] in its profane sense as not simply the absence of dirt but also brilliance and luminosity (cf. English "sparkling clean"). So the Ugaritic word, *thr* refers to brilliance and luminosity (cf. *ṭāhōr* in Exodus 24:10).[62] The idea of cultic holiness (purity) then is based analogically on the profane notion of cleanliness, both in its negative connotation as free of dirt and in its positive connotation of brilliance.[63] Both connotations are germane to the experience of deities: theophanies characteristically transpire in places regarded as clean from a cultic perspective, spaces ideally uncontaminated by human sin or impurity; theophanies are often marked by the brilliance of the deity's presence.

Descriptions of the experience of the divine holiness yield further information. Divine holiness in cult (theophany, literally "divine appearance") is experienced and expressed as shaking (Isaiah 6:4) and other physical effects that induce awe and fear in humans. As CAT 1.4 VII indicates, the presence of a major deity induces the same reaction of dread and fear. Commonly students of ancient religion Rave understood this experience of the holy in terms of awe and fear. In the modern Western discussion of religion, this idea dates to the theologian Rudolf Otto, who characterized this confrontation with the divine as *mysterium tremendum et fascinosum*. The opening page of *Treasures of Darkness*, a seminal study of Mesopotamian religion by the great Sumerologist Thorkild Jacobsen, follows Otto explicitly:

> Basic to all religion—and so also to ancient Mesopotamian religion—is, we believe, a unique experience with power not of this world. Rudolph Otto called this confrontation "Numinous" and analyzed it as the experience of *mysterium tremendum et fascinosum*, a confrontation with a "Wholly Other" outside of normal experience and indescribable in its terms: terrifying, ranging from sheer demonic dread through awe to sublime majesty; and fascinating, with its irresistable attraction, demanding unconditional allegiance. It is the positive human response to this experience in thought (myth and theology) and action (cult and worship) that constitutes religion.[64]

A similar view of the divinity as numinous has been forwarded recently by R. de Vito:

> [W]e must reckon with the possibility of another use of *ilum* in the onomasticon, one articulating the human response to the numinous qualities of a temple (e.g., Meslam), certain localities (e.g., Apih), or a deceased loved one (e.g., *abum*, *aḫum*). The numinous aspect of these phenomena is expressed in the word *ilum* "god": "Meslam-is-(indeed)-God," "(The)-City-is-(indeed)-God," "Apih-is-

(indeed)-God," "(The-deceased)-Father/Brother-is-(indeed)-God." But what does "god" mean in this usage?

While *Ersatznamen* [replacement names] of this type do not predate the Early Sargonic period, Fara period names show that the use of *ilum* in this sense is a possibility present from the beginning. Expressing an "earlier," more fundamental level of meaning, in these names *ilum* points beyond particular divine beings, such as Šamaš, to a realm of power incommensurate with the human and to which the gods, together as a class, belong. The very use of the determinative *dinger*, a lexical classifier, shows that the scribes of Mesopotamia engaged in a systematic effort to classify the phenomena of their world at a quite early date. Yet this should not obscure the fact that the recognition of the existence of a whole category of beings as distinct "gods" is a logical advance dependent upon a prior awareness of the underlying reality of the category, a dimension or realm of divine power, which is "more" than the particular gods who substantiate it.[65]

This notion of the divine holiness and its associated numinous characteristic are well attested in the Bible and other Middle Eastern texts.[66] The "holy voice" of the deity, whether belonging to Yahweh or Baal, signals a theophany that may wreak destruction (Psalm 29) or revelation (as in Numbers 7:89) and induces flight and fear on the part of the god's enemies (CAT 1.4 VII 29). Similarly, sanctuaries can be regarded as awe-inspiring, like the deities who own and inhabit them.[67]

Jacobsen and others make the experience of Otto's *mysterium* the cornerstone for understanding religion or the divine. However, qualification is warranted. Because such experience is mediated by a human experience and language, it is not by definition entirely "Wholly Other." It may be recognizable in the natural effects of the rain-storm or dream experience at night. In these experiences the completely "other" partakes of the here and now. Moreover, as the opening parts of this section indicate, divinity throughout the ancient Middle East is also experienced personally and not as entirely other. Indeed, anthropomorphism is a hallmark of the classic deities of the pantheon as opposed to divine monsters in many Mesopotamian myths of primordial conflict.[68] The view of ancient Middle Eastern religion (and consequently divinity) fostered by Otto's notion of *mysterium* captures one side of the perception of the divine. The *mysterium* makes its appearance in the terrestrial realm, in nature, dreams, and other purely "this worldly" locales. K. van der Toorn comments:

> One would be wrong, however, to suppose that the dichotomy between the material and the spiritual world was as natural to them as it seems to us. Occasional doubts could not rob them of the conviction that the gods dwelled in the same universe as they did and were to a large extent subject to the same forces and moved by the same reasonings.
>
> Our uneasiness stems partly from the opposition of the reality as directly perceived by the senses and a spiritual reality only reached by faith or some sort of mystical experience. This was not how the Mesopotamians conceived of their gods. To them they were the personifications of various aspects of nature and culture, very much present in daily experience.[69]

The *mysterium* was simultaneously "other" and not "other," and this combination helps make it, to repeat Otto's expression, *tremendum et fascinosum*.[70]

The "this-worldly" quality of holiness is not merely a theoretical matter. Deities and their holiness are not only served by their servants, priests, and kings; deities also serve priests and kings, and, by definition, the public sacred spaces serve both as well. The holiness of both deities and the public places where they were celebrated is not only a vague, ill-defined experience of the numinous (although it may have seemed to be that as well). As S. Guthrie has emphasized, holiness delimits and expresses the power of those who maintain such spaces.[71] Guthrie stresses that in Israel holiness attaches to the elite and the monarch; the point may apply as well to Ugarit. He notes how the radiance of the deity became associated with the power of the king: "Holiness here is ideology, and designed to serve a particular social system."[72] In his discussion of sacred order, W. E. Paden comments in a related vein: "Power and order are intertwined and mutually conditioning elements of religious world-building. Each is a premise of the other. The gods presuppose the very system which invests them with their status as gods, even though the world-order may itself be perceived as a creation of the gods."[73] Thus, the holiness of a place expressed altogether this worldly relationship of power and status.

Israelite texts also mention the holy beings collectively as a divine body or assembly led by Yahweh, their king. Psalm 89:6–8 praises Yahweh:

> So the heavens praise Your wonders, O Yahweh,
> Your fidelity also in the assembly of the Holy Ones.
> For who in the heavens can be compared to Yahweh,
> Who among the sons of god can be likened to Yahweh
> A god dreaded in the great council of the Holy Ones,
> And feared of all them that are round him?

The initial sentence characterizes the heavenly beings as Holy Ones assembled in a congregation (*qāhāl), similar to a human congregation. The first part of the question identifies the heavenly hosts as "sons of god," an expression for divine beings. The second part of the question describes this body as an assembly or council of holy ones collected around Yahweh. Zechariah 14:5 assumes a similar view of Yahweh's military hosts: "And Yahweh my god will come, with all holy ones with You."

Holiness in ancient Israel developed "apartness," a further nuance.[74] The origins of this particular connotation are unclear, but they might be assigned to the development of priestly notions about separation of the holy from the profane, represented systematically, for example, in Genesis 1. The Israelite priesthood apparently came to define divine holiness in even more specific terms as a separation from death and sex. The different priestly lines during this period found their own primary images of Yahweh (whether older or newer ones) incompatible with some of the older images, so they chose not to preserve them and thereby functionally censored them. Indeed, the presentation of Yahweh generally as sexless and unrelated to the realm of death would appear to have been produced precisely by a priesthood whose central notion of Yahweh as holy would view this deity as fully removed from realms of impurity, specifically, sex and death.[75] Several prohibitions govern the impurity of sexuality[76] and death (Numbers 19:11, 14–19; 31:19).

Priests were restricted in their selection of a spouse specifically because of the issue of holiness (Leviticus 21:7). Priests were specially restricted also in their contact with the dead.[77] Unlike the other priests, the chief priest is even more restricted, not being permitted contact with any dead (Leviticus 21:11–12) and permitted to choose as a wife only a woman who has not yet had children (*bětûlâ*, Leviticus 21:13–14). The chief priest is identified with the holiness of the divine sanctuary.[78] Holier than the holy of holies, the deity of the priesthood would have epitomized the fullest possibilities of sacredness and separation in terms of sexuality and death. It may be that older mythologies involving divine death and sex did not survive, not only because the priesthood would have actively censored such views (although such a situation is theoretically possible) but also because such mythologies did not cohere with the priestly tradition's normative understanding of the divine (nor the deuteronomic view of the divine), and so they fell into disuse in these traditions.[79]

4. Immortality

> For once I myself saw with my own eyes
> the Sibyl at Cumae hanging in a cage,
> and when the boys said to her,
> "Sibyl what do you want?"
> she replied, "I want to die."
>
> T. S. Eliot, *The Waste Land*

With these words from Petronius's *Satyricon* T. S. Eliot prefaced his now famous poem *The Waste Land*. From the perspective of humanity, death may seem a great personal destruction to be avoided; from the immortal Sibyl's viewpoint, nondeath was an inescapable fate, an undeniable fact. Some ancient Middle Eastern statements contrast divine timelessness with human mortality, for humanity cannot avoid death, except in the most exceptional of cases. One fundamental property of deities is their continuity in the cosmos, whether in the form of eternal life or divine death.

If we glance briefly at some Mesopotamian texts, we see expressions of the view that deities are free from death. A classic expression derives from a well-known passage from Gilgamesh (OB version):

> When the gods created humanity,
> They assigned death to humanity,
> But life they kept in their own hands.[80]

And some lines later:

> Who, my friend can scale heaven?
> Only the gods [live] forever under the sun.
> As for humanity, their days are numbered,
> Whatever they do is wind.[81]

According to M. G. Kovacs,[82] here Gilgamesh recites proverbs to his dear friend Enkidu about human mortality. (We may be reminded of the motifs of "under the sun" and human pursuits as "wind" in Ecclesiastes.) In contrast, the gods enjoy nondeath, that is, uninterrupted life.[83] As a later section of the Gilgamesh reminds readers, death is indeed the fate of humanity.[84] Even for Gilgamesh, regarded as two-thirds divine and one-third human,[85] death is the ultimate end. Or, to cite a Hittite writer: "Life is bound up with death, and death is bound up with life. Mortal man doesn't live forever. The days of his life are numbered."[86] In sum, death separates humanity from divinity.

The Ugaritic texts generally assume the same concept of divine deathlessness. Individual deities may be called *'lm*, "eternal." Shapshu simply bears the title "eternal" (*'lm*, 2.42.7), Rapiu is called "eternal king" (*mlk 'lm*,[87] 1.108.1, 21, 22), and El's wisdom is labeled "for eternity" (*'d 'lm*,1.3 V 31; 1.4 IV 42). Keret's son also expresses the viewpoint that gods are not expected to die (1.16 I 14–23. II 36–44).[88] Anat's promise to Aqhat to make him eternal like the gods (1.17 V 28–29) is rejected by him as implausible:[89]

I'll have you count years with Baal,	*'aššprk 'm b'l šnt*
Count months with El's offspring.	*'m bn 'il*[90] *tspr yrhm*

Finally, deities are timeless because they do not age in these texts. They are, in a sense, frozen in time, whether they are presented as younger, like Baal and Anat, or older, like El and Athirat.

Divine death then is not a norm in ancient literatures. However, J. Z. Smith provides a helpful qualification to modern presuppositions about the eternal life of deities:

> Despite the shock this fact may deal to modern Western religious sensibilities, it is commonplace within the history of religions that immortality is not a prime characteristic of divinity: gods die. Nor is the concomitant of omnipresence a widespread requisite; gods disappear. The putative category of dying and rising deities thus takes its place within the larger category of dying gods and the even larger category of disappearing deities. Some of these divine figures simply disappear; some disappear only to return in the near or distant future; some disappear and reappear with monotonous frequency.[91]

The force of Smith's critique cannot be denied; indeed, to be dead means to be defunct. Smith's generalization here might divert attention from the differences regarding divine death in various regions.

In Ugarit, even deities who are said to be dead are not permanently so. Apparently decimated by Anat in 1.6 II Mot re-appears on the scene in 1.6 VI and resumes his conflict with Baal. Yamm, too, is said to be dead (1.2 IV 32, 34) after his defeat and apparent dismemberment at Baal's hands, yet he seems to re-appear, possibly for renewed conflict with his nemesis, in the broken opening of 1.4 VII.[92] The parade example of a divine death in the Ugaritic texts is Baal himself. Of course, like Mot and perhaps Yamm, Baal does not remain permanently dead, for never in the Ugaritic texts is divine death a permanent condition.

The larger fund of Mesopotamian literary texts shows more exceptions in the deaths of gods than Ugaritic or Israelite literatures. In W. G. Lambert's words, "the gods could not die in Sumero-Babylonian thought in the sense of getting old and eventually dying of natural causes. But they could die a violent death."[93] There are three types of divine death in Mesopotamian literature: (1) older gods killed in stories of divine succession, (2) divine rebels; and (3) divine monsters.[94] (The exception to these three categories is Tammuz; as Lambert notes, he is neither old nor decrepit nor rebellious.) Deities in these three categories do not generally receive cult, and one may infer that a dead god lacks a separate cult. In other words, these figures are defunct.[95]

Moreover, these ancient deaths may serve a further function: to describe the cosmos in the (Mesopotamian) present. The deaths of these gods show how the world and humanity are connected to the divine realm, even though not divine. Hence, it is the blood of the dead rebel Qingu (sometimes spelled Kingu) that provides the blood of humanity (Enuma Elish 6:32–33),[96] and it is the carcass of the slain divine monster Tiamat that provides the substance of the cosmos (Enuma Elish 4:137–138, 5:45–65).[97] The deaths of Yamm (Sea) and Mot (Death) in the Ugaritic Baal Cycle likewise signal the relation of cosmic waters and death to the created order and experience of human beings. These deaths transpire in the context of narratives, as ways of describing the likenesses and differences of humanity and the world to divinity. (I avoid the word "explain" because I do not want to imply that myths are mainly explanations or that their authors and transmitters thought of them primarily in such terms; myths instead are descriptive of their reality, their experience of the world.) Instead of undermining the notion that death delimits divinity from humanity, these deaths describe by analogy the partial divinity of humanity and the world as well as their separateness.[98] The deaths of these gods make their divine matter usable, and they connect the created order to the gods. So even in the cases of deities, death still delimits the divine from the created order, which includes humanity. These dead gods then are fully consistent with the broader conceptualization that death distinguishes deities from humanity.

The case of Dumuzi/Tammuz is not exceptional for Mesopotamia, as Lambert's comment might suggest. Dumuzi is only one of a number of early disappearing "fertility" divinities (for example, Damu and Ninazu).[99] These other's were not regarded as ancient figures but as part of the present order of nature.[100] The same point has been claimed for the Ugaritic god Baal, because the Baal Cycle describes his descent to the underworld and presumes later his return to life. The surviving narrative describes Baal's divine death at considerable length, and it is clear that the deaths of Yamm and Mot do not present the same problem for the audience: Baal's death is a threat to the audience, whereas the deaths of Yamm and Mot mark the victory of life for the audience. For a long time scholars have claimed that both Tammuz and Baal belong to the category of "dying and rising gods." J. Z. Smith has extensively criticized this category;[101] the following chapter of this study discusses the highly diverse characters of the figures imputed to this category, as well as the different cultural contexts underlying the presentation of their deaths in narratives and rituals.[102] For Baal, only a narrative rendering survives; the seventy or so ritual texts from Ugarit are silent about any ritual background to the narrative presentation of Baal's death. To anticipate the next chapter, note here that the only ritual text pertinent to the presentation of Baal is not one mourning his death but the death of the human king in CAT 1.161. Hence, the narrative incorporates the presentation of the human king's demise into the picture of the divine king's death. The narrative encodes the information from the ritual in direct contrast to the older claim that the myth is a libretto or text for the ritual. Baal's death needs to be seen in the context of a narrative that presents his kingship as the basis of a cosmic political order.

The kingship of this warrior storm-god operates simultaneously on the three levels of nature, humanity, and divinity. On the natural level, Baal's death is associated with drought in the late summer and returning rains in the early fall. On the human and divine levels, the death signifies a loss of bounty and concomitant well-being, and his life heralds the restoration of life (so CAT 1.4 VII 49–52). Baal's death also reinforces his weakness in evidence elsewhere in the Baal Cycle; he is a weak monarch who needs the other deities. Kingship itself on all levels is precarious. Baal's rule, with its moments of strength and weakness, may parallel the Ugaritic dynasty's vulnerability to foreign powers (Egypt and Hatti) as well as to internal threats to dynastic continuity by heirs, succession, or rebellion, as the narrative of Kirta presents the problems of kingship. Accordingly, Baal's kingship gives expression to death and life on many levels; even in the narrative of his death, Baal's return to life reinforces the generalization that deities are deathless. Even his death lacks the permanence of human death. In the Ugaritic material deities, even Baal, are by definition living for the human communities that maintain their cult. Their deaths lack the finality of human death, and as Gilgamesh and Petronius remind their audiences, deities differ from humans in matters of life and death.

As in Ugaritic literature, in Israelite texts divine death is the exception rather than the rule. The notion of "dead gods" is absent from the extant corpus of Israelite texts, with the exception of Psalm 82,[103] which describes a divine council scene where Yahweh denounces the other gods as failing in their divine duties. Accordingly, Yahweh declares them to be "dead."[104] The psalm closes with a (prophetic?) call for Yahweh to demonstrate his power over the earth. In this text, the concept of "dead gods" serves a polemical purpose against the older traditional notion that other gods were the divine patrons of other nations while Israel was Yahweh's portion in this division of the cosmos (cf. Deuteronomy 32:8–9, reading "sons of God" with LXX and Dead Sea Scrolls[105]). Within the context of Psalm 82, the gods traditionally believed to represent the divine patrons of the other nations are declared now to be dead. In this case, "dead" means defunct. Yet what separates this Israelite composition about dead gods from their treatment in Ugaritic or Mesopotamian literature is the polemical purpose to which the concept is put. Stated differently, the Israelite usage involves an inner-cultural polemic aimed at nonindigenous deities (or ones perceived to be so). This insider/outsider dimension inherent in Psalm 82's polemic plays no apparent role in either the Ugaritic or Mesopotamian material.

Ezekiel 28 may be mined for this idea that deities do not die. Death is the way in which the denounced prince of Tyre will be shown to be human and not a god (New Jewish Publication Society version):

> Will you still say, "I am a god"
> Before your slayers,
> When you are proved a man, not a god,
> At the hands of those who strike you down?

Habakkuk 1:12 also seems to make this assumption about divinity: "You, O Lord, are from everlasting; My holy God, You never die."[106] Eternal life is commonly attributed to God. Psalm 90:2 reflects on the eternity of God versus noneternity of human beings. Another reflection of divine eternity involves the idea of God as the lord of human life and death (1 Samuel 2:6). Prayers requesting long life are addressed to and answered by the gods, precisely because they themselves have life in abundance.[107] Thus, it is the job of the gods to provide continued life. As the Idrimi inscription prays, "May (the gods) keep him alive and preserve him" (*li-bal-li-ṭu-ú-šu lin-na-ṣa-ru-šu*).[108]

An extended reflection on time involves "eternity" (*'ôlām*) in Ecclesiastes (Qohelet) 3:11. The verse may be translated literally (and quite woodenly):

> Everything he [God] made beautiful in its time; also *'ôlām* He gave in their heart, without humanity ever reaching the work which God made, from first to last.

The word *'ôlām* has been taken generally in four ways:[109]

1. "Eternity," based on the common BH usage, including Ecclesiastes 1: 4, 10, 2:16, 3:14, 9:6, and 12:5 (so LXX; ibn Ezra);
2. "That which is hidden, concealed," based on the BH usage of this root[110] (cf. possibly Ugaritic *ǵlmt*, "darkness" [?])[111] and supported by the Targum;
3. "Knowledge," based on Arabic *'lm*; and
4. "World," based on the later Hebrew meaning of this word."[112]

The first meaning "eternity" has the virtue of contextual support[113] in addition to clear etymological support. The initial clause characterizes divine creation in terms of time. This creation includes humanity. Yet, according to this reading of the second clause, humanity has eternity built into it. Hence, the contradiction of human life: humanity partakes both of the time-conditioned creation and the timelessness of divinity. This paradoxical nature of humanity means that we can intuit the divine plan yet cannot grasp it entirely. The second meaning likewise has some etymological and contextual support. The second half of the verse notes humanity's inability to comprehend the divine plan; hence, this plan and the deity remain "concealed" or "hidden" from human perception. The third and fourth solutions, lack etymological or contextual support. Other efforts based on emendation[114] or elastic semantic reach[115] seem poorly supported by either etymology or context.

It may be plausible to propose a double-reading of the word based on the first two meanings, the ones best supported etymologically, contextually, and text-critically. At work may be a sort of wordplay involving the different meanings of the same word or "root" in Hebrew derived from the coalescence of two originally different roots. This approach to originally different roots requires further explanation, because most Semitic scholars detect the meaning of one original root or the other in any given context, but not both. The original stock of consonants in the Semitic languages was approximately thirty letters (the exact number is a matter of debate). Ugaritic shows a coalescence of a very few original consonants, including primary *w-/y-*. (In contrast, Hebrew, Aramaic, and Phoenician show the "loss" of six or seven letters coalesced into some of the remaining twenty-two or twenty-three letters.) As a result, two originally different roots appeared to ancient speakers of these languages as a single word. The multiple meanings of two originally different roots that came to resemble one another through historical changes likely represented the meanings and connotation of a single word.[116] It may be argued that the original roots of *$'lm$ and *$ǵlm$ have coalesced in Hebrew, and the meanings of the two were used as related Hebrew words. Drawing on these two sets of meanings in Hebrew, the author perhaps plays on them: God has set an eternity in humanity that is also hidden (a note that the book sounds in its final verse, also with the root *$'lm$). Ecclesiastes 3:11 presents this irony to humanity, namely, that the source for human realization of human limits lies within humanity's very own constitution. We can only intuit that which we cannot experience: eternity.

5. Postscript: Divine and Human Life (Or, My Breakfast with Shulamit)

In closing this chapter, I hazard some general observations about the traits of West Semitic deities. One morning (Oct. 15,1996) my (then) four-year-old daughter Shulamit and I were sitting at the kitchen table. As she slurped down her Lucky Charms (just as I had some thirty years earlier), she told me that parents are strong. I asked her what else parents are. She told me that parents have big noses, they know a lot, they love each other, and they love their kids. Shulamit is aware that parents are stronger and bigger than she is, that parents are gendered and relational, that parents have knowledge she does not possess (only a matter of time). And Shulamit is aware that parents will die. She told me (yes, on another breakfast occasion) that when she has children and her children grow up, I will die. She has a relative chronology in her mind as to how long her parents will live. (Whether she perceives that parents are holy in any sense will depend on time). It doesn't take a genius to realize that even in a modern Western society images of divinity derive in large measure from the family unit, and most of the images for deities reflect this unit and its living conditions.

My conversations with Shulamit help to place the preceding discussion into some perspective, although I offer these comments only tentatively. Many characteristics of divinity correspond to the great problems of human existence, with their attendant contradictions. For example, concerning to divine strength and power, D. Pardee comments: "[E]ach deity was more powerful than any human and capable, therefore, of affecting the life of any human being."[118] Characteristics of deities ultimately relate to human characteristics, actions, capacities and incapicities. For now I will only sketch out preliminarily how four characteristics of divinity[119] correspond to problems of human existence as well as its contradictions:

human problems	*human contradictions*	*divine characteristics*
powerlessness	human power, but experience of suffering and evil people	strength, size
lack of prosperity/ infertility	experience, intuition of divine presence, but common experience of divine absence	sexuality/love

| unholiness | knowledge and experience of self as both wrong (sinning) and whole (holy) | holiness |
| mortality | limited time, but intuiting eternity | eternity |

These characteristics suggest at once a great divide looming between humanity and divinity and an intimate bond linking them. For the ancients at Ugarit, to understand divinity is to extrapolate from the human condition to express reality that cannot be entirely described; and to understand humanity is in turn to make some sense of divinity that can be sensed only in part.

The modern critique of religion as a human artifact is in part confirmed and undermined by the preceding survey. On one hand, the deities are rendered in the image and likeness of their adherents. On the other hand, the treatment of the deities clearly shows an awareness that divinity is not the same as humanity. Moreover, the discussion of anthropomorphism in section 2 indicates that divinity is not simply humanity writ large. Instead, although anthropomorphism remains the norm, reflection on it shows a recognition that more than mere "wish-fulfillment" was involved. This countertrend, though, is hardly confined to Israel; it is evident in Mesopotamia and Ugarit. The ancients struggled with the limits of their understanding of divinity, not simply assuming that it was a distorting mirror of themselves on a larger scale. It was a mystery of something beyond themselves as well, to which they had a limited access through their experience.

This description of divine mystery applies as well to Israelite material. The extant Bible exhibits no "unique" feature in descriptions of the divine. I will turn to Israelite monotheism at the end of this book, and I elaborate other features or combination of features specific to ancient Israel. Yet this is an issue of religious particularity, not an objective measure of Israelite uniqueness; by this token we could look for features of Babylonian, Assyrian, Ugaritic, or Egyptian uniqueness.[120] Clearly such quests for Israelite uniqueness, evidently driven by post-biblical concerns, are quixotic. Accordingly, the quest for specific unique traits for Yahweh appears to be theology dressed up as history or history of religions. However, this is hardly the end of the issue. The point of a theological tradition, whether in the Bible or later, is to come to understand and to know the deity to which it is dedicated. Therefore, historians of religion and theologians alike may be interested in posing the issue in terms of Yahweh's particular profile. As the survey in this chapter indicates, this issue does not involve a question of distinctive characteristics for Yahweh as much as a unique combination of characteristics and a reduction in divine characteristics, in short a convergence of the valued divine roles in the figure of Yahweh. Despite the vestiges of more divine characteristics in early Israelite polytheism, Yahweh of Israelite monotheism has no divine peers, fewer divine subordinates, no sex (probably), no death, no family, but this deity maintained all the expected roles of divine protection and blessing. As a result, monotheistic Yahwism perhaps then resulted in a deity more concealed in character, more revealed in function.

6

The Life and Death of Baal

While smooth Adonis from his native rock
Ran purple to the sea, supposed with blood
Of Thammuz yearly wounded.

> John Milton, *Paradise Lost*,
> Book I, 450–52

Chapter 5 describes the characteristics expected of deities in the biblical world. One of these traits is immortality, or inability to die. However, the "dying and rising gods" in West Semitic religion are an exception to this rule. This category of divinity received great currency after the work of Sir James George Frazer (1854–1941), but more recently J. Z. Smith, H. Barstad, and other scholars have seriously questioned it. Despite their trenchant critiques, the category continues both in scholarly literature and in nonscholarly work.[1] For historians of religion, the death of "the dying and rising god" may have passed,[2] but the category has enjoyed a certain afterlife in biblical studies. Some highly respected scholars have used the category in their research on Israelite religion. For example, T. N. D. Mettinger understands Baal of Ugarit, Adonis, and Melqart as "dying and rising gods."[3] Mettinger also takes Yahweh's title, "the living god" (*'ĕlōhîm ḥayyîm*), as an anti-Baal epithet in the latter's capacity as a "dying and rising" god.[4] According to J. Day, "Baal's death and resurrection" lies behind the re-use of "the imagery of a dying and rising fertility god" in Hosea 5:12–6:3.[5] Day also reads the imagery of national death and resurrection in Hosea 13–14 against this same background, as Hosea 13:1 mentions Baal.[6] Mettinger and Day assume the validity of the category of "dying and rising gods," yet neither discusses its origins or limits.[7]

Because highly reputable scholars continue to use the category of "dying and rising gods," I would like to address its viability with six main aims: (1) to review Frazer's category of "dying and rising gods," (2) to point out the main defects in the category, (3) to investigate the differences among the different figures subsumed under the category, (4) to suggest an alternative interpretation to one crucial example of "dying and rising" gods, (Baal of Ugarit), (5) to offer further reflections about the presentation of Baal, and (6) to address the lack of conflict mythology involving Death and Israel's national deity. To anticipate the discussion that follows, this investigation casts serious doubt on the category Frazer proposed. Many of the figures assigned to this category are related to natural fertility, but otherwise they differ significantly. Furthermore, there is no hard evidence for a ritual background behind the "rising" of these figures. Because the category is fraught with difficulty, its origins deserve further examination. W. Robertson Smith and W. Mannhardt provided Frazer with the initial impetus for the category; Frazer's classical background perhaps contributed to its further systematization. In comments on ancient Near Eastern religions, classical authors sometimes equated different deities. This category of "dying and rising gods" was not well grounded in the primary evidence. As a result, interpreting either biblical passages or the Baal Cycle against the background of this putative category becomes a dubious procedure. It would seem more productive to interpret the various gods in the context of the cultures to which they belong before constructing a comparative category. The test case here is Baal of Ugarit. To the credit of Mettinger and Day, their comments connect funerary motifs with some of the figures involved, thereby pointing, in my mind, in the direction that the analysis of Baal's death and return to life in the Baal Cycle should take. Finally, the discussion focuses on the literary production of this mythology and its absence in biblical literature.

1. Frazer's Hypothesis about "Dying and Rising Gods"

In the wake of Frazer's work, it has been commonplace to characterize Baal as "a dying and rising god." Frazer's view can be traced back to the first edition of *The Golden Bough* (1890) and then in *Adonis Attis Osiris* (1906), which was incorporated as part 4 of the third edition of *The Golden Bough* (1911–1915).[8] In its time this work was immensely popular, its influence spreading beyond scholarly circles, into the wider culture, as reflected in such works as T. S. Eliot's famous poem *The Waste Land*.[9] The work was considered a beautifully written text, a powerful synthesis that offered massive explanatory power to an age seeking general evolutionary explanations for the origins and development of human civilizations.[10] Based on wide-ranging comparisons and assumptions, Frazer connected the cycle of vegetation with the mythologies of Egyptian Osiris, Sumerian Dumuzi/Akkadian Tammuz (his name given in Ezekiel 8:14), late Anatolian Attis and the late classical Adonis.[11] Writing of Tammuz (Dumuzi), Frazer asserts:

> In the religious literature of Babylonia Tammuz appears as the youthful spouse or lover of Ishtar, the great mother goddess, the embodiment of the reproductive energies of nature. The references to their connexion with each other in myth and ritual are both fragmentary and obscure, but we gather from them that each year Tammuz was believed to die, passing away from the cheerful earth to the gloomy subterranean world, and that every year his divine mistress journeyed in quest of him. . . . The stern mother of the infernal regions . . . reluctantly allowed Ishtar . . . to depart, in company probably with her lover Tammuz, that the two might return together to the upper world, and that with their return all nature might revive.[12]

Similarly, in his remarks about Adonis, Frazer suggests that: "the ceremony of the death and resurrection of Adonis must have been a dramatic representation of the decay and revival of plant life."[13]

Frazer generalizes about the "dying and rising gods" in the following way:

> Nowhere, apparently, have these rites been more widely and solemnly celebrated than in the lands which border the Eastern Mediterranean. Under the names of Osiris, Tammuz, Adonis, and Attis, the peoples of Egypt and Western Asia represented the yearly decay and revival of life, especially vegetable life, which they personified as a god who annually died and rose again from the dead. In name and detail the rites varied from place to place: in substance they were the same. The supposed death and resurrection of this oriental deity, a god of so many names but of essentially one nature, is now to be examined.[14]

The deities were thought to be the incarnations of the spirit of fertility or, more specifically, the spirit of particular crops such as corn. Referring specifically to Adonis, Frazer writes:

> [T]he annual death and revival of vegetation is a conception which readily presents itself to men in every stage of savagery and civilisation; and the vastness of the scale on which this ever-recurring decay and regeneration takes place, together with man's intimate dependence on it for subsistence, combine to render it the most impressive annual occurrence in nature, at least within the temperate zones. It is no wonder that a phenomenon so important, so striking and so universal, should, by suggesting similar ideas, have given rise to similar rites in many lands. We may, therefore, accept as probable an explanation of the Adonis worship which accords so well with the facts of nature and with the analogy of similar rites in other lands. Moreover, the explanation is countenanced by a considerable body of opinion among the ancients themselves, who again and again interpreted the dying and reviving god as the reaped and sprouting grain.[15]

Accordingly, these gods' narratives and rituals epitomized the cycle of natural fertility, which moved from life to death and then from death to life. Rituals connected with vegetation celebrated the drama of the gods' death and resurrection. This theory has four key elements: the divine status of the figures, their death and their return to life, a correspondence of this thematic cycle to the seasonal cycle, and a series of rituals that provide a cultic context for the recitation and performance of this thematic material.

The preface to the first edition of *The Golden Bough* credits the notion of the "slain god" to W. Robertson Smith, Frazer's friend and mentor in anthropology as well as the person to whom he dedicated the volume: "Indeed the central idea of my essay—the conception of the slain god—is derived directly, I believe from my friend. But it is due to him to add that he is in no way responsible for the general explanation which I have offered of the custom of slaying the god."[16] Frazer speaks quite correctly, as Robertson Smith's influence is evident in his work. In the first edition of *Lectures on the Religion of the Semites* (1889), Robertson Smith speaks of Baal in these terms in a section labeled the "annual death of the god": "The interpretation of the death of the god as corresponding to the annual withering up of nature . . . was naturally suggested by Baal-worship. . . . [I]n Baal-worship, when the death of the god becomes a mere cosmical process, and the most solemn rites that ancient religions knew sank to the level of scenic representation of the yearly revolutions of the seasons . . ."[17] Robertson Smith also speaks of Adonis (= Tammuz for Smith) as the incarnation of the spirit of vegetative fertility. Robertson Smith therefore seems to be Frazer's original source for seeing Adonis, Tammuz, and Baal as parts of the vegetative cycle.

Robertson Smith apparently influenced another feature of Frazer's thought on this subject. The comparison between the annual cycle of life and death represented by Baal and Jesus' death and resurrection was made by Robertson Smith in the first edition of his *Lectures* in 1889, a year before the first edition of *The Golden Bough*. The comparison was deleted from subsequent editions. In contrast, Frazer avoided such a comparison in the first edition of *The Golden Bough*, but beginning with the second edition, he explicitly compares Jesus and "dying and rising gods."[18] Frazer extended Robertson Smith's thought on the subject. The creation of the category of "dying and rising gods," as well as the greater range of gods brought under this rubric, seems to reflect Frazer's own systematization of Robertson Smith's more nuanced differentiation of these gods. Although Robertson Smith himself cites Frazer at times on such matters,[19] his discussions depart markedly from what Frazer offers. For example, Osiris does not appear in these terms in Robertson Smith's volume. Furthermore, Frazer included non-Semitic deities such as Dionysius in the category.

Frazer's approach was superimposed on Baal of Ugarit shortly after the early publication of Ugaritic texts. Scholars such as F. F. Hvidberg, T. H. Gaster, and G. Widengren characterized Baal as "a dying and reviving god."[20] In this category Gaster included the figures of Tammuz, Osiris, Telepinu, Attis, Adonis, and Persephone.[21] Hvidberg was clearly influenced by Frazer, and Gaster sympathized with Frazer's magnum opus enough to deem it worthy of an abridgment, brought out in 1959 under the title *The New Golden Bough*.[22] Like Frazer, Gaster posited a seasonal background to the mythology of these figures. Furthermore, rituals celebrated the deaths and reviving of these figures according to the seasons.[23] This view of Baal as a "dying and rising god" has enjoyed some currency in more recent scholarship.[24]

The final two tablets of the Baal Cycle (CAT 1.5–1.6) certainly seem to provide evidence for Baal as a "dying and rising god." Although the myth does not preserve an account of Baal's death or return to life, there is little doubt that these events transpire in some portion of the lost narrative, for El's messengers report how they discovered the god dead (1.5 VI 8–10) and Anat gives his corpse a proper burial (1.6 I). Later in the narrative Baal re-appears (1.6 V). This reappearance is anticipated by El's dream-vision, which calls the god *ḥy*, "alive," in the expression, *ḥy 'al'iyn b'l* ("Mighty Baal lives") in CAT 1.6 III 2, 8, 20; this expression has been taken as a reference to Baal's resurrection.[25] The description of Baal's death and the allusions to his return to life as well as his reappearance in the narrative provided *prima facie* evidence for Baal as "a dying and rising god."[26] I examine this claim in section 2. Two subsidiary arguments for Baal as a "dying and rising god" derive from other Ugaritic sources. Ritual evidence for Baal as a "dying and rising god" could theoretically be founded on CAT 1.17 VI 28–33. In this passage, Anat offers the hero Aqhat "non-death" (*bl mt*) in exchange for his bow. In describing the offer, Anat compares her offer of life to Baal when *b'l* is "brought to life" or "brings to life" (*yḥwy*). If the verb were passive, then it could be taken as an allusion to Baal's resurrection.[27] Furthermore, the figure of Arsay, one of Baal's three "daughters" or "women," seems to provide ancillary evidence for Baal as a "dying and rising god." Arsay's name literally means "Earthy," but it could plausibly be understood as "Netherworldly."[28] The latter interpretation would make good sense in view of the equation of this goddess with Allatum,[29] an underworld figure in Mesopotamian myth.[30] Baal's other two "women" bear either a meteorological name or title: Tallay means "Dewy" and she has the epithet "daughter of showers" (*bt rb*); and some commentators take Pidray's appelation, *bt 'ar*, as "daughter of moisture."[31] Accordingly, these two females seem to be connected with Baal's meteorological functions, whereas Arsay's characteristics might be taken to point to some chthonic aspect of Baal.

2. Problems with the Category

In his own lifetime Frazer's work was called into question for several reasons. Over the course of the quarter century when the three editions of *The Golden Bough* appeared (1890, 1900, and 1911–1915), the work met with increasing opposition from anthropologists. First of all, commentators criticized what Frazer called his "comparative method."[32] Although the response to the first edition was relatively respectful, the second and third editions' increase in suspect comparisons outraged a number of anthropologists,[33] and explicit comparisons of "primitive" rituals with Jewish and Christian practices introduced into these later editions sparked further controversy.[34] Frazer's work was controversial in wider intellectual circles as well. Following the appearance of the second edition, William James met Frazer in Rome and noted what he regarded as his overly rationalist interpretation. In a letter of Christmas 1900, James wrote that Frazer "thinks that trances, etc., of savage soothsayers, oracles and the like are all *feigned*! Verily science is amusing!"[35] In 1930, about a decade before Frazer's death, the philosopher Ludwig Wittgenstein (1889–1951) took an interest in Frazer's work, and beginning in 1931 he began to make notes on *The Golden Bough*.[36] Wittgenstein's observations are replete with acute criticisms of the work's presuppositions and methodological difficulties. Commenting on Frazer's comparisons of rituals across cultures, Wittgenstein wrote:

> The most noticeable thing seems to me not merely the similarities but also the differences throughout all these rites. It is a wide variety of faces with common features that keep showing in one place and in another. And one would like to draw lines joining the parts that various faces have in common. But then a part of our contemplation would still be lacking, namely what connects this picture with our own feelings and thoughts. This part gives the contemplation its depth.[37]

Frazer's procedure of noting similarities across cultures, Wittgenstein rightly suspected, reveals more of Frazer's own assumptions and perhaps less of the cultures'. Specialists outside of anthropology were critical of Frazer's derivative understanding in their fields. Writing later on Frazer's influence on ancient Near Eastern scholars (including T. H. Gaster), Cyrus Gordon remarked: "[T]he great mass of scholarly writing on Baal, who is supposed to die for the rainless summer and return to life for the rainy winter, misses the point of ancient Near Eastern religion as a reflection of Near Eastern climate."[38]

Within Frazer's lifetime, many anthropologists generally eschewed his comparative enterprise in favor of studying religion within its cultural setting. The anthropological approach developed by Frazer's protégé B. Malinowski and Frazer's acquaintance E. E. Evans-Pritchard concentrated on fieldwork within current cultures and tended to work methodologically toward interpreting features of religion within specific societies.[39] The comparative approach of *The Golden Bough* unavoidably suffered. In abstracting features of specific motifs from their cultural and historical contexts (sometimes misinterpreted or poorly attested), Frazer produced categories that otherwise never existed. This approach might be called "patternism," an approach to texts that reigned in ancient Near Eastern studies during the middle of this century. Since 1970, such an approach entered a period of decline in the face of more sophisticated analyses informed by anthropology, the history of religions, and folklore studies. Whatever the similarities between Baal and other ancient Near Eastern figures (and here I am thinking of the concern for death and agricultural fertility, kingship, and perhaps the role of the female familial relation in regenerating life), they require examination within their specific cultural contexts. Indeed, the survey in the following section suggests that cultural attitudes and ritual activity involving death in Mesopotamia and Egypt influenced the formulation of mythic motifs involving Dumuzi and Osiris; similar results might be expected for Baal.

Within the field of anthropology, Frazer's comparative approach never recovered, and the comparative agenda was left to historians of religion to pursue. However, comparative study of religion has followed anthropology in avoiding comparisons of religious features apart from their cultural settings. Moreover, historians of religion learned many negative lessons from Frazer and others; one was the need to be far more aware of modern suppositions.[40] Frazer's work was deeply affected by his concern for two later cultures, Christianity and the classical world. As noted the category of "dying and rising gods" represented Frazer's attempt to explain the death and resurrection of Jesus Christ, a connection Frazer himself made. Frazer's further inspiration for the category of "dying and rising gods" apparently was classical literature, his point of departure for *The Golden Bough* and "his first love," according to Frazer's devoted, uncritical biographer, R. Angus Downie.[41] *The Golden Bough* notes many equations made by classical writers between Greek and Middle Eastern deities. Frazer cites classical identifications of various "dying and rising gods," sometimes without reference to a particular writer, sometimes by name.[42] For example, Frazer cites *De Dea Syria* 7's well-known correlation between Adonis of Byblos and Osiris.[43] In classifying these figures, Frazer perhaps followed the lead of the classical authors whom he read. Many classical authors interpreted Middle Eastern deities in part through identifications between gods of different regions. Indeed, many identifications of deities were made by classical authors who, like Frazer, were outsiders to the religions they discuss. These equations in the classical period reflected the observations of learned people who sought to define foreign practices and beliefs they themselves did not share, much less understand from experience. Moreover, Frazer engaged in the negative psychological interpretations of the classical authors he quotes.[44] At one point Frazer sounds the very negative notes that his citation of Plutarch makes about Osiris. In short, Frazer's impulse to abstract and compare deities from different cultures seems to replicate classical tendencies to classify ancient Near Eastern deities and to provide them with a negative psychological interpretation.[45] This sort of comparative approach, whether in its ancient classical form or Frazer's modern tomes, generated asbtract generalizations and assumed their validity.

3. The So-Called Dying and Rising Gods

In his survey of "dying and rising gods," J. Z. Smith finds a bewildering number of differences among them.[46] In this section, I briefly repeat Smith's survey and supplement it with further information now available. The following survey focuses on the putative similarities of Baal and Dumuzi, Osiris, Melqart, and Adonis. Other figures sometimes invoked in this discussion, such as Attis and Marduk, are not discussed here. Readers may consult J. Z. Smith's general discussion as well as P. Lambrechts's work on Attis[47] and T. Frymer-Kensky's treatment of material thought to support Marduk's death and resurrection in the "Marduk Ordeal Text."[48] I would stress that the rituals and mythologies that mention these deities are complex, and my goal is to summarize the evidence to address Frazer's basic claims. Frazer's ritualist assumptions and his profiles of the figures involved often cannot be sustained, but the wider themes of kingship and its mortuary custom, as well as natural fertility, do obtain in the corpora associated with most of these figures.

Osiris

The mythology of Osiris[49] is known at considerable length thanks to Plutarch's *De Iside et Osiride* (ca 100 C.E.).[50] According to M. Lichtheim,[51] the fullest indigenous account appears in the "great Hymn to Osiris" on the stela of Amenmose (eighteenth dynasty). This mythology revolves around Osiris's struggle with, and death at the hands of, his brother Seth, followed by the recovery and rememberment of Osiris's body parts by his sister, Isis. Osiris revives in the underworld when his son Horus avenges his death. That this turn of events corresponds to natural fertility has been inferred from texts and iconography associating Osiris with the sprouting of grain. Iconography likewise shows grain sprouting from the coffin of Osiris, as he is to awaken to new life thanks to the rays of the sun above.[52] It has been often claimed that the story of the struggle between Osiris and Seth identifies the former with the fertility of the Nile and the valley that the river regularly inundated.[53] Osiris apparently dies and revives (if only in the underworld), and these mythological events were thought to correspond to the revival of nature. Here are conspicuous similarities between Osiris and Baal. Both are associated with natural fertility. Furthermore, both suffer a violent death at the hands of another god, and the aftermaths of their deaths involve the intervention of their sisters.

However, problems attend comparisons of Osiris and other figures. In an important study of Osiris, J. G. Griffiths is highly critical of Frazer's category.[54] Griffiths accepts the older criticism, made by A. H. Gardiner and H. Kees, that Osiris, unlike Baal, does not undergo any return to life. Instead, Osiris journeys to the netherworld where he becomes king. With no resurrection or rising for Osiris, a major cornerstone of Frazer's theory fails in the face of primary evidence. The comparison of Osiris and Baal likewise meets problems. Osiris' defeat, in the form of a violent dismemberment, comes at the hands of Seth, who was identified with Baal in the New Kingdom period. Indeed, Osiris seems quite the opposite of Baal in that the former was considered the dead king of the netherworld. Accordingly, J. C. de Moor compares Osiris not with Baal but with Mot, the Ugaritic god of Death.[55] Indeed, Osiris has been understood fundamentally as a funerary deity.[56] Frazer[57] and many Egyptologists observed that the "mythology" of Osiris was influenced by Egyptian mortuary cult. At many points Griffiths notes the conceptual relations between the presentation of Osiris and royal funerary practices and beliefs.[58] He argues that it "is in the royal funerary rites that the cult of Osiris achieves an early ascendancy."[59] Of particular interest is Griffiths's view that the "Osiris myth . . . grew out of the royal funerary ceremonial."[60] For example, the Pyramid texts present Osiris as the prototype of burial and mummification for the king.[61] Moreover, Osiris stands for the deceased king while Horus, Osiris's son, stands for the living king. In his relationship to royal funerary practice, Osiris is hardly alone among the figures Frazer discussed; several in this section show the impact of royal mortuary cult on their mythology.

Dumuzi/Tammuz

A good deal of Sumerian pastoral poetry and love songs celebrates the marriage of the shepherd Dumuzi to the goddess Inanna while mythological texts and laments mourn his death.[62] The narratives about Dumuzi describe his death—for example, how the *galla*-demons come and haul him off to the underworld. In *Inanna's Descent to the Netherworld*, the goddess is furious with Dumuzi's lack of deference when she returns accompanied by the *galla*, so she allows them to take him to the netherworld. Dumuzi's "resurrection" had been long denied,[63] but a fragment at the end of *Inanna's Descent of the Underworld* has given new life to this view of Dumuzi. The crucial line reads: "You (Dumuzi), half the year! Your sister (Geshtinanna), half the year!"[64] Despite the line's fragmentary context, S. N. Kramer conceded the point in 1966: "[O]n realizing that as a shepherd-god, his presence is needed on earth in order to insure the fecundity of the flocks, she [Inanna] decreed that he stay in the Netherworld only half the year, and that his doting sister Geshtinanna take his place the other half."[65]

Dumuzi seems to conform to Frazer's category of "dying and rising gods." Dumuzi's character and his relationship to Inanna are tied to natural fecundity. With Dumuzi dead, nature clearly stops producing. Dumuzi is also regarded as a divinity of some sort. Yet what kind? Dumuzi's quasi-divine status is evident from his complaint that he has the misfortune of "walking among men,"[66] but his life of shepherding and his prayers to deities[67] also suggest his human status. B. Alster, preceded by Kramer, claimed that Dumuzi was a deified king.[68] This view has been supported by the Sumerian king list, which mentions two rulers named Dumuzi. In a review of the evidence, Alster suggested that "Dumuzi as the husband of Inanna exemplifies the pattern of a mortal who becomes the husband of a goddess, like Enmerkar and Inanna, Lugalbanda and Ninsun."[69] Alster also denied the older view that Dumuzi was originally a vegetation god. Instead, Alster attributed the correlation of Dumuzi's disappearance to the hot season (coinciding with the seasonal termination of milk production by flocks) to his secondary association with Damu, "originally an independent deity and a true vegetation deity."[70]

Problems also are inherent in the ritual underpinnings supporting Frazer's approach to Dumuzi. Although his death is mourned, no known ritual text celebrates his return to the land of the living. The closest evidence for the figure's manifestation appears embodied in his form as the "astral Dumuzi," to use D. A. Foxvog's expression.[71] In the Akkadian myth of Adapa,[72] Tammuz is said to be located with Anu in heaven. For the mortal Adapa, who in heaven chances upon Dumuzi incognito, Dumuzi is absent:

> Tammuz and Gizzida were standing at Anu's door.
> When they saw Adapa, they cried "(Heaven) help (us)!
> "Fellow, for whom are you like this?
> "Adapa, why are you dressed in mourning?"
> "Two gods have disappeared from the land,
> "So I am dressed in mourning."
> "Who are the two gods who have disappeared from the land?"
> "Tammuz and Gizzida."[73]

Both associated with the underworld, the two gods could be mourned. A number of other texts refer to the "astral Dumuzi," including an OB hymn to Inanna.[74] According to Foxvog, these references support the notion that Dumuzi appears in astral form, monthly not annually. Furthermore, this astral form does not represent a return to the world. Indeed, Adapa presents himself as mourning for a disappeared Dumuzi, and it may be telling that Adapa does not recognize Tammuz. However, the astralization of the deceased Dumuzi may reflect an alternative notion of "resurrection," of becoming one "like the stars." Such a concept perhaps derived from the royal cult.[75]

Finally, it may be assumed that Dumuzi was regarded as returning from the realm of death, but the form that Dumuzi's resurrection from the underworld takes is unknown. At the end of *Ishtar's Descent to the Netherworld*, Ishtar refers to the day when Dumuzi (Tammuz) "comes up to me" (*ellâni*).[76] The verb points not to Dumuzi's "resurrection" but to his participation in a ritual in which the dead were invoked and then temporarily manifest. Indeed, the context at the end of *Ishtar's Descent to the Underworld* explicitly connects the day of Dumuzi's ascent with the ascent of the dead. Akkadian *elû* also corresponds to the title of necromancers, *mušēlû eṭemmi/ṣilli*, "one who makes the ghost/shade ascend." In summary, the nature of Dumuzi's "resurrection" is unknown, and, perhaps equally important, it appears to go uncelebrated in any ritual manner. Even if "resurrection" were the proper term to characterize Dumuzi's half-year on earth every year, it appears to be a concept without ritual context. This seems to be a "theology" designed to make sense out of Dumuzi's annual death: if he "dies" every year, then he must return to life every year as well.

Perhaps to understand better the background of Dumuzi's death, we should return to the correspondence between the use of the verb *elû* in *Ishtar's Descent to the Underworld* and the religious necromancy. Behind the picture of Dumuzi's death may lie the influence of royal funerary cult. The evidence from festivals points to the intertwining of funerary practices for human kings and the presentation of Dumuzi as the disappearing god. The composition known as "In the Desert by the Early Grass" explicitly links the death of Dumuzi with the funerary cult of the Ur III dynasty.[77] The link between divine and human kings goes further. In both the Old Babylonian and Ur III periods, Ur attests rituals for the disappearing god, Ninazu, in conjunction with rituals for the deceased kings.[78] M. E. Cohen writes:

> A second type of festival involving the netherworld was also observed throughout many cities of Mesopotamia. This festival was based upon the cult of the disappearing god, occasionally becoming intertwined with observances for deceased kings—rulers identified with those disappearing deities. In most cities it was Dumuzi . . . who had gone to the netherworld, while at Ur it was Ninazu.[79]

Beyond these festival observances, we may also note the "astral Dumuzi," which may be informed by royal mortuary cult as well. Foxvog suggests the possibility that Shulgi may have been the tacit subject lying behind the description of Dumuzi in the OB hymnal already noted.[80] If correct, it would point to the influence of royal mortuary concepts on the presentation of the astral Dumuzi. The literary presentation of Dumuzi may then reflect the imprint of royal mortuary custom.

Finally, it is important to note differences between Dumuzi and Baal. Dumuzi is no great god like Baal, nor is he a storm-god, nor does he engage in mortal combat as part of the description of the struggle between life and death. Even Dumuzi's relations to nature involve the flock and not nature more generally. In discussion of the two figures,[81] Cohen cites M. Astour's view[82] that Mot is identified with the ripe grain that was cut and winnowed. This view is overstated, but if any Ugaritic deity is presented as suffering the sort of death associated (if only on the level of imagery) with grain, it is not Baal but Mot, the god of Death. Both Ugaritologists and Mesopotamian specialists have observed the correspondence here with Mot. Gaster, the most creative proponent of Frazer's approach, recognized this problem. For although he assumes Baal to be a "dying and rising" figure, he notes that Mot, not Baal, is "dismembered and reassembled."[83] Similarly, A. Livingstone has discussed the dismemberment of Mot in connection with the death of Dumuzi.[84] Given this comparison, it is difficult then to identify Baal with the grain in any meaningful sense according to Frazer's analysis.

To summarize, Dumuzi/Tammuz "dies" in a manner that correlates in general terms with the seasonal cycle. Moreover, Dumuzi is only one of a number of disappearing "fertility" divinities (for example, Damu and Ninazu).[85] So one may argue that early Mesopotamian religion attests to divinities who disappear in accordance with the seasons. However, major pieces in Frazer's category are missing

for Dumuzi/Tammuz. The manner of Dumuzi's return from the underworld is unknown, and he would appear to be a divinized human. Finally, comparison with
Baal is highly problematic. In a constructive vein, the Mesopotamian material
points to a relationship between rituals devoted to disappearing gods and royal
ancestors. A comparable impact is proposed for Baal in section 4.

Melqart

Since the time of Frazer, Melqart has been drawn into the discussion of "dying
and rising gods."[86] A long line of scholars, including M. Clermont-Ganneau,[87] R.
de Vaux, E. Lipínski,[88] J. Teixidor,[89] C. Bonnet,[90] J. C. Greenfield,[91] and S. Ribichini,[92] have noted mostly Hellenistic period (or later) Phoenician and Punic
inscriptions (CIS i 227, 260–262, 377, 3351, 3352, 3788, 4863–4872, 5903, 5950
[= KAI 93], 5953 [= KAI 90], 5979, 5980, 6000,[93] as well as KAI 44, 70 and
161), which refer to persons (cultic personnel)[94] as "the raiser of the god" (*mqm/
mqym 'lm*).[95] The question of the god's identity in these expressions seems to have
been established by the fourth-century Phoenician inscriptions from Larnax tes
Lapethou in north-central Cyprus (henceforth LL).[96] According to Greenfield, "a
survey of the *mqm 'lm* material demonstrates a clear relationship with Melqart, as
can be seen by a survey of the names of dedicants of the inscriptions."[97] In the LL
inscriptions alone, Melqart appears by name (II:2,[98] 3, 7). The proponents of *mqm/
mqym 'lm* as a reviver of the god allow for the possibility that the god is viewed
as asleep, not dead, a view that would parallel Elijah's taunt of Baal's prophets in
1 Kings 18:27b: "Call with a loud (lit., great) voice if he is a god . . . [p]erhaps he
is asleep and will awake." Certainly, such sleep (if correct) may denote death.[99]

A number of questions have been raised about the meaning of the title *mqm/
mqym 'lm* to support the idea of divine resurrection.[100] In his original publication
of LL III, A. M. Honeyman reckoned that the title *mqm 'lm* refers literally to "the
cult-supervisor" (literally, "establisher of the gods").[101] Honeyman appeals to other
Phoenician uses of *'lm* for this generic sense (e.g., *ksp 'lm*, "temple treasury").[102]
H. P. Müller has recently argued for *mqm/mqym 'lm* as a cultic officiant who induces
a ritual theophany, not a ritual return from death.[103] Further the speaker of this
inscription refers in line 5 to Osiris as "my lord" (*'dny*). This title might seem
incompatible with devotion to Melqart, if both Osiris and Melqart are to be reckoned in the putative list of "dying and rising gods." Even if the claim that *mqm
'lm* were to refer to a cultic role such as "raiser of the god," no information establishes the ritual and conceptualization for this cultic role. Moreover, no text provides information about the putative death of the god. For both claims the texts
are silent. There is simply insufficient evidence to prove the case or to dismiss it
entirely.

Herakles

Scholars commonly identify Melqart with Herakles based on ancient equations.[104]
KAI 47, a second-century Greek-Phoenician inscription from Malta, supports the
identification between Herakles and "Melqart, lord of Tyre" (*mlqrt b'l ṣr*). Philo of

Byblos is said to make this identification (*PE* 1.10.27).[105] *De Dea Syria* 3 likewise mentions the "Herakles at Tyre" who "is not the Heracles whom the Greeks celebrate in song. The one I mean is much older and is a Tyrian hero."[106] Some texts have been used to support the idea of the Tyrian Herakles as a "dying and rising god." Josephus twice records the same account derived from Menander of Ephesus. In book VIII of the *Antiquities of the Jews*, Josephus refers to *egersis* in connection with Heracles.[107] The passage in question describes the activities of Hiram of Tyre (*Antiquities* VIII, 5, 3, para. 146). The context is provided from paragraph 144 through the pertinent line in paragraph 146 from R. Marcus's translation:

> These two kings are also mentioned by Menander, who translated the Tyrian records from the Phoenician language into Greek speech, in these words: "And on the death of Abibalos, his son Eiromos [Hiram] succeeded to his kingdom, who lived to the age of fifty-three and reigned thirty-four years. He it was who made the Eurychoros (Broad Place) embankment and set up the golden column in the temple of Zeus. Moreover, he went off and cut timber from the mountain called Libanos for the roofs of the temples, and pulled down the ancient temples and erected new ones to Heracles and Astarte; and he was the first to celebrate the awakening of Heracles in the month of Peritius (*prōtos te tou Herakleous egersin epoiēsato en tō Peritiō mēni*)"[108]

Josephus provides no context for the phenomenon of "the awakening of Herakles," and scholars are quite divided over its significance. Furthermore, some commentators take the passage as a reference to the erection of a temple.[109] This interpretation, for example, is the thrust of H. St. J. Thackeray's view in his translation of Josephus, *Against Apion* I.119, which uses the same language about Herakles:

> I will, however, cite yet a further witness Menander of Ephesus. This author has recorded the events of each reign, in Hellenic and non-Hellenic countries alike, and has taken the trouble to obtain his information in each case from the the national records. Writing on the kings of Tyre, when he comes to Hirom he expresses himself thus: "On the death of Abibalus the kingdom passed to his son Hirom, who lived fifty-three years and reigned thirty-four. He laid the embankment of the Broad place, dedicated the golden pillar in the temple of Zeus, went and cut down cedar wood on the mount called Libanus for timber for the roofs of temples, demolished the ancient temples, and built new shrines dedicated to Heracles and Astarte. That of Heracles he erected first, in the month of Peritius (*prōton te tou Herakleous egersin epoiēsato en tō Peritiō mēni*)."[110]

The authenticity of Josephus's information has been long supported by a Roman period Greek inscription from Philadelphia (Amman). The inscription is partially broken: a man named Maphtan calls himself, in F. Abel's term, "excitateur d'Hercule" (*egerse[iten tou] Herakleou[s]*).[111] But *egersis* need not involve death as such. Moreover, even if "awakening" of the god were the correct interpretation of *egersis*, no context is provided for this "awakening." And equally important for any argument for a "dying and rising god," the tradition is silent on the putative death of the god. The evidence came secondhand to Josephus, and it is hard to know what to make of these texts' context as a source for understanding the cult of Herakles.

Information hailing from the western end of the Mediterranean at Gades (modern Cadiz) on the southwestern coast of Spain suggests a tradition of the god's death. Sallust mentions a source attesting to the god's sepulchre in the Gades temple.[112] J. B. Tsirkin points further to the description of the iconography of the Herakleion gates at Gades known from Silius Italicus, which include the burning of the hero, with "the great soul soaring up in flames to the stars."[113] Tsirkin understands this scene as a representation of the god's death and resurrection. It is by no means assured that Tsirkin is correct either in his interpretation of his Latin source or in his assumption that the interpretation of this source represents the indigenous Punic understanding rather than a Roman interpretation of the iconography. Yet, even if Tsirkin were correct on both counts, we do not know whether the traditions at the opposite ends of the Mediterranean basin were uniform. We do not know about the basic eastern tradition of the god's death. However, I am inclined to accept the possibility of a Phoenician tradition of the god's death because it is rendered in terms that may recall the Phoenician practice of cremation.[114] Even if one assumes there was a god's "death," one cannot assume that any "resurrection" was involved. Furthermore, the ritual context is inadequately known.

Adonis

Adonis has long been cited as the paradigm case of a "dying and rising god."[115] Given the Semitic character of the name Adonis (cf. Ugaritic *'adn*, Phoenician *'dn*, BH *'adôn*, "lord"), it is usually thought that Adonis was originally a Phoenician god from Byblos.[116] There are, however, no extant indigenous descriptions of Adonis. One of the fuller classical witnesses is *De Dea Syria* 6, a second-century C. E. text that recounts how Adonis's death is celebrated at the sanctuary in Byblos:

> As a memorial of his suffering [i.e., his death because of a boar] each year they beat their breasts, mourn and celebrate, and celebrate their rites. Throughout the land they perform solemn lamentations. When they cease their breast-beating and weeping, they first sacrifice to Adonis as if to a dead person, but then, on the next day, they proclaim that he lives and send him into the air.[117]

This account is perhaps the closest one resembling a death and resurrection, but even here the passage is hardly clear.[118] Other sources provide further information about Adonis, especially his relationship with the goddess Aphrodite (thought by many to refer to Astarte), as well as the various local traditions and rituals associated with him. However, no descriptions present a death and resurrection. Unlike rituals for Osiris, Dumuzi, and Baal, some rituals devoted to Adonis center on the demise of vegetation in the form of special gardens devoted to the cultivation of cereals and vegetables in earthen pots, which wilted under the heat of the summer sun shortly after being planted. These rituals accentuate Adonis's death; there is no hint of rebirth.[119] J. Z. Smith too rejects Adonis as a rising god. He claims that the classical accounts of Adonis neither mention nor describe his rising from death and that only accounts fashioned by Christian writers introduce the theme of Adonis's resurrection.[120]

Finally, Frazer's survey of Adonis was highly selective, addressing only those aspects of the tradition that comport with the features he abstracted from other "dying and rising gods." Hence, M. Detienne is extremely critical of Frazer's silence on some of the most important material about Adonis:

> [Y]et we have only to read the myth of Adonis in the version given by Panyassis of Halicarnassus (who was related to Herodotus), to see at once that Adonis— like so many others dealt with in this way—has been surreptitiously taken out of his true context and distorted by scholars applying an unchecked comparative method in which they are so carried away by the resemblances they believe they have discovered that they ignore the differences which might have set them on the right path.[121]

The "right path" for Detienne involves examining all the cultural information encoded in the different versions of Adonis myth. And this inquiry shows the highly selective character of Frazer's treatment. The structuralist strategies of interpreting mythology in Detienne's hands have the effect of showing a great deal of information Frazer ignored. If this deficit of Frazer's work may be regarded in a more positive light, it would suggest that the themes he highlighted are major notes to be observed.

Adonis's Semitic background has been the subject of major discussion. Despite the considerable differences between Baal and Adonis, valiant efforts have been made to reconstruct the West Semitic background of the Adonis traditions based on the textual evidence about Baal attested at Ugarit.[122] In the most substantive modern effort, N. Robertson interprets the Baal Cycle as the outgrowth of rituals he detected in the Adonis traditions.[123] Robertson reconstructs an ancient ritual background by using the classical explanations (*aitia*) given for the traditions associated with Adonis. Robertson extends this approach to the Baal Cycle. For him, the Baal Cycle contains reflexes of Baal/Adonis rituals: the winnowing of Mot in CAT 1.6 II corresponds to a threshing rite of the gardens of Adonis, which flourished, only to expire in the summer.[124] Although some Adonis traditions may be related to the Late Bronze Age Ugaritic traditions of Baal, it is not the Baal Cycle, but other narratives about Baal (notably CAT 1.12) that—if actually related—represent the clearer Ugaritic antecedent to the classical narrative about the boar goring Adonis.[125] Although the Adonis traditions reflect some earlier material, these traditions have amalgamated material from a variety of sources deriving from different time periods and may not represent a direct reflection of the Baal Cycle.

Even more problematic, Adonis shares relatively few traits with Baal. After all, Baal is a storm god, warrior, and major figure of the pantheon. Unlike Osiris and Baal, but perhaps like Dumuzi, Adonis is a mortal. J. Z. Smith characterizes Adonis as good-looking and young, "inefficient as a hunter," but "deemed a paragon of anti-heroic behaviour." If any of the figures I have thus far discussed share any family resemblance with Adonis, it is Dumuzi. Dumuzi and Adonis stand out as humans or perhaps deified humans, young figures (both possibly associated with a major goddess) who are not warriors. In contrast to these figures, Baal and Osiris are major gods. The ritual lamentation devoted to Dumuzi and Adonis and specific links with vegetation distinguish them further from Baal and Osiris. With the similarities between Dumuzi and Adonis, one might ask whether the cults of Dumuzi and Adonis (and Melqart?) were historically related, a view Frazer himself suggested.[126] It is evident that the cult of Dumuzi spread from Mesopotamia to Syria-Palestine during the first millennium, as reflected in Ezekiel 8:14.[127] Isaiah 17:9–11 also seems to reflect a Judean cult of Tammuz or Adonis.[128] Or one might ask if the disappearing fertility god behind the Adonis traditions was instead Damu, because one of the El-Amarna letters from Byblos (EA 84:31) refers to AN.DA.MU-*ia*, which has been usually taken as *ᵈda-mu-ia*, literally "my Damu."[129] Finally, despite the possibility of a historical relationship between Adonis and Dumuzi, Detienne warns that the further trajectories of the Adonis traditions in Greek material remove this figure far beyond recognition with any particular Middle Eastern god.[130]

An Unknown Phoenician God

The argument for a Phoenician "dying and rising god" has been built further on a Phoenician inscription from the Etruscan site of Pyrgi (KAI 277) dating to around 500. The dating formulary gives the year, month, and day. Line 8 provides the dating formula, "the day of the burial of the god" (*bym qbr 'lm*).[131] Although this inscription suggests the death of some god, no one knows which god was involved. (The only deity mentioned by name in the inscription is the sun-god in line 5, and there is no need to connect him with the referent found in the dating formula.)[132] It is evident that *qbr 'lm* is a frozen expression with no particular relationship to the content of the rest of the inscription.[133]

Gibson proposes to identify the unnamed god with either Adonis or Melqart.[134] If Melqart could be sustained, this inscription might then be linked to the title *mqm 'lm*. However, in his treatment of the Pyrgi inscription, J. A. Fitzmyer expresses doubts: "We see no need to understand *qbr 'lm* in terms of the burial of *Adonis*, which some commentators have suggested (at least as a possibility)."[135] Fitzmyer's reservations about this evidence are appropriate. G. A. Knoppers has recently offered a very strong challenge to the theory of "a dying and rising god" in this inscription. Following a proposal of W. F. Albright, Knoppers suggests that *'lm* in the Pyrgi inscription refers to "a recently deceased person for whom Thebariye Velinas [the king named in the inscription] built this shrine."[136] Knoppers points to evidence of Etruscan divination of the deceased, which would comport with his view of *'lm*. He summarizes his overall interpretation of the inscription:

> The much-debated phrase, "the day of the burial of the deity," thus refers to the day on which the deceased was buried. His *bt* becomes both tomb and temple, mausoleum and shrine. On his death the person would become deified, hence clarifying the intent of the closing phrase, "as to his years during which the god

(resides) in his temple, (may they be as many) years as these stars." In accordance with Etruscan burial beliefs and customs, the spirit of the dead is to be in his house forever. Recognizing the funerary character of the Pyrgi lamina therefore not only resolves ambiguities, but also reveals a hitherto undisclosed unity of purpose and design in the text.[137]

Beause of the uncertainty of the referent of '*lm*, it is impossible to substantiate a Phoenician cult devoted to "a dying god" in this inscription, as some scholars inspired by Frazer proposed. Moreover, even if a Frazerian view of "the god" did prove to be one of the "dying and rising gods," the text provides no context for a ritual about the death. And the text is certainly silent on any issue of resurrection.

To conclude this survey, the figures identified as "dying and rising gods" share limited commonality. It is evident that several of the figures are regarded as dying or disappearing in a manner related to seasonal phenomena. To a limited degree, it is possible to regard at least Dumuzi and a number of other minor Mesopotamian figures as disappearing or dying "fertility" divinities (even though Dumuzi's divinization was secondary and his association with fertility was due to amalgamation with some of these figures). I think Frazer was quite right to draw attention to the concern for natural fecundity, even if its character varied (crops versus animals; clearly seasonal or not); and he was correct to note the divinity of most of the figures involved, even if the character of that divinity varies significantly. Finally, the kingship of many of the characters is no minor point. The mythic dramas involve the different divine or divinized members of the royal, cosmic family. In these dramas, the action revolves around males, whereas females play a largely subsidiary role (here the traditions concerning Dumuzi and Inanna are an exception). Kingship, at least of Osiris and Baal, however different, denotes power, and here a king is paradigmatic; in the ancient Near Eastern texts goddesses do not die.[138]

Frazer's survey also manifests major problems in method and data. Four major difficulties stand out for my purposes here. First, Frazer's method assumes a category applicable across thousands of miles and years as well as a multitude of cultures. The data are spread not only all over the ancient Near East and classical world; they also range widely in date, from the third millennium[139] through the late classical period. Second, the figures in Frazer's theory vary widely in character. Although many of these figures are associated with natural fertility, they otherwise differ tremendously: some (Osiris) do not "rise" (it is unclear if any do), some are storm-gods (Baal, Hadad-Rimmon, Melqart [?]) whereas others are not (Osiris), and still others may not even be gods (Dumuzi, Adonis [?]). Many of them are poorly documented for the purposes of this category. Third, the ritual background posited for these figures is absent from indigenous Levantine evidence. Some ritual background is evident in the Egyptian and Mesopotamian records, but the ancient West Semitic cultures are virtually mute about ritual information pertaining to these figures.

Fourth, and finally, some of the best evidence pertaining to "dying and rising" derives from late classical authors, who often received their information secondhand. The Phoenician texts cited in support of this category are relatively late and poorly understood. Without a clearer knowledge of these texts' background, they hardly qualify as compelling evidence. The use of evidence from the first millennium to assess data from the second is potentially anachronistic and misleading. Although to dismiss out of hand possible support from Phoenician-Punic or Greek evidence, as meager as it may be, would be unwise, caution about comparing this late material with the second-millennium evidence about Baal. In short, evidence about these gods can offer no positive conclusion about the cult of gods in earlier periods. Even if all of this evidence referred to a single Phoenician god who "dies and rises," the indigenous understanding of the phenomenon may have been quite different from what the account of *De Dea Syria* suggests. The late classical authors were not credible witnesses to contemporary religions foreign to them; the same point applies all the more to foreign religions that preceded them.

Finally, the problem with this entire survey is that it meets Frazer's category largely on its own terms. Frazer may be credited for drawing attention to certain themes that recur at least in part in a number of the different figures' mythologies, but the question equally important for understanding these gods is the social or political encoding specific to each culture. Frazer's category takes insufficient account of the figures within their own cultures, which have their own complex histories. Indeed, the label "dying and rising gods" presupposes that the deities are the focal point of the category. Instead, what truly drives the similarities Frazer observed, as far as the present evidence reasonably shows, is the continuity of life in the face of death in the natural, human, and divine spheres, as well as the royal funerary cult as the cultural context for the experience and expression of this theme. A significant feature of some of these deities is the apparent incorporation of information drawn from nature and funerary practice. I have noted the impact of mortuary practice and belief on the descriptions of Dumuzi and Osiris. The descriptions of Melqart's death by fire may have drawn on the Phoenician practice of cremation.[140] A similar cultural dynamic may be involved in the case of Ugaritic Baal.

4. Foundations for a Theory of Baal's Death and Return to Life

To begin, it is important to note the limits of the Baal Cycle's information about Baal's death and return to life. The extant Baal Cycle never recounts Baal's return to life. Therefore, any attempt to render a reconstruction of Baal's death and return to life should make no assumption about the nature of the latter.[141] Furthermore, this narrative presentation of the god may not derive from a specific ritualistic understanding of Baal as a "dying and rising god." Indeed, given the ritual underpinnings of Frazer's work (and the work of his intellectual heir in the ancient Near Eastern field, T. H. Gaster), the absence of the god's death or his revivification from any of the seventy or so[142] ritual texts is significant. As S. Ackerman rightly notes, "[W] do not know how (or if) this Ugaritic mythology which describes Baal's death and the associated mourning was commemorated in the Late Bronze Age Canaanite cult."[143] Baal's death and return to life may not themselves reflect ritual involving Baal. Instead, the narrative is a literary statement incorporating ritual notions; it is difficult to situate the text in a ritual context. To my mind, this lack of evidence does not prove absence, but the burden of demonstration for Baal as a "dying and rising god," with its attendant ritual background, falls on those who argue for it.

If Baal is not a "dying and rising god" (and perhaps no god is), then another approach is required. Criticizing the long-reigning paradigm of "dying and rising gods" hardly lays to rest the evidence in the Baal Cycle. More recent scholarship tends toward a revised label of "disappearing gods" associated with fertility. The category of "disappearing gods" is common now in ancient Near Eastern scholarship[144] and among historians of religion.[145] J. Z. Smith's comment is pertinent: "The putative category of dying and rising deities thus takes its place within the larger category of dying gods and the even larger category of disappearing deities. Some of these divine figures simply disappear; some disappear only to return in the near or distant future; some disappear and reappear with monotonous frequency."[146] Compared to the category Frazer created, this one seems more descriptive and makes fewer assumptions. Smith's attempt to provide a better grounded category of "disappearing gods" finds support in a comparison with the closest second-millennium analogues to Baal, the Anatolian disappearing deities. One might argue that Baal shares less with Dumuzi, Tammuz, and Adonis than with the Hittite disappearing gods, the Storm-god and his son, Telepinus.[147] About a dozen different Hittite divinities, mostly not storm-gods, appear as "disappearing deities."[148] Only some versions concern the procession of seasons, and none involves death. In the versions of the Telepinus myth,[149] the storm-god departs in anger from the realm of human culture and agriculture and goes to the steppe and sleeps. As a result, vegetation and animals no longer produce. Desperate, Telepinus's father the Storm-god sends out divine search parties to find the god, including the sun-god. Finally, the Bee finds him and wakes him from his sleep with a sting. A discussion ensues, and after a break in the text, the ritual prayer to the god attempts to assuage his anger. After the ritual, the narrative resumes with the return of Telepinus, which issues in his care for the king and queen and the fertility of crops and animals.

Six basic similarities obtain between this version and the Baal Cycle. First, the two deities are similar in type: Baal is a major storm-god like Telepinus and his father. Second, both gods are also responsible for nature as well as both humanity and divinities. CAT 1.4 VII 50b–51 presents Baal's claim that applies to both "gods and men." Similarly, the absence of Telepinus from the land brings hunger of both humans and gods: "The pasture and the springs dried up, so that famine broke out in the land. Humans and gods are dying of hunger."[150] Accordingly, the disappearance of these storm-gods correlates with the withering of vegetation. Telepinus's absence due to his journey and sleep causes the destruction of vegetation, and his return restores fertility.[151] Baal's absence causes in El's lament for the peoples (1.6 I), and his return is presaged by El's oracular dream that shows the impending return of the land's fertility (1.6 III). General well-being of the society is also a concern of this text. The Hittite material mentions the king and queen. A similar concern for royalty may be implicit in the Baal Cycle.[152]

Third, the narratives describe the god's absence, which issues in a divine search for him (1.6 IV). The Ugaritic texts likewise attest to the search for the disappearing god. In an important study, S. B. Parker demonstrates that 1.16 III contains a command to go about (*sb*; cf. *sbn* in 1.5 VI 3) the heavens and earth to search for Baal, since the god's meteorological effects are lacking (lines 3–5).[153] The search for Baal in lines 3–5 matches 1.5 VI 3–5 quite closely and suggests a shared theme of the disappearing god and the search for him. Fourth, both searches involve the sun-deity (1.5 V–VI). Fifth, the searches take place in the steppe, including the mountains (see 1.5 VI).

Sixth, and finally, Baal's disappearance in the form of a descent to the underworld may seem unusual for a disappearing storm-god, but even on this point the Hittite material affords some help, as the disappearance of the Storm-god of Nerik includes his descent to the underworld:

> The Storm God of Nerik became angry and went down into the pit. He [went] into the dark [four corners] and [. . .] to(?) the bloody, bloodstained, . . . [. . .]mortals.
>
> "Let them summon [him . . .]. Let him turn himself [. . .] to the Dark Earth. Let him come [. . .]. Let him open the gates of the Dark Earth [. . .]. Before him/it [let . . .]. Let them [bring(?)] the Storm God of Nerik up from the Dark Earth.[154]

This particular presentation seems to be related to the offerings made to the pit[155] in the Hittite text.

By the same token, the differences between the Baal Cycle and the Hittite material are to be recognized as well. In contrast to the Hittite disappearing gods, Baal's disappearance assumes the form of human death, complete with burial and funerary offerings, carried out by Anat and El (CAT 1.5 VI–1.6 I). The Hittite disappearing gods may sleep, but they do not seem to undergo death. Furthermore, the Hittite material does not seem to be preoccupied with the god's kingship as such; it is driven by the ritual concerns of appeasing the absent god. In contrast, central to the Baal Cycle as a whole is the kingship of the god (and, I suggest, the kingship of the Ugaritic dynasty whom Baal served as royal patron). Finally, the Baal Cycle encodes the Ugaritic dynasty's fragility in the figure of Baal and his death. In contrast, the Hittite dynasty never suffered from the sort of political vassalage or domination which it imposed on Ugarit.

What strongly stands out in the Baal Cycle, to restate the obvious, is the place of dying as a subcategory of disappearance in the Baal Cycle. J. Z. Smith, I think, flattens the significance of this point: "Despite the shock this fact may deal to modern Western religious sensibilities, it is commonplace within the history of religions that immortality is not a prime characteristic of divinity: gods die."[156] Smith believes that his point might be shocking to modern readers of ancient myths; it would have been problematic to many of ancient Ugarit as well (so T. J. Lewis, personal communication). The son of Kirta asks whether gods can die (CAT 1.16 I 14–15, 17–18, 20–23; cf. virtually the same speech in II 36–38, 40, 43–44):[157]

"In your life, O father, I rejoice,	*bḥyk 'abn 'ašmḥ*
In your non-death, we exult . . .	*blmtk ngln*

So, father, shall you die like mortals? . . .		*'ap 'ab kmtm tmtn*
How can it be said that Kirta is a son of El,		*'ikm yrgm bn 'il krt*
Progeny of the Beneficent and Holy One?		*šph ltpn wqdš*
So can gods die,		*'u'ilm tmtn*
The Beneficent's progeny not live?"		*šph ltpn lyh*

In West Semitic cultures deities with active cultic devotion die rarely, if ever (unlike cosmic divine enemies such as Yamm and Mot, whose deaths would be welcome to a human audience). Baal's demise is therefore all the more striking. E. Hornung reports only rare occurrences of divine death in the vast wealth of Egyptian texts, and even these make no explicit statements that a god died.[158] In Mesopotamia, not only Dumuzi suffers death; the gods of old die as well. Yet these cases represent a major exception in the ancient Near East rather than a "commonplace," to use J. Z. Smith's characterization.

As a result, it is necessary to take account of the motif of dying in the Baal Cycle and to provide some means of locating it within the society of ancient Ugarit. When scholars look for similar language for Baal's death and funerary conditions, they turn to the royal funerary text, CAT 1.161, which shows important links with the Baal-Mot section of the Baal Cycle (CAT 1.5–1.6). From these connections one may posit that the royal cult of the dead made a profound impact on the literary presentation of Baal. A helpful parallel to the Baal-Mot section is provided by CAT 1.161:[159]

Superscription

1	Document for the sacrifice of the shades (?):	*spr.dbh.zlm*

Section I: Invocation of Predecessors

2	You are summoned, O Rephaim of the un[derworld],[160]	*qr'itm[.]rp'i.'a[rs]*
3	You are invoked, O Council of Di[danu].	*qb'itm.qbs.d[dn]*
4	Summoned is Ulkn, the Raph[ite],	*qr'a.'ulkn.rp['a]*
5	Summoned is Trmn, the Raph[ite].	*qr'a.trmn.rp['a]*
6	Summoned is Sdn and Rd[n],	*qr'a.sdn.wrd[n]*
7	Summoned "Bull Eternal" (?),	*qr'a.tr.'llmn[ ]*
8	Summoned are the Ancient Rephaim.	*qr'u.rp'im.qdmym[ ]*
9	You are summoned, O Rephaim of the Underworld,	*qr'itm.rp'i.'ars*
10	You are invoked, O Council of Didanu.	*qb'itm.qbs.dd[n]*
11	Summoned is King Ammithtamru,	*qr'a.'mttmr.m[l]k*
12	Summoned is King Niqma[ddu] as well.	*qr'a.'u.nqmd[.]mlk*

Section II: Ammurapi's Ritual Lamentation for King Niqmaddu

13	O throne of Niqmaddu, be bewept,	*ks'i.nqmd[.]'ibky*
14	And may he (Ammurapi) cry at his (Niqmaddu) footstool.	*w.ydm'.hdm.p'nh*

15	Before him (Niqmaddu) may he beweep the roy[al] table,	*lpnh.ybky.tlhn.ml[k]*
16	Indeed, may he swallow his tears in misery:[161]	*w.ybl'.'udm'th/'dmt.*
17	Indeed, misery upon misery!	*w.'dmt.'dmt*

Section III: Ritual Descent of the Sun-Goddess and King Ammurapi

18	Burn/go down, O Sun,	*'išhn.špš.*
19	Indeed burn/go down, O Great Light!	*w.'išhn/nyr.rbt.*
	Above Sun cries out:	*'ln.špš.tsh*
20	"After your [lo]rd(s)[162] from[163] the throne,	*'atr.[b]'lk.l.ks<'i>h[164].*
21	After your lord(s) to the under-world descend,	*'atr/b'lk.'arṣ.rd.*
22	To the underworld descend and be low in the dust:	*'arṣ/rd.w.špl.'pr.*
23	Beneath[165] Sdn and Rdn,	*tht/sdn.w.rdn.*
24	Beneath 'Bull Eternal' (?),	*tht.tr/'llmn.*
	Beneath the Ancient Rephaim.	*tht.rp'im.qdmym*
25	Beneath King Ammithtamru,	*tht.'mttmr.mlk*
26	Beneath King Niq[maddu] as well."	*tht[166].'u.nq[md].mlk*

Section IV: Offering on Behalf of King Ammurapi

27	One and an offe[ring],	*'šty.wt['y.]*
	[Two and] an offer[ing],	*[tn.]w.t'[y]*
28	Three [and] an offering,	*tlt.[w].t'yl[.]*
	[Four] and an offer[ing],	*['arb'].w.t'[y]*
29	Five and an offering,	*hmš.w.t'y.*
	Six [and] an offering,	*tt[w.]t'y*
30	Seven and an offering:	*šb'.w.t'y.*
31	You shall present a bird.	*tqdm 'ṣr*
32	Peace, peace to Ammur[api], and peace to his house,	*šlm šlm[167].'mr[p'i]/w.šlm.bth[168].*
33	Peace to [Tha]ryelli, peace to her house,	*šlm.[t]ryl[169]/šlm.bth.*
34	Peace to U[ga]rit, peace to her gates!	*šlm.'u[g]rt/šlm.tġrh*

Line 1 is an extra-textual rubric or superscription introducing the sacrificial text. This title shows that the text is a record or document indicating sacrifice, perhaps for the dead if *ẓlm* means "shades."[170] Whether *dbḥ* is singular or plural cannot be determined only on the basis of form. Superscriptions of ritual texts (1.148.1, 1.162.1[171]) perhaps use the singular form even when the ritual involves multiple offerings, as in 1.161.27–31.

Section 1, consisting of lines 2–12, invokes the names of two groups: the dead ancient tribal heroes (lines 4–7) framed by the designations Rapi'uma of the Underworld (cf. biblical Rephaim) and the Council of Didanu (lines 2–3, 8–10) and two more recent deceased monarchs, Ammithtamru and Niqmaddu (lines 11–12). The Rephaim here appears to be a general designation for the line of deceased ancestors. The parallel designation, the "Council of Didanu," refers to the same group, but they are identified with the figure of Didanu. Didanu is known from Old Babylonian records, specifically the Genealogy of the Hammurapi Dynasty, as one of the ancient heroes of the West Semitic royal line of Hammurapi. The royal line of Ugarit evidently derived from the same line. The Ugaritic and Babylonian dynasties evidently traced their lineages back to an ancient hero, Didanu. In addition to the ancient tribal heroes named in lines 4–7, the historical kings, Ammithtamru and Niqmaddu, are invoked to summon their presence in the ritual. From the perspective of the ritual participants, these figures dwell in the netherworld, as suggested by the phrase "Rapi'uma of the Underworld." The singular verbal forms in lines 4–7 and 11–12 morphologically could be imperatives or suffix indicatives, but the second-person plural forms in lines 2–3 and 8–10 appear to preclude the first option.[172] The forms could be either active[173] or passive suffix indicative forms.[174] On the theory that all four sections address participants in the ritual, the forms seem to be passive "performative perfects," despite the claim sometimes made that the G-passive is poorly attested and therefore suspect here.[175] In fact, the G-passive is a regular form for Ugaritic.[176] The alternation between singular and plural verbal forms, if passives, would correspond to the number of the nouns in the same lines.

Section II, lines 13–17, contains a number of debated items. The subjects of the verbs are perhaps the biggest problem. T. J. Lewis, J. G. Taylor, and M. Dietrich and O. Loretz take the furniture as the second-person subjects of the verbs in lines 13–16. For Pardee, the subject is impersonal. According to either view, the royal furniture pieces are invoked to weep for their deceased lord, Niqmaddu III, the last named figure in the first section and predecessor of the living king, Ammurapi, mentioned in the final section of the ritual. The point of the commands is mourning for the king to whom the furniture belongs. In other words, King Ammurapi is to lament for his predecessor on the royal furniture.[177] Accordingly, Ammurapi the subject of the verbs in lines 14–16. Line 17's threefold mention of *'dmt*, "misery," is here divided, as suggested by *w-*. A superlative is involved here, akin to BH *melek mĕlākîm*, "king of kings" (e.g., Ezekiel 26:7), and *šîr haššîrîm*, "the song of songs" (Song of Songs 1:1). It is possible, however, that a threefold use is intended (cf. *qādôš* in Isaiah 6:3, possibly signifying superlative degree),[178] but this tack is complicated, in view of the placement of the *w*-preceding the third occurrence of *'dmt*.

Section III, lines 18–26, begins by invoking the sun-goddess either to burn (according to Pardee) or "to bow down" (as adopted by Lewis). In lines 19b–26, Shapshu calls either the recently deceased King Niqmaddu[179] or the living king, Ammurapi,[180] to descend to the underworld to be with his deceased predecessors. The narrative rubric here precisely matches 1.6 II 22–23. At this point the sun-goddess appears as a participant in this ritual. She is commanded by and in turn addresses the main ritual participant, King Ammurapi.

Section IV, lines 27–34, begins with a series of offerings. The listing of seven offerings in lines 27–30a is formulaic; no verb may be involved in these lines, only a series of nouns.[181] Elsewhere such series function as temporal modifiers to verbs (CAT 1.4 VI 24–32; 1.14 III 2–4, 10–12, etc.),[182] and it is assumed here that the number + *t'y* essentially means that "x-times as an offering." T̲'y could be an incense-offering,[183] but the context in CAT 1.40 suggests a more generic sense.[184] If so, then the bird might be the animal for the sacrifice, *t'y* is a general word for offering, and *šlm* is the name of the sacrifice. In this case, only in lines 30b–31a is the command completed: these offerings are to be given as a peace offering in the form of a bird. The goal of the intended ritual is peace for the royal household and Ugarit. Considering the royal background of the names listed in the third section, one may suppose that the royal family is involved. Furthermore, because the final section is devoted to a blessing of peace for Ammurapi, his household, and Ugarit more generally, King Ammurapi is possibly the ritual participant summoned to make the offering.

B. A. Levine and J. M. de Tarragon have noted in some detail four major features that this funerary text shares with the Baal-Mot (Death) section of the Baal Cycle (1.5–1.6), especially 1.5 VI–1.6 I.[185]

1. In the Baal Cycle, El and Anat both mourn the fallen Baal. To lament him properly, El descends from his throne to his footstool and then from his footstool to the dust and then utters words of lamentation (1.5 VI 11–25a). After Anat's similar lamentation (1.5 VI 31, 1.6 2–10), Anat conducts the proper burial practice of Baal's corpse (1.6 I 10–18a). CAT 1.161 reflects a similar complex of funerary practices. The family of the deceased king engages in the funerary liturgy in order to lament him. Moreover, lines 14–15 call on the royal table and footstool to engage in lamentation by weeping, a superlative means of signaling the sorrow expressed by the royal participants who customarily use these pieces of furniture. As Levine and de Tarragon note, the "appurtances *swallow* their tears [CAT 1.161.15–16], just as Anath *drinks* her tears [CAT 1.6 I 9–10]."[186]

2. In the ritual the king, whether the deceased Niqmaddu[187] or the living Ammurapi[188] (the latter more favored by the parallel), is to locate his ancestors in the netherworld. In the myth Anat, Baal's sister, locates him in the underworld.[189] Levine and de Tarragon note the precise wording shared by the two texts, as well as that of Jacob's words spoken in mourning the loss of Joseph:

   Liturgy: *'atr b'lk 'arṣ rd,*
   "After your lord(s) (*b'l*) to the underworld descend." (1.161.20–21)

   Myth (1): *'atr b'l 'ard b'arṣ*
   "After Baal (*b'l*) I will descend into the underworld." (1.5 VI 24b–25)

   Myth (2): *'atr b'l nrd b'arṣ//'mh trd nrt 'ilm špš,*
   "After Baal (*b'l*) we will descend into the underworld."
   To him descends[190] the Divine Light, Shapshu.[191] (1.6 I 7b–9a)

   Family Legend: *kî-'ērēd 'el-běnî 'ābēl šě'ōlâ,*
   "For I will descend to my son in mourning to Sheol." (Genesis 37:35)

The liturgy calls on the family member, the king, to make the ritual descent, where as in the myth Anat, the sister of the deceased, declares her intention to make the descent to the underworld (on the basis of this similarity, I am inclined to see the living king as the addressee, although this king, Ammurapi, is not mentioned explicitly until line 31). The point of the relationship between family funerary ritual and the literary setting of the Baal Cycle is expressed in the designation of the deceased king: the ritual calls the human king *b'l*, where as myth focuses on *b'l*, the divine king.[192]

3. As indicated by Anat's words to Shapshu in 1.6 I 7b–9a (quoted in myth 2), the sun-goddess is to accompany the mourning family member in the ritual descent. Levine and de Tarragon comment:[193] "In the myth, the descent into the netherworld is accomplished by a goddess. In the ritual, it is acted through recitation." As myth 2 shows, 1.6 I 7 incorporates the plural *nrd*,[194] indicating that Anat intends to be joined by Shapshu, and the following line explicitly mentions the sun-goddess's role of accompaniment in the ritual descent. In the myth it is Shapshu and Anat who descend together and haul off Baal's corpse from the underworld to render it a proper burial (1.6 I 10b–18a). In the ritual Shapshu is seen as participating in the ritual directions to make the ritual descent into the underworld (1.161.18–19). The directions may even direct her to "burn bright" (*'išḥn*) in order to provide illumination into the underworld. Or, if this verb is to be taken in the sense of descent, then it would cohere with the sun-goddess's well-known night journey through the underworld (see 1.6 VI 45a–53). Accordingly, she plays the role of intermediary between the realms of life and death. It may not be amiss to note the same formula introducing her speeches in the myth and the ritual: *'ln špš tṣḥ*, "On high Shapshu cries out" (1.6 VI 22b–23a; 1.161.19).

4. Less noticed, both the funerary liturgy (CAT 1.161.27, 30) and the mythological presentation (1.6 I 18b–29 [or 31?]) end the funerary customs with a series of offerings.

From these comparisons,[195] one may conclude that information drawn from the royal funeral has influenced the presentation of Baal's death and return to life. The impact of royal funerary custom on the Baal-Mot narrative is not a matter only of general funerary practice; it is also encoded in specific wordings and motifs. Baal is modeled on the perceived fate of Ugaritic kings who die and descend to the Underworld; in their case, they may temporarily come to life. This picture is based on analogy with human existence, much as other mythological presentations of deities are modeled on human experience. For example, El has an oracular dream in 1.6 III; this, too, is modeled on the human experience (cf. Kirta's dream in 1.14 I). The liturgy that made its impact on the Baal Cycle's presentation of Baal's death and return to life was not a ritual devoted to mourning the god's death but a ritual describing the lamentation for deceased human royalty.[196] The most thematically proximate text, one of the Panammu inscriptions (KAI 214.21), suggests that the person(s) returned to "life" is a deceased king who may eat and drink with the great West Semitic storm-god;[197] it is not the god who returns to life.

In Ugarit's cultural context, Baal's fate may reflect his affinity to the condition of Ugarit's dynasty, both the deceased king and his living successor. The members of the dynasty were known to die, and they supposedly had a continued existence in the afterlife.[198] Moreover, their successors continued the dynasty and its role in Ugarit. CAT 1.161 witnesses to these aspects of royal life. The text, at once mourning the deceased king and identifying his living successor, ultimately celebrates the link between the two; indeed, the text's list of ancestors highlights the dynastic continuity between the deceased and living kings. Baal's death and return to life may represent a theological reflection on reality that incorporates the known conceptualization of Ugarit's monarchy.[199] Baal's death reflects the demise of Ugaritic kings, but his return to life heralds the role of the living king to provide peace for the world. Death is the form that the disappearance of Baal takes. The storm-gods of Hatti disappear, sleep, and return as they wish; the process was viewed as their choice, and ritual propitiation was thought to be required to ensure their return. In contrast, Baal does not choose to disappear. And as a divine king, his inexorable disappearance takes the form of royal death. In contrasting the narratives concerning Telepinus's sleep and Baal's death, there are two ways to indicate the absence or disappearance of the god; one indicates divine will in the matter, where as the second suggests the absence of divine choice.[200] The special form of disappearance Baal's death takes coheres on the literary level with the weakness the god manifests throughout the cycle.[201] This divine death likewise coheres on the natural and human levels with the weakness or annual failing of agricultural fertility and the potential threats faced by human society and by the maintainer of societal order, the Ugaritic monarch.

5. The Conceptual Ideology in Baal's Life and Death

In this approach to the Baal-Mot section of the Baal Cycle (1.5–1.6), it may be possible to offer a brief synthesis of the picture of reality the Baal Cycle offered for ancient Ugaritic. The central unifying thematic of the cycle is Baal's kingship, which affects the natural, human, and divine levels of reality.[202] The text plays out the action on the divine level, yet behind this stage are the concerns for humanity and nature. Hence, Baal's kingship, ostensibly related in a story about the divine struggle for kingship, plays out on all three levels simultaneously. Baal's rule manifests the weather to produce the rains for crops and animals and therefore satisfy humanity's needs for food and deities' needs for human offerings. Baal's rule lies at the heart of the great chain of relations between nature, humanity, and divinity. This kingship is precarious, subject to threat, and apparent on all three levels; it may be schematized in the following manner:[203]

KINGSHIP

divine level	order and conflict
human level	life and death
nature level	abundance and dessication

All three levels of reality are intertwined and affect one another. Baal's kingship provides a defining intelligibility to all of reality as understood in ancient Ugaritic society. The royal funerary ritual encoded in the Baal Cycle may signal the historical threats to dynasty from external strains posed by the empires of Egypt and Hatti or from the internal difficulties a monarchy faces. (Dynastic woe is the central problematic of the entire text of Kirta in 1.14–1.16.) Accordingly, Baal is representative of kingship, both in its strength and its weaknesses, including the moment of weakness of royal succession when the old king has died and the new king is about to begin his reign. In a sense, Baal displays the "baal-ship" of the old and new kings, of the dynastic line in life as well as death. Thus, kingship is fragile, in need of help and nurturing from many major deities. The presentation of Baal as a relatively weaker figure needing extensive divine assistance is consistent with his presentation throughout the cycle. Indeed, Baal is no super-conquering god like Marduk in Enuma Elish or Yahweh in so much Israelite poetry. The evocative picture of reality in the Baal Cycle encoded cultural information known to the society of ancient Ugarit; this chapter has stressed only the funerary aspects of this information. Yet many other sorts of information were incorporated in this text and synthesized a whole, well-ordered narrative that provides a place for ancient human experience known to ancient Ugarit.

The preceding discussion indicates the contributions and drawbacks of Frazer's theory. Frazer highlighed the major themes in a wide array of ancient literatures, yet his agenda was costly. Although Frazer highlighted the crucial themes of natural fertility and the divinity of some of the figures involved, he wound the themes into a new mythology of "dying and rising gods." The source for much of this new creation was the classical literature that provided him with a model as he linked different figures and attributed a negative psychological mindset to their ancient worshippers. Frazer's new mythology was cast in the new idiom of the nascent anthropology and assumed the mantel of its authority. Part of the intellectual baggage of this field was a relationship between myth and ritual that has recently come under attack. For decades the dominant paradigm for reading the Baal Cycle was to see it as the libretto for a cultic or ritual drama. There is, in fact, no evidence for such a ritual background for the Baal Cycle. Instead, this text was a literary achievement that incorporated motifs known from ritual, but it is itself not located against a ritual setting.[204] The relationship between myth and ritual that Frazer and his intellectual heirs assumed has been probed thoughtfully in the work of A. Livingstone. For example, Livingstone has questioned the ritual background to the Dumuzi myths: "[I]t is absolutely certain that the myths did not originally belong to the rituals, and the rituals did not originally mean the myths."[205] Furthermore, a cultic drama replaying the myth also seems unlikely for the Dumuzi traditions; Livingstone asserts that "religious or cult drama in the sense of a conscious enactment of myth is not involved."[206]

More constructively, the survey of figures points to the influence of natural phenomena and mortuary cult on their mythological presentation. In discussing Adonis, Frazer touches on the question of these very influences: "Thus their views of the death and resurrection of nature would be coloured by their views of the death and resurrection of man, by their personal sorrows and hopes and fears."[207]

In the case of Baal, these words might be modified. Although the Ugaritic view of nature affected the presentation of Baal as a storm-god, a further influence on the presentation of Baal's death and return to life was royal funerary ritual. The same has been suggested for Osiris and Melqart-Herakles. Livingstone offers a formulation about Dumuzi and nature that applies equally to Baal: "It is possible that the idea of the death of Dumuzi . . . [was] a mythical metaphor for the death of vegetation."[208] The deaths of Dumuzi, Osiris, and Baal indeed made sense as "mythical metaphors" that encoded natural and human processes. These processes informed the mythic metaphor, and they lent intelligibility and meaning to the different visions of reality incorporated in the religious narratives modern scholars call myths. Frazer and his intellectual successor, T. H. Gaster, generalized about ritual as the bridge connecting nature and myth. Ritual is only one of many social phenomena encoded in literature. And in the case of Baal, the ritual standing between nature and myth was not a complex procedure celebrating the death and resurrection of the god but royal funerary ritual.

6. The Mythology of Death and the God of Israel

This discussion of Baal holds considerable import for understanding biblical evidence about death and the underworld. The argument that the mythological presentation of Baal and the god of Death in the Baal Cycle is largely a literary one deriving some of its imagery from royal mortuary ritual should be consistent with biblical presentations of the chief deity of Israel and Death personified. Let me spell out this working hypothesis. Iron Age Israel shows clear evidence of the storm-battle imagery of Baal's mythology.[209] Indeed, biblical tradition shows a reliance on the particulars of Baal's mythology. In this category may be placed biblical references to the cosmic enemies such as Leviathan, Sea, and Tannin (discussed in chapter 1). Moreover, Psalm 48:3 identifies Mount Sapan, Baal's home in the Ugaritic texts, with Zion. Scholars generally accept the view that these details point to the continuity and modification of older traditions about Baal.[210] In view of such shared specifics, one may ask why the Bible lacks a comparable mythology of the chief-god with respect to the underworld and the god of Death. Like the Baal Cycle, the Bible is replete with speculations about the nature of the underworld and the god of Death; perhaps the best-known biblical texts are Isaiah 28:15, 18; Jeremiah 9:20; Habakkuk 2:5; and Psalm 49.[211] Unlike the Baal Cycle, the Bible contains few references to, much less any substantial mythology about, the conflict between the chief deity of Israel and the god of Death.[212] Although the Bible does mention a divine victory over Death—though barely (Isaiah 25:8; cf. Revelation 21:4)—there is no mythological presentation of this conflict.[213] The absence of this conflict is all the more striking because of the Bible's massive complex of storm-battle imagery shared with the Ugaritic texts. The disparity might be attributed to the idea that the god of Israel has nothing to do with the realm of Death.[214] Yet this is only partially correct. Certainly Yahweh is said to defeat death (Isaiah 25:8). There may be a deeper cause, one that involves the nature of this mythology as well as its social context in Ugarit and Israel. In the West Semitic world, the mythology of death may not have involved the chief deity in a conflict. However, in the Baal Cycle the presentation of Baal and Mot may have been a literary production that modified an older mythology lacking such conflict. Indeed, the many structural similarities and verbal resonances between the Baal-Mot and Baal-Mot sections of the cycle (1.1–1.2 and 1.4 VIII–1.6, respectively) lend themselves to a theory that the latter section, using the traditional mythology of the underworld and the god of Death,[215] was modeled on the former one under the further influence of a royal mortuary cult. If the theory is correct, the Ugaritic monarchy influenced the development of this particular form of the mythology of death at Ugarit. As far as the record presently indicates, Late Bronze Age West Semitic did not generally develop this sort of mythology except at Ugarit.

Accordingly, the chief god's conflict with Death may be absent in ancient Israel because West Semitic tradition perhaps did not generally contain and therefore transmit a broad mythology of death into the Iron Age. In other words, the dynasties of Israel and Judah may never have developed a mythology of Death as the Ugaritic monarchy did. The dominant priestly and deuteronomic theologies in the Iron II period in Judah may have inherited some dissociation between Israel's chief deity and the realm of death.[216] Perhaps then death and the underworld in the Bible, insofar as they appear in Israelite material without a mythology of conflict, offer limited corroboration for the argument that the Ugaritic presentation of Baal's death and re-appearance in the cosmos was fundamentally a literary production. In any case, the evidence does not support a ritual approach to the complex of material grouped under the category of "dying and rising gods," at least for Ugarit and Israel. An attempt to resuscitate Frazer's category must drastically modify its basic criteria, perhaps so much so that Frazer would barely recognize it.

PART III

THE ORIGINS OF MONOTHEISM
IN THE BIBLE

7

El, Yahweh, and the Original God of IsraEL and the Exodus

Who is This King of Glory?

Psalm 24:8

1. El in the Bronze Age

The name of the god El[1] is the same as the word for "god" in many West Semitic languages. This fact might be taken as evidence that as head of the West Semitic pantheon, El was regarded as the pre-eminent god (or, perhaps, divinity "incarnate"). The best guess for the etymology of both the word "god" and the name of El has been *'y/wl, "to be strong,"[2] but other proposals have been made. The noun may be a "primitive" biradical form meaning "chief" or "god."[3] The name of El occurs clearly first in personal names attested at Ebla, and then Mari and Amarna.[4] In contrast, the evidence in other Mesopotamian personal names is contested. These cases may involve the generic term "god," not the proper name of El. Because of the lack of evidence for El's cult in Mesopotamia, the second view may be preferable.[5]

The most extensive Bronze Age source about El comes from Ugarit. The texts there attest to the word 'il over five hundred times, in its generic use, in the name of the god, or in proper names. In the Ugaritic mythological narratives, El appears as the divine patriarch par excellence. His role as 'ab, "father," applies to the pantheon that is his royal family. The deities are generically referred to as dr 'il, literally "the circle of El," but perhaps better translated, "El's family" (CAT 1.15 III 19). Athirat is El's elderly wife with whom he has produced the pantheon, generically (but not all inclusively) referred to as "Athirat's seventy sons." As divine progenitor, El is sometimes called 'il yknnh, "El who created him/her." As the divine patriarchal authority, El oversees the actions of the pantheon, presented as a royal assembly in 1.2 I. He issues decisions and exercises authority over the other deities, including Athirat, Baal, and Anat. His authority is expressed in his title, "king" (mlk). The same notion seems to underlie his epithet, "bull" (tr): like the chief and most powerful of animals, El is the chief of the deities. His fatherly disposition toward his family is captured in his larger appellation, "Kind El, the Compassionate" (*lṭpn 'il dp'id*).[6]

Both texts and iconography present El as an elderly bearded figure, enthroned sometimes before individual deities (CAT 1.3 V; 1.4 IV–V), sometimes before the divine council (CAT 1.2 I). In 1.10 III 6 he is called *drd<r>*, "ageless one." His advanced age is apparently expressed also in his title, *'ab šnm*, "father of years," although the meaning of the second word is debated. In 1.4 V 3–4 Athirat addresses El: "You are great, O El, and indeed, wise; your hoary beard instructs you" (*rbt 'ilm lḥkmt šbt dqnk ltsrk*). In 1.3 V and 1.4 V, Anat and Athirat both affirm the eternity of El's wisdom. Anat's threats in 1.3 V 24–25 and 1.18 I 11–12 likewise mention El's gray beard. El's great age is suggested by the royal blessing at the end of 1.108.27, asking that the king's rule last "in the midst of Ugarit, for the days of the sun and moon, and the pleasant years of El."

As the divine patriarch, El enjoys a range of social activities. According to CAT 1.114, he is the head of his own male social association or club (*mrzḥ*), on analogy with well-to-do men of Ugarit (3.9). Like human patriarchs, El sustains a drunken bout in 1.114; this one is so severe that it results in hallucinations. El's *mrz'* (thought by many scholars to be a biform of *mrzḥ*) appears in 1.21 II 1, 9, evidently in connection with the dead. The broken condition of the text's larger cycle (?) of 1.20–1.22 makes it difficult to understand El's role, but perhaps he served as the host of the dead at the *mrz'* held at his home, modeled on the human cult of the dead. And 1.23 presents El's sexual activity with two women (whose identities are unknown). It has been debated whether this text describes his virility or his impotence, overcome by the coaxing of the two females.[7] In either case, the text graphically describes his "hand," a euphemism for penis, as becoming "as long as the Sea" (discussed in chapter 5, section 1). El also expresses interest in sexual relations with Athirat when she meets him in 1.4 IV.

El's home is conceptualized in both terrestrial and cosmic terms. According to the Baal Cycle (CAT 1.3 V 8–12, 1.4 IV 21–24), it is located in the waters of the "double-deeps," at a mountain (whether the home lies at the mountain's base or top is unclear). His residence is described by a series of terms that suggest a tent; this view is confirmed by a description of Elkunirsa's residence as a "tent." A ritual text, an incantation against the bite of a snake, places El's abode at a point where the upper and lower cosmic oceans meet (1.100.3). The further association of El's activity at the edge of the sea in 1.23 may be related to the location of El's abode. It is unknown if this point applies also to Athirat's title, "Lady Athirat of the Sea" (*rbt 'aṭrt ym*) or to her domestic chores at the water's edge described in 1.4 II 6.[8]

El's status vis-à-vis Baal has been a matter of debate. Some scholars have argued that Baal's promotion to the head of the pantheon took place at El's expense.[9] This view has been severely contested, yet El and Baal's relationship is fraught with tension and intrigue. El backs the god Sea (Yamm) for divine kingship against his rival Baal (CAT 1.1). This act seems to reflect El's animosity toward Baal, who may have been regarded as an outsider to El's family, as suggested by the Storm-god's title, "son of Dagan." In the Baal Cycle, El supports the god Athtar for divine kingship. Athtar is evidently one of El's sons and he shows a number of astral features.[10] The motif of El's patronage of other divine creatures hostile to Baal assumes a different form in 1.12. Common to all of these texts is a a generational conflict that possibly reflects two (competing?) forms of divinity, one an astral conceptualization (El and his children) and the other a sky conceptualization (Baal).

El attends not only to his divine family but also to the human family. In the story of Kirta, El shows solicitous care for this king, appearing to him in an incubation-dream and granting his request for the blessing of progeny. Just as El engendered the divine family, so too El produced the human family. El bears two titles exemplifying his relationship to humanity: *'ab 'adm*, "father of humanity," and *bny bnwt*, usually translated "creator of creatures". A West Semitic text written in Hurrian-Hittite was discovered in Anatolia. This text presents the figure of El under the name Elkunirsa, which is to be understood as *'il qny 'arṣ*, "El creator of the earth," a title that survives in Genesis 14:19 and KAI 26 A III:18. El's role as creator is never portrayed in the mythological texts; and from their perspective, this activity of his seems to be belonged to the distant past. He is depicted as creating a special creature to cure the sickness of King Kirta (CAT 1.16 V).

2. El in Iron Age Phoenicia

When we turn to the issue of El's cult in the Iron Age Levant outside of Israel, we enter highly disputed territory. The demise of El among Israel's neighbors has been espoused, most recently by K. van der Toorn: "El is a common Northwest Semitic god to whom the devotion is largely rhethoric in the first-millennium B.C.E. Having turned into a *deus otiosus*, his place was gradually taken by Baal-shamem or Baal-shamayin."[11] B. A. Levine, however, has defended the position that El's cult perdured into the first millennium West Semitic religion.[12] Some Phoenician data may support the later view, but the evidence is quite sparse and far-flung. I mentioned already the Phoenician title *'l qn 'rṣ* from Karatepe (KAI 26A III:18). The same title appears in a neo-Punic inscription (KAI 129:1). A Hellenistic period inscription from Umm el-'Awamid also contains the name El. Philo of Byblos[13] attests to Phoenician El. According to Philo of Byblos, Ouranos's children included Elos (West Semitic El), Baetylos, Dagon, and Atlas. Tyrian El is evidently described in Ezekiel 28.[14] This chapter describes the home of Tyrian El in terms similar to descriptions of El's abode found in the Ugaritic texts. The wisdom ascribed to Tyrian El also recalls El in the Ugaritic texts.

Furthermore, M. L. Barré suggests that Phoenician Bethel is to be understood as a hypostasis of El, which would represent further Phoenician evidence for the cult of El in the Iron II period.[15] But Vander Toorn[16] has challenged this notion that Bethel is a Phoenician hypostasis of El. He argues that Bethel is an Aramean and not a Phoenician deity; this view requires further confirmation. Indeed, second-millennium proper names from Ugarit containing the element "house of god/El"[17] apparently favor Bethel as a god indigenous to the coast. Furthermore, Philo of Byblos (*PE* 1.10.15–17)[18] provides evidence for a cult of Bethel in Phoenicia. Barré suggests that Baetylos appears as Elos's brother because he is a hypostasis of El.

The Phoenician and Punic inscriptions attesting to Baal Hamon may represent data for the continued cult of El in Phoenician cities, assuming that Baal Hamon is to be identified with El, as B. Landsberger, F. M. Cross, and S. M. Olyan argue.[19] Cross sees the name of El's mountain behind the epithet *bʿl ḥmn*, "lord of the Amanus," and follows Landsberger in viewing it as a title of El in the Phoenician-Punic world. According to Cross, the title *bʿl ḥmn* would fit El, as his home is located in the Amanus. Moreover, the iconography of Baal Hamon comports with that of El. Although Olyan regards the identification as "secure,"[20] the bases for the identification have met severe criticism. E. Lipiński asserts: "Now, this assumption is not supported by the slightest evidence and must be rejected as sheer fantasy."[21] Some problems with the evidence for the identification have been voiced. According to J. Day, the equation of Kronos with Baal Hammon does not prove that Baal Hamon was El, for Kronos was equated with both El and Baal.[22] Furthermore, the iconography of Baal Hamon may comport with that of El as known at Ugarit, but this is no guarantee of the identification. Finally, the attestation of both *ʾamn* and *ḥmn* in Ugaritic (the latter in proper names and in a Hurrian text discovered at Ugarit) seems to represent a difficulty for identifying *ḥmn* with the Amanus. M. Cogan and P. Xella prefer to take *ʾamn* as Mount Amanus, but not *ḥmn*.[23] Cross attempts to reconcile this problem by claiming that *ḥmn* specifically refers to Mount Amanus whereas *ʾamn* in CAT 2.33.16 is a different mountain though "in the same general region."[24]

Roman evidence recently marshaled by L. E. Stager in support of the equation of El and *bʿl ḥmn* is equally subject to difficulties. Accepting the equation of *bʿl ḥmn* with El, Stager takes the throne-name of the Roman emperor, Elegabalus (203–222 C.E.), as a Latinized form of the West Semitic *ʾEl Jebel*, "El of the mountain."[25] Elegabalus, a Syrian, brought a statue of Tannit to Rome. He took a vestal virgin for a wife and identified her with the goddess Tannit and himself with the god Elagabal. Stager suggests: "Their marriage, then, replicated that of the heavenly couple, Baʿal Hamon (alias Elagabal) and Tanit. Thus these Phoenician deities became part of the imperial cult in Rome."[26] The name Elegabalus does not give the specific name of El's mountain. Furthermore, the name Elegabalus may be translated as "the god of the mountain" and could be identified with a god besides El, thus vitiating Stager's reconstruction.

Whereas Cross's argument might appear prima facie to be a case of special pleading, and Stager's interpretation viable but not necessary, one fact favors the claim that Ugaritic *ḥmn* is Mount Amanus. The place-name *pʿrḥmn* appears in a Phoenician seal dating to the eighth century. According to P. Bordreuil,[27] *pʿrḥmn* is to be understood as the town Pagras of the Amanus region, corresponding to the modern village of Bagras located in the Amanus. In view of this evidence, the sources from Ugarit that give the spelling *ḥmn* and *ʾamn* should be reconsidered. As I noted, *ḥmn* appears in a Hurrian text and some proper names from Ugarit, whereas *ʾamn* is attested in a single Ugaritic text. The disparate character of these sources may suggest that *ḥmn* and *ʾamn* represent two spellings for the same mountain, a phenomenon not without parallel among geographical names in the texts from Ugarit.[28] In short, the interpretation of titles may be just as problematic as the interpretation of proper names, and using them in the name of historical reconstruction is likewise a hazardous task.[29] However, the identification of Baal Hamon with El remains possible and may be joined to the evidence from Ezekiel 28 and Philo of Byblos for the cult of El in the Phoenician world.

3. El in Iron Age Aram and Tranjordan

Aramaic evidence for the god El from the eight century is less equivocal but more sparse. Panammu, king of Samal, mentions El in a list of deities (KAI 214:1, 2, 11, 18). The so-called Sefire inscription is a treaty text with a list of divine witnesses; these include El (KAI 222A:11). Like the Phoenician evidence, the Transjordanian material for the cult of El has been debated vigorously. Ammonite personal names attest to the element *'l*, but it is unclear whether El is the referent. That El continued to have cult in the first millennium might be suggested by the Deir 'Alla inscriptions (and by their possible connections with those biblical books, such as Job, which show a similar use of divine titles).[30] B. A. Levine argues that the Deir 'Alla inscriptions show an El cult separate from the cult of Yahweh in the Iron Age.[31] Two questions surrounding this interpretation involve genre and date. Do the Deir 'Alla texts and the book of Job reflect literary usage that predates the Iron II period and therefore does not constitute evidence for El's cult in this period and region? Or do these texts reflect traditional cultic titles of El Shadday that were at home at one or more cultic sites in Transjordan? If the Deir 'Alla inscription represents a later copy of an older text, as a number of scholars suppose,[32] then its date cannot be determined. In this case, the text could not be used as evidence for the cult of El in Iron Age Transjordan.[33]

Finally, two other pieces of evidence pertain. Although van der Toorn denies that cult was devoted to El in the first millennium, he notes the appearance of El in the papyrus Amherst 63, and he concludes that "El and Baal-Shamayin were at least known to the colonists of Syene."[34] The context of El in papyrus Amherst 63 is a prayer, which implies a cult, and the parallel of the prayer with Psalm 22 suggests a cult that is near or perhaps even in Israel. Therefore, this text might constitute not only a literary attestation to El but a cultic one. Finally, Cross and Tigay have noted that the divine element *'l* dominates the theophoric elements in the Edomite onomasticon, which suggests El's cult; W. E. Aufrecht has noted the same feature in the Ammonite onomasticon.[35] Although state cults of the first-millennium Levant had patron deities other than El, this situation did not issue in the immediate loss of El's cult. After all, Baal was the dynastic god of Ugarit, but this fact did not result in the loss of El's cult at Ugarit. The evidence for El's cult in the first millennium is ambiguous, as van der Toorn observes, but this difficulty of evidence hardly settles the issue. Indeed, the apparent evidence for El in epigraphic South Arabian texts[36] might also warrant caution against dismissing first-millennium Levantine evidence for the cult of El.

4. El in Iron Age Israel

Outside of proper names, the word *'ēl* occurs about 230 times in the Hebrew Bible. It usually occurs as an appellative designating a foreign deity (Ezekiel 28:2) as well as Israel's chief deity. Most commonly, the word is used with other elements (such as the definite article or a suffix). It appears as a proper name of the deity in some poetic books, such as Psalms (5:5, 7:12; 18 [= 2 Sam 22]:3, 31, 33, 48; 102:25), Job, and Second Isaiah (Isaiah 40:18; 43:12; 45:14, 22; 46:9; cf. 42:5). A common assumption is that El's cult did not exist in Israel except as part of an identification with Yahweh. For ancient Israel, this question depends on whether Yahweh was a title of El[37] or secondarily identified with El. Besides the grammatical objections sometimes raised against this view, the oldest biblical traditions place Yahweh originally as a god in southern Edom (possibly in northwestern Saudi Arabia), known by the biblical names of Edom, Midian, Teman, Paran, and Sinai.[38] This general area for old Yahwistic cult is attested in the Bible (Deuteronomy 33:2; Judges 5:4–5; Psalm 68:9, 18; Habakkuk 3:3)[39] as well as in inscriptional sources. Evidence from Kuntillet 'Ajrud, a southern shrine preserving inscriptions written by visiting northerners, also attests to "Yahweh of Teman."[40] These facts argue against designation identification of Yahweh as originally a title of El. How were Yahweh and El related? Biblical evidence necessarily occupies a central place in this discussion. In at least one instance, biblical material points to the cult of El in the Iron I period in Israel. C. L. Seow notes El language and characteristics reflected in aspects of the cult of Shiloh.[41] The tent tradition associated with Shiloh (Psalm 78:60; Joshua 18:1; 1 Samuel 2:22) conforms to the Ugaritic descriptions of El's abode as a tent. The narrative elements of the divine appearance to Samuel in incubation-dreams, the divine gift of a child to Hannah, and the El name of Elqanah (suggesting an El worshipper?),[42] also cohere with the view that El was the original god of the *bêt 'elōhîm* there (Judges 18:31; cf. 17:5). It is probably no accident that Psalm 78 repeatedly uses El names and epithets in describing the rise and fall of the sanctuary at Shiloh.[43]

Traditions concerning the cultic site of Shechem may also illustrate the cultural process behind the Yahwistic inclusion of old cultic sites of El. In the city of Shechem the local god was *'ēl bĕrît*, "El of the covenant" (Judges 9:46; cf. 8:33; 9:4).[44] According to many scholars, this word *'ilbrt* apparently appears as a Late Bronze Age title for El (CAT 1.128.14–15).[45] In the patriarchal narratives, the god of Shechem, *'ēl*, is called *'elōhê yiśrā'ēl*, "the god of Israel," and is presumed to be Yahweh. In this case, a process of reinterpretation may be at work. In the early history of Israel, when the cult of Shechem became Yahwistic, it continued the El traditions of that site. As a result, Yahweh received the title *'ēl bĕrît*, the old title of El.[46] Finally, Jerusalem may have been a cult place of El, assuming the connection of El Elyon and El "creator of the earth" in Genesis 14:8–22 to this site.[47] This record illustrates the old transmission of West Semitic/Israelite traditions. Israelite knowledge of the religious traditions about other deities did not only reflect contact between Israel and her Phoenician neighbors in the Iron Age. In addition, as a function of the identification of Yahweh-El at cultic sites of El, such as Shiloh, Shechem, and Jerusalem, the old religious lore of El was inherited by the priesthood in Israel. At a variety of sites, Yahweh was incorporated into the older figure of El, who belonged to Israel's original West Semitic religious heritage.

Other biblical evidence for El might be taken to suggest that the cult of El perdured into the Iron II period. Whatever one is to make of *'ĕlōhîm* in the "E source" or various "El epithets" in the "priestly source," these materials might be interpreted as evidence for the cult of El in the Iron II period within Israel.[48] The usage in the book of Job and Psalm 18 (= 2 Samuel 22), may point in this direction as well. The distinction between El and Yahweh in Israel may include not only biblical texts but also Iron II epigraphic evidence. It is not necessary to interpret *'l* in the Kuntillet 'Ajrud inscriptions as "God" and assume the identification with Yahweh, as M. Weinfeld has done.[49] Weinfeld translates one inscription where *b'l* and *'l* occur in the following manner: "[W]hen God shines forth (= appears) the mountains melt . . . Baal on the day of w[ar] . . . for the name of God on the day of w[ar]."[50] It is unclear whether *'l* here should be translated as El. Similarly, Hebrew proper names with the element *'l* should not therefore always be attributed to Yahweh, as W. D. Whitt has recently argued.[51] J. Tigay's important study of inscriptional onomastica is compatible with the historical reconstruction that early Israelite tradition identified El with Yahweh. Israelite inscriptions include 557 names with Yahweh as the divine element, 77 names with **'l*, a handful of names with the divine component **b'l*, and no names referring to the goddesses Anat or Asherah. Tigay argues that the element **'l* in proper names represented a title for Yahweh. Just as no cult is attested for Anat or Asherah in Israelite religion, no distinct cult is attested for El except in his identity as Yahweh. It is unclear whether *'l* in all these instances is to be understood as a generic reference to Yahweh.

At some point, a number of Israelite traditions identified El with Yahweh or presupposed this equation. The Hebrew Bible rarely distinguishes between El and Yahweh or offers polemics against El. West Semitic El lies behind the god of the patriarchs in Genesis 33:20 and 46:3 (and possibly elsewhere). Later tradition clearly intended that this god be identified as Yahweh. For example, the priestly theological treatment of Israel's early religious history in Exodus 6:2–3 identifies the old god El Shadday with Yahweh:

> And God said to Moses, "I am Yahweh. I appeared to Abraham, to Isaac, and to Jacob, as El Shadday, but by my name Yahweh I did not make myself known to them."

This passage shows that Yahweh was unknown to the patriarchs. Rather, they are depicted as worshippers of El. In Israel El's characteristics and epithets became part of the repertoire of descriptions of Yahweh. Like El in the Ugaritic texts, Yahweh is described as an aged, patriarchal god (Psalm 102:28; Job 36:26; Isaiah 40:28; cf. Psalm 90:10; Isaiah 57:15; Habakkuk 3:6; Daniel 6:26; 2 Esdras 8:20; Tobit 13:6, 10; Ben Sira 18:30), enthroned amidst the assembly of divine beings (1 Kings 22: 19; Isaiah 6:1–8; cf. Psalms 29:1–2, 82:1, 89:5–8; Isaiah 14:13; Jeremiah 23:18, 22; Zechariah 3; Daniel 3:25). Later biblical texts continued the notion of aged Yahweh enthroned before the heavenly hosts. Daniel 7:9–14, 22 describes Yahweh as the "ancient of days," and "the Most High." He is enthroned amid the assembly of heavenly hosts, called in verse 18 "the holy ones of the Most High," *qaddîšê 'elyônîn* (cf. 2 Esdras 2:42–48; Revelation 7). This description for the angelic hosts derives from the older usage of Hebrew *qĕdōšîm*, "holy ones," used for the divine council (Psalm 89:6; Hosea 12:1; Zechariah 14:5; cf. KAI 4:5, 7; 14:9, 22; 27:12; see chapter 5, section 3).

The tradition of the enthroned bearded god appears also in a Persian period coin marked *yhd*, "Yehud." The iconography belongs to a god, possibly Yahweh. D. V. Edelman has studied the depictions of deities and symbols on coins from the Persian period through the Hasmonean period.[52] She concludes that the late Persian period coins are the first to show any avoidance of depiction of gods other than Yahweh in noncultic contexts; as this single example indicates, Yahweh is evidently represented. Based on this part of Edelman's study and the reference in Judges 17 to an image, apparently of Yahweh, one might be inclined to suggest that ancient Israel tolerated some images of Yahweh outside of the national shrines and condemned images of other deities. In short, the prohibition of images of other deities seems to reflect a general worship of Yahweh that discouraged worship of other deities.

El and Yahweh are rendered with a similar compassionate disposition toward humanity. Like El, Yahweh is a father (Deuteronomy 32:6; Isaiah 63:16, 64:7; Jeremiah 3:4, 19; 31:9; Malachi 1:6, 2:10; cf. Exodus 4:22; Hosea 11:1) with a compassionate disposition, many times expressed as "merciful and gracious god," *'ēl-raḥûm wĕḥannûn* (Exodus 34:6; Jonah 4:2; Joel 2:13; Psalms 86:15; 103:8; 145:8; Nehemiah 9:17). Both El and Yahweh appear to humans in dream-visions and function as their divine patron. Like El (CAT 1.16 V–VI), Yahweh is a healing god (Genesis 20:17; Numbers 12:13; 2 Kings 20:5, 8; Psalm 107:20; cf. the personal name, *rĕpā'ēl*, in 1 Chronicles 26:7). Moreover, the description of Yahweh's dwelling-place as a "tent" (*'ōhel*) (e.g., Psalms 15:1; 27:6; 91:10; 132:3), called in the Pentateuchal traditions the "tent of meeting" (*'ohel mô'ēd*) (Exodus 33:7–11; Numbers 12:5, 10; Deuteronomy 31:14, 15), recalls the tent of El. The tabernacle of Yahweh has *qĕrāšîm*, usually understood as "boards" (Exodus 26–40); Numbers 3:36; 4:31), whereas the dwelling of El is called *qrš*, perhaps "tabernacle" or "pavilion" (CAT 1.2 III 5; 1.3 V 8; 1.4 IV 24; 1.17 V 49). Furthermore, the dwelling of El is set amid the cosmic waters (CAT 1.2 III 4; 1.3 V 6; 1.4 IV 20–22; 1.17 V 47–48), a theme evoked in descriptions of Yahweh's abode in Jerusalem (Psalms 47:5; 87; Isaiah 33:20–22; Ezekiel 47:1–12; Joel 4:18; Zechariah 14:8). Other passages include motifs that can be traced to traditional descriptions of El (Deuteronomy 32:6–7). The eventual identification of Yahweh and El within Israel perhaps held ramifications for the continuation of other deities as well. It has been argued that Asherah became the consort of Yahweh as a result of his identification with El.[53] The history of astral deities in ancient Israel may have been affected by the identification of El and Yahweh, a point discussed in detail in chapter 3. Perhaps originally associated with El, they became part of the divine assembly subordinate to Yahweh.

5. Was El Israel's Original God?

The information in the preceding section makes this question reasonable, despite the apparent complications that this reconstruction may pose for later theology. Moreover, it is a reasonable hypothesis because of one basic piece of information: the name of Israel contains not the divine element of Yahweh but El's name, with the element **'ēl*. If Yahweh had been the original god of Israel, then its name might have been **yiśrâ-yahweh*, or perhaps better **yiśrâ-yāh* in accordance with other Hebrew proper names containing the divine name. This fact would suggest that El not Yahweh was the original chief god of the group named Israel. The distribution of El and Yahweh in personal names in many so-called early poems likewise points in this direction.[54] Proper names do pose difficulties when used to reconstruct religious history,[55] yet when used in conjunction with other evidence, proper names offer admissible evidence. Israel is a very old name, apparently known both at Ebla and Ugarit.[56] When the name began to refer to the historical phenomenon of a people in the Iron I highlands, perhaps it no longer referred to the god to whom it was devoted.

Biblical texts do attest to Yahweh and El as different gods sanctioned by early Israel. For example, Genesis 49:24–25 presents a series of El epithets separate from the mention of Yahweh in verse 18. This passage does not show the relative status of the two gods in early Israel, only that they could be named separately in the same poem.[57] More helpful is the text of the Septuagint and one of the Dead Sea Scrolls (4QDeut\[j\]) for Deuteronomy 32:8–9, which cast Yahweh in the role of one of the divine sons,[58] understood as fathered by El, called Elyon in the first line:[59]

When the Most High (Elyon) allotted peoples for inheritance,
When He divided up humanity,
He fixed the boundaries for peoples,
According to the number of the divine sons:
For Yahweh's portion is his people,
Jacob His own inheritance.

The traditional Hebrew text (MT) perhaps reflects a discomfort with this polytheistic theology of Israel, for it shows in the fourth line not "sons of El" but "sons of Israel." This passage, with the Septuagint and Dead Sea Scroll reading, presents a cosmic order in which each deity received its own nation. Israel was the nation which Yahweh received, yet El was the head of this pantheon and Yahweh only one of its members. This reading points to an old phase of Israel's religion when El held a pre-eminent position apart from the status of Yahweh. Apparently, originally El was Israel's chief god, as suggested by the personal name, Israel. Then when the cult of Yahweh became more important in the land of early Israel, the view reflected in Deuteronomy 32:8–9 served as a mode to accommodate this religious development.

If El was the original god of Israel, then how did Yahweh come to be the chief god of Israel and identified with El? We may posit three hypothetical stages (not necessarily discrete in time or geography) to account for the information presented so far:

1. El was the original god of early Israel. As noted, the name Israel points to the first stage. So do references to El as a separate figure (Genesis 49, Psalm 82).[60]
2. El was the head of an early Israelite pantheon, with Yahweh as its warrior-god.[61] Texts that mention both El and Yahweh but not as the same figure (Genesis 49; Numbers 23–24, discussed in the next section; Psalm 82) suggest an early accommodation of the two in some early

form of Israelite polytheism. If Psalm 82 reflects an early model of an Israelite polytheistic assembly, then El would have been its head, with the warrior Yahweh as a member of the second tier (see chapter 2, section 2). Yet the same psalm also uses familial language: the other gods are said to be the "sons of the Most High." Accordingly, Yahweh might have been earlier understood as one of these sons.

3. El and Yahweh were identified as a single god. If El was the original god of Israel, then his merger with Yahweh, the southern divine warrior, predates the Song of Deborah in Judges 5, at least for the area of Israel where this composition was created. In this text Yahweh, the divine warrior from the south, is attributed a victory in the central highlands. The merger probably took place at different rates in different parts of Israel, in which case it was relatively early in the area where Judges 5 was composed, but possibly later elsewhere. Many scholars place the poem in the pre-monarchic period,[62] and perhaps the cult of Yahweh spread further into the highlands of Israel in the pre-monarchic period infiltrating cult sites of El and accommodating to their El theologies (perhaps best reflected by the later version of Deuteronomy 32:8–9). The references to El in Numbers 23–24 (discussed in the following section) and perhaps Job appear to be further indications of the survival of El's cult in Transjordan. Beyond this rather vaguely defined pattern of distribution, it is difficult to be more specific.

El as a separate god disappeared, perhaps at different rates in different regions. This process may appear to involve Yahweh incorporating El's characteristics, for Yahweh is the eventual historical "winner." Yet in the pre-monarchic period, the process may be envisioned—at least initially—in the opposite terms: Israelite highland cult sites of El assimilated the outsider, southerner Yahweh. In comparison, Yahweh in ancient Israel and Baal at Ugarit were both outsider warrior gods who stood second in rank to El, but they eventually overshadowed him in power. Yet Yahweh's development went further. He was identified with El:[63] here the son replaced and became the father whose name only serves as a title for the son.[64]

This paradigm of convergence of divine identities succeeded the older paradigm of divine succession in the ancient Middle East (for example, Ea's replacement by his son Marduk in Enuma Elish). Indeed, the erasure of the father, with his transformation into the son, was a requisite condition for the monotheistic identity of the son. Many, if not all, features of the father and son could be incorporated into the one divine leader of the pantheon, or some features could be displaced in some contexts to divine features of the "Name" (discussed in chapter 4, section 5) or the guardian angel of Israel, who represents and stands under the power and authority of the One. With a distinct father-god erased, the son's identity as son was also erased. And then there was only One. This point has further ramifications. Chapter 1 of this study notes the relationship of the cosmic forces as enemies to the warrior-gods Baal in the Ugaritic texts and Yahweh in the Bible and also as the beloved of El or the pets of Yahweh. When El and

Yahweh were no longer distinguished, there was no longer a triangle of relations, pitting the head god and his beloved monstrous enemies against the young warrior-god. In biblical terms, this triangle is part of an order swept aside, leaving only Yahweh with such enemies. Like El, the enemies are reduced. El becomes Yahweh (or vice versa), and what stands at the end of the biblical convergence of divinity is one head god. In effect, the head god has become tantamount to godhead.

6. The Question of Yahweh's Original Character

A closer look at Yahweh's origins is warranted. According to many scholars, Yahweh originated at the southern sites of Seir/Edom/Teman/Sinai (known from biblical passages cited earlier), located by many scholars today in the northwestern Arabian penisula east of the Red Sea.[65] The cult of Yahweh then found a home in highland sites such as Shiloh. According to an incisive study by J. D. Schloen,[66] some vestiges of the historical process may be found in Judges 5. Some form of direct cultural contact may account for the adoption of Yahweh in Judah,[67] but it is not clear that the worship of Yahweh spread then from the south to the central and northern highlands. Perhaps a further form of contact such as trade was the impetus behind the establishment of the cult of Edomite Yahweh in the central highlands. Judges 5:6 mentions trade as part of the problem leading to the conflict described, and the preface to the hymn in verses 4–5 provides the traditional litany of places where Yahweh marches from, namely, Seir, Edom, and Sinai. Furthermore, we may note the enigmatic line in verse 14: "From Ephraim came they whose roots are in Amalek" (NJPS: *minnî 'eprayim šoršām ba'ămāléq*). This verse shows not simply a neutral mention of Amalek but a positive indication of kinship between the tribe of Ephraim and Amalek, known as a southern group in biblical tradition (e.g., associated with Edom in Genesis 36:16 and the Negeb in Numbers 13:29). In the time of Saul, the Amalekites are mentioned as enemies of Israel according to 1 Samuel 15:2–3, and the later tradition transmitted a negative view of Amalek (Exodus 17:8–16; Deuteronomy 25:27–28).[68] Such a neutral reference to Amelekites in Judges 5:14 has a ring of authenticity and suggests cultural contact between the indigenous inhabitants of the central hill-country associated with Ephraim and the southern group of Amalek. Judges 12:15 mentions a place-name, "Pirathon, in the territory of Ephraim, on the hill of the Amalekites" (NJPS).[69] Were the Amalekites some of the traders mentioned in verse 6, who then settled in the central hill-country? Finally, Judges 5:24 mentions Jael, "wife of Heber the Kenite." Like a number of other groups, such as the Midianites and the Amalekites, the Kenites (Judges 1:16, 4:11; 1 Samuel 27:10, 30:29) are placed by biblical tradition to the south of Judah, precisely the area of ancient Yahwistic cult. This datum in verse 24 lends credence to possible "Kenite" influence in the central highlands, not just in the south.[70] In short, biblical data suggest a series of relationships between the central highlanders and southern caravaneers in the Iron I period. Perhaps trade, enhanced by some kingship ties, provided the mechanism by which a far southern tradition of the deity in Se'ir/Edom/Sinai/Teman/Midian came to be celebrated originally at northern sites such as Shiloh and Bethel.[71] This tradition came to be transmitted during the Iron II period in royal theology, evidenced by Habakkuk 3.[72]

What was Yahweh's original character? Many scholars, including W. F. Albright, F. M. Cross, D. N. Freedman, and more recently J. C. de Moor, M. Dijkstra, and N. Wyatt,[73] identify Yahweh as a title of El. Other scholars, such as T. N. D. Mettinger, note how this view contradicts the early biblical evidence for Yahweh as a storm-and warrior-god from the southern region of Edom.[74] What was the precise nature of this storm? The presumed original location of Yahwistic cult in the far southern region (in southern Edom or the Hegaz), if correct, does not seem propitious as a home for a storm-god such as Baal, because this region has relatively low annual rainfall in contrast to the high rainfall for the Levantine coast. Judges 5:4–5 reflects a god that provide rains, but does this rain necessarily reflect the standard repertoire of a coastal storm-god, or does the passage reflect the storm and flash floods of desert areas? And if the rain does reflect the natural rains associated with a coastal storm-god, then might the depiction in Judges 5 reflect a secondary adaptation of the god's presentation to the coastal-highland religion? Battle and precipitation may have been features original to Yahweh's profile, but perhaps Yahweh's original character approximated the profile of Athtar, a warrior- and precipitation-producing god associated with mostly inland desert sites with less rainfall. Perhaps this profile was rendered secondarily in the highlands in the local language and imagery associated with the coastal storm-god.[75] Such a deity would have characteristics of both power and fertility, but with a different set of associations from Baal. The momentous evidence provided by the Ugaritic texts may have steered research toward El and Baal to seek Yahweh's original profile; this direction may be partially misleading. In fact, part of the original profile of Yahweh may be permanently lost, especially if the earliest biblical sources reflect secondary developments in the history of this deity's profile.

7. Was El the Original God of the Exodus?

The preceding two sections show some of the difficulties in understanding Israel's chief gods in the Iron I perod. It has been assumed that Yahweh was the original god of Israel, but this assumption has perhaps been created by the biblical presentation of early Israel. For later generations of Israelites, there was no difference between El and Yahweh, and for them there was no reason to see their earliest religious history in any other terms. However, the review of the evidence here suggests a more complex history of God in early Israel. In the traditional view, the people in the land who may have been called Israel could have had El as their god, but Yahweh was still the original chief god of the Israelite people who came out of Egypt.[76] But some evidence presents problems for this traditional view. Indeed, C. F. A. Schaeffer has written, followed by N. Wyatt[77] and me,[78] that El may have been the original god connected with the Exodus from Egypt and that this event was secondarily associated with Yahweh when the two gods coalesced. Numbers 23:22 and 24:8 (cf. 23:8) associate the Exodus not with Yahweh but with the name of El: "El who freed them from Egypt has horns like a wild ox." (This description also evokes El's attribute animal at Ugarit, the ox, reflected in his title

"Bull El."[79]) The poems in Numbers 23–24 contain the name of Yahweh (23:8, 21; 24:6), but it is considerably rarer than the name of El (23:8, 19, 22, 23; 24:4, 8, 16, 23). Indeed, El is attested almost three times as often as Yahweh. Accordingly, B. A. Levine seems correct in suggesting that these poems preserve an old repertoire of El tradition, now synthesized with references to Yahweh.[80] If so, these texts contain a valuable witness to El as the god of the Exodus, at least in one of the Israelite traditions.

This reconstruction may be supported by older information concerning the Exodus. The various Egyptian names in Shilohite lineage (Moses, Phinehas, Hopni, and Merari) may point to the Egyptian background of the Levitical Shilohite priesthood.[81] As J. M. Powis Smith asserted in 1918: "The name of 'Phinehas,' the son of Eli, priest at Shiloh, is Egyptian and points to some Egyptian connections with the Levitical priesthood of Yahweh at Shiloh, the northern shrine."[82] The later parallel etiologies in Exodus 2 and Judges 17 apparently echo the Egyptian background of the Shilohite priestly line. Moses names his son *gēršōm* because Moses was a *gēr* in the land of Egpyt. The original Levitical setting for the name echoes Judges 17:7. The Levite is described as a *gār-šām*. The son's naming makes sense if Moses was a *gēr-šām*, "in the land of Egypt" being a secondary specification. The older context of the etiology perhaps was the notion of the Levite as a *gēr* attached to sanctuaries. Levites were recognized as landless and thus retained the status of dependent sojourner.[83] Because of Seow's study and the Egyptian names, one could claim that the god of the putative figure Moses and the Levitical priesthood in Shiloh was El. Indeed, Exodus 6:2–3 reflects the notion that Israel's original god was El Shadday, who was later identified with Yahweh.[84] This passage could represent an attempt to reconcile the discrepancy by appealing to their identification. If the general line of interpretation is correct, El, not Yahweh, was the original god of the Israelites who came out of the land of Egypt. Only later, under the impetus of contact with the southern tradition of Edom, does Yahweh come to be associated, and then assimilated, with El.

If this approach is correct, then early biblical tradition preserves an association of the Exodus primarily with El and not Yahweh. T. J. Lewis, in his comprehensive review of the evidence, asks hypothetically:

> If, for the sake of argument, one assumes that El was the original god of the exodus, one then wonders how Yahweh was welcomed into the fold. What function would Yahweh have provided if worshippers look to El to fight their battles? Maybe two gods were thought to be better than one (although biblical tradition says that El and Yahweh are one and the same, not separate deities). Or, perhaps El's strength was waning (although there is no evidence of such) and a successor to the throne was needed. . . . Perhaps just as [in the Ugaritic texts] Baal comes to the fore and El recedes when it comes to a dynastic deity who fights for the nation, so the traditions of Yahweh as divine warrior come to the fore over those of El as the needs of the society changed from those of a small family group to those of a nation.[85]

As these remarks suggest, the divine profile manifest in the Exodus may have looked originally more like the presence of the deity in the patriarchal narratives, the family god or "god of the fathers" who accompanies the family on its journeys.

Indeed, it is perhaps no accident that El names and titles proliferate in the older patriarchal narratives.[86] Accordingly, the divine warrior profile in the Exodus narrative may reflect not an original description of the god involved but a secondary application (albeit an early one) of Yahweh's identity as a divine warrior. Like so many other religious features, such a distinction was perhaps lost in the early stages of Israel's religious development. Instead, the old profile of the god of the Exodus may have been then the family god, a characterization that fits El eminently well. In contrast, Yahweh's original profile as deity may be, at least in part, irretrievably lost.

8

The Emergence of Monotheistic Rhetoric in Ancient Judah

Who knows one?

A Passover Song

This chapter turns to the question of biblical monotheism. Many scholars claim great antiquity for biblical monotheism. W. F. Albright, Y. Kaufman, C. H. Gordon, H. Orlinsky, J. C. de Moor, W. H. C. Propp, and others have viewed monotheism as an original feature of Israel, at least from Sinai onward.[1] Other scholars more recently have sought to identify monotheism as a feature of Israelite religion throughout the period of the monarchy and often suggest the possibility of an earlier dating.[2] These scholars claim Yahweh as the sole ruler of his assembly, arguing that monotheism is implied. This argument appears weak not simply because one might sense possible Christian or Jewish apologetics behind such claims; indeed, this in itself is no objection. Instead, the claim associates monotheism with the form of Israelite polytheism that knew only the Supreme Ruler and various "minor" divine figures who serve the One. For example, Exodus 15 asks if the God of Israel has a counterpart among the deities. Habakkuk 3:5 presents Resheph and Deber as part of Yahweh's theophanic retinue; both are well-known West Semitic gods. Psalm 29 calls the divine beings to join in praise of Yahweh. Similarly, Job 1–2 presents divine beings coming before God, including "the satan."[3] The "astral religion" of later monarchic Judah likewise maintains the Judean national god at the head of a pantheon of lesser astral divinities.[4] Some scholars may regard the religious outlook of such passages as "*de facto* monotheism,"[5] leaving room for deities who serve the Supreme Power. Moreover, such biblical texts do not deny the power of other deities outside this "local" framework. This approach also tends to ignore biblical criticisms against polytheism and the claims of most scholars that Israel knew the cult of "Yahweh and his asherah."[6] Thus, claims of "practical monotheism,"[7] "*de facto* monotheism," "virtual monotheism," or even "monolatry" overlook the biblical evidence to the contrary, retrojecting onto "biblical Israel" a singularity of divinity that the Bible itself does not claim for ancient Israel. Indeed, claims for this sort of monotheism not only beg the question by such qualifications as "de facto" or "virtual"; they also rely on argument by omission, assuming that biblical texts lacking mention of other deities may be used to reconstruct such putative forms of worship. Accordingly, to use biblical texts to ground monotheism, or even monolatry, historically before the seventh century is difficult.

A second group of scholars, including T. J. Meek,[8] date the emergence of monotheism around the time of the "Exile" (587–538). Faced with the prospect of overwhelming earthly powers, Judeans exalted their deity in absolute terms. There is no doubt that this camp has an easier task in criticizing those who hold an early date for monotheism. In *Hebrew Origins*[9] (1936), Meek attacked Albright's view, both for its lack of early evidence for monotheism and because of the clear, later attestation of monotheistic declarations in the sixth-century prophets. In 1938 Meek put his objections about definition to Albright in a letter:

> Since returning home I looked up the dictionary definitions of henotheism, monolatry, and monotheism, and I feel more convinced than ever that you are using monotheism in a sense not supported by the dictionaries. By monotheism in my book [*Hebrew Origins*] I mean exclusive belief in and worship of one god and the denial of even the existence of other gods, which when believed in are merely figments of the imagination, with no reality at all. Our difference seems to be largely one of definition, but it is unfortunate when people define words in different ways.[10]

Meek had a good point. Much of Albright's definition had little to do with the meaning of monotheism per se. In 1940 he presented monotheists in his well-received volume *From the Stone Age to Christianity* in these terms:

> If . . . the term "monotheist" means one who teaches the existence of only one God, the creator of everything, the source of justice, who is equally powerful in Egypt, in the desert, and in Palestine, who has no sexuality and no mythology, who is human in form but cannot be seen by human eye and cannot be represented in any form—then the founder of Yahwism was certainly a monotheist.[11]

This definition is interesting, as it partially focuses on some features of Yahweh noted in preceding chapters, such as anthropomorphism and the general lack of sexuality. However, this definition was problematic. As this quotation suggests, Albright's sum representation of monotheism was drawn from many different documents of the Bible to create into a single original picture. Even more problematic for Albright's position, the Bible as a whole simply does not teach the existence of only one God. Other aspects of the Israelite deity that Albright took to be signs of old monotheism, such as multiple divine abodes, power in a multitude of locales, and the god's role as a creator god, were paralleled in fully polytheistic religions. Finally, it was evident to Albright that the biblical sources even for what he regarded as monotheism dated to the monarchic period, much later than the putative time of Mosaic monotheism.[12]

Despite these drawbacks, Albright firmly believed in the historical reality of Sinai monotheism. In 1943 he wrote to his former student G. Ernest Wright that the first edition of his book *From the Stone Age to Christianity* conceded too much to his critics.[13] For example, he thought that he could base Mosaic monotheism on the first of the Ten Commandments (in Exodus 20:3 and Deuteronomy 5:7), that the Israelites "shall have no other gods besides me" (*'al pānay*). Albright thought he could defend this translation based on the Punic use of *'l(t) pn-*, "besides," in the Marseilles tariff (KAI 69:3),[14] and that such a meaning could be used to establish monotheism. In the second edition of his book, Albright added this point.[15] On the first question, Albright had a point; the use is attested in Punic, but whether it demonstrated monotheism was in fact problematic. In retrospect, the question is why Albright took such great historical and textual leaps. He had tremendous faith in the ultimate antiquity of the tradition lying behind the biblical texts. For Albright, the biblical narrative was essentially historical, even though he conceded the lateness of the biblical texts involved.[16] Did Albright's religious sensibilities affect his judgment on this issue? Did Albright the believer perhaps subconsciously convince Albright the historian despite the lack of historical evidence?[17]

The debate between Albright and Meek solved nothing for a number of reasons. As long as the debate over definition went unresolved, so scholarly discussion of the historical issues went unresolved. However, there was a deeper problem. Scholars on both sides of the divide seemed hardly interested in addressing their opponents' more constructive points. Albright, for example, did not address the fundamental question concerning later monotheistic formulations. Assuming for a moment that Israel was basically monotheistic from an early time, as Albright claimed, then why did its monotheistic faith appear in clearer, less ambiguous forms in the seventh and sixth centuries? And Meek, for all his well placed concerns over definition, did not truly turn to the question raised by the particularly distinctive forms of Israelite polytheism in the biblical record, considerably less ample than the pantheons in the record of other ancient Near Eastern literatures.[18] Finally, neither camp attempted to situate the issues in terms of Judah's larger social structure and situation in the seventh and sixth centuries. Meek's basic point remains valid, yet the relatively late emergence of the rhetoric of monotheism may become clear set against the background of discourse about divinity during the late Judean monarchy. This chapter begins an exploration of these issues with a survey of the clear and explicit monotheistic declarations in the Bible.

1. Defining Monotheism

To begin, we need to define the terms of discussion.[19] Most interpreters include two kinds of expressions in clearly monistic claims. The first involves a claim of exclusivity that proclaims Yahweh "alone" (**lěbadd-*) or no god "apart from, besides" Yahweh (**zûlat-*). Monotheistic exclusivity is not simply a matter of cultic observance, as in the First Commandment's prohibition against "no other gods before me" in Exodus 20:3 and Deuteronomy 5:7. It extends further to an understanding of deities in the cosmos (no other gods, period).[20] The second involves statements claiming that all other deities are "not" (*'ên*), "nothings" (*'ĕlîlîm*), or "dead" (*mētîm*).

The first category includes the following passages as examples of monotheism, with the expression, "alone" (*lĕbadd-*):[21]

> Deuteronomy 4:35: "Yahweh alone is God, there is none beside Him."
>
> 2 Kings 19:15, 19 = Isaiah 37:16, 20: "You alone are God of all the kingdoms of the earth, . . . You alone (O Yahweh) are God."
>
> Nehemiah 9:6: "You alone are Yahweh."
>
> Psalm 86:10: "You are God alone."

All but the first of these statements belong to prayers. Monotheism here belongs to the rhetoric of praise. Deuteronomy 4:35 is part of a speech of Moses to the Israelites. Accordingly, it is a "sermon" or the like, which belongs to the rhetoric of persuasion. A similar rhetorical approach obtains in the monotheistic formulation with *zûlat-*:

> 2 Samuel 7:22 = 1 Chronicles 17:20: "there is no god except You according to all that we have heard with our ears."

In this instance we again see the rhetoric of praise. One must be careful, for terms of exclusivity need not always represent the existence of only one [e.g., *zûl-* in 1 Samuel 21:10]). However, I accept the generally accepted view that these terms of divine exclusion represent monotheism.

The second category essentially denies the reality of other deities. One way to express monotheistic exclusivity in this manner involves the sentence predicate, 'ên, "(there is) not":

> Deuteronomy 4:39: "Yahweh is god in heaven above and on earth below; there is no other" ('ên 'ôd).
>
> 1 Samuel 2:2: "There is none beside You" ('ên biltĕkā).[22]
>
> Jeremiah 16:19, 20: "To You the nations shall come,/From the ends of the earth . . . Shall a man make gods for himself/And they are no gods?"[23]

The first case is part of a larger speech including the monotheistic claim of Deuteronomy 4:35.

For the criterion of other gods regarded as "nothings" or "dead," the following passages conform:

> Psalm 96:5 = 1 Chronicles 16:26: "For all the gods of the nations are nothings" ('ĕlîlîm).
>
> Psalm 82:7: "Therefore like a mortal you shall die (*mwt*),/like one of the princes you shall fall."

The first passage shows a clever pun made between the other 'ĕlōhîm (gods) and 'ĕlîlîm (nothings). Again, the effect is rhetorical, designed as much to persuade and reinforce as it is to assert. The language of divine death, as we saw in chapter 6, belongs to a slightly different rhetoric. It depicts the old order of Israelite polytheism passing to the new order of monotheism.

With other statements, it is important to be careful. Some scholars would accept as monotheistic passages that condemn the veneration of other deities, without commenting on their existence. One might then include the First Commandment (Exodus 20:3 and Deuteronomy 5:7) or Deuteronomy 32:12, 15b–21, and 37–39.[24] Or one might be tempted to add the Shema of Deuteronomy 6:4 to the list of monotheistic claims:

šěma' yiśrā'ēl yhwh 'ělōhēnû yhwh 'ěḥād

Hear, O Israel! The Lord is our God, the Lord alone. (New Jewish Publication Society version, New Revised Standard Version.)

Hear, O Israel! The Lord is our God, the Lord alone! (New American Bible)

The possible interpretation of monotheism here hinges especially on the semantics of *'ěḥād*, literally "one." The question is the significance of this "one-ness." It might be interpreted as a statement of exclusivity ("the only one"). All three translations cited render the term "alone," perhaps suggesting to readers a monotheistic interpretation, and such a view might seem plausible given a comparison with Zechariah 14:9 (which NJPS in fact cites in its note to Deuteronomy 6:4):

And Yahweh shall be king over all the earth;
on that day Yahweh will be one and His name shall be one.

Zechariah 14:9 envisions only one deity ruling the world, and it would seem also to envision worship of Yahweh only.[25] Yet does this (Hellenistic period?) passage apply to the Shema? Indeed, it is difficult to gauge to what degree the monotheistic interpretation of the Shema is due to later readings of the verse.[26] G. von Rad regarded the translation "alone" in Deuteronomy 6:4, as an expression aimed at excluding the cult of another god, such as Baal.[27] J. H. Tigay has a similar view: "For all its familiarity, the precise meaning of the Shema is uncertain and it permits several possible meanings. The present translation indicates that the verse is a description of the proper relationship between YHVH and Israel: He alone is Israel's God. This is not a declaration of monotheism, meaning that there is only one God."[28] Therefore, in discussing monotheism, one must exclude the reality of other gods. Other biblical statements might be admissible in a discussion of monotheism, but it is preferable to restrict the discussion to examples that clearly articulate monotheism, not those that simply exclude veneration of other deities.[29]

Most of the references to monotheism, derive from the exilic period or later.[30] Jeremiah 16:19, 20, if original and not secondary, point to the late pre-exilic period.[31] Perhaps exceptional are 1 Samuel 2:2 and Psalm 82, as their dates are unknown; a date in the late monarchy for these compositions remains a possibility. Some scholars claim that some references in the Deuteronomistic History predate the exile, but other scholars have dated the sections containing the monotheistic sentiments to the exile or later. Of course, it is difficult to know which dating is correct, but on the whole the late monarchy and exile seem to represent the general period for the emergence of monotheistic rhetoric. B. Halpern rightly suggests that it is unlikely that Second Isaiah was an innovator of monotheistic discourse: "Had Second Isaiah, Cyrus' Judahite spin-doctor, not had Jeremiah's (and Deuteronomy's) voice crying on his own arrival from the steppe, his explicit monotheistic claims would have fallen on deaf ears, and probably set them ringing to boot."[32] Monotheistic rhetoric probably emerged shortly before the exile.

2. The Relative Infrequency and Rhetorical Purpose of Monotheistic Statements

Because of the post-biblical importance of monotheism, the relative rarity of its expression in the Bible is quite striking (even if more controversial examples were to be included). Indeed, the relatively few instances are spread over the whole of the so-called Deuteronomistic History (Joshua through 2 Kings), the post-exilic historical works of Ezra-Nehemiah, the two books of Chronicles, and a few other biblical books. The outstanding exception is "Second Isaiah," dated to the removal of members of the Judean elite to Babylon in 587–538.[33] This part consists of Isaiah 40–55 (in scholarly circles called "Second Isaiah"). The section's author(s) wants to sublimate his own identity, which is why no author is presented in it. Many scholars today believe that a "Second Isaiah" meant to circulate separate from the "First Isaiah" never existed. And, indeed, I use quotation marks around "Second Isaiah." Textually there is only one book of Isaiah.[34]

The distribution of monotheistic declarations in the Hebrew Bible prompts some observations. Because of the concentration of monotheistic declarations in "Second Isaiah," this work demands its own examination, a task undertaken in in chapter 10. To understand the monotheistic statements in "Second Isaiah," one must recognize them as part of the work's rhetoric. Indeed, biblical claims of monotheism are generally rhetorical. Israelites continued to worship deities other than Yahweh both before and possibly after the exile. We may assume on the basis of available evidence that the ruling priestly groups of the post-exilic theocracy maintained a Yahwistic monolatry expressed in its rhetoric of monotheism, but such a historical conclusion does not justify claims for an entirely "monotheistic culture."[35] Because of the relative rarity of monotheistic claims and the ongoing presence of polytheism in ancient Israel, no one can confirm a clear evolution from monarchic monolatry (the worship of only one god, e.g., Exodus 22:19) to a new stage of religion called monotheism (belief in and worship of only one deity).[36]

Monotheistic statements do not herald a new age of religion but explain Yahwistic monolatry in absolute terms. As rhetoric, monotheism reinforced Israel's exclusive relationship with its deity. Monotheism is a kind of inner community discourse[37] establishing a distance from outsiders; it uses the language of Yahweh's exceptional divine status beyond and in all reality ("there are no other deities but the Lord") to absolutize Yahweh's claim on Israel and to express Israel's ultimate fidelity to Yahweh. Monotheism is therefore not a new cultural step but expresses Israel's relationship with Yahweh. C. Seitz insightfully asserts:

> This is not a sublime monotheism capable of differentation from a more concrete henotheism—rather it is henotheism of a particularly potent stripe. The other elohim that continue to claim allegiance from humanity have detachable names

and detachable existences—to the degree that YHWH insists that they do not exist at all and envisions a time when representatives of the nations will make the confession once enjoined of Israel only.[38]

Monotheistic statement attempted to persuade Judeans still unconvinced of this perspective. Perhaps these declarations represent the efforts of a minority of "monotheists" to persuade a majority of Judeans who held Yahweh as the head of a larger group of divinities or divine powers. Perhaps the main point of such statements was not simply to move the later into the "monotheistic camp" but to convince them of the reality of Yahweh's power in the world.

3. The Prior Context of Judean Discourse about Divinity

To situate monotheistic language in seventh-and sixth-century Judah, one must ask about the context for this discourse. What forms did Judean discourse for divinity assume? The period of the monarchy sustained various forms of Israelite polytheism, noted in part 1 in this book. Unless we assume that prophets did not know what they were talking about, their criticisms of polytheism suggest that Judean society in the late monarchy enjoyed a range of polytheistic options. One end of the spectrum reflected cultic devotion to a variety of deities. The other end of the spectrum focused its devotion on Yahweh with his few servant-gods. What is apparently evident from biblical criticisms of the asherah[39] is a middle "ditheistic" model of the divine couple in charge of the four-tiered pantheon evolving to a single figure surrounded only by minor powers, which are wholly subordinate to that divinity's power.[40] In all of these models, Yahweh was the king of the heavenly host of deities. As a result of the editing of later monotheists, only scattered references to a number of other deities who belong to the middle levels of the pantheon have survived.[41] Indeed, the Bible hardly provides an objective or complete picture of Israel's religion, because of significant editorial selection. Fortunately, biblical criticisms of polytheism preserve some vestiges of information about polytheism into the late monarchic period.[42] Furthermore, most scholars believe that inscriptional evidence of "Yahweh and his asherah" and Baal at Kuntillet 'Ajrud has provided extra-biblical evidence for polytheism. Iconographic representation of what may be an Iron Age Judean goddess and archaeological evidence of female pillar figurines dating to the same period have been added to this reconstruction.[43] Even if we did not know of the biblical references to other deities, this extra-biblical evidence alone suggests a polytheistic situation. In fact, the biblical critiques of polytheism suffice to show that various forms of polytheism represented the range of religious devotion to the cult of the national god. In other words, the later dominant paradigm of a single national god with divine workers was only one version of devotion available in Iron Age Israel. Only later was the process of telescoping divinity into a single divine king with his servants completed.

The few remaining biblical monotheistic references remain because they could be easily interpreted in conformity with later stricter monotheism of the postexilic period. For example the form of older Israelite (reduced) polytheism known from Psalm 82 casts Yahweh in an explicit divine council scene not as its head, who is instead left decidedly mute or left undescribed (which is probably the reason it survived the later collapsing of the different tiers). Psalm 82[44] begins:

> God (*'ĕlōhîm*) stands in the assembly of El/divine assembly (*'ădat 'ēl*),
> Among the divinities (*'ĕlōhîm*) He pronounces judgment.

Here the figure of God takes his stand in the assembly. The name God was understood in the tradition, and perhaps at the time of the text's original composition as well, to be none other than Yahweh; the name of El seems to be involved with the expression "assembly of El" (preferable to "divine assembly," given El's title, Elyon, in verse 6). In any case, the assembly consists of all the gods of the world, for all these other gods are condemned to death in verse 6:

> I myself presumed that You are gods,
> Sons of the Most High (Elyon),
> Yet like humans you will die,
> And fall like any prince.

A prophetic voice emerges in verse 8, calling for God (*'ĕlōhîm*) to assume the role of judge of all the earth:

> Arise, O God, judge the world;
> For You inherit all the nations.

Here Yahweh in effect assumes the task of all gods to rule their own nations. Verse 6 calls all the gods "sons of Elyon," probably a title of El at an early point in biblical tradition (Genesis 14:18–20). If this supposition is correct, Psalm 82 preserves a tradition that casts the god of Israel not in the role of the presiding god of the pantheon but as one of his sons. Each of these sons has a different nation as his ancient patrimony (or family inheritance) and therefore serves as its ruler. Then verse 6 calls on Yahweh to arrogate to himself the traditional inheritance of all the other gods: all the nations.

This family view of the divine arrangement of the world is preserved also by the version of Deuteronomy 32:8–9 in the Greek texts of the Septuagint and the Dead Sea Scrolls:[45]

> When the Most High (Elyon) allotted peoples for inheritance,
> When He divided up humanity,
> He fixed the boundaries for peoples,
> According to the number of the divine sons:
> For Yahweh's portion is his people,
> Jacob His own inheritance.

The traditional Hebrew text (MT) perhaps reflects a discomfort with this polytheistic theology of Israel, for it shows not "divine sons," but "sons of Israel."[46] Yet the texts of the Septuagint and the Dead Sea Scrolls show an Israelite polytheism that clearly focuses on the central importance of Yahweh for Israel within the larger scheme of the world, yet this larger scheme provides a place for all the other gods in the world. Moreover, even if this text is quite mute about the god who presides over the whole arrangement, it does maintain a place for such a god who is not Yahweh. The title of Elyon ("Most High") seems to denote the figure of El (called El Elyon in Genesis 14:18–22); he is presider par excellence not only at Ugarit but also in Psalm 82.

The author of Psalm 82 wishes to depose this older theology, as the Israelite God is called to assume a new role as judge of all the world. Yet at the same time, Psalm 82, like Deuteronomy 32:8–9, preserves the outlines of the older Israelite theology it is rejecting. From the perspective of this older theology, Yahweh did not belong to the top tier of the pantheon. Instead, in early Israel the god of Israel apparently belonged to the second tier of the pantheon; he was not the presider god but one of his sons. This older picture, assumed in Deuteronomy 32:8–9 and criticized in Psalm 82, presupposes the model of roughly equal national gods for all of the seventy nations of the world, a notion reflected also in the Ugaritic motif of the seventy sons of El and Athirat (CAT 1.4 VI 46).[47] It is true that these expressions of older national theology survive only because they could be conformed to the later monotheistic paradigm: the figure of "the Most High" ('*elyôn*) in Psalm 82 could be read as a reference to Yahweh, and the Masoretic change in Deuteronomy 32:8–9 marks a shift to a monotheistic reading. However, analyzed not in terms of the later monotheism but in terms of the earlier national situation, these two passages offer an important witness to the old monarchic period theology of the national god. In these two cases the Bible preserves only a limited number of "snapshots" of pre-exilic religion, not a complete "tape." Accordingly, given the later textual editing "out" (and "down") of Israelite polytheism, the minimal evidence the Bible does provide should be viewed probably as only the tip of the iceberg. What little evidence we do have, implies that a number of different possibilities existed in the larger context of the national religion. As long as the nations continued and stood in roughly comparable status in Judah's eyes, the religious view of the world represented in the national theology was feasible. The next section explores this royal ideology in greater detail.

4. The National God and Royal Ideology

The royal theology and religious practice served as a basic matrix to support the national god.[48] Royal psalms present this support in a contrast between two sets of powers. On one side are Yahweh and his "anointed," the Judean king, who rule together from Jerusalem (Psalm 2), viewed ideologically as the center of the world (cf. Psalms 46, 48, and 87). In contrast, all the other kings and their nations, ideally, are to submit to the authority of Yahweh and his human regent on earth. The parallel of the cosmic and earthly levels in the royal worldview then consists of the divine and human kings centered at Zion against the divine and human enemies in the world. Yahweh the divine warrior-king parallels the human king ruling in Jerusalem, and the cosmic enemies hostile to Yahweh parallel the human enemies opposed to the Judean monarch. Both are to be defeated and submissive to the royal rule imposed by the Supreme King and carried out by his human counterpart.

This fundamental paradigm of cosmic and human royal power drew on a wider fund of West Semitic myth tradition represented in Ugaritic texts.[49] Three overlapping types of royal theology contain "mythic imagery"[50] (much of it known from the Baal Cycle): (a) action parallel between the divine king, Yahweh, and the human king; (b) the metaphorical granting of divine power to the human king in the language of the West Semitic conflict myth of Baal and Yamm, as well as the attribution of divine titles to the human king; and (c) possibly the king as "divine," 'ĕlōhîm. Because these types differ in some ways, perhaps we should speak of royal theologies[51] and examine the background of each one separately.[52] The identification of human and divine kings in battle together represents a theme running through a good deal of biblical texts surviving from the monarchy. According to 1 Samuel 25:28, the king is said to fight Yahweh's wars. The parallelism between divine and human kings is explicit in the royal psalms (Psalms 2; 89:5–18//19–37; cf. 72:8). It is commonplace to observe that Psalm 18 = 2 Samuel 22, verses 8–19 describe Yahweh in terms associated with Baal's battle (CAT 1.2 IV; cf. 1.4 VII 8–9, 38–39), fighting for the king and saving him from destruction while verses 29–45 depict Yahweh's enabling the monarch to conquer his enemies in battle.[53] Habakkuk 3 employs the conflict-myth in defense of the king. The poem tells how Yahweh has come in his storm-theophany (verses 4–11) to trample the enemy-nations (verse 12) and to save the people and his "anointed" (verse 13), the king. The divine force is arrayed against Yamm and River (verse 8), and his theophanic vanguard includes not only the theophanic light with the Sun and Moon (verse 11) but also destructive divine forces including Resheph (verse 5). Accordingly, this text provides an instance of Yahweh's action in battle with the attendant divine astral bodies and accompanying destructive divinities.[54] This poem bears a further importance, as it illustrates divine powers subservient to Yahweh, the warrior-king, in a context supportive of the monarchy.[55] As the warrior-god battles the cosmic enemies, his earthly counterpart, the human king, may fight enemies on the terrestrial level. Often the stress falls on Yahweh fighting on behalf of the king, but sometimes the text accents the king's own action aided by his divine patron. The royal theology of parallels between the heavenly and earthly realms extended also to identifying historical enemies with cosmic enemies known from the Ugaritic texts as Baal's or Anat's enemies.[56] It is well-known that Sea and River in Isaiah 11:15 appear in conflated form with the seven-headed dragon in a description of Egypt. Rahab stands for Egypt (Isaiah 30:7; Psalm 87:4), the River for Assyria (Isaiah 8:5–8; cf. 17:12–14), Tannin for Babylon (Jeremiah 51:34). It is no wonder that apocalyptic literature used this imagery so extensively, as mythical enemies had long served as emblems of historical enemies.

Another action parallel between Yahweh and the king may be seen in Psalm 89. This psalm parallels the victorious power of Yahweh in verses 5–18 with the divine favor that Yahweh bestows upon the Davidic monarch in verses 19–37. The parallelism between Yahweh and the king changes, however, in verse 26, and a different sort of notion appears: Yahweh extends his power to the monarch in language associated in Ugaritic with the god, Baal: "I will set his hand on Sea and his right hand on Rivers."[57] The power of the Judean king given to him by Yahweh, the divine warrior-king, is so great that some of Yahweh's own power over the cosmic enemies extends to the human king. As many commentators[58] have observed, Sea and River are titles of Baal's enemy in the Baal Cycle. The Baal Cycle describes a circumscribed or limited exaltation of the storm-god.[59] This limited exaltation of Baal may correspond in some manner to Ugarit's limited political circumstances, as F. Stolz suggests.[60] The cycle was developed under the royal aegis of the dynasty of Niqmaddu at Ugarit,[61] ruling in the shadow of the larger powers of Egypt and Hatti.[62] Descriptions of the king couched in the language of the West Semitic storm-god hail from the Levantine littoral, Egypt and Mari. These passages indicate that political entities as varied as Egypt, the Levantine coast, and Mari utilized the imagery of the West Semitic storm-god to dramatize royal power and legitimacy. It appears reasonable to suppose that, like other sites in the heartland of cult devoted to Baal, such as Mari and the Levantine littoral, as well as the periphery in Egypt, Ugarit also knew the political use of the language of Baal for its king.

The use of the West Semitic conflict myth to reinforce human kingship appears in a variety of texts hailing from Mari to Egypt. A letter from Nur-Sin of Aleppo to Zimri-Lim of Mari informs the king, quoting Adad (Baal), that "when you ascended the throne of your father, I gave you the weapon with which I slew Sea."[63] In some of the Amarna letters, the pharaoh is compared with "Baal in the heavens" (EA 108:9; 147:14; 149:7; 159:7; 207:16). Some Egyptian texts, such as the poetical stele of Tutmoses III,[64] dress the king in the storm imagery of Baal. The imagery in these cases does not construct parallelism between the divine and human kings. In perhaps the most dramatic biblical instance, according to Psalm 89:26, the human king's power is to extend to Sea, the cosmic enemy of Baal in the Ugaritic texts and the sometimes hostile, sometimes compliant cosmic force in the Bible:[65] "And I [Yahweh] shall set his hand [the Judean's king's] on Yam(m), and on River(s) his right hand."[66] Rather, it crosses the boundaries of this parallelism by making the king into a figure of his patron storm-god.[67] It is possible that the language was not merely a figurative ornament.[68] Rather, to use older metaphysical language, the human king was perhaps thought to "participate in" the power of the divine king. The image of the Davidic monarch receiving martial power from Yahweh also underlies the second metaphor in a post-exilic verse, Zechariah 12:8: "On that day the Lord will put a shield about the inhabitants of Jerusalem so that the feeblest among them on that day shall be like David, and the house of David shall be like God, like the angel of the Lord at their head."[69]

The idea of divine power being granted to the human king may lie behind two titles applied to the "messianic" figure in Isaiah 9:5.[70] This person is called both *'ēl gibbôr*, "warrior-god," and *'ăbî'ad*, "eternal father." Both of these titles draw on the tradition of Yahweh's titles as *'ēl gibbôr* (Isa 10:21)[71] and *'āb* (Deuteronomy 32:6; Jeremiah 3:19, 31:7–9). Finally, *'ēl gibbôr* may be viewed as the heightening of the royal title of *gibbôr* (Psalm 45:5).[72] W. L. Holladay objects to the view that the titles in Isaiah 9:5 indicate that the king is receiving divine titles.[73] Like other commentators,[74] he argues that the titles are throne names[75] given to the king as part of a coronation ode upon his accession. More specifically, the titles supposedly represent sentence names, which reflect no more a divine attribution to the monarch than any theophoric names given to anyone in ancient Israel. The content of the names therefore would refer only to God and not to the king. A. Laato refers to Holladay's view:

So how could Isaiah use a divine name for a king? After all, he made a clear distinction between God and man (see e.g. 2:22, 31:3). HOLLADAY solves the problem by claiming that the second (as well as the third) title is theophoric, that is, it refers to a quality of Yahweh, not a man (cf. ישעיהו for example). Naturally the king's authority entirely depended on Yahweh's power. Nevertheless, in the Yahweh doctrine the idea that a person may have divine power in relation to other people was not impossible. According to Ex 7:1, Moses was made into a god for the Pharaoh. In a similar way Yahweh wants to give the new-born prince divine rule over Assyria.[76]

Furthermore, these names are not theophoric as any other Israelite names are. Although the element *gibbôr* is productive in West Semitic names in Neo-Assyrian as well as Neo-Babylonian and Late Babylonian texts, it does not appear in Israelite proper names.[77] Consequently, it is preferable to understand '*ēl gibbôr* not as a common proper name, as Holladay proposes, but as a title like other divine titles.[78] Similarly, '*ăbî'ad*, though susceptible to interpretation as a sentence name, is equally intelligible as "eternal father." Furthermore, the heightened language applied to the king suits the setting Holladay posits for this passage, a coronation ode, as well as Psalm 45, which likewise exhibits exceptionally heightened language for the king (see later). Indeed, the setting Holladay proposed distinguishes these titles from any other names with theophoric elements. If these names are throne-names in the manner Holladay suggested, the names may nonetheless mark the special character of their recipient.[79] There is no impediment to the view that these two phrases were titles with heightened mythic content applied to the monarch. The background of these titles may be neither Egyptian nor Akkadian throne-names,[80] but West Semitic tradition.[81] Isaiah 9:5 does not bear directly on the long-standing question of whether or not the Israelite king was considered "a divine being" like the Ugaritic figure, Keret. Rather, these titles reflect a transfer of titles to the human king from his patron god, Yahweh. The first title has been traced further to the god El,[82] although the record of this god as a warrior is otherwise poor.[83] In this case, the word '*ēl*, "god," may not derive rom the proper name of El but would represent the generic noun "god." The title would better suit a god such as Baal. The second title, '*ăbî'ad*, "eternal father," is more apt to El, however. It is El who is the divine father par excellence, and this title may have stemmed ultimately from this god. Characteristics associated with two different gods in Ugaritic literature are attributed to Yahweh elsewhere in the Bible.[84] Attribution of divine titles in Isaiah 9:5, especially '*ēl gibbôr*, may be reflected in the metaphorical usage in Zechariah 12:8.[85]

The heightened usage of Isaiah 9:5 perhaps raises the old scholarly issue over the status of the king, a question that hinges on the exegesis of a few biblical passages and some Ugaritic parallels.[86] Many scholars have take Psalm 45:7 as evidence for the royal theology of the king as "divine" ('*ĕlōhîm*):[87] *kis'ăkā 'ĕlōhîm 'ōlām wā'ed*, "your throne, O divine one, (is) forever and ever."[88] The versions generally render the syntax in this manner.[89] Such ambiguity may be as old as the text, and the interpretation of '*ĕlōhîm* as God perhaps contributed to the survival of such an otherwise bald biblical reference to the king's divinity. Criticism of this view has been voiced. The lack of clear parallels to the king as '*ĕlōhîm* has represented a major impediment according to J. A. Emerton[90] and P. Mosca.[91] The "muted reflex"[92] of the notion in Zechariah 12:8 may reflect, however, the background of a "high" royal theology, which applied *'ĕlōhîm* to the monarch.[93] The description of the king as *'ĕlōhîm* in Ezekiel 28:14 may represent a polemic against this notion of the monarchy.[94] H. J. Kraus also compares 2 Samuel 14:17, 20, where David's ability to judge makes him *kĕmal'ak hā'ĕlōhîm*, "like the angel of God."[95] C. F. Whitley offers a further argument for the king as *'ĕlōhîm* by noting points of contact between Psalms 89 and 45:7–8:

> Ps 89 . . . provides an instructive comparison with Ps 45,7–8. Thus in Ps 89,10.21 Yahweh has chosen David from amongst the people (בחור מעם) and anointed him (משחתיו) with holy oil. So in Ps 45,8 we read >>*Elohim* . . . anointed thee—משחך—with the oil of gladness above thy companions—מחברך-<<. Again in Ps 89 the Messiah's throne (כסאו) and that of his seed shall endure as long as (ועד-עולם) the sun and moon (v. 29, 37–38). Similarly in Ps 45,7 we find >>thy throne<<(כסאך) *Elohim* is forever and ever (עולמועד). . . . Such comparisons indicate that the *Elohim* of Ps 45,7 and the Davidic figure of Ps 89 are not only similar but identifiable.[96]

J. R. Porter bases his own argument for the king as *'ĕlōhîm* on a comparison of 2 Samuel 14 and Genesis 3:

> [A]t 2 Sam. xiv. 17, David is called the Angel of God because he is able *lišmōa' haṭṭôb wĕhārā'*: this recalls Gen. iii. 22 *lāda'at ṭôb wārā'*, and it was precisely this knowledge which placed Adam among the *'ĕlōhîm*. Thus it is hardly correct that an address to the king as God finds no close parallel elsewhere in the Old Testament.[97]

Emerton objects to this view, noting that the notion of the knowledge of good and evil appears in nonroyal contexts such as Deuteronomy 1:39 and 2 Samuel 19:36 and that comparison of David with an angel does not indicate identity with a divine being.[98] However, other elements reflecting royal influence may be discerned in Genesis 2–3, and the nonroyal examples of this type of knowledge may have derived from royal usage. Moreover, the lack of references to the monarch as *'ĕlōhîm* may not constitute a definitive criterion, especially if such "high" royal theology were considered inappropriate in later periods.

Furthermore, the use of *'ĕlōhîm* for the monarch may represent not an ontological claim but a description intended to heighten the power of the king by rhetorically raising him to divine status. K. W. Whitelam speaks to this point: "Widely expressed attempts to explain away such explicit language as due to textual corruption, ellipsism or grammatical niceties have not proved wholly convincing. It needs to be asked to what extent the audience or audiences of royal rituals would have drawn such careful distinctions in the use of language."[99] In conclusion, interpreting *'ĕlōhîm* for the king in Psalm 45:7 is certainly debatable but plausible on the bases of the versional support; the basic intelligiblity of the syntax; the sense of the idea within ancient Israel, perhaps as a reflex of its West Semitic/Israelite heritage; and its support among many modern commentators. However, the lack of scholarly consensus on this interpretation precludes it as an independent witness to the notion of the king as *'ĕlōhîm*, but it comports with information otherwise known of royal theology and seems to constitute one of the several mythic ideas applied to the king.

The battles associated with the West Semitic conflict myth are not the only mythological background for royal warfare in Israel. The bloody battle, represented in Ugaritic tradition by the goddess Anat, may provide an insight into the mythos behind the biblical ban (BH *ḥerem*; Ugaritic **ḥrm*) utilized by Iron Age Levantine monarchies (Israel, Judah, and Moab). The same root applies to Anat's warfare in CAT 1.13:[100]

> Destroy under the ban (*ḥrm*) for two days,
> Sh[ed blood (?)] for three days,
> go, kill for fo[ur] days . . . !

The 1.13 text has verbal connections with Anat's battle in 1.3 II, and it may be that her battling not only in 1.13 but also in 1.3 II may have been considered an example of the ban. Anat's battles, at least in 1.3 II, suggest how the deity was seen to conduct **ḥrm* warfare: first, she slays her enemies in battle; then, she takes captives back to her house/temple; and finally, she devours them. Moreover, 1.3 II may be the most sustained depiction of the ban rendered from the divine perspective. The idea of **ḥrm* as divine battle underlies not only Anat's warfare but also the ban language in the Moabite stele (KAI 181), as well as Israelite battles described as *ḥerem*. In both Moab and Israel this language was used for warfare against royal enemies. The Mesha stele is explicit in the royal use of *ḥerem*. In 1 Kings 20:42, following Ahab's defeat of Ben-hadad, Ahab spares his life. An unnamed prophet meets the king of Israel and announces to him: "Thus said the Lord: 'Because you have set free the man whom I doomed [literally, the man of my *ḥerem*], your life shall be forfeit for his life and your people for his people.' "[101] J. Lust notes of this verse, "The reader is supposed to know that the king of Israel had to consider his defeated antagonist, the king of Damascus, as *ḥrm* to the Lord."[102] Similarly, Samuel, after anointing Saul, commands him to "utterly destroy" (RSV)—that is **ḥrm*—the Amalekites (1 Samuel 15:3). One may assume that the king had not finished the job. Later literature, especially Isaiah 34, applies the bloody language to Yahweh. Isaiah 34 has been connected with "Second Isaiah," and if dated concurrently, the *ḥerem* mythos as represented in verses 2 and 5 of this chapter outlasted the monarchy in Israel. Not surprisingly, given the royal background of the *ḥerem* language in Deuteronomic account of royal battle, this language is applied in this chapter to Edom, a traditional enemy, in verse 5. To judge from Anat's "herem," it is possible that behind Yahweh's *ḥerem* warfare lies the mythos that when the king defeats and slaughter his enemies, Yahweh is understood as fighting for the king and destroying his enemies in battle, and then slaughtering the enemy captives following battle. As the major deployers of warfare, Iron Age monarchs were well-served by the mythos of *ḥerem*-warfare. Like other mythological concepts that they used to characterize and legitimize their imperial goals, descriptions of *ḥerem*-warfare impute the desire for warfare to the deity whom the king serves.

All of these forms of royal theology focus on the power of the national god; all other deities pale in comparison.[103] This traditional royal theology exalted Yahweh as the national god who sponsored the rule of the monarch. One result was a tolerance of foreign gods regarded as the divine kings of other nations. Moreover, as long as such gods remained in the foreign domain, the national theology was adequate for those monarchic period figures opposed to the cult of what they may have regarded as foreign deities on native soil. Hence, Elijah, a great prophetic figure of the ninth century, looks like a monotheist for the later biblical tradition. So too the eighth-century prophets, Amos and Hosea, oppose the cult of other deities in Israel, but they do not speak about foreign gods in their own territory. These prophetic voices might be regarded as monolatrous, but because of their polemic against others in ancient Israel, they may not have spoken for most people in ancient Israel. In other words, it is not clear that most ancient Israelites during the monarchy either were monolatrous or regarded all other deities as foreign. Indeed, the prophetic polemics point in the opposite direction.

In short, the developments issuing in clear expressions of biblical monotheism involved many changes spanning centuries. With the heightened importance of the national god and the centrality of the national shrine in Jerusalem, eventually both human and divine power coalesced into one central authority, serving both human monarch and divine king. Furthermore, clashes between the cults of Israel's national deity and other deities (whether indigenous or foreign) from the eighth century onward would legitimate innovation over traditional conservatism of regional cult, which probably tolerated variety in worship of other deities as long as the top tier remained occupied by the national god. The further and possibly corresponding monarchic period tendency to coalesce the imagery of various deities into the figure of the national deity[104] (what I call "convergence"[105]) perhaps reflects the wider tendency of national authority to concentrate divinity in a central cosmic figure, one that reinforces the terrestrial focus point of worship in Jerusalem, the home of both temple and monarchy. The so-called reform movements of Hezekiah and Josiah involved massive social and political strategies that implemented innovations in the name of reform.[106] All these developments within Israelite society and religion contributed to the form of Yahwistic worship that emerges in monotheistic formulations, which seem to emerge distinctly only in the late monarchy and exile. Indeed, it is in the seventh and sixth centuries, reflected especially in "Second Isaiah," when such universal divine claims are unambiguous. In this period the older national theology I have described no longer appeared tenable.

5. The Social and Historical Context of Monotheism

Why did monotheistic statements emerge in the seventh and sixth centuries? What about the situation of these centuries engendered this type of discourse? Why did Judeans so express this vision of divinity during the late monarchy and the exile? What were the changing circumstances of Israel's existence, either within itself or vis-à-vis other nations? I wish to propose and explore a number of aspects of Judean culture in this time period as possible historical corollaries to the development of monotheistic discourse. Because of the dauntingly scanty evidence for ancient Israelite religion, it is impossible to prove "causes" for such discourse, but some aspects of Judah's social structure and historical circumstances correspond in time-frame to the emergence of monotheistic statements and suggest some working hypotheses.

The first involves an aspect of changing social dynamics in this period. The theological intelligibility of a single deity correlates well with the perspective of Judean social structure at the end of the seventh century and afterward. Although the language of council continues strongly in biblical texts after the exile, the root metaphor of the divine family has been eclipsed. What generally remained is a system headed by the chief god, his consort, lesser or subordinate deities (some as members of his retinue), astral bodies, and servant-messengers, which later Israelite tradition reduced further and then regarded as a sort of monotheism. This later monotheism assumes that divinity is tantamount to an individual figure. In contrast, Ugaritic and early Israelite polytheism involves both a series of individuals and a series of relations among the various deities. As noted at the end of chapter 4, polytheism at Ugarit expressed divine singleness or cohesion through a series of family relationships. Accordingly, I proposed the following working hypothesis in chapter 4 for ancient Ugarit: conceptual religious unity was expressed most strongly in the identification of the divine council as a divine family, a single family of deities whose connectedness is marked by their familial relations. A corollary hypothesis for Judah may be offered: the strongest form of social identity at Ugarit was the family.[107] Therefore, it stands to reason that the polytheistic family may have provided the most "natural" expression of the singleness or coherence of divinity. In early Israel, a similar family structure long obtained, probably through the period of the monarchy. Throughout this period Israelite texts attest to *naḥălâ* for family patrimony and other indicators of lineage maintenance. However, by the seventh century the lineage system of the family had perhaps eroded, thanks to a variety of factors, including the deleterious effects of royal power on traditional patriarchal authority the purchase of family lands by a growing upper class, and the devastating effects of warfare on the countryside.[108] This process culminated in the exilic period, with the loss of land that would diminish the traditional strength of family and inheritance. The post-exilic structure called the *bêt 'ābôt* ("fathers' house")—as opposed to the older and more traditional form known as the *bêt 'āb* ("father's house")—has been thought to be a further witness to the decline of the traditional family structure.[109] Israelite texts dating to roughly the same period as the earliest clear expressions of monotheism (seventh and sixth centuries) proclaim that the righteousness of parents cannot save their children (Ezekiel 14:12–23). This change in perspective might be reflected also in the claims of sixth-century prophets (Jeremiah 31:29–30; Ezekiel 18, cf. 33:12–20) and deuteronomic literature (Deuteronomy 24:16)[110] that children would no longer be punished for the sins of the fathers.[111] A culture with a diminished lineage system, one less embedded in traditional family patrimonies due to societal changes in the eighth through sixth centuries,[112] might be more predisposed both to hold to individual human accountability for behavior and to see an individual deity accountable for the cosmos. (I view this individual accountability at the human and divine levels as concomitant developments.) Accordingly, later Israelite monotheism was denuded of the divine family, perhaps reflecting Israel's weakening family lineages and patrimonies.[113]

The second major corollary to the emergence of monotheistic statements in the seventh and sixth centuries involves Judah's situation in the world that it faced for the first time in this period. This point has been made well by J. H. Tigay: "The need to emphasize the monotheistic idea in this period was probably due to the increased exposure of Israel to the triumphant Assyrian and Babylonian empires, which attributed their victories, including victories over Israel, to their gods."[114]

First in the face of the great empires and then in exile, Israel stands at the bottom of its political power, and it exalts its deity inversely as ruler of the whole universe, with little regard for the status of the older deities known from the pre-exilic literary record.

These two features constitute the larger landscape of monotheistic discourse and help to explain its intelligibility in this time period. Israel's political and social reduction in the world (first because of the rise of empires in the eighth and seventh centuries and then because of the "Exile" in 587–538) further altered its social structure in a manner that had a serious impact on its traditional theology. We have already seen the traditional theology in Deuteronomy 32:8–9 affirming that all the nations had their own patron-gods, with Yahweh as Israel's. Moreover, we have seen how this idea was expressed in conflictual terms in the royal worldview of the "royal psalms" (usually included are Psalms 2, 18, 20, 21, 45, 72, 89, and 110).

The reduction of Judean kingship, especially following Josiah and the subsequent loss of Judean kingship, changed the parallel or mirroring worldview known from the royal psalms. The rise of the Neo-Assyrian and Babylonian empires issued in a serious religious reflection on Yahweh's power over the nations. The loss of identity as a nation changed Israel's understanding of the national god. Looming empires made the model of a national god obsolete. Moreover, the rise of supra-national empires suggested the model of the super-national god. As a result, the figures of Assur and Marduk assumed such proportions, the super-gods whose patronage of empires matches their manifestation as the sum-total of all the other deities. As noted in chapter 5 (sections 1 and 2), Mesopotamian authors are exploring the nature of all divinity in relation to a single major god. The response from Israel followed suit in one respect. The events leading to the Judean exile of 587 extended Israel's understanding of its deity's mastery of the world even as the nation was being reduced. This shift involves a most crucial change in different Judean presentations of the relationship between the mundane and cosmic levels of reality (or, put differently, between the immanence and transcendance of divinity).[115] As Judah's situation on the mundane level deteriorated in history, the cosmic status of its deity soared in its literature. The timing of the emergence of Israelite monotheism in the late Iron Age and exilic period fits Karl Jaspers's the "Axial Age," a period in world history (ca. 800–200) that "witnessed the emergence of revolutionary new understandings of human understanding," including the awareness of "the separation between transcendant and mundane spheres of reality."[116]

Some scholars locate this shift to monotheism in the Persian period.[117] The date of "Second Isaiah" at the beginning of the Persian period might lend support in this direction, and the other biblical texts in question have likewise been dated to the Persian period by some scholars. Accordingly, the emphasis on a single divine power of good in Zoroastrianism has been thought to provide a model for the monotheism expressed in the Bible. I have reservations about this theory, apart from the dating of the biblical texts in question.[118] The first question involves the Persian model. Zoroaster (Zarathustra) preached a dualism pitting Ahura Mazda, the spirit of good, along with his six Amesha Spentas ("Bounteous Immortals"), against a spirit of evil named Angra Mainyu, later spelled Ahriman.[119] This dualism does not truly resemble biblical monotheism. Indeed, a principle of evil, for example in the form of Belial, Satan, or the devil, began to appear only in the latest biblical works and in the other Second Temple literature.[120] Furthermore, the language of biblical monotheism appears to represent, at least in its formulations, developments of older language exalting the national god. Proponents of the Persian period setting for biblical monotheism rarely, if ever, address these issues. On the other hand, this is not to say that Persian religious tradition did not reinforce monotheistic rhetoric in this period or influence some biblical presentations of divinity. Some years ago A. L. Oppenheim claimed that the "eyes and ears" of the Persian king served as the model for "the satan" in the book of Job 1–2.[121] One might concede that the Zoroastrian notion of the good god reinforced the Judean notion of monotheism, as later developments would.[122] Yet it was not Judean monotheism's main progenitor. In fact, internal and external changes in Judah's situation in the seventh and sixth centuries correspond to the timing of monotheistic statements presented at the outset of this chapter. Thus far, what we have seen of monotheism, especially in section 1, appears in the form of declarations. The expression of monotheism also extended to monotheistic descriptions and narratives; these are explored in the next chapter.

9

The Formation of Monotheistic Theologies in Biblical Literature

O Lord, our Lord,
How majestic is Your Name throughout the earth!

Psalm 8:2 = 10

The preceding chapter discusses royal theologies as a backdrop to the emergence of monotheistic rhetoric. This chapter addresses three monotheistic adaptations to the older model of the Israelite national god: (1) a priestly model, (2) the form of the figure of wisdom personified in female terms, and (3) apocalyptic imagery, with its clear reminiscences of old monarchic theology. All three involve old mythic material that spoke powerfully and was reused in new and varying circumstances. Mythic narratives and imagery were the chosen forms not only of educated classes such as the monarchy or priesthood. Rather, these groups likely drew upon these materials precisely because they were well known among the educated and uneducated, rich and poor.[1] After the treatment of these "monotheistic" presentations of the Israelite national deity, I will address the so-called demise of myth in Israel. Like the preceding chapters, this survey uses the Ugaritic mythological texts as a primary source.

1. Creation, Paradise, and the Priesthood

The preceding chapter illustrates how the monarchy used old mythic material known also in the Ugaritic texts. The monarchy was not alone in this regard. A priestly text, Genesis 1 shows a modification of old mythic material known from Israel and the rest of the ancient Near East.[2] This creation story combines two different visions of the cosmos: the first and older view that a cosmos is the stage where divine wills engage in conflict; and the second and largely priestly notion that the cosmos is a holy place analogous to a sanctuary.[3] The discussion of the royal ideology in the preceding chapter demonstrates the fundamental notion of the cosmos as a stage of conflict between cosmic powers, usually with the chief warrior-deity and divine royal patron slated against cosmic powers. The ancient Near Eastern text perhaps cited most often as an example of the cosmos as a locale for conflict between divine wills is the Babylonian classic known from its first two words, Enuma Elish ("When on high . . .").[4] In the cosmic world of this text, deities face off in battle like the royalty who patronized the epic and their enemies; then in the wake of this divine conflict creation emerges. The cosmos of the epic corresponds to the human world in three ways: (1) the enemies of the divine king, Marduk, and their human counterparts can threaten the world; (2) both kings, divine and human, reign from Babylon at the center of the world; and (3) the temple of the god is the cosmic center linking both divine and human dominion.

A number of West Semitic texts likewise allude to the cosmic conflict between the storm-god and his enemies, as noted at length in section 3 of chapter 8. The use of the conflict story to reinforce human kingship appears in a variety of texts, hailing from the city of Mari on the Euphrates river all the way to Egypt. The political use of the conflict between storm-god and cosmic enemies passed into Israelite tradition. Yahweh is not only generally similar to Baal as a storm-god. Yahweh inherited the names of Baal's cosmic enemies such as Leviathan, Sea, Death, and Tannin, as well as the name of Baal's home on Mount Saphon, which is secondarily identified with Zion in Psalm 48:3. With this evidence, it would appear that Yahweh's titles, "Rider of the heavens" (Deuteronomy 33:26; Psalm 104:3) and "Rider of the Steppes" (Psalm 68:5), echo Baal's own title, "Rider of the Clouds."[5] The political use of this conflict language also passed into ancient Israel. The biblical parallel between Yahweh, the divine king, and the Davidic ruler, the human king, may be seen in Psalm 89. The parallelism between Yahweh and the king changes, however, in verse 26, and a different sort of notion appears: Yahweh promises to extend his power to the monarch in language associated in Ugaritic with the god Baal: "I will set his hand on Sea and his right hand on Rivers."[6] In contrast, Genesis 1 depicts God as an omnipotent deity relative to comparable biblical passages treating creation of the cosmos.[7]

Moreover, the first creation story in Genesis 1:1–2:4a points beyond conflict to a vision of a holy universe, which adds to the older model of the universe as a site of conflict. This priestly narrative presents the cosmos as the divine holy place, even while it shows its debt to the old model of the cosmos as battlefield. Genesis 1 manifests the marks of the old royal model of the cosmos, but the story modifies this vision of the cosmos in three ways. First, as I noted, Enuma Elish and various biblical texts connect creation with divine conflict. Psalm 74:12–17 makes the divine conflict the basis for the establishment of the sun, moon and stars as well as the boundaries of the earth. In contrast, Genesis 1 shows only a hint of this old tradition. At the opening of Genesis 1, the audience expects the conflict, as the "mighty wind," or possibly "divine spirit" (*rûaḥ ʾĕlōhîm*), hovers over the face of the cosmic waters. Rather than conflict, Genesis 1 has God speak or make, and creation happens. With but a word, without conflict, God effects the opening of creation. In omitting the divine conflict, Genesis 1 marks a paradigm shift in the presentation of creation.[8]

Second, the old language of human rule, associated with royal model of creation as conflict, still appears in Genesis 1:[9] humanity is to "rule" (**rdh*) over the terrestrial creation (verse 28) as a human governor on earth corresponding to the

King of Kings in heaven.[10] Genesis 1 alters this royal motif in that the king on earth is not the Israelite king but all humanity. The creation of the human person in Genesis 1:26, in the "image" and "likeness" of God, represents a major shift from the old royal model. The idea of "the image" of the gods was, in ancient Near East, applied to the king.[11] It was the king who was the image of the deity. The creation of humanity in the divine image represents an ancient Near Eastern idea that has been repackaged in its priestly context. More specifically, the ancient Near Eastern material compared to the biblical passage reflects the notion of the king as "the image" of the deity.[12] Like Genesis 1:26–28, Egyptian material shows the application of this royal idea to humanity more generally. W. H. Schmidt and M. Fishbane[13] note the instructions of King Meri-ka-re:[14] "They who have issued from his body are his images."[15] Genesis 1:26 changes this idea. For humanity, understood as the participant in the cosmic Sabbath, is to be the holy image of God on earth.

If these three features of Genesis 1 represent alterations to the royal model of creation involving divine conflict, then what is the new priestly vision of reality? Often noted in Genesis 1 are the correspondences between the first and second sets of three days culminating in the seventh day.[16] This order is more than an orderly construction; it is a religious order and has a moral character. It is imbued by the word of God and seen as good. This universe intimates a priestly blueprint for human existence in three ways long recognized by scholars. The divine resting (*šbt) on the seventh day anticipates the priestly institution of the Sabbath in Exodus 20 and 31. Furthermore, Genesis 1:14 states that the lights in the firmament are to mark the times for feast-days, weeks, and years, a central feature for maintaining priestly cult. Finally, the division of the universe into heavens, earth, and seas and the assignment of the animals to these spheres foreshadow another priestly prescription, the system of dietary requirements (later called kashrut, or the practice of "keeping kosher").[17] These three themes point to the priestly service and holiness that are to characterize this new creation.

In Genesis 1, creation is no longer primarily a conflict; it is the result not of two wills in conflict but of One Will expressing the word issuing in the good creation. This One Will places humanity in this creation. The life of this creation is to be holy, moral, and good, and perhaps even priestly. One may suggest that the cosmos in Genesis 1 was to be understood as a holy place, such as a sanctuary.[18] The relation between Temple and creation was well-known. The Temple in Jerusalem, decorated with the motifs of the cosmos and the Garden of Eden, mirrored the cosmos. Biblical descriptions of creation and temple-building have influenced one another and constitute, in J. D. Levenson's view, a "homology."[19] Psalm 78:69 expresses this view metaphorically: "He built his sanctuary like the high heavens, like the earth which he has founded for ever."[20] In Psalm 78 temple-building is rendered in terms of creation.[21] Psalm 150:1 likewise expresses this idea in poetic parallelism:

Praise God in His sanctuary;
Praise Him in the sky, His stronghold.[22]

In this case the divine sanctuary and the sky are poetic parallel terms that explain one another, perhaps implying that the heavens constitute the divine sanctuary.

The sense of cosmos as sanctuary may lie behind Genesis 1 or may be evoked by it. Furthermore, the implicit evocation of kashrut in Genesis 1, if correct, may also suggest the notion of cosmos as temple. W. Houston has argued that the practice of kashrut arose in ancient Israel in the priestly protection of temple purity and holiness.[23] If this is right, Genesis 1's delineation of realms in the universe according to animals may evoke temple practice and in turn a vision of the world as a kind of temple. In any case, creation is built as a moral, good, ordered holy place, and humanity is placed in this holy site to imitate the rest, order, and holiness of the Deity in whose image humanity is made.

Genesis 1 does not use conflict as the main element in its vision of the cosmos and the place of humanity in it. Instead, the priestly holiness of time and space overshadows the component of conflict.[24] This view made sense of a world in which monarchy no longer protected Israel. This outlook would serve Israel well in exile and beyond when responsibility for community order passed from the Davidic dynasty to the priesthood of Aaron. Indeed, Genesis 1 has often been dated to the exilic or post-exilic period.[25] Genesis 1 reflects this change: to the royal model has been added a priestly model. The politics of creation have changed. There is still a king in this world, but it is the King of Kings, the One Will who rules heavens and earth alike, with no serious competition, and this King in Heaven is to be followed by humanity ruling on earth. There is no single royal agent on earth whose human foes mirror the cosmic foes of the divine king. Moreover, this king is the Holy One enthroned over the cosmos.[26] Thus, the vision of humanity in Genesis 1 anticipates the divine election of Israel as the prototypical servant of Sabbath.

With these theological moves evident, Genesis 1 creates a "monotheistic poetics." As I noted in chapter 1, Genesis 1 minimizes the cosmic waters as divine enemy. In this passage the lack of any conflict, or even any personification of the cosmic oceans or waters, is designed to heighten the picture of a powerful God who but speaks and the divine will is accomplished. So too the passing generic reference to the *tannînîm* in Genesis 1:21 conveys the notion that this God's power is incomparable, beyond any other power, beyond opposition. Not only is the conflict role eliminated in Genesis 1; even the old role of cosmic forces as domesticated has been muted by downplaying them, even depersonalizing them. These cosmic monsters are no longer primordial forces opposed to the Israelite God at the beginning of creation. Instead, they are creatures like other creatures rendered in this story. The narrative encloses the order of the divine creation around these monstrous enemies and by omission transforms them into another part of creation. In short, the change of these divine enemies into creatures involves a lexicon of creation. This reading also works for the sun and the moon, called only "the greater light" and "the lesser light" (Genesis 1:16), titles that were not necessarily polemical as such but quite traditional (cf. "great light," *nyr rbt*, for the Ugaritic sun-goddess in CAT 1.161.19,[27] and "light of the heavens," *nrt šmm*, for the Ugaritic moon-god in 1.24.16, 31). Genesis 1 does not present these figures as divinities. Instead, like the sea creatures, they are located within the created order. Here ambiguity between Creator and creatures is resolved; there is no middle ground left in Genesis 1's "monotheistic poetics." Such a depiction drains power from any old forces of opposition and leaves God as the only power in the universe.

The priestly context defines not only the character of humanity, but redefines traditional Israelite notions of the deity. Genesis 1:26 inverts Ezekiel 1:26, which itself represents a deliberate attempt to stress the transcendent character of Yahweh by reducing the anthropomorphic presentation of Yahweh in the heavenly divine council well-known from Ugaritic and biblical texts (especially Isaiah 6). Ezekiel 1:26 conveys the prophet's vision of the divine with the language of "image" of the human person ("an image like the appearance of a human," *dĕmût kĕmar'ēh 'ādām*), whereas Genesis 1:26–28 presents a vision of the human person in the likeness of the divine. Unlike Ezekiel 1:26, which reduces Yahweh to human terms in an anthropomorphic portrait (albeit a considerably more limited one than that in prior prophetic texts), Genesis 1:26–28 magnifies the human person in divine (or perhaps mythic) terms.[28] This application of prior royal theology to humanity represents a characteristic priestly notion[29] designed to reinterpret mythological notions about the monarchy in the face of its demise. Moreover, given the use of *dĕmût*, "likeness" and *ṣelem*, "image" for statues,[30] in Genesis 1:26–28 this vocabulary may represent an implicit polemic aimed against the making of images. Clearly humanity serves as the living image of the Israelite deity, and it is perhaps implicit then that images of of man-made objects constitute lifeless symbols of dead gods. Such a polemic emerges explicitly in the monotheistic rhetoric of "Second Isaiah" (discussed in the next chapter).

The imprint of priestly concerns has been detected also in Ezekiel 28.[31] Whereas older West Semitic motifs may be perceived in biblical paradise traditions, Israelite innovations in the paradise traditions[32] perhaps included the identification of the garden with the temple [33] and the naming of paradise as Eden,[34] a term that echoes the feasting in the Temple in Psalm 36:9 (cf. Jeremiah 51:34; Nehemiah 9:25).[35] Other features of the Jerusalem temple likewise evoke elements in Genesis 2–3, including the cherubim, palm trees, the divine presence, and the waters below the Temple.[36] One of the rivers in paradise (Genesis 2:10) is known as Gihon, the same name as the main spring of Jerusalem; whatever the precise origin of the name in Genesis 2:10, such similarity suggests the paradisial connotation of Jerusalem and its temple.[37] Indeed, Isaiah 51:3 makes this connection on the metaphorical level: Yahweh will restore the "wilderness"//"desert" (NJPS) of Zion like the garden of Eden. These innovations in the Israelite notion of paradise suggest that the Temple served in part as a model for the name and description of Eden.

Ezekiel 28 may contain both royal and priestly "myth-making." J. van Seters claims that the figure in Ezekiel 28:12–19 is the monarch,[38] whereas R. R. Wilson sees in this passage priestly polemical redaction making this figure into a priest.[39] Following M. H. Pope and others, Wilson assumes that the priestly editor(s) of Ezekiel 28 inherited the motif of the fall,[40] implying that, like the expulsion motif in Genesis 3, the fall in Ezekiel 28 predated its priestly tradents. Wilson begins his analysis of the editorial history of Ezekiel 28 with the list of precious stones in verse 13 to be worn by a figure in the garden of God. The stones are especially suggestive of the high priest's breastplate. Although van Seters may be correct in observing the originally royal character of the figure, in the priestly redaction of the material, the figure seems to bear a priestly character.[41] Wilson assumes that the "garden of God" is synonymous with the temple and that the figure is one who wears the stones, specifically the high priest who exercised his authority in the temple. According to verse 14, the cherub was "with" (so LXX; cf. MTT 'att) this figure; for Wilson, this is the high priest who entered the Holy of Holies and faced the cherubim throne of Yahweh. Yet MT 'att in verse 14 suggests that the object of polemic is the cherub itself. If Wilson's analysis of the chapter as reflecting an inner priestly polemic at the redactional level is correct, then the apparent object of polemic in the reading of MT 'att might be the cherub iconography of the Jerusalem temple. If so, the passage may represent an inner priestly (northern?) polemic directed against the Jerusalem cult. Accordingly, Wilson views Ezekiel 28 as reusing the old fall from the divine mountain as an inner Israelite critique of the priesthood. Ezekiel 28 would then represent an example of priestly reuse of traditional mythic material.

Although many motifs known from Ugarit and Mesopotamia resonate in the biblical descriptions of paradise,[42] the biblical narratives reflect a number of innovations. The paradise traditions show evidence of various levels of myth-making in ancient Israel, including royal and priestly elements. The identification of temple and paradise implicitly provide a privileged place for the sacrificial cult maintained by the Aaronid priesthood in the temple. Indeed, one might hypothesize that the figure of the high priest superseded the monarch as the prototypical denizen of paradise. Concurrently, the monarch in conflict with other worldly powers and protected by the Divine King gives way to the One Power served in a cosmos-sanctuary by a priestly Israel with no other deities in view.

2. Wisdom and the Levites

Another examples of mythic material used by specific sectors of society for monotheistic purposes may involve the imagery of Wisdom personified. Proverbs 1–9 presents a divine invitation from the female personification of Wisdom. In the past, a number of scholars compared the figure of Wisdom to the Canaanite goddess Asherah.[43] The "tree of life," which recalls the tree of the asherah,[44] appears in Israelite tradition as a metaphorical expression for Wisdom (Proverbs 3:18; cf. 11: 30, 15:4; Genesis 3:22; Revelation 2:7). Like the symbol of the asherah, Wisdom is a female figure, providing life and nurturing. Proverbs 3:18 may be especially pertinent: "She is a tree of life to those who lay hold of her; those who hold her fast are made happy" (*'ēṣ-ḥayyîm hî' lammaḥăzîqîm bāh wĕtōmĕkêhā mĕ'uššār*). This verse closes a small unit consisting of verses 13–18 and forms a conspicuous chiasm with verse 13. This verse opens with "Happy the one who finds wisdom" (*'ašrê ' ādām māṣā' ḥokmâ*). The unit begins and ends with same root, *' šr*, "to be happy," specifically with *'ašrê*, "happy," in verse 13 and *mĕ'uššār*, "made happy," in verse 18. The inside terms of the chiasm are *ḥokmâ*, "wisdom," and *'ēṣ-ḥayyîm*, "a tree of life." Finally, the terms *'ašrê* and *mĕ'uššār* perhaps allude to the asherah,[45] the tree symbolizing life and well-being. Here we may see a move to "monotheize" the imagery of the Asherah in a wisdom framework. B. Lang has suggested that the female figure of Wisdom functions as an image of "the divine patroness of the Israelite school system."[46] If so, Proverbs 1–9 uses the old mythic language associated with Asherah in the service of the particular social horizons of wisdom-scribes.[47] Accordingly, this use may represent a wisdom modification in the direction of monotheism. If Proverbs were a Levitical product, as perhaps suggested by verbal links with Deuteronomy,[48] then one might argue further that the female personification of Wisdom is the divine patron of the Levitical duties of teaching and writing, as these roles are attributed to the Levites.[49]

3. Apocalyptic Literature: The Case of Daniel 7

As we have seen, the monarchy was not the only segment of Israelite society that used the creation-conflict to describe divine power. Nonroyal texts also refer to the divine conflict between Yahweh and cosmic forces at the time of creation to illustrate Yahweh's ancient powers. Psalm 74:12–17 and Isaiah 51:9–10a are often cited as two classic biblical examples.[50] This conflict is set not only set in the primordial past but in the future as the definitive moment of Yahweh's salvation of Israel. Isaiah 27:1 may be the most poignant instance of this theme: "In that day the Lord with his hard and great and strong sword will punish Leviathan the fleeing serpent, and he will slay the dragon that is in the sea." The apocalyptic visions of Daniel 7 and Revelation 13 present the beasts of the Sea whom Yahweh, the divine warrior, will ultimately sweep away. The political link between these beasts and world empires was no late invention but echoed the mirroring of divine and human kings and the cosmic and human enemies known already in the second millennium.

Post-exilic apocalyptic preserved the conflictual nature of the forces in the cosmos but with the human king removed from the equation.[51] Daniel 7 expresses the conflict in largely cosmic terms, with the four beasts rising out of the cosmic sea. Whereas these beasts reflect the four empires on earth, the human counterpart to Yahweh is no human king but a persecuted community that can take solace only in divine help.[52] Here are the political vestiges of the old royal theology. Such a portrait, though less overtly political than Daniel 7 and the apocalyptic tradition, nonetheless covertly adapts to the new order on the earthly level and adjusts its religious vision accordingly. Like Daniel 7, Genesis 1 magnifies Judah's deity over the whole cosmos, despite what takes place in Judah's historical experience.

In summary, the monarchy and the descendent discourse of the apocalyptic, as well as the different priestly lines, used mythic concepts to advance their messages. These concepts specifically reflect the social location of their users. Both Ugaritic and Israelite royal and scribal-priestly groups constituted the primary literary preservers of mythic material,[53] and they were both in a position to use ancient mythic material to suit their own ends. Indeed, the extant texts of these groups grounded their claims of divine sanction by appealing to mythic imagery. For scribal-priestly groups, this reuse of mythic material assumed a monotheistic cast.

4. From "Canaanite Myth" to Biblical Monotheism?

It is often claimed that part of the development of biblical monotheism involved a rejection of myth. In addressing the "demise" of myth in ancient Israel, I should reiterate some basic points. It is true that myth as narrative centered on Yahweh or other divine beings is poorly attested, but mythic imagery is abundant in the Bible. And even if the number of myths included all narrative mentioning any divine being under the rubric of myth, that extant Israelite mythic material (and the key word is extant) still does not include lengthy narratives describing only the divine realm and its inhabitants, like Enuma Elish or the Baal Cycle. Moreover, many biblical passages involving mythic material show a temporal shift. Mythic imagery is used to describe the present in prayers and the future in apocalyptic.⁵⁴ This state of affairs points to a central question in the discussion of myth: why is mythic imagery so prevalent in biblical literature whereas the amount of attested myth is, properly speaking, relatively minimal?

Since the discovery of the Ugaritic texts, this question has been framed in a number of ways. Some scholars have questioned whether Israelite literature included epic (with Yahweh as the central character).⁵⁵ Citing the Ugaritic texts as examples of the epic genre,⁵⁶ S. Talmon argues that the absence of the epic from Israelite literature reflects a conscious purging of this genre because of the poly-theistic components associated with it.⁵⁷ Without providing a historical setting for his proposal, Talmon argues that the Pentateuch had a "normative character" bear-ing on the absence of "epic" elements in other parts of the Hebrew Bible.⁵⁸ It would not appear, however, that the epic genre had negative connotations; nor is it clear that the Pentateuch exercised a "normative character" on Israelite literature generally. Indeed, U. Cassuto identified several epic elements and compositional techniques specifically within the Pentateuch:⁵⁹ "These are indications of poetic versions that antedated the Biblical sections, and several elements of which were absorbed by the prose portrayals of the Torah."⁶⁰ Later texts deal with these "epic" elements as a problem of anthropomorphism, and the issue may have involved not the polytheistic content of epic, but polytheism⁶¹ more generally. Indeed, Deuter-onomy 4:15–16 links the issue of not seeing the "form" of Yahweh with the pro-hibition against the creation of "graven images."

Like Talmon, D. Damrosch sees an anti-Canaanite purpose behind biblical prose materials,⁶² but he views the issue of genre in terms quite different from those Talmon advanced. According to Damrosch, the biblical prose narratives of the Pentateuch and the Deuteronomistic History were modeled on Mesopotamian models that combine and transform older, traditional genres.⁶³ For Damrosch, bib-lical narratives also drew heavily from models known from Mesopotamian litera-ture, Gilgamesh and Genesis 2–11 as his key examples.⁶⁴ Although he speaks of "the early Yahwistic merging of prose chronicle and poetic epic,"⁶⁵ Damrosch's argument implies that older West Semitic poetic models were not adopted in ancient Israel to describe its national stories. It does indeed appear that the form of myth was not continued in the extant forms of national prose epic from the period of the monarchy and afterward. Rather, in the cases of extant prose histories, other models tended to displace the old West Semitic model of poetic myth, according to Damrosch.

Talmon erroneously links the lack of myth in Israel to the prose form of the Pentateuch. In later periods polytheism apparently exercised for priestly groups one theological guideline or constraint not on the form of myth as Talmon argues, but rather, the content of myth-making may have been affected by priestly concern about polytheism (although "lesser" divine beings were not excised from later mythic images or narratives). Damrosch's approach implies that the lack of poetic myth in the biblical corpus may serve as the basis for a general judgment on the West Semitic form of myth in ancient Israel. However, extra-biblical literature indicates that myth survived as a literary phenomenon in ancient Israel, just not in the extant biblical canon. Therefore, the absence of myth from the extant national narratives of ancient Israel may indicate the purposes only of their authors or tradents. Furthermore, Damrosch does not address the fact that, even if only vestiges of the older models of myth survived in extant biblical literature, mythic imagery so suffuses Israelite culture that it survived in genres involving discourse about Israel's deity. A more complex diachronic model is required to address the general absence of myth from the biblical corpus.

First of all, two stages of avoiding and muting anthropomorphism (and thus mythic language)[66] are discernible, one at the outset of known Israelite texts and another perhaps in the eighth to sixth centuries.[67] In the first stage, early levels of biblical literature exhibit many points of contact with Ugaritic literature in describing the storm-god in his meteorological procession, but Yahweh is not as personified of in the oldest biblical poetry as Baal is in Ugaritic tradition. The depiction of Baal's conflict with Yamm (CAT 1.2 IV) is discernibly more anthropomorphic than any biblical descriptions of Yahweh's conflict against cosmic enemies. The Ugaritic texts describe gods locked in hand-to-hand combat. There is a corresponding tendency in the images of the heavenly armies belonging to the entourage of Yahweh in early texts (implied in Judges 5) as well as in the later texts such as Joel, 2 Baruch 8 and 22:6, and 2 Enoch 29:3. Whereas the entourage is explicitly connected with Baal in Ugaritic literature (CAT 1.5 V 6–8), the armies appear more independent of Yahweh in biblical and intertestamental literature. Yahweh does not appear personified in the battles waged by the heavenly armies led by the divine angelic warriors. Similarly, the love of the various members of the Ugaritic pantheon is graphic by comparison to divine sex in the Bible. Indeed, it has been argued that the Hebrew Bible shows no example of sex or death in the case of Yahweh comparable to the sexual behavior and death in Ugaritic poetry.[68] This claim may be modified by reiterating the point (made in chapter 5, section 2) that one or two biblical passages may allude to divine sex or genitalia. Even if so, the biblical texts in question are nonetheless considerably less graphic or as direct as Baal's copulation with a heifer "seventy-seven times"// "eighty-eight times" (CAT 1.5 V 19–21). Parenthetically, given its priestly background, Ezekiel 16:9 may represent a "metaphorical construal" rather than a general notion of the deity (although if this image were generally known in earlier Israel, it may not have beeen considered "only" metaphorical). J. Barr distinguishes between less indicative anthropomorphisms in metaphors and more indicative divine descriptions in theophanies.[69] This approach likely applies to the sexual metaphor in Ezekiel 16:9. Even if one were to assume a "more literal" character for this verse, it is quite muted compared to divine sexual scenes attested in the Ugaritic text. In a similar vein, Ugaritic mythology describes or presumes theriomorphous deities in a manner largely absent from extant Israelite texts. Baal's mating with a heifer presupposes the view of him as a bull, and El himself is called "bull" (tr). Anat is described in flight, and iconography preserved from Ugarit depicts her as a bird.[70] Divine theriomorphous depictions in Israelite literature are rare and slight by comparison, surviving only in a handful of metaphors and titles (Numbers 24:8; cf. Genesis 49:24 [?]; Psalm 132:2, 4). The West Semitic literary tradition was quite anthropomorphic, and the Israelite literary tradition reduced this anthropomorphism to some extent.

The second stage occurred from the eighth to the sixth centuries. Earlier works such as the "Yahwist" show, in the words of H. Bloom, "uninhibited anthropomorphism,"[71] but later works further mute anthropomorphism. Two brief examples may illustrate the point. First, Yahweh had no "form" according to Deuteronomy 4:12, 15.[72] The language of divine "form" is found explicitly in Psalm 17:15, and it has been traced to the use of the divine "form" in the story of Baal's battle against Yamm (CAT 1.2 IV 26).[73] Second, the vision of the divine in Ezekiel 1 deliberate attempts to stress the transcendent character of Yahweh by reducing the anthropomorphic presentation of Yahweh in the heavenly divine council. The second stage did not hold sway generally in Israelite culture, as many Second Temple and rabbinic texts, especially apocalyptic literature, indicate the popularity of myth throughout the history of ancient Israel.

What were the reasons for the reduction of myth in biblical works? Three suggestions may be offered. First, the inclusion of other divine images may have been influenced by concerns about monolatry, as commentators have long claimed. It is striking that one example of new mythic material, the personification of Wisdom, involves a female figure. Jerusalem, too, is presented as a mythic sort of female personification (Ezekiel 16 and 23).[74] What was the impetus for such mythic figures? In view of the divine language and imagery associated with both figures, perhaps both figures represent substitutions for divine female figures. G. von Rad once termed the figure of Wisdom in Proverbs 9:1–9 "as a contrast [*Kontrastbild*] and a defence against" customs associated with a goddess.[75] This view appears plausible, given the presence of at least Astarte in Israel during the period of the monarchy. The language of Jerusalem and Wisdom personified may have usurped imagery associated generally with goddesses, perhaps specifically with the asherah (with the possible concomitant demise of the goddess Asherah in ancient Israel) and applied it to the figure of Wisdom as a "counter-advertisement" to the cults of Astarte and the Queen of Heaven.[76] Hence, new myths may in part represent replacements in service to monotherstic representations of divinity.

Second, because later biblical literature shows fewer mythic characterizations of Yahweh than early biblical tradition,[77] it may be suspected that the absence of literary myth occurred primarily within those circles responsible for the production of the extant national narratives. Even the apparent discrepancy between West Semitic myth and the first stage of Israelite literature may reflect later influences rather than some original feature of Israel that distinguished it from its neighbors. The sources for the first stage are unfortunately inaccessible to modern students of Ugaritic and Israelite literature. It is not difficult to imagine, however, that the second stage may have influenced what survived from the first. Perhaps some of the possible, older images of Yahweh (for example, having a consort) did not have survive generally in the later Israelite cult. The different priestly lines during this period found their own primary images of Yahweh (whether older or newer ones) sufficiently incompatible with some of the older images and chose not to preserve them, thereby functionally censoring them. Indeed, the presentation of Yahweh generally as sexless and unrelated to the realm of death was apparently produced by a priesthood who viewed this deity as fully removed from realms of impurity, especially sex and death.[78] Holier than the holy of holies, the deity of the priesthood would have epitomized the fullest possibilities of sacredness and separation. Older views perceived to be incompatible with this presentation of the deity may have been modified precisely by those priestly groups responsible for the redaction and transmission of so much of the extant biblical texts.

Finally, other sources for this de facto "censorship" should be considered. Perhaps other concerns or traditions of written transmission guided the absence of myth or muting of anthropomophism. What was omitted from the biblical corpus may have stemmed not only from general religious features of ancient Israel. Other factors—for example, the role of scribalism in the formation of Israel's religious tradition—likely contributed to the presentation of Yahweh as divine scribe (Exodus 31:18; 34:1; Deuteronomy 4:13; 5:22). Other sociological factors may have influenced divine images in the Bible.[79] The priestly lines that so heavily marked the composition, transmission, and redaction of the extant biblical materials may have diminished notions of the divine council and divine messengers not only out of a specific concern for monolatry or the national story of Israel as such but also because these notions did not cohere with their preferred notions about Yahweh.

In closing, old myths could be transformed in form or content or both, at times transferring roles of other gods to Yahweh or creating subordinate divine female figures possibly to replace goddesses. These changes constitute aspects of the newly emergent Judean monotheistic theologies. New Israelite mythic imagery and narrative evoked the present or the future, not so much the distant past.[80] These changes largely represent internal Israelite developments that also fostered a monotheistic outlook. As the royal and priestly uses of myth indicate, myths address problems within Israelite society and are not simply reflections of Israel's putative early "anti-Canaanite" and original monotheistic stance.[81] Some surviving myths appear filtered through the lenses of the priestly groups responsible for the transmission of the extant biblical corpus. Finally, given the wide disparity in the treatments of myth versus mythic imagery, mythic imagery was treated in as negative a way as many myths were in the biblical corpus. Despite the critical attitude toward myth, Israel and its later religious successors in both Jewish and Christian traditions creatively transmitted and transformed mythic narrative as well as imagery to express a vision of the monotheistic God.[82]

The new monotheistic language and its rhetoric proved flexible in differing historical contexts and for different social segments of Judean society. As this chapter illustrates, the users of monotheistic rhetoric modified older mythic imagery into the discourse of a single deity. In short, biblical monotheism included transformations of Canaanite myth. Put differently, biblical monotheism constituted part of Israelite's own foundational myth comparable in some respects to Canaan's own myths. The last chapter is reserved for the portion of the Bible that contains the most and the boldest monotheistic statements and presentation of deity in order to convince its audience of Judean victory in the era of foreign empires; that portion is Isaiah 40–55, also called "Second Isaiah."

Monotheism in Isaiah 40–55

We shall not cease from exploration
And the end of all our exploring
Will be to arrive where we started
And know the place for the first time.

T. S. Eliot, *Four Quartets*

This final chapter turns to the parade example of biblical monotheism, chapters 40–55 of the book of Isaiah. As chapter 8 notes, this portion of the Bible is attributed not to the prophet Isaiah but to an unnamed author speaking in the prophet's voice around the end of the exile of Judah in Babylon (dated to 587–539). Because this section has been viewed as a separate work, scholars have called it "Second Isaiah." Perhaps quotation marks around this term is a good idea, for it is unclear that the author or redactors of this section intended for it to be read or regarded separately from the prophet's own words. In a time when nothing seemed possibly good for the Judean elite held in captivity in Babylon, the rhetoric of "Second Isaiah" soars, evoking a god capable of all things. Before delving into the particulars of this work, we may note how this work, like Genesis 1 and Daniel 7 described in chapter 9, modifies the old royal theology in many respects. First, the Judean king vanishes from the picture, and in turn Yahweh freely uses the royal means available to exercise the divine will on behalf of Israel: Cyrus the Persian becomes Yahweh's "anointed" in the new divine plan of salvation for Israel and the nations (Isaiah 45:1). Second, Israel itself, instead of the Judean king, becomes the new servant who is to mediate blessing. Israel is the new bearer of the old royal "eternal covenant" (2 Samuel 23:5) now to the nations (Isaiah 55: 3).[1] Third, and perhaps most important in "Second Isaiah," Yahweh is not only politically exalted as Israel is politically demoted. Yahweh becomes more than the god above all other gods: the existence of other gods is denied and two images central to "Second Isaiah's" presentation of Yahweh, the warrior-king and creator,[2] are melded and scored in the text to counter the perceived reality of other deities and therefore the putative stupidity of cultic devotion to their images. Interestingly, Yahweh as cosmic creator and warrior in "Second Isaiah" addresses the issue of loss of land and king. Yahweh is not just the god of Israel (both as land and people), but of all lands and nations. This persuasive section of the Bible is to move Judeans in exile from their current situation to a new outlook. One part of this outlook is a new vision of their god.

1. The Polemical Context of Isaiah 40–55

Chapter 8 emphasizes the rhetorical aspects of monotheistic statements. This point applies also to "Second Isaiah." Monotheistic claims within this part of Isaiah are not isolated formulations like the Shema (Deuteronomy 6:4). Instead, they are embedded in a larger literary context focused on two or three themes; these themes drive the context, and the monotheistic claims are a piece of this context, not necessarily its highpoint or single purpose. The context may be both polemical and rhetorical, as L. Alonso Shökel notes it is "directed to and against" the audience.[3] Equally applicable is R. Alter's discussion of "prophetic poetry": "What are the principal modes of prophetic poetry? The overarching purpose is reproof (and not, I would contend, prediction), and this general aim is realized through three related poetic strategies: (1) direct accusation; (2) satire; (3) the monitory evocation of impending disaster.[4] As we will see, these three "poetic strategies" work on a double level as they work "to and against" an audience. Isaiah 40–48, unlike a Jeremiah and Ezekiel, is enacting the reversal of accusation and disaster; the audience is enabled to separate itself from the content of the accusation, the satire, and the impending disaster. On one hand, Isaiah 40–48 takes aim at outsider, that is non-Israelite, neo-Babylonian polytheism and one of its accompanying characteristics, the production of idols. On the other hand, the context is further rhetorical as it aims at persuading insiders, namely Judeans, about reality—or more in the religious idiom of the passage, about the nature of God and Israel.

Monotheistic statements in Isaiah 40–55 are confined to what scholars have identified as the first of the two major sections of the work (Isaiah 40–48, 49–55): 43:10–11; 44:6, 8; 45:5–7, 14, 18, 21; 46:9. Each is addressed briefly.

1. Isaiah 43:10–11 situates its monotheistic claims within a context of divine aid:

> Before Me no god was formed,
> And after Me none shall exist—
> None but me, the Lord;
> Beside Me, none can grant triumph.

Here one point driving the monotheistic declaration that Yahweh is the only god is the claim that He is the only one who can help Israel. Yahweh is the one who returns the captives from Babylon (verse 14).
2. Isaiah 44:6 and 8 also uses monotheistic statement to declare the new event dawning upon Israel:

> I am the first and I am the last,
> And there is no god but Me . . .
> Is there any god, then, but Me?
> There is no other god; I know none.

This divine self-declaration stands in juxtaposition to a critique of image-making (verses 9–20). Accordingly, the implicit contrast involves Yahweh, who is a god full of power and vitality, and the images of the other nations that have no power and no life.

3. Isaiah 45:5–7, 14, 18, 21 presents the longest string of monotheistic statements:

> I am the Lord and there is none else;
> Beside me, there is no other god.
> I engird you, though you have not known me,
> So that they may know, from east to west,
> That there is none but me.
> I am the Lord and there is none else . . .
> Surely God is in you, and there is none else,
> There are no other gods . . .
> I am Yahweh, and there is none else . . .
> Am I not Yahweh?
> And there are no other gods besides Me;
> A just god and savior—
> There is none besides Me.

These statements are preceded by the divine choice of Cyrus, itself a brand new event signaling a change in world history (verses 1–4). Following these monotheistic statements is a call to the heavens to yield its fertility, as Yahweh is the great creator of all, especially humanity (verses 8b-12).

4. The final monotheistic formulations appears in Isaiah 46:9:

> For I am God, and there is none else,
> I am God, and there is none like me.

This chapter begins with a satire on the processions carrying the images of the other gods, Bel and Nebo (Marduk and Nabu), contrasted with Yahweh carrying Israel (verses 1–4). Then Yahweh asks if any god is comparable, as the others are made by smiths (verses 5–7). These themes stand as the introduction to verse 9's claim of incomparability.

Looking back at the contexts of these statements, one perceives a number of connected themes, all designed to persuade Israel of the reality of Yahweh in the world. Monotheistic statements are embedded in thematic contexts involving three basic claims: (1) Yahweh as creator of the world and master of its present; (2) Yahweh chooses Israel now for good just as Yahweh chose Israel for good in the past and just as Yahweh chose to punish Israel in the past; and (3) Israel should recognize Yahweh as its god because there are no other gods, as their images are empty idols. Generally, "Second Isaiah" juxtaposes a number of passages about deities as lifeless idols made by human hands with other sections describing Yahweh as the cosmic creator (for example, Isaiah 40:18–20 with 12–14, 21–22; 45:16 with 18) or Israel's creator (Isaiah 44:9–20 with 21, 25; or, Isaiah 46:1–2 with

3–4). These juxtapositions seem to presume an underlying connection, with a polemical contrast at work: images are ultimately lifeless as they are made by human hands and their creation by humanity shows them to be truly dead deities. In contrast, humanity does not make Israel's deity; instead, Yahweh created the living world, including Israel. As a result, Yahweh the creator is shown to be the living god, unlike the putatively divine competitors who are created. To situate this rhetoric in its concrete setting, one must examine its context more precisely. I would like to to examine what I would call the outsider context—namely, the polemical conceptualization about images or what Israel calls idols—and then turn to the insider rhetoric—namely, the traditional texts that "Second Isaiah" used and adapted to articulate the new expression of Yahweh's exclusive claims on reality.

2. The Outsider Context (Polemic)

What was the object of the polemic? What was the outsider context? One way to approach these questions is to inquire into the appeal of images. Images were common throughout the ancient Near East.[5] Most images are small, standing 10–30 cm in height. For instance, the statuettes in *ANEP* 480–482, 484, and 494–497 range from 10.5 to 28 cm but *ANEP* 483 is 38 cm. The larger sort are rarer; there is, for example, the immense headless bronze statue of Queen Napirasu from Susa (thirteenth century), weighing 1800 kilograms. The front and back were cast separately and welded together over a bronze core. In general though, this one is exceptional, perhaps due to techonological constraints. According to G. Roeder and L. Aitchison,[6] metal workers did not have the furnaces or pots needed to melt and pour large quantities of fused metal for large casts.

Apart from the technological issues, what did the cult statues represent? What were they considered to be and do? How did they represent a threat and an object of biblical polemic? First and foremost, images denote presence. A. L. Oppenheim says: "Fundamentally, the deity was considered present in its image if it showed certain specific features and paraphernalia annd was cared for in the appropriate manner, both established and sanctified by the tradition of the sanctuary."[7] The image stands as the divine recipient of sacrifice and as the god manifest in ceremony. The statue would receive two meals per day, the first in the morning and the other in the evening. In mythic representations, "the human race was created solely to serve the gods by providing food and drink."[8]

Second, cult images served a function of substitution. Such an idea may be argued by analogy to the many cult statues known from Mesopotamia representing human devotees. A. Spycket and W. W. Hallo trace the human votive statue back to the end of the third millennium.[9] The widespread practice of human votive statuary may underlie vows made to deities to offer precious metal made in human form. The wife of the Hittite king, Hattusilis III, vowed a life-sized statue of him in order to protect him: "I will go (and) make for Lelwanis, my lady, a silver statue of Hattusilis—as tall as Hattusilis himself, with its head, its hand (and) its feet of gold—moreover I will hang it it (with ornaments)."[10] Similarly, in CAT 1.14 IV 40–43, King Kirta offers a vow to Asherah at her sanctuary at Tyre that:

If I take Huraya into my palace,
And have the girl enter my court,
Her two parts I'll make silver,
Her third part I'll make gold."[11]

We might not place much importance on such vows for the purposes of understanding cult statues. The promise of donation is merely an inducement to get the
deity in question to grant a request, a simple *quid pro quo*. Yet the form the donation takes is not simply a lump of precious metal; it assumes the form of the
human to be devoted to the deity. The gift is designed first to please the deity
with its wealth, but secondarily it is established in the deity's temple to remind
the deity of the devotion of the persons in question and to induce the deity to be
positively disposed toward them. Human cult statues then suggest a cultic presence,
a certain substitution of the human when the human is not present. Clearly human
cult statues are not the same phenomenon as divine cult statues, for the divine
cult statues represent the deity's local and full manifestation, even identity, according to T. Jacobsen's "ontological" formulation. Yet, like divine cult statues,
human cult statues offer an anthropomorphic statement of cultic identity of those
not fully presnt.

Third, images provide recognition. In other words, the cult statue created
ritually the recognition of divine presence. The cult statue represents the devotees'
devotion to the god, as it allows them to make themselves ritually present to the
god and to manifest their own recognition of the god. Perhaps other cult items
can lend insight into the setting and sensibility of cult statues. For example, Mesopotamian kudurru stones, which range in date from the fourteenth to seventh
centuries; are ovoid stones often of black limestone, customarily labeled as "boundary stones" to mark land ownership. V. Hurowitz has argued recently that this
designation is partially misleading. In a recent monograph devoted to the Hinke
Kudurru,[12] Hurowitz defines a kudurru "as a durable monument placed in a temple
before a god with the purpose of perpetually informing the god of the grant and
invoking divine assistance in guarding the privileges against repeal or infringe-
ment." Like cult statues, kudurru stones are cultic representations made of natural
materials. Whereas the kudurru and its claims are to be recognized by the deity,
the cult statue inversely shows that the community recognizes the god and its
claims. The cultic function in both cases is recognition in the form of presentation
and presence.

Finally, images mark "identity with a difference." This aspect of cult images
is more difficult to nail down, and the secondary literature shows many different
formulations. H. Schützinger, for example, sees in the image and its god an "equal-
ity of essence."[13] K. van der Toorn suggests "an extension of the divine personal-
ity."[14] I. Winter proposes that the "material form was animated, the representation
not standing for but actually manifesting the presence of the subject represented,"
while M. Dick compares the "real presence" of Jesus in the Eucharist.[15] A. Berlejung prefers "substantial connection," "since it implies the possibility of dissolving
the connection."[16] She observes that the gods could leave the image and the
temple. Many of these formulations refer to the work of T. Jacobsen on this subject.
Jacobsen suggests that "the god *is* and at the same time time *is not* the cult statue."[17]

Jacobsen's formulation nicely expresses the difficulty. On one hand, the statues are referred to as gods or goddesses. Jacobsen points to two Babylonian royal inscriptions where the reference to Marduk is to the statue of the god (Agumkakrime of Babylon, 1602–1585, and Nebuchadnezzar I, 1124–1103). W. W. Hallo adds two letters of Hammurapi (ca. 1792–1750) describing the transport of goddesses of Emutbal to Babylon by boat. The "goddesses," first called *ištarātu* and then *ilāti*, were cult statues.[18] On the other hand, Jacobsen points to other features showing that the god is distinguished from the cult statue. For example, the deity is known to be manifest in astral bodies or other manners. To explain the apparent contradiction, Jacobsen applies the language of manifestation or theophany to the cult statue as an expression of presence:

> In saying that the cult statue is the form of the god filling with specific divine content we do not wish to suggest the image of a vessel filled with a different content, or even of a body with a god incarnate in it. We must think, rather, in terms of a purely mystical unity, the statue mystically becoming what it represents, the god, without, however, in any way limiting the god, who remains transcendent. In so "becoming," the statue ceases to be merely earthly wood, precious metals and stones, ceases to be the work of human hands. It becomes transubstantiated, a divine being, the god it represents.[19]

Yet it is clear that the statue is not coterminous with the deity. Jacobsen himself points to the Sippar cult relief of the Babylonian king Nabu-apal-iddina (885–852).[20] In this text the cultic emblem of the sun-god, Shamash, is said to have its mouth washed "before Shamash" (*ma-ḫar* ᵈ*UTU*).[21] That is, in the mouth-opening ritual (*mīs pî*) that provides transition[22] of the cult statue or emblem from workshop to the Ebabarra temple, the divine emblem is not tantamount to the deity. In all, these texts suggest a "sacramental communion" presuming real divine presence, yet not identified in whole with the deity's reality.

These ideas about cult statues would remain general if not for the texts attesting to the *mīs pî*, or mouth washing ceremony, and the related *pit pî* or mouth-opening ritual.[23] These rituals accompany the production of cult statues, from workshop to induction into the temple. The ritual establishes the proper procedure, and therefore the purity of the cult statue, and transform the statue into the representation of the god. Or, in the words of one version, "Without mouth-opening this image does not smell incense, eat food or drink water."[24] In short, the image in the ritual represents the god as recipient of cult. The tablets for this ritual date to the first millennium, but it is possible that the ritual derives from an earlier period, for the incantations in the texts are in Sumerian. The oldest references are Sumerian administrative texts from the Ur III dynasty (2113–2006) referring to provisions for the ritual of opening the mouth of a statue of Gudea (2150), the dead, deified ruler of Lagash. In addition to evidence from the neo-Sumerian period, mouth-washing is also attested in the Middle Babylonian period.

The tablets show some geographical range, as they derive from Asshur, Nineveh, Nimrud, Babylon, Sippar, Nippur, Uruk, Sultantepe, and Hama, but the primary ritual tablets from Nineveh and Babylon contain instructions for the first day. The Nineveh version gives only an incomplete impression for the second day and may be supplemented by the Babylonian version. This version makes no references to mouth-opening as such. Instead, the mouth-washing ritual mentioned fourteen times included mouth-opening (*pit pî*), and the mouth-washing is assumed to encompass mouth-opening in this version. Mouth-washing, normally a purification ritual, was not restricted to cult statues; it was used also for divine symbols (e.g., the ushkaru crescent of the moon-god) and cultic accoutrements, some even for the king.[25] The Babylonian version adds a long list of astral deities in the sacrifices. The Nineveh version mentions only "the gods of the night."[26] The Nineveh version begins with a series of preparations unknown in the Babylonian version. In all, the ritual locations and processions mentioned in these two main versions suggest variously ten or eleven phases of the ritual. Each phase involve its own ritual actions and incantations. A. Berlejung divides the phases into three main parts, consisting of preparations, ritual proper, and induction of the statue, corresponding to the Ea sections (sections 1–4), the Ea-Asallahi-Shamash sections (5–6), and the enthronement in the temple (7–11).[27] Berlejung's division is based on the indigenous division of the text, and she opposes both M. Dick and P. Bogen's division into stages borrowed straight from van Gennep (preliminal rites, or rites separating individual from current status; liminal rites, reshaping intended to prepare the individual for new status; and postliminal rites, reintroduction of the changed individual). Despite some of the problems with mapping this schema straight onto the *mīs pî* ritual, some of van Gennep's categories remain useful here. Separation, preparation for new status, and reintroduction can be mapped onto the ritual at a number of points. The bulk of the ritual concerns the new status of the materials now understood as "the god," who is "reintroduced," or, more properly in this case, inducted into the sanctuary (according to the Babylonian version). Separation may be viewed in the disavowals of human involvement. Berlejung summarizes the ritual aims: to secure the image's complete purity, to annihilate all traces of human involvement in production of the image, to activate the senses of the image, to determine the destiny of the image, to integrate the god into the community of the divine brothers, to transfer the *me* to their bearer, and to lead the image into its realm.[28]

The first day begins with preparations in the city, countryside, and temple (Nineveh version, lines 1–54). Purification rites provide the setting of the following rituals. Materials used are all ingredients with well-known purifying properties for both deities and humans. The scene then moves to the workshop. In the workshop, Ea, Asalluhi, and the statue are all fumigated and libated, and already the statue is referred to as *ilu*, "god," not only as a "statue." At this point the statue can be addressed in the second person as a god; at this point its ears and heart function. In the Babylonian version the priest carries out the mouth-washing, the god now receives its first offering, and the incantation follows. A procession moves from the workshop to the river, where another incantation is recited. At the river bank there are repeated appeals to count the divine image with its brothers, the gods.[29] The procession then proceeds from the river bank into the orchard. Then the god is seated, turned to the east ("toward the sunrise"). At the river, meal is thrown into the river, beer is libated, and several purifications and offerings are made. The Nineveh version adds a request for the inclusion of the image among the brother gods.[30] Here the first day of the ritual procedure ends.

On day two, the ritual resumes at the orchard. Three seats are set for Ea, Shamash, and Asalluhi, set off by a curtain. Then they receive offerings, accompanied by several incantations, including "Born in heaven by his own power," and "On the day when the god was created." After the priest retires, the craftsmen who played a role in the image's manufacture are to declare: "I did not make him (the statue), Ninagal (who is) Ea (god) of smith made him." With that action the eye of the image is open. The priest then recites a long string of incantations, with the following titles: "In your growing up, in your growing up . . . ," "Statue born in a pure place," "Statue born in heaven," "Ninildu, great carpenter of Anu," "Exalted garment, . . . garment of white linen," "Exalted tiara," "Bright throne," "In heaven you shall not stand." Afterward the offerings of the image and the great gods are removed. After this central section, the procession marches from the orchard to the temple gate, with more incantations and offerings. From the gate there is a further procession to the sanctuary niche. There the priest is to take the hand of the god and lead him in, and then repeat the incantation called "My King in the goodness of heart," until they arrive in the shrine. There in the divine abode (niche), the image (that is the god) takes his seat, with the verbal accompaniment of two more incantations. At the side of the shrine a canopy is erected and an offering prepared for Ea and Marduk. With the offering completed, the washing of the mouth is performed. The image is purified, followed by the incantation "Asar [Marduk], God Being, son of Eridu" seven times. The Babylonian version adds a further, final step at "the quay of the *Apsû*." The final result of the rituals is a mechanism for divine communion with humans: hearing and seeing the deity, being heard and seen by the deity. The ritual constitutes a sacramental communion, suggested by M. Dick's comparison with the "real presence" of Jesus in the Eucharist.

In a contrast of the rhetoric of the *mīs pî* with Isaiah 40–48, a sharper profile of the biblical polemic emerges. We may note four general contrasts. First, and most basic, the Mesopotamian material claims divinity for the statue whereas "Second Isaiah," especially in some of the monotheistic statements, ridicules the notion. The creation of the image is presented as a heavenly birth, in the titles of two texts, one the prayer called "Statue bo[rn] in heaven" (Nineveh version, line 190, also B 54), and the other the name of the incantation, "Incantation, On the day when the god was created" (Babylonian version, line 47). The image is also addressed as a divinity: "You are counted [with the gods], your [br]others" (Nineveh version, line 165); "[From today] may your destiny be [coun]ted as divinity, and [with the gods,] your [br]others you are counted" (Nineveh version, lines 167–168). In contrast, "Second Isaiah" stresses the earthly manufacture of the images by detailing both the process of their creation in the workshop and the other uses to which their wood is put (e.g., Isaiah 44:12–17). "Second Isaiah" also poses the impossibility of comparing such an image to the Israelite God (Isaiah 40:18). Such cannot provide benefit to worshippers (Isaiah 44:9), a sine non qua of divinity (as noted in chapter 5).

Second, the *mīs pî* claims that the statues are not made only by human hands. At the beginning of day two, the artisans deny their involvement: "I did not make him (the statue), Ninagal (who is) Ea (the god) of the smith made him" (Babylonian version, line 52; cf. Nineveh version, lines 181–182: "I did not make [it] Ninildu who is Ea the god of the carpenter [made him . . .]," *anāku la ēpuš.. Ninildu Ea ilu ša nagāri[. . .]*). A presentation of a synergy of divine and human manufacture appears in one incantation that accompanies the ritual (STT 200, line 11): "in heaven he was made, on earth he was made" (*ina šamê ibbanu ina erṣeti ibbanu*). Similarly, the incantation, "When the god was made," in line 19 reads: "The statue is the creation of god and human!" (*[ṣa]lam [bun]nanê ša ilī u amēli*).[31] In contrast, "Second Isaiah" over and over claims human agency in the production of images. In fact, the most technical and technological language in the Bible for manufacturing an image derives from Isaiah 40:19–20 and 41:6–7, in order, among other things, to heighten the point of human production of images. After comparing Isaiah 40:12–26 with Genesis 1, R. Alter notes:

> Despite the reminscences of Genesis (to which mention of the host of heaven at the end should be added), the dominant imagery of the poem is actually technological, in part as a rejoinder to the paltry technology of idol-making which the poet denounces. God weighs, measures, gauges, plumbs, but these activities cannot operate in the opposite direction: no man can plumb the unfathomable spirit of the Lord.[32]

This contrast is already in the polemical material of Jeremiah 10, as noted by M. Dick:[33] the verb, "to make" (***ʿśh) is applied to both the images (*maʿăśēh*) and Yahweh's act of creation (**ʿśh* in verse 12).

Isaiah 41:6–7 further highlights the human agency behind the images by contrasting the craftsmen with Yahweh, specifically by employing wordplay involving three Hebrew words or roots; (1) with the root **ʿzr*, "to help": craftsmen assist each other, but Yahweh assists Israel (Isaiah 41:10, 13, 14); (2) with the root **ḥzq*, "to be strong, to strengthen": workers fortify each other, but Yahweh fortifies Israel (Isaiah 41:9); (3) with the root **ʾmr*, "to say, speak": craftsmen speak to each other, but Yahweh speaks to Israel (Isaiah 41:9). The issue of who is made versus who is a maker is matched by "Second Isaiah's" use of the word *ʾēl* or "god": Yahweh is truly *ʾēl* (Isaiah 46:9) versus idol claimed as *ʾēl* (Isaiah 46:6). In summary, images are lifeless as they are made by human hands, and their creation by humanity shows them to be truly lacking in reality or life. In contrast, humanity does not make Israel's deity; rather, Yahweh created the living world, including Israel (Isaiah 44, especially verse 21).

Third, the images, like the gods, are attributed anthropomorphic senses: "Without mouth-opening this image does not smell incense, eat food or drink water" (STT 200).[34] Note the claim in "Second Isaiah" that the images cannot "look nor think" (Isaiah 44:9), nor offer benefit (Isaiah 44:10). This background may help to explain in part the satire of Isaiah 44:15–17 where the image-maker, tired from his labors, uses part of the wood for the statue and part for fuel for fire to warm himself and cook some food. Dick would extend the point in suggesting that the long listing of wood in Isaiah 44:9–20 may reflect an awareness of the indigenous ritual "in its broadest outline and [may] be mocking its seeming unnatural sequence."

Finally, the procession and induction into the temple of the images may raise an additional point about "Second Isaiah," in particular Isaiah 46:1–2. On one hand, the ritual reflects a common feature, the procession of statues. On the other hand, Isaiah 46 mocks the procession, but it is not satisfied with the simple criticism of Jeremiah 10:5: "They have to be carried, for they cannot walk." Isaiah

46:1–2 goes further, presenting a picture of captivity not by Babylonians but for Babylonians and their gods, who burden their carriers:

> Bel is bowed, Nebo is cowering,
> Their images are a burden for beasts and cattle;
> The things you would carry [in procession]
> Are now piled as a burden
> On tired [beasts].
> They cowered, they bowed low as well,
> They could not rescue the burden (or: "him who carried [them]"),
> And they themselves went into captivity.

The ritual presents a processional act of entry into sanctuary in Babylon versus Isaiah 46's description of a processional act exiting from Babylon. (There may be more to the polemic than taking a general aim at processions. W. W. Hallo compares Nabonidus's attempts to remove Babylonian gods to safety against the imminent approach of Cyrus.[35]) The action of carrying becomes the entry-point for another positive claim about Yahweh: You carry idols (Isaiah 46:1) while I, Yahweh will carry you (Isaiah 46:3–4).[36] C. Franke observes: "The Babylonian gods must be carried, but Yahweh carries (the point of comparison centers on the word *ns'*). While Yahweh carries a burden, by contrast the Babylonian gods are a burden."[37] Yahweh's carrying suggests further the difference in Israel's and Babylon's fortunes. Franke insightfully notes: "The descent and exile of Babylon are contrasted with the ascent and liberation of Jacob/Israel."[38]

3. Insider Referentiality and Isaiah 44

The comparison of Mesopotamian material with "Second Isaiah" provides a helpful outsider context. Such a comparison makes it easier to understand the depth of the threat of images and the ideas associated with them. Like the conquering and exiling power of Babylon, so too the very fact of its religious proximity to Judean exiles would be powerful. Yet "Second Isaiah" does not draw solely on ideas well-known in the larger world of Mesopotamia. The work is indebted also to the author's (or authors') own Israelite traditions. From the context of "Second Isaiah," we can infer that the author and the audience were familiar with the important themes of cosmic creation, Exodus material, and royal covenantal formulary. We might infer further, from the placement of this text under the rubric of the book of Isaiah, that this author and audience are familiar also with an older corpus of Isaiah material or tradition. Therefore, to locate the rhetoric of monotheism, we may refer both to older traditional (now biblical) materials and then to the older Isaiah corpus of "First Isaiah."[39] Various polemical contrasts appear in all of the passages expressing monotheism in Isaiah 40–48. To do justice to their poetics, it would be necessary to examine all of them individually. I have selected only one example, Isaiah 44. I regard Isaiah 40–55 as interlocking sections with different themes woven through major parts of the whole, and, accordingly, chapter 44 may be analyzed either on its own or in conjunction with the preceding and following units or in terms of the themes issuing from earlier chapters and flowing through it (in short, poetry as symphonic).

The chapter opens with a speech addressed to "Jacob, my servant" in a manner designed to contrast with the end of the preceding chapter. Commenting on the phrase, "And now, hear" (*wĕ'attâh šĕma'*) in Isaiah 44:1, ibn Ezra restates the verse to mean: "This evil I have brought upon you for your sanctuaries, but now hear the good which I will do for you."[40] Here ibn Ezra is acknowledging the contrast marked by the particle *wĕ'attâ*, "and now," as opposed to the past punishment mentioned at the end of the last chapter. So, on one hand, we may see continuity with the preceding chapter, but we may begin also with this point. Verses 1–8 and 21–44 constitute two sections addressed by God to Jacob/Israel. Together they frame the long description of images in verses 7–20. Two semantic contrasts first alert us to the framing device of verses 1–8 and 21–44 around verses 7–20:

1. "To make" (**'śh*): idols in verses 13, 15, 17, 19 versus Yahweh the creator in verses 2 and 24.
2. "To craft" (**yṣr*): "idol crafters" in verse 9 versus Yahweh as one "who crafts you from the womb" in verses 2 and 24.[41]

The contrasts do not end with the semantic field of production:

3. "To fear" (**pḥd*): idol-makers are afraid in verse 11 versus Israel told in verse 8 "do not fear."[42]
4. "Witness" (**'ēd*): Israel is Yahweh's witness (verse 8), which contrasts with the witness of the idols in verse 9.
5. "To know" (**yd'*): Israel knows who the only God is (verse 8), whereas image-makers do not (verses 18, 19).
6. "To be glorified/beauty" (**p'r*): Yahweh is "glorified" through Israel (verse 23), whereas images are made according to the "beauty" (*tip'eret*) of humans (verse 13).
7. "Wood" (*'ēṣ*) + "forest" (*ya'ar*): wood is cut down in order to serve both as wood for the statue and fuel for burning (verse 14; see also *'ēṣ* in verse 19), whereas all the trees of the forest praise Yahweh (verse 23).
8. Recognition formulary: the craftsman declares the image: "You are my god" (*'ēlî 'attâ*, verse 17), whereas Yahweh declares to Jacob/Israel: "You are my servant" (*'abdî 'attâ*)// "You are my servant" (*'ebed-lî 'attâ*, verse 21).[43]
9. The statue is expected to be able to save (**nṣl*, verse 17), but Yahweh is the redeemer (**g'l*) of Jacob/Israel (verses 22, 23).

With titles and terms for God and Israel from earlier chapters, Isaiah 44 begins a section of consolation, telling the people, "do not be afraid." Furthermore, the passage proclaims the new life of Jacob/Israel in terms that echo and reverse the image of the withered grass said to be the people in the opening section of "Second Isaiah" (40:6–8). "Second Isaiah" often revisits earlier language, echoes and develops it, and returns to it later. In this case, the dessication mentioned first in Isaiah 40:6–8 is replaced with fertility and blessing. Hence, the subject of verse 4 is the offspring (so Targum Jonathan and Rashi, and not the spirit and blessing, so ibn Ezra[44]).

Accordingly, verse 5 marks Jacob//Israel as belonging to the Lord (rendered poetically in aba'b' fashion):

"I am the Lord's": "Jacob"
"I am the Lord's": "Israel"

This sort of quotation also ends the chapter as a whole in verses 26–28. Here again another element builds the frame. Divine prediction likewise appears in both verses 26–28 and verses 6–8, which press the case for Yahweh as the one and only real creator or god by claiming foreknowledge. In verses 6–8 Yahweh claims that he is the only god, the only divinity, and therefore the only one who could have foretold Israel's destiny. Similarly, verses 26–28 denounce the predictions of Mesopotamian experts in favor of his own "servant" and "messengers." Here is a central point. It is the word of Yahweh that stands forever, the theme that opens and closes "Second Isaiah" (40:1–11 and 55:1–5). This word then reflects Yahweh's capacity to foretell the future, a theme in Isaiah 44, which resumes earlier passages: 41:21–28, 42:9, 44:7–8, 24–28; 45:20–23; 47:13. Indeed, these passages suggest a theme throughout Isaiah 40–48. In 44:7–8 this theme is directly tied to the monotheistic claims of 44:6–8. Similarly, in 43:10–11 the monotheistic claims accompany a description of Israel as Yahweh's servant. This figure was chosen so that Yahweh may be believed and known as the only deity, one who long ago proclaimed the victory over Babylon. Yet where did the author believe this claim to have been made long ago? Who is his messenger in verse 26? I propose that "Second Isaiah" may be referencing the earlier Isaianic corpus.

Study of "Second Isaiah" has recently focused on its relations with "First Isaiah."[45] Recent studies have sought to understand "Second Isaiah" as the positive message, "the new things," corresponding to the original prophet's presentation of the "former things" versus the "latter things" (*ḥarî' šōnôt* versus *hā' ōtiyyôt lĕ' āḥôr* in 41:22–23 or *ri' šōnô* versus *qadmōniyyôt* in 43:18; cf. Isaiah 44:7).[46] Isaiah 40–55 is not meant to be the prophet's continuing voice.[47] Chapter 39 marks the passing of Isaiah from the scene: Hezekiah's death is the focus of this prose section, and he is, after all, the last king mentioned in Isaiah 1:1.[48] Accordingly, "Second Isaiah" alludes to material in Isaiah 1–39. The comfort of 40:1 reprises the opening verb of chapter 12, which concludes the first section of the book, and it echoes through the hymnic material of 49:13, 51:3, 9; 52:9. The guilt to be forgiven in 40:1 is Israel's guilt declared in Isaiah 1:4.[49] To link the future of the original prophet's message with the present of the exilic anonymous author of "Second Isaiah," the author correlated the divine word provided via the original prophetic person's experience in chapter 6 with the announcement of the divine word in chapter 40. Hence, commentators since the Middle Ages have noted the similarities between the "call narrative" of Isaiah 6 with the apparent call of Isaiah 40, both involving a divine voice commissioning a prophetic figure in the company of the divine council.[50] Yet commentators have generally missed the allusion in Isaiah 40 to the portrait of Babylon in Isaiah 13–14, the dominant section of oracles against nations, in the emphasis on Babylon's pride and oppressiveness.[51] I believe that Isaiah 40 deliberately reverses the so-called oracles against Babylon in Isaiah 13–14:

1. Isaiah 13:2: set up a sign on a high mountain
2. "Voice" (*qôl*) in Isaiah 13: 2, 4 (two times)
3. Defeat of Babylon by the Medes in Isaiah 13:17–19
4. Compassion on Jacob//choice of Israel in Isaiah 14:1
5. Return of Jacob//Israel to the land in Isaiah 14:2
6. Rest of Jacob//Israel from its hard service in Isaiah 14:3
7. Nature's celebration in song in Isaiah 14:7–8

It is only natural that Isaiah 44's allusion about Yahweh's earlier prediction should derive precisely from the predictions regarding Babylon found in Isaiah in chapters 13 and 14. Unlike so many biblical works, this one has the singular distinction of alluding to an earlier description within the same corpus. The claim is founded on the formation of the prophetic book as a whole, and it further provides a basis for the claim of Yahweh as the only god. Israel can be Yahweh's witnesses (verse 8), because Israel has access to the information provided in the corpus of Isaiah. No other god can provide such information. Contrary to Babylonian claims, their divination is worthless (verse 25), so those whom they serve are nothing; Yahweh is the first and the last and there is no god but Yahweh (verse 6).

The opening section of Isaiah 44:1–8 poses the monotheistic issue, with Israel's answer stated in verse 8: "There is no other rock; I know none" (*wě'ên ṣûr bal-yādā'tî*). How does Israel know, or how is Israel expected to know, this fact? The clue lies in the form of the answer. The answer, that "There is no other rock; I know none," introduces a new element, Yahweh the "rock." This title is not uncommon in the Psalms, but the formulation with the negative may suggest that Israel may have access to this knowledge of God by virtue of its tradition, as represented in a text such as Deuteronomy 32.[52] At first glance, Deuteronomy 32 seems an unlikely candidate for comparison with "Second Isaiah," specifically Isaiah 44:8b. Yet the image of the rock is the central leitmotif of Deuteronomy 32. Moreover, Deuteronomy 32, like Isaiah 44, is largely a polemic against other gods, with an appeal to Yahweh as creator and rescuer from a land of captivity.[53] Accordingly, we might hear in Isaiah 44:8b an echo[54] of Deuteronomy 32's use of negatives, especially *'ên*, to denounce other gods:

Verse 12: "And there was no alien god with Him" (*wě'ên 'immô 'ēl-nēkar*)

Verse 17: "Gods whom they did not know" (*'ĕlōhîm lō'-yĕdā'ûm*)

Verse 21: "They incensed Me with no gods" (NJPS; *bĕlō'-'el*)

Verse 39: "And there is no god with Me" (*wě'ên 'ĕlōhîm 'immādî*; cf. *wě'ên* in verse 4)

Deuteronomy 32 provided an ideological template for the monotheistic rhetoric that takes aim at the external threat of image-making. And we will see further possible examples of using such a text to develop monotheistic rhetoric in Isaiah 44.

We have already seen the themes of mistaken divinity spelled out in Isaiah 44:9–11. The two descriptions of the craftsmen here stress first the technical aspects of their craft (verses 12a, 13–14), followed by comments that seem more satirical than polemical (verses 12b, 15–17). In verse 12b we are told that the craftsman may get wearied with his work, and we are perhaps seeing an echoing contrast with 40:29, where Yahweh is said to give strength to a fatigued Israel (the root *'*yp*, at work in both verses).[55] In verses 15–17 we are given a wonderfully satirical dig at the nature of the god by showing what other uses the same wood may be put to. Verses 18–20 complete the polemic with straight criticism. Leaving aside the satire, these verses simply declare the lack of understanding on the part of the images' makers, perhap as *pars pro toto*, for any who would treat these images as gods.

To draw this analysis of Isaiah 44 to a close, it would appear that the ritual of the *mīs pî* and the polemic of Isaiah 40–48 are opposite in their depiction of images. The latter's understanding of false images shows the nature of true divinity. Yahweh has no image; he is the only God. Ritual, in general, is designed to incorporate and indoctrinate its participants, whereas polemic is designed to make distinctions, to separate people from practices; it involves "detraining." Monotheism offers a "reality check" that should be clear in the minds of Jacob/Israel, not part of deluded minds. In the context of "Second Isaiah," monotheism is a claim that defangs images, rendering them as lifeless depictions in the image of their human makers, or, as expressed in the words of verse 13, "like the pattern of a man, like human beauty" (*kĕtabnît 'îš kĕtip'eret 'ādām*). Monotheistic statements in themselves play a secondary role in the discourse of this chapter, and they form within all of Isaiah 40–48 one of the many thematic strands. Actually, monotheism helps to illuminate the vacuity of Babylonian images: if there is no god present in the cult statue, the cult statue is only an assemblage of materials. And, therefore, images are worthless. In summary, monotheism as a claim is related to the problem of the practice of image-making, and as I have noted already, this practice really seems to drive the passage. Why? What makes images of Babylonians such a crucial issue for "Second Isaiah"?

If we coax some passages in Isaiah 40–48, we may hear the answer. Recall Isaiah 46:1:

> Bel is bowed, Nebo is cowering,
> Their images are a burden for beasts and cattle;
> The things *you* would carry [in procession]
> Are now piled as a burden
> On tired [beasts].
> They cowered, they bowed as well,
> They could not rescue the burden,
> And they themselves went into captivity.[56] (NJPS)

The addressee is none other than "you," "the house of Jacob," as named in the following verse 3. Here the author focuses just enough light on the problem at hand to show that it is Jacob, unconvinced of Yahweh's presence, who has turned to the images of neighbors and overlords.[57] Isaiah 46:5–8, in its denunciation of "you sinners" following the address to Jacob, locates the problem with Yahweh's own people. Chapter 48:5–8 shows the point explicitly. Addressed to "the House of Jacob," the chapter declares that Yahweh foretold future events so "that you might not say, 'My idol caused them, My carved and molten images ordained them'" (verse 5). Returning to Isaiah 44, we might have assumed that only Babylonians are the craftsmen (or, at least the only adherents) of the images in verses 7–20, but the text does not confirm this assumption.[58] Indeed, the ambiguity of identity is used rhetorically for the audience to make a choice: does it want to be a deluded image-seekers (or even image-makers?), or would it choose the only god who has chosen it from the very beginning of its existence?

The polemic of biblical monotheism is therefore complex. On one level, the theme of comfort and consolation involved in the glorious new events for Israel balances the denunciation of Babylon with its attendant practices. On another level, the audience is being challenged to identify with its own heritage and not the practice of Babylon. The dynamic of polemic therefore functions on multiple levels:

> When defined as the art of combat, religious polemic would seem to be directed at the enemy, the "other side" that supports views and practices that run counter to the ideas of the polemicist. In reality, the ideal audience of the polemist is made up of those who are already in sympathy with his cause. There are, in fact, two audiences to be reckoned with: the opponents and the converts; the former are the formal audience, the latter the intended audience. The audience in name does not coincide with the audience of fact. On the part of the author there is a deliberate duplicity: while his overt claim is to defeat his enemies (using words as his weapons), his real purpose is to foster complicity between himself and his readers. The enemy audience is addressed as an oblique way of transmitting a message to his support group.[59]

The polemic here purports to reclaim a group, to delineate between the overt object of attack (Babylonian idolatry) from the implicit object of attack (Judean participation in Babylonian idolatry). We may hear then in the polemic a literary polarity, one carried out explicitly elsewhere in Isaiah 40–48 between Zion and Babylon, the literary antipodes also of Psalm 137. The audience is to determine for itself to which entity it belongs.

4. Reading for Monotheism

As demonstrated by Second Isaiah (as well as Psalm 137), the loss of the monarchy and land as defining marks of Judean identity issued in a probing search for a reworked identity. This process of probing, involved an examination of Israel's older traditions. Older texts helped to provide a background for interpretation of this new reality of Yahweh as the only deity in the cosmos. Monotheistic claims made sense in a world where political boundaries or institutions no longer offered any middle ground. In its political and social reduction in the world, Israel elevated the terms of its understanding of its deity's mastery of the world. Thus, monotheism is not a new stage of religion but a new stage of rhetoric in a situation never known prior to the threat of exile. It represents not a change of religious policy but a new formulation or interpretation of religious reality delineating along cosmic lines what was no longer well delineated in the human, political lines. Such a vision would come to dominate discourse about divinity for Israel. The Judean community also molded monotheistic discourse into various forms according to their social background. Here, the rise of written prophecy, and of written Scripture more broadly,[60] aided various exilic and post-exilic Judeans in their religious quest to understand the god of Israel. (Accordingly, we might even say that text substitutes for land.) Here, the dominant voices preserved in the post-exilic period—priestly, deuteronomic, wisdom, and apocalyptic—all promoted the new vision of the one and only deity, the one to whom the religions of the Book have continued to turn for inspiration.[61]

Like the post-exilic transmitters of the biblical corpus, believers read for the monotheistic God across the wide narrative contexts of the priestly work in the Pentateuch, the major prophetic books of the sixth century, the apocalyptic of later centuries, and the presentation of Wisdom personified. As a consequence, believers participate in a process begun already in the biblical period: they read for the monotheistic God in all the attested traditions of Israel, including earlier ones that contain vestiges of the polytheistic past of Israel and its national god. With such a process of reading, believers like the ancient tradents of the Bible, erase such vestiges and construct the "historical myth" of the monotheistic God as the original historical experience of ancient Israel at Sinai and afterward. As a result, like the ancient transmitters of biblical traditions, later readers confront the complex and many biblical texts and their shaping as a single text now called the Bible, an experience that induces a single reading of a single deity whose divinity spans all of its individual texts and beyond.

Notes

Introduction

1. For the situation in the United States, see P. K. Conkin, *When All the Gods Trembled: Darwinism, Scopes and American Intellectuals* (Lanham: Rowman & Littlefield, 1998).

2. E. J. Larson and L. Witham, "Scientists Are Still Keeping the Faith," *Nature* 386 (3 April 1997), 435–36. My thanks go to T. J. Lewis for this reference.

3. See also some of the essays published in *Religion and Science*, a collection edited by W. Mark Richardson and Wesley Wildman.

4. *Aspects of Monotheism: How God Is One* (ed. H. Shanks and J. Meinhardt; Washington, DC: Biblical Archaeology Society, 1997).

5. Gnuse, *No Other Gods: Emergent Monotheism in Israel* (JSOTSup 241; Sheffield: Sheffield Academic Press, 1997).

6. Miles, *God: A Biography* (New York: Knopf, 1995). Cf. the much better informed R. E. Friedman, *The Hidden Face of God* (San Francisco: HarperSanFrancisco, 1995), which traces a similar trajectory in the Bible from divine action and speech to divine silence and hiddenness.

7. Schwartz, *The Curse of Cain: The Violent Legacy of Monotheism* (Chicago: University of Chicago Press, 1997), 176.

8. Besides Gnuse's book, see T. Frymer-Kensky, *In The Wake of the Goddesses: Women, Culture, and the Biblical Transformation of Pagan Myth* (New York: Free Press, 1992), 106; E. Gerstenberger, *Yahweh the Patriarch: Ancient Images of God and Feminist Theology* (trans. F. J. Gaiser; Minneapolis: Fortress, 1996), 110; and S. A. Geller, *Sacred Enigmas: Literary Religion in the Hebrew Bible* (London: Routledge, 1996).

9. See chapter 8 for examples. For this foundational myth in the work of a world-renowned Egyptologist, see J. Assmann, *Moses the Egyptian: the Memory of Egypt in Western Monotheism* (Cambridge, MA: Harvard University Press, 1997), 7, 39, 158, 169, 211, 218.

10. See the survey of H. Niehr, *Religionen in Israels Umwelt: Einführung in die nordwestsemitischen Religionen Syrien-Palästinas* (Die neue Echter-Bibel: Ergänzungsband zum Alten Testament: 5; Würzburg: Echter, 1998).

11. See the convenient collection of F. Pomponio and P. Xella, *Les dieux d'Ebla: Étude analytique des divinités éblaïtes à l'époque des archives royales du IIIe millénaire* (AOAT 245; Münster: Ugarit-Verlag, 1997). See further R. R. Stieglitz, "Ebla and the Gods of Canaan,"

Eblaitica: Essays on the Ebla Archives and Eblaite Language (ed. C. H. Gordon and G. A. Rendsburg; two vols; Winona Lake, IN: Eisenbrauns, 1990), 2.79–89; and A. Archi, "How a Pantheon Forms: The Cases of Hattian-hittite Anatolia and Ebla of the 3rd Millennium B.C.," *Religionsgeschichte Beziehungen zwischen Kleinasien, Nordsyrien und dem Alten Testament: Internationales Symposion Hamburg 17.-21. März 1990* (ed. B. Janowski, K. Koch, and G. Wilhelm; OBO 129; Freiburg Schweiz: Universitätsverlag; Göttingen: Vandenhoeck & Ruprecht, 1993), 3–18, esp. 7–16.

12. See the surveys in W. G. Lambert, "The Pantheon of Mari," *MARI* 4 (1985), 525–39; A. Malamat, *Mari and the Bible* (Studies in the History and Culture of the Ancient Near East 12; Leiden: Brill, 1998); and the essays in *Mari in Retrospect: Fifty Years of Mari and Mari Studies* (ed. G. D. Young; Winona Lake, IN: Eisenbrauns, 1992). See also O. Rouault, "Noms divins," *Archives royales de Mari* XVI/1 (Paris: Geuthner 1979), 251–68.

13. See the essays in *Emar: The History, Religion, and Culture of a Syrian Town in the Late Bronze Age* (ed. M. W. Chavalas; Bethesda, MD: CDL Press, 1996). For linguistic evidence, see E. J. Pentiuc, "West Semitic Terms in Akkadian Texts from Emar," *JNES* 58 (1999), 81–96, with bibliography.

14. See E. Hornung, *Conceptions of God in Ancient Egypt: The One and the Many* (trans. J. Baines: Ithaca, NY: Cornell, 1982); idem, *Idea into Image: Essays on Ancient Egyptian Thought* (trans. E. Bredeck; New York: Timken, 1992); the essays in *Religion in Ancient Egypt: Gods, Myths and Personal Practice* (ed. B. E. Schafer; Ithaca/London: Cornell, 1991); and J. Baines, "Egyptian Deities in Context: Multiplicity, Unity, and the Problem of Change," *One God or Many? Concepts of Divinity in the Ancient World* (ed. B. N. Porter; Transactions of the Casco Bay Assyriological Institute, vol. 1; Bethesda, MD: CDL Press, 2000), 9–78.

15. See the essays treating Mesopotamian religion in *Unity and Diversity* (ed. H. Goedicke and J. J. M. Roberts; Baltimore: Johns Hopkins University Press, 1975); see further works cited in chapter 5.

16. *Polytheistic Systems* (ed. G. Davis; Cosmos: The Yearbook of the Traditional Cosmology Society 5; Edinburgh: Edinburgh University Press, 1989). For the treatment of Hinduism in this book, see D. Green, "Towards a Reappraisal of Polytheism," 3–11, and K. Werner, "From Polytheism to Monism—A Multidimensional View of the Vedic Religion," 12–27; and for Greek religion, see J. G. Howie, "Greek Polytheism," 51–76. The engaging piece on Israelite monotheism is authored by J. C. L. Gibson, "Language about God in the Old Testament," 43–50.

17. See in the meantime S. Geller, "The One and the Many: An Essay on the God of the Covenant," *One God or Many? Concepts of Divinity in the Ancient World* (ed. B. N. Porter; Transactions of the Casco Bay Assyriological Institute, vol. 1; Bethesda, MD: CDL Press, 2000), 273–319.

18. Smith, *The Early History of God: Yahweh and the Other Deities in Ancient Israel* (San Francisco, CA: Harper & Row, 1990). Henceforth *EHG*.

19. Notable also as the title of M. Detienne's article, "Qu'est ce qu'un dieu," *RHR* 205 (1988), 339–44.

20. For divinity and the term "god" (n<u>t</u>r) in Egyptian, see E. Hornung, *Conceptions of God in Ancient Egypt: The One and the Many* (trans. J. Baines: Ithaca, NY: Cornell University Press, 1982), 156–57; J. Baines, " 'Greatest god' or category of gods?" *Göttingen Miszellen* 67 (1983), 13–28; idem, "On the Symbolic Context of the Principal Hieroglyph for 'god'," *Religion und Philosophie im alten Ägypten: Festgabe für Philippe Derchain zu seinem Geburstag am 24. Juli 1991* (ed. U. Verhoeven and E. Graefe; OLA 39; Leuven: Leuven University, 1991), 29–46; idem, "Egyptian Deities in Context: Multiplicity, Unity, and the Problem of Change" (proceedings of the "Unity and Diversity" conference, ed. B. Porter, in press; cited

with the author's permission); D. Meeks, "Notion de <<dieu>> et structure du panthéon dans l'Egypte ancienne," *RHR* 205 (1988), 425–46. See various comments also in *ANET* 413 nn. 10, 14; D. O'Connor and D. P. Silverman, *Ancient Egyptian Kingship* (Probleme der Ägyptologie 9; Leiden: Brill, 1995), XXIII, 9–10, 54–55, 60, 67, 81, 303. For a broad connection made between *'ĕlōhîm* and (*nṯr*, see C. H. Gordon, "The International God Elohim/Ntr," *HS* 23 (1982), 33–35.

21. See chapter 1.

22. For Mesopotamian and Israelite evidence, see M. S. Moore, "Job's Texts of Terror," *CBQ* 55 (1993), 663 nn. 4 and 5.

23. The phenomenon was relatively circumscribed in Mesopotamia. Shulgi was somewhat exceptional in this regard. For Egyptian evidence, see F. Abitz, *Pharao als Gott in den Unterweltbüchern des Neuen Reiches* (OBO 146; Freiburg Schweiz: Universitätsverlag; Göttingen: Vandenhoeck & Ruprecht, 1995). For the reflection of this language in the Amarna letters, see examples in EA 141:31–33 and 185:13–15.

24. See *'il* applied to deceased Ugaritic monarchs in CAT 1.113.13–26.

25. See *'ilm//mtm* in CAT 1.6 VI 48–49. Note also *rp'im/'ilnym* in 1.6 VI 46–47. See also BH *'ĕlōhîm* referring to the deceased in 1 Samuel 28:13 and Isaiah 8:19.

26. See *CAD* I:102–3, #7.

27. See F. A. M. Wiggermann, *Mesopotamian Protective Spirits: The Ritual Texts* (Cuneiform Monographs 1; Groningen: Styx & PP, 1992), 70.

28. See K. van der Toorn, "Worshipping Stones: On the Deification of Cult Symbols," *JNWSL* 23 (1997), 1–14; and B. N. Porter, "The Anxiety of Multiplicity," *One God or Many?* 243–48.

29. See chapter 4.

30. On this particular determinative, see R. A. Di Vito, *Studies in Third Millennium Sumerian and Akkadian Personal Names: The Designation and Conception of the Personal God* (Studia Pohl: Series Maior 16; Rome: Pontificio Istituto Biblico, 1993), 256–57.

31. See *CAD* K:46–47; Wiggermann, *Mesopotamian Protective Spirits*, 174.

32. *CAD* K:559 under *kurību.*

33. Conventionally translated somewhat misleadingly as "fates." See *CAD* S/3:16b, #2d; J. N. Lawson, "The Concept of Fate in Ancient Mesopotamia of the First Millennium: Toward an Understanding of *šimtu*" (Ph.D. diss., HUC-JIR, 1992), 3, 24–25, 72, 74 (published as *The Concept of Fate in Ancient Mesopotamia of the First Millennium: Toward an Understanding of šimtu* [Wiesbaden: Harrassowitz, 1994]). See section 2. Note also that the meaning of Akkadian *ilu* includes "good fortune, luck" (*CAD* I:101b, #5).

34. See T. Abusch, "Ishtar's Proposal and Gilgamesh's Refusal: An Interpretation of the Gilgamesh Epic, Tablet 6, Lines 1–79," *History of Religions* 26 (1986), 143–87; B. Foster, "Gilgamesh: "Sex, Love and the Ascent of Knowledge," *Love and Death in the Ancient Near East: Essays in Honor of Marvin H. Pope* (ed. J. H. Marks and R. M. Good; Guilford, CT: Four Quarters, 1987), 28, 31. See also N. Vulpe, "Irony and Unity of the Gilgamesh Epic," *JNES* 53 (1994), 275–83.

35. Erra IV:3; see B. R. Foster, *Before the Muses: An Anthology of Akkadian Literature* (two vols.; Bethesda, MD: CDL Press, 1993), 2.794. See further R. C. van Leeuwen, "The Background to Proverbs 30:4aα," *Wisdom, You Are My Sister: Studies in Honor of Roland E. Murphy, O. Carm., on the Occasion of His Eightieth Birthday* (ed. M. L. Barré; CBQMS 29; Washington, DC: Catholic Biblical Association of America, 1997), 116.

36. See *CAD* A/II:59, #1a, 2'.

37. For this point in Mesopotamia and Israelite Literatures, see F. E. Greenspahn, "A Mesopotamian Proverb and Its Biblical Reverberations," *JAOS* 114 (1994), 33–38; van Leeuwen, "The Background to Proverbs 30:4aα," 102–21.

38. See in particular chapter 5.

39. See H. Ringgren, *TDOT* 1:273. This view is entertained also by F. M. Cross, *TDOT* 1:244.

40. Brought to my attention by M. P. O'Connor.

41. So for example as listed (with more instances) in *The Dictionary of Classical Hebrew. Volume I* (ed. D. J. A. Clines, executive editor, J. Elwolde; Sheffield: Sheffield Academic Press, 1993), 259–60. Note the continuation of idiom in late Hebrew, e.g., Ben Sira 14:11 and 4Q179 (= 4QapocrLam A), Frag. I, line 1.

42. Watson, "Reclustering Hebrew *l'lyd*," *Bib* 58 (1977), 213–15.

43. See J. H. Tigay, *The JPS Torah Commentary. Deuteronomy* (Philadelphia: Jewish Publication Society, 1996), 265.

44. *UNP* 191 and n. 11.

45. See the single item listed for Amorite material for this root (***'w/yl²*) treated by R. Zadok, "On the Amorite Material from Mesopotamia," *The Tablet and the Scroll: Near Eastern Studies in Honor of William H. Hallo* (ed. M. E. Cohen, D. C. Snell, and D. B. Weisberg; Bethesda, MD: CDL Press, 1993), 319.

46. *EUT* 18. Later in his life, Pope favored this etymology.

47. Pardee (from his forthcoming edition and commentary on RS 1.001:3): "en accadien la voyelle du nom *ilu* ne semble pas être longue alors qu'en hébreu les anthroponymes comportant l'élément *'ēl-* présentent la réduction du *ṣere* en *ḥatef segol* là où cette syllabe est ouverte (par. ex. *'ĕlî' āb*)." I thank Professor Pardee for bringing these points to my attention and for permission to cite his forthcoming study.

48. See also O. Loretz, *Ugarit und der Bibel: Kanaanäische Götter und Religion im Alten Testament* (Darmstadt: Wissenschaftliche Buchgesellschaft, 1990).

49. Ludwig, "Gods and Goddesses," *The Encyclopedia of Religion*, vol. 6 (ed. M. Eliade; New York: Macmillan; London: Collier Macmillan, 1987), 59–66, esp. 61. See also the thoughtful reflections by R. Panikkar in his contribution, "Deity," *The Encyclopedia of Religion*, vol. 4 (ed. M. Eliade; New York: Macmillan; London: Collier Macmillan, 1987), 264–76. For further comparative discussions, see J. B. Carmen, *Majesty and Meekness: A Comparative Study of Contrast and Harmony in the Concept of God* (Grand Rapids, MI: Eerdmans, 1994); the essays in *God: The Contemporary Discussion* (ed. F. Sontag and M. D. Bryant; New York: Rose of Sharon Press, 1982).

50. Wiggermann, "Transtigridian Snake Gods," *Sumerian Gods and Their Representations* (ed. I. L. Finkel and M. J. Geller; Groningen: Styx, 1996), 47–48. See also Wiggermann, *Mesopotamian Protective Spirits. The Ritual Texts* (Cuneiform Monographs I; Groningen: Styx & PP, 1992), 151–52. There are many fine studies of Egyptian evidence; see the interesting study of D. Meeks and C. Fayard-Meeks, *Daily Life of the Egyptian Gods* (trans. G. M. Goshgarian; Ithaca: Cornell University Press, 1996).

51. Mullen, *The Divine Council in Canaanite and Early Hebrew Literature* (HSM 2; Chico, CA: Scholars, 1980); and Handy, "Dissenting Deities or Obedient Angels: Divine Hierarchies in Ugarit and the Bible," *Biblical Research* 35 (1990), 18–35; *Among the Host of Heaven: The Syro-Palestinian Pantheon as Bureaucracy* (Winona Lake, IN: Eisenbrauns, 1994); and "The Appearance of the Pantheon," *The Triumph of Elohim: From Yahwisms to Judaisms* (ed. D. V. Edelman; Grand Rapids, MI: Eerdmans, 1996), 27–43.

52. J. D. Schloen, "The Patrimonial Household in the Kingdom of Ugarit: A Weberian Analysis of Ancient Near Eastern Society" (Ph.D. diss., Harvard University, 1995; UMI 9539430), esp. 245 n. 1 (see also pp. 4 n. 4, 165–66, 391).

53. J. Z. Smith, "The Glory, Jest and Riddle: James George Frazer and *The Golden Bough*" (Ph.D. diss., Yale University, 1969). See also his article, "Dying and Rising Gods,"

The Encyclopedia of Religion. Volume 4 (ed. M. Eliade; New York: Macmillan; London: Collier Macmillan, 1987), 521–27.

54. Levine, "The Balaam Inscription from Deir 'Alla: Historical Aspects," *Biblical Archaeology Today* (Jerusalem: Israel Exploration Society, 1985), 337–38; idem, "The Plaster Inscriptions from Deir 'Alla: General Interpretation," *The Balaam Text from Deir 'Alla Reevaluated* (ed. J. Hoftijzer and G. van der Kooij; Leiden: Brill, 1991), 58–72; see also his *Numbers 21–36* (AB 4B; New York: Doubleday, 2000), 225–30.

55. C. Seitz, *Word Without End: The Old Testament as Abiding Theological Witness* (Grand Rapids, MI: Erdmans, 1998), 255: "It is an intramural statement, made by Israel's named deity, that he alone is God."

56. Ginsberg, "Interpreting Ugaritic Texts," *JAOS* 70 (1950), 160.

57. See the critical remarks of F. Stolz, "Der Monotheismus Israels im Kontext der altorientalischen Religionsgeschichte—Tendenzen neuerer Forschung," *Ein Gott allein? JHWH-Verehrung und biblischer Monotheismus im Kontext der israeltischen und altorientalischen Religionsgeschichte* (ed. W. Dietrich and M. A. Klopfenstein; 13. Kolloquium der Schweizerischen Akademie der Geistes—und Sozialwissenschaften 1993; Freiburg Schweiz: Universitätsverlag, 1994 = repr. OBO 139; Freiburg Schweiz: Universitätsverlag; Göttingen: Vandenhoeck & Ruprecht, 1994), 33–50.

58. See *EHG*, 145–60.

59. Schloen, "The Patrimonial Household," 29. See also pp. 5, 161–62. S. N. Eisenstadt broaches these issues in his contribution, "Introduction: The Axial Age Breakthrough in Ancient Israel," to *The Origins and Diversity of Axial Age Civilizations* (ed. S. N. Eisenstadt; Albany: State University of New York Press, 1986), 127–34. However, the other material in this volume pertaining to Israel does not press this point sufficiently. See chapter 9, n. 84.

60. This section is an outgrowth of a conversation with Erich Gruen, following a lecture of mine ("The Rhetoric of Biblical Monotheism") at the University of California, Berkeley, in February 1998. I wish to thank Professor Gruen for his highly engaged and engaging interest in my lecture, and I am grateful for his efforts to make me more conscious about the modern use of the categories of monotheism and polytheism. For a critical discussion from the perspective of Egyptological studies, see J. Baines, "Egyptian Deities in Context: Multiplicity, Unity, and the Problem of Change," 9–78.

61. See F. Schmidt "Polytheisms: Degeneration or Progress?" *History and Anthropology* 3 (1987), 9–60; and J. M. Sasson, "Texts, Artifacts, and Images: Revealing Ancient Israelite Religion," *Text, Artifact, and Image. Revealing Ancient Israelite Religion* (ed. T. J. Lewis and G. Beckman; in preparation).

62. See n. 8.

63. See the overview in T. M. Ludwig, "Monotheism," *The Encyclopedia of Religion* (ed. M. Eliade; vol. 10; New York: Macmillan; London: Collier Macmillan, 1987), 75. This sort of rhetoric can be found in Schwartz's book (cited in n. 8).

64. Seitz, *Word Without End*, 255. See chapter 8.

65. For a helpful exception, see T. Frymer-Kensky, *In The Wake of the Goddesses: Women, Culture, and the Biblical Transformation of Pagan Myth* (New York: Free Press, 1992), 85–86. A further working out of Israelite polytheism might deepen some of the other claims made for monotheism. Monotheism, for example, does continue a series of "interactive forces" in nature because it continues the language of cosmic opposition; it does not banish such opposition, but holds it in check (see chapter 1).

66. For example, G. E. Wright, *The Old Testament Against its Environment* (Studies in Biblical Theology 2; London: SCM, 1950), 16–18, 78, 80; J. C. de Moor, *The Rise of*

Yahwism: The Roots of Israelite Monotheism (rev. and enlarged ed.; BETL XCI; Leuven: University Press/Uitgeverij Peeters, 1997), 91. For some of the issues as they bear on the Bible, see T. Hiebert, *The Yahwist's Landscape: Nature and Religion in Early Israel* (New York: Oxford University Press, 1996), 140–62, esp. 152–53. T. Frymer-Kensky contrasts polytheism with divinity mediating between nature and humanity with a monotheism with humanity mediating between nature and divinity (*In The Wake of the Goddesses*, 105). In general, this approach taken by Frymer-Kensky reflects the larger thrust of her interpretation of monotheism, that it is designed to make people take responsibility for the world in the wake of the demise of the other gods. I find this reading of religious responsibility very attractive, but it would not relate well to a biblical text like Psalm 82 (see Chapter 2, section 5). I am unsure why Frymer-Kensky's idea results from monotheism per se instead of deriving from specific Israelite texts.

67. G. E. Mendenhall, *The Tenth Generation: The Origins of the Biblical Tradition* (Baltimore: Johns Hopkin University Press 1973), 223. For further problems with this view, see the discussion at the end of chapter 1.

68. For representative examples of scholars who associate myth with polytheism, see Y. Kaufman, *The Religion of Israel From Its Beginnings to the Babylonian Exile* (trans. and abridged by M. Greenberg; New York: Schocken Books, 1972), 20; and more recently, P. D. Hanson, *The People Called: The Growth of Community in the Bible* (San Francisco: Harper & Row, 1986), 129. For discussions of "myth" in the Bible, see R. A. Oden, Jr., *The Bible without Theology: The Theological Tradition and Alternatives to It* (San Francisco: Harper & Row, 1987), 40–91, esp. 46–47; M. S. Smith, "Mythology and Myth-making in Ugaritic and Biblical Literature," *Ugarit and the Bible: Proceedings of the International Symposium on Ugarit and the Bible. Manchester, September 1992* (ed. G. J. Brooke, A. H. W. Curtis, and J. F. Healey; UBL 11; Münster: Ugarit-Verlag, 1994), 293–341; and the following section. For the further association of biblical narrative with biblical monotheism (as opposed to polytheistic myths), see R. Alter, *The Art of Biblical Narrative* (New York: Basic Books, 1981), 29. For a devastating critique of Alter's views, see S. B. Parker, *Stories in Scripture and Inscriptions: Comparative Studies on Narratives in Northwest Semitic Inscriptions and the Hebrew Bible* (New York: Oxford University Press, 1997), esp. 137–42.

69. Kaufman, *The Religion of Israel*, 21–59. In a similar vein see Kaufman's exaltation of monotheism in M. Greenberg, *Studies in the Bible and Jewish Thought* (Philadelphia: Jewish Publication Society, 1995), 175–88, esp. 182–83. Neither Kaufman nor Greenberg gives sufficient description to the potential positive meaningfulness of polytheism for their ancient adherents; their own exaltation of monotheism apparently prevents them from doing so. Greenberg faults comparativists for leaning too heavily on analogy for making their reconstructions of Israel's religion too similar to its neighbors' polytheistic religions. I would fault Greenberg in turn for the anachronism in making Israel's early religious history conform too readily to its later religious practice. The Pentateuchal sources' monotheism is generalized to all Israel (with some backsliders), but it seems hardly fitting to assume that early Israel was generally monotheistic. B. Uffenheimer ("Myth and Reality in Ancient Israel," *The Origins and Diversity of Axial Civilizations* [ed. S. N. Eisenstadt; Albany: State University of New York Press, 1986] 135–68) offers many helpful corrections to Kaufman on myth and monotheism in Israel (e.g., the latter's relatively long development and emergence in the exilic period), but he still generalizes too broadly about religion in Israel and the biblical corpus versus other nations and their literatures (regarding "pagan myth," divine kingship, divination). For example, on the continuity of divine kingship in Ugaritic and Israelite literature, see J. C. L. Gibson, "The Kingship of Yahweh against its Canaanite

Background," *Ugarit and the Bible: Proceedings of the International Symposium on Ugarit and the Bible. Manchester, September 1992* (ed. G. J. Brooke, A. H. W. Curtis, and J. F. Healey; UBL 11; Münster: Ugarit-Verlag, 1994), 101–12. Uffenheimer also follows Kaufman in lumping various forms of polytheism together in his analysis (see the following note). For Kaufman's work, see T. M. Krapf, *Yehezkel Kaufmann: ein Lebens- und Erkenntnisweg zur Theologie der hebräischen Bibel* (Berlin: Institut Kirche und Judentum, 1990); and *Die Priestschrift und die vorexilische Zeit: Yehezkel Kaufmanns vernachlässigter Beitrag zur Geschichte der biblischen Religion* (OBO 119; Freiburg: Universitätsverlag; Göttingen: Vandenhoeck und Ruprecht, 1992).

70. Curiously, Kaufman adverts rarely to the Ugaritic texts except where it suits his views. When Kaufman does cite Ugaritic, his line also strikes me as forcing a literal reading of mythological texts, with respect to birth and ages of deities. Theogony is surprising rare for the polytheism in the Ugaritic texts. Other features of Kaufman's description of polytheism apply poorly to the Ugaritic texts. And such a mismatch perhaps suggests caution against lumping all ancient expressions of polytheism together (see D. N. Freedman, *Divine Commitment and Human Obligation. Selected Wrtings of David Noel Freedman. Volume One: History and Religion* [ed. J. Huddlestun; Grand Rapids, MI: Eerdmans, 1997], 96; J. A. Dearman, *Religion and Culture in Ancient Israel* [Peabody, MA: Hendrickson, 1992], 37). Indeed, this approach may derive from the reductionism of seeing monotheism as a separate essence, and so too polytheism is treated as a single religious essence.

71. See CAD S/3:15b, #2b; Lawson, "The Concept of Fate in Ancient Mesopotamia of the First Millennium: Toward an Understanding of *šimtu*," 3, 24–25, 72, 74.

72. For example, Wright, *The Old Testament Against its Environment*, 16–18, 78, 80. Cf. W. F. Albright's comments on polytheism and monotheism in the modern context in *From the Stone Age to Christianity: Monotheism and the Historical Process* (sec. ed. with a new introduction; Baltimore: Johns Hopkins University Press, 1957), 288. On Albright and monotheism, see B. O. Long, *Planting and Reaping Albright: Politics, Ideology, and Interpreting the Bible* (University Park, PA: Pennsylvania State University Press, 1997), 83, 121–22, 134.

73. Wright, *The Old Testament Against its Environment*, 71–72, 73; Mendenhall, *The Tenth Generation*, 196–97. For Albright as theologian, see the reflections of his student, D. N. Freedman, *Divine Commitment and Human Obligation. Selected Writings of David Noel Freedman. Volume One: History and Religion* (ed. J. Huddlestun; Grand Rapids, MI: Eerdmans, 1997), 447, 449–51.

74. De Moor, *The Rise of Yahwism*, 71–102. The quotes appear on pp. 91 and 84. One need only examine some comparable biblical texts to realize that they do not constitute the basis for a general cultural theory of "a crisis of monotheism." I am thinking not only of the books of Qohelet (Ecclesiastes) and Job that present suffering and evil in terms comparable to what de Moor takes as evidence for the crisis of polytheism in what he calls Canaan. Other biblical texts likewise could be built into a case for a putative "crisis of monotheism." Such texts could include the expulsion of Hagar in Genesis 21 (see Genesis 16:9), the divine command to sacrifice Isaac in Genesis 22, the divine hardening of Pharaoh's heart in Exodus 4–14 and the divine rejection of Saul as king (see 1 Samuel 15:35). De Moor and others would probably defend the God of the Bible against such charges and they would not be prepared to defend the gods of Canaan in the same manner. Accordingly, it would be my contention that de Moor, like other authors who present polytheism in a negative way, does not provide a balanced view of polytheism in ancient Ugarit. I do see a fragile universe for the Ugaritic pantheon (*UBC* 104), but this does not amount in my view to a crisis of polytheism. See further chapter 5, section 2.

75. L. Boadt, "Rhetorical Strategies in Ezekiel's Oracles of Judgement," *Ezekiel and His Book: Textual and Literary Criticism and their Interrelation* (ed. J. Lust; Leuven: University Press/Uitgeverij Peeters, 1986), 192.

76. Boadt, "Rhetorical Strategies," 193.

77. J. C. L. Gibson, "The Theology of the Baal Cycle," *Or* 53 (1984 = Mitchell Dahood Memorial Volume), 202–19. See also the constructive remarks of E. L. Greenstein, "The God of Israel and the Gods of Canaan: How Different Were They?" *Proceedings of the Twelfth World Congress of Jewish Studies Jerusalem, July 29–August 5, 1997: Division A. The Bible and Its World* (ed. R. Margolin; Jerusalem: World Union, of Jewish Studies, 1999) 47*–58*.

78. W. Lambert, "Trees, Snakes and Gods in Ancient Syria and Anatolia," *BSOAS* 48 (1985), 439.

79. J. D. Levenson makes this comment with respect to the creation of the Sabbath as "*both* a mimetic reenactment of the creator God's primordial rest *and* an enduring memorial to Israel's relief from slavery after the exodus." (Levenson, *Creation and the Persistance of Evil; The Jewish Drama and Divine Omnipotence* [San Francisco: Harper & Row, 1985], 82). Ancient Near Eastern myths often reflect the human world as their ultimate concern. See J. J. M. Roberts, "Myth *Versus* History: Relating the Comparative Foundations," *CBQ* 38 (1976), 1–13; J. M. Sasson, *Ruth: A New Translation with a Philological Commentary and a Formalist-Folklorist Interpretation* (sec. ed.; Sheffield: JSOT, 1989), 220–21. See also the remarks of J. Z. Smith, *Imagining Religion: From Babylon to Jonestown* (Chicago: University of Chicago Press, 1982), 101. The question of "myth" is discussed at considerably greater length later in section 4.

80. Wright, *The Old Testament Against its Environment*, 78.

81. Cf. the discussion of text and reality in P. Ricoeur, *Figuring the Sacred: Religion, Narrative and Imagination* (trans. D. Pellauer; ed. M. I. Wallace; Minneapolis: Fortress, 1995), 42–47.

82. For a recent survey of the issues, see M. S. Smith, *The Pilgrimage Pattern in Exodus* (JSOTSup 239; Sheffield: Sheffield Academic Press, 1997), 144–79.

83. A. Rainey, "A Canaanite at Ugarit," *IEJ* 13 (1963), 43–45, and "Ugarit and the Canaanites Again," *IEJ* 14 (1964), 101. See Albright's critique in YGC 116 n. 15. See further G. del Olmo Lete, "Fenicio u Ugarítico," *AO* 4 (1986), 32–33.

84. Hillers, "Analyzing the Abominable: Our Understanding of Canaanite Religion," *JQR* 75 (1985), 253–69.

85. For linguistic issues, see W. F. Albright in YGC 116 n. 15; and more recently, B. Isaksson, "The Position of Ugaritic Among the Semitic Languages," *Orientalia Suecana* 28–29 (1989–90), 54–70. For issues involving religious literature, see Greenstein, "The God of Israel and the Gods of Canaan," 47*–58*.

86. N. P. Lemche, *The Canaanites and their Land: The Tradition of the Canaanites* (JSOTSup 110; Sheffield: JSOT, 1991), 29–52.

87. Rainey, "Who is a Canaanite? A Review of the the Textual Evidence," *BASOR* 304 (1996), 8–9.

88. Lemche, *The Canaanites and Their Land*, 52.

89. Lemche, *The Canaanites and Their Land*, 152.

90. The term Appalachia might serve as a modern analogue.

91. See the well-placed critiques by N. Na'aman, "The Canaanites and Their Land: A Rejoinder," *UF* 26 (1994), 397–418; A. F. Rainey, "Who is a Canaanite? A Review of the the Textual Evidence," *BASOR* 304 (1996), 1–15. However, Lemche responds to the first in an article, "Greater Canaan: The Implications of a Correct Reading of EA 151:49–67," *BASOR* 310 (1998), 19–24; and he answers the latter in his essay, "Where Should

We Look for Canaan? A Reply to Nadav Na'aman," *UF* 28 (1996), 767–72. See further
the remarks of D. Fleming, " 'The Storm God of Canaan' at Emar," *UF* 26 (1994), 127–
30. Fleming adds the datum of ^dIM *ša ki-na-i*, which he renders "the Storm-God of Canaan"
(Emar VI.3 446:107–108). See further R. S. Hess, "Occurrences of 'Canaan' in Late Bronze
Age Archives of the West Semitic World," *IOS* 18 (1998), 365–72; and N. Na'aman, "Four
Notes on the Size of Late Bronze Age Canaan," *BASOR* 313 (1999), 31–38.

92. Goetze, Review of Z. S. Harris, *Development of the Canaanite Dialects, Language* 12
(1941), 167–70.

93. Greenfield, "Amurrite, Ugaritic and Canaanite," *Proceedings of the International
Congress on Semitic Studies held in Jerusalem, 19–23 July 1965* (Jerusalem: Israel Academy of
Sciences and Humanities, 1969), 92–95.

94. Zadok, "On the Amorite Material from Mesopotamia," 315–333.

95. Zadok, "On the Amorite Material from Mesopotamia," 315.

96. Caubet, "Reoccupation of the Syrian Coast After the Destruction of the 'Crisis
Years'," *The Crisis Years: The Twelfth Century B.C., From Beyond the Danube to the Tigris*
(ed. W. A. Ward and M. Joukowsky; Dubuque, IA: Kendall/Hunt Publishing, 1992), 129.

97. In a blessing Keret is to be blessed among the *pḫr ddn*, "the Assembly of Didanu,"
an ancestral figure known from both CAT 1.161 and Assyrian King List A. For discussion,
see *EHG* 76–77 n. 120; *UBC* 111–14.

98. Jacobsen, "The Battle between Marduk and Tiamat," *JAOS* 88 (1968), 104–8;
UBC 106–14.

99. See M. T. Larsen, "The 'Babel/Bible' Controversy and Its Aftermath," *Civilizations
of the Ancient Near East* (ed. J. M. Sasson; four vols.; New York: Charles Scribner's Sons/
Macmillan Library Reference USA; London: Simon & Schuster and Prentice Hall International, 1995), 4.95–106.

100. See W. R. Garr, *A Dialect-Geography of Syria-Palestine, 1000–586* B.C.E. (Philadelphia: University of Pennsylvania Press, 1985), 30–32.

101. D. Sivan, *A Grammar of the Ugaritic Language* (Leiden: Brill, 1997), 47–48.

102. Keel and Uehlinger, *Gods, Goddesses and Images of God in Ancient Israel* (trans.
T. Trapp; Minneapolis: Fortress, 1998), 396. It is precisely this sort of negative evaluation
that may lead Keel and Uehlinger to underplay the indigenous background of West Semitic
astral religion. For evidence, see chapter 3, section 3.

103. *EHG* 1–26.

104. For many of these materials, see the collection of sources cited in *EHG*. For
examples of pertinent rabbinic materials, see Jacobs, "Near-Eastern Mythology in Rabbinic
Aggadah," 1–11.

105. For example, U. Cassuto, "The Israelite Epic," *Keneset* 8/3 (1943), 121–42 (Heb.)
republished in *BOS* 69–109; N. M. Sarna, *The JPS Torah Commentary. Genesis: the Traditional Hebrew Text with the New JPS Translation* (Philadelphia: Jewish Publication Society,
1989), 3.

106. See Day, "Ugarit and the Bible: Do They Presuppose the Same Canaanite My-
thology and Religion?" *Ugarit and the Bible: Proceedings of the International Symposium on
Ugarit and the Bible. Manchester, September 1992* (ed. G. J. Brooke, A. H. W. Curtis, and J. F.
Healey; UBL 11; Münster: Ugarit-Verlag, 1994), 35–52. A perusal of instances cited in the
EHG would show essentially the same point.

107. For these abodes and enemies, see chapter 1.

108. Or, their gentilic forms in CAT 1.14 IV 35, 37–38. For the forms *ṣrm* and *ṣdynm*,
see M. H. Pope, "Ugaritic Enclitic *-m.*" *JCS* 5 (1951), 125–26. Ginsberg took both forms as
gentilic, the first reflecting a contraction of the ending *-ı̄ma* from *-iyima*. Pope suggests that
the first term may be the place-name, "Tyre," and the second term is gentilic for Sidonians.

109. CAT 1.10 II 9; see YGC 118 n. 18.

110. Possible examples include (1) BH *zû* and Ugaritic *d*; (2) **yqy* in its suzerainty-vassal sense, "to obey," in CAT 1.2 I 18, 34 (*ANET* 130) and Genesis 49:10 (NJPS; cf. Proverbs 30:17; cf. Arabic **wqy* [Lane 3059]; for this root in West Semitic proper names, see S. C. Layton, *Archaic Features of Canaanite Personal Names* [HSM 47; Atlanta, GA: Scholars, 1990], 222–23); (3) **hlm* in 1.2 IV 14, 16, 21, 24 and Judges 5:22, 26, which share a number of other features; (4) *hdrt* in 1.14 III 51 and Psalm 29:2; cf. Psalms 96:9; Isaiah 35:2.

111. A. Jirku, "Kanaʿanäische Psalmenfragmente in der vorisraelitischen Zeit Palästinas und Syriens," *JBL* 52 (1933), 108–20; R. Hess, "Hebrew Psalms and Amarna Correspondence from Jerusalem: Some Comparisons and Implications," *ZAW* 101 (1989), 249–65.

112. In addition to the material generally in this book and in *EHG*, see in particular 1–7.

113. Here I am thinking of the insightful remarks about methodology made by J. Z. Smith in his "In Comparison a Magic Dwells," *Imagining Religion: From Babylon to Jonestown* (Chicago: Univesity of Chicago Press, 1982), 19–35.

114. See also the broader consideration made by Morton Smith, "The Common Theology of the Ancient Near East," *JBL* 71 (1952), 135–136.

115. See *EHG* 145–60.

116. *EHG* 1–26.

117. For the knotty methodological issues, see J. Berlinerblau, "The 'Popular Religion' Paradigm in Old Testament Research: A Sociological Critique," *JSOT* 60 (1993), 3–26, esp. 9. For now I avoid the term "elites" and its implied opposite(s).

118. Geertz, "Thick Description: Toward an Interpretative Theory to Culture," *The Interpretation of Cultures: Selected Essays* (New York: Basic Books, 1973; repr. London: Fontana, 1993), 3–30.

119. For an example, see the learned work of J. C. de Moor, *The Rise of Yahwism: The Roots of Israelite Monotheism* (rev. and enlarged ed.; BETL XCI; Leuven: University Press/ Uitgeverij Peeters, 1997), 71–102.

120. See, for example, the essays on politics and religion in volume 24/1 (1982).

121. For a range of views on history and sociology, see the essays in T. Skocpol, ed., *Vision and Method in Historical Sociology* (Cambridge: Cambridge University Press, 1984). See also the review by J. A. Goldstone, "How to Study History: The View from Sociology," *Historical Methods* 19 (1986), 82–84.

122. For the problems involved, see the essays in *Can a 'History of Israel' be Written?* (ed. L. I. Grabbe; JSOTSup 245; European Seminar in Historical Methodology 1; Sheffield: Sheffield Academic Press, 1997). I found particularly helpful the essay by H. M. Barstad, "History and the Hebrew Bible," 37–64.

123. See the relevant articles in *Bulletin of the Council of Societies for the Study of Religion* 26/3 and 27/1. For a critique of the study of religion, See T. Fitzgerald, *The Ideology of Religious Studies* (New York: Oxford University Press, 2000).

124. See Berlinerblau, "The 'Popular Religion' Paradigm," 9–15.

125. For a reprise of these issues, see the essays in Lynn Hunt, ed., *The New Cultural History* (Berkeley: University of California Press, 1989).

126. M. Wallace, "Introduction," in P. Ricoeur, *Figuring the Sacred: Religion, Narrative, and Imagination* (trans. D. Pellauer; Minneapolis: Fortress, 1995), 7–8; with a quote of Paul Ricouer, cited from "The Critique of Religion," *The Philosophy of Paul Ricoeur: An Anthology of His Work* (ed. C. E. Reagen and D. Stewart; Boston: Beacon, 1978), 219.

127. Preus, *Explaining Religion: Criticism and Theory From Bodin to Freud* (New Haven: Yale University Press, 1987).

128. Allport, *How To Think about God: A Guide for the Twentieth-Century Pagan—One Who Does Not Worship the God of Christians, Jews, or Muslims* (New York: Collier/Macmillan, 1980). See further the essays in *Religion and Reductionism: Essays on Eliade, Segal, and the Challenge of the Social Sciences* (ed. T. A. Idinopulous and E. A. Yonan; Numen 62; Leiden: Brill, 1994). See also the critique of P. Ricouer, *Freud and Philosophy* (trans. D. Savage; New Haven: Yale University Press, 1970).

129. Allport, *The Individual and His Religion: A Psychological Interpretation* (New York: Macmillan, 1950; pb. 1965), 8.

130. McFague, *Models of God: Theology for an Ecological, Nuclear Age* (Philadelphia: Fortress, 1987), 23.

131. See T. Jacobsen, *Treasures of Darkness: A History of Mesopotamian Religion* (New Haven/London: Yale, 1976), 3–5.

132. For some reflections, see H. Ott, "Does the Notion of 'Mystery'—As Another Name for God—Provide a Basis for a Dialogical Encounter between the Religions?" *God: The Contemporary Discussion* (ed. F. Sontag and M. D. Bryant; New York: Rose of Sharon, 1982), 5–17. See further in chapter 5.

133. See J. Hick, "Is God Personal?" *God: The Contemporary Discussion*, 169–79. See also chapter 5.

134. Cf. Wallace, "Introduction," 8: "In its essence, faith is a living out of the figures of hope unleased by the imagination."

135. As a slight digression, it bears mentioning that it is not by accident that mountains play an important place in biblical and pre-biblical narratives about deities. As religious metaphors for approaching the divine, mountains express more than the connection between the divine and the human, by analogy to the heavenly and the earthly; they also represent what is physically overwhelming compared to humanity, yet perceptible by humanity. Mountains are a kind of metaphor for the divine, and the texts that present the beauty and power of such mountains are telling readers some insights about the divine. Chapter 1, section 2, discusses these sacred mountains.

136. Otzen, Gottlieb and Jeppesen, *Myths in the Old Testament* (trans. F. Cryer; London: SCM, 1980).

137. The following works survey the place of myth within biblical studies: J. W. Rogerson, *Myth in Old Testament Interpretation* (BZAW 134; Berlin: de Gruyter, 1974); Oden (*The Bible without Theology*; 52–91; ibid, "Mythology," *ABD* 4:946–56; ibid, "Myth in the OT," *ABD* 4:956–60; B. Batto, *Slaying the Dragon* (Minneapolis, MN: Augsburg-Fortress, 1992), esp. chapter 1.

138. Oden (*The Bible without Theology*, 42–52) notes Christian antipathy toward myth. Christianity assumed in the past that its theology reflects on true faith while other religions tell stories or myths. Eusebius condemns what he himself calls perhaps ironically "the theology of the Phoenicians" (PE 1.10.54–55; H. W. Attridge and R. A. Oden, *Philo of Byblos. The Phoenician History: Introduction, Critical Text, Translation, Notes* [CBQMS 9; Washington: Catholic Biblical Association, 1981], 69). According to Oden, Christianity has argued that the Bible contains little or no myth because the Bible affirms a single deity while myths are stories about the gods. But a good deal of the Bible is mythic by this definition because the Hebrew Bible contains numerous references to beings beside Yahweh who are called "divine," "gods," or "sons of god/God" (e.g., Psalms 29:1; 89:7) or "holy ones" (Psalm 89: 6; Hosea 12:1; Zechariah 14:5; cf. KAI 4:5, 7; 14:9, 22; 27:12). Finally, Christian faith (1 Timothy 1:4; 4:7; Titus 1:14) has represented itself as a historical religion that regards the myths of other religions as untrue.

139. D. McGaughey, "Through Myth to Imagination," *Journal of the American Academy of Religion* 56 (1988), 57.

140. For Ewald, see Rogerson, *Myth in Old Testament Interpretation*, 27–28. This view of myth can be found in the third edition of Gunkel's Genesis commentary; see Rogerson, *Myth in Old Testament Interpretation*, 59; J. A. Wilcoxen, "Narrative," *Old Testament Form Criticism* (ed. J. A. Hayes; San Antonio: Trinity University Press, 1974), 68. Rogerson (*Myth in Old Testament Interpretation*, 59–60, 62–63) also notes Gunkel's inconsistency on this point: according to Gunkel Gen 2:2f. is a myth because God is involved. According to Rogerson, the inconsistency arose from Gunkel's use of two different definitions of myth (also observed by Otzen in Otzen, Gottlieb, and Jeppesen, *Myths in the Old Testament*, 5). In addition to the view that myths are stories about the gods (thus excluding narratives about Yahweh), he also held that myths answer questions of universal concern (hence including some narratives about Yahweh). The definition of myth as stories about deities but not the Deity of Israel implicitly underlies some of the twentieth century biblical theologies that viewed Israelite religion as historical and other ancient Near Eastern religions as largely mythic, ahistorical, and relatively devoid of theological importance except as a foil to Israelite religion. The names of G. Ernest Wright, Gerhard von Rad, and Yehezkiel Kaufman are usually invoked in this connection. See Oden, *The Bible without Theology*, 47–48; J. J. Collins, "Is a Critical Biblical Theology Possible?" *The Hebrew Bible and Its Interpreters* (ed. W. H. Propp, B. Halpern, and D. N. Freedman; Winona Lake, IN: Eisenbrauns, 1990) 4–5. For the ideological uses of Greek myth in scholarship, see B. Lincoln, *Theorizing Myth: Narrative, Ideology, and Scholarship* (Chicago: University of Chicago Press, 1999).

141. Thompson, "Myth and Folktales," *Myth. A Symposium* (ed. T. A. Sebeok; Bloomington, IN: Indiana University Press, 1965), 173: "The practical definition which I have suggested and which seems to be rather well agreed upon is that myth has to do with the gods and their actions, with creation, and with the general nature of the universe and of the earth."

142. See McGaughey, "Through Myth to Imagination."

143. The school of analytical psychology associated with the name of Carl G. Jung has shown a positive attitude toward myth. For Jung and his disciples, myths are stories reflecting different stages in the development of human consciousness. See E. Neumann, *The Origins and History of Consciousness* (Bollingen Series XLII; Princeton: Princeton University Press, 1954); S. F. Walker, *Jung and the Jungians on Myth* (New York: Garland, 1990).

144. See the essays in *Myth and Mythmaking* (ed. H. A. Murray; Boston: Beacon, 1968); J. Z. Smith, *Imagining Religion: From Babylon to Jonestown* (Chicago: University of Chicago Press, 1982), 66–71, 78–79, 87–91; Y. Bonnefoy, *Mythologies* (ed. W. Doniger; trans. G. Honigsblum; 2 vols.; Chicago: University of Chicago Press, 1991).

145. For Stith Thompson's satirical remarks on various functional approaches to myth, see his article "Myth and Folktales," 171–72.

146. Eliade, "Toward a Definition of Myth," *Mythologies* (ed. Y. Bonnefoy and W. Doniger; trans. G. Honigsblum; vol. 1; Chicago: University of Chicago Press, 1991), 5.

147. Oden, *The Bible without Theology*, 55. See also Oden, "Myth in the OT," 959–60. One aspect of Oden's second criterion, namely that the context is "almost always" oral (so also M. Simpson, "Myths and Cosmologies," *Civilizations of the Ancient Mediterranean: Greece and Rome* [ed. Michael Grant and Rachel Kitzinger; New York: Scribner's, 1988], 862), is problematic; ancient Near Eastern societies produced and transmitted both oral and written forms of myths during the same periods.

148. The fourth criterion is emphasized by J. D. Levenson, *Sinai & Zion: An Entry into the Jewish Bible* (San Francisco: Harper and Row, 1987), 102–05.

149. Oden (*The Bible without Theology*, 58) oversteps his own definition by including some nonnarrative biblical material under the label of myth (e.g., "any number of references to a cosmic mountain"). See later text for this problem.

150. Oden, *The Bible without Theology*, 58.

151. See J. J. M. Roberts, "Myth *Versus* History: Relating the Comparative Founda-tions," *CBQ* 38 (1976), 1–13; J. M. Sasson, *Ruth; A New Translation with a Philological Commentary and a Formalist-Folklorist Interpretation* (sec. ed.; Sheffield: JSOT, 1989), 220–21. See also the remarks of J. Z. Smith, *Imagining Religion*, 101. Ancient Near Eastern myths not infrequently reflect the human world as their ultimate concern. Apocalyptic provides another example of the inadequacy of the dichotomy made between myth and history in biblical studies (see chapter 9, section 3).

152. See Rogerson, *Myth in Old Testament Interpretation*, 6–7. For the later form-critical adoption of this terminology, see Rogerson, *Myth in Old Testament Interpretation*, 57–65; Wilcoxen, "Narrative," 60–79; Otzen in Otzen, Gottlieb, and Jeppesen, *Myths in the Old Testament*, 4–9. For criticism of these distinctions, see Thompson, "Myth and Folktales," 175.

153. A development bearing on the problem of myth in the Bible may be seen in the attempt in the field of biblical theology to substitute the category of story for history (J. Barr, *The Scope and Authority of the Bible* [Philadelphia: Westminster, 1980], 5; cf. Collins, "Is a Critical Biblical Theology Possible?" 10–11). This move accommodates not only the nonhistorical sources of the Pentateuch as well as the more historical works of the books of Samuel and Kings, but also different sorts of poetic works. This approach seems to bear on myth in the Bible. Indeed, myth seems to be a subcategory of J. J. Collins's ("Is a Critical Biblical Theology Possible?" 11) application of "story" to biblical narratives expressed in the following terms: "We recognize stories as 'true' or as valid expressions of reality in so far as they fit our experiences, although the fit cannot be scientifically verified . . ." Rather than use only the term "story," though, Collins ("Is a Critical Biblical Theology Possible?" 13) cautiously employs the term "fiction": "If we recognize that much biblical 'history' is fiction, in the sense of Paul Ricouer's poetic language, then we must also recognize that statements about God must be in the context of that fiction." The label "fiction" for biblical narrative in current theological discussions including those of biblical theology may indicate that myth no longer appears alien to the discussion of the Bible. It might be argued that myth constitutes one type of biblical fiction, one which focuses on divine beings or the divine realm.

154. Eissfeldt, *Kleine Schriften II* (ed. R. Selheim and F. Maass; Tübingen: Mohr [Sie-beck], 1963), 496–501; cf. J. C. L. Gibson, "Myth, legend and folklore in the Ugaritic Keret and Aqhat Texts," *Congress Volume; Edinburgh 1974* (VTSup 28; Leiden: Brill, 1975), 60–68. For a discussion of Eissfeldt's views, see Rogerson, *Myth in Old Testament Interpretation*, 146. Like the Pentateuch and the books of Joshua and Judges, Keret and Aqhat might be viewed as a myth of societal origins. In the case of Keret, it would appear that this narrative was considered the story of a distant ancestor of the dynastic line if the blessing in CAT 1.15 III is any indication. In this blessing Keret is to be blessed among the *phr ddn*, "the Assembly of Didanu," an ancestral figure known from both CAT 1.161 and Assyrian King List A. For discussion, see *EHG* 76–77 n. 120.

155. For this consensus form-critical definition of myth, see O. Eissfeldt, *The Old Testament: an Introduction* (trans. P. R. Ackroyd; New York: Harper and Row, 1965), 35; Rogerson, *Myth in Old Testament Interpretation*, 145–73; see also G. W. Coats, *Genesis: With an Introduction to Narrative Literature* (FOTL 1; Grand Rapids, MI: Eerdmans, 1983), 10. For a wider form-critical assessment, see Otzen in Otzen, Gottlieb, and Jeppesen, *Myths in the Old Testament*, 4–9.

156. Thompson, "Myth and Folktales," 169–80, esp. 173–74.

157. So noted by Oden. This point is evident not only from the most brief range of opinions cited above, but from Oden's survey of definitions of myth (see *The Bible without Theology*, 42–52).

158. For an introduction to the Ugaritic Baal Cycle, for the present see *UBC* 1–114.

159. That the categories even for the Baal Cycle are somewhat open to discussion cannot be denied. The folklorist, Heda Jason (*Ethnopoetry: Form, Content, Function* [Forum Theologicae Linguisticae 11; Bonn: Linguistica Biblica, 1977], 32), and P. J. Milne (*Vladimir Propp and the Study of the Structure in Hebrew Bible Narrative* [Bible and Literature Series 13; Sheffield: Sheffield Academic Press, 1988], 169–70) classify the Baal Cycle (and Enuma Elish) as a "mythic epic."

160. Cf. CMHE 142.

161. This distinction might be compared to W. H. Schmidt's distinction between myth as story (*Erzählung*) and mythic conceptions (*Vorstellungen*), but the term imagery seems preferable to conception as it constitutes less of an abstraction from the textual evidence. See Schmidt, "Mythos im Alten Testament," *EvTh* 27 (1967), 237–54; Rogerson, *Myth in Old Testament Interpretation*, 159–60.

162. Cf. Cross's characterization of this poem as exemplifying the old mythic pattern (CMHE 142). A. Fitzgerald (private communication) has observed that the poem does not reflect the march of the rain-wielding divine warrior since this god destroys not with a rain-bearing storm but with the dry scirocco. This feature is reflected in the language of Exodus 14:21 and 15:7.

163. Thompson, "Myth and Folktales," 175–76.

164. M. Himmelfarb, "From Prophecy to Apocalypse: The *Book of the Watchers* and Tours of Heaven," *Jewish Spirituality: From the Bible through the Middle Ages* (ed. A. Green; World Sprituality: An Encyclopedic History of the Religious Quest 13; New York: Crossroad, 1988), 145–65. For the West Semitic background of the interpreting angel, see S. Gevirtz, "Phoenician *wšbrt mlṣm* and Job 33:23," *Maarav* 5–6 (1990) = *Sopher Mahir: Northwest Semitic Studies Presented to Stanislaus Segert* (ed. E. M. Cook; Santa Monica, CA: Western Academic Press, 1990), 145–58.

1. Anthropomorphic Deities and Divine Monsters

1. For example, see E. Shils, *Center and Periphery: Essays in Macrosociology* (Chicago: University of Chicago Press, 1975); and the essays in *Centre and Periphery in the Ancient World* (eds. M. Rowlands, M. Larsen, and K. Kristiansen; Cambridge: Cambridge University Press, 1987). For similar reflections on center and periphery for Mesopotamia, see M. Liverani, "The Ideology of the Assyrian Empire," *Power and Propaganda: A Symposium on Ancient Empires* (ed. M. Trolle Larsen; Mesopotamia. Copenhagen Studies in Assyriology 7; Copenhagen: Akademisk forlag, 1979), 306–7; and P. Machinist, "On Self-Consciousness in Mesopotamia," *The Origins and Diversity of Axial Age Civilizations* (ed. S. N. Eisenstadt; Albany: State University of New York Press, 1986), 184–91. For the dialectic between center and periphery in historical writing, see P. Burke, *History and Social Change* (Cambridge: Cambridge University Press, 1992), 79–84.

2. Wiggermann, "Scenes from the Shadow Side," *Mesopotamian Poetic Language: Sumerian and Akkadian* (ed. M. E. Vogelzang and H. L. J. Vantiphout; Cuneiform Monographs 6; Groningen: Styx Publications, 1996), 207–20. See also Wiggermann, "Transtigridian Snake Gods," *Sumerian Gods and Their Representations* (ed. I. L. Finkel and M. J. Geller; Groningen: Styx, 1996), 47–48, and *Mesopotamian Protective Spirits. The Ritual Texts* (Cuneiform Monographs I; Groningen: Styx & PP, 1992), 151–52.

3. J. D. Schloen, "The Patrimonial Household in the Kingdom of Ugarit: A Weberian Analysis of Ancient Near Eastern Society" (Ph.D. diss., Harvard University, 1995; UMI 9539430), 245 n. 1 (see also pp. 4 n. 4, 165–66, 391).

4. For more on the household in myth, see the following two chapters. O. Marc offers a psychological interpretation of the home as an expression of the self, and in particular as

an image of the womb; see Marc, *The Psychology of the House* (London: Thames and Hudson, 1977). While such a Jungian interpretation imposes a broad archetypal reading on many different cultures and runs the risk of ignoring these cultures' indigenous language for the home, West Semitic cultures do use anatomical terms for architectural terms, implying a homology between the human body and home; for examples, see *UBC* 349, esp. n. 228. The two appear as analogous structures subject to external threat and protective of their internal parts. Therefore, the comparison of the human body to parts of the house as in Ecclesiastes 12 is at home in ancient Israel.

5. One contrast works poorly for the Ugaritic texts compared to Mesopotamia—the contrast between time present and time past. According to Wiggermann, time present for Mesopotamia marks the epoch of deities and time past signals the ancient era of monstrous enemies. Hence, Enuma Elish recounts the ancient past that precedes Tiamat's defeat at the hands of Marduk. The narrative is set in hoary antiquity. In marked contrast, in Ugaritic myth only one case might involve a "theogony" (1.23). See F. M. Cross, "The 'Olden Gods' in Ancient Near Eastern Creation Myths," *Magnalia Dei. The Mighty Acts of God: Essays on the Bible and Archaeology in Memory of G. Ernest Wright* (ed. F. M. Cross, W. E. Lemke, and P. D. Miller, Jr.; Garden City, NY: Doubleday, 1976), 328–38; Mullen, *The Divine Council*, 34, 45, 76, 88. Cf. the far-ranging study of N. Wyatt, "The Theogony Motif in Ugarit and the Bible," *Ugarit and the Bible*, 395–419. For later West Semitic theogony, see further K. Koch, "Wind und Zeit als Konstituenten des Kosmos in phönikischer Mythologie und spätalttestamentlichen Texte," *Mesopotamia—Ugaritica—Biblica: Festschrift für Kurt Bergerhof zur Vollendung seines 70. Lebensjahres am 7. Mai 1992* (ed. M. Dietrich and O. Loretz; AOAT 232; Kevelaer: Butzon & Bercker; Neukirchen-Vluyn: Neukirchener Verlag, 1993), 59–91.

The Ugaritic texts also lack a narrative rendering an ancient conflict between divine warriors and their cosmic enemies issuing in creation (or what F. M. Cross, his students E. T. Mullen and R. J. Clifford, and a variety of other scholars call "cosmogony"). See Cross, "The 'Olden Gods' in Ancient Near Eastern Creation Myths," 328–38; Mullen, *The Divine Council*, 34, 45, 76, 88; R. J. Clifford, "Cosmogonies in the Ugaritic Texts and in the Bible," *Or* 53 (1984 = Mitchell J. Dahood Memorial Volume), 183–201; P. D. Miller, "Aspects of the Religion of Israel," 59. See also L. Fisher, "Creation at Ugarit and in the Old Testament," *VT* 15 (1965), 313–25; N. Wyatt, "Killing and Cosmogony in Canaanite and Biblical Thought," *UF* 17 (1985), 375–81; T. Fenton, "Nexus and Significance: Is Greater Precision Possible?" *Ugarit and the Bible: Proceedings of the International Symposium on Ugarit and the Bible. Manchester. September 1992* (ed. G. J. Brooke, A. H. W. Curtis, and J. F. Healey; UBL 11; Münster: Ugarit-Verlag, 1994), 76–81.

To be sure, such old conflicts are topics of conversation. So Anat and Mot both refer to ancient enemies (1.3 III 38–46; 1.5 I 1–3, 28–30; cf. 1.82.1). An ancient cosmogony featuring El as the warrior-creator has often been claimed for the Ugaritic texts, and the idea may be supported by reference to El's weaponry in 1.65.12–14, but even this text, which is so focused on El and his household, does no more than allude to this possibility (for this text with transation, see chapter 2, section 2). There is no myth devoted to this topic, in stark contrast with the attested Mesopotamian and Israelite literary traditions. Of course, one might argue that the Ugaritic literary tradition once included such texts, but that they are no longer extant. Yet the Ugaritic text usually compared with Enuma Elish is the Baal Cycle, and they apparently differ in time-frame. Enuma Elish explicitly situates its narrative in the distant past. In contrast, the Baal Cycle presents Yamm and Mot not as subjugated foes of the past but as enemies whose struggles with Baal never seem to quite end. This is clear for Mot, who returns after seven years to renew his conflict with the storm-god (1.6 V 8–10); Yamm may also appear after his defeat at Baal's hands (1.4 VII

14). The warrior's battles over Yamm and Mot are not the stuff of high antiquity, but matters of a sort of present; whether timeless or repetitive I doubt anyone can really say (although many scholars do). I prefer to say that such conflict is represented as part of the present scheme of reality, not simply of the distant past. This presentation reflects the precarious character of the cosmic order represented by Baal's kingship (discussed in chapter 6, section 5).

The one myth considered a theogony is often called "the Birth of the Beautiful Gods" (CAT 1.23). Including the birth of two gods sired by El, this text has been regarded as the single instance of a theogony in the Ugaritic corpus. Like the Baal Cycle, this text is not explicitly set in the ancient past (although it does describe the births of gods long known, that is, Shahar and Shalim, or Dawn and Dusk). Yet the time of this text is the ritually present, as the many ritual comments of the text suggest. I cannot say whether such a "ritual present" likewise informs the narrative presentation of the Baal Cycle, even though this would fit very nicely with ritual theories of the text. Yet ritual perspective and information do not necessarily create a text for ritual performance. Accordingly, it may be preferable to investigate the Baal Cycle's temporal perspective as a literary question. The cosmic enemies may be divided according to time-frame in the Baal Cycle: most seem to belong to the ancient past, which is only a matter of passing reference, but Yamm and Mot belong to the present. Their power is manifest as much in the present cosmos as the kingship of Baal, their warrior-enemy. Cosmic enemies in the present of this sort may be an issue specific to the Baal Cycle, insofar as the text seems to view the cosmos in the present. Yet I am not aware of a classic Mesopotamian or Israelite text that represents the present threat of cosmic enemies in these terms and the help accorded the divine hero by other deities. In sum, the apparent present setting in the Baal Cycle seems to demarcate it from the Mesopotamian and Israelite texts commonly compared with it.

6. For Ugaritic evidence, see N. Wyatt, "Sea and Desert: Symbolic Geography in West Semitic Religious Thought," *UF* 19 (1987), 375–89, esp. 380–85, and Wyatt, *Myths of Power: A Study of Royal Power and Ideology in Ugaritic and Biblical Tradition* (UBL 13; Münster: Ugarit-Verlag, 1996), 19–115, esp. 26–30, 75–81. For Mesopotamian and biblical examples of the motif, see A. Haldar, *The Notion of the Desert in Sumero-Akkadian and West Semitic Religions* (Uppsala: Lundequistska bokhandeln, 1950); S. Talmon, "The 'Desert Motif' in the Bible and in Qumran Literature," *Biblical Motifs: Origins and Transformations* (ed. A. Altmann; Cambridge, MA: Harvard University Press, 1966), 31–63; idem, "*midbār*," *TDOT* 8:87–118. For the root **dbr*, see most recently E. Lipiński, "<<Leadership>> The Roots *DBR* and *NGD* in Aramaic," *"Und Mose schrieb dieses Lied auf": Studien zum Alten Testament und zum Alten Orient. Festschrift für Oswald Loretz zur Vollendung seines 70. seines Lebenjahres mit Beiträgen von Freunden, Schülern und Kollegen* (ed. M. Dietrich and I. Kottsieper; AOAT 250; Münster: Ugarit-Verlag, 1998), 501–8.

7. See A. Rainey, "The Kingdom of Ugarit," *The Biblical Archaeologist Reader* 3 (ed. E. F. Campbell, Jr. and D. N. Freedman; Garden City, NY: Doubleday, 1970), 93–94. Should we see here the religious practice of royal women? Cf. "the religion of the palace women" at Mari, discussed in W. G. Lambert, "The Pantheon of Mari," *MARI* 4 (1985), 527.

8. The word *šd* may apply not only to the center, but in its meaning "open country," it applies also to periphery (CAT 1.6 II 20; cf. 1.5 VI 6, 29).

9. See CMCOT 34–97.

10. The listing of Anat and Athtart together suggests a different figure here, as surmised by P. Bordreui, "Ashtart de Mari et les dieux d'ougarit," *MARI* 4 (1985), 545–47.

11. For the deities and these cult-sites, see D. Pardee, *Les textes para-mythologiques de la 24e Campagne (1961)* (Ras Shamra—Ougarit IV; Mémoire no 77; Paris: Editions Recherche sur les Civilisations, 1988), 210–12.

12. Very nicely observed by Wyatt, *Myths of Power*, 27–28. For further discussion of this mountain, see P. N. Hunt, "Mount Saphon in Myth and Fact," *Phoenicia and the Bible: Proceedings of the Conference held at the University of Leuven on the 15th and 16th of March 1990* (ed. E. Lipiński; OLA 44; Studia Phoenicia XI; Leuven: Department Oriëntalistiek/ Uitgeverij Peeters, 1991), 103–15; K. Koch, "Ḥazzi-Ṣafôn-Kasion: Die Geschichte eines Berg und seiner Gottheiten," *Religionsgeschichte Beziehungen zwischen Kleinasien, Nordsyrien und dem Alten Testament: Internationales Symposion Hamburg 17.-21. März 1990* (ed. B. Janowski, K. Koch and G. Wilhelm; OBO 129; Freiburg Schweiz: Universitätsverlag; Göttingen: Vandenhoeck & Ruprecht, 1993), 171–223.

13. Wyatt, *Myths of Power*, 27–28.

14. As seen by Wyatt, *Myths of Power*, 40 n. 38. See also T. Stordalen, "Echoes of Eden: Genesis 2–3 and Symbolism of the Eden Garden in Biblical Hebrew Literature," (Ph.D. diss., Norweigan Lutheran School of Theology, Oslo, 1998), 127, 132, where he notes the same word used for the land at the edge of the underworld, perhaps as a reflection of royal garden-graves at Ugarit. If so, this usage might reflect the cosmic connecting point between the royal center of the palace of the living dynasty and the royal periphery of the deceased royal ancestors in the underworld. The deceased ancestors are tied to the living even as they have passed into the realm of the underworld in the periphery. Rituals designed to communicate with the dead (such as CAT 1.161) and myths that reflect aspects of the cultic devotion to the dead (such as CAT 1.5–1.6) express contact of members of the living and deceased royal line between the center and the periphery. For these texts, see chapter 6.

15. Wyatt, *Myths of Power*, 27–115. Wyatt also identifies the temple and city as cosmic centers identified in various ways with the divine mountain and the garden.

16. The question is nicely raised by Stordalen, "Echoes of Eden," 117–32; see also D. P. Wright, "Holiness, Sex, and Death in the Garden of Eden," *Bib* 77 (1996), 305–29. Stordalen explores the question of whether 1.23.66–68a assumes a garden; it would seem based on the typology discussed that lines 68b-76 assume the notion of the sown as an enclosed garden complete with a "watchman of the sown." One problematic aspect of the text involves the command to El's wives to raise an offering in the outback, apparently for the ravenous gods (line 65–66). This command would fly in the face of the notion that monstrous forces generally do not receive cultic offerings, possibly even in a sanctuary site in the outback (*mdbr qdš*). However, it is unclear from the context whether such a command can be carried out, for no such offering is described in the narrative. In fact, such a proposed offering may be intended to forestall the monstrous gods' entry into the sown, which takes place in the following lines (lines 68–76).

17. Resheph's appearance with other deities, such as Baal, Yarih, Kothar, and perhaps Anat (under the title Rahmay) in 1.15 II 3–6 militates against classifying him easily on this side. So, too, his name in lists of deities (1.47.27 = 1.118.26) and evidently his temple (4.219.3).

18. On this expression, see M. H. Pope, "Mid Rock and Scrub, a Ugaritic Parallel to Exodus 7:19," *Biblical and Near Eastern Studies: Essays in Honor of William Sanford LaSor* (ed. G. Tuttle; Grand Rapids, MI: Eerdmans, 1978), 146–50 = Pope, *Probative Pontificating in Ugaritic and Biblical Studies: Collected Essays* (ed. M. S. Smith; UBL 10; Münster: Ugarit-Verlag, 1994), 45–50 (with "An afterthought 22/12/92 on 'Mid rock and Scrub' ").

19. S. B. Parker's recent translation of these pertinent lines renders *mdbr 'il š'iy* as "the god-awful wilderness." See *UNP* 189.

20. See A. van Selms, *Marriage and Family Life in Ugaritic Literature* (Pretoria Oriental Studies 1; London: Luzac, 1954), 63–64; and Pope, review of van Selms, *Marriage and Family Life in Ugaritic Literature*, *JBL* 74 (1955), 293–94, and *EUT* 37.

21. The word *ll* appears in Ugaritic otherwise as a time-referent in ritual texts using the expression *lll*, "at night" (1.39. 12; 1.49.9; 1.50.7; 1.106.27; cf. *ll* in the partly non-Ugaritic texts, 1.69.3 and 1.132.17, 25, as the apparent recipient of cultic devotion).

22. The tiers of the pantheon are described in detail in chapters 2 and 3.

23. See T. H. Gaster, "The Religion of the Canaanites," *Forgotten Religions* (ed. V. T. A. Ferm; New York: Philosophical Library, 1950), 121–30. Contrast the relationship between deities and realms in Mesopotamian myth; for discussion, see A. Livingstone, *Mystical and Mythological Explanatory Works of Assyrian and Babylonian Scholars* (Oxford: Clarendon Press, 1986), 71–91. See also W. Horowitz, *Mesopotamian Cosmic Geography* (Mesopotamian Civilizations 8; Winona Lake, IN: Eisenbrauns, 1998).

24. See A. Rainey, *The Scribe at Ugarit. His Position and Influence* (The Israel Academy of Sciences and Humanities Proceedings III/4; Jerusalem: Israel Academy of Sciences and Humanities, 1968), 136, esp. n. 58.

25. On this name, see W. G. E. Watson, "The Ugaritic PN *krt*," *UF* 26 (1994), 497–500.

26. For a presentation and discussion of CAT 1.161, see chapter 6, section 4. Deceased kings and heroes are discussed also in chapter 4, section 2.

27. "L'onomastique . . . montrerait sans aucun doute que les noms de personne théophores cristallisent une attitude religieuse semblable: ils demandent à la divinité, quelque soit son nom, salut et bénédiction, protection et faveur." In Caquot, "Problèmes d'histoire religieuse," *La Siria del Tardo Bronzo* (Orientis Antiqui Collectio 9; Rome: Centro per le Antichìta e la Storia dell'Arte del Vicino Oriente, 1969), 70.

28. For a caution in identifying "fertility" primarily with goddesses or a particular goddess (as opposed to gods), see J. A. Hackett, "Can A Sexist Model Liberate Us? Ancient Near Eastern 'Fertility' Goddesses," *Journal of Feminist Studies in Religion* 5 (1989), 65–76. See the well-placed caution of P. D. Miller against reducing Ugaritic religion to simply a "fertility religion" (Miller, "Aspects of the Religion of Israel," *Ancient Israelite Religion: Essays in Honor of Frank Moore Cross* [ed. P. D. Miller, Jr., P. D. Hanson, and S. D. McBride; Philadelphia: Fortress, 1987], 59).

29. For this rendering, see A. Rainey, "Gleanings from Ugarit," *IOS* 3 (1973), 51; see also *TO* 2.215; *UBC* 76. For a more generic translation, "death," see D. Pardee, "Ugarit. Texts and Literature," *ABD* 6:710. G. del Olmo Lete also takes *mt* here as the god of Death, but he interprets the third line as a further protasis; see del Olmo Lete, *Canaanite Religion According to the Liturgical Texts of Ugarit* (trans. W. G. E. Watson; Besthesda, MD: CDL Press, 1999), 95. This latter difference does not affect the interpretation of Mot here.

30. For discussion, see M. S. Smith, "Death in Jeremiah IX, 20," *UF* 19 (1988), 289–93.

31. According to some scholars, *ym* in the ritual texts, e.g., 1.102.3, 1.118.29, 1.162.11, might not be the god Yamm, but a cultic basin; so J. F. Healey, "The Akkadian 'Pantheon' List from Ugarit," *SEL* 2 (1985), 120. Or, it is a deity called "Day"; so see E. T. Mullen, *The Divine Council in Canaanite and Early Hebrew Literature* (HSM 24; Chico, CA: Scholars, 1980), 89. However, de Moor defends the identification ("The Semitic Pantheon of Ugarit," *UF* 2 [1970], 201). Support for *ym* as a cultic item is derived from the observation that the next entry in 1.47 and 1.118 (but not in 1.148) is a divinized incense burner (*'utht*). On 1.148, see D. Pardee, "RS 24.643: Texte et Structure," *Syria* 69 (1992), 153–70, esp. 158, 160.

32. Certainly not "divine Sapan," as the mountain is mentioned in line 6 of the same text. See J. F. Healey, "The Akkadian 'Pantheon' List from Ugarit," 117. Note that the offering list in 1.148 begins *dbḥ ṣpn*, apparently the sacrificial heading corresponding to the *'il ṣpn* in 1.147.1 (see the preceding note).

33. See del Olmo Lete, *Canaanite Religion*, 96, 260.

34. Pardee, "Ugarit. Texts and Literature," 709. For the lists, see J. F. Healey, "The Akkadian 'Pantheon' List from Ugarit," 115–25, and "The 'Pantheon' of Ugarit: Further Notes," *SEL* 5 (1988 = Fs. O. Loretz), 103–12.

35. P. Amiet, *Corpus des cylindres de Ras Shamra—Ougarit II: Sceaux-cylindres en hématite et pierres diverses* (Ras Shamra—Ougarit IX; Paris: Éditions Recherche sur les Civilisations, 1992) 68: "animaux attributs." Cf. "Animal attribute" in Amiet, *Art of the Ancient Near East* (trans. J. Shepley and C. Choquet; New York: Abrams, 1980), 440 no. 787. Amiet also uses "attendant animal," in "Part Five: A Lexicon" of the same work.

36. I prescind from the arguments over whether any goddess is to be considered the "mistress of animals." For discussion and references, see I. Cornelius, "Anat and Qudshu as the <<Mistress of Animals>>. Aspects of the Iconography of the Cananite Goddesses," *SEL* 10 (1993), 21–45. For a general treatment of evidence of the goddesses involved, see W. G. E. Watson, "The Goddesses of Ugarit: A Survey," *SEL* 10 (1993), 47–59. For the issue of the goddess's representation as a cow, see M. Dijkstra, "Semitic Worship at Serabit el-Khadim (Sinai)," *ZAH* 10 (1997), 89–97. Because the evidence at Ugarit is unclear, I prescind from this question as well. I would only point out the association of a domesticated species with a deity.

37. The element *tr* is not listed in F. Gröndahl, *Die Personnamen der Texte aus Ugarit* (Studia Pohl 1; Rome: Päpstliches Bibelinstitut, 1967).

38. See Amiet, *Corpus des cylindres de Ras Shamra*, 69. For examples from Ugarit, see Amiet, *Corpus des cylindres de Ras Shamra*, 68, 71, and 79 no. 146, and 73 and 81, no. 160. For the temporal extent of Levantine bull iconography, see O. Keel and C. Uehlinger, *Gods, Goddesses, and Images of God in Ancient Israel* (trans. T. Trapp; Minneapolis: Fortress, 1996), 37, 50–51, 56, 78, 82, 118–20, 130, 144–45, 158, 169, 172, 191–95, 278.

39. For the bull iconography at Bethel and the close relation of 1 Kings 12 and Exodus 32, see *CMHE* 198–99; Keel and Uehlinger, *Gods, Goddesses, and Images of God*, 191–92. On p. 194 n. 12 the authors suggest that *'glyw* in the Samaria Ostracon no. 41 should be rendered not "YW is a bull calf," but "Bull calf of YW," a view that gains in plausibility and sense from the discussion in section 6 and n. 65 there.

40. See *EHG* 51.

41. See *CAD* E:63a: *būru ek-du ša Adad* in a Middle Babylonian kudurru and ᵈAMAR *ek-du* in a list of divine symbols.

42. See K. van der Toorn, *Family Religion in Babylonia, Syria and Israel: Continuity and Change in the Forms of Religious Life* (Studies in the History and Culture of the Ancient Near East VII; Leiden: Brill, 1996), 321.

43. F. C. Fensham, "Winged Gods and Goddesses in the Ugaritic Tablets," *OA* 5 (1966), 157–64. For iconography of Anat as a bird, see M. H. Pope, "The Scene on the Drinking Mug from Ugarit," *Near Eastern Studies in Honor of William Foxwell Albright* (ed. H. Goedicke; Baltimore: Johns Hopkins University Press, 1971), 393–405 = Pope, *Probative Pontificating in Ugaritic and Biblical Studies: Collected Essays* (ed. M. S. Smith; UBL 10; Münster: Ugarit-Verlag, 1994), 17–27. On Anat's form as a bird, see further F. Gangloff and J. C. Haelewyck, "Osée 4, 17–19: Un marzeah en l'honneur de la déesse 'Anat?" *ETL* 71 (1995), 370–82. For the lion possibly as her animal (representing her warrior prowess), see Amiet, *Corpus des cylindres de Ras Shamra*, 34, 35 no. 46.

44. For the parsing of the expression, see G. A. Tuttle, "*di dit* in UG 5.2.1.8," *UF* 8 (1976), 465–66; *TO* 2:116 n. 356.

45. Insightfully noted by Pope, "The Scene on the Drinking Mug from Ugarit," 393–405.

46. Tessier, *Ancient Near Eastern Cylinder Seals from the Marcopoli Collection* (Berkeley: University of California Press, 1984), 79.

47. Tessier, *Ancient Near Eastern Cylinder Seals*, 243 nos. 476, 477.

48. Tessier, *Ancient Near Eastern Cylinder Seals*, 245 no. 480 (?), 481 (?). For the possibility also of the cow as Anat's iconography representation, see Keel and Uehlinger, *Gods, Goddesses, and Images of God*, 126, 195. The winged figure standing on a bull on one of the bronze plaques from Dan could be Anat (see A. Biran, "Two Bronze Plaques and the Ḥuṣṣot of Dan," *IEJ* 42 [1999], 53–54).

49. For Ugaritic glyptic, see Amiet, *Corpus des cylindres de Ras Shamra*, 167–76. For the wider Levantine context, see also Keel and Uehlinger, *Gods, Goddesses, and Images of God*, 76–78, 155. Mesopotamia offers a wide variety of monstrous forms. See W. G. Lambert, "Ninurta Mythology in the Babylonian Epic of Creation," *Keilschriftliche Literaturen* (ed. K. Hecker and W. Sommerfeld; XXXIII Rencontre Assyriologique Internationale; Berliner Beiträge zum Vorderen Orient 6; Berlin: Dietrich Reimer, 1986), 55–60; E. Reiner, "Magic Figurines, Amulets, and Talismans," *Monsters and Demons in the Ancient and Medieval Worlds: Papers Presented in Honor of Edith Porada* (ed. A. E. Farkas, P. O. Harper, and E. B. Harrison; Mainz: Philipp von Zabern, 1987), 27–36; Wiggermann, *Mesopotamian Protective Spirits*, 143–87. For a valuable comparative study, see T. J. Lewis, "CT 13.33–34 and Ezekiel 32: Lion-Dragon Myths," *JAOS* 116 (1996), 28–47. For Hittite and Aegean parallels, see recently C. Watkins, "Le dragon hittite Illuynkas et le géant grec Typhôeus," *CRAIBL* 1992: 319–30. Snakes of the more terrestrial variety may denote other values such as regeneration and they are depicted occasionally with the goddess. See Keel and Uehlinger, *Gods, Goddesses, and Images of God*, 53, 86, 274. Unfortunately the two uses of serpentine imagery are conflated and confused in Miles, *God: A Biography*, 32. It is arguable that a mythic battle underlies the reference to the serpent in Genesis 2; for clarification, see S. M. Olyan, *Asherah and the Cult of Yahweh in Israel* (SBLDS 34; Atlanta, GA: Scholars, 1988), 71.

50. Amiet, *Corpus des cylindres de Ras Shamra*, 71 and 78, no. 144. See also Amiet, *Corpus des cylindres de Ras Shamra*, 74 and 82, no. 166; See E. Williams-Forte, "The Snake and the Tree in the Iconography and Texts during the Bronze Age," *Ancient Seals and the Bible* (ed. L. Gorelick and E. Williams-Forte; Malibu, CA: Undena, 1983), 18–43. On this type in Mesopotamia, see Wiggermann, "Transtigridian Snake Gods," 210–11.

51. See A. Caquot, "Un recueil ougaritique de formules magiques: KTU 1.82," *SEL* 5 (1988—Fs. O. Loretz), 31–43; J. C. de Moor, *An Anthology of the Religious Texts from Ugarit* (Nisaba 16; Leiden: Brill, 1987), 175–81.

52. So in his treatment of Mesopotamian glyptic, see E. D. van Buren, "The Dragon in Ancient Mesopotamia," *Or* 15 (1946), 24–25. Cf. the massive literature on creatures of mixed form ("hybrid creatures") serving as guardians of deities' sanctuaries. See Keel and Uehlinger, *Gods, Goddesses and Images of God*, 248–53, 278–79, 290, 376.

53. Yamm in 1.3 III 38–39, etc.; 'Arsh in 1.3 III 43 and Mot in 1.4 VII 48–49, VIII 23–24, 30–32, etc.

54. Szubin, "The 'Beloved Son' in the Hebrew Bible and the 'Beloved Disciple' in the New Testament in Light of Ancient Near Eastern Legal Texts" (Abstract, Society of Biblical Literature International Conference, 1995; used with permission).

55. *UBC* 1.59–60, 150–1.

56. On this problem, see chapter 3, section 3.

57. Regarding Fire (*'išt*), see *UBC* 306 n. 158. For this divinity especially at Ebla, see also F. Pomponio and P. Xella, *Les dieux d'Ebla: Étude analytique des divinités éblaïtes à l'époque des archives royales du IIIe millénaire* (AOAT 245; Münster: Ugarit-Verlag, 1997), 201.

58. For further details to the following discussion, see M. S. Smith, "Terms of Endearment: 'Dog' (*klbt*) and 'Calf' (*'gl*) in KTU 1.3 III 44–45," "*Und Mose schrieb dieses Lieb auf. . . .*" *Studien zum Alten Testament und zum Alten Orient: Festschrift für Oswald Loretz zur Vollendung seines 70. Lebenjahres mit Beiträgen von Freuden, Schülern und Kollegen* (ed. M. Dietrich and I. Kottsieper; Münster: Ugarit-Verlag, 1998), 713–16.

59. See the discussion of the identification of Akkadian *agālu* in CAD A/1:141b.

60. The gender of this dog presumably derives from the feminine gender of *'išt* (so suggested by T. J. Lewis, personal communication).

61. D. R. West has proposed that the title *klbt 'ilm* indicates that *'išt* (usually translated as "Fire") was conceived as a cosmic dog, "a native form of Mesopotamian Lamashtu" (West, "Hekate, Lamashtu and *klbt 'ilm*," *UF* 24 [1992], 384). The basis for West's comparison is quite general: both Lamashtu and *'išt* have fiery and canine associations. Since so little is known of *'išt*, it is quite possible that *klbt* has some mythological association along the lines proposed by West. Other parallels, such as Cerberus, might leap to mind as well. For possible Akkadian parallels, see *CAD* K:71a, 2'f.

62. EA 67:16–18; 76:12–16; 84:6–10, 16–18; 90:19–26; 91:3–5; 108:25–28; 134:11–13; 201:9–16; 320:16–25; cf. 109:44–49; 130:31–38; 138:95–97. These texts are conveniently collected and discussed by J. M. Galán, "What Is He, the Dog?" *UF* 25 (1993), 174.

63. It is possible that such a metaphorical usage lies also behind *keleb*, a category of cultic personnel proscribed in Deuteronomy 23:19, and Phoenician *klbm* in the Kition plaque (CIS 86b = KAI 37, line 10; see also 86a, line 16). See F. L. Benz, *Personal Names in Phoenician and Punic Inscriptions: A Catalog, Grammatical Study and Glossary of Elements* (Studia Pohl 8; Rome: Biblical Institute Press, 1972), 331; J. C. L. Gibson, *Textbook of Syrian Semitic Inscriptions. Volume III: Phoenician Inscriptions Including Inscriptions in the Mixed Dialect of Arslan Tash* (Oxford: Clarendon, 1982), 124–25, 126–27, 130. Some scholars, however, prefer a more literal understanding of **klb* for these cultic personnel. See L. E. Stager, *Ashqelon Discovered: From Canaanites and Philistines to Romans and Moslems* (Washington: Biblical Archaeologist Society, 1991), 35, 36. For further opinions on the two sides of this discussion, see further J. Hoftijzer and K. Jongeling, *Dictionary of the North-West Semitic Inscriptions. Part One: '-L* (HdO; Leiden: Brill, 1995), 509. The issues attendant on the Kition plaque are beyond the scope of this investigation.

64. For Ugaritic evidence, Gröndahl, *Die Personennamen*, 150. For more Akkadian names with the element **kalbu*, see *CAD* K:696. For BH examples, see *BDB* 477. For Phoenician instances, see Benz, *Personal Names in Phoenician and Punic Inscriptions*, 131–32, 331.

65. See K. Koenen, "Der Name 'GLYW auf Samaria-Ostrakon Nr. 41," *VT* 44 (1994), 399 n. 5. For further examples, see *CAD* A/1:141b. The personal name *'glyw* in Samaria Ostracon 41 was also interpreted in this manner by Martin Noth, but this view is controverted. See the discussion in Koenen, "Der Name," 399 n. 5. A verbal form of **'gl* could be involved (J. Tigay, personal communication). See also the Palmyrene name *'glbwl* discussed in Koenen, "Der Name," 399 n. 2, 400 n. 15.

66. So *AHw* 141b. For other instances, see *CAD* B:342a. Note also the comment there: "OB personal names of the type *Būrija, Būratum* are probably hypocoristics of WSem. names."

67. For domesticated dogs, see CAT 1.16 I 2, 15. For examples of domesticated dogs in shepherding and hunting, see *CAD* K:71a.

68. For animals in the Bible, see the essays in *Gefährten und Feinde des Menschen: Das Tier in der Lebenswelt des alten Israel* (ed. B. Janowski, U. Neumann-Gorsolke, and U. Glessmer; Neukirchen-Vluyn: Neukirchener, 1993). See also the surveys of Firmage, "Zoology (Animal Profiles)," 1109–67; and P. Riede, " 'Denn wie der Mensch jedes Tier nennen würde, so sollte es heissen': Hebräische Tiernamen und was sie uns verraten," *UF* 25 (1993), 331–78.

69. For this point about apocalyptic, see chapters 9 and 10.

70. For a convenient summary, see A. Kapelrud, "Ba'al, Schöpfung und Chaos," *UF* 11 (1979 = C. F. A. Schaeffer Festschrift), 407–12.

71. A summary of the evidence on this figure can be found in J. Day, "Leviathan," *ABD* 4:295–96.

72. See J. Huehnergard, *Ugaritic Vocabulary in Syllabic Transcription* (HSS 32; Atlanta, GA: Scholars, 1987), 72, 185–186.

73. For this figure especially in the Bible, see W. Herrmann, "Jahwes Triumpf über Mot," *UF* 11 (1979 = C. F. A. Schaeffer Festschrift), 371–38.

74. The text-critical difficulties with the end of this line make any translation little more than a hazardous guess.

75. Among more recent threatments, see T. N. D. Mettinger, "The Enigma of Job: The Deconstruction of God in Intertextual Perspective," *JNWSL* 23/2 (1997), 1–19, esp. 14–15. My thanks go to Professor Mettinger for bringing this article to my attention.

76. For the evidence and argumentation regarding this convergence in Israelite religion, see *EHG* 21–24 and below chapter 7, section 5.

77. Furthermore, Yamm is perhaps treated as divine, if this is the figure lying behind the word *ym* included in two god-lists (1.47.30 = 1.118. 29) and equated with "Divine Sea" (*ᵈtâmtum*) in RS 20.24.29, marked with the divine determinative. There are questions, however, with this interpretation. See previous for a discussion of this issue.

78. See S. Layton, review of J. D. Fowler, *Theophoric Personal Names in Ancient Hebrew,* *JNES* 52 (1993), 69.

79. See S. Layton, review of J. D. Fowler, *Theophoric Personal Names in Ancient Hebrew,* *JNES* 52 (1993), 69.

80. Cf. I. Cornelius, "The Visual Representation of the World in the Ancient Near East and the Hebrew Bible," *JNWSL* 20 (1994), 193–218, esp. 202.

81. This point has been made repeatedly by biblical scholars. See the fine presentation of J. D. Levenson, *Creation and the Persistance of Evil: The Jewish Drama of Divine Omnipotence* (San Francisco: Harper & Row, 1988), 53–99. See more recently E. T. Mullen Jr., *Ethnic Myths and Pentateuchal Foundations: A New Approach to the Formation of the Pentateuch* (SBL Semeia series; Atlanta, GA: Scholars, 1997), 94–98.

82. Levenson, *Creation and the Persistance of Evil*, 3.

83. For the relationship between "a form of discourse and a certain modality of the confession of faith," see P. Ricoeur, *Figuring the Sacred: Religion, Narrative and Imagination* (trans. D. Pellauer; ed. M. I. Wallace; Minneapolis: Fortress, 1995), 39. In this book Ricoeur's own examples suffer from outdated information concerning biblical scholarship since von Rad and about religion since Eliade. Broader generalizations about the relationship between monotheism and biblical genre is a problematic undertaking. For example, R. Alter associates biblical narrative with biblical monotheism (as opposed to polytheistic myths), but S. B. Parker has provided a devastating critique of Alter's interpretation of biblical genres. See Alter, *The Art of Biblical Narrative* (New York: Basic Books, 1981), 29; Parker, *Stories in Scripture and Inscriptions: Comparative Studies on Narratives in Northwest Semitic Inscriptions and the Hebrew Bible* (New York: Oxford University Press, 1997), esp. 137–42.

84. Cf. also the sun-goddess's titles "Great Sun" (*rbt špš*) in 1.16 I 37 and "Light of the Gods, Shapshu" (*nrt 'ilm špš*) in 1.3 V 17, 1.4 VIII 21, 1.6 I 8, 11, 13, II 24, III 24, IV 17, 1.19 IV 47, 49.

85. See further the discussion of El's astral family in chapter 3, section 3.

86. See T. McCreesh, "A Carnival of Animals in Job," presented at a meeting of the Old Testament Colloquium held at Conception Abbey in Conception, Missouri, on February 6, 1993. For the east wind as a possible terrestrial manifestation of the god of Death, see *EHG* 53; I base this observation on the unpublished work of Aloysius Fitzgerald, who has noted the role that the east desert wind plays in many biblical passages.

87. Mendenhall, *The Tenth Generation*, 211 n. 35.

88. The exilic period has been a long-championed backdrop for this chapter. See most recently Mullen, *Ethnic Myths and Pentateuchal Foundations*, 94. However, it has also been argued that Second Isaiah is dependent on Genesis 1; see A. Kapelrud, "The Date of the Priestly Code (P)," *ASTI* 3 (1964), 58–64; M. Weinfeld, "God the Creator in Genesis 1

and in the Prophecy of Second Isaiah," *Tarbiz* 37/2 (1968), 105–32; M. Fishbane, *Biblical Interpretation in Ancient Israel* (Oxford: Clarendon Press, 1985), 325; cited and discussed in P. T. Willey, *Remember the Former Things: The Recollection of Previous Texts in Isaiah 40–55* (SBLDS 161; Atlanta GA: Scholars, 1997), 32–33; and B. D. Sommer, *A Prophet Reads Scripture: Allusion in Isaiah 40–66* (Contraversions. Jews and Other Differences; Stanford, CA: Stanford University Press, 1998), 142–45.

89. UBC 109–10.

90. Cf. Ricoeur, *Figuring the Sacred*, 47: faith "could be called 'unconditional trust' to say that it is inseparable from a movement of hope that makes its way in spite of the contradictions of experience and that turns reasons for despair into reasons for hope according to the paradoxical laws of a logic of superabundance."

2. The Divine Council

1. See the well-known article of T. Jacobsen, "Primitive Democracy in Ancient Mesopotamia," *JNES* 2 (1943), 159–72. See further G. Evans, "Ancient Mesopotamian Assemblies: An Addendum," *JAOS* 78 (1958), 114.

2. See AHw 876.

3. See E. T. Mullen, *The Divine Council in Canaanite and Early Hebrew Literature* (HSM 2; Chico, CA: Scholars, 1980), 113–20. For the iconography of the divine council, C. Uehlinger, "Audienz in der Götterwelt: Anthropomorphismus und Sociomorphismus in der Ikonographische eines altsyrichen Zylindersiegels," *UF* 24 (1992), 339–59.

4. See AHw 876–77.

5. Contra Mullen, *The Divine Council*, 117; as questioned by D. Pardee, review of Mullen, *The Divine Council in Canaanite and Early Hebrew Literature*, *JNES* 45 (1986), 65.

6. UBC 231.

7. There phrases are preceded by '*ab*, "father" (in other words El). See n. 14.

8. Cf. the possibly nondivine usage, *bt qbṣ*, in 1.79.7.

9. Cf. the possibly nondivine usage in 4.120.3.

10. Here I am following the lead of major scholars of Ugaritic studies: Caquot, "Problèmes d'histoire religieuse," 70–71; de Moor, "The Semitic Pantheon of Ugarit," *UF* 2 (1970), 216; Miller, "Aspects of the Religion of Israel," 54; and the works of Pardee cited later. This assessment of the evidence stands in opposition to the otherwise highly informative work of Mullen, *The Divine Council* (see later).

11. See G. del Olmo Lete, *Canaanite Religion*, 101. See also pp. 343, 344–65.

12. CMHE 37, 183; cf. UBC 230–31.

13. UBC 225–34. As Baal's lament to El indicates, El and Athirat have a house while Baal and his "daughters" do not (1.3 IV 48–53, V 38–44; 1.4 I 9–18, IV 50–57; cf. the same model of human household is evident in Danil's lament in 1.17 I 16–27 that he lacks a son like his brothers).

14. For discussion of various options for each word, see *EUT* 85–88; and Y. Avishur, *Studies in Hebrew and Ugaritic Psalms* (Jerusalem: Magnes, 1994), 308–29; see also Pardee, "Ugarit. Texts and Literature," 709; and the bibliography cited in CAT p. 91, sub 1.65; also N. Wyatt, "Arms and the King. The Earliest Allusion to the *Chaoskampf* Motif and Their Implications for the Interpretation of the Ugaritic and Biblical Traditions," *"Und Mose schrieb dieses Lied auf": Studien zum Alten Testament und zum Alten Orient. Festschrift für Oswald Loretz zur Vollendung seines 70. seines Lebensjahres mit Beiträgen von Freunden, Schülern und Kollegen* (ed. M. Dietrich and I. Kottsieper; AOAT 250; Münster: Ugarit-Verlag, 1998), 858–61. Pardee takes lines 1–11 and 12–19 as two syntactical units: "the text becomes essentially bipartite: lines 1–11 a divine list centered on El and Baal, lines 12–19 a statement about El's creative

abilities." I am inclined not to see such a division, but in general I am following Pardee's understanding of the words in lines 1–8 and 12–18 as outlined there and as further expressed in a personal communication (but on line 19 see later notes). Pardee's treatment of this text will appear in his forthcoming volume, *Les Textes rituels* (Ras Shamra-Ougarit; Paris: Éditions Recherche sur les Civilisations, in preparation). I remain very unsure about line 9 (which has been taken as containing divine titles) and about the specific meanings of the nouns in lines 15–19 (see later notes). Wyatt ("Arms," 858–59) takes the initial words in lines 6–8 as imperatives, unlikely given the final-*t* on *nṣbt* in line 7. Some disagreement is perhaps inevitable given the difficulties of this text (as with so many words in Ugaritic), and perhaps we do well to recall "Ginsberg's dictum" (as Marvin Pope used to call it): "[F]or the only people who have never made mistakes in Ugaritic philology are those who have never engaged in it" (Ginsberg, "Interpreting Ugaritic Texts," *JAOS* 70 [1950], 156). It is worth noting as well Ginsberg's lesser known sarcasm about the field: "Each of these texts by itself is a happy hunting-ground for philological sportsmen abounding as it does in lacunae and obscurities, while the intricate and tantalizing problems of the mutual relations of the texts themselves can afford even more ambitious nimrods of research scope for weeks and weeks of congenial activity" (Ginsberg, review of J. Obermann, *Ugaritic Mythology, JCS* 2 [1948], 139).

15. So on the basis of the apparently comparable group of divinities listed in 1.40.33–35 and 1.65.1–4 (following J. C. de Moor, "The Semitic Pantheon of Ugarit," 197, 219):

'ab bn 'il	'il bn 'il
dr bn 'il	dr bn 'il
<mphrt bn 'il>	mphrt bn 'il
tkmn [w] šnm	tkmn w šnm

On the basis of this comparison, one might be inclined to view both first lines as construct chains despite the awkward sense this would produce in the case of 1.65.1 ("El/the god of the sons of El" = El!). On the other hand, this rendering would avoid the apparent repetition of *bn 'il*. See further Mullen, *The Divine Council*, 271. For CAT 1.40, see J. C. de Moor, "An Ugaritic Expiation Ritual and its Old Testament Parallels," *UF* 23 (1991), 283–300; D. Pardee, "The Structure of RS 1.002," *Semitic Studies in Honor of Wolf Leslau: On the Occasion of His Eighty-Fifth Birthday. November 14th, 1991. Volume II* (ed. A. S. Kaye; Wiesbaden: Harrassowitz, 1991), 1181–96.

16. See D. Pardee, "Tukamuna wa Šunama," *UF* 20 (1988), 195–99.

17. The family of El in lines 1–5 is followed by three hypostases of El's qualities. The element **ḥnn* applies only to El in the proper names listed in Gröndahl, *Die Personnamen*, 136. For the element *nṣbt*, cf. the personal name *yṣb*, which Gröndahl (*Die Personnamen*, 169) derives from **nṣb*. This name belongs to the son of Krt, himself said to be *bn 'il*, "a son of El." For the meaning of *nṣbt*, Avishur (*Studies*, 313) compares Aramaic *niṣbĕtā'*, "strength, stability" (Dan 2:41).

18. One might be inclined to see a divinity here because of *'il ḫšm* (1.123.30) in the context of a series of divinities (see the next note). Instead, Pardee would render "The god who shows solicitude" and compares Mari Akkadian *ḫâšu*, "to show solicitude" (following Dietrich and Loretz); *CAD* H:147 (*ḫâšu* B, "to worry") remarks that the "Mari passages are not quite clear." Pardee's translation also assumes asyndesis unmarked by *d-*, and the change in word order may point in this direction. If this text is a prayer, however, these forms could be imperatives addressed to El: "O El, show solicitude! O El, exalt Baal Sapan. . . ." Y. Avishur has taken the text as a prayer and he renders: "El, hasten! El, save! On behalf of [Mount] Zaphon, on behalf of Ugarit" (Avishur is reading *b'd* twice; so also Wyatt, "Arms," 858–59). See Avishur, *Studies in Hebrew and Ugaritic Psalms*, 310. This translation presumes comparison with Akkadian *ḫâšu* A, "to move quickly, to rush to a goal" (*CAD* H: 146).

19. CAT reads 'add. Accordingly, de Moor ("The Semitic Pantheon," 198) compares Alalakh personal name ḫa-aš-ᵈAdad as well as ᵈAdad rapidim. Based on the reading ndd, Pardee renders: "se leve." Assuming this reading, the following phrase bʻd ṣpn (and the following prepositional phrases) may be dependent on this verb. Line 19 remains problematic for this view.

20. Scholars emend either bʻd to bʻl on the basis of the following bʻl (e.g., Pardee); or they emend the following bʻl on the basis of the preceding bʻd (e.g., Avishur, Wyatt).

21. The word mrḥ is perhaps a weapon in 1.6 I 51: "One so weak cannot run / Like Baal, nor handle the lance (mrḥ) / Like the Son of Dagan for he is prostrate." (M. S. Smith in UNP 154; see also 1.16 I 51 as rendered by E. L. Greenstein in UNP 33; 1.92.7, 12). Scholars compare BH rōmaḥ and Egyptian mrḥ. The latter reflects borrowing from a West Semitic word with the order of consonants as found in the Ugaritic word (so UT 19.1547; J. E. Hoch, Semitic Words in Egyptian Texts of the New Kingdom and Third Intermediate Period [Princeton, NJ: Princeton University Press, 1994], 139). Of course, it is possible that 'il, here, as in the following lines, is not the name of the god El, but the substantive used to denote each weapon as "divine."

22. The word nʻit seems to be a tool of some sort in 1.86.21, 4.625.2, 5, 7, 9, 11, 16, 18, and 4.632.3, 7, 11, 16 (in these texts note also mʻṣd and ḥrmtt; see also Akkadian nitu in the Akkadian texts of Ras Shamra, taken as either a weapon [so AHw 798] or tool [so CAD N/2:300]). See J. C. Greenfield, "Ugaritic Lexicographical Notes," JCS 21 (1967), 93; J. F. Healey, "Swords and Ploughshares," UF 15 (1983), 48–49. Given the other two words for weaponry in 1.65.11 and 13, I am inclined to view nʻit similarly in line 12, even if the primary meaning is a tool. Pardee renders the word, "adze" (Pardee, "Ugarit, Texts and Literature," 709). For examples from Ugarit, see A. Caquot and M. Sznycer, Ugaritic Religion (Leiden: Brill, 1980), 24, 26, plates XIII, XXI; several axes bear inscriptions (CAT 6.6–6.10).

23. The word ṣmd suggests a weapon (1.2 IV 11, 15–16, 18, 23–24; 1.6 V 3; see UBC 338–41) rather than a tool (El's "yoke"?). For this term in administrative texts, see R. M. Good, "Some Ugaritic Terms Relating to Draught and Riding Animals," UF 16 (1984), 77–80.

24. Apart from a possibly personal name, dṯn is a hapax. Based on a sacrificial view of šrp in the preceding line, one might guess that some sacrificial sense obtains in the case of dṯn (related to BH dešen? so DLU 138; but this assumes that dšn in 1.108.5 is d + šn instead of dšn; for this text, see R. M. Good, "On RS 24.252," UF 24 [1992], 155–60). However, such a view of šrp is unnecessary (see the previous note). Apparently assuming cognate with BH dešen, Gaster renders "richness" (see EUT 86). I am inclined to relate dṯn here to dṯydṯ in 1.18 I 19, taken by M. Dahood to mean "trample underfoot," but better, "beat" pace Parker (UNP 64) and cognate with BH *dwš (Dahood, Ugaritic-Hebrew Philology [BibetOr 17; Rome: Pontifical Biblical Institute, 1965], 56 no. 714) and apparently Arabic *dyṯ (see J. C. Greenfield, "Amurrite, Ugaritic and Canaanite," Proceedings of the International Conference on Semitic Studies held in Jerusalem, 19–23 July 1965 [Jerusalem: Israel Academy of Sciences and Humanities, 1969], 96 n. 18; A. Rainey, "Observations on Ugaritic Grammar," UF 3 [1971], 159, 5.12). Avishur (Studies 317) compares *dtt, "to thrust, strike hard" and renders "force." Others prefer an abstract such as "honor" (Avishur, Studies, 317, citing Obermann, Ginsberg, and comparing Gaster's "greatness" on the basis of Arabic *srf). For a discussion for a possible Eblaite precedent, see F. Pomponio and P. Xella, Les dieux d'Ebla: Étude analytique des divinités éblaïtes à l'époque des archives royales du IIIe millénaire (AOAT 245; Münster: Ugarit-Verlag, 1997), 391.

25. Ugaritic šrp is a sacrificial term (see G. del Olmo Lete, "The Sacrificial Vocabulary at Ugarit," SEL 12 [1995], 44), except in 1.6 V 14 where it is one step in Mot's destruction.

It is unclear whether a destructive or theophanic connotation would apply here. The *śĕrāpîm* of Isaiah's vision in Isaiah 6 have been related to Ugaritic *šrp* here (*EUT* 87). Would the biblical *serapîm* then be hypostases of this divine quality?

26. The best candidate for a divine attribute in these lines is *knt 'il* if *knt* derives from **kwn*, "to be" and hence means "order" or the like.

27. *ǧdyn* might be a divine attribute as well (*DLU* 155). So Gaster: "Vigour (?)"; see *EUT* 86.

28. Pardee informs me about line 19 that the "best reading of the line as a whole is {bn'il}." Accordingly, he wishes to take the final line as a verbal clause, "El builds," on which the tools (not weapons) and other items in lines 12–19 refer to El's building activity. This approach is hardly impossible, but I confess I find it unpersuasive. He does make the valid point: "If line 19 says simply 'the sons of El,' one is at a loss to explain the different syntaxes in lines 1–12 as compared with lines 12–18." Perhaps line 19 represents a final summary clause, separate from the preceding lines.

29. Cf. Mullen, *The Divine Council*, 273.

30. This overlap is noted by Pardee, "Ugarit. Texts and Literature," 709.

31. On these two figures, see D. Pardee, "Ṯakamuna wa Šunama," *UF* 20 (1988), 195–99.

32. *UBC* 231; cf. Mullen, *The Divine Council*, 114, 117, 269.

33. See Olmo Lete, "The Divine Panoply (KTU 1.65: 12–14)," *AO* 10 (1992), 254–56; Wyatt, "Arms," 858–61.

34. See *CMHE* 40–41; P. D. Miller, "El the Warrior," *HTR* 60 (1967), 411–31, and *DW* 48–58; Mullen, *The Divine Council*, 32–34, 181, 186. See also J. J. M. Roberts, "El," *IDBS* 256; A. G. Vaughan, "*il ǧzr*—An Explicit Epithet of El as Hero/Warrior," *UF* 23 (1993), 423–30 and K. van der Toorn, *Family Religion in Babylonia, Syria and Israel: Continuity and Change in the Forms of Religious Life* (Studies in the History and Culture of the Ancient Near East 7; Leiden: Brill, 1996), 327. Yet Cross and Mullen are correct to regard all other information as indicating at most that El's battles are not extant in the Ugaritic texts and that his theogonic wars lie in the distant past. Regarding Vaughan's attempt to take *ǧzr* as warrior title of El, a point made by J. D. Schloen may be noted: "In mythological texts from Ugarit, therefore, the social category indicated by the term *ǧzr* is that of an unmarried youth who is the son, not the servant, of the household head. Being unmarried, the *ǧzr* is well-suited for warfare and adventure; hence the extended meaning 'hero' or 'soldier' " (Schloen, "The Patrimonial Household in the Kingdom of Ugarit: A Weberian Analysis of Ancient Near Eastern Society" [Ph.D. diss., Harvard University, 1995], 334 n. 154).

35. W. Herrmann, "El," *DDD* 276.

36. See the further discussion in section 4.

37. On these three figures, see further chapter 3, section 1.

38. See N. Wyatt, "Baal's Boars," *UF* 19 (1987), 391–98; cf. *UBC* 113–14 n. 224.

39. Mullen, *The Divine Council*, 213, 269.

40. Amiet, *Corpus des cylindres de Ras Shamra*, 74 and 82, no. 167.

41. De Moor (*The Rise of Yahwism*, 73, 74, 79) asserts that Anat is Baal's spouse and he is therefore El's son-in-law. This scenario is plausible, but it has been seriously questioned by N. H. Walls, Jr., and P. L. Day. See Walls, *The Goddess Anat in the Ugaritic Myth* (SBLDS 135; Atlanta, GA: Scholars, 1992); Day, "Why is Anat a Warrior and Hunter?" *The Bible and the Politics of Exegesis: Essays in Honor of Norman K. Gottwald on His Sixty-Fifth Birthday* (ed. D. Jobling, P. L. Day, and G. T. Sheppard; Cleveland, OH: Pilgrim Press, 1991), 141–146, 329–32. The positions of Walls and Day partially rely on an argument from silence.

42. This point was first made *in nuce* for the Ugaritic texts in M. S. Smith, "Divine

Travel as a Token of Divine Rank," *UF* 16 (1984), 359. See also the extensive contributions of L. K. Handy, "Dissenting Deities or Obedient Angels: Divine Hierarchies in Ugarit and the Bible," *Biblical Research* 35 (1990), 18–35; *Among the Host of Heaven: The Syro-Palestinian Pantheon as Bureaucracy* (Winona Lake, IN: Eisenbrauns, 1994); and "The Appearance of the Pantheon," *The Triumph of Elohim: From Yahwisms to Judaisms* (ed. D. V. Edelman; Grand Rapids, MI: Eerdmans, 1996), 27–43. For further discussion of Handy's work, see the end of this chapter, and n. 76.

43. See N.-E. A. Anderson, "The Role of the Queen Mother in Israelite Society," *CBQ* 45 (1983), 179–94; S. Ackerman, "The Queen Mother and the Cult in Ancient Canaan," *JBL* 112 (1993), 385–401; N. Wyatt, "Asherah," *DDD* 99. For a critique of Ackerman's views, see B. Halpern, "The New Names of Isaiah 62:4: Jeremiah's Reception in the Restoration and the Politics of 'Third Isaiah'," *JBL* 117 (1998), 640 n.46.

44. In contrast, royal mothers bear the title, *mlkt* (e.g., 2.13.1, 15, 2.30.1, 2.36.1, 3, 2.68.1, 2.82.1; cf. 3.1.28). For citations, see J. C. Greenfield, "The Epithets *rbt*//*trrt* in the KRT Epic," *Perspectives on Language and Text: Essays and Poems in Honor of Francis I. Andersen's Sixtieth Birthday July 28, 1985* (ed. E. W. Conrad and E. G. Newing; Winona Lake, IN: Eisenbrauns, 1987), 35–37, esp. 36 n. 6; and C. H. Gordon, "Ugaritic *RBT/RABĪTU*," *Ascribe to the Lord: Biblical & other studies in Memory of Peter C. Craigie* (ed. L. Eslinger & G. Taylor; JSOTS 63; Sheffield: JSOT, 1988), 127–32.

45. See the following chapter.

46. Mullen, *The Divine Council*, 186 n. 122.

47. However, *'adn* here is taken as a royal title by G. del Olmo Lete, "Receta mágica para un infante enfermo (KTU 1.124)," *Sefarad* 52 (1992), 187–92 and *Canaanite Religion*, 310. See later discussion on *'adn*.

48. J. Leclant, "Astarté à cheval d'aprés les représentations égyptiennes," *Syria* 37 (1960), 1–67; R. Stadelmann, *Syrisch-Palästinensische Gottheiten in Ägypten* (Probleme der Ägyptologie 5; Leiden: Brill, 1967), 101–10; N. Wyatt, "Astarte," *DDD* 110–11.

49. For a copy of the picture, see *UBC* 107. For further discussion, see *UBC* 106; T. L. Fenton, "Baal au foudre: of snakes and mountans, myth and message," *Ugarit, religion and culture: Proceedings of the International Colloquium on Ugarit, Religion and Culture. Edinburgh, July 1994. Essays Presented in Honour of Professor John C. L. Gibson* (ed. N. Wyatt, W. G. E. Watson, and J. B. Lloyd; UBL 12; Münster: Ugarit-Verlag, 1996), 49–64.

50. For Baal as warrior: in prayer see 1.119; for incantations, see 1.93 and 1.169; in myth, 1.2 IV, 1.4 VII, 1.6 V 1–4, and 1.6 VI; and in personal names, see Gröndahl, *Die Personnamen*, 142 (under *yd*), 197 (under **dmr*).

51. M. S. Smith, "Kothar wa-Hasis, the Ugaritic Craftsman God" (Ph.D. diss., Yale University, 1985), 463. The characterization, "general factotum," was Marvin Pope's phrase. See also the summary about Kothar in Pardee, "Koshar," *DDD* 490–91. For the view of Kothar as a "Heilbringer," see P. Xella, "Il dio siriano Kothar," *Magia: Studi di Storia delle religioni in memoria di Raffaela Garosi* (ed. P. Xella; Rome: Bulzani Editore, 1976), 124.

52. See Gröndahl, *Die Personennamen*, 152.

53. For *'inš 'ilm* as deceased kings divinized as gods of the palace, see del Olmo Lete, *Canaanite Religion*, 59, 89, 113, 260. Wyatt also proposes *ǵlm* in 1.119.27 as "the Divine Assistant" and as a member of this tier; see Wyatt, *Religious Texts from Ugarit*, 417 n. 9.

54. Mullen, *The Divine Council*, 282.

55. See Mullen, *The Divine Council*, 113–20; also P. D. Miller, "Cosmology and World Order in the Old Testament: The Divine Council as Cosmic-Political Symbol," *Horizons in Biblical Theology* 9 (1987), 53–78; also Miller, "The Divine Council and the Prophetic Call to War," *VT* 18 (1968), 100–7.

56. See the references cited in n. 42.

57. For a discussion of the archaeology of the site as well as its finds (as well as further bibliography), see A. Mazar, *Archaeolog of the Land of the Bible 10,000–586 B.C.E.* (ABRL; New York: Doubleday, 1990), 446–50. For discussions of the inscriptions, see J. A. Emerton, "New Light on Israelite Religion: The Implications of the Inscriptions from Kuntillet 'Ajrud," *ZAW* 94 (1982), 2–20; M. Weinfeld, "Kuntillet 'Ajrûd Inscriptions and Their Significance," *SEL* 1 (1984), 121–30; P. K. McCarter, "Aspects of the Religion of the Israelite Monarchy: Biblical and Epigraphic Data," *Ancient Israelite Religion: Essays in Honor of Frank Moore Cross* (ed. P. D. Miller, Jr, P. D. Hanson, and S. D. McBride; Philadelphia: Fortress, 1987), 137–55; idem, "The Religious Reforms of Hezekiah and Josiah," *Aspects of Monotheism: How God is One* (ed. H. Shanks and J. Meinhardt; Washington, DC: Biblical Archaeology Society, 1997), 74–80; S. M. Olyan, *Asherah and the Cult of Yahweh in Israel* (SBLMS 34; Atlanta, GA: Scholars, 1988), 23–34; J. M. Hadley, *The Cult of Asherah in Ancient Israel and Judah: The Evidence for A Hebrew Goddess* (Oriental Publications series 57; Cambridge: Cambridge University Press, 2000); idem, "Some Drawings and Inscriptions on Two Pithoi from Kuntillet 'Ajrud," *VT* 37 (1987), 180–213; idem, "The Khirbet el-Qom Inscription," *VT* 37 (1987), 50–62; idem, "Chasing Shadows? The Quest for the Historical Goddess," *Congress Volume: Cambridge 1995* (ed. J. A. Emerton; Leiden: Brill, 1997), 169–84; S. A. Wiggins, "The Myth of Asherah: Lion Lady and Serpent Goddess," *UF* 23 (1991), 383–94; idem, *A Reassessment of 'Asherah': A Study According to the Textual Sources of the First Two Millennia B.C.E.* (AOAT 235; Kevelaer: Butzon & Bercker; Neukirchen-Vluyn: Neukirchener Verlag, 1993); M. Dietrich and O. Loretz, *"Jahwe und seine Aschera": Anthropomorphes Kultbild in Mesopotamien, Ugarit und Israel. Das biblische Bilderverbot* (UBL 9; Münster: Ugarit-Verlag, 1992); Keel and Uehlinger, *Gods, Goddesses, and Images of God in Ancient Israel*, 228–48, 332, 369–70; C. Frevel, *Aschera und der Ausschliesslichkeitanspruch YHWHs* (BBB 94; two vols.; Weinheim: Beltz Athenäum, 1995); the response to Frevel in Keel, *Goddesses and Trees, New Moon and Yahweh: Ancient Near Eastern Art and the Hebrew Bible* (JSOTSup 262; Sheffield: Sheffield Academic Press, 1998); and P. Merlo, *La dea Ašratum—Atiratu-Ašera: Un contributo alla storia della religione semitica del Nord* (Mursia: Pontificia Università Lateranense, 1998). See also the survey in S. A. Wiggins, "Asherah Again: Binger's Asherah and the State of Asherah Studies," *JNWSL* 24 (1998), 231–40. For the sake of completeness, the books of T. Binger and R. J. Pettey may be mentioned; Binger, *Asherah: Goddesses in Ugarit, Israel and the Old Testament* (JSOTSup 232; Copenhagen International Seminar 2; Sheffield: Sheffield Academic Press, 1997); Pettey, *Asherah: Goddess of Israel* (American University Studies, Series VII Theology and Religion, 74; New York: Peter Lang, 1990). On this subject, see further chapter 4, section 4.

58. This is not the place to engage into a full critique of this very widespread view, but suffice it to say that the so-called evidence does not tally into such a picture without a leap of faith. It remains quite possible that such a picture was the case in ancient Israel, but what passes for evidence hardly constitutes "hard evidence." Many may retort that few historical ancient realities enjoy such a level of "hard evidence"—and I would agree. Yet this difficulty does not compel historians to accept such conclusions; it may be better to prescind from a historical judgment in the matter (something we should perhaps do more often as a scholarly community). For further discussion, see chapters 4 and 9.

59. See N. Wyatt, "Astarte," *DDD* 112–13, esp. 111; P. Xella, "Resheph," *DDD* 702–03; G. del Olmo Lete, "Deber," *DDD* 231–32. For information on these deities from Ebla, see also Pomponio and Xella, *Les Dieux d'Ebla*, 82, 124.

60. See T. Hiebert, *God of My Victory: The Ancient Hymn in Habakkuk 3* (HSM 38; Atlanta, GA: Scholars, 1986), 4, 92–94, 123; R. D. Haak, *Habakkuk* (VTSup 44; Leiden: Brill, 1992), 83, 90. This phenomenon of military retinues in a theophanic context is noted also later in chapter 4, section 1.

61. The older treatments of Psalm 82 in this vein without reference to the Ugaritic texts include H. S. Nyberg, *Studien zum Hoseabuche: Zugleich ein Beitrag zur Klärung des Problems der Alttestamentlichen Textkritik* (Uppsala Universitets °Arsskrift 1935:6; Uppsala: Almqvist & Wiksells, 1935), 122–25; and O. Eissfeldt, "Neue Götter im alten Testament," *Atti del XIX Congresso Internazionale degli Orientalisti. Roma, 23–29 Settembre 1935-XIII* (Rome: Tipografia del Senato, 1938), 479. The best recent treatment is S. B. Parker, "The Beginning of the Reign of God. Psalm 82 as Myth and Liturgy," *RB* 102 (1995), 532–59. See also J. F. A. Sawyer, "Biblical Alternatives to Monotheism," *Theology* 87 (1984), 172–80; M. Dietrich and O. Loretz, *"Jahwe und seine Aschera": Anthropomorphes Kulbild in Mesopotamien, Ugarit und Israel. Das biblische Bilderverbot* (UBL 9; Münster: Ugarit-Verlag, 1992), 134–57; and A. Schenker, "Le monothéisme israélite: un dieu qui transcende le monde et les dieux," *Bib* 78 (1997), 442–44. Among the commentaries, see K. Seybold, *Die Psalmen* (HAT I/15; Tübingen: Mohr [Siebeck], 1996), 324–26.

62. Psalm 82 belongs to the "elohistic Psalter," thought by many scholars to have undergone a replacement of the name of Yahweh with the title "God" (*'akelōhîm*). I have reservations about this theory although it would point more clearly to Yahweh understood as the subject of this sentence.

63. T. Frymer-Kensky argues that the demise of the gods here leads to a responsibility for humans: "There are no longer any gods—and it is up to *humanity* to ensure that the foundations of the earth do not totter" (*In The Wake of the Goddesses: Women, Culture, and the Biblical Transformation of Pagan Myth* [New York: Free Press, 1992], 106). While this view makes for a powerful modern reading of the text, it is not supported by it. Instead, verse 6 summons God to fill the "power vacuum" created by the demise of all other gods. I take special note of this reading of Psalm 82 because this train of thought forms the basic point of Frymer-Kensky's reading of monotheism more generally, namely, that without other powers humanity is left to exercise great responsibility in the world. Theologically, I find the idea attactive, but I also find little biblical support for the idea that human responsibility is to replace the responsibility associated formerly with other gods.

64. 4QDeut^{q} *bny 'l*[; 4QDeut^{j} *bny 'lwhym*[; LXX *huiōn theou* (cf. LXX variants with *aggelōn* interpolated). For the evidence, see E. Tov, *Textual Criticism of the Hebrew Bible* (Minneapolis: Fortress; Assen/Maastricht: Van Gorcum, 1992), 269; J. A. Duncan, *Qumran Cave 4. IX: Deuteronomy, Joshua, Judges, Kings* (ed. E. Ulrich and F. M. Cross; DJD XIV; Oxford: Clarendon Press, 1995), 90; also BHS to Deuteronomy 32:8 note d. For older bibliography, *EHG* 30 n. 37; and A. Schenker, "Le monothéisme israélite: un dieu qui transcende le monde et les dieux," *Bib* 78 (1997), 438. For an older discussion, see O. Eissfeldt, "Neue Götter im alten Testament," 479. For further discussion, see chapters 8 and 9. L. K. Handy calls the textual variants from the Septuagint and Dead Sea Scrolls "invented text as real text" (*JAOS* 52 [1993], 157); Handy does not say why the Hebrew of Dead Sea Scrolls or the Greek variant represents an "invented text." In the absence of an explanation, it would appear that at least in this case he privileges the Masoretic text to the complete exclusion of textual variants, but it would be unfair to regard him as a "Masoretic fundamentalist."

65. Cf. the echo of Deuteronomy 32:7–9 in Ben Sira 44:2 (cf. verse 23), which reflects the understanding in MT. For discussion, see P. W. Skehan and A. A. DiLella, *The Wisdom of Ben Sira: A New Translation with Notes* (AB 39; New York: Doubleday, 1987), 498.

66. Tov, *Textual Criticism of the Hebrew Bible*, 269. Tov regards the change of *běnê 'ělōhîm*, "divine beings," in Psalm 29:1 to *mišpěḥôt 'ammîm*, "families of the people," in Psalm 96:7 as another example of such an "anti-polytheistic alteration." For the literary dependence of Psalm 96 on Psalm 29, see H. L. Ginsberg, "A Strand in the Cord of Hebrew

Psalmody," *EI* 9 (1969 = W. F. Albright volume), 45–50. Psalm 29 reflects an early expression of Israelite polytheism.

67. For example, see N. Habel, *Yahweh versus Baal: A Conflict of Religious Cultures* (New York: Bookman, 1964), 42.

68. See chapter 9 for a fuller discussion. The book of Jonah, set in the Neo-Assyrian period, apparently affirms both Yahweh as the universal god and the sailors' god. Perhaps then the Neo-Assyrian period marks the transition between the older forms of Israelite polytheism and the newer theology of monotheism. I thank T. J. Lewis for bringing this text to my attention.

69. The issues involving the development of "angels" are more complex than the presentation here suggests. For their analogy of characteristics with higher deities (size; protection, help and battle; divine communication and instruction) and with humans (praise, sacrifice), S. Meier, *The Messenger in the Ancient Semitic World* (HSM 45; Atlanta, GA: Scholars, 1989); and J. T. Greene, *The Role of the Messenger and Message in the Ancient Near East* (Brown Judaic Studies 169; Atlanta GA: Scholars, 1989). See also the very different studies of S. M. Olyan, *A Thousand Thousands Served Him* (TSAJ 36; Tübingen: J. C. Mohr [Siebeck], 1992); K. Koch, "Monotheismus und Angelologie," *Ein Gott allein? JHWH-Verehrung und biblischer Monotheismus im Kontext der israeltischen und altorientalischen Religionsgeschichte* (ed. W. Dietrich and M. A. Klopfenstein; 13. Kolloquium der Schweizerischen Akademie der Geistes-und Sozialwissenschaften, 1993; Freiburg Schweiz: Universitätsverlag, 1994), 565–81; R. Kasher, "Angelology and the Supernal Worlds in the Aramaic Targums to the Prophets," *Journal for the Study of Judaism in the Persian, Hellenistic, and Roman Period* 27/2 (1996), 168–91; I. Nowell, "The Angels Are Here," *Spirit and Life* 92/3 (1996) 16–18.

70. For a partial listing, see *The Dictionary of Classical Hebrew: Volume I: א* (ed. D. J. A. Clines, Executive Editor, J. Elwolde; Sheffield: Sheffield Academic Press, 1993), 253–54.

71. Miller, "Cosmology and World Order," 72.

72. Miller, "Cosmology and World Order," 72–73.

73. See Levenson, *Creation and the Persistence of Evil*, 131. Professor Benjamin Sommers has orally made essentially the same suggestion to me.

74. Handy, *Among the Host of Heaven*. For another treatment in this larger vein, see also J. Macdonald, "An Assembly at Ugarit?" *UF* 11 (1979), 515–26.

75. Handy, *Among the Host of Heaven*, 13–14.

76. Schloen has criticized Handy's application of Weber's notion of bureaucracy to the Ugaritic pantheon:

> Lowell Handy has, however, recently defended the proposition that the Syro-Palestininan pantheon reflects the *bureaucratic* structure of mundane society. In my view this is ananchronistic and improbable. Unlike the late-first millennium Near Eastern mythological compositions that are preserved in apocalyptic literature, the Ugaritic myths do not mention heavenly armies and grand battles. The scale is much smaller and the focus is the extended family; thus social conflict is typified by the factional rivalry for power and privilege among patrilaterals within larger patriarchal households. The Ugaritic myths accordingly validate an authority structure—based on familiar household relationships—that existed at all levels of society, from the royal family to the humblest household in the kingdom.

Schloen, "The Patrimonial Household," 400. It is not my intention, nor do I have sufficient expertise, to enter into the theoretical issues in the sociological theory of Max Weber that Handy and Schloen use. Schloen has laid the issues out on pp. 151–60. On the application of Weberian theory to Ugaritic mythology, see also L. Karkajian, "La maisonnée patrimoniale divine à Ougarit: une analyse wébérienne du dieu de la mort, Mot" (Ph.D. diss., University of Montreal, 1999). Directed by Dr. Robert David, the dissertation is now published on the internet by Presses Universitaires de Montréal at: www.pum.montreal.ca/theses/pilote/karkajian/these.html. This work came to my attention after the completion of this study.

77. For examples and discussion, see *EHG* 10.

78. See, for example, the Sumerian composition often called "Enki and the World Order." For discussion, see H. L. J. Vanstiphout, "Why Did Enki Organize the World?" *Sumerian Gods and Their Representations* (ed. I. L. Finkel and M. J. Geller; Groningen: Styx, 1996), 117–33. For bureaucracy in Mesopotamia, see the essays in *The Organization of Power: Aspects of Bureaucracy in the Ancient Near East* (ed. M. Gibson and R. Biggs; SAOC 46; Chicago: Oriental Institute of the University of Chicago, 1987).

3. The Divine Family

1. A point nicely emphasized by G. del Olmo Lete, *Canaanite Religion According to The Liturgical Texts of Ugarit* (trans. W. G. E. Watson; Bethesda, MD: CDL Press, 1999), 101. For some of these texts, see also chapter 2, sections 1 and 2.

2. Wyatt, "Baal, Dagan, and Fred: A Rejoinder," *UF* 24 (1992), 429.

3. Schloen, "The Patrimonial Household in the Kingdom of Ugarit: A Weberian Analysis of Ancient Near Eastern Society" (Ph.D. diss., Harvard University, 1995), esp. 399. See also the ranging observations of C. H. Gordon, "Father's Sons and Mother's Daughters in Ugaritic, in the Ancient Near East and in Mandaic Magic Texts," *"Und Mose schrieb dieses Lied auf": Studien zum Alten Testament und zum Alten Orient. Festschrift für Oswald Loretz zur Vollendung seines 70. seines Lebenjahres mit Beiträgen von Freunden, Schülern und* `Kollegen (ed. M. Dietrich and I. Kottsieper; AOAT 250; Münster: Ugarit-Verlag, 1998), 319–24. For households in contemporary Akkadian texts from Syria, see further the essays in *Houses and Households in Ancient Mesopotamia: Papers Read at the 40th Rencontre Assyriologique Internationale. Leiden, July 5–8, 1993* (ed. K. R. Veenhof; Leiden: Nederlands Historisch-Archaeologisch Institut te Istanbul, 1996).

4. Schloen, "The Exile of Disinherited Kin in *KTU* 1.12 and *KTU* 1.23," *JNES* 52 (1993), 209–20.

5. See also L. Karkajian, "La maisonnée patrimoniale divine à Ougarit: une analyse wébérienne du dieu de la mort, Mot" (Ph.D. diss., University of Montreal, 1999); published on the internet by Presses Universitaires de Montréal at www.pum.montreal.ca/theses/pilote/karkajian/these.html.

6. Good, "On RS 24.252," *UF* 24 (1992), 160.

7. H. A. Hoffner, *Hittite Myths* (ed. G. M. Beckman; SBL Writings from the Ancient World Series 2; Atlanta, GA: Scholars, 1990), 69. For the same parallelism of 77//88, see also CAT 1.5 V 19–22. For 77, see also Judges 8:14.

8. See M. H. Pope, "Seven, Seventh, Seventy," *IDB* 4:285–95; F. C. Fensham, "The Numeral Seventy in the Old Testament and the Family of Jerubbaal, Ahab, Panammuwa and Athirat," *PEQ* 109 (1977), 113–15; J. C. de Moor, "Seventy!" *"Und Mose schrieb dieses Lied auf": Studien zum Alten Testament und zum Alten Orient. Festschrift für Oswald Loretz zur Vollendung seines 70. seines Lebenjahres mit Beiträgen von Freunden, Schülern und Kollegen* (ed. M. Dietrich and I. Kottsieper; AOAT 250; Münster: Ugarit-Verlag, 1998), 199–203.

9. See A. Biran and J. Naveh, "The Tel Dan Fragment: A New Fragment," *IEJ* 45 (1995), 12–13; and most recently S. B. Parker, *Stories in Scripture and Inscriptions: Comparative Studies on Narratives in Northwest Semitic Inscriptions and the Bible* (New York: Oxford University Press, 1997), 46, 58.

10. J. Day, "Ugarit and the Bible: Do They Presuppose the Same Canaanite Mythology

and Religion?" *Ugarit and the Bible: Proceedings of the International Symposium on Ugarit and the Bible. Manchester, September, 1992* (ed. G. J. Brooke, A. H. W. Curtis, and J. F. Healey; UBL 11; Munster: Ugarit-Verlag, 1994), 38–39.

11. *TO* 1.214 n. k.

12. S. E. Loewenstamm compares this filial devotion with the piety demonstrated by Shem and Japhet to their drunken father, Noah, in Genesis 9:20–24. See Loewenstamm, "Ham," *Enyclopaedia Miqra'it* 3:163; and M. Garsiel, *Biblical Names: A Literary Study of Midrashic Derivations and Puns* (Ramat-Gan: Bar Ilan University, 1991), 139–40. References are courtesy of Dr. David Goldenberg.

13. Del Olmo Lete, *Canaanite Religion*, 273–74.

14. Del Olmo Lete, *Canaanite Religion*, 257.

15. Del Olmo Lete, *Canaanite Religion*, 208–09.

16. Karkajian, "La maisonnée patrimoniale divine à Ougarit."

17. See N. Walls, *The Goddess Anat in Ugaritic Myth*; and P. L. Day, "Anat: Ugarit's 'Mistress of Animals'," *JNES* 51 (1992), 186. See also Day, "Why Is Anat a Warrior and Hunter?" *The Bible and the Politics of Exegesis: Essays in honor of Norman K. Gottwald on His Sixty-Fifth Birthday* (ed. D. Jobling, P. L. Day, and G. T. Sheppard; Cleveland, OH: Pilgrim Press, 1991), 141–46, 329–32. T. J. Lewis (personal communication) has suggested to me the possibility that if Anat were the daughter of a concubine, it might explain why her mother goes unnamed in the texts; perhaps Anat reflects the situation of concubines' daughters whose father would not be obliged to arrange a full marriage. Her liminal status as unmarried, but with access to her father, El, as perhaps sexually active, but not as a wife (as a concubine herself?), may reflect this status. On concubines in the family, see the later discussion. Would Baal and Anat's mythological kinship as siblings reflect a shared status below the other children in the family of El and Athirat?

18. Frymer-Kensky, *In the Wake of the Goddess: Women, Culture, and the Biblical Transformation of Pagan Myth* (New York: Free Press, 1992), 65.

19. De Moor, *The Rise of Yahwism*, 73, 74, 79.

20. Walls, *The Goddess Anat in the Ugaritic Myth*; Day, "Why Is Anat a Warrior and Hunter?" 141–6, 329–32.

21. *ANET* 200–01. For further examples of the identification of Seth with Baal in New Kingdom Egypt, see R. Stadelmann, *Syrisch-palästinensische Gottheiten in Ägypten* (Probleme der Ägyptologie 5; Leiden: Brill, 1967), 27–47; *ANET* 249; Cornelius, *The Iconography of the Canaanite Gods Reshef and Ba'al*. The identification of Baal and Seth may be reflected in the divine name Bolchoseth found on amulets, *defixiones*, and in formularies dating to the Hellenistic-Roman period. For discussion, see J. G. Gager (ed.), *Curse Tablets and Binding Spells from the Ancient World* (New York: Oxford University Press, 1992), 266.

22. *ANET* 15. See Te Velde (*Seth, God of Confusion: A Study of his Role in Egyptian Mythology and Religion* [Problem der Ägyptologie 6; Leiden: Brill, 1967], 29–30), seconded by Walls (*The Goddess Anat in Ugaritic Myth*, 144–52) and P. L. Day ("Anat: Ugarit's 'Mistress of Animals'," 186; idem, "Why Is Anat a Warrior and Hunter?" 141–46, 329–32).

23. A. Dupont-Sommer, "Une stèle araméene d'un prêtre de Ba'al trouvée en Égypte," *Syria* 33 (1956), 79–80. cf Day, "Anat," *DDD* 72.

24. Cross (*CMHE* 17, 165–66 n. 86), Mullen (*The Divine Council*, 214), and others understand '*nn* originally as "clouds" (i.e., servants for Baal) and hence "servants." Yet R. M. Good observes that '*nn* applies to servants belonging to figures other than Baal. See Good, "Clouds Messengers," *UF* 10 (1978), 436–37; *UBC* 292–93.

25. P. Amiet, *Corpus des cylindres de Ras Shamra—Ougarit II: Sceaux-cylindres en hématite et pierres diverses* (Ras Shamra—Ougarit IX; Paris: Éditions Recherche sur les Civilisations, 1992), 68 discussing 70 and 78, no. 141–143.

26. The women who engage in sexual relations with El in 1.23 may belong to this category. See M. Dijkstra, "Astral Myth of the Birth of Shahar and Shalim (KTU 1.23)," *"Und Mose schrieb dieses Lied auf": Studien zum Alten Testament und zum Alten Orient. Festschrift für Oswald Loretz zur Vollendung seines 70. seines Lebenjahres mit Beiträgen von Freunden, Schülern und Kollegen* (ed. M. Dietrich and I. Kottsieper; AOAT 250; Münster: Ugarit-Verlag, 1998), 287.

27. For a maximal case for Athirat's maritime religious significance, see A. J. Brody, " 'Each Man Cried Out to His God': The Specialized Religion of Canaanite and Phoenician Seafarers* (HSM 58; Atlanta, GA: Scholars, 1998), 26–30. See also Baal Sapan as "patron of mariners," according to M. Dijkstra, "Semitic Worship at Serabit el-Khadim (Sinai)," *ZAH* 10 (1997), 90.

28. On *ml'ak*, see E. L. Greenstein, "Trans-Semitic Equivalency and the Derivation of Hebrew *ml'kh*," *UF* 11 (1979), 329–36; Mullen, *The Divine Council*, 210; S. Meier, *The Messenger in the Ancient Semitic World* (HSM 45; Atlanta, GA: Scholars, 1989); and J. T. Greene, *The Role of the Messenger and Message in the Ancient Near East* (Brown Judaic Studies 169; Atlanta, GA: Scholars, 1989).

29. See further the language of *nḥlt* applied to gods' homes (1.3 III 30, IV 20, VI 16; 1.4 VIII 14; 1.15 II 16); the word, **nḥl*, "heir," is very common in Ugaritic economic documents. See Pardee, "Ugarit. Texts and Literature," 713; Schloen, "The Patrimonial Household," 68. For the same vocabulary at Emar, see D. Arnaud, "Le vocabulaire du l'héritage dans les textes syriens du moyen-Euphrate à la fin de l'âge du Bronze Récent," *SEL* 12 (1995), 21–26. For an important general discussion at Ugarit, see Schloen, "The Patrimonial Household." For helpful reflections on the "home" in antiquity, see D. Cave, "The Domicile in the Study and Teaching of the Sacred," *The Sacred and the Scholars: Comparative Methodologies for the Study of Primary Religious Data* (ed. T. A. Idinipulos and E. A. Yonan; Numen LXXIII; Leiden: Brill, 1996), 156–68.

30. See Schloen, "The Patrimonial Household," esp. 41, 73. In the general approach and areas of data pertaining to this subject, Schloen follows his mentor, L. E. Stager, "The Archeology of the Family in Ancient Israel," *BASOR* 260 (1985), 1–35. See also C. Meyers, " 'To Her Mother's House': Considering a Counterpart to the Israelite *Bêt 'āb*," *The Bible and the Politics of Exegesis: Essays in Honor of Norman K. Gottwald on His Sixty-Fifth Birthday* (ed. D. Jobling, P. L. Day, and G. T. Sheppard; Cleveland, OH: Pilgrim Press, 1991), 39–51; S. Bendor, *The Social Structure of Ancient Israel* (Jerusalem Biblical Studies 7; Jerusalem: Simor, 1996); and K. Van der Toorn, *Family Religion in Babylonia, Syria and Israel: Continuity and Change in the Forms of Religious Life* (Studies in the History and Culture of the Ancient Near East 7; Leiden: Brill, 1996), 151–205. For an older appreciation of the family as the basic unit of society, see I. Mendelsohn, "The Family in the Ancient Near East," *BA* 11 (1948), 24–40. See also economic emphasis on the family unit by B. Gordon, "Lending at Interest: Some Jewish, Greek, and Christian Approaches, 800 BC–AD 100," *History of Political Economy* 14 (1982), 411.

31. See J. C. de Moor, "The Semitic Pantheon of Ugarit," *UF* 2 (1970), 188; *DLU* 100–01; Schloen, "The Patrimonial Household," 336–37.

32. The word has been taken as "patron" (*DLU* 9). The background here is familial, given the equation of this word with Akkadian *abu*, "father," in *Ugaritica* V, text 130 ii 9', and the parallelism of *'adn* with *'um* in 1.24.33–34 (DLU 9 renders *'adn* in 1.24.33 by "senör padre"). Note also the attestation of the family term *'ad* for "father" (1.23.32, 43; cf. 1.172.23; 2.26.30), from which *'adn* is derived (see *UT* 19.352; *UBC* 150 n. 58; see further *DLU* 9). For further evidence in favor of viewing *'adn* here as a familial term, see the later discussion.

33. Schloen ("The Patrimonial Household," 336, 337) translates "his two married

sons." I accept this as an interpretation (note the lack of *w-* between the two nominal units), and I prefer to preserve in translation the appositional character of the units *ṯn bnh* and *bʻlm*. Apposition obtains also in *w ʼadnhm ṯr*.

34. Ugaritic *nʻr* occurs once in a mythological text (1.114.28), but the context is unclear (see *UNP* 195). It is attested in a number of administrative texts (4.60.3; 4.179.3; 4.362.3; 4.402.2; 4.786.1; 4.788.4, 7). On the social significance of this term, see Stager, "The Archaeology of the Family in Ancient Israel," citing H. P. Stähli's definition: "a *naʻar* is an unmarried male who has not yet become a 'head of household'." In someone's household a *nʻr* is therefore a "retainer." So also Schloen, "The Patrimonial Household," 333.

35. Schloen ("The Patrimonial Household," 337 n. 1) comments: "The term *ḫpṯ is cognate to* Akk *ḫupšu*, which seems to denote a low-ranking person or dependent peasant who nonetheless has a household of his own; i.e., a client. . . . The *ḫbṯ* is thus distinguished from the *nʻrm* (l. 5) who are domestic retainers without households of their own." More research is warranted on the precise sense of these terms specifically in the Ugaritic administrative texts.

36. It is because of the consistent collocation of sons with *bʻlm* that I am not inclined to view the latter here as "workers," a translation philologically but not contextually defensible.

37. Noted already in *EHG* 51.

38. So A. H. W. Curtis, "Some Observations on 'Bull' Terminology in the Ugaritic Texts and the Old Testament," *OTS* 26 (1990), 17–31, esp. 30–31. See also *YGC* 120.

39. Concerning Dagan in the Ugaritic texts and Syro-Mesopotamia more generally, see J. F. Healey, "Dagon," *DDD*, 216–19. For Dagan at Emar, see Emar 379.5 and 383.88'. For Baal and Dagan at Ekalte/Tell Munbaqa, see W. Mayer, "Eine Urkunde über Grundstückskäufe aus Ekalte/Tell Munbaqa," *UF* 24 (1992), 263–74, esp. 272.

40. For this word, see the options discussed in M. Dietrich, "Ugaritische Lexicographie," *SEL* 12 (1995), 113–16.

41. The same figure as *rpʼu mlk ʻlm* (1.108.1)? On this figure and the *rpʼum*, see section 4.

42. F. Gröndahl, *Die Personennamen der Texte aus Ugarit* (Studia Pohl 1; Rome: Päpstliches Bibelinstitut, 1967), 86, 89.

43. Gröndahl, *Die Personnamen der Texte*, 99; cf. Pardee, "An Evaluation of the Proper Names from Ebla from a West Semitic Perspective: Pantheon Distribution according to Genre," *Eblaite Personal Names and Semitic Name-Giving: Papers of a Symposium in Rome July 15–17, 1985* (ed. A. Archi; Archivi Reali di Ebla: Studi I; Rome: Missione Archaeologica Italiana in Siria, 1988), 139 n. 90. This instance of "Genuspolarität" is not exceptional; see also the name *adānu-ummu*, "Lord is mother" (Gröndahl, *Die Personnamen*, 46) and *špšmlk*, "Shapshu is king" (Gröndahl, *Die Personnamen*, 195).

44. Pardee, "An Evaluation of the Proper Names," 131–33. The topic of popular religion at Ugarit remains relatively unexplored; for some preliminary remarks, see M. Yon, "Recherche sur la civilisation ougaritiques: fouilles de Ras Shamra 1979," *La Syrie au Bronze Récent* (Paris: Éditions Recherche sur les civilisations, 1982), 14–16.

45. See the convenient resource of J. Aboud, *Die Rolle des Königs und seiner Familie nach den Texten von Ugarit* (Forschungen zur Anthropologie und Religionsgeschichte 27; Münster: Ugarit-Verlag, 1994), esp. 123–90.

46. For the family in the ancient Middle East generally, see Schloen, "The Patrimonial Household," 216–29.

47. Pardee, personal communication (20 April 1998).

48. See Rainey, "The Kingdom of Ugarit," 88.

49. For the distribution of sacred sites, see M. Yon, "Ugarit: History and Archaeology," *ABD* 6:703. See also Yon, *The City of Ugarit at Tell Ras Shamra* (Winona Lake, IN: Eisenbrauns, 2000, in press).

50. Yon, "Ugarit: History and Archaeology," *ABD* 6:697, 700, 702; Yon, *The City of Ugarit at Tell Ras Shamra*.

51. Yon, "Ugarit: History and Archaeology," 704.

52. KAI 26; ANET 653–54. See Y. Muffs, *Love & Joy: Law, Language and Religion in Ancient Israel* (New York: Jewish Theological Seminary of America, 1992), 57.

53. KAI 24; ANET 654–55. See Muffs, *Love & Joy*, 57.

54. Compare the typology proposed by R. R. Steiglitz for what he calls "the Old Semitic core of deities," namely "a celestial set consisting of Hadda, 'Athtar, Astapil, Kabkab, Suinu, and UTU," and "a terrestrial set consisting of Il, Dagan, Hayyum, Kamish, Malik, and Rasap" (Steiglitz, "Ebla and the Gods of Canaan," *Eblaitica: Essays on the Ebla Archives and Eblaite Language. Volume 2* (ed. C. H. Gordon and G. A. Rendsburg; Publications of the Center for Ebla Research at New York University; Winona Lake, IN: Eisenbrauns, 1990], 82–83).

55. For an older, maximal investigation along these lines, see D. Nielsen, *Ras Šamra Mythologie und Biblische Theologie* (Abhandlungen fuur die Kunde des Morgenlandes XXI/4; Leipzig: 1936; repr. Nendeln, Liechtenstein: Kaus Repint Ltd., 1966). For Nielsen, the astral family was the older Semitic group while the storm-god was later. This "chronology of divinity" cannot be sustained with the oldest attested textual material. See J. J. M. Roberts, *The Earliest Semitic Pantheon: A Study of the Semitic Deities Attested in Mesopotamia before Ur III* (Baltimore/London: Johns Hopkins, 1972); F. Pomponio and P. Xella, *Les dieux d'Ebla: Étude analytique des divinités éblaïtes à l'époque des archives royales du IIIe millénaire* (AOAT 245; Münster: Ugarit-Verlag, 1997).

56. See del Olmo Lete, *Canaanite Religion*, 129, 285–86. See further pp. 199, 243, 289 n. 105. I am open to the possibility that the royal cult of infernal and astral deities reflects beliefs about the royal afterlife that involves descent to the underworld followed by some form of heavenly exaltation characterized as "astralization" (becoming one like the stars). This notion perhaps lies at the base of the "astral Dumuzi" (see chapter 6, section 3 for the discussion of Dumuzi/Tammuz in this vein) and perhaps later expressions of resurrection in Daniel 12:3. It is possible that such a conceptualization of royal afterlife also informs the apparent juxtaposition of Hadad and the king in the afterlife together in KAI 214.16, 21. On this juxtaposition, see J. C. Greenfield, "Un rite religieux aramén et ses parallèles," *RB* 80 (1973), 46–52; *EHG* 30.

57. For the readings, see CAT and Parker, *UNP* 182.

58. Also Parker, *UNP* 182.

59. See Parker, "Shahar," *DDD* 754–55; and H. B. Huffmon, "Shalem," *DDD*, 755–57. On the mythological motifs in 1.23, see Schloen, "The Exile of Disinherited Kin in KTU 1.12 and KTU 1.23," 209–20; Wyatt, "The Theogony Motif in Ugarit and the Bible," 395–419; Dijkstra, "Astral Myth of the Birth of Shahar and Shalim (KTU 1.23)," 265–87; especially 270, 274–79.

60. For a recent discussion of Yarih, see S. A. Wiggins, "What's in a Name? Yarih at Ugarit," *UF* 30 (1999), 761–79.

61. For convenience, see J. C. de Moor, "'Athtartu the Huntress (KTU 1.92)," *UF* 17 (1985) 225–30. See further M. Dijkstra, "The Myth of Astarte, the Huntress (KTU 1.92). New Fragments," *UF* 26 (1994), 113–26.

62. See section 4 for this text. The view that the stars in 1.43.2–3 represent the deified dead in the underworld may be doubted. So see the critical discussion in M. Dietrich and

O. Loretz, *"Jahwe und seine Aschera": Anthropomorphes Kultbild in Mesopotamien, Ugarit und Israel. Das biblische Bilderverbot* (UBL 9; Münster: Ugarit-Verlag, 1992), 50–51. For another indication of cultic devotion to the stars, see apparently 1.164.15.

63. B. Schmidt ("Moon," *DDD*, 587–88) argues that the moon is disparaged in 1.114 and the Ugaritic texts elevate the sun. This state of affairs would represent, according to Schmidt, "an exception to the rule in early Levantine lunar traditions." This reading of 1.114 is speculative, and even if it were correct, Schmidt reconstructs too much on the basis of it. He rejects the view of Yarih as gate-keeper, but it is hardly more speculative than his own view. Schmidt provides no real basis for his view as "more likely the case." And if anything, CAT 1.24 would hardly support any diminishment of the moon-god. The god-list of 1.118 lists Yarih well before Shapshu, again failing to support Schmidt's claim. Yet the two astral bodies may have developed separate mythologies, but this in itself does not indicate a disparity of status.

64. Dijkstra, "The Ugaritic-Hurrian Sacrificial Hymn to El (RS 24.278 = CAT 1.128)," *UF* 25 (1993), 161.

65. Emar 378.39. See D. Arnaud, *Recherches au pays d'Aštata. Emar VI, tome 3: texts sumériens et accadiens* (Paris: Editions Recherche sur les Civilisations, 1986), 373; noted and discussed in M. S. Smith, "The God Athtar in the Ancient Near East and His Place in KTU 1.6 I," *Solving Riddles and Untying Knots: Biblical, Epigraphic, and Semitic Studies in Honor of Jonas C. Greenfield* (ed. Z. Zevit, S. Gitin, and M. Sokoloff; Winona Lake, IN: Eisenbrauns, 1995), 628–29.

66. See P. Bordreuil, *Catalogue des sceaux ouest-sémitiques inscrits de la Bibliothèque Nationale, du musée du Louvre et du Musée biblique et Terre Sainte* (Paris, 1986), 75 no. 85. See also the reference to Arabs called "the people of Atarsamain" (ᵘᵃ'lu ša ᵈAtaršamain) in Assurbanipal's royal annals (for discussion, see Smith, "The God Athtar," 633, esp. n. 47).

67. See T. Jacobsen, *Treasures of Darkness: A History of Mesopotamian Religion* (New Haven/London: Yale, 1976), 140; J. J. M. Roberts, *The Earliest Semitic Pantheon: A Study of Semitic Deities Attested in Mesopotamia before Ur III* (Johns Hopkins Near Eastern Studies; Baltimore: Johns Hopkins University Press, 1972), 39–40; W. Heimpel, "A Catalog of Near Eastern Venus Deities," *Syro-Mesopotamian Studies* 4/3 (1982), 14–15.

68. See J. Gray, "The Desert God 'Attr in the Literature and Religion of Canaan," *JNES* 8 (1949), 72–83, and *The Legacy of Canaan* (VTSup 5; sec. ed.; Leiden: Brill, 1965), 170; A. Caquot, "Le dieu 'Athtar et les textes de Ras Shamra," *Syria* 35 (1958), 51; U. Oldenburg, *The Conflict between El and Ba'al in Canaanite Religion* (Supplementa ad Numen, III; Leiden: Brill, 1969), 39–45.

69. Fulco, *The Canaanite God Rešep* American Oriental Series; (New Haven, CT: American Oriental Society, 1976), 39–40. See also T. de Jong and W. H. van Soldt, "Re-dating an Early Solar Eclipse Record (KTU 1.78). Implications for the Ugaritic Calendar and for the Secular Accelerations of the Earth and the Moon," *JEOL* 30 (1987–88), 65–77; D. Pardee and N. Swerdlow, "Not the Earliest Solar Eclipse," *Nature* 363 (1993), 406. Note also G. del Olmo Lete, "Ug. ḥgb y slḥ como material sacrificial," *AO* 10 (1992), 151–52.

70. Keel and Uehlinger, *Gods, Goddesses, and Images of God*, 310–11, 312–15, fig. 308; 402; Keel, *Goddesses and Trees, New Moon and Yahweh: Ancient Near Eastern Art and the Hebrew Bible* (JSOTSup 261; Sheffield: Sheffield Academic Press, 1998), 44.

71. A. J. Brody, " *'Each Man Cried Out to His God': The Specialized Religion of Canaanite and Phoenician Seafarers* (HSM 58; Atlanta SA: Scholars, 1998), 27.

72. El is said to survive in South Arabian religion as well. U. Oldenburg, "Above the Stars of El. El in South Arabic Religion," *ZAW* 82 (1970), 187–208; J. Ryckmans, "South Arabia, Religion of," *ABD* 6:172.

73. Epigraphic South Arabian sources may support this approach to Athirat. According to A. Jamme, Athirat is the name of a Qatabanian solar goddess and spouse of the moon-god. See Jamme, "La religion sud-arabe préislamique," *Histoire des religions* 4 (publié sous la direction de M. Brillant et R. Aigrain; Paris: Bloud et Gay, 1956), 266. See also G. Ryckmans, *Les religions arabes préislamiques* (sec. ed.; Bibliothèque de Muséon XXVI; Louvain: Publications universitaires, 1951), 44. See also S. A. Wiggins, *A Reassessment of Asherah: A Study According to the Textual Sources of the First Two Millenia [sic]* B.C.E. (AOAT 235; Kevelaer: Butzon & Bercker; Neukirchen-Vluyn: Neukirchener Verlag, 1993), 161–62.

74. See Caquot, "Problèmes d'histoire religieuse," 70. Similarly, J. Ryckmans has suggested that the South Arabian cult of El was displaced by the cult of Athtar; Ryckmans, "South Arabia," 172.

75. See F. Stolz, *Strukturen und Figuren im Kult von Jerusalem* (BZAW 118; Berlin: de Gruyter, 1980), 181–218.

76. Oldenburg, *The Conflict between El and Ba'al in Canaanite Thought*, 18.

77. See P. Raabe, *Obadiah* (AB 24D; New York: Doubleday, 1996), 132–33.

78. Cf. Obadiah 3. See Raabe, *Obadiah*, 132–33.

79. G. I. Davies (*Ancient Hebrew Inscriptions: Corpus and Concordance* [Cambridge: Cambridge University Press, 1991], 492) lists 14 instances.

80. On *šlm* in Hebrew personal names, see Davies, *Ancient Hebrew Inscriptions*, 495–96, who lists 23 instances.

81. So J. H. Tigay, "Israelite Religion: The Onomastic and Epigraphic Evidence," *Ancient Israelite Religion: Essays in Honor of Frank Moore Cross* (ed. P. D. Miller, Jr., P. D. Hanson, and S. D. McBride; Philadelphia: Fortress, 1987), 164 and 166 nn. n, o, and p.

82. S. M. Olyan, *Asherah and the Cult of Yahweh* (SBLMS 34; Atlanta, GA: Scholars, 1988), 38–61; followed in *EHG* 19, as part of the larger process of convergence in Israelite religion.

83. Taylor, *Yahweh and the Sun: Biblical and Archaeological Evidence for Sun Worship in Ancient Israel* (JSOTSup 111; Sheffield: Sheffield Academic Press, 1993), 105–06, 258.

84. B. Halpern, " 'Brisker Pipes than Poetry': The Development of Israelite Monotheism," *Judaic Perspectives on Ancient Israel* (ed. J. Neusner, B. A. Levine, and E. S. Frerichs; Philadelphia: Fortress, 1987), 94, 98; idem, "Jerusalem and the Lineages in the Seventh Century BCE," 81, 83–84.

85. Taylor, *Yahweh and the Sun*, 105–06.

86. See H. Spickermann, *Juda unter Assur in der Sargonidenzeit* (FRLANT 129; Göttingen: Vandenhoeck und Ruprecht, 1982); so too in the iconographic survey of Keel, *Goddesses and Trees*, 62–109. The latter's particular emphasis on Aramean dispersion for astral imagery perhaps diverts his attention from the full force of the astral evidence in the Ugaritic texts. For the question of Assyrian influence, see the considerably more qualified study of S. W. Holloway, "The Case for Assyrian Religious Influence in Israel and Judah" (Ph.D. diss., University of Chicago, 1992).

87. See Taylor, *Yahweh and the Sun*, 105–06, 260–61.

88. See the summary of scholarly discussion in T. Hiebert, *God of My Victory: The Ancient Hymn in Habakkuk 3* (HSM 38; Atlanta, GA: Scholars, 1986), 100.

89. See the discussion in section 1.

90. The name of Dagan has been derived from Arabic **dajana*, "to be cloudy, rainy" (H. Wehr, *A Dictionary of Modern Written Arabic* [ed. J. M. Cowan; third ed.; Ithaca, NY: Spoken Languages Services, 1976], 245). See W. F. Albright, *JAOS* 40 (1920) 319; D. Marcus, "The Term 'Chin' in the Semitic Languages" *BASOR* 226 (1977), 53–60; S. E. Loewenstamm, "Did the Goddess Anat Wear Side-Whiskers and a Beard? A Reconsideration," *UF* 14 (1982), 120. F. Renfroe (*Arabic-Ugaritic Lexical Studies* [ALASP 5; Münster: Ugarit-

Verlag, 1992], 91–94) and J. F. Healey (review of F. Renfroe, *Arabic-Ugaritic Lexical Studies*, *UF* 25 [1993], 507) are critical of this etymology, given the distance in time and space.

91. Ginsberg, *ANET* 140 n. 1.

92. On this text *PE* 1.10.18–19, see H. W. Attridge and R. A. Oden, *Philo of Byblos. The Phoenician History: Introduction, Critical Text, Translation, Notes* (CBQMS 9; Washington, DC: The Catholic Biblical Association of America, 1981), 50–51. For the issue, see *EUT* 47 n. 95; Mullen, *The Divine Council*, 19–20.

93. For Demarous = *dmrn* in 1.4 VII 39, see *BOS* 2.198. See also *CMHE* 15 n. 14; cf. E. Lipiński, "The 'Phoenician History' of Philo of Byblos," *BiOr* 40 (1983), 309.

94. *EUT* 47 n. 95; Mullen, *The Divine Council*, 19–20.

95. See C. E. L'Heureux, *Rank Among the Canaanite Gods: El, Ba'al and the Repha'im* (HSM 21; Missoula, MT: Scholars, 1979), 29–30, 31–32.

96. H. Hoffner has arrived at a comparable conclusion for Kumarbi and the Storm-god, that they do not stand in a single line; instead, their succession represents one dynastic line supplanting another. See Hoffner, "Hittite Mythological Texts: A Survey," *Unity and Diversity: Essays in the History, Literature and Religion of the Ancient Near East* (ed. H. Goedicke and J. J. M. Roberts; Baltimore: Johns Hopkins University Press, 1975), 136–45. The succession of generations in the Hittite-Hurrian Kumarbi cycles might suggest the equation of Ouranos with Anu (L'Heureux, *Rank Among the Canaanite Gods*, 30–31), but Kumarbi has been equated with both El and Dagan (see L'Heureux, *Rank Among the Canaanite Gods*, 39–40, for cautions).

97. *ANET* 519. See also Hofner, "The Elkunirsa Myth Reconsidered," *RHA* 23/76 (1965), 5–16.

98. Caquot, "Le dieu 'Athtar et les textes de Ras Shamra," 55. See also H. Gese, in H. Gese, M. Höfner, and K. Rudolph, *Die Religionen Altsyriens, Atlarabiens und der Mandäer* (Die Religionen der Menschheit X/II; Stuttgart: Kohlhammer, 1970), 138.

99. Cf. the comments of J. Gray (*The Legacy of Canaan*, 170 n. 2): "The fertility function of the deity is not to be doubted, but in view of the pre-eminence of the cult of 'Attar in oases and lands bordering on the desert it seems more natural than the fertility-function of the deity in the settled lands." Such observations call for a "divinity geography" (on analogy with dialect geography) that would show distributions for the cult-sites of various West Semitic deities in the Middle and Late Bronze periods. Taken far enough, such an inquiry might show some results reflected further in Ugaritic mythology.

100. Robertson Smith, *Lectures on the Religion of the Semites: The Fundamental Institutions* (third ed.; introduction and additional notes by S. A. Cook; New York: KTAV, 1969 [original, 1927], 102 n. 2. For subsequent modifications of this contrast, see Smith, *Lectures on the Religion of the Semites*, 95–113, esp. 100, 102 n. 2.

101. M. Yon, "Ugarit: History and Archaeology," 698.

4. Pluralities, Pairings, and Other Divine Relations

1. E. T. Mullen, *The Divine Council in Canaanite and Early Hebrew Literature* (HSM 24; Chico, CA: Scholars, 1980), 213, 269. We might also note in this connection the six occurrences of "Baal" (*b'lm*, a singular plus mimation as indicated by the Akkadian RS 20.24) following *b'l ṣpn* in 1.47.5–11 1.118.54–10. It is dubious that these *b'lm* are the Baals of various sites (see Pardee's discussion, "An Evaluation of the Proper Names, from a West Semitic Perspective: Pantheon Distribution According to Genre," *Eblaite Personal Names and Semitic Name-Giving* (ed. A. Archi; Rome: Missione Archaeologica Italiana in Siria, 1988) 138 n. 79). With *b'l ṣpn* in the list, there is no reason why the following entries would not also add the geographical name if these *b'lm* are references to Baal of particular

locales. Perhaps these *b'lm* and *'il t'dr b'l* are to be compared to the "Baali-Zaphon," attested in New Kingdom Egypt (*ANET* 250). J. A. Wilson (*ANET* 250 n. 12) interprets this phrase as either a plural of majesty or a collective noun. J. C. de Moor prefers to see each *b'lm* as identical to Baal Sapan; see de Moor, "The Semitic Pantheon of Ugarit," *UF* 2 (1970), 219. Cf. S. Parpola, "Monotheism in Ancient Assyria," *One God or Many?* 174.

2. On Resheph, see W. J. Fulco, *The Canaanite God Rešep* (New Haven, CT: American Oriental Society, 1976); P. Xella, "Le dieu Rashaph à Ugarit," *Les annales archaeologiques arabes syriennes* 29–30 (1979–80), 145–62; "KTU 1.91 (RS 19.15) e i sacrifici del re," *UF* 11 (1979), 833–38; and "Resheph," *DDD* 700–03; A. Cooper, "Divine Names and Epithets in the Ugaritic Texts," *Ras Shamra Parallels III: the Texts from Ugarit and the Hebrew Bible* (ed. S. Rummel; AnOr 51; Rome: Pontifical Biblical Institute, 1981), 413–15; Y. Yadin, "New Gleanings on Resheph from Ugarit," *Biblical and Related Studies Presented to Samuel Iwry* (ed. A. Kort and S. Morschauer; Winona Lake, IN: Eisenbrauns, 1985), 259–74.

3. J. M. de Tarragon, *Le Culte à Ugarit* (Paris: Gabalda, 1980), 167. This plural usage for divine statues may underline the apparently plural form *'štrm*, attested in several dedicatory inscriptions on unprovenanced Phoenician bronze bowls. See R. Deutsch and M. Heltzer, *Forty New Ancient West Semitic Inscriptions* (Tel Aviv: Archaeological Center Publication, 1994), 69, 71, 73, 75, 77, 79 (on the assumption of authenticity); T. C. Mitchell, Review of Deutsch and Heltzer, *Forty New Ancient West Semitic Inscriptions*, *PEQ* 128 (1996), 172.

4. *ANET* 250 n. 27.

5. Donner and Röllig (*Kanaanäische und Aramaische Inschriften; Band II: Kommentar* (Wiesbaden: Otto Harrassowitz, 1973), 24. Might *'rṣ* refer, like *šmm rmm* in the preceding line of KAI 15:2, to a sacred "district," in this case perhaps figuratively to the "underworld," and hence a cemetery? See G. C. Picard, "From the Foundation of Carthage to the Barcid Revolution," *Archaeologia Viva* 1/2 (1968–69), 152.

6. Fulco, *The Canaanite God Rešep*, 47.

7. Fulco, *The Canaanite God Rešep*, 69–70.

8. See T. Hiebert, *God of My Victory: The Ancient Hymn in Habakkuk 3* (HSM 38; Atlanta: Scholars, 1986), 4, 92–94, 123; R. D. Haak, *Habakkuk* (VTSup 44; Leiden: Brill, 1992), 83, 90; and noted in chapter 2, section 4.

9. H. W. Attridge and R. A. Oden, *Philo of Byblos: The Phoenician History: Introduction, Critical Text, Translation Notes* (CBQMS 9; Washington, DC: Catholic Biblical Association of America, 1981), 50–51.

10. For a survey with bibliography, see J. N. Ford, "The 'Living Rephaim' of Ugarit: Quick or Defunct?" *UF* 24 (1992), 73–101. To my mind the most insightful study of this collective remains W. J. Horowitz, "The Significance of the Rephaim *rm. aby. btk. rpim*," *JNWSL* 7 (1979), 37–43.

11. As suggested by M. S. Smith in G. C. Heider, *The Cult of Molek: A Reassessment* (JSOTSup 43; Sheffield: JSOT Press, 1985), 127. For a discussion of the issues, see Heider, *The Cult of Molek*, 113–49.

12. This geographical identification perhaps militates against the view of M. Dietrich and O. Loretz that *rp'u mlk 'lm*, *gtr wyqr*, and *'il* (= *mlk*/Milku) are three different figures. See Dietrich and Loretz, "Rapi'u and Milku aus Ugarit: Neuere historisch-geographischen Thesen zu *rpu mlk 'lm* (KTU 1.108:1) und *mt rpi* (KTU 1.17 I 1)," *UF* 21 (1989), 123–31, esp. 126; Dietrich and Loretz, *"Jahwe und seine Aschera": Anthropomorphes Kultbild in Mesopotamien, Ugarit und Israel. Das biblische Bilderverbot* (UBL 9; Münster: Ugarit-Verlag, 1992), 39–76. In addition, the word *gtr* has been understood possibly as another name of *rp'u* in 1.108.2, since *rp'u* is called not only *mlk*; he may also be called *gtr wyqr* (see de Tarragon, *Le Culte à Ugarit*, 159, 176). The latter is also the name of the dynastic "founder."

At first glance the syntax does not suggest a personal name, Yaqaru, but another title. However, if *gtr wyqr* were a binomial name, then *yqr* could not be precluded as the name of the original dynast whom the text regards as divine, especially as *'il yqr* heads the list of dynasts in 1.113.26 (cf. *rp'i yqr* in the unclear context of 1.166.13). For the record, one possible reading for the subjects of the two clauses in 1.108.1–2 would run "Rp'u the Eternal King//"[the god of] Gtr and Yqr" unless these latter two are the objects of the verb (see del Olmo Lete, *Canaanite Religion*, 186). In either case, Rp'u is not to be identified as *gtr wyqr* (as most interpreters say), but may be the ancestral patron god of *gtr wyqr* (might then *gtr* be the father of *yqr*?). In any case, it would be tempting then to extend the equation in the following mannner: *rp'u: mlk: gtr:: rp'um : mlkm: gtrm* (cf. del Olmo Lete, *Canaanite Religion According to the Liturgical Texts of Ugarit* (trans. W. G. E. Watson; Bethesda, MD: CDL, 1999) 241). However, CAT 1.43, the one text where *gtr* and *gtrm* both appear, hardly relates the two in particular together (see the following note; for text and translation, see section 4).

13. If and how *gtrm* in 1.43 is to be identified with *rp'um* (and *mlkm*) is also unclear. Until Pardee's study (see the preceding note), many scholars equated *gtrm* with *rp'um*; this identification is held by Caquot, de Tarragon, del Olmo Lete, and Sapin. For references, see Pardee, "RS 1.005 and the Identification of the *gtrm*," *Ritual and Sacrifice in the Ancient Near East: Proceedings of the International Conference Organized by the Katholieke Universiteit Leuven from the 27th to the 20th of April 1991* (ed. J. Quaegebeur; Leuven: Uitgeverij Peeters en Departement Oriëntalistiek, 1993), 312 n. 35; G. del Olmo Lete, "The Cultic Literature of Ugarit. Hermeneutical Issues and Their Application to KTU 1.112," *Keilschriften Literaturen* (ed. K. Hecker and W. Sommerfeld; XXXII Rencontre Assyriologique; Berliner Beiträge zum Vorderen Orient 6; Berin: Dietrich Reimer, 1986), 162. Others prefer a more specific identification. J. C. de Moor takes *gtrm* as a dual refering to *gtr wyqr*; de Moor, *An Anthology of Religious Texts from Ugarit*, 170 n. 15, 187 n. 2. O. Loretz and P. Xella interpret the form also as a dual, but one referring to the statues of two *gtr*; see Dietrich and Loretz, "Jahwe und seine Aschera," 54–55. See also P. Xella, "Le deu et <<sa>> déese: l'utilisation des suffixes pronominaux avec des théonymes d'Ebla à Ugarit et à Kuntillet 'Ajrud," *UF* 27 (1995), 607–8. The grammar of the dual/plural indicative prefix form precludes a singular noun with mimation for lines 9–10: *t'rbn gtrm bt mlk*, "the *gtrm* enter the house of the king. . . ." The context could seem to suggest cult statues of some dual or plural figures. For cult statues as *'ilm*, see 1.42.23, 24 and 1.112.8. See Watson, "Notes on Some Ugaritic Words," *SEL* 6 (1989), 47. Pardee suggests that the term *gtrm* covers three deities in 1.43, namely, Shapshu, Yarih, and *gtr*. Cf. del Olmo Lete, *Canaanite Religion*, 241. With Pardee it remains feasible to hold out for the possibility that one of the *gtrm* in 1.43.9–10 could be identified with *gtr*, possibly *gtr wyqr* in 1.108.2; see Pardee, "RS 1.005 and the Identification of the *gtrm*," 312–17. In *Les textes paramythologiques*, 91–93 esp. 93 n. 62, Pardee had accepted the widely held hypothesis that *gtrm* are the *rp'um*.

14. In lines 1–5 this figure leads the musical celebration with *hbr ktr tbm*, "the goodly companions of Kothar," which I have taken as a possible reference to the *rp'um* (see Smith in D. Pardee, *Les textes para-mythologiques*, 100 n. 111).

15. See the important discussion of K. van der Toorn, "Ilib and the 'God of the Father'," *UF* 25 (1993), 379–87. Formerly most commentators had taken *'il'ib* to be the divine version of the family-god.

16. For these lists, see Healey, "The Akkadian 'Pantheon' List from Ugarit," *SEL* 2 (1985), 115–25; Lewis, *Cults of the Dead*, 56–57.

17. See the informative survey in K. Spronk, *Beatific Afterlife in Ancient Israel and in the Ancient Near East* (AOAT 219; Kevelaer: Butzon & Bercker; Neukirchen-Vluyn: Neukirchener, 1986), 3–85.

18. The following are representative: Spronk, *Beatific Afterlife in Ancient Israel and in the Ancient Near East*, and the review of M. S. Smith and E. M. Bloch-Smith, "Death and Afterlife in Ugarit and Israel," *JAOS* 108 (1988), 277–84; T. J. Lewis, *Cults of the Dead in Ancient Israel and Ugarit* (HSM 39; Atlanta, GA: Scholars, 1989); O. Loretz, "Nekromantie und Totenevokation im Mesopotamien, Ugarit und Israel," *Religionsgeschichtliche Beziehungen zwischen Kleinasien, Nordssyrien und dem Alten Testament* (ed. B. Janowski; OBO 129; Freiburg Schweiz: Universitätsverlag; Göttingen: Vandenhoeck & Ruprecht, 1993), 285–318; B. Schmidt, *Israel's Beneficent Dead: Ancestor Cult and Necromancy in Ancient Isrelite Religion and Tradition* (FAT 11; Tübingen: J. C. B. Mohr [Siebeck], 1994), 100–20, and my review in *CBQ* 58 (1996), 724–25; Bloch-Smith, *Judahite Burials and Beliefs about the Dead* (JSOT-Sup 123; Sheffield: Sheffield Academic Press, 1992). See also the articles devoted to this topic by H. Niehr, R. Wenning, J. F. Healey, K. van der Toorn, and T. Podella in *Theologische Quartalschrift* 177/2 (1997).

19. Bloch-Smith, *Judahite Burials and Beliefs about the Dead*; see also her article, "The Cult of the Dead in Judah," *JBL* 111 (1992), 213–24. See the responses in A. Cooper and B. R. Goldstein, "The Cult of the Dead and the Theme of Entry into the Land," *Biblical Interpretation* 1/3 (1993), 285–303, esp. 301 n. 37; and R. Tappy, "Did The Dead Ever Die in Biblical Judah?" *BASOR* 298 (1995), 59–68.

20. See Smith, "Kothar wa-Hasis, the Ugaritic Craftsman God" (Ph.D. diss, Yale University, 1985), 466, 468; Pardee, "Kosharoth," *DDD* 491–92.

21. So Smith, "Kothar wa-Hasis, the Ugaritic Craftsman God," 469; Pardee, "Kosharoth," *DDD* 492. On the root, the most sustained treatment remains Smith, "Kothar wa-Hasis, the Ugaritic Craftsman God," 51–81.

22. For example, *'ilhm b'lm* in 1.39.5, 9; 1.41.12; and *'iltm hnqtm* 1.102.13. On *'ilhm*, see the proposal of O. Loretz, "Die Teraphim als 'Ahnes-Götter-Figur(in)en' im Lichte der Texte aus Nuzi, Emar und Ugarit: Anmerkungen zu *'ilānu*, *ilhm/'lhym* und DIN-GER.ERIN.MEŠ/*inš ilm*," *UF* 24 (1992), 156–61. For an important older survey, see J. C. de Moor, "The Semitic Pantheon," *UF* 2 (1970), 187–228.

23. De Moor, "The Semitic Pantheon of Ugarit," 187–228, esp. 227–28.

24. See Greenstein in *UNP* 25 and 45 n.66.

25. *ANET* 15. The value of this evidence for Anat as Baal's consort has been challenged, however, by H. Te Velde (*Seth, God of Confusion: A Study of his Role in Egyptian Mythology and Religion* [Problem der Ägyptologie 6; Leiden: Brill, 1967], 29–30), seconded by Walls (*The Goddess Anat in Ugaritic Myth*, 144–52) and P. L. Day ("Anat: Ugarit's 'Mistress of Animals,'" *JNES* 51 [1992], 186). See also Day, "Why is Anat a Warrior and Hunter?" *The Bible and the Politics of Exegesis: Essays in Honor of Norman K. Gottwald on His Sixty-Fifth Birthday* (ed. D. Jobling, P. L. Day, and G. T. Sheppard; Cleveland, OH: Pilgrim Press, 1991), 141–46, 329–32. Te Velde's chief argument is that other than in this one text Anat is not called the consort of Seth. The uniqueness of this rendering of Anat as the wife of Seth might be viewed as militating in favor of its authenticity as a witness to the West Semitic tradition. However, this need not apply at Ugarit, if marriage is a rarity among the members in the second tier of the pantheon.

26. *ANET* 200–01. For further examples of the identification of Seth with Baal in New Kingdom Egypt, see *ANET* 249. A single figure from Memphis served as the prophet of Baal and Astarte (*ANET* 250 n. 13), which perhaps also illustrates the close relationship between Baal and Astarte and their cult in Memphis during New Kingdom times. The identification of Seth and Baal may be reflected in the divine name Bolchoseth, found on amulets, *defixiones*, and in formularies dating to the Hellenistic-Roman period. For discussion, see J. G. Gager (ed.), *Curse Tablets and Binding Spells from the Ancient World* (New York: Oxford University Press, 1992), 266.

27. For a full listing, including additional examples from ritual texts, see de Moor, "The Semitic Pantheon," 227–28. On the pairings in 1.100, see B. A. Levine and J. M. de Tarragon, "<<Shapshu Cries out in Heaven>>: Dealing with Snake-Bites at Ugarit," *RB* 95 (1988), 505–06.

28. Cf. F. M. Cross, "The 'Olden Gods' in Ancient Near Eastern Creation Myths," *Magnalia Dei. The Mighty Acts of God: Essays on the Bible and Archaeology in Memory of G. Ernest Wright* (ed. F. M. Cross, W. E. Lemke, and P. D. Miller, Jr.; Garden City, NY: Doubleday, 1976), 329–38; idem, *From Epic to Canon*, 74–83.

29. De Moor, "The Semitic Pantheon of Ugarit," 227–28.

30. See S. M. Olyan, *Asherah and the Cult of Yahweh in Israel* (SBLMS 34; Altanta, GA: Scholars, 1988), 10, 30, 39–40, 48, 55–56, 59.

31. Del Olmo Lete, *Canaanite Religion*, 51–52, 65 n. 57.

32. In contrast, this title is viewed as original to the "Jahwist source" by T. L. J. Mafico, "The Divine Compound Name יְהֹוָה אֱלֹהִים and Israel's Monotheistic Polytheism," *JNWSL* 221 (1996), 155–73. Mafico takes the second part of the name as representing the gods of the ancestors of various tribes as "primarily a political move employed to unite all the ethnic groups of Israel under the monarchy" (p. 161), a change he would attribute to the "Yahwist."

33. On Genesis 1's "monotheistic poetics," see the final section of chapter 1.

34. For text and translation, see Pardee, "RS 1.005 and the Identification of the *gtrm*," 301–02.

35. See M. Dietrich and O. Loretz, *..Jahwe und seine Aschera*," 39–76; Xella, "Le dieu et <<sa>> déesse," 599–610, esp. 607–08. Xella relates this usage also to examples from Ebla. See also del Olmo Lete, *Canaanite Religion*, 289 n. 109.

36. Pardee, "RS 1.005 and the Identification of the *gtrm*," 309. See also his extensive remarks in his review of M. Dietrich and O. Loretz, *..Jahwe und seine Aschera*," *JAOS* 115 (1995), 301–03.

37. See *EHG* 90–91.

38. For a discussion of the archaeology of this site as well as its finds (as well as comparable evidence at Khirbet el-Qom), see A. Mazar, *Archaeology of the Land of the Bible 10,000–586 B.C.E.* (ABRL; New York: Doubleday, 1990), 446–50. For discussions of the inscriptions, see J. A. Emerton, "New Light on Israelite Religion: The Implications of the Inscriptions from Kuntillet 'Ajrud," *ZAW* 94 (1982), 2–20; M. Weinfeld, "Kuntillet 'Ajrûd Inscriptions and Their Significance," *SEL* 1 (1984), 121–30; P. K. McCarter, "Aspects of the Religion of the Israelite Monarchy: Biblical and Epigraphic Data," *Ancient Israelite Religion: Essays in Honor of Frank Moore Cross* (ed. P. D. Miller, Jr, P. D. Hanson, and S. D. McBride; Philadelphia: Fortress, 1987), 137–55; idem, "The Religious Reforms of Hezekiah and Josiah," *Aspects of Monotheism: How God Is One* (ed. H. Shanks and J. Meinhardt; Washington, DC: Biblical Archaeology Society, 1997), 74–80; S. M. Olyan, *Asherah and the Cult of Yahweh in Israel* (SBLMS 34; Atlanta, GA: Scholars, 1988), 23–34; J. M. Hadley, *The Cult of the Goddess in Ancient Israel and Judah: The Evidence for a Hebrew Goddess* (University of Cambridge Oriental Publications series vol. 57; Cambridge University Press, 2000); idem, "Some Drawings and Inscriptions on Two Pithoi from Kuntillet 'Ajrud," *VT* 37 (1987), 180–213; idem, "The Khirbet el-Qom Inscription," *VT* 37 (1987), 50–62; idem, "Chasing Shadows? The Quest for the Historical Goddess," *Congress Volume: Cambridge 1995* (ed. J. A. Emerton; Leiden: Brill, 1997), 169–84; S. A. Wiggins, "The Myth of Asherah: Lion Lady and Serpent Goddess," *UF* 23 (1991), 383–94; idem, *A Reassessment of 'Asherah': A Study According to the Textual Sources of the First Two Millennia B.C.E.* (AOAT 235; Kevelaer: Butzon & Bercker; Neukirchen Vluyn: Neukirchener, 1993); Dietrich and Loretz, "*Jahwe und seine Aschera*", 77–133; Keel and Uehlinger, *Gods, Goddesses, and Images of God in Ancient Israel*, 228–48, 332, 369–70; C. Frevel, *Aschera und der Ausschliesslichkeitsanspruch YHWHs* (BBB 94; two vols.; Weinheim: Beltz Athenäum, 1995); the response

to Frevel in Keel, *Goddesses and Trees, New Moon and Yahweh: Ancient Near Eastern Art and the Hebrew Bible* (JSOTSup 262; Sheffield: Sheffield Academic Press, 1998); and P. Merlo, *La dea Ašratum—Atiratu—Ašera: Un contributo alla storia della religione semitica del Nord* (Mursia: Pontificia Università Lateranese, 1998). See also the survey in S. A. Wiggins, "Asherah Again: Binger's Asherah and the State of Asherah Studies," *JNWSL* 24 (1998), 231–40.

39. Gitin, "Cultic Inscriptions Found in Ekron," *BA* 53/4 (December 1990), 232. For the difficulties in using this term for the cultural features of this region in the Iron Age, see S. Bunomowitz, "Problems in the 'Ethnic' Identification of the Philistine Culture," *TA* 17 (1990), 210–22. L. E. Stager has suggested "neo-Philistine" (personal communication).

40. J. Naveh, "Writing and Scripts in Seventh Century B.C.E. Philistia: The New Evidence from Tell Jemmeh," *BASOR* 35 (1985), 8–21. The 1992 excavations at Ashqelon uncovered an inscription of a grain receipt that F. M. Cross compares in script to the inscriptions at Tell Jemmeh and Tell Shariah (information courtesy of L. E. Stager).

41. For the following information I am indebted to S. Gitin, Director of the W. F. Albright Institute in Jerusalem and co-director of the excavations at Ekron-Tel Miqne. See his article, "Seventh Century B.C.E. Cultic Elements at Ekron," *Congress on Biblical Archaeology 1990* (Jerusalem: Israel Exploration Society, 1993), 248–58. See also Halpern, "Jerusalem and the Lineages in the Seventh Century BCE: Kinship and the Rise of Individual Moral Liability," *Law and Ideology in Monarchic Israel* (ed. B. Halpern and D. W. Hobson; JSOTSup 124; Sheffield: JSOT, 1991), 46–47 n. 1.

42. The evidence for *qdš* as an epithet of Asherah is problematic since final feminine *-t* would be expected for a goddess's title (so Wyatt, "Asherah," *DDD* 100), despite the name of Qudšu in the Winchester plaque (see later). The divine council is called *'ilm*//*bn qdšm*. The first word is the common word for "gods." The second is either a general designation, "the holy ones" (*EUT* 44; cf. *qdšm*, "gods," in KAI 4:4–5), or "the sons of Qdš," i.e., Athirat (*CML*² 41, 156; J. C. de Moor, *An Anthology of Religious Texts from Ugarit* [Nisaba 16; Leiden: Brill, 1988], 32 n. 140). In the latter case, the divine council would be tantamount to the "seventy sons of Athirat" (KTU 1.4 VI 46). The word *qdš* in KTU 1.14 IV 34 is "sanctuary" and not a divine title (so *CMHE* 33 n. 124), and *qdš* in the title *ltpn w-qdš* may refer to El and not Athirat (so *EUT* 43). D. B. Redford ("New Light on the Asiatic Campaign of Horemheb," *BASOR* 211 [1973], 46) takes *qi-di[d-šu]* as a deity in *Ugaritica V*, text 137, iv a 14, but according to J. Huehnergard (*Ugaritic Vocabulary in Syllabic Transcription* [HSS 32; Atlanta, GA: Scholars, 1987], 173) the word means "sanctuary, shrine," given the Hurrian equivalent provided, *ha-ma-ar-re*, the definite form of the Hurrian noun *hamri*, "sanctuary." The Winchester plaque (I. E. S. Edwards, "A Relief of Qudšu-Astarte-Anath in the Winchester College Collection," *JNES* 14 [1955], 49–51) contains the names Qudšu-Astarte-Anat. Albright ("Some Observations on the New Material for the History of the Alphabet," *BASOR* 134 [1954], 26), Cross (*CMHE* 33–34), Olyan (*Asherah*, 40 n. 6), and R. Hestrin ("The Lachish Ewer and the 'Asherah," *IEJ* 37 [1987], 218) consider Qudšu to be an epithet of Athirat by a process of elimination, for Astarte and Anat appear after Qudšu in the inscription. Olyan calls the representation on the plaque "a triple-fusion hypostasis." Others scholars take *qdš* as a title of either Astarte or Anat, however (see discussion in Olyan, *Asherah*, 40 n. 6). For extensive criticism of the identification of *qdš* as Asherah, see S. A. Wiggins, "The Myth of Asherah, 383–89.

43. See S. Gitin, "Ekron of the Philistines. Part II: Olive Suppliers to the World," *Biblical Archaeology Review* 16/2 (March/April 1990), 59 n. 18; idem, "Cultic Inscriptions Found in Ekron," 232.

44. Gitin, "Seventh Century B.C.E. Cultic Elements at Ekron," 248–58.

45. W. R. Garr, *Dialect Geography of Syria-Palestine, 1000–586 B.C.E.* (Philadelphia: University of Pennsylvania Press, 1985), 60–61, 94.

238 Notes to Pages 73–74

46. One might use the term "Philistian" rather than "Philistine" for the culture in the area of Philistia during this period, but the potential confusion as a specific ethnic designation remains. See Bunomowitz, "Problems in the 'Ethnic' Identification of the Philistine Culture," 210–22.

47. Information courtesy of Dr. S. Gitin.

48. See CMHE 33–35. See also S. Ackermann, *Under Every Green Tree: Popular Religion in Sixth-Century Judah* (HSM 46; Atlanta, GA: Scholars, 1992), 191. For criticisms, see Wiggins, "The Myth of Asherah," 383–89.

49. See S. Gitin, T. Dothan, and J. Naveh, "A Royal Dedicatory Inscription from Ekron," *IEJ* 47 (1997), 1–16. See also A. Demsky, "The Name of the Goddess of Ekron: A New Reading," *JANES* 25 (1997), 1–5; "Discovering a Goddess," *Biblical Archaeologist Review* 24/5 (1998), 53–58. Demsky reads the enigmatic name taken as *ptgyh* by Gitin et al. as *ptnyh*, known in Greek as *potnia*, a title meaning "mistress" or "lady." Demsky suggests further that this title here may refer to Asherah.

50. We are now predisposed to such conclusions reflecting contemporary interest in the worship of goddesses, whether in prehistoric or historical times. For interesting reflection on methodological issues attending this area of research, see J. Wood, "The Concept of the Goddess," *The Concept of the Goddess* (ed. S. Billington and M. Green; London:Routledge, 1996), 8–25. She makes one particularly interesting point that the idea of the goddess drives the research agenda as Victorian anthropology was driven by Sir James George Frazer. Comparing the two, Wood comments (p. 13): "Indeed, so similar are the assumptions and the methodology of many Goddess-studies that, in her universality and persistance, the Goddess resembles Frazer's Dying god, resuscitated once again and cross dressed." Frazer's work is discussed at considerable length in chapter 6, sections 1 and 2.

51. See EHG 80–97; and C. Frevel, *Aschera und der Ausschliesslichkeitanspruch YHWHs.*

52. See Olyan, *Asherah*, 23–34.

53. See Olyan, *Asherah*, 23–34.

54. See EHG 80–97.

55. See Pardee, Review of M. Dietrich and O. Loretz, *"Jahwe und seine Aschera,"* 301–03; Frevel, *Aschera und der Ausschliesslichkeitanspruch YHWHs.* F. M. Cross too has commented: "In any case I must reject any attempt to make it a proper name." He prefers a position closer to the view of another former student of his, P. K. McCarter, that the asherah was "a conventionalized tree of life, a cult object, or a hypostasis of an aspect of 'El." Finally, he comments: "If you want syncretism in the Hebrew Bible, there is plenty of material to be found without manufacturing it" (all three quotes are taken from a letter to me dated 7 December 1998). For McCarter's view, see his articles, "Aspects of the Religion of the Israelite Monarchy" and "The Religious Reforms of Hezekiah and Josiah." Compare Keel and Uehlinger, *Gods, Goddesses, and Images of God in Ancient Israel*, 228–48, 332, 369–70; Keel, *Goddesses and Trees*; Merlo, *La dea Ašratum—Atiratu—Ašera.* The last of these contains other relevant bibliography. Keel and Uehlinger dubiously combine two views, that the symbol of the asherah lost its associations to the goddess by the eighth century, only to regain them by the second half of the seventh century.

56. See M. D. Coogan, *Stories from Ancient Canaan* (Philadelphia: Westminster, 1978), 74; Olyan, *Asherah*, 48. Šu-um appears as a divinity at Ebla; see P. Xella, "Aspekte religiöser Vorstellungen in Syrien nach den Ebla-und Ugarit-Texten," *UF* 15 (1983), 290; R. R. Stieglitz, "Ebla and the Gods of Canaan," *Eblaitica: Essays on the Ebla Archives and Eblaite Language* (ed. C. H. Gordon and G. A. Rendsburg; two vols.; Winona Lake, IN: Eisenbrauns, 1990), 2.81; F. Pomponio and P. Xella, *Les dieux d'Ebla: Étude analytique des divinités éblaïtes à l'époque des archives royales du IIIe millénaire* (AOAT 245; Münster: Ugarit-Verlag, 1997), 503–05. The element *šm is attested in second and first millennium proper names,

including Amorite names (H. Huffmon, *Amorite Personal Names in the Mari Texts: A Structural and Lexical Study* [Baltimore/London: Johns Hopkins, 1965], 248–49), Akkadian names from Ugarit (F. Gröndahl, *Die Personennamen der Texte aus Ugarit* [Studia Pohl l; Rome: Päpstliches Bibelinstitut, 1967], 193–94), and Phoenician and Hebrew names (see F. M. Cross, "Newly Found Inscriptions in Old Canaanite and Early Phoenician Scripts," *BASOR* 238 [1980], 3).

57. So noted by N. H. Walls, *The Goddess Anat in the Ugaritic Texts* (SBLDS 135; Atlanta, GA: Scholars, 1992), 117. Cf. Olyan, *Asherah*, 48. D. Fleming argues for a pairing of Baal and Athtart at Emar, but the evidence is presently meager. See D. Fleming, *The Installation of Baal's High Priestess at Emar: A Window on Ancient Syrian Religion* (HSS 42; Atlanta, GA: Scholars, 1992), 214–21, 293.

58. See TO 1.94. For Astarte in Egyptian sources, see J. Leclant, "Astarté à cheval d'après les représentations égyptiennes," *Syria* 37 (1960), 1–67.

59. *CMHE* 30.

60. Mullen, *The Divine Council*, 120.

61. For McCarter, see the discussion later in this section.

62. Olyan, *Asherah*, 48: "an early example of hypostasization in Canaanite religion, which directly associates her with Baal, as a manifestation of his name essence."

63. These scholars would identify other examples of hypostasis in Levantine religion. For further proposals, see M. Weinfeld, "Semiramis: Her Name and Her Origin," *Ah, Assyria; Studies in Assyrian History and Ancient Near Eastern Historiography Presented to Hayim Tadmor* (ed. M. Cogan and I. Eph'al; Scripta Hierosolymitana 33; Jerusalem: Magnes, 1991), 99–103, esp. 100; M. Barker, *The Great Angel: A Study of Israel's Second God* (London: SPCK, 1992), 97–102. See also Derketo as a fish in *De Dea Syria* 14 (Attridge and Oden, *The Syrian Goddess (De Dea Syria) Attributed to Lucian* [Texts and Translations 9, Graeco-Roman Religion Series 1; Missoula, MT: Scholars Press, 1976], 23). D. Pardee would apply the term "hypostasis" for various manifestations of Athtart ('*ttrt ḥr* in KTU 1.43.1, and '*ttrt šd* in KTU 1.91.10 and 1.148.18); see Pardee, "*Marziḥu, Kispu*, and the Ugaritic Funerary Cult: A Minimalist View," *Ugarit, Religion and Culture: Proceedings of the International Colloquium on Ugarit, Religion and Culture. Edinburgh, July 1994. Essays Presented in Honour of Professor John C. L. Gibson* (ed. N. Wyatt, W. G. E. Watson, and J. B. Lloyd; UBL 12; Münster: Ugarit-Verlag, 1996), 277. On the other hand, manifestations of a deity are precisely what the biblical material shows for the name-hypostasis (see section 5).

64. Attridge and Oden, *Philo of Byblos*, 54–55.

65. Olyan, *Asherah*, 48.

66. For the West Semitic and biblical evidence, see especially S. D. McBride, "The Deuteronomic Name Theology" (Ph.D. diss., Harvard University, 1969).

67. T. H. Gaster, *Thespis; Ritual, Myth, and Drama in the Ancient Near East* (New York: Norton, 1977), 156; P. G. Mosca, "Child Sacrifice in Canaanite and Israelite Religion; A Study in Mulk and מלך," (Ph.D. diss., Harvard University, Cambridge, 1975), 195–223; *EHG* 100–01; M. Barker, *The Great Angel: A Study of Israel's Second God* (London: SPCK, 1992) 97. See NJPS n. i to this verse.

68. C. T. L. Kloos, *Yhwh's Combat with the Sea: A Canaanite Tradition in the Religion of Ancient Israel* (Amsterdam: G. A. van Oorschot; Leiden: Brill, 1986) 33.

69. The eastward storm theophany in Psalm 29 moves from the Mediterranean Sea across the Lebanon, the Anti-Lebanon, and into the Syrian desert. The storm theophany of the psalm, the archaic form of the language, and the northern referents in the psalm would suit either a non-Israelite background or a northern Israelite provenance. Ginsberg, Gaster, Cross, and Fitzgerald suggest that Psalm 29 was originally a "Canaanite" hymn to Baal (for discussion, see J. L. Cunchillos, *Estudio del Salmo 29, Canto al Dos de la fertilidad-*

fecundidad. A portación al conocimiento de la Fe de Israel a su entrada en Canaan (Valencia: San Jerónimo, 1976) 163–68; A. Fitzgerald, "A Note on Psalm 29," *BASOR* 215 [1974], 61–63; J. Day, *God's Conflict with the Dragon and the Sea: Echoes of a Canaanite Myth in the Old Testament* (University of Cambridge Oriental Publications Series, 35; Cambridge: Cambridge University Press, 1985) 58). According to Fitzgerald, the higher level of alliteration achieved by substituting the name of Baal for Yahweh in this psalm shows that it was originally a "Canaanite" psalm. Furthermore, the expression *midbar qādēš* in Psalm 29:8 recalls *tk mdbr qdš*, possibly translated either as "in the midst of the holy outback" or "in the outback a sanctuary," in CAT 1.23.65. The other place-names apparently suit a Syrian site for *midbar qādēš* in Psalm 29:8 better than the traditional southern site named Kadesh (noted by many commentators; see *CMHE* 154 n. 37; cf. Day, *God's Conflict*, 60 n. 169).

70. *CMHE* 153 n. 30, 165–67; M. Weinfeld, "Divine Intervention in War in Ancient Israel and the Ancient Near East," *History, Historiography and Interpretation: Studies in Biblical and Cuneiform Literatures* (ed. H. Tadmor and M. Weinfeld; Jerusalem: Magnes; Leiden: Brill, 1986), 132–36.

71. Isaiah 63:9 attests the notion of the "face" (*pānîm*) as warrior. For discussion, see T. N. D. Mettinger, *The Dethronement of Sabaoth: Studies in the Shem and Kabod Theologies* (ConBOT 18; Lund: Gleerup, 1982), 124; *EHG* 100–01; A. Rofé, "Isaiah 59:19 and Trito-Isaiah's Vision of Redemption," *The Book of Isaiah. Le Livre d'Isaïe: Les oracles et leur relectures. Unité et complexité de l'ouvrage* (BETL 81; Leuven: University Press/Uitgeverij Peeters, 1989), 407. For the name as warrior in Judaism and Christianity in the Greco-Roman period, see the recent but flawed discussion of Barker, *The Great Angel*, 208–12. Barker claims that Revelation 19:15 presents the figure of Jesus as the hypostasis of the name, but in fact this figure receives the name of "The Word of God" (RSV). If any "hypostasis" is involved in this passage, it involves the word. Barker also includes as a "hypostasis" the notion of Jesus representing the name of the Father (John 17:6) as well as the notion of putting on the name. It is unclear if or how these phenomena are related.

72. The line is generally taken to mean that the worshippers in the temple "say glory" (NJPS, NRSV) or "cry glory" (RSV). It is possible that such a liturgical response to the coming theophany could take place, but more in keeping with the notion of biblical theophanies is not the proclamation but the appearance of glory. The apparent impediment to this interpretation in this context would be the semantics of the root **'mr*, which generally means "to say." However, "to see" is one meaning of Ugaritic **'mr* (CAT 1.3 I 22) and Akkadian *amāru*. Cross (*CMHE* 154 n. 39) cites the Ugaritic proper name, *a-mur-ᵈba'l*, "I saw Baal"; see also R. de Vito, *Studies in Third Millennium Sumerian and Akkadian Personal Names: The Designation and Conception of the Personal God* (Studia Pohl: Series Maior 16; Rome: Editrice Pontificio Istituto Biblico, 1993), 192, 279; *PTU* 320). For the verb **'mr*, see J. Barr, "Etymology and the Old Testament," *Language and Meaning: Studies in Hebrew Language and Biblical Exegesis* (OTS 19; Leiden: Brill, 1974), 5–6; T. Abusch, "Alaktu and Halakhah: Oracular Decision, Divine Revelation," *HTR* 80 (1987), 25. *Amur*-names are also attested in Mesopotamian and Eblaite personal names. See de Vito, *Studies in Third Millennium Sumerian and Akkadian Personal Names*, 192, 279; P. Fronzaroli, "Eblaic Lexicon: Problems and Appraisal," *Studies on the Language of Ebla* (ed. P. Fronzaroli; Quaderni de Semitistica 13; Florence: Istituto di Linguistica e di Lingue Orientali, 1984), 120. The form of the verb in Psalm 29:9 is perhaps then a passive-stative **qatul*. In any case, the Masoretes no longer knew the older meaning of **'mr* and interpreted this instance according to its better-known sense; interpreters have generally followed suit.

73. Other BH examples include Psalm 8:8; 2 Samuel 2:9; Isaiah 16:7; Jeremiah 18:31; Ezekiel 29:2; 35:15; Job 34:13 (arguably Numbers 16:3 as well); see J. C. de Moor and P. van der Lugt, "The Spectre of Pan-Ugaritism," *BibOr* 31 (1974), 9. The postpositive constructive is known also in Ugaritic (CAT 1.3 VI 14; 1.6 I 65; 1.14 IV 20; often recon-

structed in 1.1 III 1* on the basis of 1.3 VI 14) and Aramaic (KAI 215:17; 222 A 5; Peshitta Lev 8:21; Peshitta Num 14:21). See I. Avinery, "The Position of the Declined *kl* in Syriac," *Afroasiastic Linguistics* 3/5 (1976), 25. The usage is not restricted to place names: Psalm 8:8 uses it after two words for animals; CAT 1.6 I 65 employs it after *'arṣ*, "land," and CAT 1.14 IV 20 uses it in a temporal construction. Syriac attests *ldkr' klh*, "the whole ram" (Peshitta Lev 8:21) and *b'r'' kwlh*, "in all the earth" (Peshitta Num 14:21). For further discussion, see Avinery, "The Position of the Declined *kl* in Syriac," 25. There is no text-critical, grammatical, or poetical basis for its deletion from Psalm 29:9. Cf. *CMHE* 154 n. 39, which dismisses the form as "prosaic."

74. McCarter, "Aspects of the Religion of the Israelite Monarchy, 147.

75. See Gröndahl, *Die Personennamen*, 31, 193–94, 355.

76. See *CMHE* 11; R. S. Hess, *Amarna Personal Names* (American Schools of Oriental Research Dissertation Series 9; Winona Lake, IN: Eisenbrauns, 1993), 145–46, 212. For a personal name with *šm* as a theophoric element in an arrowhead inscription thought to date to the eleventh century, see R. Deutsch and M. Heltzer, *New Epigraphic Evidence from the Biblical Period* (Tel Aviv/Jaffa: Archaeological Center Publication, 1995), 14. Although the arrowheads discussed by F. M. Cross ("The Arrow of Suwar, Retainer of 'Abday," *EI* 25 [1996] 9*–17*) do not include this inscription, he does note the problem of forgeries of arrowheads, a problem that may apply in this instance. The photograph for the obverse is very unclear, which complicates resolution of the issue.

77. See chapter 2, section 2.

78. See B. F. Batto, "Zedeq," *DDD* 929–34.

79. The evidence from personal names at Ugarit is inconclusive; see Gröndahl, *Die Personennamen*, 148. For the element *kabid-* as a theophoric element in Ebla and Amarna personal names, see Stieglitz, "Ebla and the Gods of Canaan," 82; Pomponio and Xella, *Les dieux d'Ebla*, 174.

80. The entry of J. E. Fossum, "Glory," in *DDD* 348–52 omits discussion of the older Levantine evidence.

81. J. S. Kselman and M. L. Barré, "Psalms," *NJBC* 1.533.

82. For the biblical material, see D. P. Wright, "Holiness, Sex, and Death in the Garden of Eden," *Bib* 77 (196), 305–29. For the possibility of the notion of sacred garden lying behind the Ugaritic use of *n'm*, see also chapter 1, section 2, and chapter 5, section 3.

83. Del Olmo Lete, *Canaanite Religion*, 119 n. 123.

84. See B. A. Levine and J. M. de Tarragon, "The King Proclaims the Day: Ugaritic Rites for the Vintage (*KTU* 1.41//1.87)," *RB* 100 (1993), 97; Wyatt, *Religious Texts from Ugarit*, 353 n. 42.

85. Cross, "The 'Olden Gods' in Ancient Near Eastern Creation Myths," 330. Cross's disclaimer that the Ugaritic ritual texts do not attest to olden gods such as "heaven and earth" may now be modified by reference to 1.47.12 = 1.118.11 and 1.148.24. See further M. Hutter, "Heaven," *DDD* 388.

86. See Healey, "The Akkadian 'Pantheon' List from Ugarit," *SEL* 2 (1985), 120.

87. Jacobsen, "Foreword" in Y. Muffs, *Love & Joy: Law, Language and Religion in Ancient Israel* (New York: Jewish Theological Seminary of America, 1992), xix. For extensive discussion of divinized cult items in Mesopotamia, see G. J. Selz, "The Holy Drum, the Spear, and the Harp. Towards an Understanding of the Problems of Deification in the Third Millennium Mesopotamia," *Sumerian Gods and Their Representations* (ed. I. L. Finkel and M. J. Geller; Cuneiform Monographs 7; Groningen: Styx, 1997), 167–213.

88. These generalizations are not intended to preclude a variety of other means of conceptual unity within Mesopotamia. Another that comes to mind is the equation of the parts of Marduk's, Ninurta's, or Ishtar's body with other deities, as indicating that these deities literally embody the others. See chapter 5, section two for discussion.

89. See chapter 5, section 2 for discussion.

90. Cf. triads of deities described in familial terms in Egyptian religion. See S. Morenz, *Egyptian Religion* (trans. A. E. Keep; Ithaca, NY: Cornell University Press, 1992), 142–46. Reference courtesy of T. J. Lewis.

91. Pardee, "Ugarit. Texts and Literature," *ABD* 6:713. See further J. D. Schloen, "The Patrimonial Household in the Kingdom of Ugarit: A Weberian Analysis of Ancient Near Eastern Society" (Ph.D. diss., Harvard University, 1995), 66. Note also the central importance of the family in both Keret and Aqhat.

92. See L. E. Stager, "The Archeology of the Family in Ancient Israel," *BASOR* 260 (1985), 1–35. See also C. Meyers, " 'To Her Mother's House': Considering a Counterpart to the Israelite *Bêt 'āb*," *The Bible and the Politics of Exegesis: Essays in Honor of Norman K. Gottwald on His Sixty-Fifth Birthday* (ed. D. Jobling, P. L. Day, and G. T. Sheppard; Cleveland, OH: Pilgrim Press, 1991), 39–51.

93. For evidence and argument, see B. Halpern, "Sybil, or the Two Nations? Archaism, Kinship, Alienation, and the Elite Redefinition of Traditional Culture in Judah in the 8th–7th Centuries B.C.E.," *The Study of the Ancient Near East in the Twenty-First Century: The William Foxwell Albright Centennial Conference* (ed. J. S. Cooper and G. M. Schwartz; Winona Lake, IN: Eisenbrauns, 1996), 291–338; J. Blenkinsopp, "The Family in First Temple Israel," in L. Perdue et al., *Families in Ancient Israel* (The Family, Religion, and Culture series; Louisville, KY: Westminster John Knox, 1997), 88–92. See further K. van der Toorn, *Family Religion in Babylonia, Syria and Israel: Continuity and Change in the Forms of Religious Life* (Studies in the History and Culture of the Ancient Near East 7; Leiden: Brill, 1996), 362, 371–72.

94. J. J. Collins, "Marriage, Divorce, and Family in Second Temple Judaism," in L. Perdue et al., *Families in Ancient Israel*, 105.

95. Reference courtesy of S. Olyan. See Geller, "The God of the Covenant," 298.

96. See B. Halpern, "Jerusalem and the Lineages in the Seventh Century BCE: Kinship and the Rise of Individual Liability," *Law and Ideology in Monarchic Israel* (ed. B. Halpern and D. W. Hobson; JSOTSup 124; Sheffield: Sheffield Academic Press, 1991), 11–15. See further Halpern, "Sybil, or the Two Nations?" 295, 317–18, 323, 326; and Geller, "The God of the Covenant," 298.

97. As noted independently by Geller, "The God of the Covenant," 298. See Halpern, "Jerusalem and the Lineages in the Seventh Century BCE," 11–107. See further Halpern, "Sybil, or the Two Nations?" 291–338.

98. De Moor, "The Crisis of Polytheism in Late Bronze Ugarit," *OTS* 24 (1986), 1; and *The Rise of Yahwism: The Roots of Israelite Monotheism* (revised and enlarged edition; Bibliotheca Ephemeridum Theologicarum Lovaniensium XCI; Leuven: University Press/ Uitgeverij Peeters, 1997), 71. This is not to deny that elite members of the culture may not have explored the problems of religious existence. For further discussion, see Introduction, section 2.

99. For some preliminary reflections in this direction, see *UBC* 96–114; M. S. Smith, "Myth and Mythmaking in Canaan and Ancient Israel," *Civilizations of the Ancient Near East* (ed. J. M. Sasson; four vols.; New York: Scribner's/Macmillan, 1995), 3.2032–33; and part 2 of this work.

5. The Traits of Deities

1. For comparable reflections for Mesopotamia, see J. Black, "The Slain Heroes—Some Monsters of Ancient Mesopotamia," *Society for Mesopotamian Studies Bulletin* 15 (1988), 19–20. For a broader study of many of these characteristics in the ancient Near East, see K.

van der Toorn, "God (I)," *DDD* 352–65. See also R. C. van Leeuwen, "The Background to Proverbs 30:4aα," *Wisdom, You Are My Sister: Studies in Honor of Roland E. Murphy, O. Carm., on the Occasion of His Eightieth Birthday* (ed. M. L. Barré; CBQMS 29; Washington, DC: Catholic Biblical Association of America, 1997), 102–20; note especially his comment on p. 20: "The main purpose of the topos [of ascent to heaven] is to reaffirm the great gulf that separates humans from the divine realm and prerogatives of deity, such as immorality, superhuman knowledge, wisdom and power." None of these studies addresses at any great length the Ugaritic evidence pertaining to divine characteristics. For an important comprehensive listing with discussion, see M. C. A. Korpel, *A Rift in the Clouds: Ugaritic and Hebrew Descriptions of the Divine* (UBL 8; Münster: Ugarit-Verlag, 1990). On the issue of knowledge and wisdom, see the next note.

2. I would be inclined to include knowledge and wisdom as a fifth characteristic. However, the Ugaritic texts do not present knowledge and wisdom as general aspects of divinity. Moreover, the number of Ugaritic personal names denoting wisdom and knowledge is quite limited (see Gröndahl, *Die Personennamen*, 142–43 for *yd'; *hss does not appear in Gröndahl's listing). Instead, they are concentrated in the figures of El and to a lesser extent Kothar (based on his technological expertise). On the wisdom of El, see *EUT* 42–43; M. Dietrich and O. Loretz, "Die Weisheit des ugaritisches Gott El im Kontext der altorientalisches Weisheit," *UF* 24 (1992), 31–38. Regarding Kothar's wisdom, see Smith, "Kothar wa-Hasis, the Ugaritic Craftsman God," 85–90. To be sure, other deities such as Baal may have been thought to possess special knowledge unknown to humans; so P. Xella, "La >>sagesse<< de Baal," *Ana šadî Labāni lu allik: Beiträge zu orientalischen und mittelmeerischen Kulturen. Festschrift für Wolfgang Röllig* (ed. B. Pongratz-Leisten, H. Kühne, and P. Xella; AOAT 247; Kevelaer: Butzon & Bercker; Neukirchen-Vluyn: Neukirchener, 1997), 435–46. J. C. de Moor discusses divine "foreknowledge" as a general feature of "the great gods of Ugarit" (de Moor, *The Rise of Yahwism: The Roots of Israelite Monotheism* [sec. ed.; ETL XCI; Leuven: University Press/Uitgeverij Peeters, 1997], 85–87). Features that de Moor takes as theologically significant strike me at times as literary matters: El's caution to Yamm and his so-called unwillingness to help him heighten the tension of the narrative, to my mind. However, missing on the whole from Ugaritic myths are any general statements about the wisdom or knowledge of the deities. In contrast, a particular stress is placed on knowledge and wisdom in Mesopotamian and Israelite texts. In Gilgamesh the woman tells Enkidu: "You are wise, Enkidu, and you have become like a god" (Gilgamesh 4:34; *ANET* 75). In addition to Genesis 3:22, wisdom texts such as Job 11:7–8 and Sirach 1:3, 8 acknowledge this divine feature. For discussion, see R. C. van Leeuwen, "The Background to Proverbs 30:4aα," 107–08. See also the title "God of knowledge" (1 Samuel 2:3) echoed in 1QH 1:27, 12:10, 13:18, etc.; for additional listings, see *The Dictionary of Classical Hebrew: Volume II.* רב (ed. D. J. A. Clines, J. Elwolde, Executive Editor; Sheffield: Sheffield Academic Press, 1995), 456. Knowledge also obtains among angels (2 Samuel 14:17, cf. 1 Peter 1:12); see further R. Kasher, "Angelology and the Supernal Worlds in the Aramaic Targums to the Prophets," *Journal for the Study of Judaism in the Persian, Hellenistic, and Roman Periods* 27/2 (1996), 176. Accordingly, this category might represent an "isogloss of divinity" between Ugaritic, on the one hand, and, on the other, Mesopotamian and Israelite texts. Note also the limits on divine knowledge in the Bible, discussed by M. Carasik, "The Limits of Omniscience," *JBL* 119 (2000), 221–32.

3. Caquot and Sznycer, *Ugaritic Religion*, 23, plates VII, VIII. See also O. Negbi, *Canaanite Gods in Metal* (Tel Aviv: Tel Aviv University, Institute of Archaeology, 1976), 46; and N. Wyatt, "The Stela of the Seated God from Ugarit," *UF* 15 (1983), 271–77.

4. Caquot and Sznycer, *Ugaritic Religion*, 24, plate XIV; Negbi, *Canaanite Gods in Metal*,

114, figure 129 no. 1630. See the beautiful photograph in Amiet, *Art of the Ancient Ancient Near East*, 202 and 203, no. 78.

5. See J. J. M. Roberts, "The Hand of Yahweh," *VT* 21 (1971), 244–51, esp. 246–48; S. Norin, "Die Hand Gottes im alten Testament," *La Main de Dieu/Die Hand Gottes* (ed. R. Kieffer and J. Bergman; WUNT 94; Tübingen: Mohr [Siebeck], 1997), 54. Other essays in this volume address the broader ancient Near Eastern context of this motif.

6. Roberts, "The Hand of Yahweh," 247–48; Pardee, " 'As Strong As Death'," *Love & Death in the Ancient Near East: Essays in Honor of Marvin H. Pope* (ed. J. H. Marks and R. M. Good; Guilford, CT: Four Quarters, 1987), 65–69.

7. See M. S. Smith, "Divine Form and Size in Ugaritic and Israelite Religion," *ZAW* 100 (1988), 424–27. For some Mesopotamian evidence, see V. Hurowitz, *I Have Built You an Exalted House: Temple Building in the Bible in Light of Mesopotamian and Northwest Semitic Writings* (JSOTS 115; Sheffield: JSOT, 1992), 337.

8. See M. Delcor, "Two Special Meanings of the יד," *JSS* 12 (1967), 234–40; A. Fitzgerald, "Hebrew *yd* = 'Lore' and Beloved,' " *CBQ* 29 (1967), 368–74; *CMHE* 23 n. 56; *TO* 1.205 n. i; M. H. Pope, "The Ups and Downs of El's Amours," *UF* 11 (1979), 706; C. L. Seow, *Myth, Drama, and the Politics of David's Dance* (HSM 46; Atlanta, GA: Scholars, 1989), 110 n. 88. Cross, Pope, Seow, and others rightly argue for wordplay here, but the development underlying this wordplay may be delineated further. As these authors note, the Ugaritic word is literally "hand," but it is also a term for "love," with the further connotation of "penis." Two roots seem to underlie Ugaritic *yd*, namely, the primitive bi-consonantal **yd*, "hand" and the triconsonantal **wdd*, "love." In Ugaritic these two roots have coalesced and the meaning of the former seems to have affected the semantics of the latter (see n. 116 for BH examples of this phenomenon). The semantic connotation of "love" underlying **wdd* has evidently influenced the meaning of **yd*, "hand," by taking on the nuance of "passion" and "penis." The usage appears in the two passages cited. Ugaritic *yd* is sometimes a circumlocution for penis, as 1.23.33–35 illustrates, and 1.4 IV 38–39 likewise uses both *yd* and *'ahbt* in a sexual manner.

9. M. H. Pope and J. H. Tigay, "A Description of Baal," *UF* 3 (1971), 122.

10. See W. H. Irwin, "The Extended Simile in RS 24.245 obv.," *UF* 15 (1983), 54–57.

11. See A. Abou Assaf, *Der Tempel von 'Ain Dara* (Damaszener Forschungen 3; Mainz: Philip von Zabern, 1990), 13–16; E. M. Bloch-Smith, " 'Who is the King of Glory?': Solomon's Temple and Its Symbolism," *Scripture and Other Artifacts: Essays on the Bible and Archaeology in Honor of Philip J. King* (ed. M. D. Coogan, J. C. Exum, and L. E. Stager; Louisville, KY: Westminster/John Knox, 1994), 21–25; and in M. S. Smith, *The Pilgrimage Pattern in Exodus* (JSOTSup 239; Sheffield: Sheffield Academic Press, 1997), 85, 87. For pictures of the foot impressions, see T. J. Lewis, "Divine Images and Aniconism in Ancient Israel," *JAOS* 118 (1998), 40. For an older discussion of deities' supersize, see M. S. Smith, "Divine Form and Size in the Ugaritic and Pre-Exilic Israelite Religion," *ZAW* 100 (1988), 424–27.

12. For the following points, see E. M. Bloch-Smith, " 'Who Is the King of Glory?' " 18–31. See also her contribution in Smith, *The Pilgrimage Pattern in Exodus*, 84–85, 86.

13. However, see the discussion in the following section regarding the meaning of *šûl*, customarily regarded as the skirt of the divine robe.

14. The phrase derives from a discussion of comparable Mesopotamian material by van Leeuwen, "The Background," 105.

15. Hurowitz, in his presentation at the symposium in April 1998 sponsored by the Center for Judaic Studies. See Hurowitz, "What Goes In Is What Comes Out: Materials for Creating Cult Statues," *Text, Artifact, and Image. Revealing Ancient Israelite Religion* (ed. T. J. Lewis and G. Beckman; in preparation).

16. Schmandt-Besserat, " 'Ain Ghazal 'Monumental' Figures," *BASOR* 310 (1998), 12. For Schmandt-Besserat, such descriptions imply two heads.

17. *ANET* 62.

18. This material derives from Smith, *The Pilgrimage Pattern in Exodus*, 249–57.

19. For Mesopotamia, see P. Amiet, "La Naissance des Dieux. Approche iconographique," *RB* 102 (1995), 481–505.

20. Mullen (*The Divine Council*, 78) suggests instead that *'glt* is a goddess, in which case neither divinity would be theriomorphic.

21. Parker in *UNP* 186–87. For discussion of some terms for divine genitalia in the Ugaritic texts, see D. Pardee, "(Rather Dim but Nevertheless Appreciable) Light from (a Very Obscure) Ugaritic (Text) on (the) Hebrew (Bible)," *To Touch the Text: Biblical and Related Studies in Honor of Joseph A. Fitzmyer, S. J.* (ed. M. P. Horgan and P. J. Kobelski; New York: Crossroad, 1989), 84; Watson, "Notes on Some Ugaritic Words," 47.

22. On the attribute animals of various Ugaritic deities, see chapter 1, section 4.

23. De Moor, *The Rise of Yahwism*, 84.

24. De Moor, *The Rise of Yahwism*, 84.

25. See M. S. Smith, "Divine Travel as a Token of Divine Rank," *UF* 16 (1984), 359.

26. To be sure, de Moor offers other passages as evidence for this crisis of belief in the gods. For the problems with de Moor's view of the gods' "ineffectual foreknowledge," see n. 2. For other related matters, see the end of the last section of chapter 4. Contra de Moor (*The Rise of Yahwism*, 88–91), evil is hardly less overcome in biblical texts than in the Ugaritic texts (see chapter 1), and the presentation of Mot in the Baal Cycle hardly suggests a crisis in divinity, only the limits of Baal's kingship. The situation reflects a theology of divinity that is at once powerful even if at times precarious (*UBC* 101–10, esp. 104). Kirta's situation, which de Moor takes pains to show reflects badly on the gods (*The Rise of Yahwism*, 91–95) is hardly worse off than Job's (see Introduction, nn. 66, 74; cf. chapter 4, section 8). Some of the pessimism detected by de Moor derives from his view of the inexorable turn of the seasons to which even the gods are subject. Yet this approach depends on de Moor's view of the seasonal pattern in the Ugaritic texts, which has received substantial criticism (see *UBC* 60–75). As for "becoming too human," such a later notion for the second person of the Trinity does not seem to have produced a "crisis of faith," on the contrary.

27. See T. Jacobsen, *Treasures of Darkness: A History of Mesopotamian Religion* (New Haven/London: Yale, 1976), 234–36; A. Livingstone, *Mystical and Mythological Explanatory Works of Assyrian and Babylonian Scholars* (Oxford: Clarendon Press, 1986), 101–02, 233; idem, *Court Poetry and Literary Miscellanea* (State Archives of Assyria III; Helsinki: Helsinki University, 1989), 99; W. G. Lambert, "The Historical Development of the Mesopotamian Pantheon: A Study in Sophisticated Polytheism," *Unity and Diversity* (ed. H. Goedicke and J. J. M. Roberts; Baltimore: Johns Hopkins University Press, 1975) 191–200; idem, "Syncretism and Religious Controversy in Babylonia," *Altorientalische Forschungen* 24 (1997), 158–62; P. K. McCarter, "The Religious Reforms of Hezekiah and Josiah," *Aspects of Monotheism: How God is One* (ed. H. Shanks and J. Meinhardt; Washington, DC: Biblical Archaeology Society, 1997), 67–69; and Porter, "The Anxiety of Influence," 240–54. This sort of comparison is reminiscent of incantations invoking divine help by identifying parts of the body with various deities. For an example, see T. Jacobsen, "Mesopotamia," in H. Frankfort et al., *The Intellectual Adventure of Ancient Man: An Essay on Speculative Thought in the Ancient East* (Chicago: University of Chicago Press, 1946), 133. Such an approach does not appear in texts from Syria-Palestine. The thrust of R. S. Hendel's discussion links the former sort of text to Mesopotamian iconism. See Hendel, "Aniconism and Anthropomorphism in Ancient Israel," *The Image and the Book: Iconic Cults, Aniconism, and the*

Rise of Book Religion in Israel and the Ancient Near East (ed. K. van der Toorn; Leuven: Peeters, 1997), 208. Accordingly, the lack of such texts in Israel might be linked to its so-called aniconic tradition. If correct, some sort of similar text might be expected in Ugarit. See 1.101 discussed in section 1.

28. KAR 102, lines 10–19, quoted in Jacobsen, *Treasures of Darkness*, 235.

29. CT XXIV pl. 50, no. 47406 obv. 3–10, cited in Jacobsen, *Treasures of Darkness*, 235. See also B. Hartmann, "Monotheismus in Mesopotamien?" *Monotheismus im Alten Israel und seiner Umwelt* (ed. O. Keel; BB 14; Fribourg: Schweizeriches Katholisches Bibelwerk, 1980), 64.

30. CT 24 50, BM 47406, quoted translation taken from Lambert, "The Historical Development of the Mesopotamian Pantheon," 198.

31. Hendel, "Aniconism and Anthropomorphism in Ancient Israel," 208. McCarter sets this sort of monism within polytheism under the rubric of the "origins of monotheism" (McCarter, "The Religious Reforms of Hezekiah and Josiah," 67–69); only someone looking toward the *telos* of monotheism would view such a monism in this manner. I have preferred to relate this phenomenon to the apparent convergence of different divinities' characteristics in the figure of Yahweh (see *EHG* xxiii–xxiv, 21–24, 36–37, 146–47, 154–57); but this development constitutes neither monotheism nor even monolatry. Instead, both the Mesopotamian and Israelite phenomena involve exaltation of the national god, which in Israel's case turned out to be prerequisite to the development of monotheism. See chapter 8.

32. See the previous section for further discussion of this text. See also W. H. Irwin, "The Extended Simile in RS 24.245 obv.," *UF* 15 (1983), 54–57. See comparisons sometimes made with Song of Songs 5:10–16 (M. H. Pope and J. H. Tigay, "A Description of Baal," *UF* 3 [1971], 117–30; W. Tyloch, "Ugaritic Poems and Song of Songs," *Šulmu IV: Everyday Life in the Ancient Near East: Papers Presented at the International Conference. Poznan, 19–22 September 1989* [ed. J. Zablocka and S. Zawadzki; Seria Historia 182; Poznan: University Press of Poznan, 1993], 300–01).

33. *EHG* 97–103; B. Uffenheimer, "Myth and Reality in Ancient Israel," *The Origins and Diversity of Axial Civilizations* (ed. S. N. Eisenstadt; Albany: State University of New York Press, 1986), 164–66.

34. For a summary of the current discussion about this so-called source, see Smith, *The Pilgrimage Pattern in Exodus*, 146–59.

35. See J. J. M. Roberts, "The Motif of the Weeping God in Jeremiah and Its Background in the Lament Tradition of the Ancient Near East," *Old Testament Essays* 5 (1992), 361–74.

36. Eslinger, "The Infinite in a Finite Organical Perception (Isaiah VI 1–5)," *VT* 45 (1995), 145–73; followed by Wyatt, *Myths of Power*, 5, 342. Wyatt argues that the suffixes on the body parts named in verse 2 belong to Yahweh and not the seraphim since the suffixes are plural, but this argument ignores the distributive prepositional phrase, *lĕ'eḥād*, "to each one," applied to the seraphim in this verse.

37. One may remain open to this theory for **šûl* in verse 1 as divine genitals, but I would voice the following reservations about the arguments: (1) I am not as prepared as Eslinger is to dismiss the relevance of *šûl* as part of priestly garment in Exodus 38:33–34, 39:25–26 (the point of such a divine covering may be to mark the divine holiness on analogy with the holiness of the priesthood); (2) the other biblical contexts (as well as the cognates) sometimes involve human dress or lack thereof, and Eslinger allows for dress *or* pudenda in some passages, with the former sometimes as a hint of the latter; and (3) the typical description of the divine leader of the heavenly council elsewhere in either Ugaritic or biblical texts lacks any such reference to sexuality per se (I do not regard El and Athirat's conversation in CAT 1.4 IV–V as typical). It is to be noted that **šûl* in the meaning of

"side" is clearly attested elsewhere (e.g., in the Copper Scroll, 3Q15 1.11, 4.9) and therefore not easily dismissed. Finally a separate issue: the "feet" in verse 2 have been taken by many commentators as an euphemism for genitalia of the seraphim, but Eslinger sees Yahweh as the one with the "feet" as well as the "face" here; for a traditional approach to these body parts as belonging to the seraphim augmented by iconographical analysis, see Keel and Uehlinger, *Gods, Goddesses and Images of God*, 272–74, 401. Eslinger's view of verse 2 requires a reading of the pronominal suffixes that is elastic at best (in the article sometimes lô in verse 2 is arranged with what precedes, sometimes with what follows). For all of these reasons, the interpetation remains problematic. Despite these questions, readers should understand that despite their possible sense of propriety about biblical portraits of the divine, a divine portrait with sexual aspects is a priori not impossible or even improbable.

38. Pope, Review of M. C. A. Korpel, *A Rift in the Clouds*, UF 22 (1990), 497–502. M. Dijkstra (personal communication) has expressed reservations about the order of elements assumed by this interpretation, but I think that this point is hardly as salient as he believes.

39. The material and issues are complex and beyond the scope of this investigation. See (by year) R. S. Hendel, "The Social Origins of the Aniconic Tradition in Ancient Israel," CBQ 50 (1988), 365–82; idem, "Images of God in Ancient Israel," *Bulletin of the Anglo-Israel Archaeological Society* 8 (1988–89), 81–82; the seminal book of T. N. D. Mettinger, *No Graven Image? Israelite Aniconism in Its Ancient Near Eastern Context* (ConBOT 42; Stockholm: Almqvist & Wiksell, 1995); the thoughtful review of Mettinger's book by T. J. Lewis, "Divine Images and Aniconism in Ancient Israel," JAOS 118 (1998), 36–53; and the various responses to Mettinger's work in *The Image and the book*. The arguments for aniconism in ancient Israel rest variously on an argument from silence (i.e., the lack of excavated divine images), a dismissal of pillar figurines as divine statuary, and stelas (*maṣṣēbôt*) as aniconic symbols of deities; all three are debatable. With regard to the third, the main clear indigenous information about how stelas were perceived cultically, namely, Genesis 28, would suggest that they do not represent the deity per se, but mark the *place* of the deity's cultic presence. Specifically, the reference to *bêt-'ēl*, "the house of God," suggests that it is the place and not the deity so much that the stelas signify (the same point would apply to stelas called *baitylia* in PE 1.10.16 and other late classical sources). However, this distinction may not have obtained in some contexts. For the evidence and issues, see M. Hutter, "Kultstelen und Baityloi: Die Ausstrahlung eines syrischen religiösen Phänomens-nach Kleinasien und Israel," *Religionsgeschichtliche Bezlehungen zwischen Kleinasien, Nordsyrien und dem Alten Testament: Internationales Symposion Hamburg 17–21. März 1990* (ed. B. Janowski, K. Koch and G. Wilhelm; OBO 129; Freiburg Schweiz: Universitätsverlag; Göttingen: Vandenhoeck & Ruprecht, 1993), 87–108; K. van der Toorn, "Worshipping Stones: On the Deification of Cult Symbols," JNWSL 23 (1997) 7–10; E. Bloch-Smith, "Representations of Divinity in the Archaeological Record of Ancient Israel," *Text, Artifact, and Image. Revealing Ancient Israelite Religion* (ed. T. J. Lewis and G. Beckman; in preparation).

40. See the same vocabulary in lines 1, 12, 15, and 16 of the Tell Fakhariyah inscription, discussed in D. M. Gropp and T. J. Lewis, "Notes on some Problems in the Aramaic Text of the Hadd-Yith'i Bilingual," BASOR 259 (1985), 47. For the editio princeps, see A. Abou-Assaf, P. Bordreuil, and A. R. Millard, *La statue de Tell Fekheriyé et son inscription bilingue assyro-araméenne* (Paris: Editions recherche sur les civilisations, 1982). Accordingly, one may sense in this usage an implicit polemic against the making of images, since humanity serves as the living image of the Israelite deity while images of of man-made objects constitute lifeless symbols of dead gods. In Second Isaiah such a polemic against images is explicit. See further chapters 9, section 1, and chapter 10 in general.

41. The most recent proponent of this approach is J. C. de Moor, "The Duality in

God and Man: Gen. 1:26–27 as P's Interpretation of the Yahwistic Creation Account," *Intertextuality in Ugarit and Israel: Papers Read at the Tenth Joint Meeting of the Society for Old Testament Study and Het Oudtestamentisch Werkgezelschap in Nederland en Belgie held at Oxford, 1997* (ed. J. C. de Moor; OTS XL; Leiden: Brill, 1998), 112–25.

42. M. S. Smith, "God Male and Female in the Old Testament: Yahweh and his asherah," *Theological Studies* 48 (1987), 333–40. Cf. EHG 114 n. 138.

43. For a discussion of divine and human sexuality in this text without recourse to such explanations, see T. Frymer-Kensky, *In The Wake of the Goddesses: Women, Culture, and the Biblical Tansformation of Pagan Myth* (New York: Free Press, 1992), 142.

44. For the details in the following remarks, see EHG 97–103.

45. For the female imagery of the divine in "Second Isaiah," see especially M. I. Gruber, *The Motherhood of God and Other Studies* (South Florida Studies in the History of Judaism 57; Altanta, GA: Scholars, 1992), 3–15. Cf. B. S. Childs, *Old Testament in a Canonical Context* (Philadelphia: Fortress, 1985) 39–40.

46. See Roberts, "The Motif of the Weeping God in Jeremiah," 361–74.

47. See chapter 10.

48. For references for the following material, see EHG 99–100. See further the fine study of H. W. Jüngeling, " 'Was anders ist Gott für Menschen, wenn nicht sein Vater und seine Mutter?' Zu einer Doppelmetapher der religiösen Sprache," *Ein Gott allein? JHWH-Verehrung und biblischer Monotheismus im Kontext der israeltischen und altorientalischen Religionsgeschichte* (ed. W. Dietrich and M. A. Klopfenstein; 13. Kolloquium der Schweizerischen Akademie der Geistes-und Sozialwissenschaften 1993; Freiburg Schweiz: Universitätsverlag, 1994 = repr. OBO 139; Freiburg Schweiz: Universitätsverlag; Göttingen: Vandenhoeck & Ruprecht, 1994), 365–86.

49. De Moor, "The Duality in God and Man: Gen. 1:26–27," 112–25; see also S. D. Moore, *God's Gym: Divine Male Bodies of the Bible* (New York: Routledge, 1996), 92.

50. So the heavy-handed interpretation of H. Eilberg-Schwartz, *God's Phallus and Other Problems for Men and Monotheism* (Boston: Beacon Press, 1994); the question would be whether the homoeroticism belongs to the text or this author. There is no biblical evidence for the subordinate clause in the following claim: "these men [Moses and the patriarchs] love, in ways that are imagined as erotically and sensually, a male deity" (p. 3). Eilberg-Schwartz also writes wrongly of Israelite religion as "imagining men as wives of God." The logic for the claim is flawed: because Israel is imagined as God's lover and men are part of Israel (including ones who author such images), it is assumed that men then imagined themselves as lovers. This logic indeed manifests "the worst kind of literalism" (see the following note). See also his article, "God's Phallus and the Dilemmas of Masculinity," *Reclaiming Men: Religion and Masculinities* (ed. S. B. Boyd, W. M. Longwood, and M. W. Muesse; Louisville, KY: Westminster John Knox, 1996), 36–47 (I thank Professor Shawn Krahmer for bringing this reference to my attention). This is not to deny the potential value of psychoanalytic theory for the study of religion. See chapter 8, section 5. For further discussion of the "corporeal God" in the Bible informed by the work of Eilberg-Schwartz, see Moore, *God's Gym*, esp. 82–86.

51. Childs, *Old Testament in a Canonical Context*, 40.

52. Frymer-Kensky, *In The Wake of the Goddesses*, 189.

53. Hendel, "Aniconism and Anthropomorphism in Ancient Israel," 222–23 n. 68.

54. Eilberg-Schwartz (*God's Phallus and Other Problems for Men and Monotheism*, 71) recognizes that authority is part of the issue with these passages, but he insists on their "ambivalence" (p. 64) and "teasing uncertainty" (p. 70). Eilberg-Schwartz can always claim that scholars who deny his view are "into denial," but I see no such features in these texts. I take authority as the central issue in the prophetic passages. I see Exodus 33–34 as a

commentary on the visionary experience of Exodus 24:9–11 (Smith, *The Pilgrimage Pattern in Exodus*, 248–57), and I see this bit of old tradition also as an expression of the privileged place of Moses and the other Israelite leaders in a piece of Pentateuchal tradition now largely unpreserved and perhaps rewritten.

55. See J. K. Eakins, "Anthropomorphisms in Isaiah 40–55," *HS* 20 (1979), 47–50, with the well-noted accompanying citation of Isaiah 55:6: "Seek Yahweh while He can be found, // Call to Him while He is near."

56. See *EHG* 101, and the secondary literature cited there. See also chapter 4, n. 41.

57. It is possible that in the second translation *qdš* is to be regarded as the title of a specific deity (Athirat is the usually cited possibility here), but this view is debated. For discussion, see *UBC* 294–95; P. Merlo, "Note critiche su alcune presunte iconografie della dea Ashera," *SEL* 14 (1997), 43–64, esp. 50.

58. For the different views, see *EUT* 43; *UBC* 295 n. 135 with further literature.

59. For discussion, see chapter 4, section 7.

60. As noted by D. P. Wright, "Holiness, Sex, and Death in the Garden of Eden," *Bib* 77 (1996), 305–29.

61. These points are made in K. van der Toorn, *Sin and Sanction in Israel and Mesopotamia: A Comparative Study* (Studia Semitica Neerlandica 22; Assen: Van Gorcum, 1985), 28–29; idem, "La pureté rituelle au proche-orient ancien," *RHR* 206 (1989), 339–56. It is claimed that the Akkadian word related to the Hebrew words for "holy" and "holiness" (*qdš*) means "to be clean" (so *AHw* 891a). However, such usage is rarely, if ever, attested, according to van der Toorn (*Sin and Sanction*, 28). For some further clarifications on the Mesopotamian evidence, see M. J. Geller, "Taboo in Mesopotamia: A Review Article," *JCS* 42 (1990), 105–17.

62. For this latter meaning in Ugaritic as applied to lapis lazuli, see CAT 1.4 V 19. For discussion of both this Ugaritic passage and Exodus 24:10, see Smith, "Kothar wa-Hasis, the Ugaritic Craftsman God," 321–22.

63. For this point, see van der Toorn, *Sin and Sanction*, 23.

64. Jacobsen, *Treasures of Darkness*, 3. For a valuable appreciation of this work, see Muffs, *Love and Joy*, 61–66.

65. R. A. Di Vito, *Studies in Third Millennium Sumerian and Akkadian Personal Names: The Designation and Conception of the Personal God* (Studies Pohl: Series Maior 16; Rome: Pontificio Istituto Biblico, 1993), 256–57.

66. To be sure, Otto's *mysterium tremendum et fascinosum* has been influential in the analysis of other religions. For only one example, see R. C. Zaehner, *Hinduism* (sec. ed.; Oxford: Oxford University Press, 1966), 86.

67. See the cases discussed by Jacobsen, *Treasures of Darkness*, 16.

68. See F. A. M. Wiggerman, *Mesopotamian Protective Deities: The Ritual Texts* (Cuneiform Monographs 1; Groningen: Styx & PP, 1992), 151–54. For further discussion of such monsters, see section 4 and chapter 1.

69. Van der Toorn, *Sin and Sanction*, 23.

70. For a discussion of Otto's concept of the *mysterium tremendum et fascinosum*, see D. Merkur, "The Numinous as a Category of Values," *The Sacred and the Scholars: Comparative Methodologies for the Study of Primary Religious Data* (ed. T. A. Idinipulos and E. A. Yonan; Numen LXXIII; Leiden: Brill, 1996), 104–23.

71. For the ideological use of "holiness" of temples and other sacred spaces, see S. Guthrie, "The Sacred: A Skeptical View," *The Sacred and the Scholars: Comparative Methodologies for the Study of Primary Religious Data* (ed. T. A. Idinipulos and E. A. Yonan; Numen LXXIII; Leiden: Brill, 1996), 124–138.

72. Guthrie, "The Sacred: A Skeptical View," 135.

73. W. E. Paden, "Sacrality as Integrity: 'Sacred Order' as a Model for Describing Religious Worlds," *The Sacred and the Scholars: Comparative Methodologies for the Study of Primary Religious Data* (ed. T. A. Idinipulos and E. A. Yonan; Numen LXXIII; Leiden: Brill, 1996), 15. See also p. 13: "The rites for honoring a religious leader or a king and those for honoring a god are often hard to distinguish." So, too, myths for a deity?

74. See *BDB* 871–74.

75. T. Frymer-Kensky, *In the Wake of the Goddesses: Women, Culture, and the Biblical Transformation of Pagan Myth* (New York: Basic Books, 1992), 189–90. See also E. S. Gerstenberger, *Yahweh the Patriarch: Ancient Images of God and Feminist Theology* (trans. F. J. Gaiser; Minneapolis: Fortress, 1996), vi, 90; and Wright, "Holiness, Sex and Death," 314.

76. Sexual impurity includes menstruation (Leviticus 15:19–30; 18:19), pregnancy (Leviticus 12), a male's emission of semen (Leviticus 15:1–18). The connection between these sorts of impurity and the holiness of Yahweh is made explicitly in Leviticus 15:31.

77. For restrictions on priestly contact with the dead, see Leviticus 21:1–3, 11; 22:4b; Numbers 6:6–7. The statement in Leviticus 21:3 stands in distinct tension with 22:4b. See E. M. Bloch-Smith, "The Cult of the Dead in Judah: Interpreting the Material Remains" *JBL* 111 (1992), 222–23, who emphasizes the financial benefit gained through these prohibitions.

78. For the degrees of holiness between the people, the priesthood, and the chief priest, see J. Milgrom, "Israel's Sanctuary: The Priestly 'Picture of Dorian Gray'," *RB* 83 (1976), 390–99; reprinted in *Studies in Cultic Theology and Terminology* (Leiden: Brill, 1983), 75–84.

79. *EHG* 165.

80. OB X iii 3–5. See *ANET* 90 and W. G. Lambert, "The Theology of Death," *Death in Mesopotamia: Papers read at the XXVIᵉ Rencontre assyriologique internationale* (ed. B. Alster; Mesopotamia Copenhagen Studies in Assyriology 8; Copenhagen: Akademisk Forlag, 1980), 53; and "Some New Babylonian Wisdom Literature," *Wisdom in Ancient Israel: Essays in Honour of J. A. Emerton* (ed. J. Day, R. P. Gordon, and H. G. M. Williamson; Cambridge: Cambridge University Press, 1995), 41.

81. OB III iv 6–8 (*ANET* 79).

82. Kovacs, *The Epic of Gilgamesh* (Stanford, CA: Stanford University Press, 1989), 19 n. 6.

83. W. G. Lambert posits a literary relationship between Gilgamesh and Ecclesiastes, mediated by the inclusion of the former by scribes at Ugarit and Emar in the Late Bronze Age. See Lambert, "Some New Babylonian Wisdom Literature," 41–42. The point is mentioned here in order to highlight one social location of this sort of description of deities and humanity or at least of its transmission, namely, scribes of the Late Bronze Age through the Persian period.

84. OB Meissner ii 4'. See B. Foster, "Gilgamesh: Sex, Love and the Ascent of Knowledge," *Love and Death in the Ancient Near East: Essays in Honor of Marvin H. Pope* (ed. J. H. Marks and R. M. Good; Guilford, CT: Four Quarters, 1987), 41.

85. Tablet I ii 1 in *ANET* 73; IX ii 16 in *ANET* 88.

86. This information is taken from H. Hoffner, "Hittite Terms for the Life Span," *Love and Death in the Ancient Near East*, 53.

87. This title also applies to an Egyptian king in 2.42.9, perhaps a reflection of royal ideology that kings are eternal in a manner analogous to deities. Deceased Ugaritic kings were likewise labelled as *'il* (see 1.113.14–26). Cf. the apparent scribal exercise in 5.9 I 2–6, which requests blessing of eternity for *mnn*, either a personal name or "whomever"; if the latter were correct, it might reflect an extension of royal ideology.

88. For further discussion, see chapter 6, section 4.

89. See J. F. Healey, "The Immortality of the King: Ugarit and the Psalms," *Or* 53 (1984 = M. J. Dahood Memorial Volume) 246–47.

90. Cf. Mullen, *The Divine Council*, 19.

91. J. Z. Smith, "Dying and Rising Gods," *The Encyclopedia of Religion. Volume 4* (ed. M. Eliade; New York: Macmillan; London: Collier Macmillan, 1987), 521–22.

92. See Mullen, *The Divine Council*, 57, 91.

93. Lambert, "The Theology of Death," 64. The following points derive from Lambert, "The Theology of Death," 64–5. Note also the dead gods can have ghosts in Mesopotamian literature. See W. L. Moran, "The Creation of Man in Atrahasis I 192–248," *BASOR* 200 (1970), 54 n. 21.

94. For the divine character of such monsters, see Lambert, "The Theology of Death," 64; J. Black, "The Slain Heroes—Some Monsters of Ancient Mesopotamia," *Society for Mesopotamian Studies Bulletin* (Toronto) 15 (1988), 19–25. Such monsters are not deities in the same sense as their opponents. For some important distinctions, see Wiggerman, *Mesopotamian Protective Deities*, 158; and chapter 1.

95. See A. Livingstone, *Mystical and Mythological Explanatory Works of Assyrian and Babylonian Scholars* (Oxford: Clarendon Press, 1986) 142–45.

96. ANET 68.

97. ANET 67, 501–02.

98. Creation of the human person from the dust of the earth, a common Middle Eastern motif, signifies humanity's reality as created, but receiving the breath of life from Yahweh in Genesis 2 signals at the same time the connectedness of the human person to the divine. Genesis 1:26–28 achieves a comparable effect in a less anthropomorphic manner. To be in the divine image is to be connected somehow to the divine without actually being divine.

99. See Jacobsen, *Treasures of Darkness*, 25–27; Wiggermann, "Transtigridian Snake-Gods," 33–34, 41.

100. See Livingstone, *Mystical and Mythological Explanatory Works of Assyrian and Babylonian Scholars*, 136–41.

101. J. Z. Smith, "The Glory, Jest and Riddle: James George Frazer and *The Golden Bough*" (Ph.D. diss., Yale University, 1969), 366–75; idem, "Dying and Rising Gods," *The Encyclopedia of Religion. Volume 4* (ed. M. Eliade; New York: Macmillan; London: Collier Macmillan, 1987) 521–27. See chapter 6, section 1.

102. See the next chapter for detailed discussion.

103. On this text, see Mullen, *The Divine Council*, 118, 226–38; S. B. Parker, "The Beginning of the Reign of God. Psalm 82 as Myth and Liturgy," *RB* 102 (1995), 532–59; see also chapter 2, section 4.

104. Holloway, "The Case for Assyrian Religious Influence," 346, cites the notion of dead gods in Psalm 82 in connection with no. 30:3 in A. Livingstone, *Court Poetry and Literary Miscellanea* (State Archives of Assyria 3; Helsinki: Helsinki University, 1989): "servant of a dead god, house whose star has been disappeared from the heavens." The passage is discussed in chapter 2, section 4.

105. The passage and the different text-critical readings are discussed in chapter 2, section 4.

106. This is the translation of New Jewish Publication Society version, which notes that the Hebrew actually reads "we," "a change made by a pious scribe."

107. The parade West Semitic examples are CAT 1.108.11–12; 5.9.2–6; KAI 10:9; 26 A III 5–6; Psalm 72:5. For Akkadian and West Semitic evidence, see J. C. Greenfield, "Scripture and Inscription: The Literary and Rhetorical Element in Some Early Phoenician Inscriptions," *Near Eastern Studies in Honor of William Foxwell Albright* (ed. H. Goedicke;

Baltimore: Johns Hopkins University Press, 1971) 266–68; S. M. Paul, "Psalm 72:5—A Traditional Blessing for the Long Life of the King," *JNES* 31 (1972) 351–5; M. L. Barré, "An Analysis of the Royal Blessing in the Karatepe Inscription," *MAARAV* 3/2 (1982) 177–94. For Hittite prayers requesting long life, see H. Hoffner, "Hittite Terms for the Life Span," *Love and Death in the Ancient Near East*, 53–55.

108. S. Smith, *The Statue of Idrimi* (Occasional Papers of the British Institute of Archaeology in Anakara 1; London: The British Institute of Archaeology in Ankara, 1949), 22; cited by M. L. Barré, "An Analysis of the Royal Blessing in the Karatepe Inscription, 185 n. 28.

109. For these alternatives, see G. A. Barton, *A Critical and Exegetical Commentary on the Book of Ecclesiastes* (ICC; Edinburgh: T. & T. Clark, 1912), 105; R. Gordis, *Koheleth— The Man and His World: A Study of Ecclesiastes* (third augmented ed.; New York: Schocken, 1968), 231. The last of the four is favored by Gordis. For etymological discussion of these suggestions, see W. Leslau, *Comparative Dictionary of Ge'ez (Classical Ethiopic)* (Wiesbaden: Otto Harrassowitz, 1987), 61.

110. *BDB* 761.

111. See J. C. de Moor, *An Anthology of Religious Texts from Ugarit* (Nisaba 16; Leiden: Brill, 1987), 65 n. 297.

112. This meaning has also been claimed for Ugaritic in the expression *mlk 'lm*, "king of the universe," attested in CAT 1.108.1. See *UT* 19.1858; cf. A. Cooper, "*MLK 'LM*: 'Eternal King' or 'King of Eternity'?" *Love & Death in the Ancient Near East*, 1–7. However, the imputed meaning is apparently anachronistic.

113. So C. L. Seow, *Ecclesiastes* (AB 18C; Garden City, NY: Doubleday, 1997), 163.

114. Comparing Ecclesiastes 8:17, M. Fox emends to *'āmāl*, "labor"; see Fox, *Qohelet and His Contradictions* (JSOTSup 71; Bible and Literature 18; Sheffield: Almond, 1989), 194. Cf. B. Isaksson, *Studies in the Language of Qoheleth: With Special Emphasis on the Verbal System* (Acta Universitatis Upsaliensis Studia Semitica Upsaliensia 10; Stockholm: Almqvist & Wiksell, 1987), 79–81.

115. Barton translates "ignorance," based on the sense of "hidden" or "secret" derived from the second alternative. See Barton, *A Critical and Exegetical Commentary*, 105.

116. Ugaritic offers another example of coalescence of first **w-/y-* roots and their subsequent semantic coalescence. The word Ugaritic *yd* is literally "hand," but it is also a term for "love," with the further connotation of "penis." Two roots seem to underlie Ugaritic *yd*, namely, the primitive biconsonantal **yd*, "hand" and **wdd*, "love." See *TO* 1.205 n. i; Seow, *Myth, Drama, and the Politics of David's Dance*, 110 n. 88. In Ugaritic these two roots have coalesced and their meanings seem to have affected one another. It would seem that the semantic sense of "love" underlying **wdd* has come to exert a connotation on the literal meaning of **yd*, "hand." Accordingly, Ugaritic *yd* has the resultant nuance of penis. (The usage may be illustrated by two passages, 1.23.33–35, cited in section 1, and 1.4 IV 38–39.) From these cases it is evident that any given context may draw on the connotations of both of the older roots now coalesced into a single word.

Two Hebrew roots may serve as further illustrations. Ugaritic *'it*, a word for a sacrifice, has coalesced in BH *'iššeh* as an offering made by fire (*BDB* 77–78; cf. Ugaritic *'išt* for "fire"). More controversial is the verb *ta'ăzôb* in Psalms 16:10, often derived from the old or original (for heuristic purposes, sometimes called "Proto-Semitic" or PS for short) root **ḏb>* BH **zb*, "to put, place," as suggested by the parallelism with **ntn*, "to give." See M. Dahood, *Psalms I.1–50* (AB 16; Garden City, NY: Doubleday, 1965) 90–1. The meaning "abandon, leave" from the PS root**zb*, which merged with the root **ḏb* (both became **zb* in Hebrew) does not suit the context, and it may be argued that the original root therefore was *ʿdb > BH *ʿẓb, "put, place." For the author of this psalm, however, this distinction would not have existed; rather, the author may have associated within this one Hebrew word the range of meanings and connotations of the two original PS roots, *ʿdb and *ʿẓb.

117. Cf. the restlessness of Gilgamesh's heart and his quest for eternity. See Ninevah version III ii 10: *lib-bi la ša-li-la*. See *ANET* 81; Foster, "Gilgamesh," 33.

118. Pardee, "An Evaluation of the Proper Names," 149.

119. If knowledge and wisdom were to be included (see n. 2), they might be added in the following manner:

| ignorance | some knowledge of the world and God, but experience of disorder and unintelligibility | wisdom and knowledge |

120. See the reflections on this problem by P. Machinist, "The Question of Distinctiveness in Ancient Israel: An Essay," *Ah Assyria . . . : Studies in Assyrian History and Ancient Near Eastern Historiography Presented to Hayim Tadmor* (ed. M. Cogan and I. Eph'al; Jerusalem: Magnes, 1991) 196–212; E. L. Greenstein, "The God of Israel and the Gods of Canaan: How Different Were They?" *Proceedings of the Twelfth World Congress of Jewish Studies Jerusalem, July 29 to August 5, 1997: Division A. The Bible and Its World* (ed. R. Margolin; Jerusalem: World Union of Jewish Studies, 1999) 47*–57*; and by Lewis, "Divine Images," 53.

6. The Life and Death of Baal

1. For the scholarly research, see J. B. Tsirkin, "The Labours, Death and Resurrection of Melqart as Depicted on the Gates of the Gades' Herakleion," *RSF* 9 (1981), 21–27; T. N. D. Mettinger, *In Search of God: The Meaning and Message of the Everlasting Names* (trans. F. H. Cryer; Philadelphia: Fortress, 1988) 82–91; idem, "The Elusive Presence: YHWH, El and Baal and the Distinctiveness of Israelite Faith," *Die Hebräische Bibel und ihre zweifache Nachgeschichte: Festschrift für Rolf Rendtorff zum 65. Geburstag* (ed. E. Blum, C. Macholz, and E. W. Stegemann; Neukirchen-Vluyn: Neukirchener, 1990), 401 n. 44; "The 'Dying and Rising God': A Survey of Research from Frazer to the Present Day," *SEÅ* 63 (1998) 111–23; J. Day, "Baal," *The Anchor Bible Dictionary* (ed. D. N. Freedman; six vols.; New York: Doubleday, 1992), 1.549. See also Ackerman, *Under Every Green Tree: Popular Religon in Sixth-Century Judah* (HSM 46; Atlanta, GA: Scholars, 1992), 84, 90. For ᵈNIN.KUR at Emar as "dying and rising god," see D. Arnaud in *Bulletin de la Société Ernest Renan* 1979, 118 (discussed by D. E. Fleming, *The Installation of Baal's High Priestess at Emar* [HSS 42; Atlanta, GA: Scholars, 1992], 170). For nonscholarly literature, see D. Leeming and J. Page, *God: Myths of the Male Divine* (New York: Oxford University Press, 1996). The last item of Mettinger's cited here, which came into my hands after the completion of this chapter, provides a very serviceable history of scholarship in the twentieth century. I wish to thank Professor Mettinger for making this article available to me; in it he mentions his book in progress, tentatively entitled *Resurrection Reconsidered: Dying and Rising Gods. A Study of West Semitic Religion*. The results of the discussion in this chapter will undoubtedly require modification in light of Professor Mettinger's research.

2. J. Z. Smith, "The Glory, Jest and Riddle: James George Frazer and *The Golden Bough*" (Ph.D. diss., Yale University, 1969), 366–75; idem, "Dying and Rising Gods," *The Encyclopedia of Religion. Volume 4* (ed. M. Eliade; New York: Macmillan; London: Collier Macmillan, 1987), 521–27; idem, *Drudgery Divine: On the Comparison of Early Christianities and the Religions of Late Antiquity* (Jordan Lectures in Comparative Religion, XIV. School

of Oriental and African Studies University of London; Chicago Studies in the History of Judaism; Chicago: University of Chicago Press, 1990), 85–115, esp. 90–93; W. Burkert, *Structure and History in Greek Mythology and Ritual* (Berkeley: University of California Press, 1979), 100; J. P. Södergard, "The Ritualized Bodies of Cybele's Galli and the Methodological Problem of the Plurality of Explanations," *The Problem of Ritual: Based on Papers Read at the Symposium on Religious Studies Held at Åbo, Finland on the 13th–16th of August, 1991* (ed. T. Ahlbäck; Scripta Instituti Doneriani Aboensis; Stockholm: Almqvist and Wiksell, 1993), 175–76. For the biblical and ancient Middle Eastern fields, see the citations of J. Z. Smith, "The Glory, Jest and Riddle," 40 n. 43; and more recently, H. Barstad, *The Religious Polemics of Amos: Studies in the Preaching of Am 2, 7B–8, 4, 1–13, 5, 1–27, 6, 4–7, 8, 14* (VTSup 34; Leiden: Brill, 1984), 84 n. 45, 148–51; and N. Walls, Jr., *The Goddess Anat in the Ugaritic Texts* (SBLDS 135; Atlanta, GA: Scholars, 1992), 5–6, 68. H. Frankfort's points made in his *Kingship and the Gods: A Study of Ancient Near Eastern Religion as the Integration of Society & Nature* (Chicago: University of Chicago Press, 1948, 286–94) still stand.

3. Mettinger, *In Search of God*, 84–85.

4. Mettinger, *In Search of God*, 82–91, 214 n. 6; see Ackerman, *Under Every Green Tree*, 92. This view is debatable and is susceptible to other explanations. For example, A. Kapelrud regards the use of this title in Jeremiah 10:10 as a polemic against lifeless idols; see Kapelrud, *God and His Friends in the Old Testament* (Oslo: Universitetsforlaget, 1979), 20. B. Halpern views this title as a polemic aimed against the cult devoted to deceased ancestors; see Halpern, "Jerusalem and the Lineages in the Seventh Century BCE: Kinship and the Rise of Individual Liability," *Law and Ideology in Monarchic Israel* (ed. B. Halpern and D. W. Hobson; JSOTSup 124; Sheffield: JSOT, 1991), 73.

5. Day, "Baal," 549. Cf. O. Loretz, "Tod und Leben nach altorientalischer und kanaanäisch-biblischer Anschauung in Hos 6, 1–3," *BN* 17 (1982), 37–42. The argument regarding the imagery in Hosea 6:3 may be approached in a similar way. It, too, may reflect concepts associated not with a particular ritual devoted to a "dying and rising god." Indeed, M. L. Barré regards the pertinent language in this passage as medical in character; see Barré, "New Light on the Interpretation of Hosea VI 2," *VT* 28 (1978), 129–41; "Bullutsa-rabi's Hymn to Gala and Hosea 6:1–2," *Or* 50 (1981), 241–45. I am inclined to see an allusion to deceased ancestors (*EHG* 53; cf. McAlpine, *Sleep*, 195). Whether or not these particular alternatives (or those of the preceding note) prove correct, they do not rely on the ritual category of "dying and rising gods."

6. Apart from fuller uses of the category of "dying and rising gods," this category might also be seen as surviving vestigially in the label "vegetation god." See A. Kapelrud, *God and His Friends*, 201.

7. In fairness to Mettinger and Day, they may not assume all of the freight associated with Frazer's use of this category, nor do their remarks reflect an extended discussion of the issues. I mention these two biblical scholars in particular because of the great respect their works deservedly command.

8. See R. Ackerman, *J. G. Frazer: His Life and Work* (Cambridge: Cambridge University Press, 1987), 236.

9. Eliot acknowledges his debt to Frazer in his notes to *The Waste Land* (*The Complete Poems and Plays 1909–1950* [New York: Harcourt, Brace, 1952], 50): "To another work of anthropology I am indebted in general, one which has influenced our generation profoundly; I mean *The Golden Bough;* I have used especially the two volumes *Adonis, Attis, Osiris.* Anyone who is acquainted with these works will immediately recognize in the poem certain references to vegetation ceremonies." For Frazer's impact on Eliot, see the detailed discussion of J. B. Vickery, *The Literary Impact of* The Golden Bough (Princeton, NJ: Princeton Uni-

versity Press, 1973), 233–79. For Frazer's influence on the wider culture, see in addition to Vickery's work, J. Z. Smith, "The Glory, Jest and Riddle," 8–9.

10. For the cultural and artistic appeal of the work, see Vickery, *The Literary Impact of* The Golden Bough, 3–37 (esp. 8, 19–21, 32) and 68–138.

11. For the sake of convenience, readers may consult Frazer, *The Golden Bough: A Study in Magic and Religion* (I Volume, Abridged Edition; New York: Macmillan, 1951), 378–443.

12. Frazer, *The Golden Bough*, abridged, 391.

13. Frazer, *The Golden Bough*, abridged, 378.

14. Frazer, *The Golden Bough*, abridged, 378.

15. Frazer, *The Golden Bough*, abridged, 392.

16. Frazer, *The Golden Bough* (London: Macmillan, 1890), xi. See also Ackerman, *J. G. Frazer*, 229, 238.

17. Robertson Smith, *Lectures on the Religion of the Semites* (New York: D. Appleton, 1889), 393; quoted in T. O. Beidelman, *W. Robertson Smith and the Sociological Study of Religion* (Chicago: University of Chicago Press, 1974), 57.

18. Ackerman, *J. G. Frazer*, 168–69, 238; Vickery, *The Literary Impact of* The Golden Bough, 134–35. For a choice example, see Frazer, *The Golden Bough*, abridged, 401–02. Frazer's driving motivation to "explain" Jesus's death and resurrection against the backdrop of the category of "dying and rising gods" misses the background of Jewish resurrection. See the survey of G. Nickelsburg, "Resurrection (Early Judaism and Christianity)," *Anchor Bible Dictionary. Volume 5. O–Sh* (ed. D. N. Freedman; New York: Doubleday, 1992), 684–91; and the important study of E. Puech, *La croyance des Esséniens en la vie future: Immortalitee, résurrection, vie éternelle? Histoire d'une croyance dans le Judaïsme ancien* (two vols.; Études Bibliques 21–22; Paris: Librairie Lecoffre/Gabalda, 1993). After all, Jesus as the Christ is "the first fruits of all who have fallen asleep" (1 Corinthians 15:20; cf. 1 Thessalonians 4: 13–14). Accordingly, as for Baal, Osiris, Melqart, and Herakles before him (see section 3), Jesus's resurrection was informed by cultural mortuary traditions and beliefs about human beings and their possible afterlife. For a recent defense of comparing Osiris and Jesus, see R. G. Bonnell and V. A. Tobin, "Christ and Osiris: A Comparative Study," *Pharaonic Egypt: The Bible and Christianity* (ed. S. Israelit-Groll; Jerusalem: Magnes, 1985), 1–29 (reference courtesy of G. A. Rendsburg). The claims are based on rather general thematic similarities, with little reference to their cultural background. Curiously, the name of Frazer goes uncited in this study. I am aware of the considerably later Christian presentation of Christ's descent into the underworld and resurrection, a narrative that would seem to belie such a dismissal on my part. However, it is unclear that this Christian presentation is to be traced back to West Semitic mythology. Here one may note that one recent attempt to argue for an ancient Middle Eastern background of the Christian descent theology relies less on the West Semitic evidence of the Baal Cycle and more on Egyptian texts; see A. Cooper, "Ps 24:7–10: Mythology and Exegesis," *JBL* 102 (1983), 37–60.

19. Robertson Smith, *Lectures on the Religion of the Semites* (third ed.; ed. S. A. Cook; New York: KTAV, 1927), 411 n. 4, 414 n. 2. Emphasizing the influence of Robertson Smith is not to slight the influence of other contemporary discussions, for example, by W. Mannhardt (see J. Z. Smith, "The Glory, Jest and Riddle," 371); these are beyond the scope of this investigation.

20. Hvidberg's work, *Graad og Latter i det Gmale Testmente*, was published originally as an annual University-Programme (1938) and translated into English after his death by Løkkegaard under the title, *Weeping and Laughter in the Old Testament* (trans. F. Løkkegaard; Leiden: Brill; Copenhagen: Nyt Nordisk Forlag/Arnold Busck, 1962); *Thespis* 87 (see also

p. 324); Widengren, *Sakrales Königtum im Alten Testament und im Judentum* (Stuttgart: Kohlhammer, 1955), 62–79 (cited and discussed in Mettinger, *In Search of God*, 214 n. 7). To Gaster's credit, he does not organize his analysis around the figures associated by Frazer and others with this category.

21. *Thespis*, 324.

22. See Ackerman, *J. G. Frazer*, 99, 315 n. 5. It may be noted in passing that a strong critic of Frazer's second edition of *The Golden Bough* (1899) was Gaster's father (Ackerman, *J. G. Frazer*, 170). In contrast, Gaster was very much influenced by Frazer; see Gaster's use of Frazer's materials in *Thespis*, 41, 49, 84, 217, 359, 367, 423, 424. *Thespis* more generally follows Frazer's comparative agenda (especially Frazer's ritualist underpinnings), although obviously Gaster is far more aware of the ancient Near Eastern cultures.

23. For further discussion and evaluation of Gaster's approach, see *UBC* 60–63.

24. See L. J. Greenspoon, "The Origin of the Idea of Resurrection," *Traditions in Transformation: Turning Points in Biblical Faith* (ed. B. Halpern and J. D. Levenson; Winona Lake, IN: Eisenbrauns, 1981), 247–321; N. Robertson, "The Ritual Background of the Dying and Rising God in Cyprus and Syro-Palestine," *HTR* 75 (1982), 314–59.

25. For discussion and criticism, see Barstad, *The Religious Polemics of Amos*, 84 n. 45. As mentioned in note 141, the formula may not mean so much that Baal has returned from death, but that he is present to the world, and his power is now operative in it.

26. *Thespis*, 156.

27. This is the force of Gaster's translation (*Thespis*, 347–48). This passage is discussed in section 4. For an alternative, see nn. 192, 197.

28. For Ugaritic *'arṣ* as both "earth" and underworld," see *UBC* 176.

29. *Ug V* 44–45; noted in *CMHE* 56 n. 49; *TO* 1.79.

30. According to W. G. Lambert, "The Theology of Death," *Death in Mesopotamia: Papers read at the XXVIe Recontre Assyriologique internationale* (ed. B. Alster; Mesopotamia; Copenhagen Studies in Assyriology 8; Kopenhagen: Akademisk forlag, 1980), 64, this goddess may be the spouse of Alla. For Allatum, see also the treaty of Ramses II with Hattusilis (*ANET* 205) and Emar '383.11'.

31. See *CML*² 72, 142.

32. In a letter dated November 8, 1889, written to his publisher, George Macmillan. See Ackerman, *J. G. Frazer*, 95.

33. Ackerman, *J. G. Frazer*, 47, 78, 85, 99, 158. For an interesting reflection on Frazer and the comparative agenda in anthropology, see Smith, "The Glory, Jest and Riddle," 404–42.

34. Ackerman, *J. G. Frazer*, 98, 167–74, 236.

35. James's italics; quoted in Ackerman, *J. G. Frazer*, 175.

36. For this information see R. Rhees, ed., *Ludwig Wittgenstein: Remarks on Frazer's Golden Bough* (trans. A. C. Miles; Atlantic Highlands, NJ: Humanities Press, 1979), v.

37. Rhees, *Ludwig Wittgenstein*, 13e.

38. Gordon, "Canaanite Mythology," *Mythologies of the Ancient World* (ed. S. N. Kramer; Chicago: Quadrangle, 1961), 184. Cf. *Thespis*, 109. For other criticisms by experts in the various fields of ancient Near Eastern studies, see the studies cited by J. Z. Smith, "The Glory, Jest and Riddle," 400 n. 43.

39. This point is made even in the saccharine biography of R. A. Downie, *Frazer and the Golden Bough* (London: Gollancz, 1970), 85–92; see also Ackerman, *J. G. Frazer*, 87, 105, 256. On Malinowski's relationship with Frazer, see Ackerman, *J. G. Frazer*, 172, 266–69. For one anecdote reflecting Evans-Pritchard's acquaintance with Frazer in 1926, see Ackerman, *J. G. Frazer*, 334 n. 2. For cultural reasons behind this sea-change in anthropology following the First World War, see Ackerman, *J. G. Frazer*, 100. He views the all-

embracing detail of Frazer's method as a function of the British Empire's dominance within the world, and along with it, British (and other European) scholars' belief in their capacity to cover the entire world intellectually. With the decline of the empire came the decline of such a comparative enterprise: "[W]e no longer have the cultural self-confidence that underlay the entire enterprise of anthropology."

40. For discussion, see J. Z. Smith, "The Glory, Jest and Riddle," 404–42; idem, "Dying and Rising Gods," 521; cf. Ackerman, *J. G. Frazer*, 233.

41. Downie, *Frazer and the Golden Bough*, 93. See also Ackerman, *J. G. Frazer*, 17–34.

42. Frazer, *The Golden Bough*, abridged, 378, 381, 384, 421, 422, 456.

43. H. W. Attridge and R. A. Oden, *The Syrian Goddess (De Dea Syria) Attributed to Lucian* (SBL Texts and Translations 9; Missoula, MT: Scholars, 1976), 14–15. The Vulgate version of Ezek 8:14 used the name of Adonis to translate BH Tammuz. Origen likewise identified Adonis and Tammuz.

44. Frazer, *The Golden Bough*, abridged, 430–1.

45. See the reference to Catullus in Frazer, *The Golden Bough*, abridged, 406. See also 414–15 for an explicit expression of Frazer's prejudices for ancient Greece and against Middle Eastern cultures.

46. J. Z. Smith, "Dying and Rising Gods," 521–27 (see also the other authors mentioned in n. 2).

47. J. Z. Smith, "Dying and Rising Gods," 523–24. For more on Attis and the problems of the classification of him as a "dying and rising god," see P. Lambrechts, "Les fêtes phrygiennes be Cybèle et d'Attis," *Bulletin de l'Institut belge de Rom* 27 (1952), 141–70; idem, *Attis, van herdersknaap tot god* (Amsterdam: Noord-Hollandische Uit. Mig., 1967); M. J. Vermaseren, *Cybele and Attis: The Myth and the Cult* (London: Thames and Hudson, 1977), 92, 112; Södergard, "The Ritualized Bodies of Cybele's Galli and the Methodological Problem of the Plurality of Explanations," 169–93. Attis is said to be dead but not resurrected; he is not a divinity.

48. Frymer-Kensky, "The Tribulations of Marduk. The So-called 'Marduk Ordeal Text'," *JAOS* 103 (1983), 131–41 (reference courtesy of V. Hurowitz). The political background of this text, namely, the death and return to life of the deity in order to express the return of his statue to Babylon in 669 (according to Frymer-Kensky), may serve as a valuable analogue to Baal's death and return to life: Baal's death may reflect Ugarit's weakness relative to the great empires and his return to life refers to his ongoing cult at Ugarit. In Marduk's case, the text reflects a rather specific, temporary condition, whereas Ugarit's was longer lasting.

49. For summary and bibliography on Osiris, see M. Heerma van Voss, "Osiris," *DDD* 649–51. The older standard work is J. G. Griffiths, *The Origins of Osiris and His Cult* (Numen 40; Leiden: Brill, 1980).

50. See E. Hornung, "Ancient Egyptian Religious Iconography," *Civilizations of the Ancient Near East* (ed. J. M. Sasson; four vols.; New York: Scribner's/Macmillan Library Reference USA, 1995), 3:1718. I am grateful to T. J. Lewis for bringing this reference to my attention.

51. Lichtheim, *Ancient Egyptian Literature. Volume II: The New Kingdom* (Berkeley: University of California Press; 1976), 81.

52. See Hornung, "Ancient Egyptian Religious Iconography," 3:1718, figure 11 (brought to my attention by T. J. Lewis). See further the reserved commentary of Griffiths, *Origins of Osiris and his Cult*, 163–70.

53. See the discussion in L. H. Lesko, "Ancient Egyptian Cosmogonies and Cosmology," *Religion in Ancient Egypt: Gods, Myths, and Personal Practice* (ed. B. E. Shafer; Ithaca,

NY: Cornell University Press, 1991), 92–93. This view, common since Breasted, is disputed by Griffiths, *Origins of Osiris and His Cult*, 151–63.

54. Griffiths, *Origins of Osiris and his Cult*, 29. See also J. Z. Smith, "Dying and Rising Gods," 524.

55. De Moor, *An Anthology of Religious Texts from Ugarit* (Nisaba 16; Leiden: Brill, 1987), 88 n. 430. See also F. Løkkegaard, "A Plea for El, the Bull, and Other Ugaritic Miscellanies," *Studia Orientalia Ioanni Pedersen: Septuagenario A. D. VII Id. Nov. Anno MCMLIII a Collegis Discipulis Amicis Dedicata* (Hauniae: Einar Munksgaard, 1953), 230–31.

56. See D. Silverman, "Divinity and Deities in Ancient Egypt," *Religion in Ancient Egypt: Gods, Myths, and Personal Practice* (ed. B. E. Schafer; Ithaca, NY: Cornell University Press, 1991), 426.

57. Ackerman, *J. G. Frazer*, 168–69, 238. For a choice example, see Frazer, *The Golden Bough*, abridged, 401–02.

58. Griffiths, *The Origins of Osiris and his Cult*, 3–5, 17, 22, 24, 35, 51–62, 84.

59. Griffiths, *The Origins of Osiris and his Cult*, 5.

60. Griffiths, *The Origins of Osiris and his Cult*, 35.

61. Griffiths, *The Origins of Osiris and his Cult*, 51–62, 84. See also J. Z. Smith, "Dying and Rising Gods," 525.

62. Regarding Dumuzi generally, see T. Jacobsen, *The Treasures of Darkness: A History of Mesopotamian Religion* (New Haven: Yale University Press, 1976), 25–73; B. Alster, "Tammuz," *DDD* 828–34. See also A. Livingstone, *Mystical and Mythological Explanatory Works of Assyrian and Babylonian Scholars* (Oxford: Clarendon Press, 1986), 136–39, 156–66. For the early iconography of Dumuzi, see W. G. Lambert, "Sumerian Gods: Combining the Evidence of Texts and Art," *Sumerian Gods and Their Representations* (ed. I. L. Finkel and M. J. Geller; Cuneiform Monographs 7; Groningen: Styx Publications, 1997), 4.

63. See S. N. Kramer, "Sumerian Literature and the Bible," *Studia et Orientalia Edita a Pontificio Instituto Biblico ad celebrandum Annum ex quo conditum est institutum 1909—VII Mai–1959. Volumen III. Oriens Antiquus* (AB 12. Rome: Pontificio Istituto Biblico, 1959), 198–99 n. 1; E. M. Yamauchi, "Tammuz and the Bible," *JBL* 84 (1965), 290.

64. S. N. Kramer, "Dumuzi's Annual Resurrection: An Important Correction to 'Inanna's Descent," *BASOR* 183 (1966), 31. For a translation of the section, see also T. Jacobsen, *The Harps That Once . . . : Sumerian Poetry in Translation* (New Haven: Yale University Press, 1987), 232. For another substitution of this type, cf. W. G. Lambert, "A New Babylonian Descent to the Netherworld," *Lingering Over Words: Studies in Ancient Near Eastern Literature in Honor of William L. Moran* (ed. T. Abusch, J. Huehnergard and P. Steinkeller; HSS 37; Atlanta, GA: Scholars, 1990), 289–300.

65. Kramer, "Dumuzi's Annual Resurrection," 31.

66. BM 100046, line 22, published by S. N. Kramer, "The Death of Dumuzi: A New Sumerian Version," *Anatolian Studies* 30 (1980), 5–13.

67. For example, see BM 96692, published by S. N. Kramer, "A New Dumuzi Myth," *RA* 84 (1990), 143–49.

68. Kramer, "The Dumuzi-Inanna Sacred Marriage Rite: Origin, Development, Character," *Actes de la XVIIe Rencontre Assyriologique Internationale. Université Libre de Bruxelles, 30 juin–4 juillet 1969* (ed. A. Finet; Duculot/Gembloux: Comité belge de recherches en Meesopotamie, 1970), 136.

69. Alster, "Tammuz," *DDD* 829.

70. Alster, "Tammuz," *DDD* 828.

71. Foxvog, "Astral Dumuzi," *The Tablet and the Scroll: Near Eastern Studies in Honor of William H. Hallo* (ed. M. Cohen, D. C. Snell, and D. B. Weisberg; Bethesda, MD: CDL Press, 1993), 103–08. See also Alster, "Tammuz," *DDD* 830.

72. See *ANET* 101, 102.

73. Translation from B. Foster, *Before the Muses: An Anthology of Akkadian Literature* (two vols.; Bethesda, MD: CDL Press, 1993), 1.432. For discussion, see F. A. M. Wiggermann, "Transtigridian Snake-Gods," *Sumerian Gods and Their Representations* (ed. I. L. Finkel and M. J. Geller; Cuneiform Monographs 7; Groningen: Styx Publications, 1997), 41–42.

74. Foxvog, "Astral Dumuzi," 106–07.

75. See Foxvog, "Astral Dumuzi," 108; and in this section. For the royal setting for this aspect of royal cult, see chapter 3, section 3, n. 56.

76. For the passage, see *CAD* E:122a, 2'. The following points derive from S. Paul, " 'Emigration' from the Netherworld in the Ancient Near East," *Immigration and Emigration within the ancient Near East: Festschrift E. Lipiński* (ed. K. van Lerberghe and A. Schoors; OLA 65; Leuven: Peeters/Departement Oriëntalistiek, 1995), 225–26. See Alster, "Tammuz," *DDD* 833; and K. van der Toorn, *From Her Cradle to Her Grave: The Role of Religion in the Life of the Israelite and Babylonian Woman* (Biblical Seminar 23; trans. S. J. Denning-Bolle; Sheffield: JSOT, 1994), 124. The corresponding Sumerian verb e_{11} applies in *Ishtar's Descent to the Underworld* to Inanna. Note the latter use of *'ly* for going up from the grave in a late Herodian inscription; see F. M. Cross, "A Note on a Burial Inscription from Mount Scopus," *IEJ* 33 (1983), 244–45.

77. I owe this point to J. Klein. For a translation, see Jacobsen, *The Harps That Once*, 56–84, with the explicit mention of Ur III rulers on p. 78. See also Jacobsen's discussion in *Treasures of Darkness*, 66; and Wiggermann, "Transtigridian Snake-Gods," 41.

78. M. E. Cohen, *The Cultic Calendars of the Ancient Near East* (Bethesda, MD: CDL Press, 1993), 465–81.

79. Cohen, *The Cultic Calendars of the Ancient Near East*, 465.

80. Foxvog, "Astral Dumuzi," 108.

81. Cohen, *The Cultic Calendars of the Ancent Near East*, 477.

82. Astour, "The Netherworld and Its Denizens at Ugarit," *Death in Mesopotamia: Papers Read at the XXVIᵉ Rencontre Assyriologique Internationale* (ed. B. Alster; Mesopotamia Copenhagen Studies in Assyriology 8; Copenhagen: Akademisk Forlag, 1980), 230–31.

83. Gaster, *Thespis*, 325.

84. Livingstone, *Mystical and Mythological Explanatory Works of Assyrian and Babylonian Scholars*, 162.

85. See Jacobsen, *Treasures of Darkness*, 25–27; Wiggermann, "Transtigridian Snake-Gods," 33–34, 41.

86. For documentation regarding this god, see C. Bonnet, *Melqart: Cultes et mythes de l'Heraclès tyrien en méditerranée* (Studia Phoenicia VIII; Bibliothèque de la faculté de philosophie et lettres de Namur 69; Leuven: Uitgeverij Peeters/Presses universitaires de Namur, 1988). For further questions as to his identity, see Bonnet, "Melqart est-il vraiment le Baal de Tyr?" *UF* 27 (1995), 695–701.

87. Clermont-Ganneau, "L'egersis d'Heraclès et le reveil des dieux," *Recueil d'archéologie orientale* 8 (1924), 149–67.

88. Lipiński, "La fête de l'ensevelissement et de la résurrection de Melqart," *Actes de la XVIIe Rencontre Assyriologique Internationale, Université Libre de Bruxelles, 30 juin–4 juillet 1969* (ed. E. Finet; Publications du comité belge de recherches historiques, épigraphiques et archéologiques en Mésopotamie 1; Brussels: Université Libre de Bruxelles, 1970), 30–58.

89. Following Lipiński (see previous note), but with reservations, Teixidor, *The Pagan God: Popular Religion in the Greco-Roman Near East* (Princeton, NJ: Princeton University Press, 1977), 35.

90. C. Bonnet, "Le culte de Melqart à Carthage: Un cas de conservatisme religieux," *Studia Phoenicia IV. Religio Phoenicia: Acta Colloquii Namurcensis habiti diebus 14 et 15 De-*

cembris anni 1984 (ed. C. Bonnet, E. Lipiński, and P. Marchetti; Namur: Société des Études Classiques, 1986) 214–15; idem, *Melqart.*

91. See references in J. C. Greenfield, "*Larnax Tes Lapethou* III Revisited," *Studia Phoenicia V. Phoenicia and the East Mediterranean in the First Millennium B. C.: Proceedings of the Conference Held in Leuven from the 14th to the 16th of November 1985* (ed. E. Lipiński; OLA 22; Leuven: Uitgeverij Peeters, 1987), 398.

92. Ribichini, "Melqart," *DDD* 563–65, and see the further secondary literature cited there.

93. Bonnet, "Le culte de Melqart à Carthage, 215 n. 28.

94. See KAI III.62. CIS i 377:4–6 shows that the office could be held by father and son. The role did not preclude the holding of another office such as judge (see Berger *RHR* [1914] 1, line 5) or priest (RES 553.3–4). See also Bonnet, "Le culte de Melqart à Carthage," 216.

95. In some cases the title appears in apposition with "the title *mtrḥ 'štrny*, <<Astartean bridegroom>>, alluding in all likelihood to a function in the *hieros gamos*" (Greenfield, "*Larnax Tes Lapethou* III Revisited," 399; Greenfield's italics). The text is clear, for example, in the case of one inscription from Rhodes (KAI 44). For criticisms of this view, which will be left aside in my further discussion, see J. C. L. Gibson, *Textbook of Syrian Semitic Inscriptions. Volume III: Phoenician Inscriptions including Inscriptions in the Mixed Dialect of Arslan Tash* (Oxford: Clarendon Press, 1982), 146.

96. Originally published by A. M. Honeyman, "Larnax Tes Lapethou: A Third Phoenician Inscription," *Le Muséon* 51 (1938), 285–98. For the issue of the date, see Greenfield, "*Larnax Tes Lapethou* III Revisited," 395. The following information draws heavily from Greenfield, "*Larnax Tes Lapethou* III Revisited," 397–99.

97. Greenfield, "*Larnax Tes Lapethou* III Revisited," 398. The words, *mqm 'lm mlt*, in CIS i 5980 have been interpreted as "the one who raises the god, Melqart" (Bonnet, "Le culte de Melqart à Carthage," 215 n. 28). This view of *mlt* is debated. For references, see J. Hoftijzer and K. Jongeling, *Dictionary of the Northwest Semitic Inscriptions. Part Two: M–T* (HdO; Leiden: Brill, 1995), 1003.

98. *'tpnmlqrt* in line 2 has been taken as a PN, but P. Schmitz (personal communication) argues that it is an appositive of specification, meaning "in the presence of Melqart."

99. See T. H. McAlpine, *Sleep, Divine & Human, in the Old Testament* (JSOTSup 38; Sheffield: JSOT Press, 1987), 233 n. 13.

100. See the considered remarks of Gibson, *Textbook of Syrian Semitic Inscriptions. Volume III,* 145–47.

101. Honeyman, "Larnax Tes Lapethou," 288, 297. So also P. Magnanini, *Le iscrizioni fenicie dell'oriente: Testi, Traduzioni, Glossary* (Rome: Istituto di Studi del Vicino Oriente Universita' degli Studi di Roma, 1973), 183.

102. Contra Greenfield ("*Larnax Tes Lapethou* III Revisited," 397–98), LL III.6 may suggest that *'lm* could refer to a goddess: *bbt 'lm 'štrt*. The simplest rendering is "in the house of the goddess, Ashtart" (see Honeyman, "Larnax Tes Lapethou," 297).

103. H. P. Müller, "Der phonizisch-punische *mqm 'lm* im Licht einer althebräischen Isoglosse," *Or* 65 (1991), 116–22.

104. In an article responding to my review (*JAOS* 110 [1990], 590–92) of her book, *Melqart,* C. Bonnet marshalls evidence to demonstrate the equation of Baal of Tyre with Melqart, about which I expressed reservations for the *Phoenician mainland.* The very late inscription from Arados that Bonnet cites (Melqart, 114–15; "Melqart," 697) can be used to support this equation, but it is not altogether clear and it is very late. It hardly helps for the Iron Age, or perhaps considerably later. See further Smith, "Melqart, Baal of Tyre and Dr. Bonnet," *UF* 28 (1996), 773–75. However, future discoveries may prove Bonnet's position.

105. For text and translation, see H. W. Attridge and R. A. Oden, *Philo of Byblos. The Phoenician History: Introduction, Critical Text, Translation, Notes* (CBQMS 9; Washington, DC: Catholic Biblical Association of America, 1981), 52, 53. Philo of Byblos identifies them further with Demarous, known from the Ugaritic texts as a title of Baal (see Attridge and Oden, *Philo of Byblos*, 90 n. 118). Unfortunately, equations of deities hardly guarantee equations of functions and features in different cultures.

106. For text and translation, see H. W. Attridge and R. A. Oden, *The Syria Goddess (De Dea Syria) Attributed to Lucian* (SBL Texts and Translations 9, Graeco-Roman Religion series 1; Missoula, MT: Scholars, 1976), 10, 11.

107. For a more extended commentary on the data in this paragraph, with a view to support the idea of the death and resurrection of Melqart-Herakles, see Bonnet, *Melqart*, 33–40.

108. R. Marcus in H. St. J. Thackeray and R. Marcus, *Josephus V. Jewish Antiquities, Books V–VIII* (Loeb Classical Library; London: William Heinemann; Cambridge, MA: Harvard University Press, 1934), 649–51.

109. Both positions are presented by Marcus in Thackeray and Marcus, *Josephus V. Jewish Antiquities, Books V–VIII*, 651 n. a. See also Müller, "Der phonizisch-punische *mqm 'lm* im Licht einer althebräischen Isoglosse," 114–15 (reference courtesy of T. N. D. Mettinger).

110. Thackeray, *The Life/Against Apion* (Loeb Classical Library; London: William Heinemann; Cambridge, MA: Harvard University Press, 1926), 209–11.

111. F. Abel, "Inscriptions de Transjordane et de haute Galilée," *RB* n. s. 5 (1908), 573. See also the discussions in Clermont-Ganneau, "L'egersis d'Heraclès et le reveil des dieux," 149–67; Teixidor, *The Pagan God*, 35; Gibson, *Syrian Semitic Inscriptions. Volume III*, 145–46.

112. Tsirkin, "The Labours," 21.

113. Tsirkin, "The Labours," 22–23, citing Nonnos' *Dyonisiaka* XI 358.

114. See the previous citation.

115. The following remarks about Adonis on the Greek side are based largely on M. Detienne, *The Gardens of Adonis: Spices in Greek Mythology* (trans. J. Lloyd; Atlantic Highlands, NJ: Humanities Press, 1977). For the West Semitic side, see E. Lipiński, *Dieux et déesses de l'univers phénicien et punique* (OLA 64; Leuven: Uitgeverij Peeters/Departement Oosterse Studies, 1995), 90–105; S. Ribichini, "Adonis," *DDD* 7–10; B. Soyez, *Byblos et la fête des Adonis* (EPRO 60; Leiden: Brill, 1977).

116. Loretz, "Vom Baal-Epitheton *adn* zu Adonis und Adonij," *UF* 12 (1980), 287–92; K. Spronk, *Beatific Afterlife in Ancient Israel and in the Ancient Near East* (AOAT 219; Kevelaer: Butzon & Bercker; Neukirchen-Vluyn: Neukirchener, 1986), 194; de Moor, *An Anthology*, 90 n. 435. For Adonis at Byblos, see *De Dea Syria* 6 (Attridge and Oden, *The Syrian Goddess*, 12, 13).

117. Attridge and Oden, *The Syrian Goddess*, 12, 13.

118. J. Z. Smith ("Dying and Rising Gods," 522) believes that Adonis is represented in statuary form in this passage despite no explicit mention of such.

119. J. Z. Smith, "Dying and Rising Gods," 522.

120. J. Z. Smith, "Dying and Rising Gods," 522.

121. Detienne, *Gardens of Adonis*, 1–2.

122. See *Thespis* 129; S. Ribichini, *Adonis: Aspetti 'Orientali' di un mito greco* (Studi Semitici 55; Rome: Consiglio Nazionale di Ricerche, 1981); see also O. Loretz, "Vom Baal-Epitheton *adn* zu Adonis und Adonij," 287–92.

123. Robertson, "The Ritual Background of the Dying and Rising God in Cyprus and Syro-Palestine," *HTR* 75 (1982), 314–59.

124. On this point Robertson ("The Ritual Background of the Dying and Rising God in Cyprus and Syro-Palestine," 347) incorrectly says that "[e]veryone agrees that the manner of [Mot's] death reflects the threshing and the winnowing of grain." See J. F. Healey, "Burning the Corn: New Light on the Killing of Motu," *Or* 52 (1983), 251.

125. D. B. Redford, "The Sea and the Goddess," *Studies in Egyptology Presented to Miriam Lichtheim* (ed. S. Israelit-Groll; two vols.; Jerusalem: Magnes, 1990), 2.828.

126. Frazer, *The Golden Bough*, abridged, 378. Note W. G. Lambert's comments about cultural influence in his discussion of the Dumuzi-Tammuz traditions, "A New Babylonian Descent to the Netherworld," 290:

> The story of the rape of Persephone in Greek myth is a very close parallel, and from a more comprehensive study of ancient mythology from the Aegean to India, it seems that many such similarities are due both to a common intellectual heritage going back at least to Neolithic times and to interaction of places and areas on one another in prehistoric and historic times.

127. See J. Gray, "Baal," *IDB* 1:329; Ackerman, *Under Every Green Tree*, 79–92.

128. This is an old suggestion to be found, for example, in T. Cheyne's commentary on Isaiah. See also Mettinger, *In Search of God*, 84; Ackerman, *Under Every Green Tree*, 83. This cult may have influenced the cult of Hadad-Rimmon (Zech 12:10–11); on this figure, see J. C. Greenfield, "The Aramean God Ramman/Rimmon," *IEJ* 26 (1976), 195–98. For the medieval cult of Ta'uz conducted by the Sabeans of Harran, see Livingstone, *Mystical and Mythological Explanatory Works of Assyrian and Babylonian Scholars*, 162.

129. The possibility was brought to my attention by Karel van der Toorn. On the passage, see Ackerman, *Under Every Green Tree*, 83. Following Albright, Ackerman assumes that Damu is Dumuzi. It would appear that the two are distinguished, yet sometimes identified. See Jacobsen, *Treasures of Darkness*, 25–27, 63–73. For EA 84:31, cf. N. Na'aman, "On Gods and Scribal Traditions in the Amarna Letters," *UF* 22 (1990), 248–50.

130. Detienne, *The Gardens of Adonis*, 128.

131. See J. A. Fitzmyer, "The Phoenician Inscription from Pyrgi," *JAOS* 86 (1966), 294; Gibson, *Textbook of Syrian Semitic Inscriptions. Volume III*, 151–59; G. N. Knoppers, " 'The God in His Temple': The Phoenician Text from Pyrgi as a Funerary Inscription," *JNES* 51 (1992), 105–20; P. C. Schmitz, "The Phoenician Text from the Etruscan Sanctuary at Pyrgi," *JAOS* 115 (1995), 562, 565; Hoftijzer and Jongeling, *Dictionary of the Northwest Semitic Inscriptions. Part Two: M–T*, 984.

132. Cf. the plausible, but quite speculative, discussion of Knoppers, " 'The God in His Temple'," 111–2.

133. As suggested to me by P. Schmitz.

134. Gibson, *Textbook of Syrian Semitic Inscriptions. Volume III*, 158.

135. Fitzmyer, "The Phoenician Inscription from Pyrgi," 294.

136. Knoppers, " 'The God in His Temple,' " 116.

137. Knoppers, " 'The God in His Temple,' " 120.

138. Tikva Frymer-Kensky reminds me of Persephone in Greek tradition. See W. Burkert, *Greek Religion* (trans. J. Raffan; Cambridge, MA: Harvard University Press, 1985), 159–60.

139. In addition to the Sumerian material, note also the claims made by R. Amiran for an Early Bronze depiction from Arad: a stick figure shows two postures, standing and lying down, with corn for an ear and roots for feet. Amiran regards the figure as a depiction of the death and resurrection of a fertility god. See Amiran, "A Cult Stele from Arad," *IEJ* 22 (1972), 86–88; cf. A. Mazar, *Archaeology of the Land of the Bible 10,000–586 B.C.E.* (Anchor Bible Reference Library; New York: Doubleday, 1990), 137. See also D. Schmandt-

Besserat who entertains such possibilities for Pre-Pottery Neolithic B material from 'Ain Ghazal; see Schmandt-Besserat, "'Ain Ghazal 'Monumental' Figures," *BASOR* 310 (1998), 14.

140. Bonnet, *Melqart: Cultes et mythes de l'Heraclès tyrien en méditerranée*, 173; M. S. Smith and E. Bloch-Smith, "Death and Afterlife in Ugarit and Israel" (review article of K. Spronk, *Beatific Afterlife in Ancient Israel and in the Ancient Near East*), *JAOS* 108 (1990), 591.

141. Older attempts to take *ḥy 'al'iyn b'l* ("Mighty Baal lives") in CAT 1.6 III 2, 8, 20 as a reference to Baal's resurrection have scant support. H. Barstad comments: "The usefulness, and even possibility, of isolating one formula like *ḥy 'aliyn b'l* and giving it a content of such wide-reaching consequences as has been done is dubious, to say the least." Barstad, *The Religious Polemics of Amos*, 150–51. As noted, the formula may not mean so much that Baal has returned from death, but that he is present to the world and his power is now operative in it.

142. The count derives from D. Pardee, "The Structure of RS 1.002," *Semitic Studies in Honor of Wolf Leslau: On the Occasion of his Eighty-Fifth Birthday. November 14th, 1991* (ed. A. S. Kaye; two vols.; Wiesbaden: Harrassowitz, 1991), 2.1181 n. 2: "There are approximately thirty reasonably well-preserved ritual texts in the Ugaritic language, and another forty or so fragmentary texts." The count continues to rise. RS 1992.2014, an incantation similar to RIH 78/20, has appeared in translation and notes by D. Pardee in W. W. Hallo, ed., *The Context of Scripture: Volume I. Canonical Compositions from the Biblical World* (Leiden: Brill, 1997), 327–28. Approximately sixty-six new Ugaritic texts from Urtennu's family archive have been reported (as well as three hundred Akkadian texts). See M. Dietrich and O. Loretz, "Neue Tafelfunde der Grabungskampagne 1994 in Ugarit," *UF* 26 (1994), 21.

143. Ackerman, *Under Every Green Tree*, 86.

144. It is interesting that Gaster (*Thespis*, 270–376) discusses this type, but he did not include Baal under this rubric, preferring instead what he called "the comprehensive type."

145. J. Z. Smith, "Dying and Rising Gods," 521.

146. J. Z. Smith, "Dying and Rising Gods," 521–22.

147. A. Kapelrud, *Baal in the Ras Shamra Texts* (Copenhagen: Gad, 1952), 38–39; Gaster, *Thespis*, 215; S. Parker, "KTU 1.16 III, the Myth of the Absent God and 1 Kings 18," *UF* 21 (1989), 295–96; idem, *The Pre-biblical Narrative Tradition: Essays on the Ugaritic Poems Keret and Aqhat* (SBL Resources for Biblical Studies 24; Atlanta, GA: Scholars, 1989), 186–87. The following study is not available to me: George C. Moore, "The Disappearing Deity Motif in Hittite Texts: A Study in Religious History" (B.A. thesis, Oxford, Faculty of Oriental Studies, 1975).

148. For this information about CTH 323–336, see G. Beckman, "Mythologie. A. III. Bei den Hethitern," *Reallexikon der Assyriologie* 8:566–67. My thanks go to G. Beckman for providing me with his article.

149. H. Hoffner, *Hittite Myths* (ed. G. Beckman; SBL Writings from the Ancient World 2; Atlanta, GA: Scholars, 1990), 14–20.

150. Hoffner, *Hittite Myths*, 15–20.

151. ANET 126–27; Hoffner, *Hittite Myths*, 14–17. Ritual texts from Emar, such as Emar 446:47–57, show a similar concern for life and death. Cohen (*The Cultic Calendars of the Ancient Near East*, 356) describes a series of rituals in Emar 446:

> On the 15th of the month before ninkur, there were special sacrifices at the ox stalls, at the horse stables, and in the garden of the *birikku* of Ba'al. There was also a special ceremony involving seeding: an offering was made to Dagan-Lord-

of-the-Seeds and then the diviner strewed seeds over the ground, either symbol-
ically planting the first seeds of the season or reading the signs for the upcoming
planting season from the pattern of the scattered seeds.

The text in question has many breaks. For this reason Cohen's translation (*The Cultic
Calendars of the Ancient Near East*, 358) of the pertinent passage is cited in full:

> On the 15th they bring Šaggar down to the oxen's stalls (and) they slaughter (an
> ox?). They slaughter a sheep at the horses' stables. In the same month, (during)
> the evening, they take out (the statues of the gods (?). They slaughter one sheep
> in the presence of the men who ... then first a sheep at the garden of the ...
> (structure) of Ba'al, (and then) [a sheep for] Dagan-Lord-of-the-Seeds. The divin-
> ers toss seeds about onto the ground.

As the breaks and question-marks indicate, many details about these rituals are unknown.
See further D. Fleming, "New Moon Celebration Once a Year: Emar's *Hidašu* of Dagan,"
Immigration and Emigration within the Ancient Near East: Festschrift E. Lipiński (ed. K. van
Lerberghe and A. Schoors; OLA 65; Leuven: Peters/Department Oriëntalistiek, 1995), 62.
Cohen's inferences about the ritual of the seeds are reasonable. The title of Dagan here
seems to connect him to the concern about seeds in this context. By further inference one
might draw Baal into this discussion. It would seem plausible to regard the rituals represented here as concerned for natural fertility and as trying to secure the support of Baal and
Dagan in engendering it. What further relevance this text may hold for understanding Baal
cannot be determined at present, but the evidence of the Baal Cycle alone indicates the
importance of Baal for natural fertility.

152. For this point in the latter text, see *UBC* 105–14.

153. Parker, "KTU 1.16 III, the Myth of the Absent God and 1 Kings 18," *UF* 21
(1989), 283–96.

154. Hoffner, *Hittite Myths*, 22–23.

155. Hoffner, "Second Millennium Antecedents to the Hebrew 'ÔB," *JBL* 86 (1967),
385–401, esp. 389–92. For a critique of Hoffner's interpretation of BH '*ôb* as "pit," see T. J.
Lewis, *Cults of the Dead in Ancient Israel and Ugarit* (HSM 39; Atlanta, GA: Scholars,
1989), 57–58.

156. J. Z. Smith "Dying and Rising Gods," 521–22.

157. Mot informs Baal at the end of his speech demanding Baal's descent into the
underworld: "And you will know, O god, that you are dead" (1.5 V 16–17; cf. Ps 82:7a).
Kings occupy a zone between divinity and humanity. Ideally speaking, Kirta cannot die
since he is a "son of El," the cliché used in the Baal Cycle for divinities. After all, as
indicated in the last of the remarks made by Kirta's son, deities do not die and Kirta belongs
to their rank. Yet Kirta is indisputably mortal. The text of Kirta here faces a similar problem
as the medieval political theory of the "king's two bodies" (E. H. Kantorowicz, *The King's
Two Bodies: A Study in Medieval Political Theology* [Princeton, NJ: Princeton University Press,
1957)] brought to my attention by T. Frymer-Kensky): "the King has in him two bodies,
viz., a Body natural, and a Body politic. His Body natural ... is a Body mortal. ... But his
Body politic is a Body that cannot be seen or handled" (p. 7, quoting Edmund Plowden);
"The King's Two Bodies thus form one unit indivisible, each being fully contained in the
other. ... Not only is the body politic 'more ample and large' than the body natural, but
there dwells in the former certain truly mysterious forces which reduce, or even remove,
the imperfections of the fragile human nature" (p. 9). "The king is a twinned being, human
and divine (49)." The political life of the king is ritually expressed in this doctrine: the
king in his social-political role literally embodies the dynasty in its all various functions

and its putative qualities, including its eternity, yet in his own personal self is as mortal as any other person. The text of Kirta poses the problem of the clash of the "king's two bodies" in narrative form. Just as for Kirta, for the medieval king, time exposed the underlying difficulty of the king's dual natures, as Kantorowicz (*The King's Two Bodies*, 171; see further p. 271) observes:

> [T]he king was . . . a "temporal being," strictly "within Time," and subjected, like any ordinary human being, to the effects of time. In other respects, however, that is, with regard to things *quasi sacrae* or public, he was unaffected by Time and its prescriptive power; like the "holy sprites and angels," he was beyond Time and therewith perpetual or sempiternal. The king, at least with regard to Time, had obviously "two natures"—one which was temporal and by which he conformed with the conditions of other men, and another which was perpetual and by which he outlasted and defeated all other beings.

It remains only to mention that the origins of this theology are profoundly Christological, as Kantorowicz's discussion amply documents; this Christology is in turn indebted ultimately to the West Semitic royal ideology as reflected in the text of Kirta and the so-called royal psalms (Psalms 2, 72, 89).

158. Hornung, *Conceptions of God in Ancient Egypt: The One and the Many* (trans. J. Baines; Ithaca, NY: Cornell University Press, 1985), 152.

159. Readings are based on D. Pardee, "Poetry in Ugaritic Ritual Texts," *Verse in Ancient Near Eastern Prose* (ed. J. C. de Moor and W. G. E. Watson; AOAT 42; Kevelaer: Bercker & Butzon; Neukirchen-Vluyn: Neukirchener, 1993), 208–10; Pardee's partial readings with partial brackets are not distinguished here. For the poetic divisions, see Pardee, "Poetry in Ugaritic Ritual Texts," 208–10. Issues of interpretation have been reviewed in some detail in Lewis, *Cults of the Dead*, 5–46; and P. Bordreuil and D. Pardee, "Les textes en cunéiformes alphabétiques," *Une bibliothèque au sud de la ville: Les textes de la 34e campagne (1973)* (Ras Shamra-Ougarit VII; Paris: Éditions Recherche sur les Civilisations, 1991), 151–63; these issues are not repeated here. B. Schmidt's innovations, both grammatical and interpretational, are often misinformed. See Schmidt, *Israel's Beneficent Dead: Ancestor Cult and Necromancy in Ancient Israelite Religion and Tradition* (FAT 11; Tübingen: J. C. B. Mohr [Siebeck], 1994), 100–20; and the review of M. S. Smith in *CBQ* 58 (1996), 724–25. For bibliography, see Bordreuil and Pardee, "Les textes en cunéiformes alphabétiques," 152; Pardee, "Poetry in Ugaritic Ritual Texts," 208–10; Schmidt, *Israel's Beneficent Dead*, 100–20. Whether or not Emar 6.452 proves a comparable text remains to be seen (brought to my attention by T. J. Lewis). For now see W. T. Pitard, "Care of the Dead at Emar," *Emar: The History, Religion, and Culture of a Syrian Town in the Late Bronze Age* (ed. M. Chavalas; Bethesda, MD: CDL Press, 1996), 130–37.

160. The vocative may take the accusative as in Arabic. The only form that poses problems for this reconstruction is *ks'i* in line 13, which may however reflect loss of final ending (hence **ks'i'a*). For discussion of the problem, see J. G. Taylor, "A Long-Awaited Vocative Singular Noun with Final Aleph in Ugaritic (KTU 1.161.13)?" *UF* 17 (1986), 315–18.

161. A number of writers compare Arabic *'adima*, "to be wanting, lacking, needy, destitute." W. W. Hallo (personal communication) has suggested the possibility of a threefold repetition of *'dmt*, "how long?" Hallo compares BH *'ad-mātay* and Akkadian *adi mati*, used in lament literature (for the Akkadian expression, see *CAD* A/1:119a).

162. A singular may be involved; if so, it would refer, in my mind, to Niqmaddu.

163. Grammatically, "to" is another feasible interpretation, but the funerary ritual calls for descent from the throne and probably not to a throne located in the underworld, nor

is the throne invoked here. See Lewis, *Cults of the Dead*, 13; J. G. Taylor, "A First and Last Thing to Do in Mourning: *KTU* 1.161 and Some Parallels," *Ascribe to the Lord: Biblical & Other Studies in Memory of Peter C. Craigie* (ed. L. Eslinger and G. Taylor; JSOTSup 647; Sheffield: Sheffield Academic Press, 1988), 153; M. Dietrich and O. Loretz, "Grabbeigaben für verstorbenen König: Bemerkungen zur Neuausgabe von RS 34.126 = KTU 1.161," *UF* 23 (1991), 106.

164. Pardee ("Poetry in Ugaritic Ritual Texts," 209) reads *ksh* and suggests that the reading should be *ks'i*. Or the reading is perhaps *ks'ih*.

165. Dietrich and Loretz ("Grabbeigaben," 106): "zusammen mit."

166. Reading with Pardee ("Poetry in Ugaritic Ritual Texts," 209) for *thm*.

167. It would be possible to take the first instance of *šlm* here with the previous line in the meaning of "peace-offering," except that the word with this meaning is usually spelled *šlmm*. As a result, it seems preferable to take the word here with this line. Given the structure of lines 32–34, however, one might suspect here a dittography. In any case, the second use of *šlm* here may be understood as a blessing. Cf. *šlm* in 1.123.1–3, taken as "Hail" plus DN in the vocative (so del Olmo Lete, *Canaanite Religion*, 343).

168. For *b'at*, Pardee ("Poetry in Ugaritic Ritual Texts," 210) reads as another possibility *bnh*, "her/his sons." Parallelism favors Pardee's rendering here.

169. Others are less confident as to the reading of the final letter, which Pardee marks with partial brackets. As a result, Lewis (*Cults of the Dead*, 10) offers this possibility as well as an alternative, *['a]ry[h]*, "his kinsmen."

170. The translation "shades" may be wishful thinking on the part of its supporters because all three root letters of geminate roots would appear in the consonantal writing in Ugaritic. Lewis, *The Cult of the Dead*, 11, discusses this problem at great length. The alternatives are hardly more attractive or free of difficulties. Could a cultic statue (**ẓalmu*) of the recently deceased king be involved (a query put to me by S. Tinney)?

171. Cf. the plural construct form presumably in 1.91.2, assuming that lines 3–20 of this text involve a list of sacrificial rituals (e.g., del Olmo Lete, *Canaanite Religion*, 257).

172. See M. H. Pope, "Notes on the Rephaim Texts from Ugarit," *Essays on the Ancient Near East in Memory of Jacob Joel Finkelstein* (ed. M. de Jong Ellis; Memoirs of the Connecticut Academy of Arts and Sciences 19; Hamden, CT: Archon, 1977), 177.

173. W. Pitard, "RS 34.126: Notes on the Text," *MAARAV* 4/1 (1987), 75–86; B. A. Levine and J. M. de Tarragon, "Dead Kings and Rephaim: the Patrons of the Ugaritic Dynasty," *JAOS* 104 (1984), 652; D. Sivan, *A Grammar of the Ugaritic Language* (HdO1/28; Leiden: Brill, 1997), 114.

174. Lewis, *Cults of the Dead*, 7–8; Pardee, "Poetry in Ugaritic Ritual Texts," 208–09.

175. See Schmidt, *Israel's Beneficent Dead*, 112–13.

176. See UT 9.31; D. Marcus, "The Qal Passive in Ugaritic," *JANES* 3 (1970), 102–11; D. Sivan, *A Grammar of the Ugaritic Language*, 126–28. For the G-stem passive in West Semitic languages generally, see also R. J. Williams, "The Passive *qal* Theme in Hebrew," *Essays on the Ancient Semitic World* (ed. J. W. Wevers and D. B. Redford; Toronto: University of Toronto Press, 1970), 43–50.

177. Pardee, "Epigraphic and Philological Notes," *UF* 19 (1987), 211–6.

178. Levine and de Tarragon call the three words "a rare triplication"; see Levine and de Tarragon, "Dead Kings and Rephaim," 652. On this possibility for Isaiah 6:3, I am indebted to Professor Levine.

179. So Bordreuil and Pardee, "Les textes," 158.

180. See Lewis, *Cults of the Dead*, 43. Given the implicit command to Ammurapi in the preceding section, that he is to lament for the dead king, I am inclined to see Ammurapi as the addressee in this section as well. The parallel wording with other texts also militates in favor of this view. A third possibility, namely, the royal furniture, is contextually plausible,

but the parallel wording would militate against this view. For a thorough, critical review, see D. T. Tsumura, "The Interpretation of the Ugaritic Funerary Text KTU 1.161," *Official Cult and Popular Religion in the Ancient Near East: Papers of the First Colloquium on the Ancient Near East—The City and Its Life held at the Middle Eastern Culture Center in Japan (Mitaka, Tokyo). March 20–22, 1992* (ed. E. Matsushima; Heidelberg: Universitätsverlag C. Winter, 1993), 40–55, esp. 45–52. As this discussion indicates, no view is without its difficulty.

181. Unless the forms are taken as denominative verbs, with Lewis, *Cults of the Dead,* 9, 26–27; and apparently Pardee, "Poetry in Ugaritic Ritual Texts," 209.

182. See D. Freedman, "Counting Formulas in Akkadian Epics," *JANES* 3/2 (1970–71), 65–81.

183. See Lewis, *Cults of the Dead,* 27.

184. UT 19.2715; J. M. de Tarragon, *Le culte à Ugarit d'après les textes de la pratique en cuniformes alphabétiques* (Cahiers de la Revue Biblique 19; Paris: Gabalda, 1980), 58, 75 n. 11.

185. Levine and de Tarragon, "Dead Kings and Rephaim," 649–59, esp. 656–58. See also Lewis, *Cults of the Dead,* 41–43; and G. A. Anderson, *A Time to Mourn, A Time to Dance: The Expressions of Grief and Joy in Israelite Religion* (University Park, PA: Pennsylvania State University Press, 1991), 60–67. I would favor Lewis's view that it is Ammurapi who is told to descend aided by the illumination of Shapshu.

186. Levine and de Tarragon, "Dead Kings and Rephaim," 657. The authors' italics.

187. See Bordreuil and Pardee, "Les textes," 158.

188. See n. 180.

189. Levine and de Tarragon, "Dead Kings and Rephaim," 657.

190. The prepositional phrase '*mh* could be translated "with her" or "to him." The preposition '*m* commonly means "with" in the sense of accompaniment (e.g., 1.1 IV 14; 1.3 III 24, 25, IV 11–12; 1.5 I 22–23, 24–25, V 8, 10–11, 20) and so it might be thought that '*mh* is to be rendered "with her," namely, Anat. Accordingly, **yrd* '*m* might seem to mean "to descend with" (as opposed to "to descend to"); see D. Pardee, "The Preposition in Ugaritic," *UF* 7 (175), 350, *UF* 8 (1976), 279 (see also 317–8). Yet '*m* is not uncommon with verbs in the sense of "to, toward": **ytn pnm* '*m* in 1.1 IV 21–22; 1.2 I 4, 14, 19; 1.3 III 37, IV 21; 1.4 V 23, VIII 1–4; 1.5 I 9–10, II 14–15, in some cases parallel with *tk* (e.g., 1.2 I 19; 1.5 II 14–15); and **lsm* '*m* in 1.3 III 19 (cf. 1.1 IV 11 and commonly reconstructed elsewhere in the same formulas). Finally, it is to be noted that **yrd l-* means "to descend from" (*UF* 7 [1975], 350), and no other preposition with **yrd* means "descends to." Therefore, **yrd* '*m* may mean "descend to." Note Pardee's comments on the overlap between *l-,* "to," and '*m,* "with" in *UF* 8 (1976), 317–18. Accordingly, Baal might seem to be the object of the preposition in order to indicate Shapshu's role in accompanying Anat to the underworld to locate his corpse.

191. This clause is narrative and not direct discourse, although on purely grammatical grounds it would be possible to render it so ("To him you will descend, O Divine Light, Shapshu"). The sense is indicated from the following clause beginning with '*d* (1.6 I 9). This is a subordinating conjunction that begins clauses governed by a preceding independent verb, in this case *trd.* Anderson (*A Time to Mourn,* 63–64) divides the lines differently, rendering: "We [Anat and Shapshu] are descending into the netherworld, to the place of Baal/The torch of the gods, Shapshu, descended." This division is unlikely, as "into the netherworld" is parallel to "to Baal." (His translation omits the prepositional phrase '*mh.*) Furthermore, parallels in 1.161.20–21 and Gen 37:35 makes it unlikely that '*atr b'l* is to be understood literally as "to the place of Baal."

192. It is this language of the dead king that may lie behind the allusion to *b'l* in 1.17 VI 30 and not the Storm-god, Baal, as generally thought. See n. 197.

193. Levine and de Tarragon, "Dead Kings and Rephaim," 657.

194. Based on 'ard in the parallel in 1.5 VI 25, some scholars emend to 'ard, but the emendation is not necessary. It could be argued that the context with both Anat and Shapshu would comport with the plural form.

195. The description of Anat descending and fetching the corpse of Baal may also help to locate the *Sitz im Leben* of CAT 1.161; the comparison of the two texts would point to CAT 1.161 as a funerary text on behalf of the most recently deceased king, Niqmaddu, as argued by Lewis (*The Cult of the Dead*, 32), and perhaps not a text commemorating his death, as suggested by Levine and de Tarragon ("Dead Kings and Rephaim," 654). In the narrative (1.6 I 11–15), the sun-goddess Shapshu loads the body onto Anat so that she can provide Baal with an appropriate burial and funerary offerings. These narrative details presume the sun-goddess's capacity to aid in locating the deceased and it may also presuppose a role of the sun-deity in bringing up the deceased in the ritual of necromancy. This role is known for Shamash in Mesopotamian ritual of necromancy (see I. Finkel, "Necromancy in Ancient Mesopotamia," *AfO* 29–30 [1983–84], 1–17; Lewis, *The Cults of the Dead*, 38) and the same may lie behind the narrative account of Shapshu's setting Baal's corpse on Anat's shoulders in 1.6 I 14–15. These texts may help to provide some indication as to the result of the descent in CAT 1.161, namely, the making ritually present, conceived as the raising of the deceased from the underworld in order to receive the offerings made in lines 27–31. Does this use of *'ly in 1.6 I 15 echo the language of necromancy (*elû*), noted in the case of Dumuzi (see n. 76)?

196. CAT 1.113 may also bear on the royal cult of the dead (see D. Pardee, *Les textes paramythologiques de la 24ᵉ campagne (1961)* [Paris: Éditions Recherche sur la Civilisations, 1988], 170–78), as attested in 1.3 I and 1.17 VI. The front of the text describes musical instrumentation, either described as n'm, "goodly," or perhaps played by a figure called n'm. The back of the text contains a king list originally containing at least thirty-two names and perhaps as many as fifty-two (Pardee, *Les textes paramythologiques*, 173). Despite the differences in details among the texts in question (Pardee, *Les textes paramythologiques*, 170–78), it would appear that the royal cult of Ugarit invoked the dead ancestors (CAT 1.161) and perhaps this cult is reflected in the musical instrumentation in CAT 1.113. CAT 1.3 I and 1.17 V 28–33 apparently drew on this imagery. A further connection among these texts might involve 1.108, if the figure of rp'u who plays music in this text is to be identified with n'm or is to be viewed as the eponymous tribal figure corresponding or related to the royal figure of n'm. This figure of rp'u leads the musical entertainment of the ḫbr ktr ṯbm, who may be the Rephaim as suggested by M. S. Smith (in Pardee, *Les textes paramythologiques*, 100 n. 111).

197. This crucial insight about this text was made by J. C. Greenfield, "Une rite religieux araméen et ses parallèles," *RB* 80 (1973), 46–52. Accordingly, I am prepared to entertain the possibility that the b'l mentioned in 1.17 VI 28–33 is not the god Baal but the figure of the deceased human "lord."

198. For this problem in Egypt and Mesopotamia, see W. W. Hallo, *Origins: The Ancient Near Eastern Background of Some Modern Western Institutions* (Studies in the History and Culture of the Ancient Near East VI; Leiden: Brill, 1996), 152, 196–210 (esp. 203), 229.

199. See n. 157 for the comments regarding Kirta. Like Kirta, the description of Baal embodies the enigma of royal death and eternity. Baal, the patron of Ugaritic kings, undergoes a death congruent with the conceptual tension understood between the divine character of kings and the dynasty and their well-known mortal nature. Yet Baal is a major god, and no major deity with a current cult remains dead in mythological narratives. On many of these texts and their royal background, see esp. J. F. Healey, "The Immortality of the King: Ugarit and the Psalms," *Or* 53 (1984), 245–54.

200. For this view of sleep, see B. Batto, "The Sleeping God: An Ancient Near Eastern Motif of Divine Sovereignty," *Bib* 68 (1987), 153–77. For divine sleep and death, see also McAlpine, *Sleep*, 135–49, 181–99; Mettinger, *In Search of God*, 88–89. McAlpine and Mettinger also note some differences in the uses of these two sorts of language. As McAlpine shows, sleep is hardly attributed only to the figures in Frazer's category. He demonstrates that sleep is described as the daily activity of many main deities in Mesopotamian literature (McAlpine, *Sleep*, 183–86) and of Yahweh (m. Ma'aser Sheni 5.15; McAlpine, *Sleep*, 194–95, 233 n. 15). As McAlpine observes, most of these examples of divine sleep run not on an annual cycle. The biblical language regarding Yahweh's sleep (e.g., Psalms 44:24–25, 78:65, 121:3–4) involves not annual sleep/death as for Dumuzi but divine sleep during an occasion of human need. McAlpine strongly criticizes atttempts to amalgamate these different sorts of divine sleep that he nicely lays out (*Sleep*, 194–95).

201. For documentation of this point, see UBC 104–05.

202. For further discussion of many of the following points, see UBC 96–114. My thanks go to T. Frymer-Kensky, B. Levinson, and J. Tigay for discussion of these points.

203. See R. A. Simkins, *Creator & Creation: Nature in the Worldview of Ancient Israel* (Peabody, MA: Hendrickson, 1994), 121–72.

204. For full discussion, see UBC 60–87, 96–100.

205. Livingstone, *Mystical and Mythological Explanatory Works of Assyrian and Babylonian Scholars*, 162–63.

206. Livingstone, *Mystical and Mythological Explanatory Works of Assyrian and Babylonian Scholars*, 167.

207. Frazer, *The Golden Bough*, abridged, 396.

208. Livingstone, *Mystical and Mythological Explanatory Works of Assyrian and Babylonian Scholars*, 167.

209. For some discussion, see chapter 1, sections 5 and 6. For more evidence, see the summary in EHG 49–50, 52.

210. For example, see J. C. Greenfield, "The 'Cluster' in Biblical Poetry," *Maarav* 5–6 (1990), = *Sopher Mahir: Northwest Semitic Studies Presented to Stanislaus Segert* (ed. E. M. Cook; Santa Monica, CA: Western Academic Press, 1990), 159–68, esp. 160.

211. For a survey of the biblical evidence with Ugaritic parallels, see N. J. Tromp, *Primitive Conceptions of Death and the Nether World in the Old Testament* (BibetOr 21; Rome: Pontifical Biblical Institute, 1969); Greenspoon, "The Origin of the Idea of Resurrection," 247–321; and Cooper, "Ps 24:7–10: Mythology and Exegesis," 54.

212. I wish to thank Joseph Everson for bringing this issue to my attention in a conversation in the mid-1980s.

213. Greenspoon is correct to see concepts in the Baal Cycle as background to later concepts of resurrection, but this has little bearing on the deity as a "dying and rising god"; see Greenspoon, "The Origin of the Idea of Resurrection," 247–321. Indeed, in his extensive reconstruction of continuity from the Baal Cycle's presentation of Baal's death and descent to the underworld to biblical tradition, Greenspoon shows no clear examples of warrior language for God when it comes the mythology of Death. Instead, both the Baal Cycle and biblical material on resurrection appear to be influenced by West Semitic concepts of human afterlife. See further the example of royal "resurrection" in the Panammu inscription (KAI 214.21), discussed in section 4. See also the discussion of this problem in n. 1 of chapter 9.

214. For some of the biblical scholars holding this view, with further discussion, see Tromp, *Primitive Conceptions of Death and the Nether World in the Old Testament*, 197–213.

215. For details, see UBC 17–19. For background for the proposed literary development of the cycle, see UBC 29–36.

216. For the priesthood's reaction, see in chapter 5, section 3. For deuteronomistic theology against the Rephaim, see chapter 4, section 2. For the historical setting for these developments, see the important studies of B. Halpern, " 'Brisker Pipes than Poetry': The Development of Israelite Monotheism," *Judaic Perspectives on Ancient Israel* (ed. J. A. Neusner, B. A. Levine, and E. S. Frerichs; Philadelphia: Fortress, 1987), 77–115; "The Baal (and the Asherah) in Seventh Century Judah: Yhwh's Retainers Retired," *Konsequente Traditionsgeschichte: Festschrift für Klaus Baltzer zum .65 Geburstag* (ed. R. Bartelmus, T. Krüger, and H. Utzschnieder; OBO 126; Freiburg Schweiz: Universitätsverlag; Göttingen: Vandenhoeck & Ruprecht, 1991), 115–54; "Jerusalem and the Lineages in the Seventh Century BCE: Kinship and the Rise of Individual Liability," *Law and Ideology in Monarchic Israel* (ed. B. Halpern and D. W. Hobson; JSOTSup 124; Sheffield: Sheffield Academic Press, 1991), 11–107; idem, "Sybil, or the Two Nations? Archaism, Kinship, Alienation, and the Elite Redefinition of Traditional Culture in Judah in the 8th–7th Centuries B.C.E.," *The Study of the Ancient Near East in the Twenty-First Century: The William Foxwell Albright Centennial Conference* (ed. J. S. Cooper and G. M. Schwartz; Winona Lake, IN: Eisenbrauns, 1996), 291–338.

7. El, Yahweh, and the Original God of IsraEL and the Exodus

1. Basic bibliography on El includes: F. M. Cross, "El," *TDOT* 1:242–61; CMHE 3–75; *EUT*; Pope, "Ups and Downs in El's Amours," *UF* 11 (1979 = C. F. A. Schaeffer Festschrift), 701–08; reprinted in Pope, *Probative Pontificating in Ugaritic and Biblical Literature: Collected Essays* (ed. M. S. Smith; UBL 10; Munster: Ugarit-Verlag, 1994), 29–39; idem, "The Status of El at Ugarit," *UF* 19 (1989), 219–29; reprinted in Pope, *Probative Pontificating in Ugaritic and Biblical Literature*, 47–61; W. Herrmann, "El," *DDD* 274–280. The following description of El in the Ugaritic texts is indebted to these works.

2. Cross, *TDOT* 1:242–61. See the discussion at the beginning of the Introduction, section 1.

3. See Herrmann, "El," *DDD* 274.

4. See I. J. Gelb, "Mari and the Kish Civilization," *Mari in Retrospect: Fifty Years of Mari and Mari Studies* (ed. G. D. Young; Winona Lake, IN: Eisenbrauns, 1992), 134, 149, 158, 193; R. S. Hess, *Amarna Personal Names* (ASOR Dissertaton Series 9; Winona Lake, IN: Eisenbrauns, 1993), 237.

5. See R. A. Di Vito, *Studies in Third Millennium Sumerian and Akkadian Personal Names: The Designation and Conception of the Personal God* (Studia Pohl: Series Maior 16; Rome: Pontificio Istituto Biblico, 1993), 235–36.

6. See most recently, J. F. Healey, "The Kind and Merciful God: On Some Semitic Divine Epithets," *"Und Mose schrieb dieses Lied auf": Studien zum Alten Testament und zum Alten Orient. Festschrift für Oswald Loretz zur Vollendung seines 70. seines Lebensjahres mit Beiträgen von Freunden, Schülern und Kollegen* (ed. M. Dietrich and I. Kottsieper; AOAT 250; Münster: Ugarit-Verlag, 1998), 349–51.

7. The discussion between M. H. Pope and F. M. Cross extended over decades. See *EUT* 37–41; "Up and Downs in El's Amours," *UF* 11 (1979 = C. F. A. Schaeffer Festschrift), 701–08; reprinted in Pope, *Probative Pontificating in Ugaritic and Biblical Literature*, 29–39; idem, "The Status of El at Ugarit," 219–29. See F. M. Cross, "El," *TDOT* 1:246–48; CMHE 24. The debate turns largely on the word *mmnnm*. For discussion and Cross's more recent view of *mmnnm*, see S. M. Olyan, *Asherah and the Cult of Yahweh in Israel* (HSM 34; Atlanta, GA: Scholars, 1988), 42 n. 12. As indicated in his letter of December 7, 1998 to me, Cross may finish an article on this text, so I do not cite his current view of *mmnnm*.

8. On the tent of El, see *CMHE* 36–39; *CMCOT* 35–57; *UBC* 188–89. For new information on the West Semitic tent tradition, see D. Fleming, "Mari's Large Public Tent and the Priestly Tent Sanctuary," *VT* 50 (2000), in press. For a maximal case for Athirat's maritime religious significance, see A. J. Brody, *"Each Man Cried Out to His God": The Specialized Religion of Canaanite and Phoenician Seafarers* (HSM 58; Atlanta, GA: Scholars, 1998), 26–30.

9. El's role as warrior is not the only aspect of his possibly displaced by Baal. Other features of his were perhaps also acquired by Baal. This is argued for Mount Sapan by J. C. de Moor, "Ugarit and Israelite Origins," *Congress Volume. Paris 1992* (ed. J. A. Emerton; VTSup 61; Leiden: Brill, 1995), 231–32.

10. Chapter 3, section 3, examines the evidence for El's astral family, including Athtar.

11. See K. van der Toorn, "Anat-Yahu, Some Other Deities, and the Jews of Ele-phantine," *Numen* 39 (1992), 87.

12. See B. Levine, "The Balaam Inscription from Deir 'Alla: Historical Aspects," *Biblical Archaeology Today* (Jerusalem: Israel Exploration Society, 1985), 326–39. M. Barker (*The Great Angel: A Study of Israel's Second God* [London: SPCK, 1992], 17–27) also expresses this view.

13. *PE* 1.10.44 4.16.11. See H. W. Attridge and R. A. Oden, *Philo of Byblos. The Phoenician History: Introduction, Critical Text, Translation, Notes* (CBQMS 9; Washington, DC: Catholic Biblical Association of America, 1981), 62–63, 86 n. 85. See also *PE* 1.10.18–27, 29.

14. *EHG* 25; cf. O. Loretz, "Der Wohnort Els nach ugaritischen Texten und Ez 28, 1–2.6–10," *UF* 21 (1989), 259–67.

15. Barré, *The God-List in the Treaty between Hannibal and Philip V of Macedonia* (Baltimore/London: Johns Hopkins, 1983), 48–49. The possible implication of this reasoning is that Anat-Bethel in the treaty of Esarhaddon with Baal II of Tyre is Asherah. See P. K. McCarter, "Aspects of the Religion of the Israelite Monarchy: Biblical and Epigraphic Data," *Ancient Israelite Religion: Essays in Honor of Frank Moore Cross* (ed. P. D. Miller, Jr, P. D. Hanson, and S. D. McBride; Philadelphia: Fortress, 1987), 147.

16. Van der Toorn, "Anat-Yahu, Some Other Deities and the Jews of Elephantine," 87. Specifically, he argues that Bethel and Anat-Bethel are not at home in Phoenicia, as they are not otherwise attested in Phoenician material.

17. See S. C. Layton, *Archaic Features of Canaanite Personal Names in the Hebrew Bible* (HSM 47; Atlanta, GA: Scholars, 1990) 56.

18. Attridge and Oden, *Philo of Byblos*, 46–49.

19. Landsberger, *Sam'al* (Ankara: Druckerei der Türkischen historischen Gesellschaft, 1948), 47 n. 117; *CMHE* 26–28; Olyan, *Asherah*, 52–53.

20. Olyan, *Asherah*, 52. Ackerman (*Under Every Green Tree*, 125) writes that the identification "is in no doubt."

21. Lipiński, "The 'Phoenician History' of Philo of Byblos," *BiOr* 40 (1983), 309.

22. Day, *Molech: A God of Human Sacrifice in the Old Testament* (University of Cambridge Oriental Publications 41; Cambridge: Cambridge University Press, 1989), 38–40.

23. Cogan, " '... From the Peak of Amanah'," *IEJ* 34 (1984), 255–59; Xella, *Baal Hammon; Recherches sur l'identité et histoire d'un dieu phénico-punique* (Collezione di Studi Fenici 32; Rome: Consiglio Nazionale delle Ricerche, 1991), 163. See also Y. Yadin, "Symbols of Dieties at Zinjirli, Carthage and Hazor," *Near Eastern Archeology in the Twentieth Century: Essays in Honor of Nelson Glueck* (ed. J. A. Sanders; Garden City, NY: Doubleday, 1970), 215–16, 228 n. 67. Cf. G. del Olmo Lete, "Pervivencias cananeas (ugaríticas) en el culto fenicio—III," *Sefarad* 51 (1991), 99–114.

24. *CMHE* 27.

25. Stager, "Eroticism & Infanticide at Ashkelon," *Biblical Archaeology Review* 17/4 (1991), 35–53, 42, 45, 72 n. 19

26. Stager, "Eroticism & Infanticide at Ashkelon," 45.

27. Bordreuil, *Catalogue des sceaux ouest-sémitiques inscrits de la Bibliothéque Nationale, du Musée du Louvre et du Musée biblique et Terre Sainte* (Paris: Bibliothéque Nationale, 1986), 21–22.

28. For example, the Ugaritic name for Memphis is spelled both ḫkpt and ḥqkpt (see *UT* 19.860).

29. D. Pardee, "An Evaluation of the Proper Names from a West Semitic Perspective: Pantheon Distribution According to 'Genre," *Eblaite Personal Names and Semitic Name-Giving* (ed. A. Archi; Rome: Missione Archaeologica Italiana in Siria, 1988), 119–51.

30. For connections between these inscriptions and biblical texts, see J. A. Hackett, "Religious Traditions in Israelite Transjordan," *Ancient Israelite Religion*, 125–36. Another proposal locates Job in the middle Euphrates where Aramaic was spoken in the first millennium; it was also contiguous to areas inhabited by Arab tribes. See J. C. Greenfield, "The Language of the Book," *The Book of Job* (New York: KTAV, 1980), xvi; "Philological Observations on the Deir 'Alla Inscriptions," *The Balaam Text from Deir 'Alla Re-evaluated: Proceedings of the International Symposium Held at Leiden 21–24 August 1989* (ed. J. Hoftijzer and G. van der Kooij; Leiden: Brill, 1991), 120.

31. Levine, "The Balaam Inscriptions from Deir 'Alla: Historical Aspects," 326–39.

32. See Greenfield, "Philological Obsrvations on the Deir 'Alla Inscriptions," 120.

33. The evidence of El proper names in Edomite material suffers from similar difficulties of interpretation. See J. R. Bartlett, *Edom and Edomites* (JSOT/PEF Monograph Series 1; Sheffield: JSOT Press, 1989), 190.

34. Van der Toorn, "Anat-Yahu," 87.

35. Cross, "The Epic Traditions of Early Israel: Epic Narrative and the Reconstruction of Early Israelite Institutions," *The Poet and the Historian: Essays in Literary and Historical Biblical Criticism* (ed. R. E. Friedman; Chico, CA: Scholars, 1983), 37; Tigay, "Israelite Religion: The Onomastic Evidence," *Ancient Israelite Religion*, 171, 187 n. 66; Aufrecht, "The Religion of the Ammonites," *Ancient Ammon* (ed. B. Macdonald and R. W. Younker; Leiden: Brill, 1999), 158–60.

36. See U. Oldenburg, "Above the Stars of El. El in South Arabic Religion," *ZAW* 82 (1970), 187–208; J. Ryckmans, "South Arabia, Religion of," *ABD* 6:172.

37. A recent example of this approach can be found in de Moor, *The Rise of Yahwism,* esp. 223–60; see also *CMHE* 71–75.

38. See the following among recent commentators (with earlier references) by order of year: L. E. Axelsson, *The Lord Rose up from Seir: Studies in the History and Traditions of the Negev and Southern Judah* (ConBOT 25; Lund: Almqvist & Wiksell, 1987), esp. 56–65; E. A. Knauf, *Midian: Untersuchungen zur Gechichte Palästinas und Nordarabiens am Ende des 2. Jahrtausends v. Chr.* (Wiesbaden: Harrassowitz, 1988), 43–63; T. N. D. Mettinger, "The Elusive Essence: YHWH, El and Baal and the Distinctiveness of Israelite Faith," *Die Hebräische Bibel und ihre zweifache Nachgeschichte* (ed. E. Blum et al.; Festschrift für R. Rendtorf; Neukirchen-Vluyn: Neukirchener 1990), 393–417; K. van der Toorn, *Family Religion in Babylonia, Syria and Israel: Continuity and Change in the Forms of Religious Life* (Studies in the History and Culture of the Ancient Near East VII; Leiden, 1996), 281–86; and F. M. Cross, *Epic and Canon: History and Literature in Ancient Israel* (Baltimore: Johns Hopkins University Press, 1998), 45–70. The Septuagint, Demetrius, Josephus, and a possible number of other sources favor this Arabian location according to A. Kerkeslager, "Jewish Pilgrimage and Jewish Identity in Hellenistic and Early Roman Egypt," *Pilgrimage and Holy Space in Late Antique Egypt* (ed. D. Frankfurter; Leiden: Brill, 1998), 99–225, esp. 150–210. For a

recent attempt to find the "original Sinai" at Jebel el-Lawz in northwestern Saudi Arabia (based on a suggestion of F. M. Cross), see H. Blum, *The Gold of Exodus: The Discovery of the True Mount Sinai* (New York: Simon & Schuster, 1998); see the review of R. S. Hendel in *Biblical Archaeology Review* 25/4 (1999), 54, 56.

39. CMHE 101–02, 105.

40. McCarter, "Aspects of the Religion of the Israelite Monarchy," 137–55.

41. Seow, *Myth, Drama, and the Politics of David's Dance* (HSM 44; Atlanta, GA: Scholars, 1989), 11–54. I do not share Seow's view that the sojourn of the ark at Shiloh was a factor in Yahweh's acquisition of El's characteristics.

42. Seow takes the name of his father, Yeroham, as a hypocoristic of *yrhm'l*, which, if correct, would also suggest—albeit indirectly—the cult of El at Shiloh. Proper names are notoriously problematic indicators of religious practice, but combined with other data, they may be used to defend reconstructions of religious practice or tradition. See section 5 on this point.

43. Seow argues that the title of *yhwh ṣĕbā'ôt*, the name of the god of Shiloh (1 Samuel 1:1–3), derives from a god who presided over the divine hosts of the divine council, and following T. N. D. Mettinger, Seow surmises that the best candidate for such a concept would be El. If El were originally the god of Shiloh and Yahweh were not originally a title of El, then the title *yhwh ṣĕbā'ôt* would be secondary.

44. Or possibly, "the god of the covenant." If this is correct, still the evidence weighs slightly in favor of seeing El as this god. T. J. Lewis, "The Identity and Function of El/Baal Berith," *JBL* 115 (1996), 401–23.

45. The word may refer to the god Ilabrat according to M. Dijkstra, "The Ugaritic-Hurrian Sacrificial Hymn to El (RS 24.278 = KTU 1.128)," *UF* 25 (1993), 157–62, esp. 161.

46. For the complex issues surrounding this material, see Lewis, "The Identity and Function of El/Baal Berith," 401–23.

47. Cf. Yahweh Elyon in 1 Kings 9:8, Psalms 7:18, 47:3, 97:9. See the classic treatment of G. Levi della Vida, " "El 'Elyon in Genesis 14:18–20," *JBL* 63 (1944), 1–19.

48. For recent discussions, see R. W. L. Moberly, *The Old Testament of the Old Testament: Patriarchal Narratives and Mosaic Yahwism* (OBT; Minneapolis, MN: Fortress, 1992), 44; Garr, "The Grammar and Interpretation of Exodus 6:3," 385–408.

49. See Weinfeld, "Kuntillet 'Ajrud Inscriptions and Their Significance," *SEL* 1 (1984), 126.

50. Weinfeld, "Kuntillet 'Ajrud Inscriptions and Their Significance," 126.

51. Whitt, "The Divorce of Yahweh and Asherah," *SJOT* 6 (1992), 49 n. 51. For a listing of personal names with **'l* as the theophoric element, see G. I. Davies, *Ancient Hebrew Inscriptions; Corpus and Concordances* (Cambridge: Cambridge University Press, 1991), 278–83.

52. Edelman, "Tracking Observance of the Aniconic Tradition through Numismatics," *The Triumph of Elohim: From Yahwisms to Judaisms* (ed. D. V. Edelman; Grand Rapids, MI: Eerdmans, 1996), 185–225.

53. Olyan, *Asherah and the Cult of Yahweh*, 38–61; followed in *EHG* 19. For discussion of Yahweh and Asherah possibly as consorts, see also chapter 4, section 4.

54. See de Moor, *The Rise of Yahwism*, 267.

55. Pardee, "An Evaluation of the Proper Names," 119–51.

56. For the name at Ebla, see M. Krebernik, *The Study of the Ancient Near East in the Twenty-First Century: The William Foxwell Albright Centennial Conference* (ed. J. S. Cooper and G. Schwartz; Winona Lake, IN: Eisenbrauns, 1996), 46. The comparison of Ugaritic *yšr'il* in CAT 4.623.3 with the biblical name Israel was brought to my attention by the late Gösta Ahlström.

57. The point is laid out in *EHG* 16–17.

58. 4QDeut*q*: *bny 'l[*; 4QDeut*j*: *bny 'lwhym[*; LXX *huiōn theou* (cf. LXX variants with *aggelōn* interpolated). For the evidence, see E. Tov, *Textual Criticism of the Hebrew Bible* (Minneapolis: Fortress; Assen/Maastricht: Van Gorcum, 1992), 269; J. A. Duncan, *Qumran Cave 4. IX: Deuteronomoy, Joshua, Judges, Kings* (ed. E. Ulrich and F. M. Cross; DJD XIV; Oxford: Clarendon Press, 1995), 90; noted also BHS to Deuteronomy 32:8 note d. For older bibliography, *EHG* 30 n. 37; and A. Schenker, "Le monothéisme israélite: un dieu qui transcende le monde et les dieux," *Bib* 78 (1997), 438. For an older discussion, see O. Eissfeldt, "Neue Götter im alten Testament," 479. For further discussion, see chapters 7 and 8.

59. Cf. El Elyon in Genesis 14:18–20, 22 noted in section 4.

60. See the discussion of Psalm 82 in chapter 2, section 2 and in the following chapter. Psalm 82 distinguishes the figure of the standing Yahweh from the presiding, seated divinity, evidently El Elyon to judge from the reference to Elyon in verse 6. For a tortured attempt to argue for the two deities as a single figure, see Wyatt, *Myths of Power*, 357–65; this view is driven perhaps in part by the author's presupposition that Yahweh was originally a form of El (cf. Albright, *From the Stone Age to Christianity*, 296–97).

61. To be credited with this point is the otherwise problematic work of Barker, *The Great Angel*, 17–25. Barker's attempt to trace the separate status of El and Yahweh through-out the Iron II period down through the Father and the Son in Christianity is brave but fraught with methodological issues. Barker misses a great deal of the early Israelite evidence for El (e.g., the name of Israel, Genesis 49; Numbers 23–24) that would have bolstered her case. Barker wishes to see El continue quite late, especially based on reading *'ēl* as "El" in "Second Isaiah." This interpretation is unconvincing, since *'ēl* seems often to mark the contrast with other gods, hence "god," or it can be seen in some contexts simply as a title for Yahweh (see chapter 10). Barker does not demonstrate that *'ēl* in Second Isaiah refers to a god separate from Yahweh. Barker also conflates the issue of *běnê 'ēlîm*, "sons of gods," with the issue of the Son in the New Testament. From a history of religions perspective, the "sons of gods" is a generic reference to deities, which biblical texts use to refer to the low level of the ruled divinities, who serve the Supreme Ruler (see Psalm 29:1, Job 1–2). In contrast, "the Son" would belong to the second tier of the pantheon. Typologically, the mediating step between early Israelite polytheism of El-Baal-Yahweh and later Christian thought of Father-Son might involve the re-application of Baal imagery to hypostases (cf. Isaiah 30) and angelic beings, perhaps including the figure of "the Son of Man" in Daniel 7. Yet this development is exceptionally complicated. Barker touches on a great deal of pertinent evidence, but it requires considerably greater sifting and discernment. Barker also throws the royal language of sonship into the mix, as this complex is also significant for Christian interpretation of Jesus and it deploys sonship language. Yet here again Barker does not sort out the relationships of this royal complex to other uses of "son" in relation to divinity. Barker's work essentially draws out implications from J. A. Emerton's old insight concerning the relationship between Ugaritic presentation of El and Baal, on the one hand, and "the Ancient of Days" and "the Son of Man" in Daniel 7 (Emerton, "The Origin of the Son of Man Imagery," *JTS* 9 [1958], 225–42; see also *CMHE* 17, 345 n. 8). Barker unfortunately overlooks the well-known and best treatment on the monarchy as the medium of this mythological complex to post-exilic apocalyptic, namely, P. Mosca, "Ugarit and Daniel 7: A Missing Link," *Bib* 67 (1986), 496–517. I do not deny that the different complexes of material Barker presents affected the interpretation of the reality of Jesus, only that their relationship to one another as Barker presented is at best nebulous. The compli-cations are immense and far beyond the scope of this study.

62. Following the lead of W. F. Albright, F. M. Cross, D. N. Freedman, and others. See

Albright, "The Earliest Forms of Hebrew Verse," *JPOS* 2 (1922), 69–86; "Some Additional Notes on the Song of Deborah," *JPOS* 2 (1922), 284–85; "The Song of Deborah in the Light of Archaeology," *BASOR* 62 (1936), 26–31; *From the Stone Age to Christianity: Monotheism and the Historical Process* (sec. ed. with a new introduction; Baltimore: Johns Hopkins University Press, 1957), 14; and *YGC* 13; Cross and Freedman, *Studies in Ancient Yahwistic Poetry* (Missoula, MT: Scholars, 1950 [repr.1975]), 5; Freedman, *Pottery, Poetry and Prophecy: Studies in Early Hebrew Poetry* (Winona Lake, IN: Eisenbrauns, 1980), 147–50; L. E. Stager, "Archaeology, Ecology and Social History: Background Themes to the Song of Deborah," *Congress Volume: Jerusalem 1986* (ed. J. A. Emerton; VTSup 40; Leiden: Brill, 1988), 221–34 (with references to the earlier supporters of this view); and J. C. de Moor, "The Twelves Tribes in the Song of Deborah," *VT* 43 (1993), 483–93, and *The Rise of Yahwism*, 267, 292. See also J. D. Schloen, "Caravans, Kenites, and *Casus Belli*: Enmity and Alliance in the Song of Deborah," *CBQ* 55 (1993), 18–38; van der Toorn, *Family Religion*, 281–86; and the recent survey of K. Koch, "Jahwäs Übersiedlung vom Wüstenberg nach Kanaan: Zur Herkunft von Israel's Gottesverständnis," *"Und Mose schrieb dieses Lied auf": Studien zum Alten Testament und zum Alten Orient. Festschrift für Oswald Loretz zur Vollendung seines 70. seines Lebensjahres mit Beiträgen von Freunden, Schülern und Kollegen* (ed. M. Dietrich and I. Kottsieper; AOAT 250; Münster: Ugarit-Verlag, 1998), 440–70. For the evidence based solely on grammatical considerations, see D. A. Robertson, *Linguistic Evidence in the Dating of Early Hebrew Poetry* (SBLDS 3; Missoula, MT: Scolars, 1972), 153–54. I hasten to add that I do not accept early datings of all other poems thought to be similarly early. For the problems, see my discussion in *The Pilgrimage Pattern in Exodus* (with contributions by Elizabeth M. Bloch-Smith; JSOTSup 239; Sheffield: Sheffield Academic Press, 1997), 219–26.

63. Such an identification of deities of different character is hardly exceptional in the ancient Middle East. Here we may note Amun-Re in Late Bronze Age Egypt. For the "fusion" of multiple deities, see Olyan, *Asherah*, 10 n. 29. The Judean context that leaves Yahweh-El as the only major deity is partially exceptional in this case. Whether there is a more precise analogy for the southern warrior-god merging with the highlands patriarchal god requires further investigation.

64. Here religious change becomes manifest in a paradigm that Sigmund Freud would have understood. Here the application of Freudian theory to Israelite religion by H. Eilberg-Schwartz would have been more promising (see chapter 5, section 2). See Eilberg-Schwartz, *God's Phallus and Other Problems for Men and Monotheism* (Boston: Beacon Press, 1994).

65. See the references in n. 38.

66. Schloen, "Caravans, Kenites, and *Casus Belli*," 18–38, taking up the lead of Stager, "Archaeology, Ecology and Social History," 221–34. See also Stager, "Forging an Identity: The Emergency of Ancient Israel," *The Oxford History of the Biblical World* (ed. M.) D. Coogan; New York; Oxford University Press, 1998), 142–48.

67. For contact between Judeans and Calebites and Kenites, see Axelsson, *The Lord Rose up from Seir*. For an argument for Saul's importation of the cult of Yahweh due to his Edomite background, see van der Toorn, *Family Religion*, 285–86.

68. See G. L. Mattingly, "Amalek," *ABD* 1:169–71. Judges 6–8 presents the Midianites and Amalekites in a negative light. Either one can attribute such a negative view to a later retrojection or perhaps more plausibly to some kernel of tradition that recalls the tensions between the Isralite highlanders and the southern caravaner groups. Such a record of conflict does not undermine the evidence for positive relations. For Midian in early Israelite tradition, see further G. E. Mendenhall, "Midian," *ABD* 4:815–17; Cross, *From Epic to Canon*, 60–70.

69. For this positive evidence, see Schloen, "Caravans, Kenites and *Casus Belli*," 27.

Schloen would also see a reference to Midian behind MT *middîn* in v 10. Whether an emendation is warranted, or a verbal allusion is intended, the connection seems plausible given the reference to traders (*hōlĕkê ʿal-derek*) here.

70. See *CMHE* 200. For the old "Kenite hypothesis" that worship of Yahweh was mediated to the Israelites via the Kenites, see the discussion of van der Toorn, *Family Religion*, 283–84. For further information concerning the Kenites, see B. Halpern, "Kenites," *ABD* 4:17–22. See further Cross, *From Epic to Canon*, 45–70.

71. It is often mentioned in the secondary literature that the Egyptian place-name *yhw3*, apparently located in the Negev-Sinai region, may derive from the name, Yahweh, e.g. Mettinger, "The Elusive Essence," 404; van der Toorn, *Family Religion*, 283; but see the discussion of H. Goedicke, "The Tetragrammaton in Egyptian?" *The Society for the Study of Egyptian Antiquities Journal* 24 (1994), 24–27. The theory in its current form goes back to R. Giveon, "Toponymes Ouest-Asiatiques à Soleb," *VT* 14 (1964), 244. Without some further evidence apart from place-names, it is difficult to place too much weight on this information. Moreover, etymological questions about the evidence have been raised (see Halpern, "Kenites," 20). For these reasons it is not given greater prominence here.

72. See T. Hiebert, *God of My Victory: The Ancient Hymn in Habakkuk 3* (HSM 38; Atlanta, GA: Scholars, 1986), 129–49; R. D. Haak, *Habakkuk* (VTSup 44; Leiden: Brill, 1992), 16–20.

73. See Albright, Cross, Freedman, de Moor, and Dikjstra as reported and summarized in K. van der Toorn, "Yahweh," *DDD* 910–13. See in particular *CMHE* 60–75; Cross, *TDOT* 1:260. See also de Moor, *The Rise of Yahwism: The Roots of Israelite Monotheism* (BETL XCI; Leuven: University Press/Uitgeverij Peeters, 1990), 237–39. Note also Wyatt, *Myths of Power*, 332, 357 n. 2 for Yahweh as a southern Palestinian form of El. How this view dovetails with Wyatt's efforts at an Indo-European etymology for Yahweh is unclear. For criticism of this general approach, see van der Toorn, "Yahweh, 1722."

74. For example, Mettinger, "The Elusive Essence," 393–417, esp. 410. This view is preferred also by K. van der Toorn, "Yahweh," *DDD* 916–17.

75. For these aspects of the god, see M. S. Smith, "The God Athtar in the Ancient Near East and His Place in KTU 1.6 I," חיים ליונה *Solving Riddles and Untying Knots: Biblical, Epigraphic, and Semitic Studies Presented to Jonas C. Greenfield* (ed. Z. Zevit, S. Gitin and M. Sokoloff; Winona Lake, IN: Eisenbrauns, 1995), 627–40. I do not see such a view as precluding a derivation of the name from **hwy*, "to blow" (of the wind), an etymology that at the present seems the least objectionable of the current theories; see E. A. Knauf, "Yahwe," *VT* 34 (1984), 467–72; cited favorably by van der Toorn, "Yahweh," 915–16; and Mettinger, "The Elusive Presence," 410. The diversity of scholarly views points to the great uncertainty on this point.

76. Among recent commentators, see Mettinger, "The Elusive Essence," 411: "YHWH is the God of the exodus."

77. Wyatt, "Of Calves and Kings: The Canaanite Dimension in the Religion of Israel," *SJOT* 6 (1992), 78–83. I do not accept a number of the arguments forwarded by Wyatt.

78. Smith, "Yahweh and the Other Deities of Ancient Israel: Observations on Old Problems and Recent Trends," *Ein Gotte allein? JHWH-Verehrung und biblischer Monotheismus im Kontext der israelitischen und altorientalischen Religionsgeschichte* (ed. W. Dietrich and M. A. Klopfenstein; OBO 139; Freiburg: Universitätsverlag; Göttingen: Vandenhoeck & Ruprecht, 1994), 207–08.

79. Discussed in chapter 1, section 4.

80. See Levine, "The Balaam Inscription from Deir ʿAlla: Historical Aspects," 337–38; "The Plaster Inscriptions from Deir ʿAlla: General Interpretation," *The Balaam Text from*

Deir 'Alla Re-evaluated (ed. J. Hoftijzer and G. van der Kooij; Leiden: Brill, 1991) 58–72. I am highly indebted to Levine for his seminal research on El traditions in early biblical literature, especially in Transjordanian material. See especially his commentary, *Numbers* (2) 21–36 (AB 4B; New York: Doubleday, 2000), 243–75.

81. P. K. McCarter believes that the Egyptian names of the Levitical priesthood "suggest that a portion of the tribe of Levi may have lived in Egypt at some time." See McCarter, "Exodus," *Harper's Bible Commentary* (ed. J. L. Mays; San Francisco, CA: Harper & Row, 1988), 134.

82. Smith, "Southern Influences upon Hebrew Prophecy," *AJSL* 35 (1918), 8. See also Albright, "The Evolution of the West Semitic Divinity 'An-'Anat-'ttâ," *AJSL* 41 (1925), 84 n. 1. NJPS 410 n.d.

83. See Stager, "The Archaeology of the Family in Ancient Israel," 26; "Archaeology, Ecology, and Social History," 230–31. This status may suggest the (secondary?) derivation of *lēwî* from **lwy*, "to attach" (here to a sanctuary [?]). It is evident that the tradition of the exodus was transmitted through various Levitical santuaries including Dan, which is reflected in Judges 17–18 (*CMHE* 197–99).

84. For El Shaddai in P, see W. R. Garr, "The Grammar and Interpretation of Exodus 6:3," *JBL* 111 (1992), 385–408.

85. Quoted with permission from Lewis's unpublished book manuscript on the religion of Israel to be published by Doubleday in its Anchor Bible Reference Library series. I wish to thank Professor Lewis for access to his manuscript.

86. See Cross's seminal work in this regard by *CMHE* 3–12, 46–60.

8. The Emergence of Monotheistic Rhetoric in Ancient Judah

1. For references to Albright, Kaufman, and de Moor, see chapter 1, section 2. See C. H. Gordon, "Indo-European and Hebrew Epic," *Eretz Israel* 5 (1958 = B. Mazar volume), *15 n. 42, where the patriarchal narratives are attributed "the monotheistic principle." The formulation of H. Orlinsky ("The Hebrew Origins of Monotheism: Abraham and Moses," *Monotheism and Moses* [ed. R. J. Christen and H. E. Hazelton; Lexington, MA: D. C. Heath, 1969], 59) likewise associates the patriarchs with a sort of practical monotheism. Propp's views are expressed in his unpublished essay, "Monotheism and 'Moses'" (my thanks to Professor Propp for his permission to cite this piece). For a recent appreciation of this approach, see also Tigay, *The JPS Torah Commentary*: Deuteronomy דברים (Philadelphia: Jewish Publication Society, 1996), 433–35. See, with important qualifications, P. K. McCarter, "The Religious Reforms of Hezekiah and Josiah," *Aspects of Monotheism: How God is One* (ed. H. Shanks and J. Meinhardt; Washington, DC: Biblical Archaeology Society, 1997), 73–74; K. van der Toorn, "Yahweh," *DDD* 918. For a critique of de Moor's work in this area, see N. Wyatt, *Myths of Power: A Study of Royal Power and Ideology in Ugaritic and Biblical Tradition* (VBL 13; Münster: Ugarit-Verlag, 1996), 326–27.

2. See B. Uffenheimer, "Myth and Reality in Ancient Israel," *The Origins and Diversity of Axial Civilizations* (ed. S. N. Eisenstadt; Albany: State University of New York Press 1986), 144, with important modifications of Kaufman's theories. See further introduction, section 2. See also P. Sanders, *The Provenance of Deuteronomy 32* (OTS 37; Leiden: Brill, 1996), 426–29.

3. See C. Breytenbach and P. L. Day, "Satan," *DDD* 726–32 (with further bibliography). See further E. Pagels, *The Origins of Satan* (New York: Random House, 1996).

4. See chapter 3 for discussion.

5. See Tigay, *The JPS Torah Commentary*, 433.

6. See chapter 4, section 3.

7. An old distinction, for example, made by G. A. Barton, *The Religion of Ancient Israel* (New York: A. S. Barnes, 1961; original, 1928), 94–105, 123.

8. Meek, *Hebrew Origins* (New York: Harper & Row, 1936), 204–28. See also D. Baly, "The Geography of Monotheism," *Translating & Understanding the Old Testament: Essays in Honor of Herbert Gordon May* (ed. H. T. Frank and W. L. Reed; Nashville: Abingdon, 1970), esp. 267. Despite his critique of Albright, Baly locates the requisite features of monotheism historically in the desert experience and the experience of God at Sinai; accordingly, Baly's view shares a number of points with Albright's.

9. Meek, *Hebrew Origins*, 204–28.

10. Letter dated January 22, 1938, American Philosophical Society Albright Personal Corresp. 1936–38. For their exchange in print, see also their contributions to *Monotheism and Moses* (ed. R. J. Christen and H. E. Hazelton; Lexington, MA: D. C. Heath, 1969). Albright added a little-known rejoinder in this volume (pp. 78–79), which identifies later claims against all deities with earlier claims against specific cults (1 Kings 18:27, 2 Kings 1:6).

11. Albright, *From the Stone Age to Christianity: Monotheism and the Historical Process* (sec. ed.; Baltimore: Johns Hopkins University Press, 1946), 271.

12. Albright, *From the Stone Age to Christianity*, 257.

13. Letter dated January 31, 1943, American Philosophical Society Albright Personal Corresp. 1943.

14. See J. Hoftijzer and K. Jongeling, *Dictionary of the North-West Semitic Inscriptions. Part Two: M–T* (HdO 21/2; Leiden: Brill, 1995), 919, f.

15. Albright, *From the Stone Age to Christianity* (sec. ed.; 1946), 367; see also the 1967 printing on p. 297 n. 29.

16. Albright, *From the Stone Age to Christianity*, 197.

17. See B. Long, "Mythic Trope in the Autobiography of William Foxwell Albright," *BA* 56/1 (1993), 36–45; and *Planting and Reaping Albright: Politics, Ideology, and Interpreting the Bible* (University Park, PA: Pennsylvania State University Press, 1997), 156–57. Readers interested in Albright and his legacy may peruse D. N. Freedman, "W. F. Albright as an Historian," *The Scholarship of William Foxwell Albright. An Appraisal: Papers Delivered at the Symposium "Homage to William Foxwell Albright." The American Friend of the Israel Exploration Society. Rockville, Maryland, 1984* (ed. G. van Beek; HSS 33; Atlanta, GA: Scholars, 1989), 33–43; P. Machinist, "William Foxwell Albright: The Man and His work," *The Study of the Ancient Near East in the Twenty-First Century* (ed. J. S. Cooper and G. M. Schwartz; Winona Lake, IN: Eisenbrauns, 1996), 385–403 (with further bibliography); the essays in *BA* 56/1 (1993) devoted to Albright and his work. See also M. S. Smith, *Untold Stories: The Bible and Ugaritic Studies in the Twentieth Century* (Peabody, MA: Hendrickson, 2001).

18. Some possibilities for this issue are raised in *EHG*.

19. For important basic works on monotheism in ancient Israel, see *Monotheismus im alten Israel und seiner Umwelt* (ed. O. Keel; BB 14; Fribourg: Schweizeriches katholisches Bibelwerk, 1980); *Gott, der Einzige: Zur Enstehung des Monotheismus in Israel* (Quaestiones Disputatae 104; Freiburg/Basel/Vienna: Herder, 1985) (reference courtesy of W. Propp); *Ein Gott allein? JHWH-Verehrung und biblischer Monotheismus im Kontext der israeltischen und altorientalischen Religionsgeschichte* (ed. W. Dietrich and M. A. Klopfenstein; 13. Kolloquium der Schweizerischen Akademie der Geistes-und Sozialwissenschaften 1993; Freiburg Schweiz: Universitätsverlag, 1994 = repr. OBO 139; Freiburg Schweiz: Universitätsverlag; Göttingen: Vandenhoeck & Ruprecht, 1994). See also B. Uffenheimer, "Myth and Reality in Ancient Israel," 164–66; A. Schenker, "Le monothéisme israélite: un dieu qui transcende le monde et les dieux," *Bib* 78 (1997), 436–38. Uffenheimer stresses the Israelite deity's

ontological transcendance from creation. Schenker emphasizes a conceptual distinction of Yahweh's transcendance over and above other deities. At the outset of the discussion, I favor a more pedestrian approach based on the terms employed in the texts. I am unsure whether Schenker's definition of monotheism might not also apply to some reduced forms of Yahwistic polytheism described in chapter 3. Moreover, mention of other deities for other peoples or in the Decalogue implies a de facto acceptance of polytheism for non-Israelites; this is not monotheism. I am not sure I understand what it means to have "une conception simultanément monothéiste et polythéiste" (p. 445). Despite these qualms, Schenker is absolutely correct to view monotheism in the larger polytheistic context. Finally, the authors in these works who express their view on the date of Israelite monotheism situate it in the context of the exile and, in some cases, possibly a bit earlier as well. As the discussion indicates, I share this view of matters. There are dissenters presently to this view (J. C. de Moor, W. H. C. Propp; see later), but their approach hinges on a slippery definition of monotheism and flies in the face of evidence for polytheism in ancient Israel in the Iron Age.

20. Statements of incomparability are not included; such hyperbole is known also in Mesopotamian texts. Note also 2 Kings 5:15 (anachronistic?).

21. For discussion, see Tigay, *The JPS Torah Commentary*, 439. Cf. Psalm 73:19; the interrogative formulations in 2 Samuel 22:32//Psalm 18:32.

22. For variants, see T. J. Lewis, "The Textual History of the Song of Hannah: 1 Samuel II 1–20," *VT* 44 (1994), 27–29.

23. See Tigay, *The JPS Torah Commentary*, 529 n. 3; and B. Halpern, "The Names of Isaiah 62:4: Jeremiah's Reception in the Restoration and Politics of 'Third Isaiah,'" *JBL* 117 (1998), 623–43, esp. 632. Cf. the claim by Tigay (p. 529 n. 5) that Jeremiah 2:11 and 5:7 are monotheistic. Whether or not these passages are included does not affect the argument made here.

24. For the application of this definition to Deuteronomy 32, see P. Sanders, *The Provenance of Deuteronomy 32*, (OTS 32; Leiden: Brill, 1996), 426–29.

25. See Tigay, *The JPS Torah Commentary*, 76.

26. See the considered remarks of Tigay, *The JPS Torah Commentary*, 440.

27. Von Rad, *Deuteronomy: A Commentary* (trans. D. Barton; OTL; London: SCM, 1966), 63.

28. Tigay, *The JPS Torah Commentary*, 76. See also his fine discussion on pp. 438–40.

29. Note the well-placed considerations of J. C. L. Gibson, "Language about God in the Old Testament," *Polytheistic Systems* (ed. G. Davis; Cosmos: Yearbook of the Traditional Cosmology Society 5; Edinburgh: Edinburgh University Press, 1989), 43–50.

30. See Schenker, "Le monothéisme israélite," 447–48. On the issue of possible Persian influence, see the final section of this chapter.

31. Tigay, *The JPS Torah Commentary*, 529 n. 3; and Halpern, "The Names of Isaiah 62:4," 632.

32. Halpern, "The Names of Isaiah 62:4," 632.

33. For over a century commentators have argued for a Babylonian provenance (the notable exception was C. C. Torrey) for the following reasons:

1. Command to depart from Babylon in 48:20 and "redeemed of Zion" will depart (51:11).
2. Allusion to Babylonian gods (Bel = title of Marduk, Nebo = Nabu, son of Marduk, in Isaiah 46:1). The image of the two carried in Akitu (New Year) festival in the spring. Isaiah 46 as allusion to this procession? So see C. Stuhlmueller, *Creative Redemption in Deutero-Isaiah* (AnBib 42; Rome: Pontifical

Biblical Institute, 1970), 75–77, with parallels between the Akitu and Isaiah 40:3–5 and 52:7–19.

3. Allusion to Babylonian astrology, divination, and magic (44:24–25, 47:12–13).
4. Allusions to Babylon (Isaiah 47).
5. Cuneiform royal titulary said to be applied to Jacob/Israel. See, for example, R. Kittel, "Cyrus und Deuterojesaja," *ZAW* 18 (1998), 149–64, who compares "Second Isaiah" with Cyrus inscriptions, both being dependent on "Babylonian court style; S. M. Paul, "Deutero-Isaiah and Cuneiform Royal Inscriptions," *JAOS* 88/1 (1968) = *Essays in Honor of E. A. Speiser* (ed. W. W. Hallo; New Haven, CT: American Oriental Society, 1968), 181–86: "beloved, servant, shepherd"; "to be called by name"; royal role of liberate prisoners/open eyes; being called from the womb (also in Jeremiah): to proclaim neither world domination (as in Mesopotamian royal inscription), but world salvation.
6. Akkadian loanwords in "Second Isaiah."

While the dominant view since Duhm accepts a Babylonian provenance, recently H. M. Barstad has pushed for a Judean setting. See Barstad, *A Way in the Wilderness: The <<Second Exodus>> in the Message of Second Isaiah* (JSS Monograph 12; Manchester: University of Manchester, 1989); *The Babylonian Captivity of the Book of Isaiah 40–55* (The Institute of Comparative Research in Human Culture. Oslo; Oslo: Novus forlag, 1997); "On the So-Called Babylonian Literary influences in Second Isaiah," *SJOT* 2 (1987), 90–110; "Akkadian 'Loanwords' in Isaiah 40–55—And the Question of Babylonian Origin of Deutero-Isaiah," *Text and Theology: Studies in Honour of Professor Dr. Theol. Magne Sæbø Presented on the Occasion of His 65th Birthday* (ed. A. Tångberg; Oslo: Verbum, 1994), 36–48; see also Seitz, *Word Without End: The Old Testament as Abiding Theological Witness* (Grand Rapids, MI: Eerdmans, 1998). The main value of Barstad's research is to show many weaknesses in the arguments made for a Babylonian setting. Barstad also shows continuity of life in the land during the exile and the ideological purpose that the idea of a land emptied of its people served the interests of those taken to Babylon (*The Myth of the Empty Land: A Study of the History and Archaeology of Judah During the "Exilic" Period* [Symbolae Osloenses Fasc. Suppl. XXVIII; Oslo: Sandinavian University, 1996]). While all this may be true, it does not disprove a Babylonian provenance or establish a Palestinian one for "Second Isaiah."

Barstad's critique requires scholars not only to question the old arguments for "Second Isaiah" 's Babylonian background, but also to reconsider the entire historical (or historicist) approach to the issue. I argue at the end of section two in the final chapter that the Babylonian-Jerusalem polarity is a literary construct, as in Psalm 137, another exilic period composition. (The book of Ezekiel illustrates the real-life communication between home community in Judah and the Babylonian community.) The operative geographical perspective is Zion-Jerusalem in Isaiah 40:1–11 (verses 9, 11): the journey is bring the people from there (verse 11) to here. It is a commonplace to argue that this journey represents a "Second Exodus," and I suggest that ultimately both journeys are modeled on a more basic pattern, used literarily elsewhere in the Bible, namely, the pilgrimage to the sanctuary site. Yet such an interpretive move does not remove the further question of historical setting. Despite the many good criticisms Barstad makes of the traditional scholarly view of "Second Isaiah" 's Babylonian setting, such criticism does not demonstrate a Palestinian background, and I think it is still quite feasible to argue for a Babylonian provenance. Indeed, specific passages in "Second Isaiah" would have little force in a Palestinian provenance, but would suit very well a Babylonian setting (e.g., Isaiah 46:1–4).

34. See the careful study of H. G. M. Williamson, *The Book Called Isaiah: Deutero-Isaiah's Role in Composition and Redaction* (Oxford: Clarendon Press, 1994); also Seitz, *Word*

Without End. See also the many fine essays in *The Book of Isaiah. Le Livre d'Isaïe: Les oracles et leur relectures unité et complexité de l'ouvrage* (ed. J. Vermeylen; BETL LXXXI; Leuven: University Press/Peeters, 1989); and *Studies in the Book of Isaiah: Festschrift Willem A. M. Beuken* (ed. J. van Ruiten and M. Vervenne; BETL CXXXII; Leuven: University Press/ Uitgeverij, 1997). For further issues, see B. D. Sommer, *A Prophet Reads Scripture: Allusion in Isaiah 40–66* (Contraversions. Jews and Other Differences; Stanford, CA: Stanford University Press, 1998), 73–107; and R. L. Schultz, *The Search for Quotation: Verbal Parallels in the Prophets* (JSOTSup 180; Sheffield: Sheffield Academic Press, 1999).

35. I do not agree with N. P. Lemche's reconstruction of "a general development towards a practical monotheism in the ancient Orient," but he does note rightly the literary character of Israelite monotheism: "the unique element is the literary investment that monotheism has acquired in the Old Testament" (Lemche, "From Prophetism to Apocalyptic: Fragments of an Article," *In the Last Days: On Jewish and Christian Apocalyptic and Its Period* [ed. K. Jeppesen et al.; Aarhuis: Aarhus University, 1994], 102). However, the "literary investment" may not be the only "unique element." It is too easy to assume a "practical monotheism" and treat it as commensurate with the more restrictive monotheism expressed in "Second Isaiah" and other biblical texts. Israelite monotheism's further "achievements" (to use Lemche's term) were its restrictive and explicit character and the normative status it achieved in the post-exilic community. Here the category of "practical monotheism" of a sort is held, ironically enough, by those scholars who see monotheism as hardly unique to Israel and perhaps late (so Lemche) and those scholars who see monotheism as unique and early (so Tigay).

36. This lack of clear development is evident in reconstructions that move from "*de facto* monotheism" to explicit monotheism. See the following discussion.

37. Seitz, *Word Without End*, 255: "It is an intramural statement, made by Israel's named deity, that he alone is God."

38. Seitz, *Word Without End*, 255.

39. See chapter 4, section 4, for discussion.

40. See chapter 2, section 4, for discussion.

41. Note the formulation of Wyatt (*Myths of Power*, 325): "Because of 'historical drag', we find gods persisting who in all conscience, from the point of view of a systematic theology, should have been pensioned off years ago."

42. For a survey of late monarchic polytheism in Jeremiah 7 and 44 and Ezekiel 8, see S. Ackerman, *Under Every Green Tree: Popular Religion in Sixth Century Judah* (HSM 46; Atlanta, GA: Scholars, 1992), 5–99.

43. See the important book of Keel and Uehlinger, *Gods, Goddesses, and Images of God*, 177–281, 323–49 (with bibliography). For a popular survey of the archaeological evidence (with some of the iconography), see W. Dever, "Folk Religion in Early Israel: Did Yahweh Have a Consort?" *Roots of Monotheism: How God Is One* (ed. H. Shanks and J. Meinhardt; Washington, DC: Biblical Archaeology Society, 1997), 27–56.

44. The older treatments of Psalm 82 in this vein without reference to the Ugaritic texts include H. S. Nyberg, *Studien zum Hoseabuche: Zugleich ein Beitrag zur Klärung des Problems der Alttestamentlichen Textkritik* (Uppsala Universitets Årsskrift 1935:6; Uppsala: Almqvist & Wiksells, 1935), 122–25; and O. Eissfeldt, "Neue Götter im alten Testament," *Atti del XIX Congresso Internazionale degli Orientalisti. Roma, 23–29 Settembre 1935-XIII* (Rome: Tipografia del Senato, 1938), 479. The best recent treatment is S. B. Parker, "The Beginning of the Reign of God. Psalm 82 as Myth and Liturgy," *RB* 102 (1995), 532–59. See also J. F. A. Sawyer, "Biblical Alternatives to Monotheism," *Theology* 87 (1984), 172–80; M. Dietrich and O. Loretz, "*Jahwe und seine Aschera*": *Anthropomorphes Kultbild in Mesopotamien, Ugarit und Israel. Das biblische Bilderverbot* (UBL 9; Münster: Ugarit-

Verlag, 1992), 134–57; and Schenker, "Le monothéisme israélite," 442–44. Among the commentaries, see K. Seybold, *Die Psalmen* (HAT 1/15; Tübingen: Mohr [Siebeck], 1996), 324–26.

45. 4QDeut^q: *bny 'l[*: 4QDeut^j: *bny 'lwhym[*: LXX *huiōon theou* (cf. LXX variants with *aggelōn* interpolated). For the evidence, see E. Tov, *Textual Criticism of the Hebrew Bible* (Minneapolis: Fortress; Assen/Maastricht: Van Gorcum, 1992), 269; J. A. Duncan, *Qumran Cave 4. IX: Deuteronomy, Joshua, Judges, Kings* (ed. E. Ulrich and F. M. Cross; DJD XIV; Oxford: Clarendon Press, 1995), 90; noted also in BHS to Deuteronomy 32:8 note d. For older bibliography, *EHG* 30 n. 37; and A. Schenker, "Le monothéisme israélite: un dieu qui transcende le monde et les dieux," *Bib* 78 (1997), 438. For an older discussion, see already O. Eissfeldt, "Neue Götter im alten Testament," 479. For further discussion, see chapters 7 and 8.

46. Cf. the echo of Deuteronomy 32:7–9 in Ben Sira 44:2 (cf. verse 23), which reflects the understanding in MT. For discussion, see P. W. Skehan and A. A. DiLella, *The Wisdom of Ben Sira: A New Translation with Notes* (AB 39; New York: Doubleday, 1987), 498.

47. See M. H. Pope, "Seven, Seventh, Seventy," *IDB* 4:285–95; F. C. Fensham, "The Numeral Seventy in the Old Testament and the Family of Jerubbaal, Ahab, Panammuwa and Athirat," *PEQ* 109 (1977), 113–15; J. C. de Moor, "Seventy!" *"Und Mose schrieb dieses Lied auf": Studien zum Alten Testament und zum Alten Orient. Festschrift für Oswald Loretz zur Vollendung seines 70. seines Lebenjahres mit Beiträgen von Freunden, Schülern und Kollegen* (ed. M. Dietrich and I. Kottsieper; AOAT 250; Münster: Ugarit-Verlag, 1998), 199–203. In the narrative of Elkunirsa, a West Semitic myth written in Hittite, Ashertu's children number 77//88. H. A. Hoffner, *Hittite Myths* (ed. G. M. Beckman; SBL Writings from the Ancient World Series 2; Atlanta, GA: Scholars, 1990), 69. See also chapters 3 and 7.

48. For an interesting but often overlooked study of the correlation between human and divine monarchy in Judah, see J. A. Winter, "Immanence and Regime in the Kingdom of Judah: A Cross-disciplinary Study of a Swansonian Hypothesis," *Sociological Analysis* 44 (1983), 147–62.

49. For a valuable survey of this topic, see T. N. D. Mettinger, *King and Messiah: The Civil and Sacred Legitimization of the Israelite Kings* (Coniectana Biblica, Old Testament Series 8; Lund: Gleerup, 1987). See also K. W. Whitelam, "Israelite Kingship. The Royal Ideology and Its Opponents," *The World of Ancient Israel: Sociological, Anthropological and Political Perspectives: Essays by Members of the Society for Old Testament Study* (ed. R. E. Clements; Cambridge: Cambridge University Press, 1989), 119–39 (which includes a discussion of the old question of the king's "divine status"); see most recently M. Dietrich and W. Dietrich, "Zwischen Gott und Volk: Einführung des Königtums und Auswahl des Königs nach mesopotamischer und israelitischer Anschauung," *"Und Mose schrieb dieses Lied auf": Studien zum Alten Testament und zum Alten Orient. Festschrift für Oswald Loretz zur Vollendung seines 70, seines Lebenjahres mit Beiträgen von Freunden, Schülern und Kollegen* (ed. M. Dietrich and I. Kottsieper; AOAT 250; Münster: Ugarit-Verlag, 1998), 215–64. For "mythical elements" in the Psalter in general, see the helpful survey of C. Petersen, *Mythos im Alten Testament: Bestimmung des Mythosbegriffs und Untersuchung der mythischen Elemente in den Psalmen* (BZAW 157; Berlin: de Gruyter, 1982).

50. For a discussion of "mythic imagery" in the Bible, see the final section of the Introduction.

51. The notion that the kings of the Davidic dynasty were "sons" of Yahweh is a fourth "royal theology" that has been compared with similar formulations in the Ugaritic narrative of Keret and Akkadian inscriptions. On the Akkadian material, see S. M. Paul, "Adoption Formulae: A Study of Cuneiform and Biblical Legal Clauses," *Maarav* 2/2 (1980),

175–79. Whether or not this sonship was expressed as a matter of "adoption" or "natural sonship" remains a controverted issue (see n. 75). In any case, the influence may have moved from royal ideology to mythology. For example, this idea of royal sonship was incorporated into the divine drama of the Baal Cycle (specifically 1.1 IV 12). In general for the application of royal language to Yahweh, see M. Z. Brettler, *God is King: Understanding an Israelite Metaphor* (JSOTSup 76; Sheffield: JSOT, 1989); and J. Tigay, "On Some Aspects of Prayer in the Bible," *AJSreview* 1 (1976), 363–79.

52. For the use of myth by the Egyptian monarchy, see V. A. Tobin, "The Creativity of Egyptian Myth: Wanderings in an Intellectual Labyrinth," *The Society for the Study of Egyptian Antiquities Journal* 18 (1988), 111–13. I wish to thank Professor Gordon Hamilton for bringing this reference to my attention.

53. Cf. the invocation of Addu to march at the side of Zimri-Lim: *i-la-ak ad-du-um i-na šu-me-li-šu*, "March, Addu, at his left side," cited by D. Charpin, "De la Joie à l'Orage," *MARI* 5 (1987), 661.

54. See T. Hiebert, *God of My Victory: The Ancient Hymn in Habakkuk 3* (HSM 38; Atlanta, GA: Scholars, 1986), 4, 92–94, 123; R. D. Haak, *Habakkuk* (VTSup 44; Leiden: Brill, 1992), 83, 90.

55. Haak, *Habakkuk*, 98–99. Hiebert's attempt to locate the "anointed" in the premonarchic period is unpersuasive; see Hiebert, *God of My Victory*, 107.

56. Described extensively in chapter 1. See also J. Day, *God's Conflict with the Dragon and the Sea: Echoes of a Canaanite Myth in the Old Testament* (University of Cambridge Oriental Publications No. 35; Cambridge: Cambridge University Press, 1985), 151–78.

57. In view of the Ugaritic evidence, one may wonder if *nĕhārôt* represents a plural of majesty or the like or implies a re-application of the mythic language to the maximal borders of the Wadi el-Arish to the Euphrates.

58. G. W. Ahlström, *Psalm 89: Eine liturgie aus dem Ritual des leidenden Königs* (Lund: Gleerup, 1959), 108–11; E. Lipiński, *Le poème royal du Psaume LXXXIX 1.5.20–38* (Cahiers de la Revue biblique 6; Paris: Gabalda, 1967), 53; J.-B. Dumortier, "Un rituel d'intronisation: Le Ps. LXXXIX 2–38," *VT* 22 (1972), 188 and n. 1; CMHE 258 n. 177, 261–62; Mosca, "Ugarit and Daniel 7," 509, 512; idem, "Once Again the Heavenly Witness of Ps 89:38," *JBL* 105 (1986), 33. Mosca ("Once Again," 33) points to other examples of "mythico-religious terms" in Psalm 89: the king is "the 'first-born' (*bĕkôr*, v 28) of 'my father' (*'abî*, v 27), and serves as the 'Most High' (*'elyôn*, v 28) with respect to earthly kings." Cf. M. Weinfeld, "Zion and Jerusalem as Religious and Political Capital: Ideology and Utopia," *The Poet and the Historian: Essays in Literary and Historical Biblical Criticism* (ed. R. E. Friedman; HSS 26; Chico, CA: Scholars, 1983), 97–98.

59. For argumentation, see UBC 104–5.

60. Stolz, "Funktionen und Bedeutungsbereiche des ugaritischen Ba'almythos," *Funktionen und Leistungen des Mythos: Drei altorientalische Beispiele* (ed. J. Assman et al.; OBO 48; Freiburg: Universitätsverlag; Göttingen: Vandenhoeck und Ruprecht, 1981), 83–118.

61. See P. D. Miller, "Ugarit and the History of Religions," *JNWSL* 9 (1981), 125. For an example of Egyptian cultural influence on the Ugaritic monarchy's iconographic self-presentation (on ivories), see B. M. Bryan, "Art, Empire, and the End of the Bronze Age," *The Study of the Ancient Near East in the Twenty-First Century: The William Foxwell Albright Centennial Conference* (ed. J. S. Cooper and G. M. Schwartz; Winona Lake, IN: Eisenbrauns, 1996), 69–70.

62. Stolz, "Funktionen und Bedeutungsbereiche des ugaritischen Ba'almythos," 83–118.

63. For discussion, see EHG 56–57; J. M. Sasson, "Mari Historiography and the

Yahdun-Lim Disc Inscription," *Lingering Over Words: Studies in the Ancient Near Eastern Literature in Honor of William L. Moran* (ed. T. Abusch, J. Huehnergard and P. Steinkeller; HSS 37; Atlanta, GA: Scholars, 1990), 444 n. 12.

64. E. Gaál, "Tuthmosis III as Storm-God?" *Studia Aegyptiaca* 3 (1977), 29–38. See also ANET 249.

65. See chapter 1 for discussion.

66. CMHE 258 n. 177; UBC 109.

67. CMHE 258 n. 177.

68. Cf. the self-comparison of Shalmaneser III with Hadad in ANET 277; D. Damrosch, *The Narrative Covenant: Transformations of Genre in the Growth of Biblical Literature* (San Francisco: Harper and Row, 1987), 55, 61, 70.

69. C. F. Whitley, "Textual and Exegetical Observations on Ps 45, 4–7," ZAW 98 (1986), 277–82.

70. For the problems in the dating of this verse, see A. Laato, *Who Is Immanuel? The Rise and Foundering of Isaiah's Messianic Expectations* (Abo: Abo Academy Press, 1988), 179–88.

71. For Yahweh as "warrior-god," see also Deuteronomy 10:17 and Jeremiah 32:18. See Mettinger, *King and Messiah*, 273.

72. J. S. M. Mulder, *Studies on Psalm 45* (Oss, the Netherlands: Offsetdrukkerij, 1972), 105.

73. See Holladay, *Isaiah, the Scroll of a Prophetic Heritage* (New York: Pilgrim, 1978), 106–108. I wish to thank Professor Holladay for bringing his discussion of this passage to my attention.

74. H. Wildberger, *Jesaja* (BKAT X/1; Neukirchen-Vluyn: Neukirchener, 1972), 381–89.

75. Holladay cites as parallel the Egyptian practice of giving throne names to the king upon his accession (Holladay, *Isaiah, Scroll of a Prophetic Heritage*, 106–09; see also Mettinger, *King and Messiah*, 287). Akkadian parallels to the language for divine adoption and Ugaritic expressions of Keret as "a son of El" complicate the assumption of direct Egyptian influence on Israelite conception of divine sonship (as argued by Mettinger, *King and Messiah*, 265). During the Late Bronze Age, Egypt and the Syro-Palestinian coast show mutual influence in the area of royal theology, which perhaps mediated some indirect Egyptian influence on later Israelite royal theology. For a similar argument for possible indirect Egyptian influence in another area of Israelite culture, see CMHE 247. For a judicious general opinion about direct Egyptian influence on Israelite culture, see K. A. Kitchen, "Egypt and Israel during the First Millennium," *Congress Volume: Jerusalem 1986* (ed. J. A. Emerton; VTSup 40; Leiden: Brill, 1988), 107–23. For a more optimistic view, see M. Görg, *Gott-König-Reden in Israel und Ägypten* (BWANT 105; Stuttgart: Kohlhammer, 1975).

76. Laato, *Who Is Immanuel?*, 193.

77. S. C. Layton, *Archaic Features of Canaanite Personal Names in the Hebrew Bible* (HSS 47; Atlanta, GA: Scholars, 1990), 134. Gabriel is a well-known proper name (Daniel 8:16; 9:21; Luke 1:19; for a defense of Gabriel as a sentence-name meaning "El is my strong one" as well as other views, see Layton, *Archaic Features*, 131–34).

78. Or more specifically as "El titles"; see Layton, *Archaic Features*, 133 n. 124.

79. For an Ugaritic mythological example, see CAT 1.1 IV 25, discussed by Wyatt, " 'Jedidiah' and Cognate Forms as a Title of Royal Legitimation," *Bib* 66 (1985), 112–25; del Olmo Lete, *Canaanite Religion*, 180.

80. So Laato, *Who Is Immanuel?*, 192–93.

81. See del Olmo Lete, *Canaanite Religion*, 176–81. The best Ugaritic example is CAT 7.63.1–9, discussed on pp. 176–77.

82. Cross (*CMHE* 16) relates both titles to El.

83. See the discussion of this issue in chapter 2, section 2.

84. Deuteronomy 32:8–9; 2 Samuel 22 (Psalm 18):14–16. For discussion, see *EHG* 21.

85. For discussion of the relations between Psalm 45:7 and to Zechariah 14:8, see Whitley, "Textual and Exegetical Observations."

86. Ugaritic evidence has played a role in the debate over the king as "divine" (see Mettinger, *King and Messiah*, 273). The relevance of Keret (specifically CAT 1.14 I 17–23) to this category may not hinge on whether one views *bn 'l* and *qdš* as specific designations for El (and/or Athirat), i.e. "the son of El" and "the Holy One," or general terms, "a divine son," and "a holy one." It may arguable that in the biblical material *bn 'l(m)* is a general designation, "a divine being" (see Psalm 29:1).

87. See H. Schmidt, *Die Psalmen* (HAT 15; Tübingen: Mohr [Siebeck], 1934), 86; W. O. E. Oesterley, *The Psalms; Translated with Text-Critical and Exegetical Notes* (London: SPCK, 1962), 252–53; Kraus, *Psalms 1–59*, 451–52, 455. The range of opinions on this verse may be found in Mulder, *Studies on Psalm 45*, 33–80. Mulder objects to the king as *'ĕlōhîm* in this verse because *'ĕlōhîm* elsewhere in the psalm is God. This objection requires a flat reading of the highly charged language in this psalm. The ambiguity of *'ĕlōhîm* heightens the relationship between God and the monarch in this psalm, which Mulder otherwise views as a central point of the composition.

88. Many commentators construe *'ĕlōhîm* as the nominal predicate of *kis'ăkā* (see B. Duhm, *Die Psalmen* [KAT XIV; Freiburg/Leipzig/Tübingen: J. C. B. Mohr (Paul Siebeck), 1899], 129; A. K. Kirkpatrick, *The Book of Psalms* [Cambridge: Cambridge University Press, 1957], 247–48; J. R. Porter, "Psalm XLV. 7," 51–53; Mosca, "Once Again the Heavenly Witness of Psalm 89:38," 34–35; RSV). M. J. Dahood (*Psalms I: 1–50* [AB 16; New York: Doubleday, 1966], 269) translates the first half of v 7: "The eternal and everlasting God has enthroned you!" This translation assumes the revocalization *kissē'ăkā*, a denominative D-stem verb from *kissē'*, "throne." The suggestion is inspired in part by parallelism with *bērakĕkā 'ĕlōhîm* in v 3. The otherwise unattested denominative **ks'* and such distant parallelism constitute poor grounds for Dahood's suggestion. Indeed, it may be noted that C. A. and E. G. Briggs (*A Critical and Exegetical Commentary on the Book of Psalms*, [2 vols.; ICC; Edinburgh: T. & T. Clark, 1906], 1.383) render v 7b as parallel to *bērakĕkā 'ĕlōhîm* in v 3. Following G. R. Driver ("The Modern Study of the Hebrew Language," *The People and the Book* [ed. A. S. Peake; Oxford: Clarendon Press, 1925], 115–16), J. A. Emerton ("The Syntactical Problem of Psalm XLV.7," *JSS* 13 [1968], 58–63) makes the clause into an implicit comparison: "thy throne is (like the throne of) God." This view is followed also by Mulder, *Studies on Psalm 45*, 33–80; and Mettinger, *King and Messiah*, 265, 273. For criticism of this interpretation, see Mosca, "Once Again," 35 n. 24.

89. The Targum makes God the explicit addressee. The Greek versions translate *ho theos*, which may refer either to the king (so C. and E. Briggs, *A Critical and Exegetical Commentary on the Book of Psalms*, 1:387) or God (Mulder, *Studies on Psalm 45*, 48). The Briggses (*A Critical and Exegetical Commentary on the Book of Psalms*, 1.387) and A. Weiser (*The Psalms; A Commentary* [trans. H. Hartwell; OTL; Philadelphia: Westminster, 1962], 360) also take *'ĕlōhîm* as the king.

90. Emerton, "The Syntactical Problem of Psalm XLV.7," 58–63.

91. Mosca, "Once Again," 35 n. 24.

92. This phrase is used by Mosca ("Once Again," 35), who uses this argument for his own interpretation. He also says of the wording (according to his interpretation) "quite daring," a description that, compared to what survives of expressions of royal theology, also

applies to the Israelite king as *'ĕlōhîm*. It may be, however, that such language for the monarch was quite common within royal circles.

93. Whitley, "Textual and Exegetical Observations on Ps 45, 4–7," 282.

94. See Mettinger, *King and Messiah*, 271.

95. Kraus, *Psalms 1–59; A Commentary* (trans. H. C. Oswald; Minneapolis: Augsburg, 1988), 455; see also Mettinger, *King and Messiah*, 242–43.

96. Whitley, "Textual and Exegetical Observations on Ps 45, 4–7," 282.

97. J. R. Porter, "Psalm XLV. 7," *Journal of Theological Studies* n.s. 12 (1961), 51.

98. Emerton, "The Syntactical Problem," 58.

99. Whitelam, "Israelite Kingship," 136. Cf. M. Barker, *The Great Angel: A Study of Israel's Second God* (London: SPCK, 1992), 36.

100. For detailed discussion and notes on the Ugaritic and biblical texts concerning the "ban" (*ḥrm*), see M. S. Smith, "Anat's Warfare Cannibalism and the Biblical Herem," *The Pitcher Is Broken: Memorial Essays in Honor of Gösta W. Ahlström* (ed. L. K. Handy and S. Holloway; JSOTSup 190; Sheffield: JSOT, 1995), 368–86.

101. NJPS translation.

102. J. Lust, "Isaiah 34 and the Ḥerem," *The Book of Isaiah. Le livre d'Isaïe; les oracles et leurs relectures unité et complexité de l'ouvrage* (ed. J. Vermeylen; BETL LXXXI; Leuven: University Press/Uitgeverig Peeters, 1989), 285.

103. See Gibson, "Language about God in the Old Testament," 43–50.

104. For these factors, see F. Stolz, "Monotheismus in Israel," *Monotheismus im Alten Israel und seiner Umwelt* (ed. O. Keel; BB 14; Fribourg: Schweizeriches Katholiches Bibelwerk, 1980) 143–84; *EHG* 145–57; R. Albertz, "Der Ort des Monotheismus in der israeltischen Religionsgeschichte," *Ein Gott allein? JHWH-Verehrung und biblischer Monotheismus im Kontext der israeltischen und altorientalischen Religionsgeschichte* (ed. W. Dietrich and M. A. Klopfenstein; 13. Kolloquium der Schweizerischen Akademie der Geistes-und Sozialwissenschaften 1993; Freiburg Schweiz: Universitätsverlag, 1994), 77–96. See also the survey of A. Schenker, "Le monothéisme israélite," 436–48. I place no stock in either Israel's "nomadic background" as a factor or the present form of the biblical evidence pertaining to the Exodus.

105. *EHG* xxiii, xxiv, xxxiii, 21–24, 36–37, 145–57, 161, 163.

106. For developments in the eighth to the sixth centuries, see especially B. Halpern, "Jerusalem and the Lineages in the Seventh Century BCE: Kinship and the Rise of Individual Liability," *Law and Ideology in Monarchic Israel* (ed. B. Halpern and D. W. Hobson; JSOTSup 124; Sheffield: Sheffield Academic Press, 1991), 11–107; idem, "Sybil, or the Two Nations? Archaism, Kinship, Alienation, and the Elite Redefinition of Traditional Culture in Judah in the 8th–7th Centuries B.C.E.," *The Study of the Ancient Near East in the Twenty-First Century: The William Foxwell Albright Centennial Conference* (ed. J. S. Cooper and G. M. Schwartz; Winona Lake, IN: Eisenbrauns, 1996), 291–338. See further Halpern, " 'Brisker Pipes than Poetry': The Development of Israelite Monotheism," *Judaic Perspectives on Ancient Israel* (ed. J. A. Neusner, B. A. Levine, and E. S. Frerichs; Philadelphia: Fortress, 1987), 77–115; idem, "The Baal (and the Asherah) in Seventh Century Judah: Yhwh's Retainers Retired," *Konsequente Traditionsgeschichte: Festschrift für Klaus Baltzer zum .65 Geburtstag* (ed. R. Bartelmus, T. Krüger, and H. Utzschnieder; OBO 126; Freiburg Schweiz: Universitätsverlag; Göttingen: Vandenhoeck & Ruprecht, 1993), 115–54.

107. See chapter 3 for discussion.

108. For evidence and argument, see Halpern, "Sybil, or the Two Nations?" 291–338. See also J. Blenkinsopp, "The Family in First Temple Israel," in L. Perdue et al., *Families in Ancient Israel* (The Family, Religion, and Culture series; Louisville, KY: Westminster John Knox, 1997), 88–92. For the family in early Israel, see the references in chapter 3, note 30.

109. J. J. Collins, "Marriage, Divorce, and Family in Second Temple Judaism," in *Families in Ancient Israel*, 105.

110. Reference courtesy of Professor S. Olyan.

111. See Halpern, "Jerusalem and the Lineages in the Seventh Century BCE," 11–15. See further Halpern, "Sybil, or the Two Nations?," 295, 317–18, 323, 326. Note also the criticism of family religion in Jeremiah and Deuteronomy discussed by K. van der Toorn, *Family Religion in Babylonia, Syria and Israel: Continuity and Change in the Forms of Religious Life* (Studies in the History and Culture of the Ancient Near East 7, Leiden: Brill, 1996), 352–72.

112. See Halpern, "Jerusalem and the Lineages in the Seventh Century BCE," 11–107. See also Halpern, "Sybil, or the Two Nations?" 291–338.

113. This point is not to deny the ongoing use of images for divinity based on familial concepts (such as "father" or "redeemer"); the point involves naming other deities as family relations of Yahweh, for example, as implied in the earlier Psalm 82. For discussion of these points, see the independent discussion of Geller, "The God of the Covenant," 298.

114. Tigay, *The JPS Torah Commentary*, 433. See further W. Dietrich, "Der Eine Gott als Symbol politischen Widerstands. Religion und Politik im Juda des 7. Jahrhunderts," *Ein Gott allein? JHWH-Verehrung und biblischer Monotheismus im Kontext der israeltischen und altorientalischen Religionsgeschichte* (ed. W. Dietrich and M. A. Klopfenstein; 13. Kolloquium der Schweizerischen Akademie der Geistes-und Sozialwissenschaften 1993; Freiburg Schweiz: Universitätsverlag, 1994), 463–90; P. Machinist, "The Fall of Assyria in Comparative Ancient Perspective," *Assyria 1995: Proceedings of the 10th Anniversary Symposium of the Neo-Assyrian Text Corpus Project. Helsinki, September 7–11, 1995* (ed. S. Parpola and R. M. Whiting; Helsinki: The Neo-Assyrian Text Corpus Project, 1997), 179–95 esp. 184; and Geller, "The God of the Covenant," 316.

115. As noted in n. 1 above, Uffenheimer ("Myth and Reality in Ancient Israel," 164–66) and Schenker ("Le monothéisme israélite: un dieu qui transcende le monde et les dieux," 436–38) stress transcendance, albeit in different ways.

116. J. D. Schloen, "The Patrimonial Household in the Kingdom of Ugarit: A Weberian Analysis of Ancient Near Eastern Society" (Ph.D. diss., Harvard University, 1995), 29. See also pp. 5, 161–62.

117. This argument has a long lineage. For a recent discussion in this vein, T. L. Thompson, "The Intellectual Matrix of Early Biblical Narrative: Inclusive Monotheism in Persian Period Palestine," *The Triumph of Elohim: From Yahwisms to Judaisms* (ed. D. V. Edelman; Grand Rapids, MI: Eerdmans, 1996), 107–26. For an older argument with critique, see Albright, *From the Stone Age to Christianity*, 358–63. For another recent consideration of some of the issues, see G. Ahn, "Schöpfergott und Monotheismus: Systematische Implikationen der neueren Gatha-Exegese," *"Und Mose schrieb dieses Lied auf": Studien zum Alten Testament und zum Alten Orient. Festschrift für Oswald Loretz zur Vollendung seines 70. seines Lebenjahres mit Beiträgen von Freunden, Schülern und Kollegen* (ed. M. Dietrich and I. Kottsieper; AOAT 250; Münster: Ugarit-Verlag, 1998), 15–26. For a broader consideration of religious issues in the post-exilic period, see *The Crisis of Israelite Religion: Transformations of Religious Tradition in Exilic and Post-Exilic Times* (ed. B. Becking and M. C. A. Korpel; OTS 42; Leiden: Brill, 1999).

118. For this issue as well as other problems, see H. Niehr, "Religio-Historical Aspects of the 'Early Post-Exilic' Period," in *The Crisis of Israelite Religion*, 229.

119. See M. Boyce, "Persian Religion in the Achaemenid Age," *The Cambridge History of Judaism* (ed. W. D. Davies and L. Finkelstein; 3 vols.; Cambridge: Cambridge University Press, 1985), 1.279–307. See also her magisterial study, *A History of Zoroastrianism* (3 vols.; Leiden: Brill, 1975), 1.181–228. See also the summary E. Y. Yamauchi, "Persians," *Peoples*

of the Old Testament World (ed. A. J. Hoerth, G. L. Mattingly and E. M. Yamauchi; Cambridge: Lutterworth; Grand Rapids, MI: Baker Books, 1996), 121–23.

120. See C. Breytenbach and P. L. Day, "Satan," *DDD* 726–32 (with further bibliography). Albright dates this development to the second century BCE in Testaments of the Twelve Patriarchs (Test. Jud. 20) (see *From the Stone Age*, 362).

121. Oppenheim, "The Eyes of the Lord," *JAOS* 88 (1968), 173–80.

122. This is not to suggest a later uniformity in the Jewish presentation of monotheism in the Hellenistic and Roman periods. See L. W. Hurtado, *One God, One Lord: Early Christian Devotion and Ancient Jewish Monotheism* (sec. ed.; Edinburgh: T. & T. Clark, 1998); idem, "What Do We Mean by 'First-Century Jewish Monotheism'?" *SBLSP* 32 (1993), 348–68; and the ground-breaking book of A. H. Segal, *Two Powers in Heaven: Early Rabbinic Reports about Christianity and Judaism* (Studies in Judaism in Late Antiquity 25; Leiden: Brill, 1997). For a popular survey, see J. J. Collins, "Jewish Monotheism and Christian Theology," *Aspects of Monotheism: How God Is One* (ed. H. Shanks and J. Meinhardt; Washington, DC: Biblical Archaeology Society, 1997), 81–105. Yet even where there were some difficulties in the presentation of monotheism, the commitment to the presentation of monotheism remained deeply rooted.

9. The Formation of Monotheistic Theologies in Biblical Literature

1. Occasionally later tradition tapped into mythic material generally known but for various reasons not attested as used (as far as is known) by the monarchy, the priesthood, or other authoritative groups in ancient Israel until the Persian period. The post-exilic concept of resurrection gives the appearance of this phenomenon. L. J. Greenspoon (*Traditions in Transformation: Turning Points in Biblical Faith* [ed. B. Halpern and J. D. Levenson; Winona Lake, IN: Eisenbrauns, 1981], 247–321) stresses continuity between Ugaritic material and Israelite notions of resurrection (see chapter 6 n. 213). Ugaritic attests a cult devoted to dead royal ancestors. This cult, evident from both rituals (CAT 1.161) and mythic narratives (CAT 1.20–1.22), describes the living communicating and eating with former monarchs (for surveys, see K. Spronk, *Beatific Afterlife in Ancient Israel and in the Ancient Near East* [AOAT 219; Kevelaer: Butzon & Bercker; Neukirchen-Vlugn: Neukirchener, 1986]; T. J. Lewis, *Cults of the Dead in Ancient Israel and Ugarit* [HSM 39; Atlanta, GA: Scholars, 1989]; see further chapter 6). This idea continued in first-millennium texts, such as references to the dead ancestors in Phoenician sources or the request of the dead King Panammu to drink with the great god, Hadad (= Baal), in KAI 214 (J. C. Greenfield, "Un rite religieux araméen et ses parallèles," *RB* 80 [1973], 46–52); this text explicitly manifests the modification that the dead were thought not to dwell in the underworld but with the high gods, in a sense "in heaven." Resurrection in Israelite tradition is explicit only beginning with Daniel 12:3, sometimes thought to derive from the notion of "national resurrection" in Ezekiel 37 and Isaiah 26:17–19. All three of these texts may be viewed as responses to contemporary needs utilizing old material; resurrection in Daniel 12:3 provides hope to a community in the late Seleucid period, and Ezekiel 37 and Isaiah 26:17–19 visualize restoration from the diaspora. These texts reflect traditional mythic materials, specifically a notion presupposing the image of a person's rising from the dead, and this imagery has pre-exilic roots (e.g., evidently Hosea 6:1–3) in Israelite popular religion continuous to some degree with ideas represented on the royal level in Ugaritic material (Spronk, *Beatific Afterlife*, 293–306). Denials of notions or rituals associated with the dead (e.g., Psalm 16), appropriation of the resurrection imagery (Hosea 6:1–3; so F. I. Andersen and D. N. Freedman, *Hosea* [AB 24; New York: Doubleday, 1980], 419–21; I thank Professor John J. Collins for bringing this point to my attention) and the Israelite continuation of underworld imagery

from second-millennium antecedents witnessed in the Ugaritic texts (N. J. Tromp, *Primitive Conceptions of Death and the Nether World in the Old Testament* [Rome: Pontifical Biblical Institute, 1969]) illustrate that cultic customs associated with the dead, including some idea of resurrection, continued from Ugarit through the rabbinic period; these motifs seem to hibernate from the perspective of scholars, because the religious texts from the Bible and early rabbinic sources rarely mention them and certainly give them no sanction. The idea of resurrection may not derive from mythic material about Baal, however. Rather, it is equally arguable that ideas about Baal's death and resurrection were based on the royal cult of the dead ancestors. The same direction of influence is evidence in the Phoenician material where descriptions of Melqart's death draw on the Phoenician practice of cremation (see C. Bonnet, *Studia Phoenicia VIII: Melqart. Cultes et mythes de l'Héraklès tyrien en Méditerranée* [Leuven: Uitgeverij Peeters, 1988], 173; M S. Smith and E. Bloch-Smith, Review of Bonnet, *Studia Phoenicia VIII, JAOS* 110 [1990], 591), as argued in chapter 6. B. Lang ("Life After Death in the Prophetic Promise," *Congress Volume: Jerusalem 1986* [ed. J. A. Emerton; VTSup 40; Leiden: Brill, 1988], 144–56) examines the rise of post-exilic notions of resurrection in a linear fashion, tracing the cessation of pre-exilic ancestor worship due to a "Yahweh-only" party of the late monarchy and the post-exilic rise of resurrection due to Iranian influence. The archaeological evidence shows no change due to the "Yahweh-only" party. Instead, as E. M. Bloch-Smith has shown, attention to the dead possibly including providing food for the dead continued throughout ancient Israel (Bloch-Smith, *Judahite Burial Practices and Beliefs about the Dead* [JSOTSup 123; Sheffield: JSOT, 1992]; idem, "The Cult of the Dead in Judah: Interpreting the Material Remains," *JBL* 111 [1992], 222–23), which indicates that despite religious programs of the eighth through the sixth centuries, popular practices concerning the dead continued. See further chapter 6, section 6. Consequently, post-exilic notions of resurrections may owe more to evolving indigenous popular ideas than to Iranian influence as often suggested. For further discussion of putative Iranian influence on ancient Judean thought, see chapter 8, section 5.

2. The pre-priestly background of Genesis 1:1–2:4a is not the focus of attention here. For the theory that this text is "based upon a poetic document probably of catechetical origin," see *CMHE* 301, citing the Harvard dissertation of J. Kselman, "The Poetic Background of Certain Priestly Traditions" (1971). The bibliography on the first creation story is immense. In addition to the commentaries and works cited here, see W. P. Brown, *Structure, Role, and Ideology in the Hebrew and Greek Texts of Genesis 1:1–2:3* (SBLDS 132; Atlanta, GA: Scholars, 1993); and S. L. Jaki, *Genesis 1 through the Ages* (London: Thomas More, 1992).

3. On creation, see most recently (and the works cited therein) R. J. Clifford, *Creation Accounts in the Ancient Near East and in the Bible* (CBQMS 26; Washington: Catholic Biblical Association of America, 1994); and R. A. Simkins, *Creator and Creation: Nature in the Worldview of Ancient Israel* (Peabody, MA: Hendrickson, 1994). An excerpt based on C. Westermann's three-volume commentary on Genesis was published as *Creation* (trans. J. J. Scullion; Philadelphia: Fortress, 1974) and remains a helpful precis of pertinent information. For some further considerations of issues in this first section, see J. G. Janzen, "On the Moral Nature of God's Power: Yahweh and the Sea in Job and Deutero-Isaiah," *CBQ* 56 (1994), 458–78, esp. 460–65.

4. See B. Foster, *Before the Muses: An Anthology of Akkadian Literature* (2 vols.; Bethesda, MD: CDL Press, 1993), 1.351–402. The well-known older translation of E. A. Speiser is available in *ANET* 60–72, with additions rendered by A. K. Grayson in *ANET* 501–03. For an accessible discussion, see Clifford, *Creation Accounts*, 82–93. This epic poem has been read against the political events of the late second-millennium Babylon and the later neo-Assyrian and neo-Babylonian empires of the first millennium. For a recent dis-

cussion, see B. N. Porter, *Images, Power, and Politics: Figurative Aspects of Esarhaddon's Babylonian Policy* (Memoirs of the American Philosophical Society held at Philadelphia for Promoting Useful Knowledge 208; Philadelphia: American Philosophical Society, 1993), 115, 139–43; see also J. Oates, *Babylon* (rev. ed.; London: Thames and Hudson, 1986), 169–74. For further discussion of the theological milieu of the Babylonian version of Enuma Elish, see A. Livingstone, *Mystical and Mythological Explanatory Works of Assyrian and Babylonian Scholars* (Oxford: Clarendon Press, 1986).

5. For further evidence of Yahweh's inheritance of other features associated specifically with Baal, see *EHG* 50–55.

6. G. W. Ahlström, *Psalm 89: Eine liturgie aus dem Ritual des leidenden Königs* (Lund: CWK Gleerup, 1959), 108–11; E. Lipiński, *Le poème royal du Psaume LXXXIX* 1.5.20–38 (CahRB 6; Paris: Gabalda, 1967), 53; J.-B. Dumortier, "Un rituel d'intronisation: Le Ps. LXXXIX 2–38," *VT* 22 (1972), 188 and n. 1; *CMHE* 258 n. 177, 261–62; P. Mosca, "Ugarit and Daniel 7: A Missing Link," *Bib* 67 (1986) 509, 512; idem, "Once Again the Heavenly Witness of Ps 89:38," *JBL* 105 (1986), 33. Mosca ("Once Again," 33) points to other examples of "mythico-religious terms" in Psalm 89: the king is the "first-born" (verse 28) of "my father" (verse 27), and serves as the "Most High" (verse 28) with respect to earthly kings." See also M. Weinfeld, "Zion and Jerusalem as Religious and Political Capital: Ideology and Utopia," *The Poet and the Historian: Essays in Literary and Historical Biblical Criticism* (ed. R. E. Friedman; Harvard Semitic Studies 26; Chico, CA: Scholars, 1983), 97–98.

7. J. D. Levenson, *Creation and the Persistence of Evil: The Drama of Divine Omnipotence* (San Francisco: Harper & Row, 1988), 3–78, esp. 3–10.

8. For these points, see following a long line of continental scholarship, Levenson, *Creation*, 53–127.

9. Levenson, *Creation*, 111–20.

10. The royal model is especially pronounced in the study of B. Janowski, "Herrschaft über die Terre: Gen 1, 26–28 und die Semantik von רדה," *Biblische Theologie und gesellschaftlicher Wandel. Für Norbert Lohfink SJ* (ed. G. Braulik, W. Gross and S. McEvenue; Freiburg: Herder, 1993), 183–98. See also P. Bird, "Gen 1:27b in the Context of the Priestly Account of Creation," *HTR* 74 (1981), 138–44, esp. 140. The further issue is the degree to which the priestly account has moved away from a primarily royal background or model.

11. See the many interpreters cited by Kraus, *Psalms 1–59*, 183. Kraus rejects this view as missing the specifically priestly context of this passage, but this is to miss the borrowing and adaptation of the old royal language. For this usage of the divine image in Egyptian literature (which shows a long history of using this language for the king), see Merikare (*ANET* 417; for further discussion, see Smith, "Mythology and Myth-making," 321–22).

12. For the Mesopotamian and Egyptian evidence, see W. H. Schmidt, *Die Schöpfungsgeschichte der Priesterschrift* (WMANT 17; Neukirchen-Vluyn: Neukirchener, 1964), 136–42; H. Wildberger, "Das Abbild Gottes; Gen. I, 26–30 (2. Teil)," *ThZ* 21 (1965), 484–91; T. N. D. Mettinger, "Abbild oder Urbild? >>Imago Dei<< in traditionsgeschichtlicher Sicht," *ZAW* 86 (1974), 412–18. My thanks go to T. N. D. Mettinger for these references. See further G. A. Jonsson, *The Image of God. Genesis 1:26–28 in a Century of Old Testamament Research* (ConBOT 26; Lund: Almqvist & Wiksell, 1988).

13. Schmidt, *Die Schöpfungsgeschichte*, 139; Fishbane, *The Garments of Torah: Essays in Biblical Hermeneutics* (Bloomington: Indiana University Press, 1989), 139 n. 7.

14. *ANET* 417.

15. Schmidt (*Die Schöpfungsgeschichte*, 140) cites a similar example from a neo-Assyrian letter, but the pertinent passage has been rendered quite differently by S. Parpola (*Letters from Assyrian Scholars to the Kings Esarhaddon and Assurbanipal: Part I: Texts* [AOAT 5/1; Kevelaer: Butzon & Bercker; Neukirchen-Vluyn: Neukirchener, 1970], 112–13). See also

CAD M/1 281. for further examples, see S. W. Cole and P. Machinist, *Letters from Priests to the Kings Esarhaddon and Assurbanipal* (with contributions by S. Parpola; State Archives of Assyria XIII; Helsinki: Helsinki University, 1998), XXII n. 12.

16. Cf. J. M. Sasson, "Time . . . To Begin," *"Sha'arei Talmon": Studies in the Bible, Qumran, and the Ancient Near East Presented to Shemaryahu Talmon* (ed. M. Fishbane and E. Tov with the assistance of W. W. Fields; Winona Lake, IN: Eisenbrauns, 1992), 186.

17. See also R. D. Nelson, *Raising Up a Faithful Priest Community and Priesthood in Biblical Theology* (Louisville KY: Westminster/John Knox Press, 1993, 23, 36, 94; Blenkinsopp, *Sage, Priest, Prophet: Religious and Intellectual Leadership in Ancient Israel* (Louisville, KY: Westminster/John Knox Press, 1995), 67, 101–04.

18. Without evidence this view is argued also by Blenkinsopp, *Sage, Priest, Prophet*, 68, 104, 113. For the temple background to Genesis 1, see M. Weinfeld, "Sabbath, Temple and the Enthronement of the Lord—The Problem of the Sitz im Leben of Genesis 1:1–2: 3," *Mélanges bibliques et orientaux en l'honneur de M. Henri Cazelles* (ed. A. Caquot and M. Delcor; AOAT 212; Kevelaer: Butzon & Bercker; Neukirchen-Vluyn: Neukirchener, 1981), 501–12; Levenson, *Creation*, 78–87; B. Janowski, "Tempel und Schöpfung. Schöpfungstheologische Aspekte der priesterschriftlichen Heiligtumskonzeption," *Jahrbuch für Biblische Theologie* 5 (1990), 37–69.

19. Levenson, *Creation*, 78–87.

20. For a reading of this verse based on parallels cited in the following note, see Y. Hurowitz, *I Have Built You an Exalted House: Temple Building in the Bible in the Light of Mesopotamian and North West Semitic Writings* (JSOTSup 115; Sheffield: JSOT Press, 1992), 335–37.

21. This connection was made in the Syro-Mesopotamian world as well. See Gudea, Cylinder A, xxv, line 2: "the house's stretching out . . . was like the heights of heaven awe-inspiring" (T. Jacobsen, *The Harps that once . . . . : Sumerian Poetry in Translation* [New Haven: Yale University Press, 1987], 419). For other examples, see Hurowitz, *I Have Built*, 335–37. See also the cosmic ramifications of Baal's palace in the Ugaritic Baal Cycle (for discussion, see *UBC* 77–78).

22. The translation follows NJPS, apart from the capitalization of the first word and the lack of indentation in the second line.

23. Houston, *Purity and Monotheism: Clean and Unclean Animals in Biblical Law* (JSOTS 140; Sheffield: JSOT, 1993).

24. For correlations between social groups and their cosmologies, see M. Douglas, *Natural Symbols*, esp. 138–40, 169–71, 175–76, 195.

25. See the instructive comments of P. Bird, " 'Male and Female He Created Them': Gen. 1.276 in The Context of the Priestly Account of Creation," HTR 74 (1981), 143 n. 37, 152. The royal model also informs the picture of Israel in Isaiah 42:5–6, 55:3, as argued by many interpreters. See most recently J. G. Janzen, "On the Moral Nature of God's Power: Yahweh and the Sea in Job and Deutero-Isaiah," CBQ 56 (1994), 469–78. It may be noted further that, according to Isaiah 40–55, the universe is not only the scene of divine conflict (51:9–10a), but also a divine dwelling, specifically a tent (40:22; cf. 42:5). Cf. Isaiah 66:1: " 'The heavens are My throne and the earth is My footstool . . . ' "

26. See Levenson, *Creation*, 88.

27. Cf. also the sun-goddess' titles "Great Sun" (*rbt špš*) in CAT 1.16 I 37 and "Light of the Gods, Shapshu" (*nrt 'ilm špš*) in 1.3 V 17, 1.4 VIII 21, 1.6 I 8, 11, 13, II 24, III 24, IV 17, 1.19 IV 47, 49.

28. For this interpretation, see *EHG* 102.

29. For another example of this phenomenon in P, see M. S. Smith, *"Běrît 'ām/běrît 'ôlām: A New Interpretation of Isa 42:6,"* JBL 100 (1981), 241–43.

30. See the same vocabulary in lines 1, 12, 15, and 16 of the Tell Fakhariyah inscription, discussed in D. M. Gropp and T. J. Lewis, "Motes on some Problems in the Aramaic Text of the Hadd-Yith'i Bilingual," *BASOR* 259 (1985), 47. For the editio princeps, see A. Abou-Assaf, P. Bordreuil, and A. R. Millard, *La statue de Tell Fekheriyé et son inscription bilingue assyro-araméenne* (Paris: Editions recherche sur les civilisations, 1982).

31. For the paradise traditions, see the summary of J. van Seters and his tour de force in his book, *Prologue to History: The Yahwist as Historian in Genesis* (Louisville, KY: Westminster/John Knox, 1992), 107–34. According to D. Damrosch (*The Narrative Covenant: Transformations of Genre in the Growth of Biblical Literature* [San Francisco: Harper and Row, 1987] 121–22) and B. Batto (*Slaying the Dragon* [Philadelphia: Fortress, 1992]), the biblical picture of paradise and the "fall" represents the priestly tradition's rewriting of the Yahwistic account of Genesis 2–3. Batto argues that for this Yahwistic tradition there was neither a realm of primordial bliss for the human race nor a fall resulting from disobedience; this shaping of the narrative derived from the priestly redaction of the earlier material. He claims that Genesis 1:1–2:4a provides a "new mytho-theological framework" by which the priestly writer provided "a radically new interpretation of a fall from paradise" rather than the Jahwist's "story of inchoate creation wherein the definition of humankind vis-à-vis the deity and animalkind was but gradually worked out." Batto also uses the "fall" in Ezekiel 28 to support this view of the priestly reshaping of the material in Genesis 1–3. Batto assumes that Ezekiel 28 is dependent on Genesis 1–3 for the motif of the fall, but it may be that the motif of the fall predates its priestly reception. It is arguable that the fall with its attendant theological import in Genesis 3 was a variation on the mythic fall inherited by Israelite traditions of paradise. According to H. Bloom (D. Rosenberg and H. Bloom, *The Book of J* [New York: Grove Weidenfeld, 1991], 182, 186), J makes a major point of the original human potential for immortality. The account may function, however, to explain only why humanity is not immortal (as commentators have long noted). Consistent with Bloom's view, however, some scholars have argued for a theory of "the first man" (or "*Urmensch*") privileged to access to the original heavenly mountain of Yahweh (see Mettinger, *King and Messiah*, 268–75 D. E Callendar, Jr. *Adam in Myth and History: Ancient Israelite Perspective on the Primal Human* [HSS 48; Winona Lake, IN: Eisenbrauns, 2000]). Some trace see this idea as an element of royal theology (see the point of Porter mentioned in chapter 8, section 4). For the figure in Ezekiel 28 as royal, see van Seters, *Prologue to History*, 120). If so, it would indicate how paradise traditions reflect both royal and priestly influence.

32. Many of the following points may be found in Levenson, *Sinai & Zion*, 111–37; M. S. Smith, *Psalms: The Divine Journey* (Mahwah, NJ: Paulist, 1987), 44–47. The old Israelite elements may have included the amalgamation of three divine mountains into a single divine mountainous abode. Paradise incorporates three divine mountains known from Ugaritic tradition: (1) the home of the heavenly council located on the top of a mountainous abode like Mount Olympus; (2) the abode of the god El situated at the meeting-point of divine waters called "rivers" or "deeps"; and (3) the temple/palace home of the storm-god Baal on his heavenly mountain (H. N. Wallace, *The Eden Narrative* [HSM 32; Atlanta, GA: Scholars, 1985], 70–88 following in the main Cross, *CMHE* 36–39). The mountains of El and the divine assembly may not have been identified in Ugaritic tradition as is commonly claimed by Cross and others. Ezekiel 28 shows reflexes of the heavenly mountain, and Genesis 2–3 contains the element of the rivers. Israelite myth-making transformed these traditions, at least compared with the information provided by the Ugaritic texts, in amalgamating these various abodes into a single divine abode. It is also arguable that some elements known from the Ugaritic texts were deleted in Israelite tradition; the description of the waters of El's abode never appears in biblical descriptions of the divine mountain, but only in language for the underworld (see *EHG* 22–24, 33–34 n. 57). Genesis

2–3 diminishes the heavenly placement of Eden insofar as Eden is not situated explicitly on the holy mountain of God. Other motifs in the biblical paradise traditions may have further contacts in West Semitic literature. Like Genesis 3, CAT 1.23 may contain the motif of the divine refuge guarded by a divine figure: born of divine parents, the "gracious gods" are expulsed into the desert for seven or eight years, and finally find refuge in a cultivated reserve with a divine guardian. According to de Moor ("East of Eden," *ZAW* 100 [1988], 106), CAT 1.100 and 1.107 "seem to presupppose a Canaanite tradition about the garden of Eden." Despite de Moor's departures from less controversial approaches to these texts (see B. A. Levine and J. M. de Tarragon, "<<Shapshu Cries out in Heaven>>: Dealing with Snake-Bites at Ugarit (KTU 1.100, 1.107)," *RB* 95 [1988] 481–518, esp. 505–18; D. Pardee, *Les textes para-mythologiques de la 24e Campagne (1961)* [Ras Shamra-Ougarit IV; Paris: Editions Recherche sur Civilisations, 1988], 223–25, 255–56), they should prompt reconsideration of the assumptions about Mesopotamian influence on the biblical traditions of paradise. The direction of influence is unclear; nor is it evident that these paradise traditions were not part of the stock of mythology common to Mesopotamia and the Levant.

33. For the relations between temple and paradise, see Levenson, *Creation*, 82–99, esp. 93; M. Ottoson, "Eden and the Land of Promise," *Congress Volume: Jerusalem 1986* (ed. J. A. Emerton; VTSup 40; Leiden: Brill, 1988), 179, 188. For the narrative relationship between paradise in Genesis and the Tabernacle narrative in Exodus, see M. Fishbane, *Text and Texture: Close Readings of Selected Biblical Texts* (New York: Schocken, 1979), 8–13; R. H. Moye "In the Beginning: Myth and History in Genesis and Exodus," *JBL* 109 (1990) 577–98.

34. Rather than an Akkadian loan *edinu*, "steppe" (popularized by E. A. Speiser, *Genesis* [AB 1; New York: Doubleday, 1964] 16, 19), the BH word Eden ('*ēden*) means "fertility, abundance, luxuriance." The root of the word "Eden" first appears in the Baal Cycle in reference to the storm-god, Baal-Hadad (J. C. Greenfield, "A Touch of Eden," *Acta Iranica deuxième série, volume IX. Orientalia J. Duchesne-Guillemin Emerito-oblata* [Leiden: Brill, 1984], 219–24; A. Millard, "The Meaning of Eden," *VT* 34 [1984], 103–06; Ottoson, "Eden and the Land of Promise," 177). It is the word that describes what his rains do for the earth; Baal fertilizes ('*dn//y'dn* [!]) the earth with his rain (*mṭrh*) in CAT 1.4 V 6–7. The word appears later, in line 4 of the Tell Fekheriyeh inscription (see A. Abou-Assaf, P. Bordreuil, and A. Millard, *La Statue de Tell Fekherye et son inscription bilingue assyro-araméenne* [Etudes Assyriologiques 10; Paris: Recherche sur les civilizations, 1982], 23, 62). This text describes Hadad, that is Baal, as the god who makes the earth fertile (*m'dn*). Eden may be thought then to be the terrestrial sacred mountain fertilized by the storm-god and in this sense a "garden." For the date of the association of the divine mountain with Eden, see Wallace, *The Eden Narrative*, 85–86.

35. Cf. Psalm 36:7–10 with its allusions to *harĕrê 'ēl* and *tĕhôm rabbâ* in verse 7 constitute an example of what Greenfield calls "clusters" (Greenfield, "The 'Cluster' in Biblical Poetry," 159–60). See also F. C. Fensham, "The Term *'dn* in Keret 14:32–34 (KTU 1.14: II:32–34) and a Few Other Other Occurrences in Ugaritic Reconsidered," *JNWSL* 15 (1989), 87–90.

36. G. W. Ahlström, *Aspects of Syncretism in Israelite Religion* (Lund: Gleerup, 1963) 44–45 n. 1; J. Levenson, *Theology of the Program of Restoration of Ezekiel 40–48* (HSM 10; Missoula, MT: Scholars, 1976), 25–34; J. Strange, "The Idea of After Life in Solomon's Temple in Ancient Israel: Some Remarks on the Iconography," *PEQ* 117 (1985), 35–40; Wallace, *The Eden Narrative*, 85–86; Smith, *Psalms: the Divine Journey*, 44–47.

37. Levenson, *Sinai & Zion*, 130. For different views, see C. Westermann, *Genesis 1–11: A Commentary* (trans. J. J. Scullion; Minneapolis, 1984), 218.

38. Van Seters, *Prologue to History*, 119–22.

39. Wilson, "The Death of the King of Tyre: The Editorial History of Ezekiel 28," *Love and Death in the Ancient Near East: Essays in Honor of Marvin H. Pope* (ed. J. H. Marks and R. M. Good; Guilford, CT: Four Quarters, 1986), 211–18, esp. 215–16.

40. The divine fall from heaven reflects an ancient mythic motif. The fall is not to be El's, however. Rather, the clearest attestations of this very difficult motif are related of Athtar in Ugaritic texts and the possibly related astral figure, Shahar ben-Helal, in Isaiah 14. For discussion, see P. K. Craigie, "Helal, Athtar and Phaeton (Jes 14, 12–15)," *ZAW* 85 (1973), 223–25; P. D. Hanson, "Rebellion in Heaven, Azazel, and Euhemeristic Heroes in 1 Enoch 6–11," *JBL* 96 (1977) 195–233; H. Page, *The Myth of Cosmic Rebellion: A Study of Its Reflexes in Ugaritic and Biblical Literature* (VTSup 65; Leiden: Brill, 1996).

41. Van Seters' criticisms of Wilson's proposal are hardly telling against a redactor who may have altered the figure from an originally royal one into a priest (see *Prologue to History*, 131–32 n. 45; see also Callender, *Adam in Myth and History*, 87–135).

42. Parallels with Gilgamesh have been invoked to illustrate some of the oldest features of the Israelite paradise myth, e.g., Cassuto, "The Israelite Epic," in Cassuto, *Biblical and Oriental Studies, Volume 2: Biblical and Ancient Oriental Texts* (trans. I. Abrahams; Jerusalem: Magues, 1975), 106. According to Gilgamesh XI:195 (*ANET* 95), Utnapishtim dwells "at the mouth of the rivers" (*ina pî narāti*), a description that many scholars have compared with the location of El's abode in the Ugaritic texts "at the confluence of the two rivers" (*mbk nhrm*) and with the detail of the four rivers in Genesis 2 (see Wallace, *The Eden Narrative*, 76–77, 85–86, Calender, *Adam in Myth and History*, 78). When Gilgamesh meets Utnapishtim, the ancient sage relates how Enlil granted him immortality (XI 193–194; *ANET* 95). Utnapishtim is said to have joined the assembly of the gods (XI:7; *ANET* 93), a notion presumed of dwelling on the divine mountain in Ezekiel 28. The hero Gilgamesh could have eaten a plant of rejuvenation prior to its being snatched by a snake. For treatments of the parallels between Mesopotamian literature and Genesis 2–3, see Westermann, *Genesis 1–11*, 213–75; Wallace, *The Eden Narrative*, 71–72, 104, 119–20; W. G. Lambert, "Old Testament Mythology in its Ancient Near Eastern Context," *Congress Volume: Jerusalem 1986* (ed. J. A. Emerton; VTSup 40; Leiden: Brill, 1988), 138–39; van Seters, *Prologue to History*, 120–27. For a comparison of the stones and trees in the Garden of Eden and in Gilgamesh IX 5, 47–51, see H. P. Müller, "Parallelen zu Gen 2f. und Ez 28 aus dem Gilgamesch-Epos," *ZAH* 3 (1990), 167–78. For various points of comparison between Adam and Adapa, see J. J. M. Roberts, "Does God Lie? Divine Deceit as a Theological Problem in Israelite Prophetic Literature," *Congress Volume: Jerusalem 1986* (ed. J. A. Emerton; VTSup 40; Leiden: Brill, 1988) 212; G. Erickson, "Adam och Adapa," *STK* 66 (1990), 122–28; H. P. Müller, "Drei Deutungen des Todes: Genesis 3, der Mythos von Adapa und die Sage von Gilgamesch," *Altes Testament und christlicher Glaube* (ed. I. Baldermann et al.; Jahrbuch für Biblische Theologie 6; Neukirchen-Vluyn: Neukirchener, 1991), 117–34; and Callender, *Adam in Myth and History*, 75–84.

43. For discussion, see *EHG* 94–95. For discussion of this goddess, see chapter 4, section 4.

44. Cf. the olive tree of Astarte; see R. Hanson, *Tyrian Influence in the Upper Galilee* (Meiron Excavation Project 2; Cambridge, MA: American Schools of Oriental Research, 1980), 37; P. Naster, "Ambrosiai Petrai sur les monnaies de Tyr," *Studia Phoenicia IV: La religion phénicienne* (Leuven: Uitgeverij Peeters; Namur: Presses universitaires de Namur, 1986), 361–71.

45. A wordplay first brought to my attention by A. Ceresko.

46. See Lang, *Wisdom and the Book of Proverbs: A Hebrew Goddess Redefined* (New York: Pilgrims, 1986). Cited and endorsed by S. A. Meier, "Women and Communication in the Ancient Near East," *JAOS* 111 (1991), 543.

47. For a recent discussion of the material culture pertinent to scribalism in ancient Israel, see D. W. Jamieson-Drake, *Scribes and Schools in Monarchic Judah: A Socio-Archeological Approach* (Sheffield: Almond, 1991). According to Jamieson-Drake, scribes may be better regarded as professional administrators.

48. This view has been advocated by John M. Miller ("The Malachi Circle and the Book of Proverbs" [unpublished manuscript, gratefully cited with permission]), based on parallels between Proverbs, on the one hand, and Deuteronomy and Malachi, on the other hand. The latter two works have been long traced to a Levitical background. For the Levitical background of Deuteronomy, see S. D. McBride cited in R. R. Wilson, *Prophecy and Society in Ancient Israel* (Philadelphia: Fortress, 1980), 18 n. 36, 156–66, 222; McBride, "Biblical Literature in its Historical Context: The Old Testament," *Harper's Bible Commentary* (ed. J. L. Mays; San Francisco: Harper & Row, 1988), 20, 21. Concerning the Levitical background of Malachi, see McBride, "Biblical Literature in its Historical Context: The Old Testament," 23; J. M. O'Brien, *Priest and Levite in Malachi* (SBLDS 121; Atlanta, GA: Scholars, 1990).

49. See M. S. Smith, "The Levitical Compilation of the Psalter," *ZAW* 103 (1991), 258–63. Ben Sira (Ecclesiasticus) continues and amplifies the female personification of Wisdom. Ben Sira 1:20 draws on the image of Wisdom as a tree of life: "To fear the Lord is the root of wisdom, and her branches are long life." Ben Sira 24:12–17 likewise describes Wisdom as different types of trees. Ben Sira 4:13 and Baruch 4:1, echoing Proverbs 3:18, use the image of holding fast to Wisdom. Narrative (within direct discourse) concerning Wisdom appears in Ben Sira 10, and Wisdom of Solomon 10 narrates past acts by Wisdom. This wisdom material shows the transformation of mythic imagery into narrative form. There have been attempts to retroject this narrative to the older biblical passages about Wisdom (for criticisms of this approach, see G. von Rad, *Wisdom in Israel* [trans. J. D. Martin; Nashville: Abingdon, 1972], 160 n. 17). This material, like royal psalms, may show the impact of a group's interests or background in creating mythic material. The majority of biblical critics might be followed in viewing this material in terms of "wisdom circles." The social background involved may not simply be "wisdom circles." Rather, like Proverbs, Ben Sira may have been a priestly product (S. Olyan, "Ben Sira's Relationship in the Priesthood," *HTR* 80 [1987], 261–86). The narrative of the female figure of Wisdom in this work may have served to legitimate his priestly concerns. By the same token, Baruch 4 and Wisdom of Solomon 10 indicate that the notion of personified wisdom circulated more widely.

50. CMHE 137; Clifford, *Creation Accounts*, 154–56, 168–72.

51. The apocalyptic sections of Daniel represent further well-known examples of the use of mythic material to express a political agenda. See J. Emerton, "The Origin of the Son of Man Imagery," *Journal of Theological Studies* 9 (1958), 225–42; J. J. Collins, *The Apocalyptic Vision of the Book of Daniel* (HSM 16; Missoula, MT: Scholars, 1977), 95–105; idem, "Apocalyptic Genre and Mythic Allusions in Daniel," *Journal for the Study of the Old Testament* 21 (1981), 89–93; P. Mosca, "Ugarit and Daniel 7: A Missing Link," *Biblica* 67 (1986), 496–517. For the Ugaritic background of the name of Daniel, see J. Day, "The Daniel of Ugarit and Ezekiel and the Hero of the Book of Daniel," *VT* 30 (1980), 174–84.

52. For discussion, see R. R. Wilson, "From Prophecy to Apocalyptic: Reflections on the Shape of Israelite Religion," *Semeia* 21 (1981), 79–95; and J. J. Collins, *Daniel: A Commentary on the Book of Daniel* (ed. F. M. Cross; Hermaneia; Minneapolis: Fortress, 1993), 286–94. For the best treatment of the thematic continuities from royal theology to apocalyptic, see P. Mosca, "Ugaritic and Daniel 7: A Missing Link," *Bib* 67 (1986), 496–517.

53. For the priestly and royal patronage of the Baal Cycle, see the colophon in CAT

1.6 VI 54–56. For discussion, see A. Rainey, *The Scribe at Ugarit. His Position and Influence* (Proceedings of the Israel Academy of Sciences and Humanities, Vol. III, No. 4; Jerusalem: Israel Academy of Sciences and Humanities, 1968), 127–28. The priestly transmission of the other literary texts from Ugarit are also indicated in colophons (1.6 VI 58; cf. 1.17 VI 55).

54. Gunkel, *Schöpfung und Chaos in Urzeit und Endzeit. Eine religionsgeschichtliche Untersuchung über Gen 1 und Ap Joh 12* (sec. ed.; Göttingen: Vandenhoeck und Ruprecht, 1921).

55. See S. Mowinckel, "Hat es ein israelitisches Nationalepos gegeben?" *ZAW* 53 (1953), 130–54; U. Cassuto, "The Israelite Epic"; C. Conroy, "Hebrew Epic: Historical Notes and Critical Reflections," *Bib* 61 (1980), 1–30; Watson, *Classical Hebrew Poetry*, 83–86. For a helpful discussion of the hermeneutical problems involved, see Damrosch, *The Narrative Covenant*, esp. 51–87. Damrosch's genetic explanation for the prose epic hinges on Israelite use of Mesopotamian prose models (see esp. pp. 41, 43, 46). While intriguing, Damrosch does not address West Semitic mythic antecedents to biblical myth and mythic material.

56. Talmon, "Did There Exist A Biblical National Epic?" *Proceedings of the Seventh World Congress of Jewish Studies; Studies in the Bible and the Ancient Near East* (Jerusalem: World Union of Jewish Studies, 1981), 50–53. Talmon does not specify which Ugaritic texts he has in mind; to judge from his remarks one might assume that he means the Baal Cycle, Keret, Aqhat, and other texts usually cited as Ugaritic "mythological texts" (see the texts in CAT 1.1–1.24).

57. Talmon, "Did There Exist A Biblical National Epic?" 55–58. Talmon's view has a long scholarly lineage (see O. Eissfeldt, *The Old Testament: An Introduction* [trans. P. R. Ackroyd; New York: Harper and Row, 1965], 35).

58. Talmon, "Did There Exist a Biblical National Epic?" 55. More relevant is Talmon's point regarding the shift from poetry to prose in the later shaping of Israelite literature, especially if it were to be construed as a shift from oral compositions (set down in writing) to written compositions.

59. Cassuto, "The Israelite Epic," 76–80.

60. Cassuto, "The Israelite Epic," 80.

61. Cf. Eissfeldt, *The Old Testament*, 36.

62. Damrosch, *The Narrative Covenant*, 46.

63. Damrosch, *The Narrative Covenant*, 41, 43. As Damrosch (*The Narrative Covenant*, 159 n. 13) notes, his argument depends on the dating of the biblical materials, and for this argument he observes that he remains unable to adjudicate the issue. Indeed, linguistic arguments such as the neo-Assyrian loan *abarraku* behind BH *'abrēk* (Genesis 41:43) suggest a date after major cultural contact between Israel and the neo-Assyrians. Similarly, the thematic connection between the story of baby Moses in the ark (Exodus 2) and the Sargon Birth legend suggests a neo-Assyrian date. See W. W. Hallo, *The People of the Book* (Brown Judace Studies 225; Atlanta, GA: Scholars, 1991), 39, 48.

64. Damrosch, *The Narrative Covenant*, 88–143.

65. Damrosch, *The Narrative Covenant*, 263.

66. On the topics of myth and mythic material, see Introduction, section 4. It might be argued that the creation of an anti-mythic deity constituted in some sense a new mythic image for Yahweh.

67. See chapter 5, section 2; also EHG xxiv, 150–52.

68. For more recent authors in this vein, see for example, A. H. W. Curtis, *Ugarit (Ras Shamra)* (Cities of the Biblcial World; Cambridge: Lutterworth, 1985), 121; M. C. A. Korpel, *A Rift in the Clouds: Ugaritic and Hebrew Descriptions of the Divine* (Münster: UGARIT-Verlag, 1990), 125–27; EHG 163–65.

69. Barr, "Theophany and Anthropomorphism in the Old Testament," *Congress Volume: Oxford 1959* (VTSup 7; Leiden: Brill, 1960), 31–38.

70. See M. H. Pope, "The Scene on the Drinking Mug from Ugarit," *Near Eastern Studies in Honor of William Foxwell Albright* (ed. H. Goedicke; Baltimore: Johns Hopkins University Press, 1971), 393–405; M. Weinfeld, "Semiramis: Her Name and Her Origin," *Ah, Assyria: Studies in Assyrian History and Ancient Near Eastern Historiography Presented to Hayim Tadmor* (ed. M. Cogan and I. Eph'al; Scripta Hierosolymitana 33; Jerusalem: Magnes, 1991), 99–103. See also Derketo as a fish in *De Dea Syria* 14 (Attridge and Oden, *The Syrian Goddess (De Dea Syria) Attributed to Lucian* [Texts and Translations 9, Graeco-Roman Religion Series 1; Missoula, MT: Scholars Press, 1976], 23).

71. Bloom in Rosenberg and Bloom, *The Book of J*, 301.

72. See S. Mowinckel, "Det kultiske synspunkt som forskningsprincipp i den gammeltestamentlige videnskap," *NTT* 25 (1924), 20; translated in M. R. Hauge, "Sigmund Mowinckel and the Psalms," *SJOT* 2 (1988) = *The Life and Work of Sigmund Mowinckel* (ed. H. M. Barstad and M. Ottoson), 62.

73. See *CMHE* 33 n. 151. The comparison is not without difficulties since the biblical word-pair indicates "face" for *pānêkā* while Ugaritic scholars take *pnth* as "his joints," which is semantically more proximate to BH *těmûnâ and Ugaritic *tmnt (see H. L. Ginsberg, "The Victory of the Land-God over the Sea-God," *JPOS* 15 [1935], 332 nn. 18–19). For another suggestion, see J. C. de Moor, "The Anatomy of the Back," *UF* 12 (1980), 425–26. Ps 17:15 involves the experience of seeing the form of the god, probably a morning vision following a night of sleep-incubation in the temple or the like; cf. the late Egyptian tale of Setne Khamwas and Si-osire, which describes the appearance of the form of Thoth in a dream-vision (M. Lichtheim, *Ancient Egyptian Literature: Volume III: The Late Period* [Berkeley: University of California Press, 1980], 146; S. B. Parker, *The Pre-biblical Narrative Tradition: Essays on the Ugaritic Poems Keret and Aqhat* [SBLRBS 24; Atlanta, GA: Scholars, 1988], 101–05, 155).

74. The literature on this subject is enormous. See the survey of F. W. Dobbs-Allsopp, "The Syntagma of *bat* Followed by a Geographical Name in the Hebrew Bible: A Reconsideration of Its Meaning and Grammar," *CBQ* 57 (1995), 451–70.

75. Von Rad, *Wisdom in Israel*, 167.

76. And perhaps the goddess Asherah and her tree or pole called by the same name. For discussion of Asherah in Israel, see chapter 4, section 4.

77. See also linguistic examples cited in *EHG* 100.

78. For a more detailed discussion, see chapter 5, section 2.

79. For a possible Egyptian analogue, see J. Baines, "Egyptian Myth and Discourse: Myths, Gods, and the Early Written and Iconographic Record," *JNES* 50 (1991) 103–05; cf. V. A. Tobin, "The Creativity of Egyptian Myth: Wanderings in an Intellectual Labyrinth," *The Society For The Study of Egyptian Antiquities Journal* 18 (1988), 107.

80. Narrative set in the present (see Zechariah 3–5) would not qualify as a myth for Oden (see the Introduction, section 4). Cf. Baines, "Egyptian Myth and Discourse," 99.

81. Damrosch, *The Narrative Covenant*, 46, 122.

82. For some examples from Jewish tradition, see Jacobs, "Elements of Near-Eastern Mythology in Rabbinic Aggadah," *JJS* 28 (1977), 1–11. As Jacobs ("Elements of Near-Eastern Mythology in Rabbinic Aggadah," 2) observes, b. B. Bat. 74b attests Yamm's title in the form, *śar šel yam*, "Prince of the sea":

When God desired to create the world, He said to the Prince of the sea, "Open your mouth and swallow up all the waters of the world!" The latter answered, "Lord of the universe, I have enough with my own!" Whereupon God trampled on him and slew him, as it is said, "By his power He beat down the sea, and by his understanding He smote Rahab."

The parade example of West Semitic myth from the NT is Revelation 21:1–4, which includes the disappearance of sea, the appearance of the new Jerusalem, the bride "adorned for her husband," and the disappearance of death. Indeed, this passage approximates the sequence of the three main parts of the Baal Cycle.

10. *Monotheism in Isaiah 40–55*

1. More recently, see B. D. Sommer, *A Prophet Reads Scripture: Allusion in Isaiah 40–66* (Contraversions. Jews and Other Differences; Stanford, CA: Stanford University Press, 1998), 84–86, 112–19. This move is reflected also in the priestly view of the eternal covenant in Genesis 9, 17 and Exodus 31 (cf. Jeremiah 32:40, 50:5; Ezekiel 16:60); see M. S. Smith, "Běrît 'ām/běrît 'ôlām: A New Proposal for the Crux of Isa 42:6," *JBL* 100 (1981), 241–43. For Second Isaiah more generally, see the references in chapter 8, note 34.

2. Clearly a precondition for this form of monotheism then is the attribution of both creation and war to Yahweh. Both, however, predate the expressions of monotheism in the seventh and sixth centuries. For this reason, the more local explanation for monotheism lies in the specific conditions of this later situation.

3. Alonso Shökel, "Isaiah," *The Literary Guide to the Bible* (ed. R. Alter and F. Kermode; Cambridge, MA: Belknap Press, 1987), 174.

4. R. Alter, *The Art of Biblical Poetry* (New York: Basic Books, 1985), 141.

5. For the following information, see A. Fitzgerald, "The Technology of Isaiah 40:19–20 + 41:6–7," *CBO* 51/3 (1989), 426–46.

6. Roeder, *Ägyptische Bronzefiguren* (two vols.; Staatliche Museen zu Berlin, Mitteilungen aus ägyptischen Sammlung 5–6; Berlin: Staatliche Museen, 1956), 2.516; Aitchison, *A History of Metals* (two vols.; New York: Interscience, 1960), 1.189. These references derive from Fitzgerald, "The Technology," 427–29.

7. Oppenheim, *Ancient Mesopotamia: Portrait of a Dead Civilization* (ed. E. Reiner; rev. ed.; Chicago: University of Chicago Press, 1977), 184.

8. W. G. Lambert, "Donations of Food and Drink to the Gods," *Ritual and Sacrifice in the Ancient Near East: Proceedings of the International Conference Organized by the Katholieke Universiteit Leuven from the 17th to the 20th of April 1991* (ed. J. Quaegebeur; OLA 55; Leuven, 1993), 198. For mythological discussion of sacrifices, see Sumerian Enki and Ninmah, Babylonian Atra-Hasis Epic and Enuma Elish IV:11, V:115, and VI:33–340; all discussed by Lambert, "Donations of Food and Drink to the Gods," 191–201.

9. Hallo, "Cult Statue and Divine Image: A Preliminary Study," *Scripture and Context II: More Essays on the Comparative Method* (ed. W. W. Hallo, J. C. Moyer, and L. G. Perdue; Winona Lake, IN: Eisenbrauns, 1983), 1–17, esp. 4–11.

10. *ANET* 394; reference in E. L. Greenstein, *UNP* 43 n. 37.

11. *UNP* 20.

12. Hurowitz, *Divine Service and Its Rewards: Ideology and Poetics in the Hinke Kudurru* (Beer-Sheva Studies by the Department of Bible and Ancient Near East X; Beersheba: Ben-Gurion University of the Negev, 1997), 3.

13. Schützinger, "Bild und Wesen der Gottheit im alten Mesopotamien," *Götterbild, in Kunst und Schrift* (ed. H. J. Klimkeit; Studium universale 2; Bonn, 1984), 61–80.

14. Van der Toorn, *Sin and Sanction in Israel and Mesopotamia: A Comparative Study* (Studia Semitica Neerlandica 22; Assen/Maastricht: Van Gorcum, 1985), 165 n. 168.

15. Winter, " 'Idols of the King': Royal Images as Recipients of Ritual Action in Ancient Mesopotamia," *Journal of Ritual Studies* 6 (1992), 17. For Dick, see nn. 20, 23.

16. Berlejung, "Washing the Mouth: The Consecration of Divine Images in Mesopotamia," *The Image and the Book: Iconic Cults, Aniconism, and the Rise of Book Religion in Israel and the Ancient Near East* (ed. K. van der Toorn; Biblical Exegesis & Theology 21; Leuven: Peeters, 1997), 46 n. 3. In support of her view, she cites: (1) the Esarhaddon inscription: "there appeared in the sky and on the earth favorable signs for the restoration of (the statues of the) gods and the building of sanctuaries" (see *CAD* E:32a, 2'b; note especially the *D*-stem of *edēšu*, "to renew"); (2) the sun-disk inscription of Nabû-apla-iddina (885–852), discussed in Jacobsen (note 17); and (3) Ebeling A.418: text for delapidated statue in need of reinstitution: "If the work of the god [statue] becomes delapidated and suffered damage").

17. Jacobsen, "No Graven Image," *Ancient Israelite Religion: Essays in Honor of Frank Moore Cross* (ed. P. D. Miller, P. D. Hanson, and S. D. McBride; Philadelphia: Fortress, 1987), 18 (Jacobsen's italics).

18. Hallo, "Cult Statue and Divine Image," 11–12.

19. Jacobsen, "No Graven Image," 22–23.

20. Jacobsen, "No Graven Image," 21–23; see also Hallo, "Cult Statue and Divine Image," 13; C. B. F. Walker and M. B. Dick, "The Induction of the Cult Image in Ancient Mesopotamia: The Mesopotamian *mīs pî* Ritual," *Born in Heaven, Made on Earth: The Creation of the Cult Image* (ed. M. B. Dick; Winona Lake, IN: Eisenbrauns, 1999), 58–59.

21. Column iv, line 24, published as no. 36 by L. W. King, *Babylonian Boundary Stones and Memorial Tablets in the British Museum* (London, 1912).

22. The phrase "rite of transition" is used by P. Boden, also mentioned by Berlejung, "Washing the Mouth," 47 n. 7.

23. The main editions to date for the Babylonian version (esp. BM 45749): S. Smith, "The Babylonian Ritual for the Consecration and Induction of a Divine Statue," *JRAS* (1925), 37–60 pl ii–iv; E. Ebeling, *Tod und Leben nach Vorstellungen der Babylonier* (Berlin: de Gruyter, 1931); Walker and Dick, "The Induction," 55–122, esp. 72–83 and 84–96. For Nineveh edition (esp. K6324) see H. Zimmern, *Beiträge zur Kenntnis der babylonischen Religion* (Leipzig, 1901); C. B. F. Walker, "Material for a Reconstruction of the *mīs pî* Ritual" (B. Phil. thesis in Oriental studies, Oxford, 1966), 3–22; Cf. W. R. Mayer, "Seleukidische Rituale aus Warka mit emesal-Gebeten," *Or* ns 47 (1978), 431–58.

The main studies are given by date: H. Zimmern, "Das vermutliche babylonische Vorbild des Pehta und Mambuha der Mandäer," *Orientalische Studien. Theodor Nöldeke zum 70. Geburstag (2.3.1906)* (ed. C. Bezold; two vols.; Giessen, 1906), 2.959–67; G. Meier, "Die Ritualtafel der Serie 'Mundwaschung,' " *AfO* 12 (1937–39), 40–45, pls. i–ii; Oppenheim, *Ancient Mesopotamia*, 185–86; T. Jacobsen, "The Graven Image," 15–32; M. Dietrich and O. Loretz, *Jahwe und seine Aschera: Anthropomorphisches Kultbild in Mesopotamien, Ugarit und Israel. Das biblische Bilderverbot* (UBL 9; Münster: UBL, 1992), 24–37; T. Podella, *Das Lichtkleid JHWHs: Untersuchungen zur Gestalthaftigkeit Gottes im Alten Testament und seiner altorientalischen Umwelt* (FAT 15: Tübingen: J. C. B. Mohr [Siebeck], 1996), 108–09; V. Hurowitz, "Isaiah's Impure Lips and Their Purification in Light of Akkadian Sources," *HUCA* 60 (1989), 39–89, esp. 48–49, 53; idem, " 'Aśeh lĕkā pesel (Thou Shall Make Thyself an Idol)," *Beth Mikra* 40 (1995), 337–47; P. Boden, "The Mīs Pî: A Ritual of Transition" (Ph.D. diss., Johns Hopkins University, 1998); A. Berlejung, *Die Theologie der Bilder: Herstellung und Einweihung von Kultbildern in Mesopotamien und die altestamentliche Bilderpolemi* (OBO 162; Freiburg Schweiz: Universitätsverlag; Göttingen: Vandenhoeck & Ruprecht, 1998); idem, "Washing the Mouth," 45–72; idem, "Der Handwerker als Theologie: Zur

Mentalitäts-und Traditionsgeschichte eines altorientalischen und alttestamentlichen Berufstands," *VT* 46 (1996), 145–68; M. B. Dick, "Prophetic Parodies of Making the Cult Image," *Born in Heaven, Made on Earth*, 1–53. The *mīs pî* incantations (Sultantepe incantations [henceforth STT], 198–208) are addressed in Walker, "Material for a Reconstruction of the *mis pî* Ritual"; for STT 200 in particular, see Walker and Dick, "The Induction," 96–100. The text and translation are cited according to the edition of Walker and Dick; they are in the process of preparing a technical edition for the series State Archives of Assyria (Helsinki: Helsinki University Press). I am particularly grateful to Professors Dick and Hurowitz for their help with this material.

24. STT 200 etc. 42–44; Berlejung, "Washing the Mouth," 47; cf. Psalm 135, Jeremiah 10:5; as noted by Walker and Dick, "The Induction," 114.

25. See Hallo, "Cult Statue and Divine Image," 3 n. 15.

26. Cf. the well-known "Prayer to the God of the Night," in *ANET* 390–91.

27. Berlejung, "Washing the Mouth," 51–68.

28. Berlejung, "Washing the Mouth," 71.

29. Berlejung, "Washing the Mouth," 57.

30. Berlejung, "Washing the Mouth," 57.

31. These passages are addressed by Walker and Dick, "The Induction," 114. See Esarhaddon IV R 25b 59: "creation of the gods, work of humans" (pointed out to me by V. Hurowitz).

32. Alter, "Introduction," *The Literary Guide to the Bible* (ed. R. Alter and F. Kermode; Cambridge, MA: Belknap Press, 1987), 33–34.

33. Dick, "Prophetic Parodies," 16–20.

34. Walker and Dick, "The Induction," 114.

35. Hallo ("Cult Statue and Divine Image," 14–15) compares Nabonidus's attempts to remove Babylonian gods to safety against the imminent approach of Cyrus. See P.-A. Beaulieu, *The Reign of Nabonidus King of Babylon 556–539 B.C.* (Yale Near Eastern Researches 10; New Haven: Yale University Press, 1989), 220–24. For disputes about image-making in competing neo-Babylonian cults and their possible relevance to image polemics in Second Isaiah, see V. Hurowitz, "חקות העמים הבל הוא (Jer 10:3) in Light of Akkadian *parṣu* and *Zaqīqu* referring to Cult Statues," *JQR* 89 (1999), 277–90. For the wider context of competition among neo-Babylonian cults and its pertinence to monotheistic discourse in Second Isaiah, see P. Machinist, "Mesopotamian Imperialism and Israelite Religion: A Case from the Second Isaiah," *Symbiosis, Symbolism and the Power of the Past: Canaan, Ancient Israel and Their Neighbors from the Late Bronze Age Through Roman Palestine* (ed. W. Dever and S. Gitin, in preparation).

36. C. Franke, *Isaiah 46, 47, 48: A New Literary-Critical Reading* (Biblical and Judaic Studies from UCSD 3; Winona Lake, IN: Eisenbrauns, 1994), 98: "These two [Bel and Nebo//Jacob/Israel] are compared in that both are carried, borne up. The contrast is in the agents who carry. In the case of Bel and Nebo, it is the animals in. 1–2 or the people in vv. 6–7 who must carry them. The People of Israel by contrast are carried by their God."

37. Franke, *Isaiah 46, 47, 48*, 98.

38. Franke, *Isaiah 46, 47, 48*, 263; see also p. 72.

39. See the seminal work by B. D. Sommer, *A Prophet Reads Scripture*. His work touches little on the example explored here. See also P. T. Willey, *Remember the Former Things: The Recollection of Previous Texts in Isaiah 40–55* (SBLDS 161; Atlanta, GA: Scholars, 1997).

40. M. Friedländer, *The Commentary of Ibn Ezra on Isaiah. Vol. I. Translation of the Commentary* (London, 1873; New York: Philipp Feldheim, nd), 198.

41. Cf. **p‘l*: Isaiah 44:15 image-maker makes a god versus Yahweh's making in Isaiah 43:13.

42. R. J. Clifford, "The Function of Idol Passages in Second Isaiah," *CBQ* 42 (1980), 463. For further discussion of Isaiah 44, see K. Holter, *Second Isaiah's Idol-Fabrication Passages* (Beiträge zur biblischen Exegese und Theologie 28; Frankfurt: Peter Lang, 1995), 127–212.

43. Clifford, "The Function of Idol Passages in Second Isaiah," 463.

44. Friedländer, *The Commentary of Ibn Ezra on Isaiah. Vol. I*, 199.

45. See the careful study of H. G. M. Williamson, *The Book Called Isaiah: Deutero-Isaiah's Role in Composition and Redaction* (Oxford: Clarendon Press, 1994); also C. R. Seitz, *Word Without End: The Old Testament as Abiding Theological Witness* (Grand Rapids, MI: Eerdmans, 1998), 168–93. See also the many fine essays in *The Book of Isaiah. Le Livre d'Isaïe: Les oracles et leur relectures unité et complexité de l'ouvrage* (ed. J. Vermeylen; BETL LXXXI; Leuven: University Press/Peeters, 1989); and *Studies in the Book of Isaiah: Festschrift Willem A. M. Beuken* (ed. J. van Ruiten and M. Vervenne; BETL CXXXII; Leuven: University Press/Uitgeverij, 1997). For intertextual study of "Second Isaiah" more generally, see Willey, *Remember the Former Things*. This work does not address Isaiah 44. According to Sommer (*A Prophet Reads Scripture*, 71–74), "Second Isaiah" references First Isaiah less than other prophetic section such as Jeremiah, but his work also notes literary allusions to First Isaiah in "Second Isaiah."

46. C. Seitz, "The Divine Council: Temporal Transition and New Prophecy in the Book of Isaiah," *JBL* 109/2 (1990), 229–47; cf. R. J. Clifford, "The Unity of the Book of Isaiah and Its Cosmogonic Language," *CBQ* 55/1 (1993), 1–17.

47. Unless one accepts the first-person reading of the objecting voice in 40:6b–7 as at Qumran; See D. L. Petersen, *Late Israelite Prophecy: Studies in Deutero-Prophetic Literature and in Chronicles* (SBLDS 23; Missoula, MT: Scholars, 1977), 20. The third-person reading of MT represents the more difficult reading (or *lector difficilior*); see Seitz, "The Divine Council," 234–35, 237.

48. C. R. Seitz, "How is the Prophet Isaiah Present in the Latter Half of the Book? The Logic of Chapters 40–66 within the Book of Isaiah," *JBL* 115 (1996), 219–40.

49. R. J. Clifford, *Fair Spoken and Persuading: An Interpretation of Second Isaiah* (New York: Paulist, 1984), 1.

50. See Seitz, "The Divine Council," 229–47.

51. See C. Begg, "Babylon in the Book of Isaiah," *The Book of Isaiah. Le Livre d'Isaïe: Les oracles et leur relectures unité et complexité de l'ouvrage* (ed. J. Vermeylen; BETL LXXXI; Leuven: University Press/Peeters, 1989), 121–25; cf. Sommer, *A Prophet Reads Scripture*, 74.

52. For a balanced treatment of this poem's background, see P. Sanders, *The Provenance of Deuteronomy 32* (OTS 32; Leiden: Brill, 1996). Sanders favors a pre-exilic date, perhaps the ninth or eighth century.

53. Note also in Deuteronomy 32:10 the theme of *midbār* (cf. Isaiah 40); and in 32:36 *wĕ'al-'ăbādāyw yitneḥām* (cf. Isaiah 40).

54. For discussion of this term, see Sommer, *A Prophet Reads Scripture*, 66–67. Whether more is involved cannot be determined.

55. Clifford, *Fair Spoken and Persuading*, 112 n. 10.

56. For the difficulties, see Clifford, "The Function of Idol Passages in Second Isaiah," 455 n. 19:

Bel bows down; Nebu dips low.	kr' bl qrs nbw
On beasts and cattle are they borne,	lḥyh wlbhmh nś't
Carried as a loan on weary animals.	mwswt ms' l'yph
They dip low; they bow down together.	qrsw kr'w yḥdw

Clifford takes *hāyû 'ăṣabbêhem*, "they were their idols," as a gloss secondarily incorporated into the text understood as the idiom, **hyh l-*, "to become."

57. On this question, see D. W. van Winkle, "Proselytes in Isaiah XL–LV?: A Study of Isaiah XLIV 1–5," *VT* 47 (1997), 341–59. I do not believe that proselytes are the issue here.

58. Franke, *Isaiah 46, 47, 48*, 263: "The passages in which the people are criticized for being stubborn and far from justice, that is, rebels, are related to the theme of idolatry. While many scholars look upon the polemic against idols as mocking the foolish Babylonians for their worship of mere wood and metal objects, in these two poems it is far more serious. The charges of idolatry are directed at Jacob/Israel. It is the Israelites, not the Babylonians, who are criticized for making and worshipping idols. DI is not addressing his message to the Babylonians, nor is he concerned with their future. This poet is concerned that the exiles might once again jeopardize their chance to escape from oppression, just as they did at Mt. Sinai by their lack of true righteousness and their making and worshipping idols." See pp. 32, 52–55.

59. "Religious Polemics," *Leiden Institute for the Study of Religions (LISOR) Newsletter* 1997/1:8–9.

60. For some of the issues concerning scribes and literacy in ancient Israel, see D. W. Jamieson-Drake, *Scribes and Schools in Monarchic Judah: A Socio-Archeological Approach* (Sheffield: Almond, 1991); I. M. Young, "Israelite Literacy: Interpreting the Evidence," *VT* 48 (1998), 239–53. For the emergence of written prophecy especially in the sixth century, see Sommer, *A Prophet Reads Scripture*. See also the fine survey of W. M. Schniedewind, "Orality and Literacy in Ancient Israel," *Religious Studies Review* 26/4 (2000), 327–32. The literature on these topics is vast and beyond the scope of this work.

61. See the important reflections of S. A. Geller, *Sacred Enigmas: Literary Religion in the Hebrew Bible* (London: Routledge, 1996), esp. 168–94.

Index of Texts

Index of Subjects